iOS 7
by Tutorials

By the raywenderlich.com Tutorial Team

Christine Abernathy, Soheil Moayedi Azarpour, Colin Eberhardt, Charlie Fulton, Matt Galloway, Greg Heo, Matthijs Hollemans, Felipe Laso Marsetti, Jeremy Olson, Pietro Rea, Cesare Rocchi, Marin Todorov, Chris Wagner

iOS 7 by Tutorials

Christine Abernathy, Soheil Moayedi Azarpour, Colin Eberhardt, Charlie Fulton, Matt Galloway, Greg Heo, Matthijs Hollemans, Felipe Laso Marsetti, Jeremy Olson, Pietro Rea, Cesare Rocchi, Marin Todorov, Chris Wagner

Copyright ©2013 Razeware LLC.

ISBN: 978-0-9896751-0-9

Table of Contents

Dedications

"To God first, my loving husband James, my awesome Mum, encouraging Dad, and all family and friends who are the reason every day's a delight."

–Christine Abernathy

"Specially to my wife, Elnaz, for her support and encouragement and my wonderful son, Kian."

–Soheil Azarpour

"To my lovely wife Susan, and children, Jessica, Lauren, Abbie and William."

–Colin Eberhardt

"To my savior and Lord Jesus Christ with whom all things are possible, and to the amazing boys and wife I am blessed to have."

- Charlie Fulton

"To my family and friends for all their encouragement and support."

–Matt Galloway

"To my family, for their support; and to the nerds in #tutorialteam for all the laughs and the trouts."

–Greg Heo

"To the crazy ones, the misfits, the rebels and the troublemakers."

–Matthijs Hollemans

"To God, thank you for the blessed life I get to live every day. To my beautiful girlfriend Nathalie, I love you my little Magikarp! And, to my amazing nephews Leo and Tiziano :)"

- Felipe Laso Marsetti

"To my very best friend and the love of my life, Mindy Olson."

–Jeremy Olson

"To my wonderful wife Emily. Thank you for listening to my crazy ideas and supporting me no matter what."

–Pietro Rea

"To my wife, my kid and Bob Dylan".

–Cesare Rocchi

"To my parents - ever so supportive and loving. To Mirjam."

–Marin Torodov

"To my amazing, always supportive wife Sam and our perfect baby boy Hayden"

–Chris Wagner

Introduction

By Ray Wenderlich

iOS 7 delivers one of the most massive and exciting set of changes that we've seen so far as developers.

The new design direction of iOS 7 means a massive disruption in the App Store is underway. Customers will be looking for apps that "fit in" with the new iOS 7 style and make use of the new technology. This means tons of great opportunity for you – the type of opportunity seen only once 3 to 5 years!

On top of the new design direction, iOS 7 brings a ton of new APIs and frameworks to learn about. However, trying to get a handle on all the new technology while trying to get your apps updated at the same time can be quite challenging!

That's why ever since the first day of WWDC, the Tutorial Team and I have been hard at work researching all of the new APIs and distilling them into a form that makes it quick and easy for you to get up to speed. That way you can focus on what you do best – making great apps!

So get ready for your personal tour through the amazing new features in iOS 7. By the time you are done, your iOS knowledge will be completely up-to-date, and you'll be ready to take advantage of the amazing new opportunities that iOS 7 brings.

Sit back, relax, and prepare for some fun and high quality tutorials!

About this book

This is our third book in the iOS by Tutorials series. We started with *iOS 5 by Tutorials* back in 2011, and the book was so popular that we've made a book for the new APIs of each major iOS version ever since. It's been quite a ride!

Each year, we aim to take a critical look at what we did the previous year and determine what we can do better. This year, we decided to increase our focus on three aspects: design, engagement, and practice.

Increased focus on design

One of the most important features of iOS 7 is the new minimalistic design style that brings an increased focus on content, typography, and animation.

We wanted our book to reflect this new design direction, so this year the book includes five new elements on design:

1. **Designing for iOS 7 chapter**. We teamed up with guest author Jeremy Olson, an Apple design award winner who has had several apps in the top 100 of the App Store. Jeremy wrote the first chapter of the book, "Designing for iOS 7", which will give you an overview of what it takes to make your app look and feel great on iOS 7. And the best part is it's written with a programmer audience in mind!

2. **Chapters on design-oriented APIs**. iOS 7 comes with many other APIs that help you create your app in the "iOS 7 style", such as UIKit Dynamics and custom view controller transitions. We've taken special care on these topics so you can add these cool new techniques to your toolbelt and give your apps a sense of liveliness and fun.

3. **Transitioning to iOS 7 chapters**. One of the biggest questions many developers will have while transitioning their iOS 6 apps to iOS 7 involve how to deal with the many technical challenges that arise along the way. We made this topic front and center in this book, and included three detailed chapters that shows you this very process step by step using practical examples.

4. **Custom designed sample projects**. In previous years, most of our sample projects were designed by ourselves; a team of programmers with a lot of heart and technical prowess…but not necessarily the best designers in the world. So this year, we teamed up with designer Jamie Syke, who designed each of the sample projects in our book to fit in well with the iOS 7 style. We hope that the example designs give you some inspiration for your own apps.

5. **A redesigned book cover**. You might have noticed the book cover itself looks different this year! We hope you like it – Jamie designed it to reiterate the focus we're placing on design in this book.

Increased focus on engagement

In our previous books we've noticed that we were so eager to pack in a ton of useful material, our books and chapters were sometimes overly long. For example, both iOS 5 and iOS 6 by Tutorials were too big to fit in a single printed volume!

We know your time is valuable, and we don't want to take more time than necessary to cover a new topic. So this year we made more of an effort to keep our chapters concise and readable, so you can master new topics as quickly as possible.

Note that this book is still long, since we didn't want to sacrifice on the number of topics covered or the level of technical detail. However, you will notice that most chapters are shorter and more to the point than before.

One exception to this is Chapter 2, "Transitioning to iOS 7". This was such an important topic that we really took our time there and went into great detail. We think you'll enjoy the result.

Increased focus on practice

Following a tutorial is one thing, but applying its concepts yourself is completely different. This year, we wanted to do more to help you make the transition from following along with the tutorials to applying the knowledge in your own apps.

As such, for the first time we are including challenges at the end of every chapter. The challenges have been designed to help you practice the material you just learned, with hints to walk you through the process.

If you get stuck, don't worry - we have included the solutions to the challenges with the book so you can check your answers. But try not to cheat! ☺

Note that this is the first time we're trying challenges in our books, so we're curious about the difficulty level. Were they too easy? Too hard? Just about right? Let us know so we can improve next time!

We hope you enjoy the challenges, and that they help you solidify the material.

Did we succeed?

After you finish reading this book, please let me know if you think this new focus on design, engagement, and practice has helped to improve the book. You can email me anytime at ray@raywenderlich.com.

We hope you enjoy this book, and we can't wait to see your new iOS 7 apps!

What you need

To follow along with the tutorials in this book, you need the following:

- **A Mac running OS X Mountain Lion or later**. You need a Mac running OS X Mountain Lion or later so you can install the latest version of Xcode.

- **Xcode 5 or later**. Xcode is the main development tool for iOS. You need to use Xcode 5 or later in this book, because Xcode 5 is the first version of Xcode that supports Sprite Kit and iOS 7 development. You can download the latest version of Xcode for free on the Mac app store here:
  https://itunes.apple.com/app/xcode/id497799835?mt=12

- **One or more devices (iPhone, iPad, or iPod Touch) running iOS 7 or later, and a paid membership to the iOS development program [optional]**. For most of the chapters in the book, you can run your code on the iOS 7 Simulator that comes with Xcode. However, there are a few chapters later in the book that require a real device for testing (and sometimes multiple devices).

- **A Mac with OS X Mavericks Server [optional]**. To follow along with the Continuous Integration chapters, you will need a Mac running OS X server. See those chapters for more details.

If you don't have the latest version of Xcode installed already, be sure to do that before continuing with the book.

Who this book is for

This book is for intermediate or advanced iOS developers who already know the basics of iOS development but want to upgrade their skills for iOS 7.

If you're a complete beginner, you can still follow along with the book because the instructions are always in a step-by-step manner, but there may be some missing gaps in your knowledge. You might want to go through our *iOS Apprentice* series before you go through this book, which covers the basics of Objective-C and iOS development:

http://www.raywenderlich.com/store/ios-apprentice

How to use this book

This book can be read from cover to cover, but we don't recommend using it this way unless you have a lot of time and are the type of person who just "needs to know everything". (It's okay, a lot of our tutorial team is like that, too!)

Instead, we suggest a pragmatic approach – pick and choose the subjects that interest you the most, or the ones you need for your projects, and jump directly to those chapters. Most chapters are self-contained, so you can go through them in non-sequential order.

Looking for some recommendations of important chapters to start with? Here's our suggested Core Reading List:

• Chapter 1, "Designing for iOS 7"

• Chapter 6, "Transitioning to iOS 7: Quick Start"

• Chapter 9, "What's New in Xcode 5"

• Chapter 16, "Networking with NSURLSession"

• Chapter 17, "Beginning Multitasking"

That covers the "Big 5" topics of iOS 7, and from there you can dig into other topics that are particularly interesting to you.

Book overview

iOS 7 has a host of killer new APIs that you'll want to start using in your apps right away. Here's what you'll be learning about in this book:

Section I: Design

In this section, you will learn how to design your apps to look great on iOS 7, along with the practical nuts and bolts of doing so. You will also learn about the new APIs in iOS 7 that are related to design, like UIKit dynamics, custom view controller transitions, and Text Kit.

Here's a quick overview of the chapters in this section:

1. **Chapter 1, Designing for iOS 7**: Before you dive into the code, you'll learn how to design your apps to fit in well with the new iOS 7 style.

2. **Chapter 2, UIKit Dynamics**: You'll learn how to create user interfaces that feel real by adding physics behaviors like gravity, attachments (springs), and forces.

3. **Chapter 3, Custom View Controller Transitions**: You'll learn how to use your own custom animations when switching between view controllers in your apps.

4. **Chapter 4, Beginning Text Kit**: You'll learn how to support dynamic type in your apps and make text fields with exclusion paths and dynamic text highlighting.

5. **Chapter 5, Intermediate Text Kit**: You'll learn how the Text Kit rendering system works, and apply your knowledge to create your own eBook reader.

6. **Chapters 6-8, Transitioning to iOS 7, Parts 1-3**: You'll learn the nuts and bolts of taking an app designed in the skeuomorphic iOS 6 style and converting it to the new minimalistic iOS 7 style.

Section II: What's New in Xcode 5

In this section, you'll learn about the new features in Xcode 5 that are useful when making *any* type of app. In particular, you'll learn about unit testing, source control, continuous integration, and more.

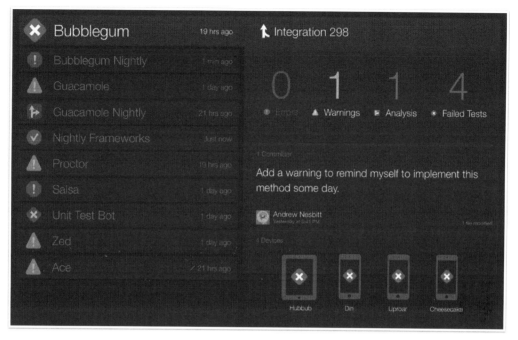

Here's a quick overview of the chapters in this section:

9. **Chapter 9, What's New in Xcode 5**: Get a quick overview of the new features in the Xcode development environment itself, like asset catalogs and image slicing.

10. **Chapter 10, What's New in Objective-C and Foundation**: Get a quick overview of new language features like modules, and important new Foundation APIs you should be aware of.

11. **Chapter 11, Unit Testing in Xcode 5**: Xcode 5 includes a new unit testing framework called XCUnit. Learn how to use it to add unit tests to your apps.

12. **Chapter 12, Beginning Source Control in Xcode 5**: Learn how to maintain your project under source control in Xcode 5 and upload your project to GitHub.

13. **Chapter 13, Intermediate Source Control in Xcode 5**: Learn about some more advanced features of source control in Xcode 5 like branching, merging, and resolving conflicts.

14. **Chapter 14, Beginning Continuous Integration in Xcode 5**: Learn how to set up a continuous integration server and create a simple automated bot to build and run your project.

15. **Chapter 15, Intermediate Continuous Integration in Xcode 5**: Learn how to set up a beautiful web-based scoreboard and automatically distribute your builds to TestFlight.

Section III: Major New Features

In this section, you'll learn about the biggest and most important new features and frameworks in iOS 7 not already covered in this book. For example, you'll learn about a new way to write networking code, a new way to keep your app's data up to date, and much more.

Here's a quick overview of the chapters in this section:

16. **Chapter 16, Networking with NSURLSession**: Learn how to write networking code with the new NSURLSession suite of classes, which are a great alternative to NSURLConnection and other similar third-party networking libraries.

17. **Chapter 17, Beginning Multitasking**: Learn how to keep your app's data up to date in the background with background fetching.

18. **Chapter 18, Intermediate Multitasking**: Learn how to download large files in the background and get notified of updates with silent push notifications.

19. **Chapter 19, JavaScriptCore Framework**: Learn how you can mix JavaScript with your native code in real time from your apps.

20. **Chapter 20, AirDrop**: Learn how to share data in an even simpler way with Apple's new AirDrop support, built right into a UIActivityViewController.

21. **Chapter 21, Peer-to-Peer Connectivity**: If you want even more control, learn how to drop down into the peer-to-peer connectivity framework, which gives you complete control of the process of discovering and sharing information with nearby devices.

Section IV: Minor New Features

In this section, you'll learn about some minor improvements to existing APIs you know and love, such as AVFoundation, MapKit, and Core Location.

Here's a quick overview of the chapters in this section:

22. **Chapter 22, What's New in AVFoundation**: Learn about the new bar code detection, video zooming, and speech synthesis capabilities in AVFoundation.

23. **Chapter 23, What's New in MapKit**: Learn about the new directions, snapshot, and camera features in MapKit.

24. **Chapter 24, What's New in Core Location**: Learn how to make an iOS app that acts as a beacon broadcasting a location, and a companion app to use the beacon.

Section V: Bonus Chapters

And that's not all – on top of the above, we have some bonus chapters for you!

These bonus chapters come as an optional PDF download, which you can download for free here:

• http://www.raywenderlich.com/store/ios-7-by-tutorials/bonus-chapters

We hope you enjoy the bonus chapters!

25. **Chapter 25, Beginning Inter-App Audio**: Learn how to connect the audio output of one app to the audio input of another app to create a suite of connected audio apps.

26. **Chapter 26, Intermediate Inter-App Audio**: Take a deeper dive into Core Audio, including what audio graphs are and how to wire one up to process audio.

27. **Chapter 27, What's New in PassKit, Part 1**: Learn how to make your passes look great in the new iOS 7 style.

28. **Chapter 28, What's New in PassKit, Part 2**: Learn about pass bundles, QR codes, how to use beacons to activate passes, and more.

29. **Chapter 29, Introduction to iAd**: Learn how to integrate iAd into your apps, whether it be banner ads, interstitials, or pre-roll video ads.

Book source code and forums

You can get the source code for the book here: http://www.raywenderlich.com/store/ios-7-by-tutorials/source-code

We've also set up an official forum for the book at raywenderlich.com/forums. This is a great place to ask any questions you have about the book or about iOS 7 in general, or to submit any errata you may find.

We hope to see you on the forums! ☺

PDF Version

We also have a PDF version of this book available, which can be handy if you ever want to copy/paste code or search for a specific term through the book as you're developing.

And speaking of the PDF version, we have some good news!

Since you purchased the physical copy of this book, you are eligible to buy the PDF version at a significant discount if you would like (if you don't have it already). For more details, see this page:

- http://www.raywenderlich.com/store/ios-games-by-tutorials/upgrade

License

By purchasing *iOS 7 by Tutorials*, you have the following license:

- You are allowed to use and/or modify the source code in the iOS 7 by Tutorials in as many apps as you want, with no attribution required.

- You are allowed to use and/or modify all art, images, or designs that are included in *iOS 7 by Tutorials* in as many apps as you want, but must include this attribution line somewhere inside your app: "Artwork/images/designs: from iOS 7 by Tutorials book, available at http://www.raywenderlich.com".

- The source code included in iOS 7 by Tutorials is for your own personal use only. You are NOT allowed to distribute or sell the source code in *iOS 7 by Tutorials* without prior authorization.

- This book is for your own personal use only. You are NOT allowed to sell this book without prior authorization, or distribute it to friends, co-workers, or students; they would need to purchase their own copy.

All materials provided with this book are provided on an "as is" basis, without warranty of any kind, express or implied, including but not limited to the warranties of merchantability, fitness for a particular purpose and non-infringement. In no event shall the authors or copyright holders be liable for any claim, damages or other liability, whether in an action of contract, tort or otherwise, arising from, out of or in connection with the software or the use or other dealings in the software.

All trademarks and registered trademarks appearing in this guide are the property of their respective owners.

Acknowledgements

We would like to thank many people for their assistance in making this possible:

- **Our families**: For bearing with us in this crazy time as we worked all hours of the night to get this book ready for publication!

- **Everyone at Apple**: For developing an amazing operating system and set of APIs, for constantly inspiring us to improve our apps and skills, and for making it possible for many developers to have their dream jobs!

- And most importantly, **the readers of raywenderlich.com — especially you**! Thank you so much for reading our site and purchasing this book. Your continued readership and support is what makes this all possible!

About the authors

Christine Abernathy is an Engineer on the Developer Advocacy team at Facebook. In this role, she is focused on helping grow the mobile developer ecosystem with emphasis on Android, iOS, and the mobile web.

Soheil Azarpour is an iOS developer. He has worked on several iOS applications for clients and his own. His hobby is coding. He enjoys making apps, hanging out with his family, and watching movies.

Colin Eberhardt has been writing code and tutorials for many years, covering a wide range of technologies and platforms. Most recently he has turned his attention to iOS. Colin is CTO of ShinobiControls, creators of charts, grids and other powerful iOS controls.

Charlie Fulton is a full time iOS developer. He has worked with many languages and technologies for many years, and is currently specializing in iOS development. In his spare time, Charlie enjoys hunting, fishing, gaming and hanging out with his family. He likes to slap people with fish in IRC.

Matt Galloway is the founder of SwipeStack, a mobile development company based in London, UK which create apps for clients and also a few of their own. He is also author of Effective Objective-C 2.0 and writes on his blog at http://www.galloway.me.uk/

Greg Heo is an indie developer and tech partner at Ferocious Apps. He likes caffeine, codes with two-space tabs, and can be found at his standing desk at all hours of the day.

Matthijs Hollemans is an independent designer and developer who loves to create awesome software for the iPad and iPhone. He also enjoys teaching others to do the same, which is why he wrote The iOS Apprentice series of eBooks. In his spare time, Matthijs is learning to play jazz piano (it's hard!) and likes to go barefoot running when the sun is out. Check out his blog at http://www.hollance.com.

Felipe Laso Marsetti is an iOS developer working at Lextech Global Services. In his spare time Felipe enjoys learning new languages and frameworks, playing violin or guitar, cooking and also video games. You can follow him on Twitter as @Airjordan12345, ADN as @iFeli, or on his blog at http://ife.li.

Jeremy Olson is the founder of Tapity, which has made Grades (a 2011 Apple Design award winner), and Languages (recently released, and got into the top 10). You can follow him on Twitter as @jerols or check out his work at: http://tapity.com/

Pietro Rea is an iOS developer based out of New York City. He started writing code in high school and is currently specializing in Objective-C and iOS. He currently develops mobile apps for the Huffington Post. Check out his blog: http://www.pietrorea.com

Cesare Rocchi is a speaker, writer, UX designer and developer specializing in web and mobile applications. He began working on interactive applications while he was a researcher in the academia. He runs Studio Magnolia, an interactive studio that creates compelling web and mobile applications. He blogs at http://upbeat.it.

Marin Todorov is an independent iOS developer and publisher, with background in various platforms and languages. He has published several books, written about iOS development on his blog, and authored an online game programming course. He loves to read, travel, and ... write code. Visit his web site: http://www.touch-code-magazine.com.

Chris Wagner currently works as the lead iOS developer at Infusionsoft and started "programming" by playing with QBASIC and the Lego Mindstorms kit (thanks Dad). After graduating with a Computer Systems Engineering degree from ASU he worked as a Java web app developer before moving on to leading multiple iOS development teams.

About the editors

Chris Belanger was the editor for this book. He has been a coder for over a quarter century, which makes him feel kind of old. He's also a prolific writer, dabbles in electronic and organic music composition, and occasionally even manages to get real work done as a developer of real-time control systems.

Greg Heo was a tech editor for this book. He is an indie developer and tech partner at Ferocious Apps. He likes caffeine, semicolons, and the Oxford comma.

Mic Pringle was a tech editor for this book. He is a Yorkshire-born developer with a passion for aesthetics and the user experience. Currently working at The Infinite Kind, he's been handcrafting exquisite iOS apps since 2011. When not knee-deep in Objective-C, he enjoys spending time with his wife and daughter, as well as attending the odd football match.

Ray Wenderlich was the final pass editor for this book. He is an iPhone developer and gamer, and the founder of Razeware LLC. Ray is passionate about both making apps and teaching others the techniques to make them. He and the Tutorial Team have written a bunch of tutorials about iOS development available at http://www.raywenderlich.com.

About the artists

Jamie Syke designed the sample projects for this book. Jamie is a User Interface and Web Designer who has spent the last 6 years honing his skills in Manchester, UK. His focus has been on creating clean, functional designs with a emphasis on user experience. He currently works as Lead Designer for online ticketing platform Fatsoma and is available for freelance work at http://syke.co.

Vicki Wenderlich created many of the illustrations in this book. Vicki discovered a love of digital art three years ago, and has been making app art and digital illustrations ever since. She is passionate about helping people pursue their dreams, and makes free app art for developers available on her website, http://www.vickiwenderlich.com.

Section I: Design

In this section, you will learn how to design your apps to look great on iOS 7, along with the practical nuts and bolts of doing so. You will also learn about the new APIs in iOS 7 that are related to design, like UIKit dynamics, custom view controller transitions, and Text Kit.

Chapter 1: Designing for iOS 7

Chapter 2: UIKit Dynamics

Chapter 3: Custom View Controller Transitions

Chapter 4: Beginning Text Kit

Chapter 5: Intermediate Text Kit

Chapter 6: Transitioning to iOS 7 – Quick Start

Chapter 7: Transitioning to iOS 7 – What's New with Auto Layout

Chapter 8: Transitioning to iOS 7 – Advanced Topics

Chapter 1: Designing for iOS 7

By Jeremy Olson

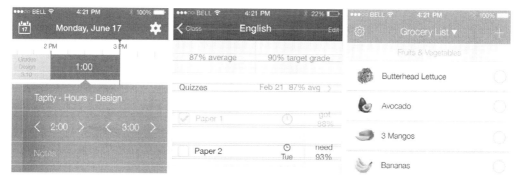

The new design of iOS 7 is a dramatic change from the skeuomorphic style of iOS 6. Love it or hate it, it was a much needed shake up. It changes everything, and customers are going to look for and expect apps that fit in with this new design style.

The best part about the new design in iOS 7 is that it represents a huge opportunity for small developers. The massive players who once dominated the App Store are going to have a tough time transitioning to iOS 7 without alienating millions of iOS 6 users or completely rethinking their apps from the ground up — something established players are often slow to do.

The nimble guys are going to win here, making this possibly the most exciting time to be building apps.

But this doesn't mean that success is going to fall into your lap. An overnight success takes about a year of hard work, as they say. Tens of thousands of developers are going to be jumping onto the iOS 7 bandwagon, all hoping for fame and fortune. How will you be different?

As always, the number one differentiator will be an app designed not only to be usable but also enjoyable to use. With a drastic de-emphasis on heavy visuals, delighting users on iOS 7 will be a much different task than on iOS 6.

Personally, I have designed a lot of apps in iOS 6 (including an Apple Design Award winner) and the new design of iOS 7 has me really excited. It brings tons of opportunities for new looks and new ideas, and my goal in this chapter is to give you a solid starting point to designing apps that look great in iOS 7.

This chapter starts out with the basics and then moves on to help you design apps that stand out from the crowd — and push the platform forward.

Developers are designers, too

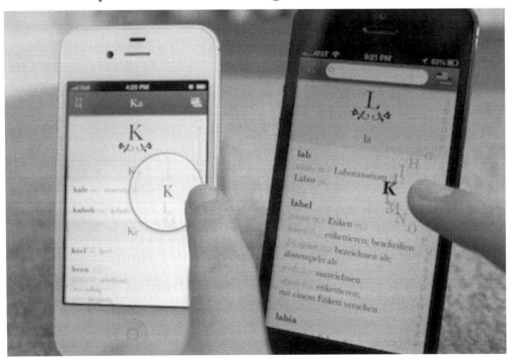

I designed the screen on the left for an app called Languages. As the developer was playing with the code, he came up with the much improved version on the right.

Since this entire book is about code, I'm assuming you, dear reader, are primarily a developer as opposed to being a designer. That's okay! Although I am primarily a designer, I'm also a closet coder as well; I think it's always good to dabble outside your comfort zone once in a while.

My favorite coders are ones who display at least a smidgen of a design instinct. Why? Because development is so closely related to design — and, inevitably, coders end up making plenty of design decisions whether they realize it or not.

This becomes even more important when working with iOS 7 and its emphasis on things like transitions and dynamics — things a designer can't easily communicate through mockups. Developers are going to end up doing a lot of those design experiments themselves. That's a good thing, though, because developers have a lot of great ideas too, and design is definitely a skill that can be learned.

Now that iOS 7 has taken the spotlight off of visually rich interfaces, maybe this will be a good opportunity for developers to start doing more interface design themselves. Reading this chapter is a great way to get started!

Say Hello to design

As a developer, you're probably used to thinking about how to *implement* your app — should I use a `UITableView` or a `UICollectionView` to display this list of items; should I use iCloud or roll my own sync solution?

You are about to explore a whole new world that goes far beyond implementation.

Design is a world where you think about what an app should *do*, how it should *behave*, how it should *look*, and even how it should make the user *feel*. It's a world where you free yourself from the bonds of logic to explore the endless possibilities of what an app could be.

That's really the essence of design: it's an expedition where you explore the possible ways your app could look and work. As you explore, you consider which ideas help realize your goals along with the goals of the users you are designing for.

It's a lot of fun and it's a nice break from the technically-oriented world of code, since you probably still spend most of your time there.

Why design?

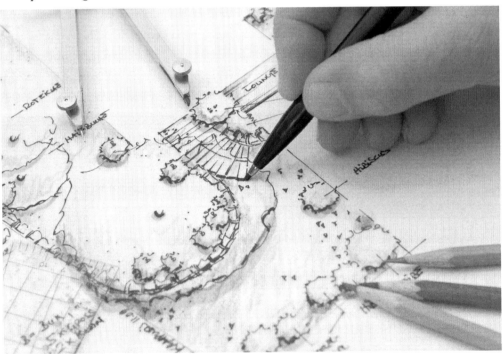

If you're like many developers, as soon as you have a basic idea of what you want to build, your first instinct is to dive into Xcode and begin coding.

But just like your code can really benefit from some initial planning before you start coding like which data structure to use, or whether to go with plists or Core Data, your user interface can really benefit from some initial planning too.

You want to be thinking about things like navigation, layout and interaction early on in the process. Sure, you can always go back and refactor, but it'll certainly take a lot more time and effort than identifying issues early in the blueprint stage where you simply change things on paper.

You need to think of design as something to consider early in the process. It's not as simple as building an initial version with "programmer art" and then slapping on a coat of paint right before launch.

Don't get me wrong; Xcode is a great tool to explore more detailed design decisions like animations and transitions, and it's a great way to find out if your "big picture" design decisions have any merit. But design isn't about tools. Rather, I'm talking about a way of thinking that focuses on user goals, ease-of-use and delight, rather than mere implementation.

What can you expect from spending more time on design?

- **More downloads.** Users have come to expect thoughtfully designed apps and are more likely to download them, not to mention that your App Store screenshot is probably *the number one factor* in a customer's decision to download your app — or to keep browsing.

- **More reviews.** The press gets hundreds of emails a day and has no time to look at poorly designed apps. Well-designed apps stick out from the crowd.

- **Higher chance of being featured.** Apple's culture revolves around design; good luck getting your app featured without reflecting that design culture. All of the apps I've designed have been featured by Apple, which I attribute primarily to a heavy and upfront focus on design.

Designing for iOS 7 is different

My team realized that redesigning our upcoming app Hours for iOS 7 was a worthwhile investment.

Designing for iOS 7 is different. Apps designed for iOS 6 will soon look like dinosaurs unless their interface is overhauled. Apps specifically designed for iOS 7 will have an edge in the market because:

• **Users** will come to expect apps that fit in with the iOS 7 environment.

• **The press** won't want to cover apps that look old.

• **Apple** will be more likely to feature apps that embrace their new design principles.

The best designers don't merely follow trends; they need to create apps that feel comfortable in the environment in which they're used — in this case, that's iOS 7. This will be tricky, since iOS 7 is the most opinionated version of iOS ever released. It even feels limiting in some ways; things that you were free to do before — heavily stylized buttons, rich metaphors, and the like — just don't fit in any more.

A cynic would imagine the App Store a year from now, filled with apps that look essentially the same except for their color — flat, textureless, and boring:

That was sort of how I felt when I first encountered iOS 7. Since then, I have become quite optimistic about the future of design in Apple's latest offering in the following ways:

- **New focus:** The whole point in stripping down the visuals is to focus on the content and interactions. That's something you don't always get from glancing at the screenshots.

- **Diversity will come:** The best iOS 7 apps will *not* simply mimic the look of apps like Settings and Calendar. The best apps will use the new design language as a starting point and then innovate on top of that, just as the best apps did in iOS 6. As the platform matures, so will the visual diversity in apps.

So let's unpack this thing together and discover what constitutes a great app in iOS 7.

The key to iOS 7 design: focus

FOCUS

As I began to design apps for iOS 7, I tried to think about what word ties everything together. I would now say that the key word is *focus*.

Contrary to popular belief, iOS 7 is not about flat design; it contains a surprising number of non-flat elements and is in fact *more* three-dimensional than previous versions of iOS in many ways. Instead, iOS 7 is about removing distractions to focus on the three key concepts Apple uses to describe their new design philosophy:

1. **Clarity:** focus on the basics of graphic design to deliver focused functionality

2. **Deference:** focus on content

3. **Depth:** focus on the interactions

These fundamental concepts drive much of the structure of this chapter as I believe the best iOS 7 apps will take these three principles and interpret them in their own unique way.

Focus on function

Great app design starts long before taking out your sketchbook or firing up Photoshop; instead, it starts with the question "Who is this app for — and what problem does it solve?"

App definition statement

An app definition statement is just what it sounds like: a one-sentence definition of who the app is for and what it does for them.

For my app, Hours, the statement went something like this:

"An app for professional business people to take the pain out of keeping track of their billable hours."

Or, simply, *"Taking the pain out of time tracking."*

An app that does everything is an app that does nothing

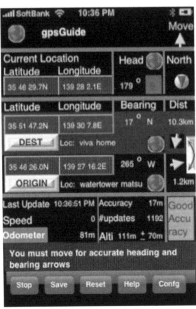

This kind of statement helps you focus on solving one problem really well. If you can't come up with one sentence that describes the essence of your app, your app is probably too big and will end up being impossible to implement well — and even harder for users to understand and share with their friends.

An app designed for everyone is an app designed for no one

A design statement also saves us from the trap of designing for "everyone". When you design for everyone, you design for no one. But if you design with one particular group of people in mind and make sure that it works really well for them, chances are it will also work for other groups of people, since empathizing with a particular group breeds thoughtful design.

Use this statement as a litmus test for every feature, button, and interaction in your app — if it doesn't work towards the goal set in your definition statement, kill it.

Focus on the basics

Since iOS 7 de-emphasizes heavy user interface elements such as rich textures, gradients, and chrome, you need to make sure you nail the basic principles of graphic design as that's pretty much all you have to work with. Steven Bradley puts it thusly:

"The thing is when you strip away the skeuomorphic ornamentation and realism, what you're left with is the fundamentals. Unfortunately too many flat designs focused solely on the flat and skipped the part about fundamental design principles."

Let's not fall into that trap. While I can't adequately cover all the fundamentals of design, I can at least talk about some basic graphic design principles to get you started.

Contrast

Contrast is the visual difference between two elements; this could be through color, texture, or other elements of style. The text on the left has high contrast because the color of the text is very different than the color of the background, making it very visible. The text on the right has very low contrast with its background, making it nearly invisible. Notice how your eye is automatically drawn to the box on the left. The drawing power of high contrast elements should be used to advantage in your designs.

Contrast is a very powerful tool and must be used discriminately. If there are too many high contrast elements on the screen, the user's eye won't know where to go.

Contrast can be used for:

- **Highlighting:** Call out the elements that matter the most for the task at hand and de-emphasize the less important elements.
- **Eye candy:** Provide visual vibrancy and weight to the design as a whole.
- **State:** Show which elements are active or can be tapped.
- **Readability:** Ensure that text is easy to read.

Take a look at the screenshot below. There is obviously something amiss in the user interface; but what *exactly* is wrong — and how you would fix it?

Jot down anything you notice that seems off about this design before you keep reading. Hint: it has to do with contrast!

Here is an annotated version of the screenshot with the problems I noticed:

It is unclear which block is active since they both bear the same visual weight.

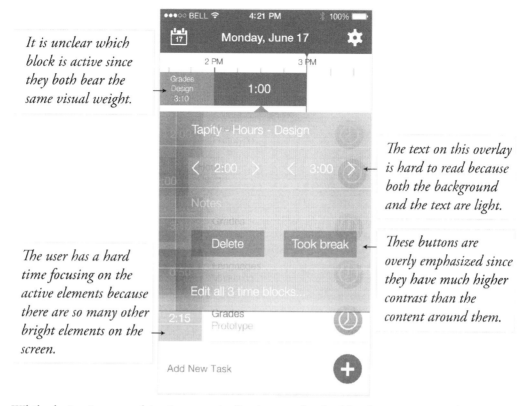

The text on this overlay is hard to read because both the background and the text are light.

The user has a hard time focusing on the active elements because there are so many other bright elements on the screen.

These buttons are overly emphasized since they have much higher contrast than the content around them.

While design is very subjective, certain fundamental rules like the proper use of contrast, are very objective and should never be broken.

The next page shows another version of the same design that has contrast applied appropriately:

We have desaturated the color of the inactive block to make it clear which block is active.

We have raised the contrast (and thus, the readability) of the text by darkening the background. This higher contrast also draws the users eye to this part of the screen.

By putting a dark overlay above the inactive content, we keep the user focused on the content that matters and make it clear that the elements below cannot be interacted with right now.

Ahh…that looks much better! This new design is much more aesthetic, professional — and functional.

Repetition

Repetition is just what it sounds like: the same object or style repeating itself. If two things are related, they should share a similar visual style. A UI that lacks repetition will look confusing because humans use patterns to make sense of the world.

Again, take a look at the following screenshot. Yes, it looks unprofessional, but why?

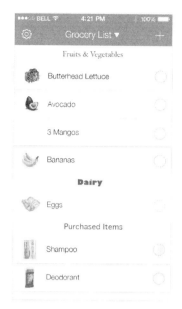

As before, jot down anything you notice that seems off before reading on. Hint: it has a lot to do with repetition!

Here is an annotated version of the screenshot with the problems I noticed:

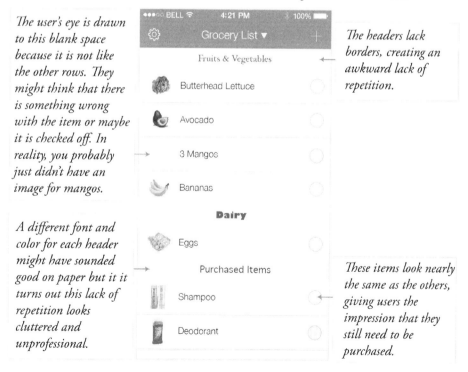

The user's eye is drawn to this blank space because it is not like the other rows. They might think that there is something wrong with the item or maybe it is checked off. In reality, you probably just didn't have an image for mangos.

The headers lack borders, creating an awkward lack of repetition.

A different font and color for each header might have sounded good on paper but it it turns out this lack of repetition looks cluttered and unprofessional.

These items look nearly the same as the others, giving users the impression that they still need to be purchased.

This screen has some repetition so it doesn't *completely* confuse users, but it lacks professionalism and looks disorganized at first glance.

Adding a little repetition goes a long way:

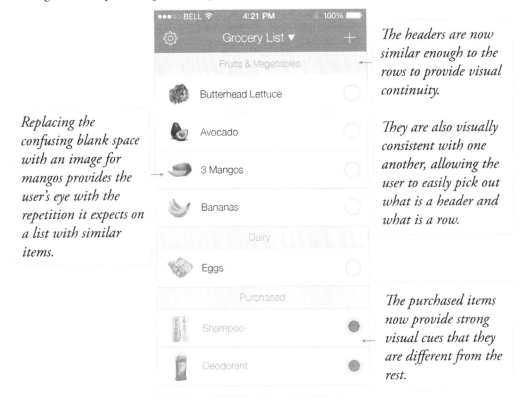

Replacing the confusing blank space with an image for mangos provides the user's eye with the repetition it expects on a list with similar items.

The headers are now similar enough to the rows to provide visual continuity.

They are also visually consistent with one another, allowing the user to easily pick out what is a header and what is a row.

The purchased items now provide strong visual cues that they are different from the rest.

Appropriate use of repetition makes this app much easier to skim visually and pull out the required information — not to mention much more professional looking in general.

Alignment

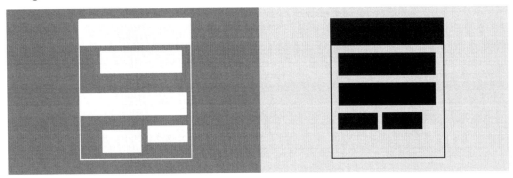

Alignment is about lining up objects with each other to visually connect them in a coherent way. This is one of the areas that *any* programmer would do well to study up on because alignment errors are probably the most common issues I see when programmers implement design.

The basic idea of alignment is that no element should ever be placed on the screen arbitrarily; every element should be visually connected to at least one other element. This could mean one of two things:

• **Edge alignment:** one or more edges line up vertically or horizontally.

• **Center alignment:** centers line up vertically or horizontally.

Take a look at the screenshot below and see if you can identify some alignment issues (you may find it useful to print this out and draw lines):

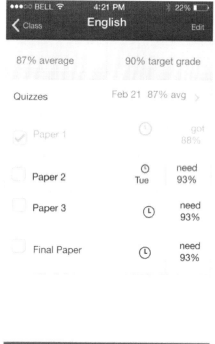

From a distance, the screen above might look okay, but if you look closely, you'll notice that the errors in alignment make the screen look disheveled and amateurish.

Here's what I came up with:

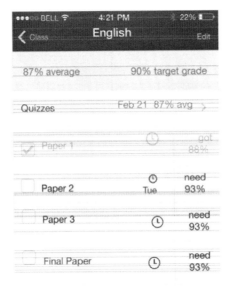

The red lines indicate horizontal alignment. Most elements on the screen are not precisely aligned to any other element, resulting in an unhealthy number of lines. What makes matters worse is that the lines don't seem to have any consistent pattern or equal spacing.

This line exercise is tremendously helpful, especially when you're just beginning to hone your eyes to pixel perfect alignment. If your vertical or horizontal alignment looks like the example above, don't fret — alignment isn't rocket science. A few pixel nudges here and there and voila:

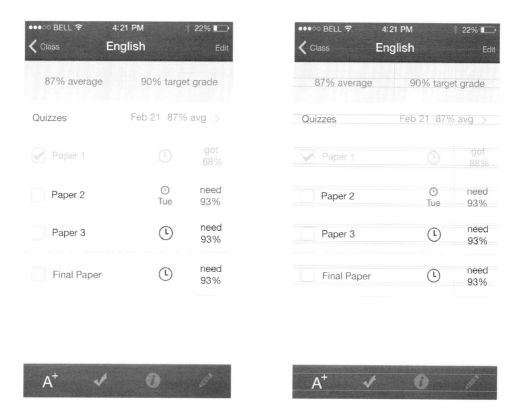

Notice how the properly aligned design not only has far fewer red lines but also spaces the lines in even patterns that will be easy on the eyes of users.

Proximity

Proximity says that if elements are related, they should be close together. If elements are not related, they should be farther apart on the screen.

Developers are often very concerned about using the screen as efficiently as possible and filling up every pixel of the screen with *stuff*. While this might be efficient, it also generates a confusing mess because whitespace — the space on the screen without *stuff* — is your most powerful tool for organizing elements into logical sections, helping your user to effortlessly make sense of the content.

See if you can identify the proximity issues on the screen below:

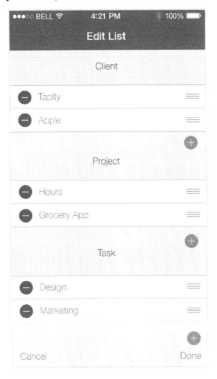

Here's what I came up with:

It's clear that improper proximity of unrelated items can make things very confusing. How would you solve these problems? Here's my take at a solution, although there are always lots of different ways to solve design issues:

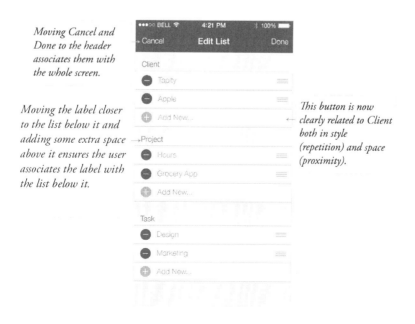

The functions of the elements of an app are far clearer when everything is grouped properly!

Typography

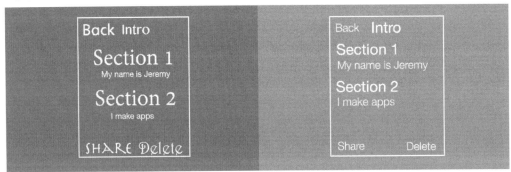

In iOS 7's minimalistic aesthetic, typography takes center stage and can even be a defining factor in your app's personality. Steve Jobs famously made typography a core design consideration way back in the original Macintosh system; that legacy continues at Apple and in iOS today.

Here are some general rules of thumb to consider when using typography in your app:

• **Use a maximum of three font styles.** A font style is a combination of font-family, such as Times or Helvetica, color, size, and modifiers like bold and italic. Don't use more than two or three font styles on one screen and try to stick to three or four styles in your whole app to maintain consistency.

• **Use centered text sparingly.** Sometimes you absolutely need to center text, such as on the Navigation Bar title, but as a rule of thumb it's best to avoid it whenever possible. Text layouts that are left- or right-justified generally look more professional.

• **Keep your font choices simple.** Fonts like **Impact** have their place, but super stylized fonts generally don't lend themselves to legible user interfaces.

• **Plan ahead for resizing of text.** The Dynamic Type feature of iOS 7 permits users to scale the system-wide text size using the Settings app. Be sure to test your app with all font sizes available to users and be sure to offer the optimal experience for each one. To learn more, see Chapter 5, "Beginning Text Kit".

• **Use serif fonts for large blocks of text.** Fonts such as Georgia or Times New Roman have little embellishments or serifs on most of the letters and help draw the reader's eye along the text. Generally, if you have a lot of text in a single block, serif fonts make the text much more readable.

- **Use sans serif fonts for small amounts of text.** Sans serif fonts like Helvetica Neue, Apple's preferred font in iOS 7, don't have embellishments on letters; they look cleaner and lend themselves well to smaller pieces of text such as headings and controls.

- **Use contrasting font-families on the same screen.** If you use Helvetica Neue in your app, don't use Calibri on the same screen; they're far too similar and look like visual errors to the user. If you are going to be using two different font families on the same screen, make them very different.

- **Use variations of one font-family on the same screen.** If your primary font is very versatile — such as Helvetica Neue — you can stick to that one font most of the time and just use variations such as light, **bold**, *italic,* and varying colors and sizes to accomplish your typographical goals.

Although that's a sizeable list of things to keep in mind, it barely scratches the surface of typography. Your overarching goal is **consistency**; your app will *feel* wrong if the font sizes are inconsistent or only some headings are bolded. Your use of typography should add to the character of your app and help convey the content — without getting in the way.

What is wrong with the typography on the screen below?

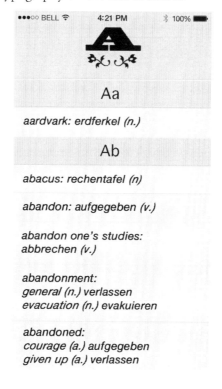

Here are some of my thoughts:

This font dominates the screen. Too big, bold, and crazy.

This sans serif font is close enough to Helvetica to look similar but different enough to look like a mistake.

Bold and italics should never be used for the main font.

Helvetica doesn't fit with the classic paper background.

The word and definition blend together because they are the same font style.

Here is my proposed solution:

The size keeps the look of a heading without dominating the screen.

Now all fonts are just variations of Baskerville, giving the app a more coherent feel.

Baskerville, a serif font, works much better with the textured background and compliments the classic feel.

Words and definitions are now distinguished by different font-styles, making it much easier to skim.

This app has become far prettier and more usable just by changing the typography.

At this point, you've learned about the five basics of design: contrast, repetition, alignment, proximity, and typography. Remember – focusing on the basics is especially important in iOS 7, because when you strip away the ornamentation, the design basics and the user's content are all that's left.

To learn more about these basic design principles, I highly recommend *The Non-Designers Design Book* by Robin Williams.

Focus on the content

One of the fundamental tenets of iOS 7 design is what Apple calls *deference*: de-emphasizing the chrome around the content in order to emphasize the content itself. This seems like a no-brainer but is actually quite tricky to get right – so we're dedicating a large portion of this chapter to this topic.

Remove unnecessary details

Great design is more about subtraction than addition. While cool ideas are important, it is often more important — and exponentially more difficult — to kill those cool ideas in order to keep the app focused.

De-emphasize chrome

"Chrome" refers to the bits of your app that aren't part of the content themself, such as the navigation bar and the tab bar. iOS 7 greatly discourages the use of chrome, with some apps even going so far as to remove it altogether. When reducing the amount of chrome in your design, consider the following points:

Is chrome needed?

Reconsider if you even really *need* chrome in the first place. Could the content *be* the navigation?

Apple's Reminders app removes all signs of chrome, allowing the user to navigate with the content alone. Instead of tapping a back button, users tap on the bottom deck of cards to go back a level; the animation of the cards make this new navigation paradigm easy to understand.

Use simple backgrounds

Instead of heavy textures, use simple, transparent backgrounds that hint at the content underneath; Apple's frosted glass effect is a really nice example of this. Play with color variations or subtle textures to add uniqueness or branding to your chrome.

Apple tends to make the chrome in their iOS 7 apps the same color as the app's primary background in an attempt to make the chrome disappear. This may work in some cases but keep in mind that doing this could very well have the opposite effect because it causes the chrome to visually blend with the content, making it harder distinguish the two. When chrome and content look the same, they both look equally as important – defeating the purpose of hiding the chrome. In other words, a contrasting background for chrome may not always be a bad thing.

Notice how the Status Bar is always blended with the Navigation Bar; always strive to blend these two elements together in a tasteful way.

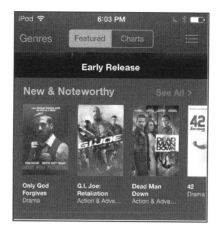

Hide the chrome when possible

Think about ways that you can hide any chrome that isn't being used. Safari uses this to great advantage, as it's an example of an app where you want the user to be intensely focused on the content and not be distracted by the navigation UI.

Safari in iOS 7 hides its already minimal chrome as you begin to scroll down a website (left) and reveals it again when you scroll up or tap the top bar (right).

Simplify UI elements

iOS 7 challenges you to question every background, texture, shadow and border. The idea is to eliminate any unnecessary ornamentation so the user can focus on the elements that really matter. While ornamentation can be useful, using it sparingly will help your apps feel more at home in iOS 7.

Because iOS 7 interfaces tend to be so minimal, any extra visual weight such as gradients, borders, or realistic detail draws tremendous attention; therefore use these elements only when you need to call out certain items by giving them a bolder visual treatment.

Borderless buttons

My initial reaction to Apple's directive to design borderless buttons was an emphatic "No!". However, it turns out that borderless buttons work really well in certain places, such as navigation bars. In a simplified navigation bar background, borders just add visual noise and are unnecessary — as long as you make it clear which elements can be tapped or interacted with. Apple typically uses color to indicate interactivity on the navigation bar; I'll cover that in more depth a little later on.

Most buttons and widgets below the navigation bar still generally require borders to differentiate between interactive and non-interactive items, as shown below:

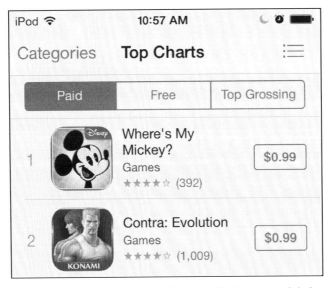

The borders Apple uses in iOS 7 tend to be thin but distinct. Apple's buttons generally use transparent backgrounds for their unselected state and simple colored backgrounds for their selected state. Experiment with things such as border weight, background color, transparency, the radius of the rounded corners, or subtle shadows and textures when seeking a unique button style for your app.

Using color to indicate interactivity

Apple mentions the use of color to indicate interactivity in an app. This works on occasion, such as in the navigation bar, but even Apple is inconsistent in applying this principle so take it with a heavy grain of salt. For example, in the Clock app below, the red color on the navigation bar indicates that the Edit and + buttons are interactive, but on the tab bar the red color instead indicates which tab is selected:

Apple uses color to indicate interactivity in an attempt to make it clear what is and isn't interactive without using borders around buttons. However, don't feel obliged to follow this rather inconsistent guideline if the interactivity of your app's elements is clear — even without the use of color.

Minimize realistic details and skeuomorphism

A mockup (left) of how the popular *Limelight* app (right) might look in iOS 7

I've read enough design arguments about skeuomorphism to cover a few lifetimes, so I won't open that can of worms too far. However, I do want to crack the lid ever so slightly and talk about the role of skeuomorphism in iOS design.

What is skeuomorphism? Well, there's quite a bit of debate on that topic. To put it simply, skeuomorphism takes design cues from the real world and applies them to your digital designs.

Skeuomorphism is by no means absent in iOS 7. For example, the buttons in iOS 7 are still skeuomorphs even without their familiar gradients and glares, as buttons are elements that exist in the real world.

iOS 7 re-vamps skeuomorphic elements by de-emphasizing realistic details like faux leather, gradients, and shadows. Mind you, it doesn't eliminate them altogether! The light look and feel of iOS 7 means that apps with a heavy-looking UI such as Grades or Tweetbot will have a hard time fitting in. However, I'm quite sure that the hit iOS 7 apps will contain plenty of textures, metaphor, and realism; they'll just look quite different from the heavily detailed apps of iOS 6.

Skeuomorphism is one of the many tools in a designer's toolbox. It isn't going away; you'll just have to explore new ways of using it in this minimalistic environment.

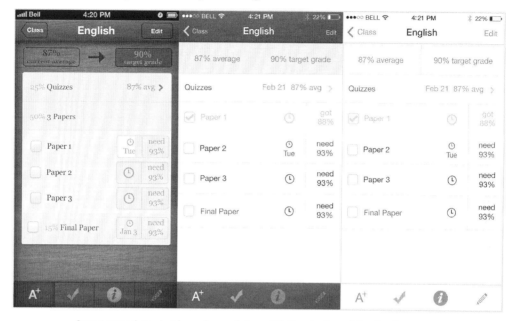

Some experiments I have been doing with the design of Grades for iOS 7.

The best apps will find a sweet spot between the old, heavily detailed styles, and the new minimalist look; you can still maintain a sense of uniqueness with subtle visuals without going overboard.

Make content king

Now that you have de-emphasized the UI, how can you emphasize the content?

Use the whole screen

Avoid unnecessary UI elements that only serve to frame the content; you want to give your content as much room as possible so that it takes center stage in your app.

Make the content define the screen

Yahoo's weather app does a great job at defining the entire feel of the app based on the current weather using gorgeous photography. Apple's blurred glass effect is perfect for allowing the graphical content to shine through the whole screen.

The various screens of Yahoo's weather app, where the content defines the design.

Make it visually interesting

The station art in iTunes Radio changes perspective as you scroll it across the screen. iOS 7 minimizes overbearing visual UI in order to maximize content — so take the opportunity to make your content visually interesting.

iTunes Radio eschews flashy UI elements, and instead adds embellishment to the content itself.

Focus on interactions

App design is about to undergo a radical shift in direction. Previously, apps could stand out based on eye-popping visuals. But with iOS 7, photorealistic wood, buttons that pop out of the screen, and rich icons are a lot less relevant.

So how do you stand out on iOS 7? How do you create an app with a delightful personality without mind-blowing graphics? In short, app design in the new paradigm will be less about how your app looks and a lot more about how it works and feels. I think the de-emphasis of visuals in iOS 7 will generate a renaissance of innovation in touch interaction design.

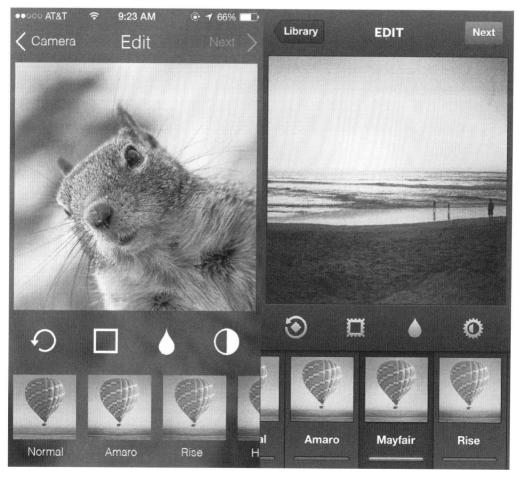

Juxtaposing the unofficial Instagram for iOS 7 mockup (left) next to Instagram for iOS 6 (right) highlights the use of much simpler visuals.

Simpler visuals make it easier to quickly experiment with novel animations, transitions, and interaction patterns, as resizing and morphing simple shapes is at least a thousand times easier than dealing with textures and bevels. The next round of standout apps will leverage that one feature alone to create interactions you've never experienced before.

Touch is magic

Touch is magic: it tricks you into thinking that you are manipulating physical objects instead of moving pixels around a screen. Apple knows this fact well; it's why the very first iPhone had 1:1 scrolling and bouncy effects.

A computer can be cold, but making that computer a window into a physical world that the user can manipulate creates friendly, familiar, and immersive experiences. However, any lag or hiccup in the delivery of that experience immediately shatters the illusion; the magic show ends with a puff of smoke.

Didn't iOS 7 kill metaphor and realistic details? Actually, no, it didn't. While the prominence of realistic visuals is discouraged, realism is strongly encouraged through user interaction and dynamic physical effects. In fact, iOS 7 has a physics engine built in for the sole purpose of creating interfaces that feel more "real".

Great design will happen a lot less frequently in Photoshop and a lot more often in tools like Xcode and Quartz Composer; these tools allow you to explore how the app *feels*, not just how it looks.

Direct manipulation

Direct manipulation is the idea of performing functions in real-time by interacting with objects on the screen, rather than tapping a button in one place and seeing the result in another. Swiping to scroll, pinching to zoom, and dragging and dropping objects are all examples of direct manipulation.

iOS 7 Photos doesn't have the arrow buttons anymore to move between photos; instead, the natural swipe action alone takes care of that task.

When looking through pictures, which feels more natural and satisfying — tapping the arrow button or swiping the current picture over to see the next one? To ask the question is to answer it. Humans are very tactile creatures — successful designers create interfaces that reflect that.

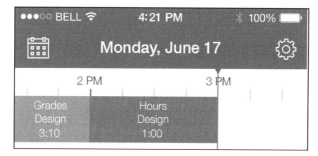

Realism extends to the way that people visualize data. People visualize time as a linear, connected entity, not as disparate items in a list.

Realistic interfaces require objects for the user to manipulate, so you need to turn your abstract functions into physical objects. For example, my team had to think about how we were going to represent time entries in our Hours app. Instead of representing time as entries in a list, Hours treats time as a physical block on a timeline. This makes it easier to visualize — and manipulate — the individual time elements.

Physics and animation

What a shame it would have been for Apple to nail 1:1 scrolling but not follow through with the inertia and bounciness you have come to know and love. Direct manipulation goes hand in hand with physics and animation; the goal is to make the interactions feel *real*.

In the future, apps that neglect physics will quickly feel stale and static. UI designers have only begun to explore the use of physics in touch user interfaces, but here are several ideas to get you started:

The iOS 7 lock screen will bounce differently based on how high it is when you let it go

- **Dynamics:** Instead of thinking about digital animations, think in terms of physical principles. When you push a ball on a physical surface it doesn't start at one speed and maintain that speed until it reaches its destination. Instead, the ball accelerates as you begin pushing it and then decelerates as friction brings it to a stop. When an object falls 10 feet it bounces higher than it would if it fell two feet. Your interface should behave the same way; fortunately, Apple's new UIKit Dynamics API makes this easy for you. To learn more, check out Chapter 3, "UIKit Dynamics and Motion Effects".

- **Continuity:** Instead of thinking about each screen as a clean slate, start thinking about which items should persist from screen to screen and how you can realistically animate them from one state to the next through actions such as moving, resizing, zooming, or morphing.

- **Bounciness:** It's not just for scrolling anymore. Depending on how flexible you want your digital objects to feel, bounciness could add a fun playful touch. When an object expands, does it expand linearly from one size to another or does it expand to be a little oversized, based on the momentum of the animation, then shrink back down to the final size? When you zoom in, do you zoom in a little further than necessary and then bounce back a bit? This animated GIF illustrates bounciness in my app Hours: http://tapity.com/quartz-composer-key-to-ios-7-design/

Working in three dimensions

Ironically, the OS that people are calling "flat" is turning out to be the most three-dimensional of all. Despite pulling back on three-dimensional effects like bevels and shines, one of the three main guiding principles of iOS 7 is **depth**.

Depth can take a few forms:

3D Effects

The addition of parallax effects make it it clear that Apple wants you to show off the three-dimensionality of your app through interesting visual effects. You can see parallax effects at work when you tilt the screen and the perspective of the UI changes relative to the degree of tile, or when the station art changes perspective as you scroll through station art in iRadio.

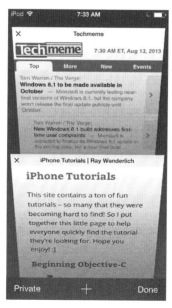

Parallax adds a level of dimensionality to interfaces by responding to the physical orientation of the device.

To learn more about adding parallax effects to your app, check out Chapter 3, "UIKit Dynamics and Motion Effects".

Layers

Tilt your iPhone and you will see that the icons are not actually sitting on the background — the parallax effect reveals they're floating above it instead. Bring up Control Center and the frosted glass makes it very apparent that Control Center is a layer above all the icons. Think about your interface in layers and use 3D effects to make the purpose of the layers clear to your user.

The frosted-glass effect provides a subtle layering effect to Control Center.

Zooming user interfaces

It's evident from the way the screen zooms into apps when you tap their icon, to the way Photos zooms into years, then collections, then moments, then photos, that Apple has fully embraced the zooming interface paradigm. They've made it incredibly easy to do so in your apps as well. I think some of the coolest UI innovation will come from developers who experiment with this concept and take it to a level not yet dreamed of.

The zooming interface paradigm is alive and well in iOS 7; tapping an icon zooms in to the appropriate application.

Gestures and navigation

Apps like Clear have only scratched the surface of using touch to navigate apps. Clear eliminated nearly all of the UI and replaced it with swipe and pinch gestures; it's quite fun to use once you learn the appropriate gestures.

Clear: where gestures are the UI.

However, some functions might not map well to gestures; unnatural gestures are hard to remember and no fun to use. Also, users are likely to forget unfamiliar gestures for apps that aren't used at least daily. Experiment with gestures and include them where it makes sense, but don't arbitrarily make buttons the enemy in favor of control-free gesture-driven UI.

iOS 7 introduced a new pattern: swipe to go back. You can still tap the back button but swiping can be a lot easier, especially on the iPhone 5's taller screen.

While there are some exceptions, gestures can be compared to keyboard shortcuts. They can make life more convenient for the power user who knows them, but generally they shouldn't be the only way to do something.

Personality

To stand out, your iOS 7 app must have a unique and delightful personality. Looks are still important, but how the app feels and works is equally, if not more, critical in defining the personality of your app.

In addition, an app's personality can be developed through:

- **Audio:** Audio is a vast, unexplored territory with a few pioneers like Tapbots, who include subtle clicks and beeps in their apps.
- **Words:** Who would have thought an error message could make someone's day? Witty or humorous copy can be one of the best ways to exude personality.
- **Icons:** Your app's icon is generally the first impression the user has of your app. Since it lives in digital perpetuity on the user's home screen, it's worth the investment in time and energy to get it right. The icon should capture the app's personality in miniature.

Personality really comes down to all the little details that turn a good app into a great one. The drive to perfect every pixel, optimize every interaction, and sprinkle the app with thoughtful touches, from delightful animations to witty error messages; these are the things that turn good apps into great apps.

Check out littlebigdetails.com for lots of great "little details" that make a big difference in the overall user experience. Charming users gets harder with every digital generation; apps with winning personalities are the apps that become blogged about, talked about, read about, and most importantly — downloaded.

Make a dent in the universe

"Not going to lie. iOS7 has made me really excited about work again. Really cool stuff in the pipeline (at least I think so)."

— Mark Jardine, designer of Tweetbot

This is possibly the most exciting time in years to be an app designer. As Marco Arment pointed out, the App Store is fertile ground again. This radical design shift means that the next few years will see a new crop of top apps in each category. These apps will put a unique twist on Apple's principles of clarity, deference, and depth to create user interfaces no one has ever seen before.

The best part of this is that **you** could create these apps! No, it won't be easy pickings. Yes, the competition will be fierce. But now is a better time than any to buckle down and pour your blood, sweat, and tears into something great, something that maybe — just maybe — will let you make your own dent in the universe.

Challenges

For the first time in our iOS by Tutorials series, we are including one or more challenges at the end of each chapter.

We have tried to make each challenge short and simple, and we provide you with step-by-step hints along the way. We highly recommend you do these challenges – it's a great way to practice what you learned in the chapter.

This chapter just has one challenge – to take an iOS 6 app, and redesign it for iOS 7. Enjoy!

Challenge 1: Redesign this app!

The screenshot below shows an iOS 6 app. It's in pretty poor shape and needs your help:

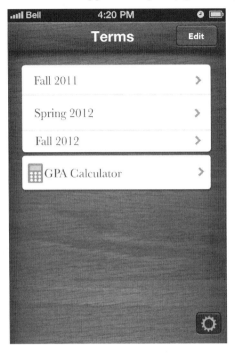

Your challenge is to apply everything you have learned about contrast, repetition, alignment, proximity, typography and Apple's new design principles to not only fix this app's issues, but redesign it for iOS 7.

You have lots of choices on how to redesign the app. You can use Xcode itself, a program like Photoshop, or simply with a piece of paper and some colored pencils.

Before you start on your new design, try to identify all the problems with the original design. Here are a few hints to get you started:

• Do you notice any issues with alignment?

• Are related concepts grouped together?

• Would any of the "rules of thumb" of typography apply here?

• What would the app look like if ornamentation was removed?

The resources for this chapter include the solution I came up with, but note that design is by its very nature wholly subjective; there's no single solution to this challenge. When you're done, be sure to visit the book's forums to share and compare your solutions with others: http://www.raywenderlich.com/forums

Chapter 2: UIKit Dynamics and Motion Effects

By Colin Eberhardt

You have probably come to realize that iOS 7 is something of a paradox; while you're being encouraged to do away with real-world metaphors and skeuomorphism, Apple encourages you at the same time to create user interfaces that *feel* real.

What does this mean in practice? The design goals of iOS 7 encourage you to create digital interfaces that react to touch, gestures, and changes in orientation as if they were physical objects far beyond a simple collection of pixels. The end result gives the user a deeper connection with the interface than is possible through skin-deep skeuomorphism.

This sounds like a daunting task, as it is much easier to make a digital interface *look* real, than it is to make it *feel* real. However, you have some nifty new tools on your side: UIKit Dynamics and Motion Effects.

UIKit Dynamics is a full physics engine integrated into UIKit. It allows you to create interfaces that feel real by adding behaviors such as gravity, attachments (springs) and forces. You define the physical traits that you would like your interface elements to adopt, and the dynamics engine takes care of the rest.

Motion Effects allows you to create cool parallax effects like you see when you tilt the iOS 7 home screen. Basically you can harness the data supplied by the phone's accelerometer in order to create interfaces that react to changes in phone orientation.

When used together, motion and dynamics form a powerhouse of user experience tools that make your digital interfaces come to life. Your users will connect with your app at a deeper level by seeing it respond to their actions in a natural, dynamic way.

Getting started

UIKit dynamics can be a lot of fun; the best way to start learning about them is to jump in feet-first with some small examples.

Open Xcode, select **File / New / Project ...** then select **iOS\Application\Single View Application** and name your project **DynamicsPlayground**. Once the project has been created, open **ViewController.m** and add the following code to the end of viewDidLoad:

```
UIView* square = [[UIView alloc] initWithFrame:
                                CGRectMake(100, 100, 100, 100)];
square.backgroundColor = [UIColor grayColor];
[self.view addSubview:square];
```

The above code simply adds a square UIView to the interface.

Build and run your app, and you'll see a lonely square sitting on your screen, as shown below:

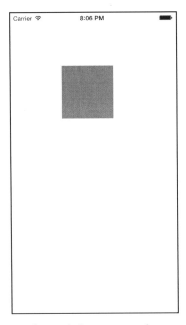

If you're running your app on a physical device, try tilting your phone, turning it upside-down, or even shaking it. What happens? Nothing? That's right — everything is working as designed. When you add a view to your interface you expect it to remain firmly stuck in place as defined by its frame — until you add some dynamic realism to your interface!

Adding gravity

Still working in **ViewController.m,** add the following instance variables:

```
UIDynamicAnimator* _animator;
UIGravityBehavior* _gravity;
```

Add the following to the end of `viewDidLoad`:

```
_animator = [[UIDynamicAnimator alloc]
                            initWithReferenceView:self.view];

_gravity = [[UIGravityBehavior alloc] initWithItems:@[square]];
[_animator addBehavior:_gravity];
```

I'll explain this in a moment. For now, build and run your application. You should see your square slowly start to accelerate in a downward motion until it drops off the bottom of the screen, as so:

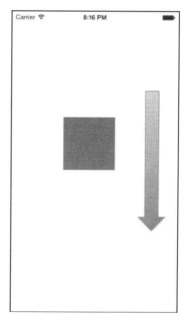

In the code you just added, there are a couple of dynamics classes at play here:

- `UIDynamicAnimator` is the UIKit physics engine. This class keeps track of the various behaviors that you add to the engine, such as gravity, and provides the overall context. When you create an instance of an animator, you pass in a reference view that the animator uses to define its coordinate system.

- UIGravityBehavior models the behavior of gravity and exerts forces on one or more items, allowing you to model physical interactions. When you create an instance of a behavior, you associate it with a set of items — typically views. This way you can select which items are influenced by the behavior, in this case which items the gravitational forces affect.

Most behaviors have a number of configuration properties; for example, the gravity behavior allows you to change its angle and magnitude. Try modifying these properties to make your objects fall up, sideways, or diagonally with varying rates of acceleration.

> **NOTE:** A quick word on units: in the physical world, gravity (g) is expressed in meters per second squared and is approximately equal to 9.8 m/s^2. Using Newton's second law, you can compute how far an object will fall under gravity's influence with the following formula:
>
> **distance = 0.5 × g × time^2**
>
> In UIKit Dynamics, the formula is the same but the units are different. Rather than meters, you work with units of thousands of pixels per second squared. Using Newton's second law you can still work out exactly where your view will be at any time based on the gravity components you supply.
>
> Do you really need to know all this? Not really; all you really need to know is that a bigger value for **g** means things will fall faster, but it never hurts to understand the math underneath.

Setting boundaries

Although you can't see it, the square continues to fall even after it disappears off the bottom of your screen. In order to keep it within the bounds of the screen you need to define a *boundary*.

Add another instance variable in **ViewController.m**:

```
UICollisionBehavior* _collision;
```

Add these lines to the bottom of viewDidLoad:

```
_collision = [[UICollisionBehavior alloc]
                              initWithItems:@[square]];
_collision.translatesReferenceBoundsIntoBoundary = YES;
```

```
[_animator addBehavior:_collision];
```

The above code creates a collision behavior, which defines one or more boundaries with which the associated items interact.

Rather than explicitly adding boundary co-ordinates, the above code sets the `translatesReferenceBoundsIntoBoundary` property to YES. This causes the boundary to use the bounds of the reference view supplied to the `UIDynamicAnimator`.

Build and run; you'll see the square collide with the bottom of the screen, bounce a little, then come to rest, as so:

That's some pretty impressive behavior, especially when you consider just how little code you've added at this point.

Handling collisions

Next up you'll add an immovable barrier that the falling square will collide and interact with.

Insert the following code to `viewDidLoad` just after the lines that add the square to the view:

```
UIView* barrier = [[UIView alloc]
                    initWithFrame:CGRectMake(0, 300, 130, 20)];
barrier.backgroundColor = [UIColor redColor];
[self.view addSubview:barrier];
```

Build and run your app; you'll see a red "barrier" extending halfway across the screen. However, it turns out the barrier isn't that effective as the square falls straight through the barrier:

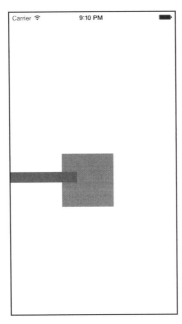

That's not quite the effect you were looking for, but it does provide an important reminder: dynamics only affect views that have been associated with behaviors.

Time for a quick diagram:

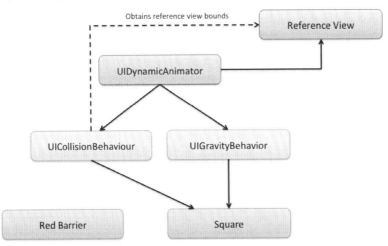

`UIDynamicAnimator` is associated with a reference view that provides the coordinate system. You then add one or more behaviors that exert forces on the items they are associated with. Most behaviors can be associated with multiple items, and each item can be associated with multiple behaviors. The above diagram shows the current behaviors and their associations within your app.

Neither of the behaviors in your current code is "aware" of the barrier, so as far as the underling dynamics engine is concerned, the barrier doesn't even exist.

Making objects respond to collisions

To make the square collide with the barrier, find the line that initializes the collision behavior and replace it with the following:

```
_collision = [[UICollisionBehavior alloc]
                            initWithItems:@[square, barrier]];
```

The collision object needs to know about every view it should interact with; therefore adding the barrier to the list of items allows the collision object to act upon the barrier as well.

Build and run your app; the two objects collide and interact, as shown in the following screenshot:

The collision behavior forms a "boundary" around each item that it's associated with; this changes them from objects that can pass through each other into something more solid.

Updating the earlier diagram, you can see that the collision behavior is now associated with both views:

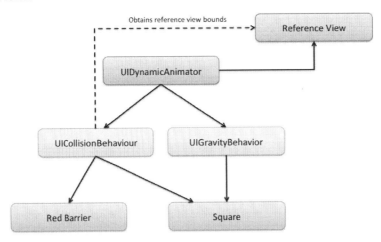

However, there's still something not quite right with the interaction between the two objects. The barrier is supposed to be immovable, but when the two objects collide in your current configuration the barrier is knocked out of place and starts spinning towards the bottom of the screen.

Even more oddly, the barrier bounces off the bottom of the screen and doesn't quite settle down like the square – this makes sense because the gravity behavior doesn't interact with the barrier. This also explains why the barrier doesn't move until the square collides with it.

Looks like you need a different approach to the problem. Since the barrier view is immovable, there isn't any need to for the dynamics engine to be aware of its existence. But how will the collision be detected?

Invisible boundaries and collisions

Change the collision behavior initialization back to its original form so that it's only aware of the square:

```
_collision = [[UICollisionBehavior alloc]
                               initWithItems:@[square]];
```

Next, add a boundary as follows:

```
// add a boundary that coincides with the top edge
CGPoint rightEdge = CGPointMake(barrier.frame.origin.x +
                               barrier.frame.size.width,
```

```
                                    barrier.frame.origin.y);
    [_collision addBoundaryWithIdentifier:@"barrier"
                                fromPoint:barrier.frame.origin
                                  toPoint:rightEdge];
```

The above code adds an invisible boundary that coincides with the top edge of the
barrier view. The red barrier remains visible to the user but not to the dynamics engine,
while the boundary is visible to the dynamics engine but not the user. As the square falls,
it appears to interact with the barrier, but it actually hits the immovable boundary line
instead.

Build and run your app to see this in action, as below:

The square now bounces off the boundary, spins a little, and then continues its journey
towards the bottom of the screen where it comes to rest.

By now the power of UIKit Dynamics is becoming rather clear: you can accomplish
quite a lot with only a few lines of code. There's a lot going on under the hood; the next
section shows you some of the details of how the dynamic engine interacts with the
objects in your app.

Behind the scenes of collisions

Each dynamic behavior has an `action` property where you supply a block to be executed with every step of the animation. Add the following code to `viewDidLoad`:

```
_collision.action = ^{
    NSLog(@"%@, %@",
        NSStringFromCGAffineTransform(square.transform),
        NSStringFromCGPoint(square.center));
};
```

The above code logs the `center` and `transform` properties for the falling square. Build and run your app, and you'll see these log messages in the Xcode console window.

For the first ~400 milliseconds you should see log messages like the following:

```
2013-07-26 08:21:58.698 DynamicsPlayground[17719:a0b] [1, 0, 0,
1, 0, 0], {150, 236}
2013-07-26 08:21:58.715 DynamicsPlayground[17719:a0b] [1, 0, 0,
1, 0, 0], {150, 243}
2013-07-26 08:21:58.732 DynamicsPlayground[17719:a0b] [1, 0, 0,
1, 0, 0], {150, 250}
```

Here you can see that the dynamics engine is changing the center of the square in each animation step and that an identity transform is applied.

As soon as the square hits the barrier, it starts to spin, which results in log messages like the following:

```
2013-07-26 08:21:59.182 DynamicsPlayground[17719:a0b]
[0.10679234, 0.99428135, -0.99428135, 0.10679234, 0, 0], {198,
325}
2013-07-26 08:21:59.198 DynamicsPlayground[17719:a0b]
[0.051373702, 0.99867952, -0.99867952, 0.051373702, 0, 0], {199,
331}
2013-07-26 08:21:59.215 DynamicsPlayground[17719:a0b] [-
0.0040036771, 0.99999201, -0.99999201, -0.0040036771, 0, 0],
{201, 338}
```

Here you can see that the dynamics engine is using a combination of a transform and a frame offset to position the view according to the underlying physics model.

While the exact values that dynamics applies to these properties are probably of little interest, it's important to know that they are being applied. As a result, if you programmatically change the `frame` or `transform` properties of your object, you can expect that these values will be overwritten. This means that you can't use a transform to scale your object while it is under the control of dynamics.

The method signatures for the dynamic behaviors use the term *items* rather than *views*. The only requirement to apply dynamic behavior to an object is that it adopts the UIDynamicItem protocol, as so:

```
@protocol UIDynamicItem <NSObject>

@property (nonatomic, readwrite) CGPoint center;
@property (nonatomic, readonly) CGRect bounds;
@property (nonatomic, readwrite) CGAffineTransform transform;

@end
```

The UIDynamicItem protocol gives dynamics read and write access to the center and transform properties, allowing it to move the items based on its internal computations. It also has read access to bounds, which it uses to determine the size of the item. This allows it to create collision boundaries around the perimeter of the item as well as compute the item's mass when forces are applied.

This protocol means that dynamics is not tightly coupled to UIView; indeed there is another UIKit class that adopts this protocol – UICollectionViewLayoutAttributes. This allows dynamics to animate items within collection views.

Collision notifications

So far you have added a few views and behaviors then let dynamics take over. In this next step you will look at how to receive notifications when items collide.

Open **ViewController.m** and adopt the UICollisionBehaviorDelegate protocol:

```
@interface ViewController () <UICollisionBehaviorDelegate>

@end
```

Within viewDidLoad, set the view controller as the delegate just after the collision behavior has been instantiated, as follows:

```
_collision.collisionDelegate = self;
```

Next, add an implementation for one of the collision behavior delegate methods:

```
- (void)collisionBehavior:(UICollisionBehavior *)behavior
         beganContactForItem:(id<UIDynamicItem>)item
```

```
                    withBoundaryIdentifier:(id<NSCopying>)identifier
                             atPoint:(CGPoint)p {
      NSLog(@"Boundary contact occurred — %@", identifier);
  }
```

This delegate method is fired when a collision occurs and prints out a log message to the console. In order to avoid cluttering up your console log with lots of messages, feel free to remove the _collision.action logging you added in the previous section..

Build and run; your objects will interact, and you'll see the following entries in your console:

```
2013-07-26 08:44:37.473 DynamicsPlayground[18104:a0b] Boundary
contact occurred — barrier
2013-07-26 08:44:37.689 DynamicsPlayground[18104:a0b] Boundary
contact occurred — barrier
2013-07-26 08:44:38.256 DynamicsPlayground[18104:a0b] Boundary
contact occurred — (null)
2013-07-26 08:44:38.372 DynamicsPlayground[18104:a0b] Boundary
contact occurred — (null)
2013-07-26 08:44:38.455 DynamicsPlayground[18104:a0b] Boundary
contact occurred — (null)
2013-07-26 08:44:38.489 DynamicsPlayground[18104:a0b] Boundary
contact occurred — (null)
2013-07-26 08:44:38.540 DynamicsPlayground[18104:a0b] Boundary
contact occurred — (null)
```

From the log messages you can see that the square collides twice with the boundary identifier barrier; this is the invisible boundary you added earlier. The (null) identifier refers to the reference view boundary.

These log messages can be fascinating reading (seriously!), but it would be much more fun to provide a visual indication when the item bounces.

Below the line that sends message to the log, add the following:

```
UIView* view = (UIView*)item;
view.backgroundColor = [UIColor yellowColor];
[UIView animateWithDuration:0.3
              animations:^{
    view.backgroundColor = [UIColor grayColor];
}];
```

The above code changes the background color of the colliding item to yellow, and then fades it back to gray again.

Build and run to see this effect in action:

The square will flash yellow each time it hits a boundary.

So far UIKit Dynamics has automatically set the physical properties of your items (such as mass or elasticity) by calculating them based on your item's bounds. Next up you'll see how you can control these physical properties yourself by using the `UIDynamicItemBehavior` class.

Configuring item properties

Within `viewDidLoad`, add the following to the end of the method:

```
UIDynamicItemBehavior* itemBehaviour =
        [[UIDynamicItemBehavior alloc] initWithItems:@[square]];
itemBehaviour.elasticity = 0.6;
[_animator addBehavior:itemBehaviour];
```

The above code creates an item behavior, associates it with the square, and then adds the behavior object to the animator. The `elasticity` property controls the bounciness of the item; a value of 1.0 represents a completely elastic collision; that is, where no energy or velocity is lost in a collision. You've set the elasticity of your square to 0.6, which means that the square will lose velocity with each bounce.

Build and run your app, and you'll notice that the square now behaves in a bouncier manner, as below:

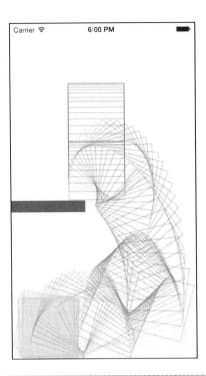

> **Note:** If you are wondering how I produced the above image with trails that show the previous positions of the square, it was actually very easy! I simply added a block to the `action` property of one of the behaviors, and every fifth time the block code was executed, added a new square to the view using the current `center` and `transform` from the square.

In the above code you only changed the item's elasticity; however, the item's behavior class has a number of other properties that can be manipulated in code. They are as follows:

- `elasticity` – determines how 'elastic' collisions will be, i.e. how bouncy or 'rubbery' the item behaves in collisions.

- `friction` – determines the amount of resistance to movement when sliding along a surface.

- `density` – when combined with size, this will give the overall mass of an item. The greater the mass, the harder it is to accelerate or decelerate an object.

- `resistance` – determines the amount of resistance to any linear movement. This is in contrast to friction, which only applies to sliding movements.

- angularResistance - determines the amount of resistance to any rotational movement.

- allowsRotation – this is an interesting one that doesn't model any real-world physics property. With this property set to **NO** the object will not rotate at all, regardless of any rotational forces that occur.

Adding behaviors dynamically

In its current state, your app sets up all of the behaviors of the system, then lets dynamics handle the physics of the system until all items come to rest. In this next step, you'll see how behaviors can be added and removed dynamically.

Open **ViewController.m** and add the following instance variable:

```
BOOL _firstContact;
```

Add the following code to the end of the collision delegate method
collisionBehavior:beganContactForItem:withBoundaryIdentifier:atPoint:

```
if (!_firstContact)
{
    _firstContact = YES;

    UIView* square = [[UIView alloc]
                      initWithFrame:CGRectMake(30, 0, 100, 100)];
    square.backgroundColor = [UIColor grayColor];
    [self.view addSubview:square];

    [_collision addItem:square];
    [_gravity addItem:square];

    UIAttachmentBehavior* attach = [[UIAttachmentBehavior alloc]
                        initWithItem:view
                                      attachedToItem:square];
    [_animator addBehavior:attach];
}
```

The above code detects the initial contact between the barrier and the square, creates a second square and adds it to the collision and gravity behaviors. In addition, you set up an attachment behavior to create the effect of attaching a pair of objects with a virtual spring.

Build and run your app; you should see a new square appear when the original square hits the barrier, as shown on the next page:

While there appears to be a connection between the two squares, you can't actually see the connection as a line or spring since nothing has been drawn on the screen to represent it.

Dynamics in real world apps

At this point in the chapter you might be under the impression that dynamics are intended for physics simulations and games. In reality, they're not.

Apple provides an entire framework designed to make 2D games called Sprite Kit that includes its own physics engine. In fact, we wrote a whole book about Sprite Kit called *iOS Games By Tutorials* – check it out if you'd like to learn more.

UIKit Dynamics is really designed for non-game applications, such as email, sports and news apps. The dynamic effects you have created so far are pretty gratuitous and would look out of place in these types of apps. Dynamics should be reserved for effects that are altogether more subtle.

The SandwichFlow app

For the rest of this chapter, you'll be working with a simple sandwich recipe application (nom!) that uses a standard table view "hub" layout. You can find the starter project in the resources for the chapter. Open it in Xcode and build and run, and you'll see the following:

Your job is to update the app to present users with the recipes stacked at the bottom of the screen. They can pull up on a recipe to take a peek at it, and when they release the recipe, it will either drop back into the stack, or dock to the top of the screen. The end result is an application with a real-world physical feel.

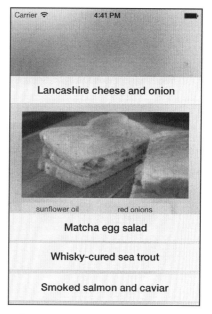

Open the starter project and take a little time to familiarize yourself with the existing codebase. The application is quite simple and makes use of Storyboards. A `UITableViewController` lists the sandwich recipes as the starting screen for the application. When a sandwich is tapped, it triggers a segue showing the recipe as a modal view controller.

Creating a custom dynamic view

The dynamic version of the application won't use a `UITableViewController` as the initial view controller; instead, it will use your custom dynamic view. The easiest way to make this change is to add a new view controller to the application.

Open **Main.storyboard** and drop a new view controller onto the storyboard:

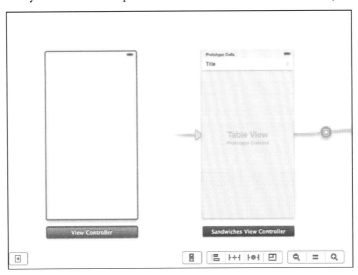

Next create a new class named `DynamicSandwichViewController` and make it a subclass of `UIViewController`. Open the newly created **DynamicSandwichViewController.m** file and update `viewDidLoad` as follows:

```
- (void)viewDidLoad
{
    [super viewDidLoad];

    // Background image
    UIImageView* backgroundImageView = [[UIImageView alloc]
      initWithImage:
        [UIImage imageNamed:@"Background-LowerLayer.png"]];
    [self.view addSubview:backgroundImageView];

    // Header logo
    UIImageView* header = [[UIImageView alloc]
      initWithImage:[UIImage imageNamed:@"Sarnie.png"]];
```

```
        header.center = CGPointMake(220, 190);
        [self.view addSubview:header];
    }
```

The above code adds a background and the sandwich image to the view controller.

The final step is to associate the view controller you added to the storyboard with this class. Open the storyboard once again and select your new view controller. In the Identity inspector, set the Custom Class to DynamicSandwichViewController, as shown below:

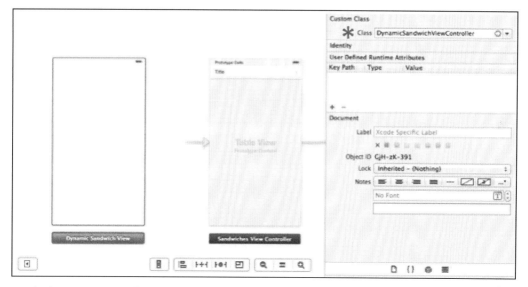

With the view controller still selected, open the Attributes inspector and check the **Is Initial View Controller** property.

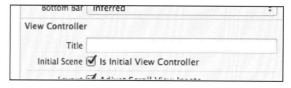

It's time to test these changes. Build and run your app, and you should see an all-new starting screen.

Adding the recipe view controllers

The new interface will display a stack of recipes at the bottom of the screen. In this next step you will create a view controller instance for each recipe and add it to the view.

You'll re-use the current sandwich recipe view controller, but in order to access it from your code, you need to add an identifier.

Open the storyboard and select the Sandwich View Controller. Switch to the Identity Inspector, and set the value of the **Storyboard ID** property to **SandwichVC**, as shown below:

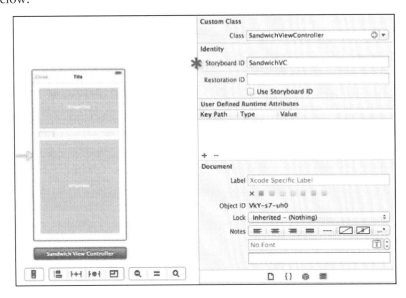

This allows you to use the `SandwichVC` identifier to access the view controller from code.

Delete the **Close** bar button from the navigation bar as well since later on you'll be replacing this action with gestures.

Open **DynamicSandwichViewController.m** and add the following imports to the top of the file:

```
#import "SandwichViewController.h"
#import "AppDelegate.h"
```

Still in the same file, add the following instance variable:

```
NSMutableArray* _views;
```

You'll use this variable to keep track of the added views. This is easier than having to iterate over all of the subviews in order to find those that you are interested in.

Add the following method to the view controller:

```
- (NSArray*)sandwiches
{
    AppDelegate* appDelegate = (AppDelegate*)
                    [[UIApplication sharedApplication] delegate];
    return appDelegate.sandwiches;
}
```

This is a simple convenience method for retrieving the sandwiches from the app delegate.

Next, add the following method:

```
- (UIView*)addRecipeAtOffset:(CGFloat)offset
            forSandwich:(NSDictionary*)sandwich {

    CGRect frameForView = CGRectOffset(self.view.bounds, 0.0,
                    self.view.bounds.size.height - offset);

    // 1. create the view controller
    UIStoryboard *mystoryboard = [UIStoryboard
                    storyboardWithName:@"Main" bundle:nil];
    SandwichViewController* viewController = [mystoryboard
        instantiateViewControllerWithIdentifier:@"SandwichVC"];
```

```
    // 2. set the frame and provide some data
    UIView* view = viewController.view;
    view.frame = frameForView;
    viewController.sandwich = sandwich;

    // 3. add as a child
    [self addChildViewController:viewController];
    [self.view addSubview:viewController.view];
    [viewController didMoveToParentViewController:self];

    return view;
}
```

This method adds a recipe to the screen at the given offset location. Consider each step of its implementation in turn:

1. Create a `SandwichViewController` instance. Notice that this uses the `SandwichVC` identifier you set earlier.

2. Set the frame of this recipe and the supply the sandwich data.

3. Add the view controller as a child and to the view.

The final step is to iterate over the recipes and use the above method to add each recipe to the view.

Within the same file, add the following code to the end of `viewDidLoad`:

```
_views = [NSMutableArray new];
CGFloat offset = 250.0f;
for (NSDictionary* sandwich in [self sandwiches]) {
    [_views addObject:[self addRecipeAtOffset:offset
                                  forSandwich:sandwich]];

    offset -= 50.0f;
}
```

This iterates over the list of sandwiches and adds a view for each one at the given offset. The hard-coded offsets aren't ideal, but a savvy developer like you can certainly use that as an exercise to find a better alternative! :]

Build and run your app; you should see the list of recipes as below:

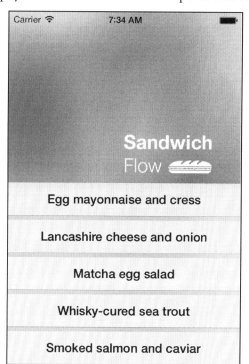

Adding some menu dynamics

Now that the re-structuring of your app is complete, you can get on with the important job of implementing dynamics in your UI.

Open **DynamicSandwichViewController.m** and add the following instance variables:

```
UIGravityBehavior* _gravity;
UIDynamicAnimator* _animator;
CGPoint _previousTouchPoint;
BOOL _draggingView;
```

There are quite a few of these; some will be familiar, and some won't. You'll discover what each one is used for as you add more code.

Add the following code to `viewDidLoad` just before the code you added earlier that adds the recipes:

```
_animator = [[UIDynamicAnimator alloc]
```

```
                                  initWithReferenceView:self.view];

_gravity = [[UIGravityBehavior alloc] init];
[_animator addBehavior:_gravity];
_gravity.magnitude = 4.0f;
```

This adds the dynamic animator and adds a gravity behavior. The `magnitude` of `gravity` is set to 4.0, making items fall more slowly than the default value of 1.0.

Next, add the following code to the end of `addRecipeAtOffset:forSandwich:`, just before the return statement:

```
// 1. add a gesture recognizer
UIPanGestureRecognizer* pan = [[UIPanGestureRecognizer alloc]
                               initWithTarget:self
                               action:@selector(handlePan:)];
[viewController.view addGestureRecognizer:pan];

// 2. create a collision
UICollisionBehavior* collision = [[UICollisionBehavior alloc]
                                  initWithItems:@[view]];
[_animator addBehavior:collision];

// 3. lower boundary, where the tab rests
CGFloat boundary = view.frame.origin.y +
                                    view.frame.size.height+1;
CGPoint boundaryStart = CGPointMake(0.0, boundary);
CGPoint boundaryEnd = CGPointMake(self.view.bounds.size.width,
                                  boundary);
[collision addBoundaryWithIdentifier:@1
                           fromPoint:boundaryStart
                             toPoint:boundaryEnd];
// 4. apply some gravity
[_gravity addItem:view];
```

Taking each step in turn, you perform the following actions:

1. Create a pan gesture recognizer associate it with the view. The `handlePan:` message is sent when a pan occurs. You'll add this method shortly.

2. Create a collision behavior for this view so it doesn't go into immediate free fall.

3. Create a boundary where this specific view controller will come to rest. It is based on the bottom edge of the current view location.

4. Finally, apply the gravity behavior to the view.

The net result of this code is that if the view associated with this view controller is moved from its current location, it will fall under the influence of gravity, eventually coming to rest at its original location.

Now to add the code that makes it move!

Within **DynamicSandwichViewController.m** add the following method to handle the pan gesture:

```
- (void)handlePan:(UIPanGestureRecognizer*)gesture {
    CGPoint touchPoint = [gesture locationInView:self.view];
    UIView* draggedView = gesture.view;

    if (gesture.state == UIGestureRecognizerStateBegan) {
        // 1. was the pan initiated from the top of the recipe?
        CGPoint dragStartLocation = [gesture
                                    locationInView:draggedView];
        if (dragStartLocation.y < 200.0f) {
            _draggingView = YES;
            _previousTouchPoint = touchPoint;
        }

    } else if (gesture.state == UIGestureRecognizerStateChanged
              && _draggingView) {
        // 2. handle dragging
        CGFloat yOffset = _previousTouchPoint.y - touchPoint.y;
        gesture.view.center = CGPointMake(draggedView.center.x,
                                draggedView.center.y - yOffset);
        _previousTouchPoint = touchPoint;

    } else if (gesture.state == UIGestureRecognizerStateEnded
              && _draggingView) {
        // 3. the gesture has ended
        [_animator updateItemUsingCurrentState:draggedView];
        _draggingView = NO;
    }
}
```

This method deals with various gesture states — hence the if-else blocks. Look at each branch in turn:

1. When the gesture begins, check if the pan was initiated near the top of the view. If so, set a flag so later gestures will know there's a pan and drag in progress. In your own apps, you might want to replace this hard-coded value of 200 points with a value derived from the view's layout.

2. If a drag is in progress, use the difference in Y locations between the previous and the current touches to offset the view's center, making it move.

3. The final case is when the drag finishes. The vital step here is messaging the animator with `updateItemUsingCurrentState`. This message informs the dynamics engine that the item state has changed and that it must update its own representation. This is similar to sending `setNeedsDisplay` to a `UIView` subclass.

Build and run your app; try to drag a recipe up the screen, and it should follow your drag action, as shown below:

Let go of the recipe, and it will fall back into place with a cute little bounce at the end.

The effect you added certainly provides a bit of realism to the application. However, there's something missing: if you rapidly swipe a view upwards, it simply falls back to the bottom of the screen once you release it. If these were real objects you should be able to 'throw' them upwards with a rapid swipe.

Time to make this app a bit more real!

Transferring velocity to dynamics

In order to achieve this effect, you need to transfer the gesture's velocity into a velocity within dynamics.

Add the following code to the end of `addRecipeAtOffset:forSandwich:`, just before the return statement:

```
UIDynamicItemBehavior* itemBehavior =
        [[UIDynamicItemBehavior alloc] initWithItems:@[view]];
[_animator addBehavior:itemBehavior];
```

This adds a dynamic item behavior for each of the recipe views. Recall from the previous section that `UIDynamicItemBehavior` allows you to change the physical properties of a dynamic item.

You'll need a way to retrieve the specific item behavior for a view when it is thrown. Add the following method to the same file:

```
- (UIDynamicItemBehavior*) itemBehaviourForView:(UIView*)view {
    for (UIDynamicItemBehavior* behaviour in
                            _animator.behaviors) {
        if (behaviour.class == [UIDynamicItemBehavior class]
            && [behaviour.items firstObject] == view) {
            return behaviour;
        }
    }
    return nil;
}
```

This iterates over the behaviors until it finds the one with the correct type (`UIDynamicItemBehavior`) associated with the given view.

The item velocity needs to be updated when the gesture ends. Add the following code to `handlePan:` just before the `updateItemUsingCurrentState:` message is sent to the animator:

```
[self addVelocityToView:draggedView fromGesture:gesture];
```

Finally, still in **DynamicSandwichViewController.m** add the following method implementation:

```
- (void)addVelocityToView:(UIView*)view
            fromGesture:(UIPanGestureRecognizer*)gesture {
    CGPoint vel = [gesture velocityInView:self.view];
    vel.x = 0;
    UIDynamicItemBehavior* behaviour =
                            [self itemBehaviourForView:view];
    [behaviour addLinearVelocity:vel forItem:view];
}
```

This takes the gesture velocity, removes the X component (you don't want those recipes flying off sideways!), locates the item behavior, and then adds the velocity to the behavior.

Fortunately, the gesture velocity is expressed in points per second, which is the same units used by dynamics — no unit conversions make for happy developers!

Build and run your app, and try to throw the recipes up with a fast swiping motion to see if they "stick":

You may have noticed that you can hurl recipes right off the top of the screen. Don't worry about that for now – you'll be fixing that shortly.

Docking views

While it is a lot of fun throwing those recipes around, your users are probably getting hungry and just want to snap the recipe to the top of the screen and get on with making their sandwich.

Add the following instance variables to **DynamicSandwichViewController.m**:

```
UISnapBehavior* _snap;
BOOL _viewDocked;
```

UISnapBehavior does what is says on the tin, and performs a "snap to point" similar to dragging items around Interface Builder. When the user releases a recipe that has been dragged, you need to determine whether the recipe has been dragged far enough in order to dock it. That state is stored in the boolean `_viewDocked`.

Add the following code to `handlePan:` in the final `else` `if` block, just before the call to `addVelocityToView:fromGesture:`

```
[self tryDockView:draggedView];
```

The above code executes the `tryDockView:` method each time the user stops dragging the view.

Next, add the following method:

```
- (void)tryDockView:(UIView *)view {
    BOOL viewHasReachedDockLocation =
                               view.frame.origin.y < 100.0;
    if (viewHasReachedDockLocation) {
        if (!_viewDocked) {
            _snap = [[UISnapBehavior alloc]
                            initWithItem:view
                          snapToPoint:self.view.center];
            [_animator addBehavior:_snap];
            [self setAlphaWhenViewDocked:view alpha:0.0];
            _viewDocked = YES;
        }
    } else {
        if (_viewDocked) {
            [_animator removeBehavior:_snap];
            [self setAlphaWhenViewDocked:view alpha:1.0];
            _viewDocked = NO;
        }
    }
}
```

This method checks whether the view has been dragged close to the top of the screen. If it has, and the view is not yet docked, it creates a `UISnapBehaviour` which snaps the view to the center of the screen.

If the view has been dragged away from the top of the screen and was previously docked, the code removes the snap behavior.

Add the following method to **DynamicSandwichViewController.m**:

```
- (void)setAlphaWhenViewDocked:(UIView*)view
                        alpha:(CGFloat)alpha {
    for (UIView* aView in _views) {
```

```
      if (aView != view) {
          aView.alpha = alpha;
      }
    }
  }
```

This is used to show and hide the non-docked views so that the docked recipe occupies the entire screen without being obscured by the recipes below.

Build and run your app; try docking and un-docking the recipes by dragging them close to the top of the screen and then back down, as below:

There's one final tweak required for the dynamics: the code that determines whether a view should be docked checks the Y location of the view after the gesture ends. However, if you 'throw' a view, the gesture may end *before* this point, but the view continues moving and eventually reaches this point by itself.

How are you going to detect whether a view is thrown beyond the dock location?

You could add a code block to the `action` property of one of the behaviors and repeatedly test the location at each animation step, but this sounds a bit messy. It would be much better if you could receive a message when the view passes the dock location.

Catching thrown views

Fortunately there is an easy way to do this!

In **DynamicSandwichViewController.m** add the following code to
addRecipeAtOffset:forSandwich:, just after the first boundary has been added to
the collision behavior and before gravity is added:

```
boundaryStart = CGPointMake(0.0, 0.0);
boundaryEnd = CGPointMake(self.view.bounds.size.width, 0.0);
[collision addBoundaryWithIdentifier:@2
                          fromPoint:boundaryStart
                            toPoint:boundaryEnd];
collision.collisionDelegate = self;
```

The above code creates a boundary at the top of the screen, gives it an identifier of **2** and
assigns the collision delegate to the view controller.

At the top of the same file adopt the UICollisionBehaviorDelegate via the view
controller's class extension:

```
@interface DynamicSandwichViewController ()
                              <UICollisionBehaviorDelegate>

@end
```

Finally implement the delegate method as follows:

```
- (void)collisionBehavior:(UICollisionBehavior *)behavior
      beganContactForItem:(id<UIDynamicItem>)item
   withBoundaryIdentifier:(id<NSCopying>)identifier
                  atPoint:(CGPoint)p {
  if ([@2 isEqual:identifier]) {
      UIView* view = (UIView*) item;
      [self tryDockView:view];
  }
}
```

A collision will invoke the delegate method above. This checks whether a boundary with
the identifier "2" is involved in the collision and if so, docks the recipe item.

Build and run your app; throw a view up to the top of the screen but make the gesture
stop short of the top of the screen and let the momentum of the action carry the view to
the top of the screen. Feel the physics power!

Motion effects

The final effect to explore in this chapter is from a completely different set of brand new UIKit APIs – motion effects.

Motion effects allow you to create user interfaces such as the parallax effect on the iOS 7 home screen where the background moves as the device is rotated. Typically motion effects are used in subtle ways in the background.

For your SandwichFlow application, you'll replace the background image with two images that slide over each other as the device orientation changes. Grab an iOS device to test this feature on so you experience the full effect.

Open **DynamicSandwichViewController.m** and remove the code in `viewDidLoad` that adds the background and logo images. Replace it with the following:

```objc
// 1. add the lower background layer
UIImageView* backgroundImageView = [[UIImageView alloc]
                initWithImage:[UIImage
                    imageNamed:@"Background-LowerLayer.png"]];
backgroundImageView.frame =
                CGRectInset(self.view.frame, -50.0f, -50.0f);
[self.view addSubview:backgroundImageView];
[self addMotionEffectToView:
                            backgroundImageView magnitude:50.0f];


// 2. add the background mid layer
UIImageView* midLayerImageView = [[UIImageView alloc]
  initWithImage:[UIImage imageNamed:@"Background-MidLayer.png"]];
[self.view addSubview:midLayerImageView];


// 3. add the foreground image
UIImageView* header = [[UIImageView alloc]
                initWithImage:[UIImage imageNamed:@"Sarnie.png"]];
header.center = CGPointMake(220, 190);
[self.view addSubview:header];
[self addMotionEffectToView:header magnitude:-20.0f];
```

The above code adds a number of images in layers. The easiest way to understand the layering is from the following diagram:

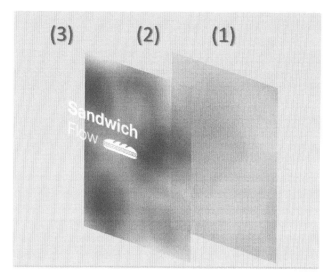

The middle layer (2) doesn't move, but layers (1) and (3) do move since you call the
`addMotionEffectToView:magnitude:` on them.

Add the method below to implement `addMotionEffectToView:magnitude:`

```
- (void)addMotionEffectToView:(UIView*)view
                    magnitude:(CGFloat)magnitude {

    UIInterpolatingMotionEffect* xMotion =
            [[UIInterpolatingMotionEffect alloc]
                    initWithKeyPath:@"center.x"
    type:UIInterpolatingMotionEffectTypeTiltAlongHorizontalAxis];
    xMotion.minimumRelativeValue = @(-magnitude);
    xMotion.maximumRelativeValue = @(magnitude);

    UIInterpolatingMotionEffect* yMotion =
            [[UIInterpolatingMotionEffect alloc]
                    initWithKeyPath:@"center.y"
    type:UIInterpolatingMotionEffectTypeTiltAlongVerticalAxis];
    yMotion.minimumRelativeValue = @(-magnitude);
    yMotion.maximumRelativeValue = @(magnitude);

    UIMotionEffectGroup* group = [[UIMotionEffectGroup alloc]
                                                    init];
    group.motionEffects = @[xMotion, yMotion];

    [view addMotionEffect:group];
}
```

The above code creates a pair of `UIInterpolatingMotionEffect` instances: one that tracks horizontal motion, the other that tracks vertical motion.

In order to create an interpolation effect you specify the keypath to the property that you want to change. You also set the maximum and minimum relative values; these values are passed in on a per-view basis so the background can move in one direction while the logo moves in the other direction.

> **Note:** The motion effect interpolation uses the same implementation as Core Animation, you can interpolate `CGRect`, `CGPoint`, doubles, integers, `UIColor` and more!

Build and run your application, tilt your device to the left and right and watch the parallax effect at work:

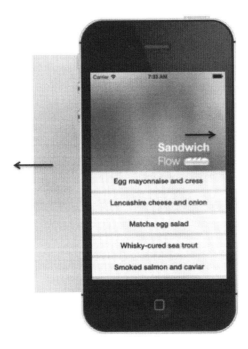

Your application is complete — perhaps you can celebrate by making a sandwich. Hopefully you have had fun playing with dynamics and motion effects and will be able to find novel uses for these features in your own applications.

Challenges

Now it's your turn to exercise your dynamics and motion effects skills with a couple of simple challenges. The solutions for each are provided, although it is worth trying them on your own first.

Challenge 1: Back to earth with a bump!

In the current application, if you pull up one of the recipes, but don't drag it close enough to the top of the screen, the gravity behavior ensures that it falls back to its original location. Each recipe 'rests' on its own collision behavior boundary, and if it falls far enough will bounce a little before it comes to rest.

Wouldn't it be cool if, at the point the recipe comes crashing down, it caused the others to jump just a little. This would give the impression that there is some real 'weight' behind these views.

And that is your challenge! When a recipe is dropped and hits the bottom boundary you need to transfer some of its velocity to the other views.

Here are a few hints to help you get started:

1. The `DynamicSandwichViewController` already has a method that is called when a collision occurs. Currently it is just used to determine when a view hits the top of the screen. This method will also be called when a view hits the bottom boundary (this has an identifier of `@1`).

2. When you have identified that a view has landed back at the bottom of the screen, you can find its velocity at the point of impact via the `UIDynamicItemBehaviour` class. You can than pass on a fraction of that velocity to the other views in order to make them bounce at the point of impact. Why not add a little bit of randomization as well, to make it feel more natural?

That was pretty simple wasn't it? It's actually a lot of fun throwing a recipe downwards to see how high you can make the others bounce when it hits the boundary!

Challenge 2: More motion

Your next challenge involves adding some further motion effects to the application. Currently when the device is tilted the background and SandwichFlow icons move creating a subtle parallax effect.

This challenge is to build on this effect, so that the recipes also move with the device, as illustrated in the image below:

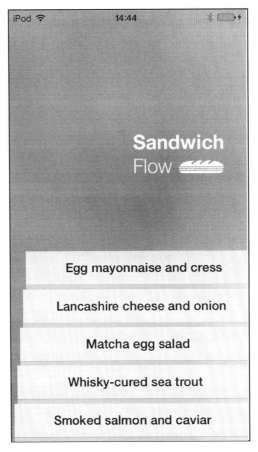

In the above image you can see that as the device is tilted, the top-most recipe moves further than the one at the bottom. As you move the phone around this gives a real sense of depth.

You can actually achieve the above effect with around 5 lines of code, so there are no hints for this challenge, just make use of the `addMotionEffectToView: magnitude:` method which you added earlier in the tutorial.

Chapter 3: Custom View Controller Transitions

By Colin Eberhardt

If you tap an item in the Messages or App Store apps in iOS 7, you'll find that the detail view controller seems to slide over the list view controller, with subtle changes in the overlapped view. Also, you can return to the previous view controller using a swipe gesture, or even pause the navigation halfway, change your mind, and swipe back again!

The good news for developers is that all of this functionality is available to you via new APIs in iOS 7 in the form of custom view controller transitions. You have full control over the animations used in your application as it transitions from one view controller to the next. You can even create your own gesture-driven transitions, called *interactive transitions*.

In this chapter you will get hands-on experience with the new iOS 7 APIs by:

- **Creating a custom present transition**. You will start by creating a very simple transition to presenting a modal view controller.

- **Creating a custom dismiss transition**. You will learn how to create a transition to dismiss the modal view controller as well, learning about of some of the new `UIView` animations such as spring and key frame.

- **Creating a navigation controller transition**. You will learn how to customize the pushing or popping of a view controller from a navigation controller, using a flip transition as an example.

- **Creating an interactive transition**. You will finally learn how to make the transition fully interactive, allowing the user to control the flip with a simple gesture.

It's time to dive straight in with a simple transition ... oh, and I hope you like cats. :]

Getting started

The best way to get started with creating your own transitions is to dive in head first. Unpack the starter project for this chapter in the **ILoveCatz.zip** file and build and run it in Xcode. You should be greeted with the following app:

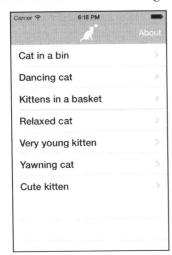  

It's an app about — you've guessed it — cats!

The application is based on the Xcode master-detail template. It is composed of three view controllers: the master page containing a list of cat pictures, the detail page showing the selected cat picture, and an About view presented modally.

The app makes use of storyboards to connect the view controllers. Take a little time to familiarize yourself with the code and the project layout.

A custom present transition

When you tap the About button in the app, the About view appears in the standard modal style of sliding up from the bottom. Your first task is to write a custom transition for this view.

There are three steps to create a custom transition in iOS:

1. **Create the animation controller.** The first step is to create a class that implements the UIViewControllerAnimatedTransitioning protocol. This class contains the code to perform the actual animation, so this class is referred to as the animation controller.

2. **Before presenting a view controller, set its transitioning delegate.** Before you present a view controller, you should set a class as its transitioning delegate (usually the presenting view controller). By doing this the delegate will get a callback asking for the animation controller to use when presenting the view controller.

3. **Return the animation controller in the callback.** Finally, implement the callback method to return an instance of the animation controller you created in step 1.

Let's get started with the first and most important step: creating the animation controller.

Creating the animation controller

Right-click on the **ILoveCatz** group in the project navigator, select **New File...**, and choose **iOS\Cocoa Touch\Objective-C class**. Name the class **BouncePresentAnimationController**, and make it a subclass of **NSObject**.

Open **BouncePresentAnimationController.h** and adopt the UIViewControllerAnimatedTransitioning protocol:

```
@interface BouncePresentAnimationController :
    NSObject <UIViewControllerAnimatedTransitioning>

@end
```

This protocol has two required methods that define your custom animation between view controllers. Later, you'll attach an instance of this class to the storyboard segue.

Open **BouncePresentAnimationController.m** and add the following method to the implementation:

```
- (NSTimeInterval)transitionDuration:
  (id <UIViewControllerContextTransitioning>)transitionContext {
    return 2.0;
}
```

This method specifies the length of the transition animation. In this case you've gone for a relatively sedate two-second animation just to make it obvious.

The `transitionContext` parameter gives you access to the *to* and *from* view controllers, the containing `UIView`, and other bits of context. You could query these properties to animate your transitions differently depending on the view controllers involved, but in this case you're using a two second transition all around.

Next is the animation itself. Add the following method:

```
- (void)animateTransition:
  (id <UIViewControllerContextTransitioning>)transitionContext {

    // 1. obtain state from the context
    UIViewController *toViewController = [transitionContext
  viewControllerForKey:UITransitionContextToViewControllerKey];
    CGRect finalFrame = [transitionContext
                finalFrameForViewController:toViewController];

    // 2. obtain the container view
    UIView *containerView = [transitionContext containerView];

    // 3. set initial state
    CGRect screenBounds = [[UIScreen mainScreen] bounds];
    toViewController.view.frame =
        CGRectOffset(finalFrame, 0, screenBounds.size.height);

    // 4. add the view
    [containerView addSubview:toViewController.view];

    // 5. animate
    NSTimeInterval duration =
                [self transitionDuration:transitionContext];
```

```
      [UIView animateWithDuration:duration
          animations:^{
              toViewController.view.frame = finalFrame;
          } completion:^(BOOL finished) {
              // 6. inform the context of completion
              [transitionContext completeTransition:YES];
          }];
  }
```

There's quite a lot going on here, so consider each step in turn.

1. Using the transition context, retrieve the view controller you're navigating to and the final frame the transition context should have when the animation is completed.

2. The views that correspond to the from- and to- view controllers are hosted within this container view throughout the animation. It's your responsibility to add the to- view to the container view.

3. Position the to- view just below the bottom of the screen.

4. Add the to- view to the container view.

5. Animate the to- view, and set its final frame to the location supplied by the transition context. Note that the animation duration comes from the first protocol method.

6. Inform the transition context when the animation completes. The framework then ensures the final state is consistent and removes the from- view from the container.

There's your first custom animation controller! It performs a two-second animation that slides the new view up from the bottom of the screen. Your next step is to link it to a storyboard segue.

Setting the transitioning delegate

UIViewController has a new property transitionDelegate that supports custom transitions. When transitioning to a view controller, the framework first checks this property to see if a custom transition should be used.

Open **MasterViewController.m** and adopt the UIViewControllerTransitioningDelegate by adding it to the class extension near the top of the file:

```
@interface MasterViewController ()
    <UIViewControllerTransitioningDelegate>

@end
```

This delegate supplies custom transitions; you'll implement the method that performs this task shortly.

Within the same file, add the following to the bottom of `prepareForSegue: sender:`

```
if ([segue.identifier isEqualToString:@"ShowAbout"]) {
    UIViewController *toVC = segue.destinationViewController;
    toVC.transitioningDelegate = self;
}
```

This detects the segue for the About screen by the segue name `ShowAbout` defined in the storyboard and sets the `transitionDelegate` property of the destination view controller.

Continuing with the wire-up process, add the following import to the top of the file:

```
#import "BouncePresentAnimationController.h"
```

This imports your custom animation controller so it's available for use.

A little further down add an instance variable that stores the animation controller:

```
@implementation MasterViewController {
    BouncePresentAnimationController *_bounceAnimationController;
}
```

And just beneath that, add the following initializer method:

```
- (id)initWithCoder:(NSCoder *)aDecoder {
    if (self = [super initWithCoder:aDecoder]) {
        _bounceAnimationController =
                        [BouncePresentAnimationController new];
    }
    return self;
}
```

This ensures that the custom animation controller is available when the storyboard initializes the `MasterViewController`.

You need to implement the `UIViewControllerTransitioningDelegate` method that supplies this animation controller. Add it as shown below:

```
- (id<UIViewControllerAnimatedTransitioning>)
    animationControllerForPresentedController:
                        (UIViewController *)presented
                    presentingController:
```

```
                                   (UIViewController *)presenting
                              sourceController:
                                   (UIViewController *)source {
        return _bounceAnimationController;
   }
```

This method simply returns your custom animation controller instance. If you had multiple view controllers wired up, you could also check the view controller presented to switch between different custom animations. In this case, the only view controller wired up with a delegate is the About one. Build and run your app; tap the About button in the navigation bar and you should see the About view controller slowly slide up from the bottom of the screen, as so:

The two-second custom transition isn't terribly exciting, but hey — it's all your own code!

Don't worry, you'll add something more exciting shortly that makes use of the new animation APIs. Before you get there, you'll need a bit of background first.

The transition APIs

The view controller transitions API is composed of a number of protocols, and just one concrete class. On first glance, the protocol naming can be a bit confusing! In this section you'll learn the responsibilities of each protocol, and walk through the process of a custom transition.

The diagram below shows the protocols and their relationships to each other:

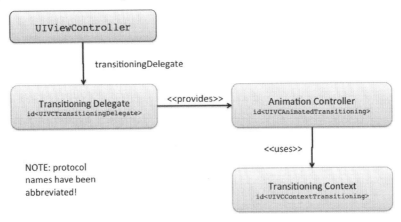

Let's consider each protocol in turn:

- `UIViewControllerTransitioningDelegate` – The transitioning delegate supplies animation controllers and interaction controllers; you'll learn about those a little later on. View controllers have a `transitioningDelegate` property, which holds a reference to an implementation of this delegate. In your ILoveCatz app, the master view controller adopts this delegate.

- `UIViewControllerAnimatedTransitioning` – The animation controllers such as your `BouncePresentAnimationController` adopt this protocol. The two required methods indicate the duration of your custom transition and perform the animation itself.

- `UIViewControllerContextTransitioning` – The context passed into the custom animation methods adopts this protocol; it supplies the information needed to perform a transition. This includes information such as the to- and from- view controllers, the frame that the to- view should have at the end of the transition, the containing view, and more. The animation controller is also responsible for informing the transitioning context that the transition has completed.

> **Note:** You do not need to implement a class that adopts the `UIViewControllerContextTransitioning` protocol; this is a class that the framework supplies to your animation controller.

One of the really useful features of the transitioning context is that it supplies the animation controller with the to- and from- view controllers. This allows you to de-couple the animation controller from the transitioning delegate.

Why is this a good idea? Take a look at the current implementation of `BouncePresentAnimationController`; notice it doesn't have any idea about master view controllers or about view controllers. This frees you to write animation controllers that are re-usable in other projects.

The transition process

Now that you have a better understanding of the classes involved, you can walk through the transition process in detail:

1. Instantiate a view controller transition as the result of a storyboard segue, or a programmatic push / pop / modal presentation.

2. The framework asks the to- view controller for its transitioning delegate.

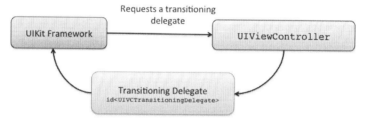

3. If the to- view controller does not have a transitioning delegate, then it uses a standard built-in transition.

4. The framework requests an animation controller for this transition by sending the `animationControllerForPresentedController: presentingController: sourceController:` message to the transitioning delegate. If the delegate returns `nil` it uses built-in transition instead.

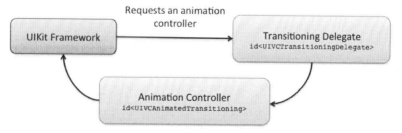

5. If an animation controller is returned, the framework gets ready for the transition and constructs a transitioning context.

6. The framework asks the animation controller how long it will take to perform its transition by sending it the `transitionDuration:` message.

7. Now for the animation! The framework sends the `animateTransition:` message to the animation controller telling it to perform its animation using the supplied transitioning context.

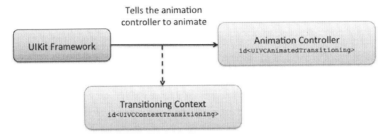

8. When the animation completes, the animation controller sends the `completeTransition:` message to the transitioning context.

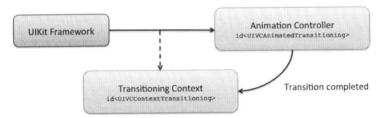

9. On completion of the transition, the framework takes care of ensuring that the view controller and view hierarchies are consistent.

The transition process might seem a bit complicated at first; there's a lot of moving parts here. If you don't fully understand the process right now, don't worry; it will make more sense as you follow this tutorial further.

Now to spice up that two-second transition animation.

Spicing up the transition

The About view slides out from the bottom of the screen, giving the impression that it overlaps and covers the view underneath. You can accentuate this effect by making the from- view fade out slightly.

Open **BouncePresentAnimationController.m** and add the following line directly underneath the line that obtains the to- view controller in `animateTransition:`

```
UIViewController *fromViewController = [transitionContext
```

```
    viewControllerForKey:UITransitionContextFromViewControllerKey];
```

This simply grabs a reference to the from- view controller.

Next, update the animation block a little further down the same method, replacing the current single line with the following two:

```
    fromViewController.view.alpha = 0.5;
    toViewController.view.frame = finalFrame;
```

This animates the from- view controller's alpha as well as the frame of the to- view controller.

Build and run your app; tap the About button and watch the from- view controller subtly fade out as it is covered by the to- view controller:

That's a bit more interesting. However, it probably won't take you long to spot a bit of an issue.

When you dismiss the view by hitting the OK button you will notice that the list of cats is still faded out:

Whoops. What's going on here?

When the transition is complete, the from- view controller remains within the view controller hierarchy; however, its view is removed from the view hierarchy.

When the transition is reversed, the view associated with the previous from- view controller is restored. The framework has no way of knowing that you changed the alpha, so it is your responsibility to change it back.

Fortunately this is easily fixed. Add the following line to the animation completion block, just before the call to completeTransition: on the transitioning context:

```
fromViewController.view.alpha = 1.0;
```

Now when you dismiss the About screen, the list of cats will be back to normal.

The transition is looking a little better, but there are a few new UIView animation methods in iOS 7 that are crying out to be used.

Still within the same method, replace the entire UIView animation call with the following:

```
[UIView animateWithDuration:duration
```

```
                       delay:0.0
    usingSpringWithDamping:0.6
     initialSpringVelocity:0.0
                     options:UIViewAnimationOptionCurveLinear
                  animations:^{
        // set the state to animate to
        fromViewController.view.alpha = 0.5;
        toViewController.view.frame = finalFrame;
    } completion:^(BOOL finished) {
        // inform the context of completion
        fromViewController.view.alpha = 1.0;
        [transitionContext completeTransition:YES];
    }];
```

The exact same properties are being animated, but this time you're using the new
UIView "using spring" animation. This animation allows you to easily create bouncy
animations that feel natural.

> **Note:** If you like bouncy animations or the words *spring* and *damping* make your
> eyes light up, check out Chapter 2, "UIKit Dynamics and Motion Effects."

The damping parameter defines how bouncy the animation will be – basically the higher
the value, the bouncier. A value less than 1.0 causes the view to 'overshoot' its final
position and oscillate. Setting a value equal or greater than 1.0 causes the view to
smoothly decelerate to its final position without oscillating.

Before running and admiring your handiwork, you should reduce the transition
duration to make it a bit snappier. Still working in the same file, replace
transitionDuration: as follows:

```
- (NSTimeInterval)transitionDuration:
  (id <UIViewControllerContextTransitioning>)transitionContext {
    return 0.5;
}
```

This reduces the transition duration to 0.5 seconds.

Build and run your app, bring up the About view, and watch it bounce around:

Admittedly, static pictures don't really do justice to transitions — especially bouncy kitten transitions! :]

A custom dismiss transition

Just like the UIViewControllerTransitioningDelegate allows you to specify an animation controller when *presenting* a view controller, it also allows you to specify an animation controller to use when *dismissing* a view controller.

In this section, you will customize the transition used when the about view is dismissed. In the process, you will learn about two new features in iOS 7: key frame animations, and UIView snapshotting.

The basic process will be quite similar to what you did last time, so let's start by creating an animation controller for the dismiss animation.

Creating the animation controller

Right-click on the **ILoveCatz** group in the project navigator, select **New File...**, and choose **iOS\Cocoa Touch\Objective-C class**. Name the class **ShrinkDismissAnimationController**, and make it a subclass of **NSObject**.

Open **ShrinkDismissAnimationController.h** and adopt the
`UIViewControllerAnimatedTransitioning` protocol:

```
@interface ShrinkDismissAnimationController : NSObject
<UIViewControllerAnimatedTransitioning>

@end
```

Open **ShrinkDismissAnimationController.m** and add the following method that
returns the transition duration:

```
- (NSTimeInterval)transitionDuration:
  (id <UIViewControllerContextTransitioning>)transitionContext {
    return 0.5;
}
```

Next, add the following method to animate the transition:

```
- (void)animateTransition:
  (id <UIViewControllerContextTransitioning>)transitionContext {
    UIViewController *toViewController =
            [transitionContext viewControllerForKey:
                       UITransitionContextToViewControllerKey];
    UIViewController *fromViewController =
            [transitionContext viewControllerForKey:
                       UITransitionContextFromViewControllerKey];
    CGRect finalFrame = [transitionContext
                    finalFrameForViewController:toViewController];

    UIView *containerView = [transitionContext containerView];

    // 1
    toViewController.view.frame = finalFrame;
    toViewController.view.alpha = 0.5;

    // 2
    [containerView addSubview:toViewController.view];
    [containerView sendSubviewToBack:toViewController.view];

    // The actual animation will go here...

}
```

This is quite similar to the implementation you added for your first animation
controller; however, there are a few differences to highlight:

1. This time the to- view controller (i.e. the master view controller in your case) is stationary while the from- view controller slides down to reveal it. Hence, the initial position for the to- view controller is the same as its final position.

2. Again, you are always responsible for adding the to- view to the container view. You want to slide out the from- view to reveal the underlying view, so the to- view is sent to the back.

For the animation itself, you'll use something a little different from the standard UIView animation and dig into another new iOS 7 feature: **key frame animations**.

Animating with Key frames

Key frame UIView animations make it easy to create animations with multiple steps. Before iOS 7 you had to chain animations together, each animation firing after the completion of the preceding one (or drop down a lower level into Core Animation). With key frame animations, you simply define a single animation with multiple steps.

Add the following code to the end of the animateTransition: implementation you added in the previous section:

```
// 1. Determine the intermediate and final frame for the from
view
CGRect screenBounds = [[UIScreen mainScreen] bounds];
CGRect shrunkenFrame =
            CGRectInset(fromViewController.view.frame,
                fromViewController.view.frame.size.width/4,
                fromViewController.view.frame.size.height/4);
CGRect fromFinalFrame =
      CGRectOffset(shrunkenFrame, 0, screenBounds.size.height);

NSTimeInterval duration = [self
                        transitionDuration:transitionContext];

// 2. animate with keyframes
[UIView animateKeyframesWithDuration:duration
          delay:0.0
     options:UIViewKeyframeAnimationOptionCalculationModeCubic
   animations:^{
          // 3a. keyframe one
          [UIView addKeyframeWithRelativeStartTime:0.0
                              relativeDuration:0.5
                                  animations:^{
            fromViewController.view.frame = shrunkenFrame;
```

```
                toViewController.view.alpha = 0.5;
    }];
    // 3b. keyframe two
    [UIView addKeyframeWithRelativeStartTime:0.5
                          relativeDuration:0.5
                                animations:^{
        fromViewController.view.frame = fromFinalFrame;
        toViewController.view.alpha = 1.0;
    }];
}
completion:^(BOOL finished) {
    // 4. inform the context of completion
    [transitionContext completeTransition:YES];
}];
```

The nested blocks make this a little hard to read, however, it's fairly straightforward. Taking each step in turn:

1. Calculate the intermediate and final frame for the from- view. The first step is to shrink it to half its size, and the second step is to move it to the bottom of the screen.

2. Initialize a key frame animation.

3. (a) Key frame one starts at a relative time of 0.0, with a relative duration of 0.5; i.e. it starts immediately and lasts for 50% of the total duration of the animation. This key-frame sets the from- view frame to its intermediate state.

   (b) Key-frame two occurs at a relative time of 0.5, with a relative duration of 0.5; i.e. it starts 50% through the animation and lasts for the remaining 50% of the total duration of the animation. This key-frame moves the from- view to its final location.

4. Once again, inform the transition context that the animation is complete.

The overall effect shrinks the view down into the bottom center of the screen with a 3D-like effect that makes it look like the view is moving away from you.

Time to wire up this transition to the animation controller!

Repeating some of the steps you used to add your first animation controller, open **MasterViewController.m** and add this import to the top of the file:

```
#import "ShrinkDismissAnimationController.h"
```

A little further down the same file add the following instance variable:

```
ShrinkDismissAnimationController
  *_shrinkDismissAnimationController;
```

Create an instance of the new animation controller by adding the following code to `initWithCoder:` right after the line that constructs your other animation controller:

```
_shrinkDismissAnimationController =
                       [ShrinkDismissAnimationController new];
```

The `UIViewControllerTransitioningDelegate` protocol provides `animationControllerForDismissedController:` to retrieve the animation controller of a dismissed view controller.

Add the following code to the bottom of the same file:

```
- (id<UIViewControllerAnimatedTransitioning>)
           animationControllerForDismissedController:
                             (UIViewController *)dismissed {
    return _shrinkDismissAnimationController;
}
```

This simply returns your new animation controller.

Build and run your app; you'll see your new animation as follows:

Oh dear. While you can certainly see the two key-frame steps, the effect isn't quite what you had planned!

What's going on here? In the image above you can see that the white frame for the view is set correctly, but the *scale* of its contents hasn't changed. Ah, that makes perfect sense: changing the frame for a view doesn't affect the view's children.

You *could* fix this by using a scale transform on the view; however, this gives you an excuse to try out another new iOS 7 feature: UIView snapshots. Hmm, it's almost as if the author *planned* it this way! :]

UIView snapshotting

UIView snapshotting is a simple yet powerful feature that allows you to snapshot an existing UIView together with its hierarchy and render it into a new lightweight UIView. You can even snapshot partial views, allowing you to perform all kinds of special effects.

Within **ShrinkDismissAnimationController.m**, add the following code just before the UIView animation:

```
// create a snapshot
UIView *intermediateView = [fromViewController.view
                              snapshotViewAfterScreenUpdates:NO];
intermediateView.frame = fromViewController.view.frame;
[containerView addSubview:intermediateView];

// remove the real view
[fromViewController.view removeFromSuperview];
```

This creates a new snapshot view then adds it the container view. This snapshot is used as a replacement for the from- view, so the real view must first be removed.

Replace the UIView animation with the following code:

```
[UIView animateKeyframesWithDuration:duration
        delay:0.0
      options:UIViewKeyframeAnimationOptionCalculationModeCubic
   animations:^{
      [UIView addKeyframeWithRelativeStartTime:0.0
                            relativeDuration:0.5
                                  animations:^{
          intermediateView.frame = shrunkenFrame;
          toViewController.view.alpha = 0.5;
      }];
      [UIView addKeyframeWithRelativeStartTime:0.5
                            relativeDuration:0.5
                                  animations:^{
          intermediateView.frame = fromFinalFrame;
```

```
            toViewController.view.alpha = 1.0;
    }];
}
completion:^(BOOL finished) {
    // remove the intermediate view
    [intermediateView removeFromSuperview];
    [transitionContext completeTransition:YES];
}];
```

This substitutes the snapshot `intermediateView` for the real from- view. In the completion block, you remove the `intermediateView` when the animation completes since it won't be needed any more.

Build and run to see the finished transition:

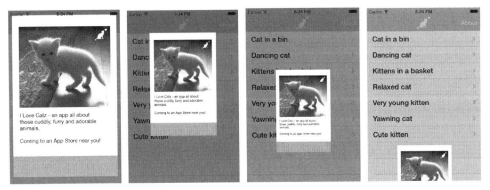

Ahh, that's more like what you had in mind. That completes your custom dismiss transition.

Navigation controller transitions

So far you've worked with modal view controller presentations, where you add a transitioning delegate to the view controller presented. This approach of setting a delegate on every single view controller gets quite tiresome when using a `UINavigationController` or a `UITabBarController`.

Fortunately, these controllers provide a simpler approach where the animation controller for a transition is supplied via the `UINavigationControllerDelegate` or `UITabBarControllerDelegate`.

In this section, you will try this out by adding a custom transition to a navigation controller. But first things first – you need an animation controller to use! This time, you will create an animation controller that flips between the two view controllers.

Adding a flip animation controller

You are going to add a new animation controller that flips over the current view controller to reveal the destination.

Right-click on the **ILoveCatz** group in the project navigator, select **New File…**, and choose **iOS\Cocoa Touch\Objective-C class**. Name the class **FlipAnimationController**, and make it a subclass of **NSObject**.

Open **FlipAnimationController.h**, modify it to adopt the `UIViewControllerAnimatedTransitioning` protocol and add a simple property, as so:

```
@interface FlipAnimationController :
                NSObject <UIViewControllerAnimatedTransitioning>

@property (nonatomic, assign) BOOL reverse;

@end
```

The `reverse` property will be used to set the direction of this transition.

Open **FlipAnimationController.m** and add the following transition duration method:

```
- (NSTimeInterval)transitionDuration:
  (id<UIViewControllerContextTransitioning>)transitionContext {
    return 1.0;
}
```

Also add the following utility method below:

```
- (CATransform3D) yRotation:(CGFloat) angle {
    return CATransform3DMakeRotation(angle, 0.0, 1.0, 0.0);
}
```

This creates a 3D transform that rotates around the Y-axis.

Finally, add the following animation implementation:

```
- (void)animateTransition:
  (id<UIViewControllerContextTransitioning>)transitionContext {

    // 1. the usual stuff ...
    UIView* containerView = [transitionContext containerView];
    UIViewController *fromVC = [transitionContext
```

```
                     viewControllerForKey:
                    UITransitionContextFromViewControllerKey];
UIViewController *toVC = [transitionContext
               viewControllerForKey:
                    UITransitionContextToViewControllerKey];
UIView *toView = toVC.view;
UIView *fromView = fromVC.view;
[containerView addSubview:toVC.view];


// 2. Add a perspective transform
CATransform3D transform = CATransform3DIdentity;
transform.m34 = -0.002;
[containerView.layer setSublayerTransform:transform];


// 3. Give both VCs the same start frame
CGRect initialFrame = [transitionContext
                     initialFrameForViewController:fromVC];
fromView.frame = initialFrame;
toView.frame = initialFrame;


// 4. reverse?
float factor = self.reverse ? 1.0 : -1.0;


// 5. flip the to VC halfway round - hiding it
toView.layer.transform = [self yRotation:factor * -M_PI_2];


// 6. Animate
NSTimeInterval duration = [self
             transitionDuration:transitionContext];
[UIView animateKeyframesWithDuration:duration
                               delay:0.0
                             options:0
                          animations:^{
    [UIView addKeyframeWithRelativeStartTime:0.0
                            relativeDuration:0.5
                                  animations:^{
        // 7. rotate the from view
        fromView.layer.transform =
                [self yRotation:factor * M_PI_2];
    }];
    [UIView addKeyframeWithRelativeStartTime:0.5
                            relativeDuration:0.5
                                  animations:^{
        // 8. rotate the to view
```

```
            toView.layer.transform =
                        [self yRotation:0.0];
        }];
    } completion:^(BOOL finished) {
        [transitionContext completeTransition:
            ![transitionContext transitionWasCancelled]];
    }];
}
```

Hey — there's some familiar looking code in this method. Taking each step in turn:

1. Obtain the usual information from the transition context.

2. Add a perspective transform to the container view – more in this a little later.

3. Give both the from- and to- view the same frame – in this case, a frame that fills the screen.

4. Using the `reverse` property, create a factor that negates the rotation angles used later on in the transition.

5. The to- view should not be visible initially. To achieve this, rotate it 90 degrees around its y-axis so that its zero-width edge is head-on.

6. Start the animation using a key-frame animation.

7. The first step of the key-frame animation rotates the from- view by 90 degrees along its y-axis. Once it has reached this angle, it will be invisible.

8. The second step reveals the to- view by rotating it 90 degrees.

Now back to step (2), this is worth a slightly more detailed explanation. You can apply a 3D transformation to a layer, and its children via the `sublayerTransform` property. The transform itself is a 4 x 4 matrix that allows you to apply any combination of rotate, skew and scale transforms to the layers.

In the code above the identity matrix is being used as the basis for the transform. The m34 matrix cell is modified to achieve the required level of perspective. You can see the effect of applying various values to this cell below:

| m34 = 0 | m34 = -0.0001 | m34 = -0.001 | m34 = -0.01 |

You can perform all kinds of interesting effects via these transformation matrices; it is well worth having a play with them!

The final step, as always, is wiring it up.

Open **MasterViewController.m** and add the following import to the top of the file:

```
#import "FlipAnimationController.h"
```

A little further down the same file add the following instance variable:

```
FlipAnimationController *_flipAnimationController;
```

Create an instance of this class by adding the following line to `initWithCoder:`, right next to where you construct the other animation controllers:

```
_flipAnimationController = [FlipAnimationController new];
```

The navigation controller delegate supplies the animation controller. To this end, update the class extension near the top of the file as so:

```
@interface MasterViewController ()
            <UIViewControllerTransitioningDelegate,
                            UINavigationControllerDelegate>
```

Now add the following to the end of the current `viewDidLoad` method:

```
self.navigationController.delegate = self;
```

This sets the host navigation controller's delegate so you can receive the new transition delegate methods.

The final step is to add the required delegate method as shown:

```
- (id<UIViewControllerAnimatedTransitioning>)
            navigationController:
                (UINavigationController *)navigationController
  animationControllerForOperation:
                (UINavigationControllerOperation)operation
            fromViewController:(UIViewController *)fromVC
            toViewController:(UIViewController *)toVC {

  _flipAnimationController.reverse =
            operation == UINavigationControllerOperationPop;
    return _flipAnimationController;
}
```

The above method requests an animation controller to navigate between the from- and to- view controllers, and receives the flip animation controller in response. Notice that the flip direction is based on whether this is a push or pop navigation.

Build and run your app; tap on a table view cell to see your new transition in action:

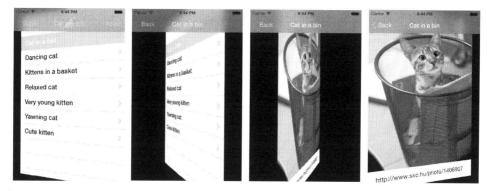

Did you notice that the navigation bar automatically performs a fade transition in parallel with your custom animation? iOS 7 is full of neat little effects like this.

Interactive transitions

The final new iOS 7 feature to implement is an **interactive transition**. These transitions allow the user to control a view controller transition with gestures.

To see an interactive transition in action, open up the Settings app on your device. Drill through the hierarchy of settings and swipe slowly from the left hand side of the screen. You'll see that you can initiate a pop transition as an alternative to the Back button, which is pretty cool.

However, what's even better is that the view tracks your finger location, allowing you to peek behind the topmost view, and if you wish, change your mind and swipe it back again.

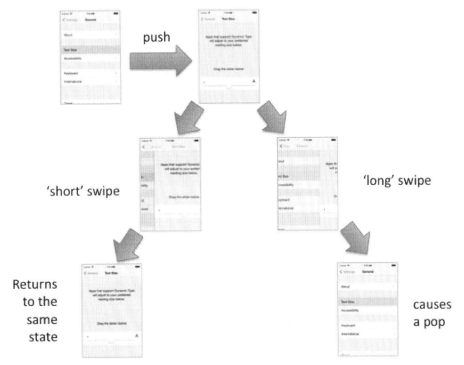

The above illustration shows how you can either complete or cancel an interactive transition by navigating to the to- view controller of return to the from- view controller respectively.

Sounds complicated? You'll be amazed to find that interactive transitions are actually really easy to implement. You are going to change the current flip transition to be interactive; to do this you won't have to change a single line of code within your animation controller — honest.

Adding an interaction controller

Interactive transitions use yet another protocol. This time it's `UIViewControllerInteractiveTransitioning`. The transitioning delegate or navigation controller delegate requests an optional interaction controller after requesting an animation controller.

As you can probably guess from its name, an interaction controller controls the animation: stepping through the animation as a gesture takes place, playing it to

completion when the interaction ends, or playing it in reverse if the navigation is cancelled.

First up, you'll create your interaction controller.

Right-click on the **ILoveCatz** group in the project navigator, select **New File…**, and choose **iOS\Cocoa Touch\Objective-C class**. Name the class **SwipeInteractionController**, and make it a subclass of **UIPercentDrivenInteractiveTransition**.

Open **SwipeInteractionController.h** and replace with the following:

```objc
@interface SwipeInteractionController :
                              UIPercentDrivenInteractiveTransition

- (void)wireToViewController:(UIViewController*)viewController;

@property (nonatomic, assign) BOOL interactionInProgress;

@end
```

`UIPercentDrivenInteractiveTransition` is the only concrete class you have encountered in the view controller transitions API, and it takes care of implementing the `UIViewControllerInteractiveTransitioning` protocol on your behalf.

In order to use `UIPercentDrivenInteractiveTransition` you must ensure that your animation controller uses a single `UIView` animation. If implemented in this way, the `UIPercentDrivenInteractiveTransition` can automatically stop, reverse, play and control the animations you provide.

Open **SwipeInteractionController.m** and add the following instance variables:

```objc
@implementation SwipeInteractionController {
    BOOL _shouldCompleteTransition;
    UINavigationController *_navigationController;
}
```

You'll see what these are used for shortly.

Add the following method just below your instance variables:

```objc
- (void)wireToViewController:(UIViewController *)viewController
{
    _navigationController = viewController.navigationController;
    [self prepareGestureRecognizerInView:viewController.view];
}
```

This method allows you to attach the interaction controller to a view controller. It obtains a reference to the navigation controller, which it uses to initiate a pop transition when a gesture occurs.

Add the following method just beneath the above method:

```
- (void)prepareGestureRecognizerInView:(UIView*)view {
    UIPanGestureRecognizer *gesture =
        [[UIPanGestureRecognizer alloc] initWithTarget:self
                            action:@selector(handleGesture:)];
    [view addGestureRecognizer:gesture];
}
```

This method adds a gesture recognizer to the view controller's view to detect a pan.

Add the following final method before you deal with the real interaction logic:

```
- (CGFloat)completionSpeed
{
    return 1 - self.percentComplete;
}
```

The completion speed is a `UIPercentDrivenInteractiveTransition` method that informs the framework how much of the animation remains when a gesture completes. Here the completion speed is simply the proportion of the remaining animation, but there is nothing stopping you from making this number bigger or smaller. For example, you could scale this up to a larger number to make the view controller snap back very quickly if an interaction is cancelled.

Now onto the real business of handling gestures and triggering an interactive transition. Add the method below:

```
- (void)handleGesture:(UIPanGestureRecognizer*)gestureRecognizer
{
    CGPoint translation = [gestureRecognizer
            translationInView:gestureRecognizer.view.superview];

    switch (gestureRecognizer.state) {
        case UIGestureRecognizerStateBegan:
            // 1. Start an interactive transition!
            self.interactionInProgress = YES;
            [_navigationController
                            popViewControllerAnimated:YES];
            break;
        case UIGestureRecognizerStateChanged: {
```

```
      // 2. compute the current position
      CGFloat fraction = - (translation.x / 200.0);
      fraction = fminf(fmaxf(fraction, 0.0), 1.0);

      // 3. should we complete?
      _shouldCompleteTransition = (fraction > 0.5);

      // 4. update the animation
      [self updateInteractiveTransition:fraction];
      break;
    }
    case UIGestureRecognizerStateEnded:
    case UIGestureRecognizerStateCancelled:
      // 5. finish or cancel
      self.interactionInProgress = NO;
      if (!_shouldCompleteTransition ||
  gestureRecognizer.state == UIGestureRecognizerStateCancelled) {
            [self cancelInteractiveTransition];
      }
      else {
            [self finishInteractiveTransition];
      }
      break;
    default:
      break;
  }
}
```

The gesture recognizer added to the view invokes the above method. Looking at each step in turn:

1. When the gesture first starts, set the `interactionInProgres` property to YES and initiate a pop navigation. You'll see shortly how the wire-up code uses this property.

2. While the gesture is in progress, compute a fraction that indicates how complete the transition is. In this case, a swipe of 200 points will cause the transition to be 100% complete, and should fully navigate to the to- view.

3. Determine whether the transition should complete if the gesture finishes at this location. In this case, if the users swipes at least halfway before releasing, then complete the transition.

4. Inform the object of the current position. This is all you need to do to ensure the animation from your animation controller plays correctly.

5. Finally, invoke the finish or cancel methods of
   `UIPercentDrivenInteractiveTransition` based on the
   `_shouldCompleteTransition` instance variable set in step 3.

As you can see, using `UIPercentDrivenInteractiveTransition` as the superclass
makes it very easy to create an interaction controller. What's more, the interaction
controller doesn't have any reference at all to your animation controller. This allows you
to freely mix and match interaction controllers and animation controllers.

Wiring it up

There's only a little bit of code left between you and your epic kitten transition.
Complete the usual wiring-up process as shown below.

Open **MasterViewController.m** and add the following import to the top of the file:

```
#import "SwipeInteractionController.h"
```

A little further down the same file add the following instance variable:

```
SwipeInteractionController *_swipeInteractionController;
```

Create an instance of this class by adding the following code to `initWithCoder:`, right
after where you construct your animation controllers:

```
_swipeInteractionController = [SwipeInteractionController new];
```

When a push navigation occurs, this interaction controller needs to add its gesture
recognizer to the pushed view. You're already detecting push and pop events to set the
direction of the flip animation controller, so add the following code to the start of
`navigationController:animationControllerForOperation:`
`fromViewController:toViewController:`

```
if (operation == UINavigationControllerOperationPush) {
    [_swipeInteractionController wireToViewController:toVC];
}
```

This is one of the new navigation controller delegate methods that allows you to supply
animation controllers. The above code simply wires up the interaction controller to any
pushed view controller.

Finally, add the following method to provide the interaction controller instance:

```
- (id <UIViewControllerInteractiveTransitioning>)
        navigationController:
```

```
          (UINavigationController *)navigationController
interactionControllerForAnimationController:
(id <UIViewControllerAnimatedTransitioning>)animationController
{
    return _swipeInteractionController.interactionInProgress ?
                          _swipeInteractionController : nil;
}
```

The framework first asks for an animation controller; if one is returned, it then asks for an interaction controller using the above method.

In the above implementation, it checks whether the interaction is in progress (i.e. it is currently handing gestures), and if so returns it.

Build and run your app; select a cat from the list, and from the detail view swipe your finger from right to left. Your view should animate as below:

A smooth swipe from right to left is effectively a pop, as if you tapped the back button. You can also hold down your finger and in a single touch event, swipe from the right to left to right to see the interaction at work.

Considering the relatively few steps involved, it's quite amazing how easy it is to create smooth, interactive custom transitions in iOS 7.

Challenge

Before moving on to the next chapter, it's time to put some of your newfound knowledge to use. The following section provides a challenge for you to try out, and in this case, it is quite a challenging one! If you do get stuck, the solution is provided.

Challenge 1: An interactive pinch-dismiss transition

The current application uses an interactive transition for back-navigation. Your challenge is to add a second interactive transition.

When the about view is dismissed it first shrinks before disappearing off the bottom of the screen. It would feel quite natural to initiate this transition using a pinch gesture:

And that is exactly what your challenge is! Add an interaction controller that allows the user to dismiss the about view using a pinch gesture.

Here are a few hints:

1. You'll need to add a new interaction controller to the app, just follow the general pattern of the existing `SwipeInteractionController`. However there will be a couple of small differences:

    a. The first is quite obvious; this interaction controller will need to make use of a pinch gesture recognizer rather than a pan gesture recognizer. You'll have to work out how to convert the current pinch state into a percentage in order to update the transition progress.

b. The second is more subtle; `SwipeInteractionController` informs the navigation controller when it should initiate a pop navigation. In this case, the interaction controller instead needs to send `dismissViewControllerAnimated:completion:` to the about view controller.

2. You will need to add the usual wire-up code to master view controller, however, as this interaction controller is being used for a dismiss transition, you need to return it via the `interactionControllerForDismissal:animator:` method which is defined on the `UIViewControllerTransitioningDelegate` delegate (Recall that the view controller that is being navigated to has the delegate which is used to supply animation and interaction controllers, and in this case, the master view controller is the to- view controller).

3. Finally, whenever an interaction controller is used, the animation controller needs to correctly inform the transitioning context whether the transition has completed or not. Update `ShrinkDismissAnimationController` so that the completion block uses the same logic as the `FlipAnimationController`.

At this point, it probably feels like your finished doesn't it? However, if you build and run you will find that as soon as you pinch the about view, it suddenly disappears!

There is something wrong here – and it is something quite subtle.

Firstly it is worth trying to narrow down the location of the issue. There are two broad areas that could be at fault, one is your interaction controller and the other is the animation controller. The two are independent and 'pluggable', so why not try combining the pinch interaction controller with the flip animation controller that is used for back-navigation? You should find that this works.

This tells you that there is something wrong with the implementation of your `ShrinkDismissAnimationController`. Probably the biggest difference between this, and the flip animation controller, is the use of `UIView` snapshotting. This animation controller removes the from- view replacing it with a snapshot.

Now hang on a minute ... the interaction controller has added a pinch gesture recognizer to the from- view controller's view, and the animation controller has just removed that same view from the hierarchy. Funnily enough, gesture recognizers don't work when their view has been detached.

EUREKA!

Earlier in this chapter I mentioned that the 'shrink' effect could be implemented using a transform instead of snapshotting. The following will provide exactly the same effect:

```
fromViewController.view.transform =
                        CGAffineTransformMakeScale(0.5, 0.5);
```

If you re-implement using transforms, you will find that the animation controller now works just fine with the newly added pinch interaction controller.

That was quite a challenge wasn't it!

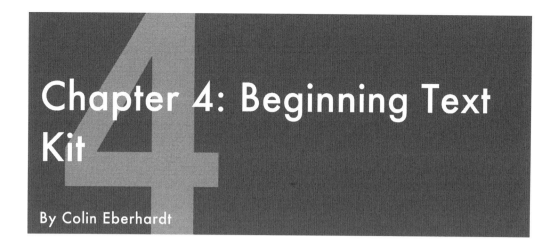

Chapter 4: Beginning Text Kit

By Colin Eberhardt

The way that text is rendered in iOS has changed a lot over the years as more powerful features and capabilities have been added. This latest iOS release brings with it some of the most significant text rendering changes yet.

In the old days before iOS 6, web views were usually the easiest way to render text with mixed styling, such as **bold**, *italics*, or even colors.

Last year, iOS 6 added attributed string support to a number of UIKit controls. This made it much easier to achieve this type of layout without resorting to rendered HTML — or so it would appear.

In iOS 6, text-based UIKit controls in iOS 6 were based on both WebKit and Core Graphics' string drawing functions, as illustrated in the hierarchical diagram below:

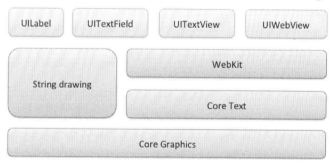

Note: Does anything strike you as odd in this diagram? That's right — UITextView uses WebKit under the hood. iOS 6 renders attributed strings on a text views as HTML, a fact that's not readily apparent to developers who haven't dug deep into the framework.

Attributed strings in iOS 6 were indeed helpful for many use cases. However, for advanced layouts and multi-line rendered text, Core Text remained the only real option — a relatively low-level and cumbersome framework.

However, this year in iOS 7 there's an easier way. With the new minimalistic design focus in iOS 7 that eschews ornamentation and focuses more on typography — such as the new `UIButton` that strips away all borders and shadows, leaving only text — it's no surprise that there's a whole new framework for working with text and text attributes: **Text Kit**.

The architecture is much tidier in iOS 7; all of the text-based UIKit controls (apart from `UIWebView`) now use Text Kit, as shown in the following diagram:

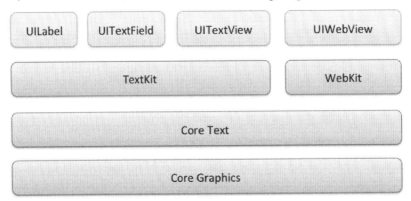

Text Kit is built on top of Core Text, inherits the full power of the Core Text framework, and to the delight of developers everywhere, wraps it in an improved object-oriented API. It's quite a sizeable framework, so this book takes two full chapters to cover Text Kit's many features.

The chapter you're reading now covers the components of Text Kit that you're likely to encounter in almost every iOS 7 application, including:

- Dynamic type

- Letterpress effects

- Exclusion paths

- Dynamic text formatting and storage

The second chapter is of great interest to those working with large, complex text layouts. It delves deeply into the core components of Text Kit, including the layout manger, text containers and text storage.

In this chapter you'll explore the various features of Text Kit as you create a simple yet feature-rich note-taking app for the iPhone that features reflowing text, dynamic text resizing, and on-the-fly text styling.

Ready to create something of note? :] Then read on to get started with Text Kit!

Getting started

The resources for this chapter includes a starter project with the user interface for the app pre-created so you can stay focused on Text Kit.

Open the starter project in Xcode and build and run the app. The app creates an initial array of `Note` instances and renders them in a table view controller. Storyboards and segues detect cell selection in the table view and handle the transition to the view controller where users can edit the selected note.

> **Note:** If you are new to Storyboards, check out Chapter 4 in *iOS 5 by Tutorials*, "Beginning Storyboards".

Browse through the source code and play with the app a little to get a feel for how the app is structured and how it functions. When you're done with that, move on to the next section, which discusses the use of dynamic type in your app.

Dynamic type

Dymamic type is one of the most game-changing features of iOS 7; it places the onus on your app to conform to user-selected font sizes and weights.

Select **Settings\General\Accessibility** and **Settings\General\Text Size** to view the new settings that affect how text is displayed in your app.

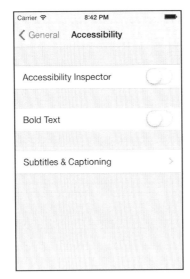
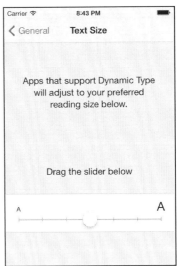

iOS 7 offers the ability to enhance the legibility of text by increasing font weight, as well as an option to set the preferred font size for apps that support dynamic text. Users will expect apps written for iOS 7 to honor these settings, so ignore them at your own risk!

In order to make use of dynamic type you need to specify fonts using styles rather than explicitly stating the font name and size. With iOS 7 a new method has been added to `UIFont`, `preferredFontForTextStyle` that creates a font for the given style using the user's font preferences.

The diagram below gives an example of each of the six different font styles:

Body	Body	Body
Caption 1	Caption 1	Caption 1
Caption 2	Caption 2	Caption 2
Footnote	Footnote	Footnote
Headline	Headline	Headline
Subhead	Subhead	Subhead

The text on the left is rendered using the smallest user selectable text size, the text in the center uses the largest, and the text on the right shows the effect of enabling the accessibility 'bold text' feature.

Basic support

Implementing basic support for dynamic text is relatively straightforward. Rather than using explicit fonts within your application, you instead request a font for a specific 'style'. At runtime a suitable font will be selected based on the given style and the user's text preferences.

Open **NoteEditorViewController.m** and add the following to the end of viewDidLoad:

```
self.textView.font = [UIFont
          preferredFontForTextStyle:UIFontTextStyleBody];
```

Then open **NotesListViewController.m** and add the following to the end of the tableView: cellForRowAtIndexPath: method, before the return statement:

```
cell.textLabel.font = [UIFont
          preferredFontForTextStyle:UIFontTextStyleHeadline];
```

In both cases you are making use of the new iOS font styles.

> **Note:** Using a semantic approach to font names, such as UIFontTextStyleSubHeadline, helps avoid hard-coded font names and styles throughout your code — and ensures that your app will respond properly to user-defined typography settings as expected.

Launch TextKitNotepad again, and you'll notice that the table view and the note screen now honor the current text size; the difference between the two is shown in the screenshots below:

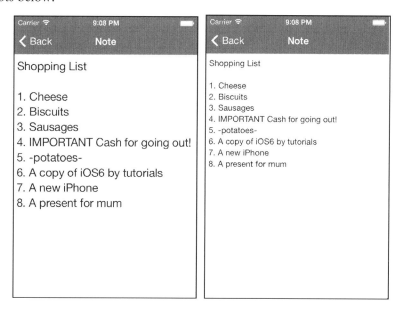

That looks pretty good — but sharp readers will note that this is only half the solution. Head back to **Settings\General\Text Size and modify the text size again. This time,** switch back to TextKitNotepad — without re-launching the app — and you'll notice that your app didn't respond to the new text size.

Your users won't take too kindly to that! Looks like that's the first thing you need to **correct in this app.**

Responding to updates

Open up **NoteEditorViewController.m** and add the following code to the end of `viewDidLoad`:

```
[[NSNotificationCenter defaultCenter]
    addObserver:self
        selector:@selector(preferredContentSizeChanged:)
            name:UIContentSizeCategoryDidChangeNotification
          object:nil];
```

The above code registers the class to receive notifications when the preferred content size is changed and passes in the method to be called (`preferredContentSizeChanged:`) when this event occurs.

Next, add the following method to **NoteEditorViewController.m**, immediately below `viewDidLoad`:

```
- (void)preferredContentSizeChanged:(NSNotification *)
  notification {
    self.textView.font =
        [UIFont preferredFontForTextStyle:UIFontTextStyleBody];
}
```

This simply sets the text view font to one based on the new preferred size.

> **Note:** You might be wondering why it seems you're setting the font to the same value it had before. When the user changes their preferred font size, you must request the preferred font again; it won't be updated automatically. The font returned via `preferredFontForTextStyle:` will different when the font preferences are changed.

Open up **NotesListViewController.m** and add the following code to the end of the `viewDidLoad` method:

```
[[NSNotificationCenter defaultCenter]
    addObserver:self
        selector:@selector(preferredContentSizeChanged:)
            name:UIContentSizeCategoryDidChangeNotification
          object:nil];
```

Hey, isn't that the same code you just added to **NoteEditorViewController.m?**
Yes, it is — but you'll handle the preferred font change in a slightly
different manner.

Add the following method to NotesListViewController.m, immediately
below `viewDidLoad`:

```
- (void)preferredContentSizeChanged:(NSNotification *)
  notification {
    [self.tableView reloadData];
}
```

The above code simply instructs `UITableView` to reload its visible cells, which updates
the appearance of each cell.Build and run your app; change the text size setting and
verify that your app responds correctly to the new user preferences.

Changing layout

That part seems to work well, but when you select a really small font size, your table
view ends up looking a little sparse, as shown in the left-hand screenshot below:

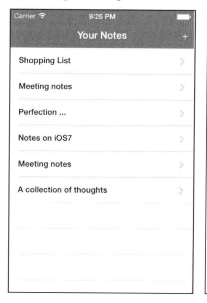
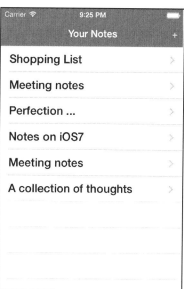

This is one of the trickier aspects of dynamic type. To ensure your application looks good across the range of font sizes, your layout needs to be responsive to the user's text settings. Auto Layout solves a lot of problems for you, but this is one problem you'll have to solve yourself.

Your table row height needs to change as the font size changes. Implementing the `tableView: heightForRowAtIndexPath:` delegate method solves this quite nicely.

Add the following code to **NotesListViewController.m,** in the table view data source section:

```
- (CGFloat)tableView:(UITableView *)tableView
        heightForRowAtIndexPath:(NSIndexPath *)indexPath {

    static UILabel* label;
    if (!label) {
        label = [[UILabel alloc]
                initWithFrame:CGRectMake(0, 0, FLT_MAX, FLT_MAX)];
        label.text = @"test";
    }

    label.font = [UIFont
            preferredFontForTextStyle:UIFontTextStyleHeadline];
    [label sizeToFit];
    return ceilf(label.frame.size.height * 1.7);
}
```

The above code creates a single shared — or **static** — instance of `UILabel` with the same font used by the table view cell. It then invokes `sizeToFit` on the label, which forces the label's frame to fit tightly around the text, and results in a frame height proportional to the table row height.

Build and run your app; modify the text size setting once more and the table rows now size dynamically to fit the text size, as shown in the screenshot below:

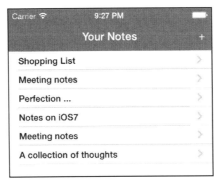

Letterpress effects

Letterpress effects add subtle shading and highlights to text that give it a sense of depth — much like the text has been slightly pressed into the screen.

> **Note:** The term "letterpress" is a nod to early printing presses, which inked a set of letters carved on blocks and pressed them into the page. The letters often left a small indentation on the page — an unintended but visually pleasing effect, which is frequently replicated in digital typography today.

Open **NotesListViewController.m** and replace the contents of `tableView:cellForRowAtIndexPath:` with the following code:

```objc
static NSString *CellIdentifier = @"Cell";
UITableViewCell *cell = [tableView
        dequeueReusableCellWithIdentifier:CellIdentifier
                             forIndexPath:indexPath];

Note* note = [self notes][indexPath.row];

UIFont* font = [UIFont
         preferredFontForTextStyle:UIFontTextStyleHeadline];

UIColor* textColor = [UIColor colorWithRed:0.175f
                       green:0.458f blue:0.831f alpha:1.0f];
NSDictionary *attrs =
@{ NSForegroundColorAttributeName : textColor,
  NSFontAttributeName : font,
  NSTextEffectAttributeName : NSTextEffectLetterpressStyle
};

NSAttributedString* attrString = [[NSAttributedString alloc]
                            initWithString:note.title
                                attributes:attrs];

cell.textLabel.attributedText = attrString;

return cell;
```

The above code creates an attributed string for the title of a table cell using the letterpress style.

Build and run your app; your table view will now display the text with a nice letterpress effect, as shown below:

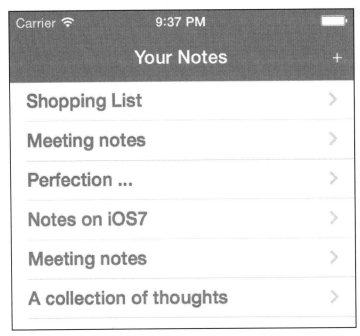

Letterpress is a subtle effect — but that doesn't mean you should overuse it! Visual effects may make your text more interesting, but they don't necessarily make your text more legible.

Exclusion paths

Flowing text around images or other objects is a standard feature of most word processors. Text Kit allows you to render text around complex paths and shapes through **exclusion paths**.

It would be handy to tell the user when a note was created; you're going to add a small curved view to the top right-hand corner of the note that shows this information.

You'll start by adding the view itself – then you'll create an exclusion path to make the text wrap around it.

Adding the view

Open up **NoteEditorViewController.m** and add the following line to the list of imports at the top of the file:

```
#import "TimeIndicatorView.h"
```

Next, add the following instance variable to **NoteEditorViewController.m**:

```
@implementation NoteEditorViewController
{
    TimeIndicatorView* _timeView;
}
```

As the name suggests, this houses the time indicator subview.

Add the code following to the very end of `viewDidLoad` in
NoteEditorViewController.m:

```
_timeView = [[TimeIndicatorView alloc]
               init:self.note.timestamp];
[self.view addSubview:_timeView];
```

This simply creates an instance of the new view and adds it as a subview.

`TimeIndicatorView` calculates its own size, but it won't do this automatically. You
need a mechanism to call `updateSize` when the view controller lays out the subviews.

Add the following code to the bottom of **NoteEditorViewController.m**:

```
- (void)viewDidLayoutSubviews {
    [self updateTimeIndicatorFrame];
}

- (void)updateTimeIndicatorFrame {
    [_timeView updateSize];
    _timeView.frame = CGRectOffset(_timeView.frame,
        self.view.frame.size.width - _timeView.frame.size.width,
        0.0);
}
```

`viewDidLayoutSubviews` calls `updateTimeIndicatorFrame`, which does two things:
it calls `updateSize` to set the size of the subview, and positions the subview in the top
right corner of the view.

All that's left is to call `updateTimeIndicatorFrame` when your view controller receives
notification that the size of the content has changed. Modify
`preferredContentSizeChanged:` in **NoteEditorViewController.m** to the
following:

```
- (void)preferredContentSizeChanged:(NSNotification *)n {
```

```
    self.textView.font = [UIFont
            preferredFontForTextStyle:UIFontTextStyleBody];
    [self updateTimeIndicatorFrame];
  }
```

Build and run your project; tap on a list item and the time indicator view will display in the top right hand corner of the item view, as shown below:

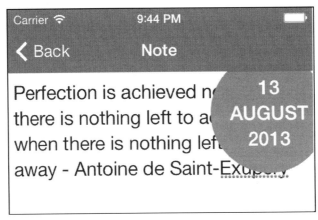

Modify the device Text Size preferences, and the view will automatically adjust to fit.

However, something doesn't look quite right. The text of the note renders behind the time indicator view instead of flowing neatly around it. Fortunately, this is the exact problem that exclusion paths are designed to solve.

Exclusion paths

Open **TimeIndicatorView.h** and add the following method declaration:

```
- (UIBezierPath *)curvePathWithOrigin:(CGPoint)origin;
```

This permits you to access `curvePathWithOrigin:` from within your view controller and define the path around which you'll flow your text. Aha — that's why the calculation of the Bezier curve is broken out into its own method!

All that's left is to define the exclusion path itself. Open up **NoteEditorViewController.m** and add the following code block to the very end of `updateTimeIndicatorFrame`:

```
UIBezierPath* exclusionPath = [_timeView
                  curvePathWithOrigin:_timeView.center];
_textView.textContainer.exclusionPaths = @[exclusionPath];
```

The above code creates an exclusion path based on the Bezier path created in your time indicator view, but with an origin and coordinates that are relative to the text view.

Build and run your project and select an item from the list; the text now flows nicely around the time indicator view, as shown in the following screenshot:

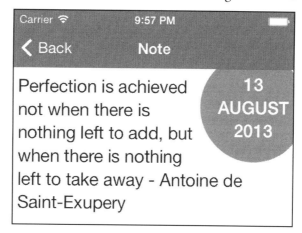

This simple example only scratches the surface of the abilities of exclusion paths. You might have noticed that the exclusionPaths property expects an instance of NSArray; therefore each container can support more than one exclusion path.

Furthermore, exclusion paths can be as simple or as complicated as you want. Need to render text in the shape of a star or a butterfly? As long as you can define the path, exclusionPaths will handle it without problem!

As the text container notifies the layout manager when an exclusion path is changed, dynamic or even *animated* exclusions paths are possible to implement — just don't expect your user to appreciate the text moving around on the screen as they're trying to read!

Dynamic text formatting and storage

You've seen that Text Kit can dynamically adjust fonts based on the user's text size preferences. But wouldn't it be cool if fonts could update dynamically *based on the actual text itself?*

For example, what if you want to make this app automatically:

• Make any text surrounded by the tilde character (~) a fancy font

• Make any text surrounded by the underscore character (_) italic

- Make any text surrounded by the dash character (-) crossed out

- Make any text in all caps colored red

That's exactly what you'll do in this section by leveraging the power of the Text Kit framework!

To do this, you'll need to understand how the text storage system in Text Kit works. Here's a diagram that shows the "Text Kit stack" used to store, render and display text:

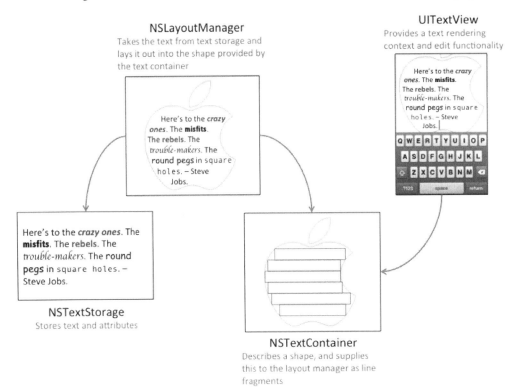

Behind the scenes, Apple creates these classes for you automatically when you create a `UITextView`, `UILabel` or `UITextField`. In your apps, you can either use these default implementations or customize any part to get your own behavior. Let's go over each class:

- `NSTextStorage` stores the text to be rendered as an attributed string and informs the layout manager of any changes to the text's contents. You might want to subclass `NSTextStorage` in order to dynamically change the text attributes as the text is updated (as you will see later in this chapter).

- `NSLayoutManager` takes the stored text and renders it on the screen; it serves as the layout 'engine' in your app.

- `NSTextContainer` describes the geometry of an area of the screen where text is rendered. Each text container is typically associated with a `UITextView`. You might want to subclass `NSTextContainer` to define a complex shape that you would like to render text within.

To implement the dynamic text formatting feature in this app, you'll need to subclass `NSTextStorage` in order to dynamically add text attributes as the user types in their text.

Once you've created your custom `NSTextStorage`, you'll replace `UITextView`'s default text storage instance with your own implementation. Let's give this a shot!

Subclassing NSTextStorage

Right-click on the **TextKitNotepad** group in the project navigator, select **New File...**, and choose **iOS\Cocoa Touch\Objective-C class**. Name the class **SyntaxHighlightTextStorage**, and make it a subclass of **NSTextStorage**.

Open **SyntaxHighlightTextStorage.m** and add an instance variable and initializer as follows:

```
#import "SyntaxHighlightTextStorage.h"

@implementation SyntaxHighlightTextStorage
{
    NSMutableAttributedString *_backingStore;
}

- (id)init
{
    if (self = [super init]) {
        _backingStore = [NSMutableAttributedString new];
```

```
        }
    return self;
    }
@end
```

A text storage subclass must provide its own 'persistence' hence the use of a
NSMutabeAttributedString 'backing store' (more on this later).

Next add the following methods to the same file:

```
- (NSString *)string
{
    return [_backingStore string];
}

- (NSDictionary *)attributesAtIndex:(NSUInteger)location
                effectiveRange:(NSRangePointer)range
{
    return [_backingStore attributesAtIndex:location
                          effectiveRange:range];
}
```

The above two methods simply delegate directly to the backing store.

Finally add the remaining mandatory overrides to the same file:

```
- (void)replaceCharactersInRange:(NSRange)range
              withString:(NSString *)str
{
    NSLog(@"replaceCharactersInRange:%@ withString:%@",
        NSStringFromRange(range), str);

    [self beginEditing];
    [_backingStore replaceCharactersInRange:range
                              withString:str];
    [self edited:NSTextStorageEditedCharacters |
NSTextStorageEditedAttributes
            range:range
      changeInLength:str.length - range.length];
    [self endEditing];
}

- (void)setAttributes:(NSDictionary *)attrs range:(NSRange)range
```

```
{
    NSLog(@"setAttributes:%@ range:%@",
            attrs, NSStringFromRange(range));

    [self beginEditing];
    [_backingStore setAttributes:attrs range:range];
    [self edited:NSTextStorageEditedAttributes
                range:range
        changeInLength:0];
    [self endEditing];
}
```

Again, these methods delegate to the backing store. However, they also surround the edits with calls to beginEditing / edited / endEditing. This is required in order that the text storage class notifies its associated layout manager when edits are made.

You've probably noticed that you need to write quite a bit of code in order to subclass text storage. Since NSTextStorage is a public interface of a **class cluster** (see the note below), you can't just subclass it and override a few methods to extend its functionality. Instead, there are certain requirements that you must implement yourself, such as the backing store for the attributed string data.

Note: Class clusters are a commonly used design pattern throughout Apple's frameworks.

A class cluster is simply the Objective-C implementation of the Abstract Factory pattern, which provides a common interface for creating families of related or dependent objects without specifying the concrete classes. Familiar classes such as NSArray and NSNumber are in fact the public interface to a cluster of classes.

Apple uses class clusters to encapsulate private concrete subclasses under a public abstract superclass, and it's this abstract superclass that declares the methods a client must use in order to create instances of its private subclasses. Clients are also completely unaware of which private class is being dispensed by the factory, since it only ever interacts with the public interface.

Using a class cluster certainly simplifies the interface, making it much easier to learn and use the class, but it's important to note there's been a trade-off between extensibility and simplicity. It's often far more difficult to create a custom subclass of the abstract superclass of a cluster.

Now that you have a custom `NSTextStorage`, you need to make a `UITextView` that uses it.

A UITextView with a custom Text Kit stack

Instantiating `UITextView` from the storyboard editor automatically creates an instance of `NSTextStorage`, `NSLayoutManager` and `NSTextContainer` (i.e. the Text Kit stack) and exposes all three as read-only properties.

There is no way to change these from the storyboard editor, but luckily you can if you create the `UITextView` and Text Kit stack programatically.

Let's give this a shot. Open up **Main.storyboard** in Interface Builder and locate the **NoteEditorViewController** view. Delete the `UITextView` instance.

Next, open **NoteEditorViewController.m** and remove the `UITextView` outlet from the class extension.

At the top of **NoteEditorViewController.m**, import the text storage implementation as follows:

```
#import "SyntaxHighlightTextStorage.h"
```

Add the following code immediately after the `TimeIndicatorView` instance variable in **NoteEditorViewController.m**:

```
SyntaxHighlightTextStorage* _textStorage;
UITextView* _textView;
```

These are two instance variables for your text storage subclass, and a text view that you will create programmatically soon.

Next remove the following lines from `viewDidLoad` in **NoteEditorViewController.m**:

```
self.textView.text = self.note.contents;
self.textView.delegate = self;
self.textView.font = [UIFont
            preferredFontForTextStyle:UIFontTextStyleBody];
```

Since you are no longer using the outlet for the text view and will be creating one manually instead, you no longer need these lines.

Still working in **NoteEditorViewController.m** , add the following method:

```
- (void)createTextView
```

```
{
    // 1. Create the text storage that backs the editor
    NSDictionary* attrs = @{NSFontAttributeName:
        [UIFont preferredFontForTextStyle:UIFontTextStyleBody]};
    NSAttributedString* attrString = [[NSAttributedString alloc]
                                initWithString:_note.contents
                                    attributes:attrs];
    _textStorage = [SyntaxHighlightTextStorage new];
    [_textStorage appendAttributedString:attrString];

    CGRect newTextViewRect = self.view.bounds;

    // 2. Create the layout manager
    NSLayoutManager *layoutManager = [[NSLayoutManager alloc]
                                                        init];

    // 3. Create a text container
    CGSize containerSize =
        CGSizeMake(newTextViewRect.size.width,  CGFLOAT_MAX);
    NSTextContainer *container = [[NSTextContainer alloc]
                                initWithSize:containerSize];
    container.widthTracksTextView = YES;
    [layoutManager addTextContainer:container];
    [_textStorage addLayoutManager:layoutManager];

    // 4. Create a UITextView
    _textView = [[UITextView alloc]
                            initWithFrame:newTextViewRect
                            textContainer:container];
    _textView.delegate = self;
    [self.view addSubview:_textView];
}
```

This is quite a lot of code. Let's consider each step in turn:

1. An instance of your custom text storage is instantiated and initialized with an attributed string holding the content of the note.

2. A layout manager is created.

3. A text container is created and associated with the layout manager. The layout manager is then associated with the text storage.

4. Finally the actual text view is created with your custom text container, the delegate set and the text view added as a subview.

At this point the earlier diagram, and the relationship it shows between the four key classes (storage, layout manager, container and text view) should make more sense:

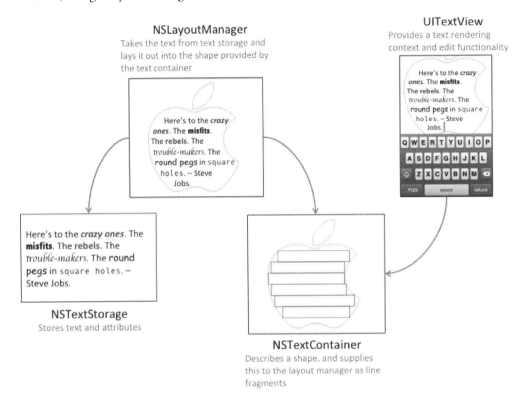

Note that the text container has a width matching the view width, but has infinite height — or as close as `CGFLOAT_MAX` can come to infinity. In any case, this is more than enough to allow the `UITextView` to scroll and accommodate long passages of text.

Within `viewDidLoad` add the following line just after the call to `viewDidLoad` on the superclass:

```
[self createTextView];
```

Next modify the first line of `preferredContentSizeChanged` to read as follows:

```
_textView.font = [UIFont
    preferredFontForTextStyle:UIFontTextStyleBody];
```

Here you simply replace the old outlet property with the new instance variable.

One last thing, a custom view created in code doesn't automatically inherit the layout constraints set in the storyboard; therefore, the frame of your new view won't resize when the device orientation changes. You'll need to explicitly set the frame yourself.

To do this, add the following line to the end of `viewDidLayoutSubviews`:

```
_textView.frame = self.view.bounds;
```

Build and run your app; open a note and edit the text while keeping an eye on the Xcode console. You should see a flurry of log messages created as you type, as below:

This is simply the logging code from within `SyntaxHighlightTextStorage` to give you an indication that your custom text handling code is actually being called.

The basic foundation of your text parser seems fairly solid — now to add the dynamic formatting.

Dynamic formatting

In this next step you are going to modify your custom text storage to embolden text ***surrounded by asterisks***.

Open **SyntaxHighlightTextStorage.m** and add the following method:

```
-(void)processEditing
{
    [self performReplacementsForRange:[self editedRange]];
    [super processEditing];
}
```

`processEditing` sends notifications for when the text changes to the layout manager. It also serves as a convenient home for any post-editing logic.

Add the following method right after `processEditing`:

```
- (void)performReplacementsForRange:(NSRange)changedRange
```

```
{
    NSRange extendedRange = NSUnionRange(changedRange,
      [[_backingStore string]
        lineRangeForRange:NSMakeRange(changedRange.location, 0)]);
    extendedRange = NSUnionRange(extendedRange,
      [[_backingStore string]
    lineRangeForRange:NSMakeRange(NSMaxRange(changedRange), 0)]);

    [self applyStylesToRange:extendedRange];
}
```

The code above expands the range that will be inspected to match our bold formatting pattern. This is required because changedRange typically indicates a single character; lineRangeForRange extends that range to the entire line of text.

Add the following method right after performReplacementsForRange:

```
- (void)applyStylesToRange:(NSRange)searchRange
{
    // 1. create some fonts
    UIFontDescriptor* fontDescriptor =
        [UIFontDescriptor
    preferredFontDescriptorWithTextStyle:UIFontTextStyleBody];
    UIFontDescriptor* boldFontDescriptor = [fontDescriptor
    fontDescriptorWithSymbolicTraits:UIFontDescriptorTraitBold];
    UIFont* boldFont =  [UIFont
        fontWithDescriptor:boldFontDescriptor size: 0.0];

    UIFont* normalFont = [UIFont
        preferredFontForTextStyle:UIFontTextStyleBody];

    // 2. match items surrounded by asterisks
    NSString* regexStr = @"(\\*\\w+(\\s\\w+)*\\*)\\s";
    NSRegularExpression* regex = [NSRegularExpression
                    regularExpressionWithPattern:regexStr
                                         options:0
                                           error:nil];

    NSDictionary* boldAttributes =
                @{ NSFontAttributeName : boldFont };
    NSDictionary* normalAttributes =
                @{ NSFontAttributeName : normalFont };

    // 3. iterate over each match, making the text bold
```

```
[regex enumerateMatchesInString:[_backingStore string]
        options:0
          range:searchRange
      usingBlock:^(NSTextCheckingResult *match,
                   NSMatchingFlags flags,
                   BOOL *stop){

    NSRange matchRange = [match range];
    [self addAttributes:boldAttributes range:matchRange];

    // 4. reset the style to the original
    if (NSMaxRange(matchRange)+1 < self.length) {
        [self addAttributes:normalAttributes
            range:NSMakeRange(NSMaxRange(matchRange)+1, 1)];
    }
}];

}
```

The above code performs the following actions:

1. Creates a bold and a normal font for formatting the text using **font descriptors**. Font descriptors help you avoid the use of hardcoded font strings to set font types and styles.

2. Creates a regular expression (or **regex**) that locates any text surrounded by asterisks; for example, in the string "iOS 7 is *awesome*", **the regular expression stored in** regExStr **above will match and return the text** "*awesome*". Don't worry if you're not totally familiar with regular expressions; they're covered in a bit more detail later on in this chapter.

3. Enumerates the matches returned by the regular expression and applies the bold attribute to each one.

4. Resets the text style of the character that follows the final asterisk in the matched string to "normal". This ensures that any text added after the closing asterisk is not rendered in bold type.

> **Note:** Font descriptors are a type of descriptor language that allows you to modify fonts by applying specific attributes, or to obtain details of font metrics, without the need to instantiate an instance of UIFont.

Build and run your app; type some text into a note and surround one of the words with asterisks. The words will be automagically bolded, as shown in the screenshot below:

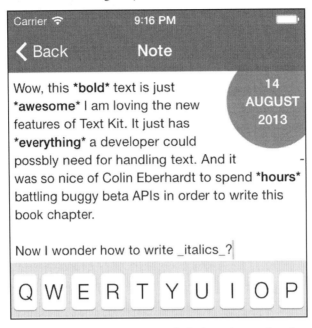

That's pretty handy — you're likely thinking of all the other styles that could be added to your text.

You're in luck: the next section shows you how to do just that!

Adding further styles

The basic principle of applying styles to delimited text is rather straightforward: use a regex to find and replace the delimited string using `applyStylesToRange` to set the desired style of the text.

Add the following instance variable to **SyntaxHighlightTextStorage.m**:

```
NSDictionary* _replacements;
```

Next, add the following method to **SyntaxHighlightTextStorage.m**:

```
- (void) createHighlightPatterns {
    UIFontDescriptor *scriptFontDescriptor =
        [UIFontDescriptor fontDescriptorWithFontAttributes:
            @{UIFontDescriptorFamilyAttribute: @"Zapfino"}];

    // 1. base our script font on the preferred body font size
```

```
UIFontDescriptor* bodyFontDescriptor = [UIFontDescriptor
    preferredFontDescriptorWithTextStyle:UIFontTextStyleBody];
NSNumber* bodyFontSize = bodyFontDescriptor.
            fontAttributes[UIFontDescriptorSizeAttribute];
UIFont* scriptFont = [UIFont
        fontWithDescriptor:scriptFontDescriptor
                    size:[bodyFontSize floatValue]];


// 2. create the attributes
NSDictionary* boldAttributes = [self
  createAttributesForFontStyle:UIFontTextStyleBody
                withTrait:UIFontDescriptorTraitBold];
NSDictionary* italicAttributes = [self
  createAttributesForFontStyle:UIFontTextStyleBody
                withTrait:UIFontDescriptorTraitItalic];
NSDictionary* strikeThroughAttributes =
            @{ NSStrikethroughStyleAttributeName : @1};
NSDictionary* scriptAttributes =
            @{ NSFontAttributeName : scriptFont};
NSDictionary* redTextAttributes =
    @{ NSForegroundColorAttributeName : [UIColor redColor]};


// construct a dictionary of replacements based on regexes
_replacements = @{
    @"(\\*\\w+(\\s\\w+)*\\*)\\s" : boldAttributes,
    @"(_\\w+(\\s\\w+)*_)\\s" : italicAttributes,
    @"([0-9]+\\.)\\s" : boldAttributes,
    @"(-\\w+(\\s\\w+)*-)\\s" : strikeThroughAttributes,
    @"(~\\w+(\\s\\w+)*~)\\s" : scriptAttributes,
    @"\\s([A-Z]{2,})\\s" : redTextAttributes};
}
```

Here's what's going on in this method:

1. It first creates a "script" style using Zapfino as the font. Font descriptors help determine the current preferred body font size, which ensures the script font also honors the users' preferred text size setting.

2. Next, it constructs the attributes to apply to each matched style pattern. You'll cover `createAttributesForFontStyle:withTrait:` in a moment; just park it for now.

3. Finally, it creates a dictionary that maps regular expressions to the attributes declared above.

If you're not terribly familiar with regular expressions, the dictionary above might look a bit strange. But if you deconstruct the regular expressions that it contains, piece by piece, you can decode them without much effort.

Take the first regular expression you implemented above that matches words surrounded by asterisks:

```
\\*\\w+(\\s\\w+)*\\*)\\s
```

The double slashes are a result of having to escape special characters in regular expressions in Objective-C with an extra backslash. If you cast out the escaping backslashes, and consider just the core regular expression, it looks like this:

```
(\*\w+(\s\w+)*\*)\s
```

Now, deconstruct the regular expression step by step:

1. (* - match an asterisk

2. \w+ - followed by one or more "word" characters

3. (\s\w+)* - followed by zero or more groups of spaces followed by "word" characters

4. *) - followed by an asterisk

5. \s - terminated by a space.

> **Note:** If you'd like to learn more about regular expressions above and beyond this chapter, check out this NSRegularExpression tutorial and cheat sheet:
>
> http://www.raywenderlich.com/30288/nsregularexpression-tutorial-and-cheat-sheet

As an exercise, decode the other regular expressions yourself, using the explanation above and the cheat sheet as a guide. How many can you do on your own?

Now you need to actually call `createHighlightPatterns` from somewhere.

Update `init` in **SyntaxHighlightTextStorage.m as follows:**

```
- (id)init
{
    if (self = [super init]) {
        _backingStore = [NSMutableAttributedString new];
        [self createHighlightPatterns];
```

```
    }
    return self;
}
```

Add the following method to **SyntaxHighlightTextStorage.m**:

```
- (NSDictionary*)createAttributesForFontStyle:(NSString*)style
                              withTrait:(uint32_t)trait {
    UIFontDescriptor *fontDescriptor = [UIFontDescriptor
     preferredFontDescriptorWithTextStyle:style];
    UIFontDescriptor *descriptorWithTrait = [fontDescriptor
         fontDescriptorWithSymbolicTraits:trait];
    UIFont* font =  [UIFont
                     fontWithDescriptor:descriptorWithTrait
                              size: 0.0];
    return @{ NSFontAttributeName : font };
}
```

The above method applies the supplied font style to the body font. It provides a zero size to `fontWithDescriptor:size:` which forces `UIFont` to return a size that matches the user's current font size preferences.

Next, replace the existing `applyStylesToRange` method with the one below:

```
- (void)applyStylesToRange:(NSRange)searchRange
{
    NSDictionary* normalAttrs = @{NSFontAttributeName:
        [UIFont preferredFontForTextStyle:UIFontTextStyleBody]};

    // iterate over each replacement
    for (NSString* key in _replacements) {
        NSRegularExpression *regex = [NSRegularExpression
                        regularExpressionWithPattern:key
                                             options:0
                                               error:nil];

        NSDictionary* attributes = _replacements[key];

        [regex enumerateMatchesInString:[_backingStore string]
                     options:0
                       range:searchRange
                  usingBlock:^(NSTextCheckingResult *match,
                              NSMatchingFlags flags,
                              BOOL *stop){
```

```
            // apply the style
            NSRange matchRange = [match range];
            [self addAttributes:attributes range:matchRange];

            // reset the style to the original
            if (NSMaxRange(matchRange)+1 < self.length) {
                [self addAttributes:normalAttrs
                range:NSMakeRange(NSMaxRange(matchRange)+1, 1)];
            }
        }];
    }
}
```

This code does pretty much exactly what it did before, but this time it iterates over the dictionary of regex matches and attributes, and applies the specified style to the matched patterns.

Build and run your app, and exercise all of the new styles available to you, as illustrated below:

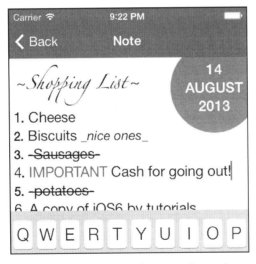

Your app is nearly complete; there's just a few loose ends to clean up.

If you've changed the orientation of your screen while working on your app, you've already noticed that the app no longer responds to content size changed notifications since your custom implementation doesn't yet support this action.

As for the second issue, if you add a lot of text to a note you'll notice that the bottom of the text view is partially obscured by the keyboard; it's a little hard to type things when you can't see what you're typing!

Time to fix up those two issues.

Reviving dynamic type

To correct the issue with dynamic type, your code should update the fonts used by the attributed string containing the text of the note when the content size change notification occurs.

Open up **SyntaxHighlightTextStorage.h** and add the following method declaration to the interface:

```
@interface SyntaxHighlightTextStorage : NSTextStorage
- (void)update;
@end
```

Next, add the following implementation to **SyntaxHighlightTextStorage.m**:

```
-(void)update {
    // update the highlight patterns
    [self createHighlightPatterns];

    // change the 'global' font
    NSDictionary* bodyFont = @{NSFontAttributeName :
      [UIFont preferredFontForTextStyle:UIFontTextStyleBody]};
    [self addAttributes : bodyFont
                 range : NSMakeRange(0, self.length)];

    // re-apply the regex matches
    [self applyStylesToRange:NSMakeRange(0, self.length)];
}
```

The method above updates all the fonts associated with the various regular expressions, applies the body text style to the entire string, and then re-applies the highlighting styles.

Finally, open **NoteEditorViewController.m** and update `preferredContentSizeChanged:` to invoke `update`:

```
- (void)preferredContentSizeChanged:(NSNotification
*)notification {
    [_textStorage update];
    [self updateTimeIndicatorFrame];
}
```

Build and run your app and change your text size preferences; the text should adjust accordingly as in the example on the next page:

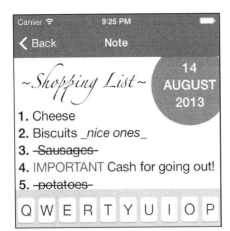 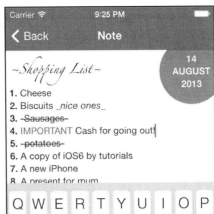

Resizing text views

All that's left to do is solve the problem of the keyboard obscuring the bottom half of the text view when editing long notes. This is one issue that iOS 7 hasn't solved for us yet!

To fix this, you'll reduce the size of the text view frame when the keyboard is visible.

Add the following instance variable to **NoteEditorViewController.m**:

```
CGRect _textViewFrame;
```

This will be used to store the current text view frame.

Within the same file update `viewDidLayoutSubviews` to make use of this newly added instance variable.

```
- (void)viewDidLayoutSubviews {
    [self updateTimeIndicatorFrame];
    _textView.frame = _textViewFrame;
}
```

And add the following to the bottom of `viewDidLoad` to set the initial frame value:

```
_textViewFrame = self.view.bounds;
```

The next step is to update this variable when the keyboard is shown. The `NoteEditorViewController` class already adopts the `UITextViewDelegate`. Add the following method to update the frame when editing begins:

```
- (void)textViewDidBeginEditing:(UITextView *)textView {
```

```
    _textViewFrame = self.view.bounds;
    _textViewFrame.size.height -= 216.0f;
    _textView.frame = _textViewFrame;
}
```

This simply reduces the height of the frame by 216 pixels, the height of the on-screen keyboard.

> **NOTE:** Yes, this is a *magic number*! You might want to handle the notification that occurs when the keyboard is shown. The data passed via this notification includes the keyboard size.

Finally, return the text view frame to its original size when editing finishes by updating `textViewDidEndEditing` as follows:

```
- (void)textViewDidEndEditing:(UITextView *)textView
{
    self.note.contents = textView.text;

    _textViewFrame = self.view.bounds;
    _textView.frame = _textViewFrame;
}
```

Build and run your app, edit a note and check that displaying the keyboard no longer obscures the text, as shown below:

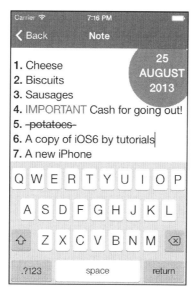

Where to go from here?

Text Kit adds many new and interesting features; ones like dynamic type will impact almost every iOS 7 application that you write. Other features, such as exclusion paths, offer opportunities for some really creative effects in your apps.

This chapter only scrapes the surface of Text Kit framework; to learn more, read on to the next chapter where you'll start to learn more about the role of the layout manager and the tremendous power it gives you.

Challenges

Before moving on to the next chapter, it's worth putting some of your newfound knowledge to use. The following section provides a few challenges for you to try out. Each challenge has a number of hints, but if you do get completely stuck, the solutions are provided.

Challenge 1: Highlighting URLs

Try extending the base list of regular expressions for dynamic styles to add a few of your own invention. Adding a regular expression to highlight URL strings, and make them 'clickable' would be a really valuable feature, and an interesting challenge!

Here are a few hints to help you along the way:

1. First you will need to construct a regular expression for locating URLs. This is quite a challenge in itself! Why not search the web and see if you can find a suitable one online?

2. The `applyStylesToRange:` method within `SyntaxHighlightTextStorage` would be a suitable place to match this regular expression. However, this time, the attributes you apply will need to contain the URL using the `NSLinkAttributeName` attribute.

3. Once you have managed to highlight URLs, you will probably discover that they are not clickable yet – this is because the `UITextView` only allows you to interact with URLs when it is no editable. In order to accommodate this, add a bar button to the Note Editor view controller which toggles the text view between its editable and non-editable state.

Challenge 2: Provide an Embedded Browser

With the current implementation, the built-in behavior is used when links are clicked – Safari is launched, leaving your notes app. It would be much better if you could keep your users within the app, displaying the web link with a `UIWebView` control, and that is the subject of your next challenge!

The `UITextViewDelegate` has had a new method added to it in iOS 7, `textView: shouldInteractWithURL: inRange:`. If you implement this delegate and return `NO`, Safari is not launched and you can add your own logic to handle when links are clicked.

Your next challenge is to use this delegate method to handle links within your app, by navigating to a view controller that hosts a `UIWebView` to render the website that the link navigates to.

Here are a few pointers:

1. You need to add a new view controller to the app, which is navigated to via the `NoteEditorViewController`. To do this, add a segue that performs a push navigation, and give it a name.

2. Provide an implementation for the view controller that exposes the URL as a property.

3. Within `NoteEditorViewController` implement the `textView: shouldInteractWithURL: inRange:` method and navigate to this newly added view controller. You can initiate this navigation by calling `performSegueWithIdentifier: sender:` with the name of the segue you added to the storyboard.

4. Finally, you need to supply the URL to the newly added view controller. You can do this by adding an implementation of `prepareForSegue: sender:` within `NoteEditorViewController`.

So – how did you do?

Chapter 5: Intermediate Text Kit

By Colin Eberhardt

In the previous chapter, you learned about the most important functionality of Text Kit, iOS 7's powerful new text rendering framework. Specifically, you learned how to support dynamic type, add letterpress effects, use exclusion paths, and create your own dynamic text formatting and storage system.

This chapter will be particularly interesting to those who are making apps that involve large, complex text layouts. You will dive more deeply into the Text Kit rendering engine itself, and learn how to use it to create your own custom text layouts.

In the process, you will build a simple iPad book app that includes the use of multiple text containers, both with and without views. Throughout the process you will delve more deeply into the way Text Kit achieves text layout. Using this knowledge you will optimize your application for performance and memory usage.

Getting started

Just like last chapter, I have created a starter project with the user interface for the app pre-created so you can stay focused on Text Kit.

Open the starter project in Xcode and build and run the app. You'll be greeted with the screen on the following page:

There's not much there right now, but that's where you and your Text Kit knowledge will come in.

The starter project is a simple modification of the Xcode master-detail template project. The detail view controller has been renamed to `BookViewController` and the master has been renamed to `ChaptersViewController`.

Most of the functionality involving communication between the master and detail view controllers has also been removed. Finally, the project also has an **Assets** group, which contains the text for the book you are going to render along with a few images.

Note: The text for the book is formatted in a markup language called Markdown, created by Daring Fireball's John Gruber. You compose and format your text using a simple plain text format, which can be converted into many other markup languages including HTML.

Markdown is designed to be readable in its native format, as the markup appears natural and doesn't compromise readability.

You can learn more about Markdown here:

http://daringfireball.net/projects/markdown/syntax

Before you start coding, it's important to review what you learned in previous last chapter about the Text Kit architecture, and then dive a little bit deeper into the layout system.

Text Kit architecture

To review from previous chapter, the following objects are constructed to support text rendering when you create a UITextView:

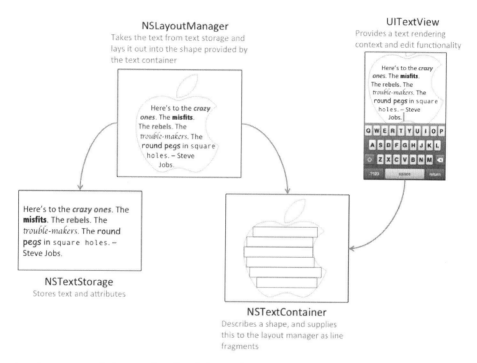

Again, the responsibilities of each of these classes are as follows:

- NSTextStorage serves as the character data repository for the text system. The format of this data is an attributed string; which is a sequence of characters and the styling attributes that apply to them. NSTextStorage is actually a subclass of NSMutableAttributedString.

- NSLayoutManager coordinates the layout and rendering of characters held in an instance on NSTextStorage. NSLayoutManager is also responsible for mapping Unicode characters to their corresponding glyphs.

• NSTextContainer defines the region of a view where text is laid out.
NSLayoutManager depends on NSTextContainer to determine where to break lines,
layout portions of text, and so on.

In order to understand the role of each of these classes, it helps to picture them in the
context of the model-view-controller design pattern, demonstrated in the image below:

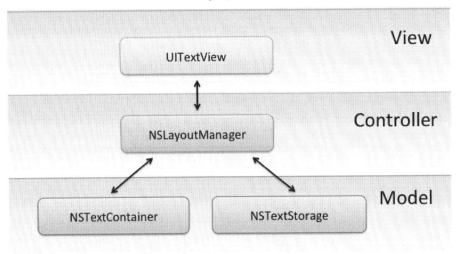

In the text rendering process, NSTextStorage provides the **model**, holding both the
text itself and the attributes that describe the associated styling. The NSTextContainer
is also considered part of the model layer, in that it describes the geometric layout of the
text on a particular view.

The NSLayoutManager is the **controller** and directs layout, glyph generation and the
rendering workflow. Finally, the UITextView (or other text-rendering UIKit control
such as UILabel) is the **view**.

If you look at the API for NSLayoutManager you will see that it is pretty complicated.
This reflects the complexity of text rendering and also the many functions that the
controller performs.

Layout configurations

In the last chapter, you created a UITextView with a custom Text Kit stack, as
illustrated:

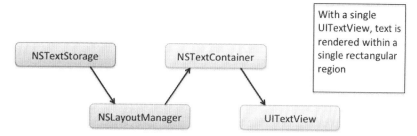

This was in order to replace the framework's `NSTextStorage` with your own custom subclass.

However, the layout manager can be associating with multiple text containers, allowing for much more complex configurations. For example, you can use multiple text containers to render text across multiple columns or pages, as illustrated below:

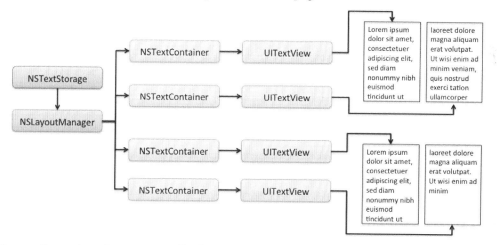

The configuration above is actually the one that you will be creating as you progress through this chapter.

Anyhow, enough of the theory, it's time to build an application!

Rendering the text

The first step in creating a working book reader is rendering the text on the screen.

`AppDelegate` will serve as the central point for application data, so open up **AppDelegate.h** and add the following property to the interface declaration:

```
@property (nonatomic, copy) NSAttributedString *bookMarkup;
```

This property will store the book markup and formatting in an attributed string.

Add the following code to `application:didFinishLaunchingWithOptions:` in **AppDelegate.m**, just before the view controllers are created:

```
NSString *path = [[NSBundle mainBundle]
                      pathForResource:@"alices_adventures"
                             ofType:@"md"];
NSString *text = [NSString
      stringWithContentsOfFile:path
                    encoding:NSUTF8StringEncoding
                       error:NULL];
self.bookMarkup = [[NSAttributedString alloc]
                                      initWithString:text];
```

The above code loads the contents of **alices_adventures.md** into an instance of `NSString`, initializes an instance of `NSAttributedString` with the contents of this `NSString`, and finally sets `bookMarkup` to the contents of the attributed string.

Create a new class by going to **File\New\File…**, choosing the **iOS\Cocoa Touch\Objective-C class** template, and clicking **Next**. Name the class `BookView`, make it a subclass of `UIView` and click **Next**. Check the box to add the new class to the **TextKitMagazine** target and finally click **Create**.

Your new view will be used to render the book text. Open **BookView.h** and add the following method and property to the interface declaration:

```
@interface BookView : UIView

@property (nonatomic, copy) NSAttributedString *bookMarkup;

- (void)buildFrames;

@end
```

The `bookMarkup` property stores the text to be rendered, while `buildFrames` creates the Text Kit components required for rendering.

Open **BookView.m** and add a private instance variable:

```
@implementation BookView
{
    NSLayoutManager *_layoutManager;
}
```

This will store an instance of the layout manager. Remember, the layout manager is the class responsible for transforming the characters in your text storage into rendered characters (i.e. glyphs) on screen.

Still in **BookView.m**, add the following implementation of buildFrames just above the @end compiler directive:

```
- (void)buildFrames
{
    // create the text storage
    NSTextStorage *textStorage = [[NSTextStorage alloc]
                    initWithAttributedString:self.bookMarkup];

    // create the layout manager
    _layoutManager = [[NSLayoutManager alloc] init];
    [textStorage addLayoutManager:_layoutManager];

    // create a container
    NSTextContainer *textContainer = [[NSTextContainer alloc]
        initWithSize:CGSizeMake(self.bounds.size.width, FLT_MAX)];
    [_layoutManager addTextContainer:textContainer];

    // create a view
    UITextView *textView = [[UITextView alloc]
                                initWithFrame:self.bounds
                                textContainer:textContainer];
    textView.scrollEnabled = YES;
    [self addSubview:textView];
}
```

If you followed along with the previous chapter, the above code should be quite familiar. It creates a UITextView with a custom "Text Kit stack" consisting of an NSTextStorage, NSLayoutManager, and NSTextContainer.

Open **BookViewController.m** and add the following imports to the top of the file:

```
#import "BookView.h"
#import "AppDelegate.h"
```

Next, add a new instance variable:

```
@implementation BookViewController
{
    BookView *_bookView;
}
```

This will keep track of an instance of the new `BookView` class you just created.

Finally, replace `viewDidLoad` with the following implementation:

```
- (void)viewDidLoad
{
    [super viewDidLoad];

    self.view.backgroundColor = [UIColor colorWithWhite:0.87f
                                                   alpha:1.0f];

    [self setEdgesForExtendedLayout:UIRectEdgeNone];

    AppDelegate *appDelegate = (AppDelegate *)
            [[UIApplication sharedApplication] delegate];

    _bookView = [[BookView alloc]
                             initWithFrame:self.view.bounds];
    _bookView.autoresizingMask = UIViewAutoresizingFlexibleWidth
                             | UIViewAutoresizingFlexibleHeight;
    _bookView.bookMarkup = appDelegate.bookMarkup;

    [self.view addSubview:_bookView];
}
```

The code above creates an instance of the new `BookView` class and assigns the markup loaded by the app delegate to its `bookMarkup` property. It also sets the edges for extended layout so that the view doesn't appear under the navigation bar.

The size for the book view will be computed when the view controller lays out its subviews. Conveniently, `viewDidLayoutSubviews` is the perfect place to instruct the book view to build itself.

In **BookViewController.m**, add the following code just below the `viewDidLoad` method:

```
- (void)viewDidLayoutSubviews
{
    [_bookView buildFrames];
}
```

Build and run your app, and behold as the text of the book renders on-screen:

Well, the text is rendered on the screen... but there's still a lot of room to improve its readability! Good thing Text Kit still has a few tricks up its sleeve.

Adding a multi-column layout

Many websites and apps make the mistake of presenting large passages of text in a line length that makes reading quite difficult. In your book reader app, there are probably in excess of 100 characters — sorry, *glyphs* — in a single unbroken line.

> **Note:** There isn't a 1:1 relationship between glyphs and characters, as a rendered glyph might actually represent more than one character in the text file. This happens, for example, when the layout manager replaces a pair of characters with a ligature. You'll discover this later when you need to find specific locations in the text, and you need to juggle the glyph and character locations separately!

Readers find long lines of text uncomfortable to read because the eye has difficulty tracking back from the end of one line to the start of the next — there's nothing more frustrating than losing your place while reading!

An optimal line length is generally around fifty to sixty characters per line. Most blogs render their text within a narrow, fixed-width section of the page, while most newspapers and magazines will use a multiple column layout to fill the page.

In your app you don't want to have a large blank margin either side of the text, nor do you want to use a huge font size, so using a multi column approach makes sense.

You will create a text view for each column of the book, and lay them out from left to right. Note you'll create all the text views at once - even beyond the two that are visible on the screen. Then you will set the book view up as a horizontal scroll view so the user can page through the book.

"Wait a minute", you might think, "creating all of these views at once sounds like a big performance problem, especially if the book is super long!" That is true, and we will discuss this more in a following section. But for now, let's go with this as it's the easiest way to get started.

Let's try this out. Open **BookView.h** and change the superclass from UIView to UIScrollView:

```
@interface BookView : UIScrollView
```

Open **BookView.m** and replace the existing buildFrames implementation with the following:

```
- (void)buildFrames {
    // create the text storage
```

```objc
    NSTextStorage *textStorage = [[NSTextStorage alloc]
                    initWithAttributedString:self.bookMarkup];

    // create the layout manager
    _layoutManager = [[NSLayoutManager alloc] init];
    [textStorage addLayoutManager:_layoutManager];

    // build the frames
    NSRange range = NSMakeRange(0, 0);
    NSUInteger containerIndex = 0;
    while(NSMaxRange(range) < _layoutManager.numberOfGlyphs) {

        // 1
        CGRect textViewRect = [self
                        frameForViewAtIndex:containerIndex];

        // 2
        CGSize containerSize =
                CGSizeMake(textViewRect.size.width,
                            textViewRect.size.height - 16.0f);
        NSTextContainer* textContainer =
            [[NSTextContainer alloc] initWithSize:containerSize];
        [_layoutManager addTextContainer:textContainer];

        // 3
        UITextView *textView = [[UITextView alloc]
                                initWithFrame:textViewRect
                                textContainer:textContainer];
        [self addSubview:textView];

        containerIndex++;

        // 4
        range = [_layoutManager
                    glyphRangeForTextContainer:textContainer];
    }

    // 5
    self.contentSize = CGSizeMake(
        (self.bounds.size.width / 2) * (CGFloat)containerIndex,
        self.bounds.size.height);
    self.pagingEnabled = YES;
}
```

You still create a single instance of `NSTextStorage` and `NSLayoutManager` as before, but now you also create several instances of `NSTextContainer` and `UITextView` based on the number of glyphs in the layout manager.

The remainder of the methods works as follows:

1. Create a frame for the view at this index; you'll implement this method shortly. Remember, you are creating all of the text views necessary to display the entire book at once, and laying out the text views one at a time from left to right.

2. Create an instance of `NSTextContainer` with a size based on the frame returned from `frameForViewAtIndex:`. Note the `16.0f` *magic number*; you decrease the height by this amount as `UITextView` adds an `8.0f` margin above and below the container.

3. Create the `UITextView` for this container.

4. Determine the glyph range for the new text container. This value is used to determine whether further text containers are required.

5. Finally update the size of the scroll view based on the number of containers created.

> **Note:** Why aren't you using the `NSTextContainer` property `heightTracksTextView` instead of manually adjusting the height of the text view? This poses a performance issue as each time a container is added, it will be re-sized to track its associated view, causing the layout manager to repeatedly layout the same text.

Now that you have to handle multiple `UITextView` instances, you'll need to compute the frame size for each one.

Add the following method to the bottom of **BookView.m**:

```objc
- (CGRect)frameForViewAtIndex:(NSUInteger)index
{
    CGRect textViewRect = CGRectMake(0, 0,
            self.bounds.size.width / 2, self.bounds.size.height);
    textViewRect = CGRectInset(textViewRect, 10.0, 20.0);
    textViewRect = CGRectOffset(textViewRect,
            (self.bounds.size.width / 2) * (CGFloat)index, 0.0);
    return textViewRect;
}
```

This method calculates a frame to be a column of half the width of the screen, reduces the margins a bit, and then sets the position to be the proper amount from the left of the view based on which column it is.

Build and run your app; the text is now rendered in two columns as shown below:

That looks a *lot* more readable — and it only took a few lines of code since Text Kit does a lot of the heavy lifting for you.

Adding text styling

Take a quick look at the text displayed in your app; you'll recognize it as the classic Alice's Adventures in Wonderland (available free thanks to the Gutenberg Project - http://www.gutenberg.org/ebooks/11).

However, check out the hash marks and other unexpected characters in the title and chapter headers; this is Markdown formatting, which was introduced in the beginning part of this chapter.

Your next task is to apply some appropriate styling to the Markdown formatting in the document.

Create a new class by going to **File\New\File…**, choosing the **iOS\Cocoa Touch\Objective-C class** template, and clicking **Next**. Name the class

MarkdownParser, make it a subclass of `NSObject` and click **Next**. Check the box to add the new class to the **TextKitMagazine** target and finally click **Create**.

Open **MarkdownParser.h** and add the following method to the interface declaration:

```
@interface MarkdownParser : NSObject

- (NSAttributedString *)parseMarkdownFile:(NSString*)path;

@end
```

Then open **MarkdownParser.m** and add the following instance variables:

```
@implementation MarkdownParser
{
    NSDictionary *_bodyTextAttributes;
    NSDictionary *_headingOneAttributes;
    NSDictionary *_headingTwoAttributes;
    NSDictionary *_headingThreeAttributes;
}
```

These will be used to store the various text attributes that are applied to the text in order to style it.

Next, within the same file, add the following init method:

```
- (id) init {
    if (self = [super init]) {
        [self createTextAttributes];
    }
    return self;
}
```

This calls the `createTextAttributes` method that you will add next:

```
- (void)createTextAttributes {
    // 1. Create the font descriptors
    UIFontDescriptor *baskerville = [UIFontDescriptor
                fontDescriptorWithFontAttributes:
        @{UIFontDescriptorFamilyAttribute: @"Baskerville"}];

    UIFontDescriptor *baskervilleBold = [baskerville
    fontDescriptorWithSymbolicTraits:UIFontDescriptorTraitBold];

    // 2. determine the current text size preference
```

```objc
UIFontDescriptor *bodyFont = [UIFontDescriptor
    preferredFontDescriptorWithTextStyle:UIFontTextStyleBody];
NSNumber *bodyFontSize =
    bodyFont.fontAttributes[UIFontDescriptorSizeAttribute];
CGFloat bodyFontSizeValue = [bodyFontSize floatValue];

// 3. create the attributes for the various styles
_bodyTextAttributes = [self
    attributesWithDescriptor:baskerville
                        size:bodyFontSizeValue];
_headingOneAttributes = [self
    attributesWithDescriptor:baskervilleBold
                        size:bodyFontSizeValue * 2.0f];
_headingTwoAttributes = [self
    attributesWithDescriptor:baskervilleBold
                        size:bodyFontSizeValue * 1.8f];
_headingThreeAttributes = [self
    attributesWithDescriptor:baskervilleBold
                        size:bodyFontSizeValue * 1.4f];
}
```

Here's an explanation of the above code, comment by comment:

1. Create two font descriptors for the Baskerville family: one normal, and one bold. Remember from the previous chapter that font descriptors are a new way in iOS 7 to specify a font that matches a collection of attributes, rather than hard-coding a particular font like in previous versions of iOS.

2. Determine the required point size of the body text; this allows you to honor the user's text size preferences without using the default font.

3. Create various attributes for the styles to be used in the document such as the body and headings, using appropriate Baskerville font and various multiplications of the user's preferred body text size.

Step (3) makes use of a simple utility method `attributesWithDescriptor: size:` that you will add next:

```objc
- (NSDictionary *)attributesWithDescriptor:
            (UIFontDescriptor*)descriptor size:(CGFloat)size
{
    UIFont *font = [UIFont fontWithDescriptor:descriptor
                                         size:size];
    return @{NSFontAttributeName: font};
```

```
        }
```

This simply creates a dictionary with a single font attribute.

Next up, it's time to add the parsing logic. Within the same file add the following method:

```objc
- (NSAttributedString *)parseMarkdownFile:(NSString *)path {
    NSMutableAttributedString* parsedOutput =
                [[NSMutableAttributedString alloc] init];

    // 1. break the file into lines and iterate over each line
    NSString *text = [NSString stringWithContentsOfFile:path
                    encoding:NSUTF8StringEncoding error:nil];
    NSArray *lines = [text
      componentsSeparatedByCharactersInSet:[NSCharacterSet
                                    newlineCharacterSet]];
    for(NSUInteger lineIndex=0; lineIndex<lines.count;
                                        lineIndex++){

        NSString *line = lines[lineIndex];

        if ([line isEqualToString:@""])
            continue;

        // 2. match the various 'heading' styles
        NSDictionary *textAttributes = _bodyTextAttributes;
        if (line.length > 3){
            if ([[line substringToIndex:3]
                        isEqualToString:@"###"]) {
                textAttributes = _headingThreeAttributes;
                line = [line substringFromIndex:3];
            } else if ([[line substringToIndex:2]
                        isEqualToString:@"##"]) {
                textAttributes = _headingTwoAttributes;
                line = [line substringFromIndex:2];
            } else if ([[line substringToIndex:1]
                        isEqualToString:@"#"]) {
                textAttributes = _headingOneAttributes;
                line = [line substringFromIndex:1];
            }
        }

        // 3. apply the attributes to this line of text
        NSAttributedString *attributedText =
```

```
                    [[NSAttributedString alloc] initWithString:line
                                          attributes:textAttributes];

        // 4. append to the output
        [parsedOutput appendAttributedString:attributedText];
        [parsedOutput appendAttributedString:
            [[NSAttributedString alloc] initWithString:@"\n\n"]];
    }

    return parsedOutput;
}
```

This method performs a relatively simplistic parsing process. Taking each step in turn:

1. The `componentsSeparatedByCharactersInSet:` method is used to split the text into an array of individual lines.

2. If the line starts with one or more 'hash' characters, the required text attributes for this level of heading are obtained. Note that this rather simplifies the process of markdown parsing, you might want to implement a more robust method for your own apps!

3. An attributed text string is constructed, which takes the current line of text and applies the attributes determined in step (2).

4. Each complete line of text is appended to the output.

Now all that's left is to make use of your parser. Open **AppDelegate.m** and add the following import:

```
#import "MarkdownParser.h"
```

Then locate the code that loads the markdown file and replace it with the following:

```
NSString* path = [[NSBundle mainBundle]
            pathForResource:@"alices_adventures" ofType:@"md"];
MarkdownParser* parser = [[MarkdownParser alloc] init];
self.bookMarkup = [parser parseMarkdownFile:path];
```

Build and run your app, and check out the snazzy new styling as illustrated below:

Once again, a little bit of Text Kit code goes a long way to making things much more readable!

Like most other areas of iOS development, there's a balance between ease of implementation and performance when working with visual elements, such as rendered text. The following section goes into more detail on performance hits, how to detect them, and how to implement performance improvements in your app.

Performance

Depending on the current font size, the application is currently rendering around 100 individual views. Since these are housed within an instance of `UIScrollView`, it means that at any point there are around 98 off-screen views that have been instantiated and are rendering text.

Not only is this is a significant waste of both CPU and memory, but it also adds to the launch time of the app as the glyphs for each view are rendered.

You could use Instruments to gather an accurate picture of memory and CPU usage, but a quick and simple alternative is to simply log messages within `UIViewController`'s `viewDidLoad` and `viewDidAppear` methods.

Open **BookViewController.m** and add the following just below the call to `[super viewDidLoad]` in `viewDidLoad`:

```
NSLog(@"viewDidLoad");
```

This simply prints the method name, along with the date and time, to the console. Add the following directly below the `viewDidLoad:` method:

```
- (void)viewDidAppear:(BOOL)animated
{
    [super viewDidAppear:animated];
    NSLog(@"viewDidAppear");
}
```

Build and run your app on your device; you'll notice it takes around 2.2 seconds to start up the application. Switch to the **Debug Navigator** pane and you'll see that the app is using around 125 MBs of memory. Yikes!

Now comment out the `viewDidLayoutSubviews` method in **BookController.m**, and build and run a second time. This time the launch is almost instantaneous and memory usage drops right down. This gives an immediate indication of the amount of memory and CPU time being wasted on those off-screen views.

A much less resource intensive approach would be to render just the visible views, creating and destroying views as required when the users scrolls. And that's exactly what you're going to do next.

Open **BookView.m** and remove the following lines of code from the `buildFrames` method.

```
// 3
UITextView *textView = [[UITextView alloc]
                         initWithFrame:textViewRect
                         textContainer:textContainer];
[self addSubview:textView];
```

As a result all the instances of `NSTextContainer` will be created, but not the `UITextView` counterparts. Add the following to the very end of the `buildFrames` method:

```
[self buildViewsForCurrentOffset];
```

We'll add this method shortly. First you need to add a few utility methods to the bottom of **BookView.m**. Start with this one:

```
- (NSArray *)textSubViews
{
    NSMutableArray *views = [NSMutableArray new];
    for (UIView *subview in self.subviews) {
        if ([subview class] == [UITextView class]) {
            [views addObject:subview];
        }
    }
    return views;
}
```

This method simply returns all the instances of UITextView that have been added as subviews of BookView.

Next add another new helper method:

```
- (UITextView *)textViewForContainer:
                    (NSTextContainer *)textContainer {
    for (UITextView *textView in [self textSubViews]) {
        if (textView.textContainer == textContainer) {
            return textView;
        }
    }
    return nil;
}
```

This method returns the owning UITextView for the NSTextContainer instance passed in, if one exists.

Finally, add one last helper method:

```
- (BOOL)shouldRenderView:(CGRect)viewFrame
{
    if (viewFrame.origin.x + viewFrame.size.width <
            (self.contentOffset.x - self.bounds.size.width))
        return NO;

    if (viewFrame.origin.x >
            (self.contentOffset.x + self.bounds.size.width * 2.0))
        return NO;

    return YES;
```

```
        }
```

This method determines whether or not a view with the given frame should be rendered, based on the current content offset of the scroll view.

It's worth noting that shouldRenderView returns YES for any frame that is within the visible portion of the scroll view, or for one frame-width on either side. This pre-loads the left and right scroll views before the user actually scrolls the view, so you're prepared in either case.

Now that you have these helper methods, you can implement the method you called earlier to build the appropriate views for the current scroll offset:

```objc
- (void)buildViewsForCurrentOffset
{
    // 1
    for(NSUInteger index = 0; index <
        _layoutManager.textContainers.count; index++) {

        // 2
        NSTextContainer *textContainer =
                        _layoutManager.textContainers[index];
        UITextView *textView = [self
                        textViewForContainer:textContainer];

        // 3
        CGRect textViewRect = [self frameForViewAtIndex:index];

        if ([self shouldRenderView:textViewRect]) {
            // 4
            if (!textView) {
                NSLog(@"Adding view at index %u", index);
                UITextView* textView = [[UITextView alloc]
                                initWithFrame:textViewRect
                                textContainer:textContainer];
                [self addSubview:textView];
            }
        } else {
            // 5
            if (textView) {
                NSLog(@"Deleting view at index %u", index);
                [textView removeFromSuperview];
            }
        }
    }
```

```
        }
    }
```

The logic here is pretty straightforward:

1. Iterate over all instances of `NSTextContainer` that have been added to the layout manager.

2. Obtain the view that renders this container. `textViewForContainer:` will return `nil` if a view is not present.

3. Determine the frame for this view, and whether or not it should be rendered.

4. If it should be rendered, check whether it already exists. If it does, do nothing; if not, create it.

5. If it shouldn't be rendered, check if it exists already. If it does, remove it.

Build and run, and you'll see that so far the code creates the first four text views; two for the visible page, and two for the page to the right.

The final step is to invoke your `buildViewsForCurrentOffset` method when the user scrolls. To do this, open **BookView.h** and adopt the scroll view protocol by adding `<UIScrollViewDelegate>` to the interface declaration:

```
@interface BookView : UIScrollView <UIScrollViewDelegate>
```

Within the `initWithFrame` method, set the delegate property to reference `self`:

```
- (id)initWithFrame:(CGRect)frame
{
    self = [super initWithFrame:frame];
    if (self) {
        self.delegate = self;
    }
    return self;
}
```

Finally, implement the delegate method that's invoked when scrolling finishes. Add the following to the bottom of **BookView.m**:

```
- (void)scrollViewDidEndDecelerating:(UIScrollView *)scrollView
{
    [self buildViewsForCurrentOffset];
}
```

Build and run your app; from the end user perspective it looks exactly the same, but if you look at the Xcode Debug Navigator you'll see it now uses a fraction of the memory it did before, and also launches in around half the time.

You can also watch the console to see the messages that are logged when views are created and destroyed:

```
2013-07-04 07:49:52.350 TextKitMagazine[7916:a0b] Adding view at index 0
2013-07-04 07:49:52.370 TextKitMagazine[7916:a0b] Adding view at index 1
2013-07-04 07:49:52.372 TextKitMagazine[7916:a0b] Adding view at index 2
2013-07-04 07:49:52.373 TextKitMagazine[7916:a0b] Adding view at index 3
2013-07-04 07:49:54.561 TextKitMagazine[7916:a0b] Adding view at index 4
2013-07-04 07:49:54.562 TextKitMagazine[7916:a0b] Adding view at index 5
2013-07-04 07:49:55.912 TextKitMagazine[7916:a0b] Deleting view at index 0
2013-07-04 07:49:55.913 TextKitMagazine[7916:a0b] Deleting view at index 1
2013-07-04 07:49:55.914 TextKitMagazine[7916:a0b] Adding view at index 6
2013-07-04 07:49:55.915 TextKitMagazine[7916:a0b] Adding view at index 7
2013-07-04 07:49:57.219 TextKitMagazine[7916:a0b] Deleting view at index 2
2013-07-04 07:49:57.220 TextKitMagazine[7916:a0b] Deleting view at index 3
2013-07-04 07:49:57.222 TextKitMagazine[7916:a0b] Adding view at index 8
2013-07-04 07:49:57.223 TextKitMagazine[7916:a0b] Adding view at index 9
2013-07-04 07:49:57.976 TextKitMagazine[7916:a0b] Deleting view at index 4
2013-07-04 07:49:57.977 TextKitMagazine[7916:a0b] Deleting view at index 5
2013-07-04 07:49:57.977 TextKitMagazine[7916:a0b] Adding view at index 10
2013-07-04 07:49:57.978 TextKitMagazine[7916:a0b] Adding view at index 11
All Output
```

This represents a tremendous gain in performance. More importantly, the app is now much more scalable. You could conceivably render a book with thousands of pages without running out of memory.

The text layout process might still take a few seconds for larger books, so you would probably want to show some sort of progress indicator to the user, and load and parse the markup on a separate thread to avoid blocking.

Adding a table of contents

With the current state of your app, the reader will quickly wear out their finger swiping madly to get to their desired chapter! Adding a table of contents is a much better idea to navigate the various chapters in the book.

Add a new class by going to **File\New\File…**, choosing the **iOS\Cocoa Touch\Objective-C class** template, and clicking **Next**. Name the class `Chapter`, make it a subclass of `NSObject` and click **Next**. Check the box to add the new class to the **TextKitMagazine** target and finally click **Create**.

Open **Chapter.h** and add the following properties to the interface declaration:

```
@interface Chapter : NSObject

@property (nonatomic, copy) NSString *title;
@property (nonatomic, assign) NSUInteger location;
```

```
@end
```

This will keep track of the title of the chapter, and the location of the chapter as an offset into the text.

Open **AppDelegate.h** and add a property to the interface declaration that exposes an array of chapters:

```
@property (nonatomic, strong) NSArray *chapters;
```

Next open **AppDelegate.m** and import the new Chapter class, just beneath the existing imports:

```
#import "Chapter.h"
```

Then add the following method to the bottom of the implementation, just above the @end compiler directive:

```
- (NSMutableArray *)locateChapters:(NSString *)markdown {
    NSMutableArray *chapters = [NSMutableArray new];
    [markdown
        enumerateSubstringsInRange:NSMakeRange(0,
                                    markdown.length)
        options:NSStringEnumerationByLines
        usingBlock:^(NSString *substring,
                     NSRange substringRange,
                     NSRange enclosingRange,
                     BOOL *stop) {
        if (substring.length > 7 &&
            [[substring substringToIndex:7]
                        isEqualToString:@"CHAPTER"]) {
            Chapter *chapter = [Chapter new];
            chapter.title = substring;
            chapter.location = substringRange.location;
            [chapters addObject:chapter];
        }
    }];
    return chapters;
}
```

This uses NSString's enumerateSubstringsInRange:options:usingBlock: method, which invokes a block for each line of the text it finds. For each line, it looks for the "CHAPTER" keyword and builds up an array of `Chapter` instances to mark their respective locations in the book based on the offset in the text.

Still within **AppDelegate.m**, add the following line to `application:didFinishLaunchingWithOptions:` just below the spot that parses the markdown file:

```
self.chapters = [self locateChapters:self.bookMarkup.string];
```

Now that you have an array of chapters, the next step is to render them as the table of contents.

Open **ChaptersViewController.m** and add the following imports to the top of the file:

```
#import "AppDelegate.h"
#import "Chapter.h"
```

Further down the same file, add a convenience method that obtains the chapter array from the app delegate:

```
- (NSArray *)chapters
{
    AppDelegate *appDelegate = (AppDelegate *)
                    [[UIApplication sharedApplication] delegate];
    return appDelegate.chapters;
}
```

The next step is to update the tableview data-source methods to display the chapters.

Still working in **ChaptersViewController.m**, update the method that informs the table view of the number of rows to display:

```
- (NSInteger)tableView:(UITableView *)tableView
                    numberOfRowsInSection:(NSInteger)section
{
    return [self chapters].count;
}
```

Next, update the method that creates the tableview cells:

```
- (UITableViewCell *)tableView:(UITableView *)tableView
        cellForRowAtIndexPath:(NSIndexPath *)indexPath
{
    UITableViewCell *cell = [tableView
```

```
                    dequeueReusableCellWithIdentifier:@"Cell"
                                      forIndexPath:indexPath];
    Chapter *chapter = [self chapters][indexPath.row];
    cell.textLabel.text = chapter.title;
    return cell;
}
```

This simply sets the text for each cell to the title of the corresponding chapter.

Build and run your app; tap on the **Chapters** button to reveal the list of chapters, as so:

However, poke all you want at the chapter entries in the list; you still won't go anywhere. The next section walks you through hooking up the chapter entries to the correct position in the text!

Adding chapter navigation

Open **ChaptersViewController.m** and locate the empty
`tableView:didSelectRowAtIndexPath:` method; replace it with the following:

```
- (void)tableView:(UITableView *)tableView
```

```
                 didSelectRowAtIndexPath:(NSIndexPath *)indexPath
{
    Chapter *chapter = [self chapters][indexPath.row];
    [self.bookViewController
            navigateToCharacterLocation:chapter.location];
}
```

This simply locates the selected `Chapter` and asks the `bookViewController` to navigate to that chapter via `navigateToCharacterLocation`. Looks like that's the next bit of code you need to implement!

Open **BookViewController.h** and add the following to the interface declaration:

```
- (void)navigateToCharacterLocation:(NSUInteger)location;
```

Then open **BookViewController.m** and add the following implementation to the bottom of the class, just above the @end compiler directive:

```
- (void)navigateToCharacterLocation:(NSUInteger)location
{
    [self.masterPopoverController dismissPopoverAnimated:YES];
    [_bookView navigateToCharacterLocation:location];
}
```

This dismisses the `chaptersViewController` and relinquishes the responsibility of navigating to the required location to the `BookView` instance.

Open **BookView.h** and add the following method to the interface declaration:

```
- (void)navigateToCharacterLocation:(NSUInteger)location;
```

Then open **BookView.m** to add the following implementation just below `scrollViewDidEndDecelerating`:

```
- (void)navigateToCharacterLocation:(NSUInteger)location
{
    CGFloat offset = 0.0f;
    for (NSTextContainer *container in
                       _layoutManager.textContainers) {
        NSRange glyphRange = [_layoutManager
                      glyphRangeForTextContainer:container];
        NSRange charRange = [_layoutManager
                        characterRangeForGlyphRange:glyphRange
                                    actualGlyphRange:nil];
        if (location >= charRange.location &&
```

```
            location < NSMaxRange(charRange)) {
                self.contentOffset = CGPointMake(offset, 0);
                [self buildViewsForCurrentOffset];
                return;
            }
            offset += self.bounds.size.width / 2.0f;
        }
    }
```

Although it may not look like it, this method is surprisingly simple. It iterates over each of the `NSTextContainer` instances associated with the layout manager and obtains the instance's glyph range. The code then performs the critical step of converting the glyph range into a character range.

For each instance of `NSTextContainer,` the code checks whether the required location is within the bounds of its characters range. If so, it applies the scroll view offset and invokes `buildViewForCurrentOffset` to build the required views.

> **Note:** Why the conversion from glyphs to characters? `NSLayoutManager` primarily deals with glyphs, whereas `NSTextStorage`, and strings in general, deal with characters. As noted earlier in this chapter, the mapping is certainly not always one-to-one, due to things such as different Unicode character sets, or font-specific features such as ligatures.

Build and run your app, and tap on one of the chapter entries; you can now successfully jump to a specific chapter in the book.

If you are an eagle-eyed software tester, you might have spotted one minor flaw with the current user interface – the chapter list retains its previous selection. Why is this a bad thing?

Put yourself in the position of an end user, they open up the chapter navigation and tap to jump ahead to Chapter VII, The Mad Hatter's Tea Party (everyone's favorite chapter!). They then read on from there for another couple of chapters. If they then re-open the chapter navigation, it gives the impression that they are still at chapter VII.

An inconsistent user interface will confuse and frustrate your users!

Fortunately this issue is very easy to fix, this is a very common use-case for table view controllers, and it has a built in feature that clears selection automatically for you. At the top of **ChaptersViewController.m** locate the line that sets the `clearsSelectionOnViewWillAppear` property (this was inserted by the Xcode project template), and set it to YES:

```
self.clearsSelectionOnViewWillAppear = YES;
```

Build and run your app, it now performs as it should :]

The presentation of the book is certainly looking much better now, but astute readers will have noticed that there are image placeholders in the book. Time to add some images to further dress up this book!

Adding images

In Text Kit, images are added to text storage as instances of `NSTextAttachment`. If you take a look at the image placeholders in the text, you'll see that they use the standard Markdown image format:

```
![Alt text](/path/to/image.png)
```

> **Note:** *Alt text* is a nod to its HTML image tag brethren, and is used as alternative to the image for accessibility.

The title page of this book contains the image tag below:

```
![Alice in Wonderland](alice.png)
```

Your parser needs to match this pattern, replacing each Markdown image tag with an instance of `NSTextAttachment` that contains the requisite image.

Open **MarkdownParser.m** and add the following code to the `parseMarkdownFile` method, just above the `return parsedOutput` statement:

```objc
// 1. Locate images
NSRegularExpression *regex = [NSRegularExpression
          regularExpressionWithPattern:@"\\!\\[.*\\]\\((.*)\\)"
                                options:0
                                  error:nil];

NSArray *matches = [regex
          matchesInString:[parsedOutput string]
                  options:0
                    range:NSMakeRange(0, parsedOutput.length)];

// 2. Iterate over matches in reverse
for (NSTextCheckingResult *result in
                          [matches reverseObjectEnumerator]) {
    NSRange matchRange = [result range];
    NSRange captureRange = [result rangeAtIndex:1];

    // 3. Create an attachment for each image
    NSTextAttachment *textAttachment = [NSTextAttachment new];
    textAttachment.image = [UIImage imageNamed:
        [parsedOutput.string substringWithRange:captureRange]];

    // 4. Replace the image markup with the attachment
    NSAttributedString *replacementString = [NSAttributedString
        attributedStringWithAttachment: textAttachment];
    [parsedOutput replaceCharactersInRange:matchRange
        withAttributedString:replacementString];
}
```

Let's look at each step in turn:

1. A regular expression is used to locate all the markdown images in the book text. You'll look at this regular expression in detail shortly.

2. A for loop is used to iterate over the matches in reverse. This might seem a bit odd, but there is a perfectly good reason for this. Since each image tag is replaced with an attachment, the overall string length will decrease. Enumerating in reverse avoids having to recalculate the ranges returned by the regular expression.

3. An NSTextAttachment instance is created for each image.

4. The image markdown is replaced with an attributed string based on this attachment.

Now, back to that regular expression, if you cast out the escaping backslashes, and consider just the core regular expression, it looks like this

```
\!\[.*\]\((.*)\)
```

Now, deconstruct the regular expression step by step:

1. \! - match an exclamation mark

2. \[.*\] - followed by some characters surrounded by square brackets, i.e. the alt-text

3. \((.*)\) - followed by some characters surrounded by round brackets, i.e. the image location. Note that extra brackets around the expression that matches the characters, (.*), this is a 'capture', which allows us to pull out the image location from the matches expression.

> **Note:** If you'd like to learn more about regular expressions above and beyond this chapter, check out this NSRegularExpression tutorial and cheat sheet:
>
> http://www.raywenderlich.com/30288/nsregularexpression-tutorial-and-cheat-sheet

Build and run your app; you should now see images nestled comfortably in your book content:

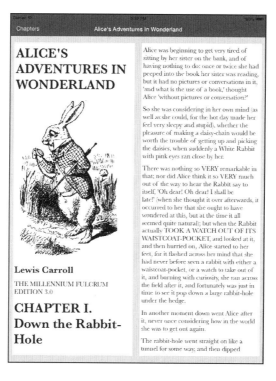

Adding dictionary lookups

Okay, you have text, you have chapters, and now you have images. Your work here is done, right?

Almost! Like most modern e-readers, you'll provide a dictionary lookup function where the user can tap any word in the book and instantly get a definition.

There are two steps to this: finding and highlighting tapped words, and then displaying the dictionary results.

Finding and highlighting tapped words

Open **BookView.m** and add the following just below the `self.delegate = self;` statement in `initWithFrame:`

```
UITapGestureRecognizer *recognizer =
   [[UITapGestureRecognizer alloc]
                     initWithTarget:self
                            action:@selector(handleTap:)];
[self addGestureRecognizer:recognizer];
```

This adds an instance of `UITapGestureRecognizer` that invokes the `handleTap` method, which you'll implement shortly.

> **Note:** `UITapGestureRecognizer` is a subclass of `UIGestureRecognizer` that looks for single or multiple taps. For the gesture to be recognized, the specified number of fingers must tap the view the specified number of times.

Add the following instance variable to **BookView.m**, just below the `_layoutManager` instance variable:

```
NSRange _wordCharacterRange;
```

This stores the character range of the word that was tapped.

Now add the following method directly below `navigateToCharacterLocation`:

```
-(void)handleTap:(UITapGestureRecognizer*)tapRecognizer
{
    NSTextStorage *textStorage = _layoutManager.textStorage;
        // 1
```

```
        CGPoint tappedLocation = [tapRecognizer
                                        locationInView:self];
        UITextView *tappedTextView = nil;
        for (UITextView *textView in [self textSubViews]) {
            if (CGRectContainsPoint(textView.frame,
                                    tappedLocation)) {
                tappedTextView = textView;
                break;
            }
        }

        if (!tappedTextView)
            return;

        // 2
        CGPoint subViewLocation = [tapRecognizer
                                    locationInView:tappedTextView];
        subViewLocation.y -= 8.0;

        // 3
        NSUInteger glyphIndex = [_layoutManager
                    glyphIndexForPoint:subViewLocation
                        inTextContainer:tappedTextView.textContainer];
        NSUInteger charIndex = [_layoutManager
                        characterIndexForGlyphAtIndex:glyphIndex];

        // 4
        if (![[NSCharacterSet letterCharacterSet]
                characterIsMember:[textStorage.string
                                    characterAtIndex:charIndex]])
            return;

        // 5
        _wordCharacterRange = [self
                    wordThatContainsCharacter:charIndex
                                    string:textStorage.string];

        // 6
        [textStorage addAttribute:NSForegroundColorAttributeName
                        value:[UIColor redColor]
                        range:_wordCharacterRange];
}
```

Here's an explanation of the above code, comment by comment:

1. First, locate the tapped instance of UITextView by iterating over all the subviews belonging to the view and check whether its frame contains the point of the tap.

2. Next, convert the tap point into the coordinate system of the respective view and subtract the text container's margin accordingly.

3. Determine the index of the tapped glyph using NSLayoutManager and convert the glyph index into a character index. This allows you to look up the corresponding character(s) in the text storage.

4. Determine whether the tapped character is a letter; it's a bit troublesome to perform dictionary lookups on spaces, numbers, and attachments!

5. Expand the character index into a word range.

6. Finally, apply a text color attribute to the word range.

The only thing missing is the method that expands a character into a word range.

Add the following just above the @end compiler directive in **BookView.m**:

```
- (NSRange)wordThatContainsCharacter:(NSUInteger)charIndex
                              string:(NSString *)string
{
    NSUInteger startLocation = charIndex;
    while(startLocation > 0 &&
        [[NSCharacterSet letterCharacterSet] characterIsMember:
            [string characterAtIndex:startLocation-1]]) {
        startLocation--;
    }
    NSUInteger endLocation = charIndex;
    while(endLocation < string.length &&
        [[NSCharacterSet letterCharacterSet] characterIsMember:
            [string characterAtIndex:endLocation+1]]) {
        endLocation++;
    }
    return NSMakeRange(startLocation,
                    endLocation-startLocation+1);
}
```

The above code calculates the word range by searching backward and forward from the selected index until it finds the non-letter characters on either side of the word.

Build and run your app and tap various words in the book; they should highlight in red, as shown:

Okay; you know that your tap event handling and word range calculations work as designed. Now you need to look up the word in the dictionary and display the results.

Displaying dictionary results

Add a new protocol by going to **File\New\File…**, choosing the **iOS\Cocoa Touch\Objective-C protocol** template, and clicking **Next**. Name the protocol BookViewDelegate and click **Next**. Check the box to add the new protocol to the **TextKitMagazine** target and finally click **Create**.

Open **BookViewDelegate.h** and replace the contents with the following:

```objc
@class BookView;

@protocol BookViewDelegate <NSObject>

- (void)bookView:(BookView *)bookView didHighlightWord:(NSString *)word inRect:(CGRect)rect;

@end
```

This informs delegates of `BookView` that a word has been tapped.

Open **BookView.h** and import this delegate:

```
#import "BookViewDelegate.h"
```

And also add a property to the interface declaration:

```
@property (nonatomic, weak)
  id<BookViewDelegate> bookViewDelegate;
```

Now open **BookView.m,** locate the `handleTap:` method and add the following to the bottom of the implementation:

```
// 1
CGRect rect = [_layoutManager
      lineFragmentRectForGlyphAtIndex:glyphIndex
                       effectiveRange:nil];

// 2
NSRange wordGlyphRange = [_layoutManager
            glyphRangeForCharacterRange:_wordCharacterRange
                  actualCharacterRange:nil];
CGPoint startLocation = [_layoutManager
              locationForGlyphAtIndex:wordGlyphRange.location];
CGPoint endLocation = [_layoutManager
            locationForGlyphAtIndex:NSMaxRange(wordGlyphRange)];

// 3
CGRect wordRect = CGRectMake(startLocation.x, rect.origin.y,
              endLocation.x - startLocation.x, rect.size.height);

// 4
wordRect = CGRectOffset(wordRect, tappedTextView.frame.origin.x,
                                 tappedTextView.frame.origin.y);

// 5
wordRect = CGRectOffset(wordRect, 0.0, 8.0);

NSString* word = [textStorage.string
                       substringWithRange:_wordCharacterRange];
[self.bookViewDelegate bookView:self didHighlightWord:word
inRect:wordRect];
```

Looking at each commented section in turn, you'll see that the code does the following:

1. Obtains the relevant line fragment for the tapped glyph.

2. Obtains the location of the first and last glyphs of the tapped word.

3. Calculates the rectangle of the selected word by using the height of the line fragment and the position of the start and end glyphs in the word.

4. Converts the resulting rectangle into the coordinate system of the `BookView` instance.

5. Adjusts the rectangle by the margin offset, and invokes the newly added delegate method.

Open **BookViewController.m** and add the following import:

```
#import "BookViewDelegate.h"
```

A little further down the file, adopt this delegate, together with the popover delegate:

Still in **BookViewController.m**, update the interface declaration to adopt both the `BookViewDelegate` and `UIPopoverControllerDelegate` protocols:

```
@interface BookViewController ()
    <BookViewDelegate, UIPopoverControllerDelegate>
```

Further down the same file, add the following line to the bottom of the `viewDidLoad` method to set the view controller as the book view's delegate:

```
_bookView.bookViewDelegate = self;
```

Next, add the following instance variable for the popover just below the `_bookView` instance variable:

```
UIPopoverController* _popover;
```

The book view delegate declares a single method that is invoked when a word is tapped.

Add the following code to the bottom of **BookViewController.m**:

```
- (void)bookView:(BookView *)bookView
    didHighlightWord:(NSString *)word inRect:(CGRect)rect {

  UIReferenceLibraryViewController *dictionaryVC =
          [[UIReferenceLibraryViewController alloc]
                                  initWithTerm: word];
  _popover.contentViewController = dictionaryVC;

  _popover = [[UIPopoverController alloc]
```

```
                    initWithContentViewController:dictionaryVC];
     _popover.delegate = self;

     [_popover presentPopoverFromRect:rect
                             inView:_bookView
            permittedArrowDirections:UIPopoverArrowDirectionAny
                           animated:YES];


  }
```

The above code creates an instance of a UIReferenceLibraryViewController, which renders the built-in iOS dictionary. This view controller is then hosted within a UIPopoverController that is 'presented' at the location of the tapped word.

The popover delegate adopted earlier allows you to detect when the popover is closed. Add the following method to **BookViewController.m** directly below the method you added above:

```
- (void)popoverControllerDidDismissPopover:
                  (UIPopoverController *)popoverController
{
    [_bookView removeWordHighlight];
}
```

This method simply informs the BookView instance that the word highlight should be removed.

Open **BookView.h** and add the following method to the interface declaration:

```
- (void)removeWordHighlight;
```

And within **BookView.m,** add the following implementation to the bottom of the class, just above the @end compiler directive:

```
- (void)removeWordHighlight
{
    [_layoutManager.textStorage
              removeAttribute:NSForegroundColorAttributeName
                        range:_wordCharacterRange];

}
```

This simply removes the highlight attribute that was previously applied to the tapped word.

Build and run your app; tap on any word in the book and you're presented with a dictionary lookup, as shown below:

Now you can finally discover what bandersnatches and borogroves are! :]

Note – you may have to download a dictionary to the simulator in order to make the look-up work. To do this, tap on the 'manage' button and select the dictionary you wish to install:

With that final feature in place, your Text Kit powered book is complete!

Challenges

You've learnt a lot of new things throughout this chapter, and now it's time to put some of this newfound knowledge into practice!

The following are a collection of challenges where you will expand on the application you have been developing, adding new features.

If you get stuck, you will find the solutions in the resources section of this chapter. But don't peek until you have at least tried to complete the challenge by yourself ;]

Challenge 1: Dynamic Type

The current book application honors the users text size preferences. However, there is one small problem – the text size is only determined when the application first starts up (you can find this code within `MarkdownParser`). This means that the user has to re-launch the application if they wish to change the text size. This is a pretty poor user experience.

Your challenge is to fix this problem, and have the application adjust its text size when the user switches back to the app after adjusting their text size preference.

Here are a few hints:

1. You need to handle the `UIContentSizeCategoryDidChangeNotification` notification. The `BookViewController` is probably the best for this logic.

2. The fonts used to render the book are created by the `MarkdownParser`. The easiest way to update this information is to simply create a new `MarkdownParser` instance and parse the markdown once again. To do this, you need to add a method to the `AppDelegate` interface, and invoke it from the `BookViewController`.

3. You need to provide the updated text to the `BookView` and tell it to re-draw.

4. Finally, as the text size has changed, the users current viewing location will not be correct. Within `BookView` you should probably reset the scroll location in the `buildFrames` method.

That was pretty simple wasn't it? However, there's something not quite right, and that brings us on to your second challenge (which is a bit harder).

Challenge 2: Maintaining the reader's location

Your book app now responds to text size changes, without the need to restart the app, but if you put yourself in the position of the user, something is not quite right.

Let's say I am just over half way through the book, enjoying the absurdity of a croquet match played with flamingos for croquet mallets and hedgehogs for balls. At this point, it is getting a little dark in my house, and my eyes are growing weary, so I want to increase the text size.

I switch to the settings screen, then switch back, the book responds, increasing its font size, but moves right back to the start of the book. I then have to try to find my reading position again. Frustrated and angry I give your app a 1-star rating in the App Store (user's can be so irrational!).

It is quite understandable that a user would get frustrated if the app causes them to lose their position, so this challenge if to fix this problem!

The app already has the logic required to navigate to a specific location, via the BookView method `navigateToCharacterLocation`. You are going to have to find a way to keep track of the current location, then re-apply it after responding to text size changes.

Here are a few hints:

1. You are going to have to add an instance variable to `BookView` to keep track of the current location, i.e. a variable that stores the character index of the first visible view.

2. You need to find a suitable point within the code to update this variable (remember the user can navigate by scrolling, or by tapping on a chapter, so this code must be executed in both cases). I would say `buildViewsForCurrentOffset` is a good candidate.

3. Determining the character index of the first visible view is a bit challenging! How about iterating over all the containers, using the `frameForViewAtIndex` method to determine its location, in order to find the text container that will be visible? You can get the character range for this container using the code you have already seen within `navigateToCharacterLocation:`.

4. Finally, you need to navigate to this location when the view is re-built following text size changes. You already have a method that will perform this, `navigateToCharacterLocation:`, it is just a matter of calling it at the right point in the code. How about near the end of `buildFrames`?

This was a bit more of a challenge wasn't it?

If you do get stuck, the solution is included in this chapter's resources. But do try to complete this challenge by yourself first!

Chapter 6: Transitioning to iOS 7 – Quick Start

By Matthijs Hollemans

If you have an app on the App Store that doesn't yet take full advantage of iOS 7's new look and feel, then you may find it quickly disregarded by new and old customers alike. Texture-rich apps with hyper realistic-looking designs simply do not fit in well with the new aesthetic. The changes are more than skin deep; there are also important differences in how users expect apps to work on iOS 7, not just how they look. If you want your apps to fit in, you need to join the revolution.

In the first chapter of this book, you learned how to make your apps feel look and feel great in iOS 7 from a design perspective. In this and the following two chapters, you'll switch to a technical perspective and take more of a hands-on, practical approach.

Specifically, you'll take an app that was written for iOS 6 — filled with lush, richly detailed textures — and transition it to the new design language of iOS 7. You'll deal with the technical aspects involved in moving to the latest version of the SDK, and you'll also consider the impact of the various design changes.

Even if you're making an app completely for scratch for iOS 7, you will find these chapters useful. They cover many of the most important aspects that have changed in iOS 7 that all developers should be aware of.

One word of warning: this chapter is long! Although we kept most of the chapters in this book short to reach our goal of engagement as mentioned in the introduction, we made an exception for this chapter.

This is because we thought of all the chapters in the book, this was the most important, and we wanted to take a complex real world example that demonstrates many of the issues you may come across when working on your own apps. Let's take a peek!

Getting started

In this chapter, you will take an app called **Treasure Hunt** that was designed for iOS 6, and update it for iOS 7.

Treasure Hunt is a social app for sharing treasure maps, so that users can engage in solving riddles and finding hidden treasures together. It's a bit like geocaching — a fun outdoor activity in which those taking part use their mobile devices to hide and find containers, known as geocaches, all over the world — but instead of GPS coordinates, it uses the age-old tradition of hand-drawn treasure maps.

This is what the app looks like on iOS 6.1:

  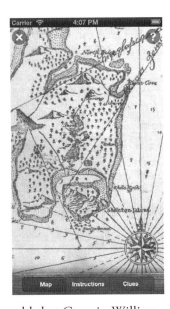

The app is not just for finding historical treasure, such as the gold that Captain William Kidd is supposed to have buried in the late 1600's. People can upload any kind of treasure map they like; it's great for birthday parties, Easter egg hunts, or any other activity where the fun lies in unraveling obscure clues to unearth some kind of hidden treasure, whether that is mountains of gold or just a bar of candy. If only they had this app in The Da Vinci Code!

> **Note:** If the above description makes you want to put the app on your phone and head out to find some gold, then you're going to be disappointed. It's only a sample project and the included treasure maps aren't real. Sorry, treasure hunters!

> If this were a real app, it would have to connect to a server to download the shared maps and coordinate the social activities. That's outside of the scope for this tutorial, so the app simply fakes the connection to the server.
>
> The important thing, however, is that Treasure Hunt demonstrates a lot of the issues that you'll come across transitioning your apps to iOS 7 — and more importantly the solutions!

The resources for this chapter include a starter project with the source code for the iOS 6 version of the app. If you want to see how Treasure Hunt worked in iOS 6, the best way is to open it in Xcode 4.6 (if you still have it installed). This will build the app against the iOS 6.1 SDK and run it on the iOS 6 simulator, giving you the most accurate view of what it looked like running in iOS 6.

If you open the app in Xcode 5, then it will build against the iOS 7 SDK instead and certain things may not work the way you'd expect — which is exactly the sort of thing that you're going to fix in this tutorial.

If you don't have Xcode 4.6 installed anymore, don't worry — you don't need it except if you're curious about how the app used to work before iOS 7. You just might notice some strangeness with the app when you run it in Xcode 5, but you'll be fixing that soon! ☺

When you're done with this tutorial, Treasure Hunt will look like this:

You will make this transition across the next three chapters:

1. **Chapter 6, Transitioning to iOS 7: Quick Start**: You are here! In this chapter, you will cover the most important aspects you need to know to get started making apps for iOS 7: table view changes, asset catalogs, tint colors, and data entry.

2. **Chapter 7, Transitioning to iOS 7: What's New with Auto Layout**: iOS 7 brings some exciting new improvements to Auto Layout that makes working with Auto Layout much easier and practical. And with the new dynamic type system that you learned about in Chapter 4, "Beginning Text Kit", using Auto Layout is now almost a necessity!

3. **Chapter 8, Transitioning to iOS 7: Advanced Topics**: As always we want to take you beyond just the basics in our books. In this chapter, we'll show you how to use blur effects, make swipe menus, and make sure your app still works on iOS 6.

You don't necessarily have to go through all three of these chapters – you can pick and choose which are the most useful to you. We recommend going through this chapter to get the basics, and then reading further if you need additional help with some tricky ports.

Why bother?

If you already have an app on the App Store and it's doing well, then why should you bother to update it for iOS 7? Well, that decision depends on a few things. If your app already has a design not too dissimilar from iOS 7, then there may be no need to rush. You can simply tweak the UI a little bit in your next update. But if your app has a skeuomorphic design filled to the brim with heavily detailed, oversaturated textures, such as Treasure Hunt, then you may want to consider the following points:

- The new subtle, unassuming and less brash UI of iOS 7 makes many existing apps look and feel out-of-place. Chances are that your UI needs a complete design overhaul in order to feel at home on iOS 7. Design is like fashion; if your app doesn't follow the latest trends, your users are going to start looking elsewhere for apps that appear up-to-date.

- Even if you don't want to update the look of your user interface, certain standard UIKit elements such as alert views, action sheets, and the on-screen keyboard now appear in the new style, which might well clash with your existing style.

- Apps compiled against the iOS 6 SDK on Xcode 4.6 run in a special emulation mode on iOS 7 that tries to preserve the old look. But as soon as you switch to Xcode 5 and build against the iOS 7 SDK, things will start to go awry in your app. The new SDK makes many changes to the metrics and visuals of the standard UI elements. You need to fix these issues anyway, so you may as well think about switching altogether.

- iOS 7 introduces new accessibility features such as Dynamic Type, which lets the user determine how big the text on the screen should be. If your app doesn't support this, users will start looking for alternatives that do.

- If your app uses custom gestures, they might conflict with the new system-wide gestures for summoning Control Center or swiping back on navigation controllers. You may need to tweak your gestures so they can co-exist on iOS 7.

- Apple as a company cares deeply about the future — and iOS 6 clearly represents the past. If you want to be noticed by Apple, then iOS 7 is where you need to be. It's unlikely that the App Store will feature any apps that do not fully embrace iOS 7 and all it has to offer. Moving to iOS 7 will greatly increase your chances of App Store success.

- The icons are different. You need a new 120×120 pixel icon that has a different corner radius. So at the very least, make sure to update your icon!

Switching to iOS 7 can be a lot of work, especially if you have a completely custom UI. Embrace the change; if you don't, you run the risk of your app becoming irrelevant — sooner than later. Your apps deserve better than that.

Back to the drawing board

One of the main themes of iOS 7 is **deference**; that the interface should get out of the way of the user. Apple has made it very clear that apps should focus on their *content*. For Treasure Hunt, the content is the treasure maps. If you have a photo manipulation app, the content is the photos. If your app is for note taking, the content is the notes. Content is king on iOS 7; UI elements should never compete with the content for the user's attention.

As you consider the transition of your app to iOS 7, it might be useful to rethink your app and consider what is *really* important to your app and what isn't. Does the user experience still make sense in an iOS 7 world? Maybe now is a good time to change the navigational structure of your app, to combine two separate screens into one, or to use gestures to directly manipulate your content rather than through buttons and sliders.

Many of the standard apps — Calendar and Photos, for example — now use a zooming paradigm for navigating through the content. You zoom in from the year to the month to the week to the day, often literally, using attractive but contextually relevant animations. When you launch an app, the app icon appears to zoom into the launch image. Conversely, closing an app invokes a zoom-out animation. Zooming is a big idea on iOS 7 and if your app can take advantage of it, you should plan to adopt the new paradigm.

The changes to the Treasure Hunt app of this chapter won't be that extensive. There will be many small tweaks in the UI, but the organization of most of the screens will remain largely the same. As you're looking to transition your own apps, you might take this as an opportunity to not just patch up the graphics, but also to dramatically increase the user experience.

First steps in Xcode 5

> **Note:** Before you open your own projects in Xcode 5, it's essential to make a backup copy first. Xcode 5 will make some format changes to your storyboard files, making it impossible to edit them in the previous version of Xcode, should you want to go back at some point. Of course, if you're using version control, this is less of an issue. Just make sure you commit your latest changes first.

Open the **Treasure Hunt** starter project in Xcode 5. If you haven't used it before, Xcode 5 looks quite similar to Xcode 4 so you should be able to find your way around quite quickly, as you'll note in the image below:

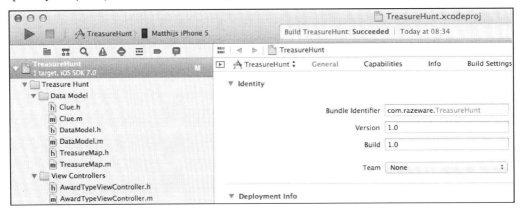

The sample project should open without any issues. Press ⌘+B to build the app (that's the **cmd** key on your keyboard together with the **B** key). You should see no warnings or error messages.

> **Note:** In the Build Settings for this app, the **Other Warning Flags** are set to –Wall –Wextra. This setting will catch most common mistakes. In addition, the Static Analyzer is always enabled. It makes sense to get as much help from the compiler as possible to catch silly programming errors.

Time to take a look at the app in iOS 7. Run the app using the **iPhone Retina (4-inch)** simulator. Choose the simulator using the scheme picker box at the top of the Xcode window:

If you also have the iOS 6 simulator installed, it looks like this:

The app looks a bit worse for wear now:

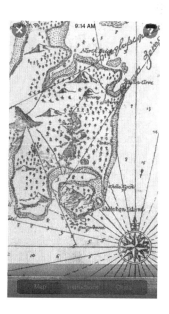

There are some obvious problems here:

- In the main screen of the app, the + bar icon is blue and the Edit label doesn't fit the bar button shape. The background of the table view cell with the torn paper is not transparent but opaque white. The selected tab bar icon is also blue, which doesn't sit well with the wooden motif.

- The Edit Map screen has a solid black bar where the status bar used to be, and the rest of its layout looks untidy.

- The third screen, known as the Map Detail screen, does have a status bar but it overlaps the actual map image making it hard to see. The toolbar doesn't look very good either; its shadow image is now a dark strip on top of the map, and the colors of the labels render them illegible.

The app has several more screens, and they all suffer from similar problems. What's worse, the richly textured design of the app no longer fits in well with the overall aesthetic of iOS 7. All other iOS 7 apps use a subtle, minimal design. This clashes with the heavy wood texture used in Treasure Hunt.

The following image of the Clue Sheet popup that lets users add clues and comments to a treasure map illustrates this mismatch between visual styles:

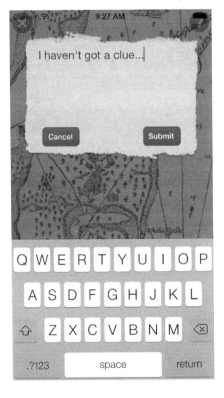

The new look of the on-screen keyboard conflicts directly with the tattered paper texture of the Clue Sheet. This just isn't very nice to look at.

Going iOS 7 only

To simplify the transition to iOS 7, let's assume the app is now iOS 7-only. The look-and-feel of iOS 7 is so different from its predecessors that it will be tricky to make your apps look good *and* be backward compatible.

> **Note:** In Chapter 8, "Transitioning to iOS 7: Advanced Topics" you will see how you can make the app also run on iOS 6.

To force the app to be iOS 7-only, you have to set the **iOS Deployment Target** to 7.0. You may be familiar with doing this in Xcode 4, but there's a new way to set this in Xcode 5 because it combines several settings screens into the one area.

Click the **TreasureHunt** icon at the top to switch from the **Target** settings to the **Project** settings. A project can contain multiple targets. The settings you change at the project level filter down to all targets unless you override them on a per-target basis:

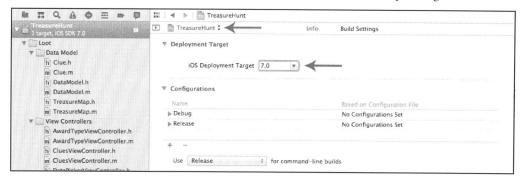

Change **iOS Deployment Target** from 6.1 to **7.0**. This makes sure the app can only run on devices that have iOS 7.0 or better.

> **Note:** The Deployment Target version number and the SDK version number are two different things. The SDK contains all the frameworks necessary to build your app. You should always use the latest version of the SDK, even if you're making apps for older versions of iOS.

> The Deployment Target indicates the versions of iOS that your app is compatible with. So you can build against the 7.0 SDK but have your Deployment Target set to 6.1 or even 5.0. Of course, when the app runs on iOS 5 or 6, it cannot use any features that were added in the 7.0 SDK.

Press ⌘+B to build the app again. Xcode will now give several warning messages:

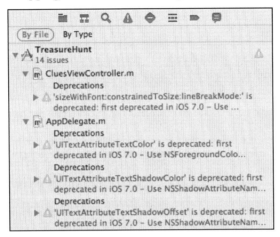

Apparently the app is using an API that's been deprecated in iOS 7. You'll take care of that later on. Other than that, there are no compilation problems, so you're still in pretty good shape.

Not so fast! This doesn't mean the app update is now ready for submission to the App Store. There are plenty of small UI problems to fix, as you saw earlier.

You'll now go through the app and fix these issues one by one. When you do this, it's easiest to remove all the custom graphics and strip the app down to its bare essentials. This allows you to focus on the more important problems first. Once everything works properly, *then* you can then add the graphics back in.

For Treasure Hunt, removing the custom graphics is simple. All the appearance customizations for the iOS 6 version of the app are performed in code and a single flag enables or disables them.

Open **TreasureHunt-Prefix.pch** (under **Other Sources**) and change the following line:

```
#define CUSTOM_APPEARANCE 1
```

to this:

```
#define CUSTOM_APPEARANCE 0
```

Build and run your app to see the difference:

This already looks more like an iOS 7 app, but it still has plenty of UI issues. Also, turning off the custom appearance means the app has lost most of its charm. Those wooden textures may be considered overkill in this new design style, but they did give the app tons of personality. This chapter will show you how to retain some of that charm even in a minimal, texture-barren world.

Notice that all the compiler warnings have now disappeared — bar one. Most of them were related to the UIAppearance API. The app no longer uses this API; you removed that dependency with the #define statement earlier. If you use UIAppearance in your own apps then be forewarned; many of the things that you were able to do with it are now deprecated or work slightly differently.

> **Note:** When you switched the Deployment Target to iOS 7, the non-Retina iPhone simulators were removed from the scheme picker. This means you cannot test your iOS 7 apps on a non-Retina iPhone simulator. This sounds draconian, but it makes sense since there aren't any low-resolution iPhone or iPod touch models (iPhone 3GS or earlier) that can run iOS 7. All iPhones that can run iOS 7 have Retina screens.

Does this mean you no longer need to supply non-Retina images for you app? It depends. If your app is for the iPad (or universal) then you still need to provide 1x versions of the graphics to support the iPad 2 and iPad mini.

Remember that the iPad can run any non-universal iPhone app in a special emulation mode. As of iOS 7 this emulation mode always uses the Retina graphics. So if your app is iPhone-only then yes, you no longer need 1x graphics. (Designers rejoice!)

If you do decide to leave out the 1x artwork for the iPhone version of your app, make sure your Retina images still adhere to the Retina **@2x.png** naming rules or UIKit won't apply the proper scaling to them.

Fixing the table views

My Maps is considered the main screen of the app, as it's the first one the user comes across; it makes sense to start your iOS 7 rework here. This screen shows the treasure maps that the local user created and shared with other **Treasure Hunt** users.

The **My Maps** screen — with the lush textures removed — looks like the following:

It doesn't look *too* bad, but there are a few small details that could be improved. Let's start with the table view. The text in the table view cells isn't supposed to be that bold. One of the most important changes that Apple made in iOS 7 is a change in the font styling; iOS 7 apps now use much thinner fonts everywhere.

Another more subtle change is the selection style of the table view cells. If you select a row, the text turns white. That used to be necessary because the default row selection color was a very saturated blue, but it has since been changed to a light gray. In Apple's own table views, the label color no longer changes when a row gets selected.

You could make these two changes by hand, but there is an easier way.

Open the **MainStoryboard.storyboard** file, found in the **Resources** group, and select the **My Maps View Controller**. This is a table view controller with a single prototype cell, shown below:

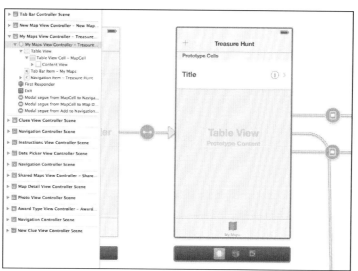

This cell adopts the **Basic** style, but since this app was made for iOS 6 it's really the **Basic** style from iOS 6. To adopt the style from iOS 7, simply change **Style** to **Custom** and then back to **Basic** again in the Attributes inspector.

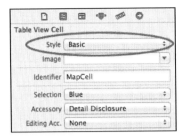

Notice that the font is now a lot thinner. It used to be `System Bold 20.0`, but now it's `System 18.0`. Apple's put their system fonts on a diet — and shrunk them a bit, too! The new font is shown below:

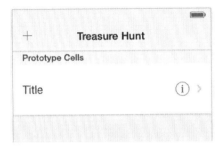

Build and run your app, and select a cell in the table. You'll see that the text label in a selected row remains black, as so:

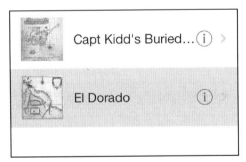

If your own apps use the built-in cell styles on prototype cells, it's a good idea to repeat this exercise for *all* of the cells on *all* of your table view controllers.

> **Note:** Did you notice that on iOS 7 the separator line between table view cells doesn't run across the entire width of the screen? This is automatic behavior on the built-in cell styles. If your app has custom cells, you can get this same effect by setting the `separatorInset` property on the individual cells, or on the entire table view. When you set the `separatorInset` on the table view, these insets are applied to the empty cells as well.

One small thing to tweak here is the height of the cells. On iOS 6 it made sense to have padding above and below the thumbnail image to accommodate the background texture, but here the extra spacing is wasted and looks out of place.

Open the storyboard once again, and in the **My Maps View Controller** select the table view, making sure to not select a cell instead. Go to the **Size inspector** (the ruler icon) and under the **Table View Size** section, change the **Row Height** from 80 to 60.

Build and run your app and have a look at the table view; the app looks much tidier with the smaller row height, as demonstrated in the following image:

Extend edges and content insets

With the increased focus on content in iOS 7, content should preferably make use of all screen space; even space underneath the navigation bar, tab bar, and toolbars. iOS 7 sets the navigation bar and the other bars to translucent so you can still make out the content of the view controllers under these bars.

This feature is already enabled for you by default. For most apps you should leave it on, but just in case you want to turn it off, you can find the options in the **Attributes** inspector for a view controller, as shown here:

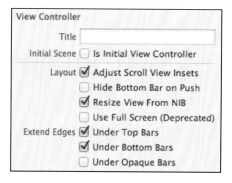

The **Extend Edges** checkboxes determine whether the content of a view controller can run beneath the top and bottom bars. Uncheck the **Under Top Bars** and **Under Bottom Bars** options, then build and run your app to see the difference:

In the image on the left, the **Extend Edges** options are enabled, which is the default setting. Notice how the bars become darker and much uglier when the **Extend Edges** options are disabled, as shown in image on the right.

It's recommended to keep both **Under Top Bars** and **Under Bottom Bars** enabled so that your app behaves like the rest of iOS 7. It might require a bit of effort on your part to make your app work properly with this option enabled, because your view controllers now need to compensate for the fact that they are partially visible below these bars. Fortunately, table view controllers make this incredibly easy. If you do decide to disable the Extend Edges options, then be consistent and make sure to do it everywhere. Your app will seem unnatural if some screens extend under the bars while others don't.

Before moving on, make sure both **Under Top Bars** and **Under Bottom Bars** are enabled on the **My Maps View Controller**.

When **Under Top Bars** is enabled, the table view literally sits under the navigation bar and the status bar. That means the top 64 points of the table view are hidden from sight. You only see an obscure version of it shining through the navigation bar. So how come you can still see the first row from the table view when you're scrolled all the way to the top? You'd expect that row to sit under the navigation bar as well.

This is where the **Adjust Scroll View Insets** setting comes in; this is also an option in the **Attributes** inspector for a view controller. The content insets for a scroll view allow you to define an extra region around the scroll view's content, like so:

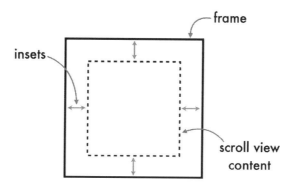

Since a table view is a descendent of `UIScrollView`, you can also use this property to add some extra space around the table view's cells. When **Adjust Scroll View Insets** is enabled and the view controller sits inside a navigation controller or tab bar controller — and in this app it sits in both — then it automatically adds the space for these bars to the table view's `contentInset` property.

To see what it looks like without insets, deselect **Adjust Scroll View Insets**, then build and run your app:

Yeah, that doesn't look so good. If you look closely at the navigation bar you'll see the top-most cell is now underneath the navigation bar. It's almost impossible to interact with this cell now. Go back to the Attributes inspector, re-enable **Adjust Scroll View Insets** — and let us never speak of this again.

Edit mode

A common feature of table views that isn't immediately obvious is swipe-to-delete. The image on the next page shows how it appears on iOS 6:

On iOS 7 this has changed dramatically. The swipe motion now feels more natural as it employs the bounce of a scroll view, and rather than placing the **Delete** button on top of the cell, it's revealed sitting underneath:

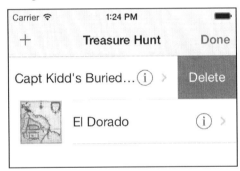

Tapping **Edit** in the navigation bar puts you in Edit mode, where things look different yet again:

There isn't much you can do here to customize how this looks, so when you tweak the visuals of your iOS 7 apps, keep in mind that they should compliment the bright red colors of the swipe-to-delete button and edit mode, not clash with them.

Asset catalogs

iOS 7 introduces a new feature to help organize your images: *asset catalogs*. An asset catalog is a special folder for your images managed by Xcode that makes it easy to associate multiple versions of an image (i.e. normal version, Retina version, 4-inch iPhone version, iPad version, etc) with a single filename.

From the Xcode menu bar, choose **File\New\File...** From the sidebar choose **Resource,** and then **Asset Catalog**.

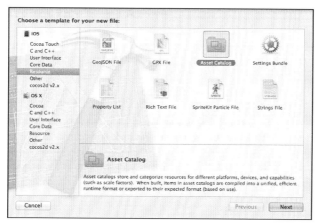

Click **Next**. Keep the default name, **Media.xcassets**, and make sure the **TreasureHunt** target is checked. Click **Create** to finish. This adds a new, blue folder in the project's file list:

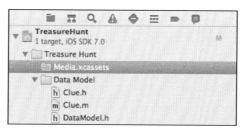

> **Note:** If you have used *folder references* before in Xcode, which also appear as blue folders, then you should be aware that an asset catalog works differently. For folder references, you are responsible for managing their contents; if you place a new file into this folder via Finder, it automatically shows up in Xcode.

> However, for asset catalogs it's recommended you make any changes using Xcode's interface and to *not* manipulate the folder structure by hand. An asset catalog contains more than just image files. For example, it also contains JSON files that describe the catalog's file structure.

One of the many changes in the design of iOS 7 is the style of tab bar icons. If you compare the existing icons on the **My Maps** screen to similar icons from built-in apps such as Phone or Music, these ones seem too wide and heavy. The new bar icons have a thin stroke — two pixels wide to match the stroke width of the font — and are very rarely filled in. You will fix this by importing new images for the tab bar icons into the asset catalog.

Select the new asset catalog, **Media.xcassets**, in the project navigator. There is a small + button at the bottom of the asset catalog pane.

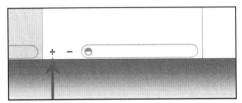

Click it and select **Import...** Navigate to the **Resources/New Images** folder that accompanies this chapter, and select all the image files inside that folder:

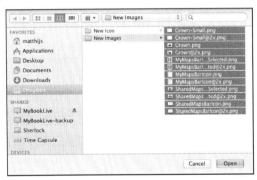

Click **Open** to finish the import. The images now show up in the asset catalog, grouped under a common name:

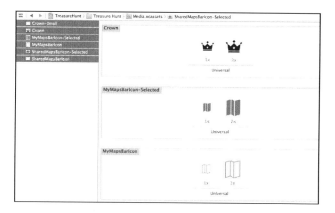

Note: If your asset catalog contains just a single item, New Images, then repeat the above procedure but this time select the individual image files from the folder, not the folder itself.

An asset catalog makes it easier to keep track of your images, while ensuring the app will load the images as efficiently as possible. You can store any images you wish in this catalog, including your app icons and launch images. Loading images from an asset catalog works no differently than it did in a pre-iOS 7 universe. When you ask UIImage to load an image file, it now looks inside the asset catalog first.

Run the app and you should see much cleaner tab bar icons:

In the built-in Apple apps, for example Music.app, it is common for the selected tab icon to be "inverted", just to make the selection clearer. You already added the required images for this. In **MyMapsViewController.m** in the **View Controllers** group, add the following line to viewDidLoad:

```
self.tabBarItem.selectedImage = [UIImage
                    imageNamed:@"MyMapsBarIcon-Selected"];
```

And add the following line to viewDidLoad in **SharedMapsViewController.m**:

```
self.tabBarItem.selectedImage = [UIImage
                    imageNamed:@"SharedMapsBarIcon-Selected"];
```

Build and run; now the selected tab has an inverted icon:

To make the app look a bit more interesting you'll replace the title text **Treasure Hunt** with an image. In **MyMapsViewController.m**, add the following line to `viewDidLoad`:

```
self.navigationItem.titleView = [[UIImageView alloc]
            initWithImage:[UIImage imageNamed:@"Crown"]];
```

This replaces the text that was in the navigation bar with the new crown image from the asset catalog. Build and run the app to see your new title bar image:

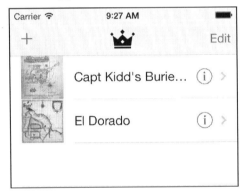

This crown shape is an integral part of the new theme for this app. You will see it appear in several more places.

Many of the images in the project were used to style the iOS 6 version of the app, but there's a handful that are also used for the iOS 7 version. So it's a good idea to put them into the asset catalog as well. First, you will clean up the project to remove the images that are no longer needed.

Right-click the **Icon** group from the project navigator and select **Delete**, **Move to Trash**. Repeat for the **Launch Images** group. Then expand the **Images** group and delete all image files except for the following and their @2x counterparts:

- CloseButton

- ClueButton

- UnknownThumb

Good riddance!

To move these remaining six images to the asset catalog, open **Media.xcassets** and press the **+** button. This time, choose the **Import from Project...** option. That opens a dialog listing all the images that are currently in the project, shown here:

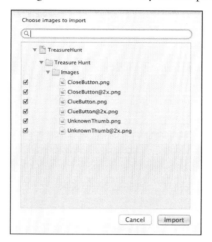

You should have all 6 items selected. Press **Import** to move these images into the asset catalog. This literally moves the files; they get removed from their original location in the file system and placed inside the Xcode-managed **Media.xcassets** folder.

The app icon

There are also new rules for the app icon in iOS 7. The height and width of the app icon have increased slightly to 120×120 pixels on the iPhone or iPod touch, 76 pixels for iPad 2 and iPad mini, and 152 pixels for Retina iPad. Icons also have a different corner radius that appears to taper off; it is no longer a pure rounded-rectangle.

Here are the iOS 6 and new iOS 7 icons for **Treasure Hunt** side-by-side:

The new icon is slightly bigger and obviously a lot flatter and more abstract, keeping with iOS 7 design principles. On iOS 7, you no longer have to reference your icons in the **Info.plist** file. Instead, you put them into the asset catalog along with all your other images.

You already removed the old icon files when you deleted the Icon group from the project. Now you will add the new icon images to the asset catalog. First, go to the **Target Settings** screen:

In the **App Icons** section, click the **Use Asset Catalog** button. This opens a dialog that lets you pick the destination asset catalog (you can have more than one in your app). Leave this set to **Media** and make sure **Also migrate launch images** is checked.

Click **Migrate** to finish. The asset catalog now has two new items named AppIcon and LaunchImage. Select the **AppIcon** group:

In Finder, go to the resources for this chapter and open the **New Icon** folder. Drag the image files onto their corresponding slots. Note that the sizes below the slots are in points, while the names of the image files are in pixels. So the file **Icon-120.png** goes into the slot that says **60 pt**. If you've killed too many brain cells converting your app to iOS 7 then you may have to whip out a calculator for this step. :]

Or if you're feeling lazy, you can just drag all of the files into the AppIcon asset and let Xcode figure it out for you.

Build and run your app; you should see a new icon on the springboard. If not, you might need to reset the simulator first. In the following chapter you will also put the launch images into the asset catalog.

Tint color

Just for fun, compare the iOS 6 version of **Treasure Hunt** with the new, cleaned-up iOS 7 version below:

 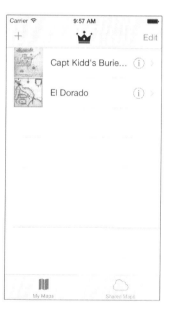

The new version certainly fits in better with iOS 7 aesthetic — but it's looking a bit bland in comparison with the extravagant textures from iOS 6. Just because iOS 7 has a cleaner, lighter design, doesn't mean your apps can't have some personality of their own. Later on you'll make some extensive changes to the look of the app, but right now you'll begin by tweaking one of the most basic but most obvious visual aspects of your app: the *tint color.*

Everything colored blue in the iOS 7 screenshot above is based on the tint color of the app. On iOS 7, the tint color is used to indicate which items can be tapped; for example, the **+** and **Edit** buttons in the navigation bar and the disclosure buttons of the table view cells are all selectable. Tinting also highlights active items, such as the icon on the currently selected tab. The tint color is used throughout an app to make the distinction between active and non-active elements. Because the UI is intended to stay out of the user's way in iOS 7, the use of a single color in your app has until now never been so important.

The tint color is blue by default, but by changing this color you can immediately give your app its own unique style with very little effort. Views inherit the tint color from their parent views, so by setting the `tintColor` property on the app's single `UIWindow` instance you effectively change the tint color for *every* view. However, in an app that uses a storyboard you can also set the tint color from Interface Builder, which is even easier.

Open **MainStoryboard.storyboard** and activate the **File inspector,** which is the first tab in the inspectors pane. Change the **Global Tint** setting to a light brown color — red 140, green 70, blue 35 — that will harken back to the old theme of wooden treasure chests:

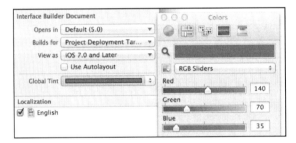

Build and run the app to see your new tint color in action:

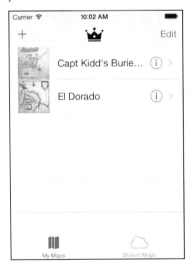

This already looks a little less stock than before. You want to make sure that when choosing a tint color it's not too dark, or else it'll be difficult to tell apart from inactive UI elements, such as black labels and gray tab bar icons.

> **Note:** Due to a bug in iOS 7, the segmented control on the Map Detail screen does not get the proper tint color. As a workaround, add the following lines to `viewDidLoad` in **MapDetailViewController.m**:
>
> ```
> self.view.tintColor = [UIColor whiteColor];
> self.view.tintColor = [UIColor colorWithRed:140/255.0f
>                        green:70/255.0f blue:35/255.0f alpha:1.0f];
> ```

Data entry forms

The **+** button from the main screen's navigation bar invokes the **New Map** screen. Here the user can create a new treasure map and, in the real-world version of this app, push it to a server so it could be shared with millions of other treasure hunters.

This screen is a typical data entry form implemented using a static table view, the kind you'll encounter in many apps. As it stands, it doesn't look very polished and it's certainly not nearly as slick as you'd expect from an iOS 7 app:

This clearly needs some work. The table view has adopted the system-provided grouped style; on iOS 6 that meant cells had rounded corners, a subtle border, and some padding around the edges, as shown on the next page.

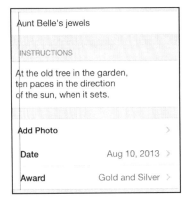

The design of the grouped style table has changed significantly in iOS 7. To help users focus on the content, Apple has decided cells should run edge-to-edge meaning the padding and the rounded corners are gone. Because of these changes, the labels and text fields embedded in the cells no longer align on their left-hand edges, as demonstrated below:

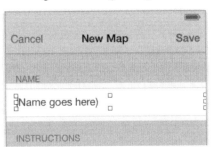

The default margins for table view cells in iOS 7 are 15 points. Prior to this release they were 20 points, although the iOS 6 version of **Treasure Hunt** reduced this to 10 points to provide extra room for the text views.

Open **MainStoryboard.storyboard** and locate the **New Map View Controller**. In the document outline expand the first table view section until you find the text field and select it. Now drag the resize handles so the text field has an X position of 15 and a width of 305. It should sit flush against the right edge of the cell, as shown below:

Back in the document outline, expand the second table view section to find the text view and select it. This time use the **Size inspector** and change the X position to 15, the Y position to 1, the **Width** to 305 and finally the **Height** to 86.

The fonts for both the text field and text view need not change; the current setting of **System 17pt** is a good size font to use on such forms.

The table view has another section that contains three rows. It's a little difficult to see these in the storyboard as not all the rows fit within the screen. You can scroll the table view inside the storyboard by selecting the view controller so that a blue outline appears around the scene, and then making a two-finger vertical swipe gesture on your mouse or track pad while the mouse pointer is over the table view.

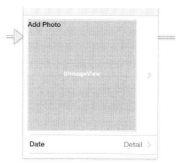

> **Note:** At the time of writing this chapter, there is a bug in Xcode where it doesn't show the bottom row of the table view in its entirety. Luckily, this only happens at design time – the row will show up OK in the app itself.

The final two rows, titled **Date** and **Award**, have a couple of issues. To start with, the font is too heavy and the highlighted text color is white. However, the main issue is that the color of the detail label is a dark blue. This clashes with the global tint color of the app, which you set to brown.

Both problems are easy to fix. As before, you simply need to force Xcode to refresh the style of the cell. For both cells, go to the **Attribute** inspector, change the **Style** option from **Right Detail** to **Left Detail**, and then change it back again to **Right Detail**.

> **Note:** It's important that you don't choose any other style before reverting back to **Right Detail**, as no other styles have the detail label. If you choose a different style, it will break the connection between the detail labels and the outlets in the view controller and you'll have to re-wire them.

Using the **Connections** inspector, double check that the detail label of the **Date** row is still set to the `dateLabel` outlet, and the detail label of the **Award** row is still set to `awardTypeLabel`. This row should also still have a push segue.

This leaves the **Add Photo** row. This cell doesn't use a system provided style; the **Style** attribute is set to **Custom**. You will have to tweak the font and positions manually.

> **Note:** The **Add Photo** row is so big because it serves two purposes. When you're creating a new treasure map, this row is initially small and simply labeled **Add Photo**. Tapping the row invokes the image picker controller that lets you choose a photo from your photo library.
>
> You'll notice the row contains both the label and the image view. If no photo is present, the image view is hidden and the `heightForRowAtIndexPath` delegate method returns 44, which is the standard height of table view cells. Once you've picked a photo, the **Add Photo** label is hidden, the image view becomes visible, and `heightForRowAtIndexPath` returns 280, which is enough to accommodate the thumbnail plus a little padding.

The font for the **Add Photo** label is currently **System Bold 16**. Change that to be **System 17**, so that it's a bit larger and no longer bold. With the **Add Photo** label still selected, click the **Editor\Size to Fit Content** menu item to resize the label to properly house its content. Set the **Highlighted** color of the label to **Default**.

Finally, change the X position of the label to 15 so it lines up perfectly with the other labels, and do the same for the image view.

Now the screen looks much better. Build and run your app to see your changes:

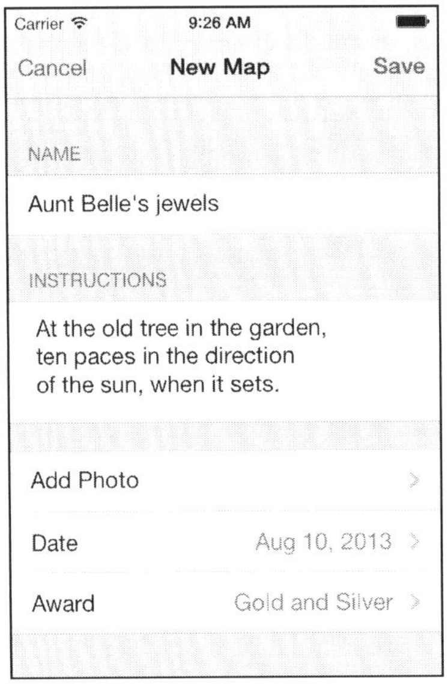

Tap the **Add Photo** row to try out the image picker. This should still function, but the image picker controller now adopts the design of iOS 7.

> **Note:** If you're running the app on the simulator and don't have any images in Photos.app, then locate the treasure map images in the **Test Data** folder of the Xcode project and drag each one onto the simulator. This will open the image in Safari. Then tap and hold the image in Safari and select the **Save Image** option from the action sheet. This will save the image into the photo library on the simulator.

Notice that the Cancel button in the image picker controller is still blue. To give this the same tint color as the rest of the app, open **NewMapViewController.m** and add the following line to `chooseFromPhotoLibrary`:

```
imagePicker.view.tintColor = self.view.tintColor;
```

Once you've picked an image, the photo row in the **New Map** screen should update and display the photo, as shown below:

Hiding the keyboard

One problem with data entry forms on mobile devices such as the iPhone is that the keyboard takes up roughly half of the available space when it's on-screen. It becomes even more frustrating when using a text view since the **return** button does not dismiss the keyboard and you need to provide another way for the user to remove the keyboard from the screen.

Treasure Hunt employs a tap gesture recognizer that dismisses the keyboard when the user taps anywhere in the navigation controller's view, which was probably the easiest way to implement the desired functionality on iOS 6.

However, iOS 7 comes with a neat little feature that you can use instead. You can tell *any* scroll view — which includes table views — that you want to hide the keyboard when the user scrolls. This is called the *keyboard dismiss mode* and it has three options: don't dismiss (the default), on drag, and dismiss interactive.

Select the table view belonging to the **New Map View Controller** in the storyboard. In the **Attributes** inspector, find the **Scroll View** section and change the **Keyboard** option to **Dismiss on drag**.

Build and run your app; bring up the keyboard over the table view and dismiss it by scrolling the view. Ahh — that's much better.

Just for kicks, set the **Keyboard** option to **Dismiss interactively** mode, and build and run your app. Now you have to drag the keyboard away with your finger, just as in Messages.app:

And that marks the end of this chapter – your app is looking much more iOS 7-like already! But there are still many issues left to fix, and they are the topic of the next two chapters.

Challenges

Now that you understand some of the most important aspects of transitioning your apps to iOS 7, it's time to practice what you just learned. There are a couple more screens in the app that need freshening up.

Challenge 1: Fix the second tab

The second tab of the app contains the **Shared Maps** screen. This is very similar to **My Maps** (the first tab) but there are some differences. Both screens are table views that list treasure maps, but whereas **My Maps** only displays the maps the user has created and uploaded, **Shared Maps** displays the maps that have been shared by everyone. Right now it looks like this:

Your challenge is to clean up the table view. Since this screen is so similar to **My Maps** it requires most of the same tweaks. As before, the font is simply too wide and heavy, and the highlighted color for the labels is wrong. The table view cells are also too tall.

When you are done, the prototype cell should look like this:

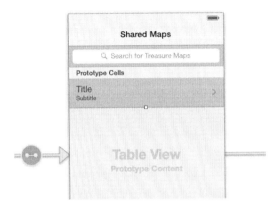

Challenge 2: Picking from a list

Tapping the **Award** row from the **New Map** screen pushes a new view controller on the navigation stack that lets you pick from a list of items:

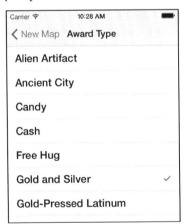

You've probably already figured out what's wrong with this view: the font is too heavy. Your first mission is to put the font on a diet but that should be a walk in the park by now. Open the storyboard, find the **Award Type View Controller**, and fix that prototype cell.

The checkmark on the currently selected item comes from the **Accessory** setting on the cell. On iOS 7 this automatically uses the tint color, so that's taken care of for you.

After your changes this screen should look much better:

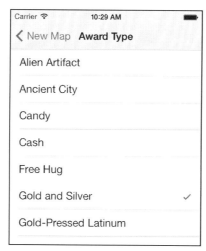

Another important principle of the iOS 7 design language is **simplification**. This screen is already pretty simple, but there's more you can do. Apple recommends that apps refrain from using titles in their navigation bars if the function of the screen is obvious. It's pretty obvious what this screen does, given you tapped the **Award** row to get here. Your job is to remove the title from the **Navigation Item**.

Build and run your app; you can immediately see that the navigation bar looks a lot less busy:

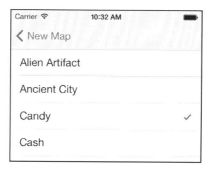

This view controller is also used to edit existing treasure maps, not just to add new ones. When you tap the detail disclosure view on a row in the **My Maps** screen, it performs the segue to the NewMapViewController, but the prepareForSegue method provides an alternate title: **Edit Map**.

With the goal of simplification in mind, it will be better to change this to just **Edit**. Find the line in the code that sets the title and change it. (Hint: it's in the method that was just mentioned.) Although shortening screen titles may seem like a small detail, it's the details that matter on iOS 7!

Chapter 7: Transitioning to iOS 7 – What's New with Auto Layout

By Matthijs Hollemans

The previous chapter gave you a glimpse of what it takes to transition an app to iOS 7. But there is more to it than fixing your table view cells, setting tint colors, and using asset catalogs.

You also need to deal with the status bar, which is no longer a separate section of the screen. And even though the user interface of your app is important, a main idea in the iOS 7 philosophy is that you focus as much as possible on the user's content instead. This chapter gives you some pointers on how to accomplish that.

Giving your apps a flexible layout became a big deal with last year's introduction of the iPhone 5 and its larger screen, but it has become even more important with Dynamic Type, a new feature of iOS 7 that allows users to determine how large they want the text in their apps to be.

As a developer you need a flexible solution for dealing with these different screen sizes and text sizes: Auto Layout. This technology has a bit of a bad reputation — it was very frustrating to use in the previous version of Xcode — but fortunately the advances in Xcode 5 more than make up for it. This chapter gets you started with the new and improved Auto Layout.

In this chapter, you continue to convert the **Treasure Hunt** app step-by-step. If you did not complete the challenges from last chapter, then pick up the starter project from this chapter's resources and follow along.

The status bar and your content

As you've seen, the `UITableViewController` class already takes care of most of the new iOS 7 features for you, especially when you place it inside a navigation controller or tab bar controller. The navigation bar, tab bar, and toolbar are all translucent, and even though the table view sits behind these bars, the content insets are adjusted to ensure the cells are always visible. If your app uses custom `UIViewControllers`, then you'll have to do some of this work yourself.

When you tap on a row with a treasure map, the **Map Details** screen appears and displays the entire treasure map image. If you were looking for treasure, this would be the most important screen of the app.

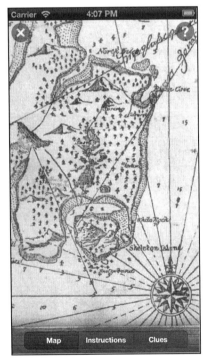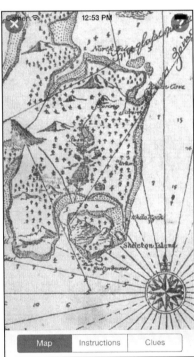

The left image shows this screen on iOS 6; the right image, iOS 7.

The most obvious issue is that the map now sits under the status bar; everything appears to have moved up by 20 points.

This is a very important change in iOS 7: the status bar is no longer a separate bar. It's now something that simply gets drawn on top of your view controllers. In previous versions of iOS, if your app displayed the status bar the height of the view controller's view was reduced to compensate — especially if it contained a navigation bar. In iOS 7, your view controllers are always supposed to fill the entire screen.

If your app has content near the top of the screen but no navigation bar, then you have a problem on your hands, as the status bar will draw on top of that content. That's exactly what's happening on the Map Detail screen. There are three possible ways to handle this:

- Move your content down by 20 points and make room for the status bar. This is the easiest solution, but it doesn't work very well if your content is embedded in a scroll view or relies on a table view.

- Implement the `prefersStatusBarHidden` method in your `UIViewController` subclass, and return `YES` to hide the status bar. The problem with this approach is that a user wants to keep the status bar visible in most non-game apps.

- Add a navigation bar on top, either by embedding the view controller inside a navigation controller, or by adding your own instance of `UINavigationBar`. The navigation bar will extend under the status bar. Your content will still sit under these two bars, but the navigation bar will blur it. This is the approach you'll take in this tutorial.

  The downside of this approach is that the navigation bar takes up valuable screen space, and iOS 7 is supposed to be about the content, not the UI. You'll see the solution to this most puzzling of conundrums later in the chapter.

Open **MainStoryboard.storyboard** and drag a **Navigation Bar** from the **Object Library** onto the **Map Detail View Controller**. Make sure you position it 20 points from the top, otherwise the status bar will draw on top of the navigation bar, and that's certainly not what you want.

Your view will look like the image on the following page:

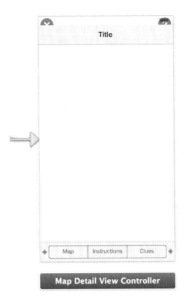

Note that the navigation bar overlaps the **X** and **?** buttons at the top. That's fine for now. You'll replace these buttons in a moment.

Just putting the navigation bar into the view controller is not enough. To see why, build and run your app and navigate to the Map screen. There is a clear gap between the navigation bar and the top edge of the screen, as so:

To fix this you need to write some code. First, you must declare the view controller to conform to the `UINavigationBarDelegate` protocol. Change the `@interface` line at the top of **MapDetailViewController.m** as follows:

```
@interface MapDetailViewController () <UINavigationBarDelegate>
```

Now add the following method:

```
- (UIBarPosition)positionForBar:(id <UIBarPositioning>)bar
{
  return UIBarPositionTopAttached;
}
```

Finally, back in **MainStoryboard.storyboard**, **Ctrl-drag** from the navigation bar to the view controller and connect the **delegate** outlet. Using the `positionForBar:` delegate method, **UIKit** determines where the navigation bar should sit within the view controller and whether its background needs to extend upward behind the status bar.

Build and run your app; the navigation bar and status bar should now appear as one unit, like so:

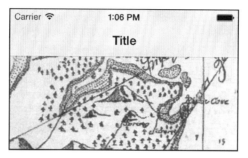

The navigation bar is translucent; the map shines through the bar, but this feature is not yet reciprocated by the toolbar at the bottom. That's because the scroll view containing the map image stops where the toolbar begins. Open **MainStoryboard.storyboard** and select **Map Detail View Controller** in the document outline. Expand the view, select the **Content View** and resize it so it covers the entire screen.

Build and run your app. You can see that your map now shines through the toolbar:

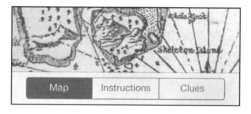

Note: You may be wondering why this didn't happen automatically. After all, the **Extend Edges** options are enabled for this view controller, so it should have resized its main view to sit under the toolbar — right? That is true, but for the **Map Detail** screen, the actual content comes from three different child view controllers. The views of these child controllers are placed inside a subview of the **Map Detail** screen: the **Content View**. UIKit doesn't automatically resize your subviews for you, only the main view!

Text instead of icons

The Map Detail screen has two buttons at the top: an **X** that closes the screen and a question mark to add clues to the map. The new navigation bar obscures these two buttons. Considering that you now have a navigation bar, it makes sense to put the buttons inside that bar instead.

In the storyboard, delete the **X** and **?** buttons from the **Map Detail** screen. In their place, drag two **Bar Button Items** from the **Object Library** onto the navigation bar. Give the one on the left the title of **Close**, and one on the right the title of **Add Clue**:

Ctrl-drag from these buttons to the view controller and connect them to the **close:** and **addClue:** actions respectively.

> **Note:** In the iOS 6 version of the app these buttons displayed icons, but here you're using just text. iOS 7 places more emphasis on text for the simple reason that icons tend to provide little context to the user, unless they're used universally for the same action. Some users might think that **?** means help instead of clue, but with the text **Add Clue** there is no confusion.

The disadvantage of using text instead of icons is that the navigation bar can feel cluttered. That's why Apple recommends leaving out the title unless it's critical in understanding the purpose of the screen. You could use the name of the treasure map as the title of this screen, but it's better to remove the title from the navigation bar altogether.

Build and run your app and take a look at your new iOS 7-style buttons:

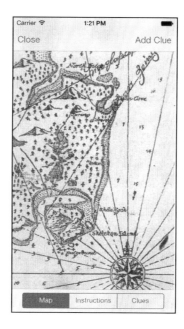

Make way for the content

Most of the time when you're studying the treasure map, you don't need access to the buttons in the navigation bar or the items in the toolbar. Whenever possible, your app should focus on the content — the image of the treasure map — and move the user interface out of the way.

To embrace the idea of users interacting with their content without distraction, you'll add a small feature that hides the bars when the user starts scrolling the image view. This is similar to what Safari does when you scroll a web page.

Using the **Assistant** editor, make outlets for the navigation bar and the toolbar in **MapDetailViewController.m**. Call them `navigationBar` and `toolbar`, respectively.

Also in **MapDetailViewController.m** update the interface declaration so that it conforms to the `UIScrollViewDelegate` protocol, as shown in the highlighted section below:

```
@interface MapDetailViewController () <UIScrollViewDelegate,
                                       UINavigationBarDelegate>

@property (nonatomic, weak) IBOutlet UIView *contentView;
@property (weak, nonatomic) IBOutlet UINavigationBar
                                           *navigationBar;
```

```
@property (weak, nonatomic) IBOutlet UIToolbar *toolbar;

@end
```

One of the child view controllers of this MapDetailViewController is called
PhotoViewController, and it has a scroll view with an image view that displays the
treasure map inside. (The other two child view controllers are CluesViewController
and InstructionsViewController, both of which you'll see more of in a moment.)

Add the following line to **MapDetailViewController.m**'s viewDidLoad:

```
photoViewController.scrollView.delegate = self;
```

This establishes the **Map Detail** screen as the delegate for the scroll view that contains
the image of the treasure map.

Now that the delegate connection has been made, you can implement the delegate
method invoked when the user begins scrolling. Add a new instance variable to
MapDetailViewController.m that will be used to keep track of the visibility of the
navigation bar and toolbar:

```
@implementation MapDetailViewController
{
  . . .
  BOOL _hideStatusBar;
}
```

Then add the following two methods:

```
- (void)scrollViewWillBeginDragging:(UIScrollView *)scrollView
{
  if (!_hideStatusBar) {
    [self hideBars];
  }
}

- (void)hideBars
{
  _hideStatusBar = YES;

  [UIView animateWithDuration:0.25 animations:^{
    [self setNeedsStatusBarAppearanceUpdate];
    self.navigationBar.alpha = 0.0f;
    self.toolbar.alpha = 0.0f;
```

```
    } completion:^(BOOL finished) {
      self.navigationBar.hidden = YES;
      self.toolbar.hidden = YES;
    }];
  }
```

When `scrollViewWillBeginDragging:` kicks off, it calls `hideBars` when the status bar is visible, which in turn sets the `_hideStatusBar` variable to `YES` and animates the alpha value of the navigation bar and toolbar to `0.0f` so that they slowly fade out.

The call to `setNeedsStatusBarAppearanceUpdate` hides the actual status bar. Calling that method causes the `prefersStatusBarHidden` method to be re-evaluated. If you return `YES` from this method, the status bar disappears.

Add the method to **MapDetailViewController.m**:

```
  - (BOOL)prefersStatusBarHidden
  {
    return _hideStatusBar;
  }
```

If you call `setNeedsStatusBarAppearanceUpdate` from within an animation block, it animates the fade over the given duration.

Build and run your app; scroll the map a little and you'll see all the user interface elements disappear, as shown below:

Of course, you also need a way to make them reappear, or the user would be forever stuck here. A common way to bring back the UI is tapping on the scroll view. Add the following to viewDidLoad in **MapDetailViewController.m**:

```
UITapGestureRecognizer *tapGestureRecognizer =
    [[UITapGestureRecognizer alloc] initWithTarget:self
                                    action:@selector(tapped:)];
[photoViewController.scrollView
                    addGestureRecognizer:tapGestureRecognizer];
```

This calls tapped: whenever the user taps on the image. Add the following methods:

```
- (void)tapped:(UIGestureRecognizer *)recognizer
{
  if (recognizer.state == UIGestureRecognizerStateEnded &&
      _hideStatusBar) {
    [self showBars];
  }
}

- (void)showBars
{
  _hideStatusBar = NO;

  self.navigationBar.hidden = NO;
  self.toolbar.hidden = NO;

  [UIView animateWithDuration:0.25 animations:^{
      [self setNeedsStatusBarAppearanceUpdate];
      self.navigationBar.alpha = 1.0f;
      self.toolbar.alpha = 1.0f;
  }];
}
```

The showBars method does the exact opposite of hideBars; it animates the reappearance of the navigation bar and toolbar. The call to setNeedsStatusBarAppearanceUpdate causes the status bar to fade back into view since _hideStatusBar is now set to NO.

Build and run your app; scroll the image to make the bars disappear, and then tap anywhere to make them reappear. Now you have the best of both worlds: a navigation bar at the top so that the content no longer clashes with the status bar, and a feature that hides both bars as soon as you start interacting with the content.

> **Note:** In the code above, you use a `UIView` animation block to animate the bars. If the **Map Detail** screen had been embedded in a `UINavigationController`, then you could have called `setNavigationBarHidden:animated:` and `setToolbarHiddenAnimated:` to slide the bars off the screen. But as that's not the case here, you have to handle the animation yourself.

Using Auto Layout for easier layout

If your app supports both the iPhone 4" and 3.5" screens or uses **Dynamic Type** (more on this in Chapter 4, "Beginning Text Kit"), you're no longer in control of how large or small the text will be in your app. This means that if you're not careful, you can run into some nasty layout problems.

Your app must always be prepared to deal with different screen sizes and/or scale its textual content up or down. To pull this off, you could end up writing a lot of manual layout code. Fortunately, **Auto Layout** can do most of the heavy lifting for you.

Auto Layout was introduced with iOS 6 as a modern alternative to manual layout or using autoresizing masks — or "springs and struts" as they're more commonly known. Auto Layout is very flexible and powerful, but it can also take a while to get used to. In fact, in previous versions of Xcode, Auto Layout was a real pain to use. In a recent iOS conference, it was even compared to a Psycho Cat!

If you tried to use it before and gave up in frustration, don't worry — you're not the only one! Auto Layout itself is pretty good, but Interface Builder didn't make it easy to fall in love with the technology. Fortunately, that's changed for the better with Xcode 5.

Auto Layout works with what are known as *constraints*, which describe the space and positioning relationships between your views. You create your layouts not by placing your views at certain positions on your screen, but instead by defining the constraints between them. Auto Layout evaluates these constraints during runtime and calculates the most efficient layout based on those constraints. However, Auto Layout can't do its job if there are too few constraints — or too many.

To prevent this from happening, the Interface Builder of Xcode 4 tried to be helpful and made sure that there were always enough constraints. Unfortunately, it was often a little *too* helpful. You could spend several minutes carefully creating your constraints and then make the tiniest of changes, for example nudging a view by a single pixel, at which point Interface Builder would decide all your constraints were no longer valid. It would throw them all away and replace them with new constraints of its own that obviously no longer did what you wanted. Extremely frustrating!

If you've used Auto Layout before then this probably sounds familiar. Many developers completely gave up on Auto Layout after running into these problems, which is a shame, because Auto Layout can be incredibly useful.

Fortunately, Apple has listened to the moaning and groaning heard the world over and now, with Xcode 5, Auto Layout is a joy to use. You can turn it on and largely ignore it. Interface Builder will no longer get in your way. On the contrary, it is quite helpful with suggestions on how to fix layouts that are invalid or incomplete.

Think constraints, not frames

So how do you use Auto Layout? First you have to change your thinking about how to layout your views. You no longer position and size your views in an explicit manner. This means that if Auto Layout is enabled, you must refrain from manually changing a view's frame in code. Doing something like this is no longer allowed:

```
myView.frame = CGRectMake(…);
```

It's Auto Layout's job to set the frame. You only influence Auto Layout's layout decisions indirectly in the manner in which you setup your constraints. That's really all you do to make your layout: you set constraints on your views.

So what's a constraint? Think of a constraint as a relationship between two views, often a view and its superview. But it can also be between two sibling views or even a view and itself, as weird as that may sound. Interface Builder offers several different types of constraints:

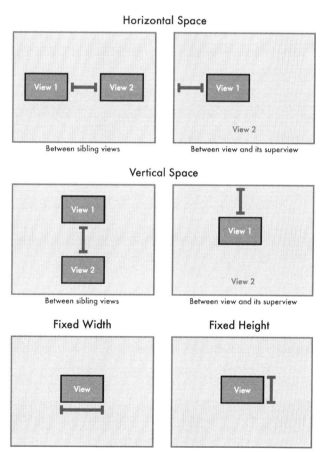

The important thing to remember is that there should always be enough constraints so the position and size of each view can be calculated. If not, Auto Layout will be unable to calculate a layout, meaning you'll get an undesired layout or the app will crash since Auto Layout can throw an exception.

Since thinking in constraints is more abstract than thinking in positions and dimensions, it's quite easy to create incomplete or invalid layouts unintentionally. In past versions of Xcode Interface Builder tried to prevent this, which made the problem even worse. With Xcode 5, however, Interface Builder just provides warnings when your layout is missing something, and provides hints and Fix-Its to resolve any issues.

OK, that's enough theory for now. Let's put Auto Layout into practice and it'll become a lot clearer how it actually works.

Enabling Auto Layout

You enable Auto Layout on a per-storyboard or per-nib file basis. Open **MainStoryboard.storyboard** and go to the **File inspector**. Check **Use Autolayout,** as shown below:

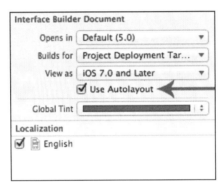

You shouldn't see much change in your storyboard, except a new menu has appeared at the bottom of the canvas:

You use these buttons to add the constraints to your views. But before you get to that, first build and run the app to see if there are any problems.

There are some obvious issues on the **Map Detail** screen; for example, the image no longer scrolls, but for the most part the app still behaves as before. You haven't added any constraints yet, so how can the app still work? Isn't it true that Auto Layout cannot compute the layout if there are not enough constraints?

Here's the clever part: for any view that has no constraints, Xcode automatically adds default constraints when it compiles the app. These *automatic constraints* give a view a fixed position and size.

That's the big difference between Auto Layout in Xcode 4 and Xcode 5; whereas Interface Builder used to force those automatic constraints upon you while you were still designing your scenes, it now waits until compile-time to fix any missing constraints. That way, you don't have to add constraints yourself if you don't have a good reason to. You can simply ignore Auto Layout except for the views that need constraints other than those added automatically.

Scrolling the scrolls

The most obvious problem with the **Map Detail** screen is that the treasure map image no longer scrolls. This is due to the following code in **PhotoViewController.m**:

```
- (void)viewWillAppear:(BOOL)animated
{
  [super viewWillAppear:animated];

  // Set the content size to the scroll view to the dimensions
  // of the image.
  self.scrollView.contentSize = self.photo.size;

  // Center the scroll view on the image.
  self.scrollView.contentOffset = CGPointMake(
    (self.photo.size.width - self.view.bounds.size.width)/2.0f,
    (self.photo.size.height -
                        self.view.bounds.size.height)/2.0f);

  // The image view is always the same size as the content area
  // of the scroll view.
  self.imageView.frame = (CGRect){ .origin = CGPointZero,
                                 .size = self.photo.size };
  self.imageView.image = self.photo;
}
```

Can you spot the statement that's causing the problem? It's the one that sets the image view's frame:

```
self.imageView.frame = (CGRect){ .origin = CGPointZero,
                               .size = self.photo.size };
```

Remember that with Auto Layout you may no longer set the frame of a view directly. This line either has no effect, or it may directly interfere with what Auto Layout is doing. Delete the offending line.

The other statement you should delete is the one that sets `self.scrollView.contentSize`. For a scroll view with Auto Layout, the content size is automatically derived from the constraints that you set on its child views.

With that handled, it's time to add some constraints! Open **MainStoryboard.storyboard** and expand the **Photo View Controller Scene** in the document outline. Select the **image view** that sits inside the scroll view. Then click on the **Pin** button at the bottom of the window:

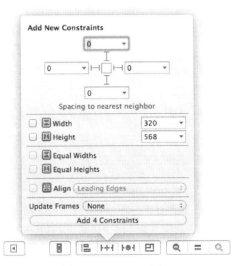

In the **Spacing to nearest neighbor** section of the popup menu that appears, click on all four red bars to select them. These red bars represent the horizontal and vertical space constraints that this image view shares with its nearest neighbor, which in this case is the image view's superview: the scroll view. Make sure the input fields are all **0**. Then click the **Add 4 Constraints** button at the bottom. This will *pin* the sides of the image view to the insides of the scroll view.

In practice, this means that the image view fills the entire content size of the scroll view; the size of that content comes from the dimensions of the image. You no longer need to set the image view's `frame` or the scroll view's `contentSize` properties by hand; Auto Layout will calculate these for you.

However, Xcode now displays some warning messages in the **Issue navigator**:

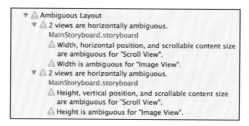

Something isn't quite right here; you can also see there's an issue when you select the image view. The orange bars surrounding the selected view represent the four constraints you've just added. However, valid constraints are colored blue. When they're orange, that indicates something is amiss in your layout.

In the document outline, a small red arrow is visible next to the **Photo View Controller Scene**. Click it to get a more detailed analysis of the Auto Layout problems, as below:

Apparently the scroll view needs some constraints too. Because you used Auto Layout for something *inside* the scroll view, you also need to supply your own constraints for the scroll view itself; Xcode will no longer add automatic constraints for that scroll view.

Before you add any constraints to the scroll view, however, first select **Photo View Controller** and in the Attributes inspector change **Status Bar** from None to **Inferred**, so that you see a little battery icon:

Now select the scroll view in the document outline and open the **Pin** menu. Click on the four red bars to select them, making sure they are all **0**. Click **Add 4 Constraints** to finish.

You can see the constraints that you just added in the document outline as below:

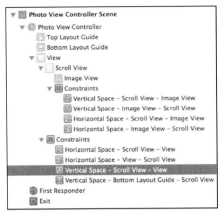

The image view has four constraints, and now the scroll view also has four constraints. Make sure that the Vertical Space constraint says "Scroll View – View" and not "Scroll View – Top Layout Guide". The reason you made the simulated status bar visible was to prevent pinning the scroll view to this Top Layout Guide.

However, this still doesn't completely fix the layout problems, as shown by the compiler warnings and the fact that the constraints are still orange. Apparently, the scroll view has **Scrollable Content Size Ambiguity**. Xcode also complains that the image view is misplaced. In the storyboard it has a size of 320×568 but the expected size is 0×0. By expected size, Xcode means the size of the view at runtime.

This is a very common warning that you can expect to see often. It indicates a discrepancy between what you told Interface Builder the size of the view would be, and what Auto Layout thinks it *should* be according to the constraints. The reason Auto Layout thinks the image view should have a height and width of 0 points is because there is no image set on the view, and under Auto Layout the size of an image view is determined by the size of its image.

To fix this warning, select the image view in the document outline and go to the **Size inspector**. Under **Intrinsic Size**, choose **Placeholder,** as so:

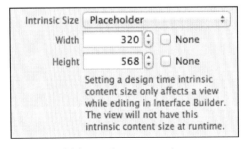

Now all the Xcode warnings should have disappeared.

Build and run your app, and try to scroll and pan the map; it should work as before.

As you've seen, with Auto Layout you need to change your approach to layout design. Manually setting frames is no longer required, but you do need to create the necessary constraints for your views. Learning which constraints to use and when is the trick to getting the most from Auto Layout.

Landscape ahoy!

Some parts of **Treasure Hunt**, notably the **Map Detail** screen, work in both portrait and landscape orientations. Unfortunately, now that you've enabled Auto Layout, the **Map Detail** screen no longer looks correct in landscape mode:

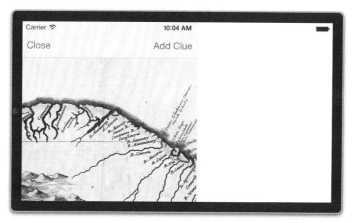

Remember that if you don't set any constraints on your views, Interface Builder adds automatic constraints that give the views a fixed position and size. That's what happened to the **Map Detail** screen's content view. When rotating to landscape, that view won't move. If you want your interfaces to be flexible and adapt to any orientation then you'll need to setup the constraints yourself.

In **MainStoryboard.storyboard**, expand the **Map Detail View Controller Scene** in the document outline and select the **content view**. The app will need to resize the view so it always fills the screen. To enable that, simply pin it to its superview on all four edges. Open the **Pin** menu, and select all the bars in the **Spacing to nearest neighbor** section. Click **Add 4 Constraints** to make the magic happen. It's a bit hard to see, but when the content view is selected, it now has four blue bars surrounding it meaning the constraints are valid.

The two other things in this screen to add constraints for are the navigation bar and the toolbar; they also need their frames adjusted for landscape mode. For the navigation bar, you want to pin just its top, left and right sides. UIKit already knows the height of the navigation bar, so these three constraints are enough to determine its full size and position.

You've already seen how to use the **Pin** popup menu to make constraints, but there is a second way. Select the **Navigation Bar** object and **Ctrl-drag** to the left, ensuring you have selected the actual navigation bar and not the Navigation Item inside it, like so:

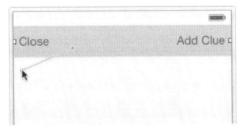

In the popup that appears, click on **Leading Space to Container**:

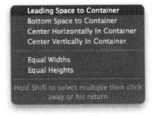

The view now gets an orange bar on the left side, which is the constraint you just added:

Why is this orange? Doesn't that indicate a problem? It sure does. There is nothing wrong with the constraint that you just added, but as soon as you add a single constraint to a view, Interface Builder expects you to add the remaining constraints as well. It only creates automatic constraints if a view has no constraints. By adding this one constraint you've told Interface Builder that you're taking responsibility for the constraints of this view, so you're going to have to add the missing constraints by hand.

> **Note:** You can still run the app even with these missing constraints, but it may not actually do what you want. So it's always best to fix the orange constraints immediately and prevent any ambiguity.

Ctrl-drag from the navigation bar again, but this time to the right, and choose **Trailing Space to Container** from the popup menu. Notice that this popup menu now has different options than before. It's contextually aware, so it will only display the options that make sense with respect to the direction of the drag action. Here you dragged to the right, so it doesn't have the leading space option, which only applies to the left edge of the view. Instead, you get Trailing Space, which applies to the right-hand edge.

You now have a new constraint on the right side of the navigation bar. Auto Layout has enough constraints to determine the X position of the navigation bar, the width, and the height. The only thing missing is a constraint for the Y position.

You might be thinking you need to add a vertical space constraint between the navigation bar and the top of the window. That's one possible approach. So far the spacing constraints you've added were all of size 0, which clamps the two views to each other. But spacing constraints can also have a size, so here you can put 20 points of space between the top of the window and the navigation bar. Although this approach would work in theory, Auto Layout now has a new feature that might be better suited to fix this issue: Top and Bottom Layout Guides.

> **Note:** On a regular view controller, such as the Map Details screen, the **Top Layout Guide** is positioned 20 points from the top of the window, right below the status bar area. The **Bottom Layout Guide** is aligned with the bottom of the window.

The main benefit of these layout guides comes from using them on a view controller that sits inside a `UINavigationController` or `UITabBarController`. The **Top Layout Guide** then sits below the navigation bar and the **Bottom Layout Guide** sits just above the tab bar or toolbar. This is very handy as the heights of these bars may change depending on the orientation of the device. So by connecting to these layout guides, your views can be positioned relative to the bars, no matter how tall they are.

In the document outline, **Ctrl-drag** from the **Navigation Bar** to the **Top Layout Guide,** as shown below:

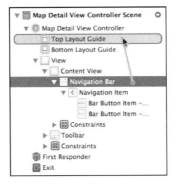

Choose **Vertical Spacing** from the popup. The navigation bar now has sufficient constraints, and its bars all turn blue to reflect this.

You also need to add constraints for the toolbar: repeat this procedure on the **Toolbar** to add a **Leading Space** constraint, a **Trailing Space** constraint and a **Vertical Spacing** constraint pinned to the **Bottom Layout Guide**. (If Interface Builder gives you a hard time with this, then Ctrl-drag onto the toolbar itself or use the Pin menu instead.)

If you ever find yourself wondering which constraints apply to a given view, you can see the list of constraints in the **Size inspector**, as shown in the screenshot below:

Build and run your app, and rotate your device or press ⌘ + **right arrow** to rotate the simulator to landscape mode. Your map view should now look like the following:

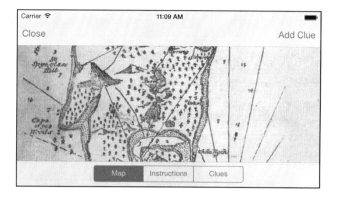

Note: Remember, you only need to add constraints for the navigation bar and toolbar because the Map Detail screen is not embedded in an instance of `UINavigationController`. If your view controller sits inside a navigation stack, then the navigation controller will already take care of the placement and sizing of the bars.

Table views and Auto Layout

The **Map Detail** screen is a very simple version of a tab bar controller, except that it uses a segmented control instead of regular tabs. Each segment is associated with its own child view controller. You've already seen the one that displays the photo of the treasure map: `PhotoViewController`. In this section you'll focus on the third segment, **Clues**.

The labels in the table view cells have gotten really messed up since enabling Auto Layout:

Yikes! First, you need to fix the **content insets** as the first cell has slipped underneath the navigation bar. You've seen this feature before; all view controllers have the **Adjust Scroll View Insets** option that makes sure the contents of a scroll view or table view don't get hidden by any bars.

However, that option only works for view controllers whose main view is a scroll view, or a descendent of a scroll view such as a table view. For the **Map Detail** screen, the actual content is provided by child view controllers; it doesn't have a scroll view of its own. For scrolling views such as this, you have to adjust the content insets yourself.

Open **CluesViewController.m** and add the following to `viewDidLoad`:

```
self.tableView.contentInset =
  UIEdgeInsetsMake(64.0f, 0.0f, 44.0f, 0.0f);
```

That is 64 points at the top – 20 for the status bar and 44 for the navigation bar – and 44 points at the bottom for the toolbar.

The reason the labels in the table view cells have incorrect sizes becomes obvious once you review the following code in `configureCell:forIndexPath:`

```
CGSize size = [self sizeForText:clue.text];
textLabel.frame = CGRectMake(20.0f, 10.0f, size.width,
                                          size.height);
```

and:

```
usernameLabel.frame = CGRectMake(20.0f, 10.0f + size.height +
                                        10.0f, 280.0f, 18.0f);
```

Setting the `frame` property no longer works under Auto Layout, so remove the above lines from the method. Also remove the `sizeForText:` method since it's no longer needed. Finally, remove `tableView:heightForRowAtIndexPath:`. You'll replace it with a much better implementation shortly.

Instead of calculating the sizes of the labels by hand, you will now let Auto Layout take care of all that for you. Head on over to **MainStoryboard.storyboard**, find the **Clues View Controller** and select the top label in the prototype cell. Use the **Pin** menu to add a top constraint of 10, and a left and right constraint of 15, as below:

The T-bar attached to the top edge is blue, meaning the Y-position of the label is okay, but there's still an orange box showing that you need to correct the size of the label.

The dashed box is the frame Auto Layout is expecting to generate at runtime. This is what Auto Layout has calculated based on the constraints you've set on the label. The solid orange box is the frame of the label as you've designed it in Interface Builder. In this case, the two don't match up.

Auto Layout expects the label to be 290 points wide because of the constraints you set, but the frame in Interface Builder is showing a width much smaller than that. The orange badge with the number +243 indicates the label should be 243 points wider, according to Auto Layout's calculations.

To fix this you could manually drag the label's handles until it fits the dashed box, but it's much easier to use the **Resolve Auto Layout Issues** menu. Click the button beside the Pin button — it looks like a TIE fighter to Star Wars geeks. :]

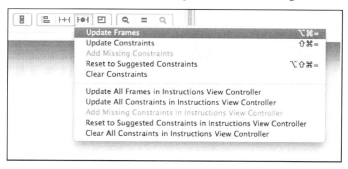

With the label selected, choose **Update Frames**. This adjusts the label's frame to match what is dictated by the constraints. Now all the constraints on the label are blue, as below:

Note that you did not set a constraint for the label's height. That's fine in this case since without that constraint Auto Layout will use the intrinsic height of the label.

> **Note:** Certain types of views, such as labels and buttons, have a size that depends on their content. If the label has a lot of text, then it needs to be wider or taller than if it only had a small amount of text. The label knows exactly how much text

it has and what its font size is, so the label can tell Auto Layout how big it wants to be.

That's what's called the *intrinsic content size*. For such views, Auto Layout can ask them how large they want to be and then it uses this size in its calculations. You do not need to give them an explicit size in Interface Builder. Of course, you can override the intrinsic size of a view by setting a width or a height constraint.

This particular label needs to be able to grow vertically if there is more than one line of text. That is why you're using the intrinsic height instead of a constraint. Auto Layout won't use the intrinsic width because the label's width is determined by the horizontal spacing constraints on either side.

Ctrl-drag from the top label to the bottom label and choose **Vertical Spacing** from the popup menu, like so:

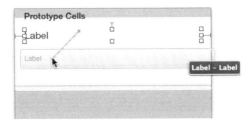

This adds an orange bar between the two labels. The space is a bit bigger than you really need, so click the bar to select it then go to the **Attributes** inspector. Constraints are objects and also have attributes. Change **Constant** to 10, so that the labels are 10 points apart, as so:

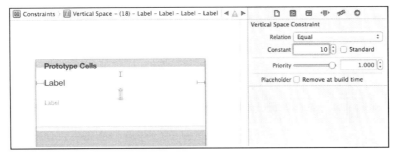

Hold down ⌘ while you click on both labels to select them together. Open the **Align** menu (left of the Pin button) and check both **Leading Edges** and **Trailing Edges**, as shown:

This will align the left and right edges of both the labels. For **Update Frames**, pick **Items of New Constraints**. You don't get any orange boxes now as Interface Builder fixes any misplaced frames for you when it adds the new constraints, as shown below:

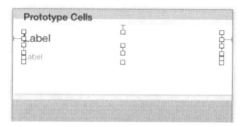

Note: You may be wondering why Auto Layout calls things on the left *Leading* and things on the right *Trailing*. It's because Auto Layout also supports languages that are not written left-to-right, such as Arabic or Hebrew. For such languages, the meaning of Leading and Trailing is reversed.

The constraints are all blue, so let's see how well this works. Build and run your app to see the effect of all your changes:

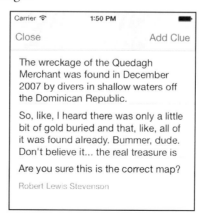

Hmm — that's not quite what you were hoping for, but it's not too far off either. The labels certainly resize to fit all the text, which is good, but the cells don't increase their height accordingly. Setting the height of table view cells is not automatic in Auto Layout; you still need to implement `heightForRowAtIndexPath` to return the actual height for each cell.

Add the new version of this method to **CluesViewController.m**:

```
- (CGFloat)tableView:(UITableView *)tableView
         heightForRowAtIndexPath:(NSIndexPath *)indexPath
{
  static UITableViewCell *cell;
  if (cell == nil) {
    cell = [tableView dequeueReusableCellWithIdentifier:
            @"ClueCell"];
  }

  [self configureCell:cell forIndexPath:indexPath];

  return [cell.contentView systemLayoutSizeFittingSize:
          UILayoutFittingCompressedSize].height + 1.0f;
}
```

Fortunately, there's no need to do any manual calculations here. Instead, you dequeue a cell and call `configureCell:forIndexPath:` to set the font and text on the labels. (You keep this cell in a static variable so you only have to make it once, the very first time that `heightForRowAtIndexPath` is called. It's a small optimization.)

The workhorse of this method is the call to `systemLayoutSizeFittingSize`. It causes Auto Layout to reevaluate all the constraints on that cell. It returns the final size for the cell, of which you return only the height, plus `1.0f` for the height of the separator line.

Is everything fixed now? Build and run your app to find out:

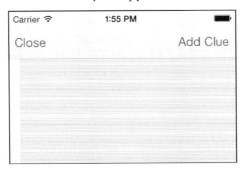

Uh oh — that looks worse, not better. The problem here is that you're always returning a height of 1.0f because there are no constraints telling the cell how tall it is. To fix that, you need to add a constraint between the bottom of the username label and the bottom of the cell. Only then does Auto Layout know that the height of the cell is *10 + height of text label + 10 + height of username label + 10.*

In **MainStoryboard.storyboard**, use the **Pin** menu to add a vertical spacing constraint of 10 between the second label and the bottom of the cell, as so:

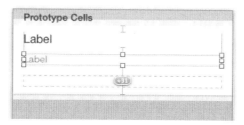

Of course, there are misplaced frames again because there's more than 10 points between the bottom edge of the label and the bottom of the cell. Select the cell and drag the bottom resizing-handle up until the cell's height is 69.

It appears you've corrected all of the Auto Layout issues. Build and run your app to see how things look:

Phew. That's a lot better, but there's still something to do here that's easily overlooked.

Setting content priorities

Think about this: the height of the prototype cell is 69 points, but at runtime, the cell height can be much larger depending on the amount of text in the top label. How does Auto Layout know how to distribute that extra height between the two labels? Does it give it all to the top label, give it all to the bottom label, do a 50-50 split, or what?

There are a number of ways Auto Layout could solve this layout issue, which technically makes it an ambiguous layout. Even though the design in Interface Builder is valid, by changing the height of the cell during runtime, you can still invalidate the layout. An ambiguous layout is unpredictable; since there are several possible solutions, Auto Layout will pick one at random and the resulting layout may not be quite what you expected.

You can actually simulate this in Interface Builder by resizing the table view cell. Drag its bottom resizing-handle downward and see which of the two labels becomes larger. Then undo and drag the handle down again. If you repeat this a few times you'll see that sometimes the top label becomes larger and sometimes the bottom label becomes larger. You should also see the following error message:

This type of issue is known as a **Content Priority Ambiguity**. Constraints have priorities, which are numbered between 1 and 1000. Auto Layout will evaluate the constraint with the highest priority first. If that constraint is invalid for the current layout, it will look at constraints with lower priorities. This allows you to make really complicated layouts. For example, using priorities you can say: "*I want these two views to stay exactly 20 points apart, but if there is no room, align them next to each other.*"

There are two special types of priorities for views with an intrinsic content size: the **content hugging priority** and the **content compression resistance priority**. The hugging priority determines how much a view should resist expanding, in other words how much it wants to prevent itself from becoming larger. The compression resistance priority is the reverse: it tells you how much the view should prevent itself from becoming smaller.

To solve this layout problem, first make the table view cell 69 points high again so that all Xcode errors disappear. Then select the bottom label. In the **Size** inspector, set the **Vertical Content Hugging Priority** to 251, like so:

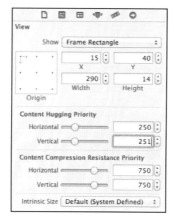

That makes it one higher than the vertical content hugging priority of the top label. Now when the cell becomes taller, Auto Layout knows that the bottom label does not want to expand and it will give all the extra space to the top label. Drag the cell's bottom resize-handle to resize it again. This time Xcode will give no warnings and all the bars remain blue. Ambiguity resolved!

> **Note:** The hugging and compression resistance priorities are only important for views with an intrinsic content size, such as labels, buttons, and image views. If you have two or more of these views connected to each other, and the width or height of the superview depends on their combined size, then you will need to play with these priorities to solve any potential layout ambiguities. Fortunately, Xcode will warn you about this in most cases.

And that wraps up this view controller – everything now resizes dynamically with Auto Layout! As you can see, Auto Layout is much improved in Xcode 5 and now you can use it with confidence in your own apps.

Challenges

There is only one challenge in this chapter but it's a big one. You will need to apply everything you learned about Auto Layout.

Challenge 1: Fixing the Instructions screen

The **Instructions** segment currently looks like the screenshot on the next page:

There's supposed to be a bold title label at the top but it's hidden beneath the navigation bar. You cannot fix this with the content insets because the main view of the InstructionsViewController is not a scroll view.

Another problem is that in landscape mode the label and the text view don't make use of the extra horizontal space:

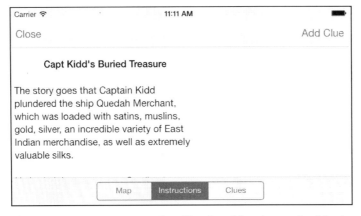

This is due to the automatic constraints that Xcode adds when it builds the app; it gives the label and the text view a fixed position and size, so they won't resize when you rotate to landscape.

Your challenge is to fix these issues by adding your own Auto Layout constraints.

- Use the **Pin** menu to add a space constraint of 80 points above the label.

- Center the label horizontally in the screen. To do this you use the **Align** menu (next to the Pin menu) and check the **Horizontal Center in Container** option.

- If there is still an orange box around the label, fix its frame using the **Resolve Auto Layout Issues** menu or **Editor\Size to Fit Content**.

The constraints on the label should look like this:

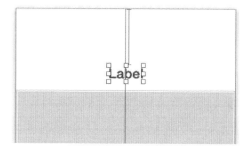

- Use the **Pin** menu to add 10 points of space between the label and the text view.

- Glue the other edges of the text view to its superview so that it will properly resize in landscape mode (add bottom, left, and right constraints of size 0).

- Remember, if the frame of the text view is mismatched (orange dashes), then use the **Resolve Auto Layout Issues** menu to fix it.

When you're done the instructions screen should look great in landscape mode as well:

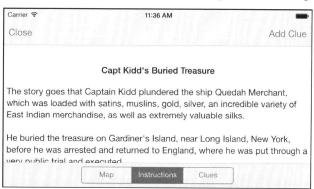

One final thing; on a map with a lot of instructions, the text may run beneath the toolbar. It would be preferable to have the last few lines be fully visible and not obscured by the toolbar. The solution is to set the **content insets** of the text view:

```
self.instructionsTextView.contentInset = UIEdgeInsetsMake(
                                    0.0f, 0.0f, 44.0f, 0.0f);
```

Chapter 8: Transitioning to iOS 7 – Advanced Topics

By Matthijs Hollemans

This final chapter on transitioning to iOS 7 looks at a variety of situations that you may encounter when migrating your own apps, such as:

• Adding an inline date picker

• Dimming the tint color

• Adding a search bar to a navigation bar

• Adding blur effects

• Supporting both iOS 6 and iOS 7

This chapter continues where the previous chapter left off. If you did not follow along, then grab the starter project from this chapter's resources.

Inline date picker

Tapping the **Date** row inside the **New Map** screen brings up the date picker. It used to look like the image on the left; a popup that appeared from the bottom of the screen. On iOS 7 however, it doesn't work at all well.

See the image on the right:

 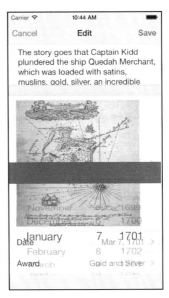

The UIDatePicker component now has a transparent background, meaning you can see the table view through it. You could change its background color to white of course, but date pickers are designed to work slightly differently on iOS 7. Apple now recommends that rather than using modal popups, you display them inline instead.

In this section you're going to change the date picker so that it looks like the following image. The **Date** row will expand when you tap it to reveal the date picker, as so:

The date picker is currently implemented using a separate child view controller, DatePickerViewController. Since this view controller is no longer needed, open the storyboard and delete the **Date Picker View Controller** scene. Also delete the source files **DatePickerViewController.h** and **DatePickerViewController.m**. Now doesn't that feel good? Throwing away old code always makes me happy.

However, your pruning effort has left **NewMapViewController.m** with some errors. To fix these errors, perform the following actions:

- Delete the #import "DatePickerViewController.h" statement.

- Delete the declaration of the _datePickerViewController instance variable.

- Delete everything inside of the showDatePicker method, but keep the method itself.

- Delete everything inside of the hideDatePicker method, but keep the method itself.

Build and run your app; it should compile without any warnings or errors.

To display the date picker inline, you'll embed an instance of UIDatePicker into a new cell in the table view, and make that cell appear only when the user taps the **Date** row. There are a couple of ways this can be accomplished.

It's entirely possible to create a new cell containing the UIDatePicker instance at the point when the user taps the **Date** row and then insert it into the table view. After the user has chosen a date, you'd then delete the new date picker row from the table view. That would certainly work, but it's not the most elegant solution. When you insert a new row, all the rows below it receive new index paths, so you may have to adjust row numbers manually depending on whether the date picker is visible or not. That's just asking for bugs. In addition, the **New Map** screen uses a static table view meaning you don't have the usual control over its data source.

Fortunately, there's an easier solution. Instead of dynamically inserting and deleting the date picker row, you are going to permanently add this row to the table view and simply hide it when it is not needed. The easiest way to hide a table view cell is to set its height to 0 points.

Open **MainStoryboard.storyboard** and find the **New Map View Controller** scene. From the **Object Library**, drag a new **Table View Cell** into the scene and place it directly below the Date row.

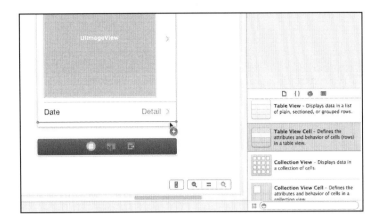

In the **Size** inspector for this cell, set the **Row Height** to 217; that's 216 points for the UIDatePicker and 1 point for the separator line. Remember that you can use the two-finger vertical pan gesture on your mouse or track pad to scroll the table view inside the storyboard so you can see this new cell in its entirety.

Drag a **Date Picker** from the **Object Library** into the new cell. For some reason the size of the date picker in Interface Builder is smaller than the runtime size, so it doesn't fit exactly. Align the date picker with the top of the cell. In the **Attributes** inspector, set the picker's **Mode** to **Date.** Now it'll display just the day, month and year.

Use the **Assistant** editor to create a new outlet for the date picker in **NewMapViewController.m**. Name it datePicker:

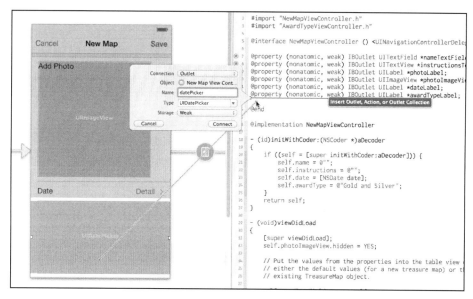

Normally this would be enough to see the date picker cell when running the app, but NewMapViewController also overrides the tableView:heightForRowAtIndexPath: delegate method so that it can adjust the size of the **Add Photo** row when the user has picked a photo. This method currently overrides the height that you set manually on the date picker's parent cell, so you need to add the if statement highlighted below:

```
- (CGFloat)tableView:(UITableView *)theTableView
          heightForRowAtIndexPath:(NSIndexPath *)indexPath
{
  if (indexPath.section == 1) {
    return 88.0f;
  } else if (indexPath.section == 2 && indexPath.row == 0) {
    return self.photoImageView.hidden ? 44.0f : 280.0f;
  } else if (indexPath.section == 2 && indexPath.row == 2) {
    return 217.0f;
  } else {
    return 44.0f;
  }
}
```

Build and run your app to see your new date picker cell in action:

You will keep track of whether the date picker cell is visible or hidden using a new instance variable. Add the following code to the top of **NewMapViewController.m**:

```
@implementation NewMapViewController
{
  BOOL _datePickerVisible;
}
```

Initially you want the date picker to be hidden. Add the following code to viewDidLoad:

```
_datePickerVisible = NO;
self.datePicker.hidden = YES;
```

This only hides the instance of UIDatePicker, not its parent table view cell. To make the entire row invisible, you need to modify the highlighted line in heightForRowAtIndexPath:

```
- (CGFloat)tableView:(UITableView *)theTableView
          heightForRowAtIndexPath:(NSIndexPath *)indexPath
{
```

```
    if (indexPath.section == 1) {
      return 88.0f;
    } else if (indexPath.section == 2 && indexPath.row == 0) {
      return self.photoImageView.hidden ? 44.0f : 280.0f;
    } else if (indexPath.section == 2 && indexPath.row == 2) {
      return _datePickerVisible ? 217.0f : 0.0f;
    } else {
      return 44.0f;
    }
  }
```

Instead of always returning `217.0f` for the row that contains the date picker, it now returns `0.0f` when the date picker is hidden from view.

Build and run your app, and verify that the date picker cell is no longer visible.

Now on to the good part: displaying the date picker, with a fancy animation, when the **Date** row is tapped. The magic happens in `showDatePicker`, which is currently empty. Replace `showDatePicker` with the following:

```
- (void)showDatePicker
{
  // 1
  NSIndexPath *dateRowIndexPath = [NSIndexPath
                          indexPathForRow:1 inSection:2];
  UITableViewCell *cell = [self.tableView
                    cellForRowAtIndexPath:dateRowIndexPath];
  cell.detailTextLabel.textColor =
                          cell.detailTextLabel.tintColor;

  // 2
  [self.datePicker setDate:self.date animated:NO];

  // 3
  _datePickerVisible = YES;
  [self.tableView beginUpdates];
  [self.tableView endUpdates];

  // 4
  self.datePicker.hidden = NO;
  self.datePicker.alpha = 0.0f;
  [UIView animateWithDuration:0.25 animations:^{
    self.datePicker.alpha = 1.0f;
  }];
```

```
// 5
NSIndexPath *pickerIndexPath = [NSIndexPath
                    indexPathForRow:dateRowIndexPath.row + 1
                          inSection:dateRowIndexPath.section];

[self.tableView scrollToRowAtIndexPath:pickerIndexPath
              atScrollPosition:UITableViewScrollPositionTop
                      animated:YES];
}
```

Here's what the above method does, step by step:

1. The detail label in the **Date** row already displays the existing date, and its font color is gray. Change its color to the global tint color to give a visual indication to the user that they're now editing this row.

2. Provide the existing date to the `UIDatePicker` instance.

3. Calling `beginUpdates` followed immediately by endUpdates causes the table view to re-layout its cells. As _datePickerVisible is now set to YES and therefore `heightForRowAtIndexPath` will return `217.0f` instead of `0.0f`, the row will slide open with an animation.

4. Fade in the `UIDatePicker` instance.

5. If necessary, scroll the table view to guarantee the date picker is fully onscreen.

Build and run your app. Tap the **Date** row and watch with amazement as the date picker slides open:

As the user changes the date using the picker, the detail label in the **Date** row needs to update in real time. Add the following method to **NewMapViewController.m**:

```
- (IBAction)dateChanged:(UIDatePicker *)datePicker
{
```

```
    self.date = self.datePicker.date;
    self.dateLabel.text = [self formatDate:self.date];
  }
```

This is an IBAction, so you'll need to hook it up. Save **NewMapViewController.m**, open the storyboard, find the **New Map View Controller** scene, select the UIDatePicker and then **Ctrl-drag** to the view controller object and select **dateChanged:** from the popup menu. Now whenever the date changes, the detail label in the **Date** row updates. Build and run your app to try it out.

You only want the date picker to be visible as long as the user is changing the date; it shouldn't remain on screen indefinitely. So there needs to be a way to hide the date picker row. In **NewMapViewController.m** replace the empty hideDatePicker method with this one:

```
- (void)hideDatePicker
{
  if (_datePickerVisible) {
    // 1
    NSIndexPath *indexPath = [NSIndexPath indexPathForRow:1
                                                inSection:2];
    UITableViewCell *cell = [self.tableView
                            cellForRowAtIndexPath:indexPath];
    cell.detailTextLabel.textColor =
            [UIColor colorWithRed:0 green:0 blue:0 alpha:0.5f];

    // 2
    _datePickerVisible = NO;
    [self.tableView beginUpdates];
    [self.tableView endUpdates];

    // 3
    [UIView animateWithDuration:0.25 animations:^{
      self.datePicker.alpha = 0.0f;
    } completion:^(BOOL finished) {
      self.datePicker.hidden = YES;
    }];
  }
}
```

The above method is essentially the opposite of showDatePicker:

1. Restore the original color of the detail label.

2. Animate the row sliding shut.

3. Fade out and hide the date picker view.

It's safe to assume that whenever the user taps on another row, they no longer want to use the date picker. This includes the **Date** row; tapping once on the **Date** row opens the date picker, tapping a second time should close it. To implement this, you need to call `hideDatePicker` from within `tableView:didSelectRowAtIndexPath:`. Modify the highlighted line in `tableView:didSelectRowAtIndexPath:` as follows:

```objc
- (void)tableView:(UITableView *)tableView
        didSelectRowAtIndexPath:(NSIndexPath *)indexPath
{
  if (indexPath.section == 0) {
    [self.nameTextField becomeFirstResponder];
  } else if (indexPath.section == 1) {
    [self.instructionsTextView becomeFirstResponder];
  }

  if (indexPath.section == 2) {
    if (indexPath.row == 0) {
      [self choosePhotoFromLibrary];
    } else if (indexPath.row == 1) {
      [tableView deselectRowAtIndexPath:indexPath animated:YES];

      // Remove this line:
      [self showDatePicker];

      // Add these lines:
      if (!_datePickerVisible) {
        [self showDatePicker];
      } else {
        [self hideDatePicker];
      }
      return;
    }
  }

  // Add these lines:
  // Also hide the date picker when tapped on any other row.
  [self hideDatePicker];
}
```

It's also a nice touch to hide the date picker when the user taps inside a text field to invoke the keyboard. Add the following statement to `viewDidLoad`:

```
[[NSNotificationCenter defaultCenter] addObserver:self
                           selector:@selector(hideDatePicker)
              name:UIKeyboardWillShowNotification object:nil];
```

This informs the notification center that the view controller is listening for the `UIKeyboardWillShowNotification,` and calls `hideDatePicker` when it's received.

Build and run your app; open the date picker and try tapping on any other cell to dismiss the date picker.

There's one more tiny detail to take care of. When the date picker is visible, it is still possible to tap on the cell, which selects it and highlights it as below:

Add Photo	>
Date	Aug 10, 2013 >

June	8	2011
July	9	2012
August	**10**	**2013**
September	11	2014
October	12	2015

Award	Gold and Silver >

That's a little ugly. Tapping in the date picker row also has the side effect of hiding the date picker, which can be confusing to the user. To fix these two problems, open **MainStoryboard.storyboard,** find the **New Map View Controller** scene in the document outline, expand the table view and select the cell containing the date picker. Make sure you select the Table View Cell, not the `UIDatePicker` inside it. In the **Attributes** inspector change **Selection** to **None**.

Also add the following method to **NewMapViewController.m**:

```
- (NSIndexPath *)tableView:(UITableView *)tableView
          willSelectRowAtIndexPath:(NSIndexPath *)indexPath
{
  if (indexPath.section == 2 && indexPath.row == 2) {
    return nil;
  } else {
    return indexPath;
  }
}
```

This instructs the table view that the row containing the date picker should not be selected. Now any extraneous taps inside the date picker row will have no effect.

It took a bit of work to place the date picker inline in the table view but this is reusable code that you should be able to drop straight into any other projects that require it. It also improves the user experience, as you no longer have to present a modal view to let users choose a date. Of course, you can also apply this technique for other types of pickers. But be sure to limit the height of the picker; if there are too many options, then it becomes confusing. As a rule of thumb, anything with a height smaller than half the screen height is okay.

Dimming the tint color

You've seen that each app has one primary color that is used for highlighting active states (tab bar, segmented control) and interactive elements (buttons). This tint color is blue by default but for Treasure Hunt you changed it to brown. Sometimes, however, you want to make it obvious to the user that certain UI elements cannot be used, for example when you're presenting a modal view such as the **Clue Sheet**. UIKit allows you to "dim" the tint color on those inactive UI elements so that they appear gray instead of tinted.

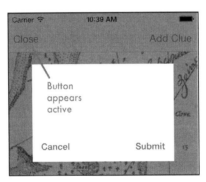

First you will patch up the appearance of the **Clue Sheet**. Open the storyboard and in the document outline expand the **New Clue View Controller Scene**. Select the view called **Content View** and use the Auto Layout **Align** menu to give it a **Horizontal Center in Container** constraint. Use the **Pin** menu to give it a top space of 64 points and a fixed width and height, like so:

Make sure that **Update Frames** is set to **Items of New Constraints**, so that Interface Builder will automatically resize and reposition the view based on these constraints, as shown in the layout below:

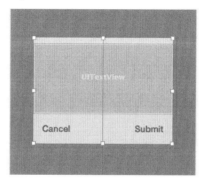

Change the background color of the **Content View** to white, but with opacity of 95%. That simulates the translucency effect of the navigation bar.

The buttons in the Clue Sheet are blue, not brown, because they were created in Xcode 4, which doesn't know about the new tint color feature. Delete the existing **Cancel** and **Submit** buttons and replace them by dragging new buttons from the **Object Library**. Notice they immediately pick up the brown global tint color:

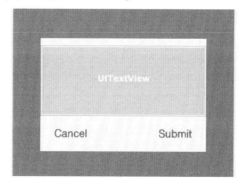

You don't have to set any constraints on these buttons, but be sure to connect the new **Cancel** button to the `cancelButton` outlet and the new **Submit** button to the `submitButton` outlet, or the **Clue Sheet** won't work anymore. **Ctrl-drag** from the view controller to the buttons to make these connections.

For some extra polish, let's give the view rounded corners. Add the following line to `viewDidLoad` in **NewClueViewController.m**:

```
self.contentView.layer.cornerRadius = 6.0f;
```

Build and run your app. Press the **Add Clue** button to bring up the clue sheet. It looks pretty good now:

When this modal view is active, the user cannot interact with any other part of the app. But the **Close** and **Add Clue** buttons in the navigation bar are still shown in the active tint color, which might confuse the user. It's better to dim these buttons to remove any doubt that these controls are unavailable.

UIKit has a new property you can leverage, `tintAdjustmentMode`. This tells the app whether to use the tint color or a dimmed shade of that color. Modify `viewDidAppear:` in **NewClueViewController.m** to the following:

```
- (void)viewDidAppear:(BOOL)animated
{
  [super viewDidAppear:animated];
  [self.textView becomeFirstResponder];

  self.view.window.tintAdjustmentMode =
                                UIViewTintAdjustmentModeDimmed;
  self.view.tintAdjustmentMode = UIViewTintAdjustmentModeNormal;
}
```

The new lines set the `tintAdjustmentMode` on the window to `UIViewTintAdjustmentModeDimmed`, which means it will turn anything that uses the tint color to a gray color. Since the **Clue Sheet** is also part of the window, you don't want its buttons to be dimmed, so you set the tint adjustment mode of the **Clue Sheet** to UIViewTintAdjustmentModeNormal, overriding the setting inherited from the window.

You need to set the window's tint mode back to normal in viewWillDisappear:, so add that method to the class as well:

```
- (void)viewWillDisappear:(BOOL)animated
{
  [super viewWillDisappear:animated];

  self.view.window.tintAdjustmentMode =
                          UIViewTintAdjustmentModeAutomatic;
}
```

Now the buttons in the navigation bar will appear disabled when the Clue Sheet appears, and return to their usual state when the Clue Sheet dismissed.

Search bar in the navigation bar

The **Shared Maps** screen (the second tab) has a search bar that is placed in the table view's header. In Apple's own apps, most notably Calendar, the search bar no longer sits at the top of the table view but is accessible through the navigation bar. As of iOS 7, you can now place the search bar inside the navigation bar, which saves space and makes search easily accessible at all times.

Open the storyboard and navigate to the **Shared Maps View Controller**. Select the search bar in the document outline and then drag it out from the table view header and down below the **First Responder**, like so:

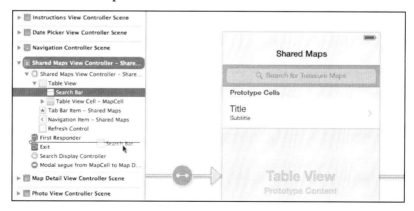

This removes the search bar from the view but the object will remain part of the view controller. When this view controller is instantiated by UIKit it will still have a search bar object associated with it. It also has a **Search Display Controller** that is connected to the same search bar.

Add the following line to `viewDidLoad` in **SharedMapsViewController.m**:

```
self.searchDisplayController
                .displaysSearchBarInNavigationBar = YES;
```

This tells the **Search Display Controller** to position the search bar within the navigation bar and to hide the **Cancel** button that would normally appear alongside the search bar.

Add the following two methods to **SharedMapsViewController.m**:

```
- (void)searchDisplayControllerWillBeginSearch:
                    (UISearchDisplayController *)controller
{
  self.searchDisplayController.searchBar
                           .showsCancelButton = YES;
}

- (void) searchDisplayControllerDidEndSearch:
                    (UISearchDisplayController *)controller
{
  self.searchDisplayController.searchBar.showsCancelButton = NO;
}
```

These are delegate methods for the **Search Display Controller**. The **Shared Maps** screen had already registered itself as the delegate but didn't implement these two methods. These simply make the **Cancel** button visible when the search begins, and hide it when the search ends.

Build and run to see the new search bar in action. Here's the **Shared Maps** screen:

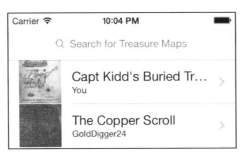

Tapping inside the search bar changes the visual focus to the search bar, as shown:

Blur effects

You have successfully updated the app so that it functions well on iOS 7 and it now looks like it belongs to the iOS 7 club. However, even though you've changed the tint color and added the crown image in various places, the app still looks very much like it came from one of the default app templates. Users upgrading from the iOS 6 version of the app will probably be a bit disappointed by the very neutral look of the new version.

In this section, you'll explore one way to give this app its own distinct personality on iOS 7. As you read in Chapter 1, "Designing for iOS 7", since iOS 7 is still so new and the design language is so different from any other iOS release, what constitutes "good iOS 7 design" will emerge over time. Presently, there's no clear direction on best design practices for this new, flat, textureless world, so some experimentation with different visual elements will be necessary for iOS 7 pioneers like you.

The use of the blur effect (i.e. "frosted glass") is prevalent in iOS 7. For example, an alert view automatically blurs the content that appears behind it. For **Treasure Hunt**, you will place a blurred, de-saturated version of the treasure maps behind the table view cells:

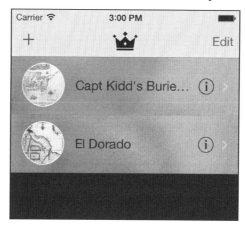

Blur is a pretty expensive effect to create in real-time, so you won't actually blur the entire treasure map photo, only the thumbnail. You don't need a high fidelity source image if you're going to blur it anyway. Often scaling down your image, blurring the smaller version, and then scaling it up again will look just as good but is a lot faster.

Unfortunately, iOS 7 does not have an easy built-in API for adding the blur effect. It would be great if you could just do [view blur]; but such an API does not exist. Instead, Apple provided sample code that demonstrates how to create blurred images. You will use that same code in Treasure Hunt.

From the **File** menu, choose **Add Files to "Treasure Hunt"**. Navigate to the **Extra Source Code** folder from this chapter's resources and select the two **UIImage+ImageEffects** source files to add them to the project. Then go to the **Target Settings** screen and under **Linked Frameworks and Libraries**, add the **Accelerate.framework** to the project as well. Build the app to make sure you don't have any errors.

You will now make a series of changes to **MyMapsViewController.m** and also to **SharedMapsViewController.m**. Both view controllers use the same customizations, so make the same changes to both source files.

First, import the new `UIImage+ImageEffects` category:

```
#import "UIImage+ImageEffects.h"
```

Then make the following changes to `viewDidLoad` in both source files:

```
self.tableView.backgroundColor = [UIColor colorWithRed:40/255.0f
                   green:20/255.0f blue:10/255.0f alpha:1.0f];

// Remove the separator lines for empty cells
UIView *footerView = [[UIView alloc] initWithFrame:CGRectZero];
self.tableView.tableFooterView = footerView;

self.tableView.separatorColor = [UIColor colorWithWhite:0.0f
                                              alpha:0.2f];
self.tableView.rowHeight = 80.0f;
self.tableView.separatorInset = UIEdgeInsetsZero;
```

This gives the table view a dark brown background and tweaks a few other parameters. Build and run; the app should look like this:

Each table view cell will get its own background image, based on a blurred version of the thumbnail for that row. Before you add the blur effect, first you will put the unprocessed thumbnail onto the cell's background, just to see how that looks. Add the following lines to `cellForRowAtIndexPath`, just before the line that returns the new cell. Remember to do this in **MyMaps-** as well as in **SharedMapsViewController.m**.

```
UIImage *backgroundImage = map.thumbnail;

UIImageView *imageView = [[UIImageView alloc]
                              initWithImage:backgroundImage];
imageView.contentMode = UIViewContentModeScaleAspectFill;
imageView.clipsToBounds = YES;
imageView.alpha = 0.8f;
cell.backgroundView = imageView;
```

Build and run; each cell now has a blown-up version of the thumbnail image in the background:

This isn't exactly pretty, but you're only a few steps away from blurry goodness. Notice that the background image is low quality. You took a 60x60 point thumbnail image and stretched it out across the width of the table. That's perfectly fine, as the user won't be able to see these imperfections anyway once the image is blurred.

Add the following method to get rid of the white blocks behind the labels:

```
- (void)tableView:(UITableView *)tableView
        willDisplayCell:(UITableViewCell *)cell
        forRowAtIndexPath:(NSIndexPath *)indexPath
{
  cell.backgroundColor = [UIColor colorWithWhite:1.0f
                                           alpha:0.2f];
  cell.contentView.backgroundColor = [UIColor clearColor];
  cell.textLabel.backgroundColor = [UIColor clearColor];
  cell.textLabel.textColor = [UIColor colorWithWhite:0.0f
                                               alpha:0.8f];
  cell.detailTextLabel.backgroundColor = [UIColor clearColor];
  cell.detailTextLabel.textColor = [UIColor colorWithWhite:0.0f
                                                     alpha:0.5f];
  cell.tintColor = cell.textLabel.textColor;
}
```

This method is part of the table view delegate protocol. It is called by the table view just before it will draw the cell on the screen. This is a good spot to customize the colors and any other properties of a standard table view cell.

Finally, to blur the background image, replace the line that sets `backgroundImage` in `cellForRowAtIndexPath` with these two lines:

```
UIColor *tintColor = [UIColor colorWithRed:140/255.0f
                  green:70/255.0f blue:35/255.0f alpha:0.2f];


UIImage *backgroundImage = [map.thumbnail applyBlurWithRadius:2
    tintColor:tintColor saturationDeltaFactor:0.8 maskImage:nil];
```

The `applyBlurWithRadius:tintColor:saturationDeltaFactor:maskImage:` method — try saying that ten times in a row — is what performs the magic. (If you want to know exactly what it does, look inside **UIImage+ImageEffects.m**.)

Build and run; you should have a nicely blurred background image behind each cell:

> **Note:** Feel free to play with the different parameters. The blur radius determines how extreme the blur is. The tint color applies an extra layer of color to the final image. Here you specify the same brown color that the app uses everywhere else, but only with 20% opacity. The saturation factor determines how much of the original color should remain in the blurred image. The closer this gets to 0, the more black & white the final image becomes.

Another common feature of iOS 7 apps is that they display thumbnails in a circular cutout (for example, headshots in the Contacts app). That effect is very easy to achieve. Add the following code to `cellForRowAtIndexPath`:

```
cell.imageView.layer.cornerRadius = 30.0f;
cell.imageView.layer.borderWidth = 1.0f;
cell.imageView.layer.borderColor = [UIColor whiteColor].CGColor;
cell.imageView.clipsToBounds = YES;
```

You set the corner radius of the image view's `CALayer` to 30 points, which is exactly half the width of the image, making it a perfect circle. The `clipsToBounds` property must be `YES` for this to work.

Build and run to see the result:

Blurring the contents of a view

In the previous section you took an existing image and blurred it. You can also take a snapshot of the contents of a view and apply the blur effect to that, which is useful for when you want to place something on top of an existing view and blur the underlying contents. That is what alert views and navigation bars do.

Even though iOS 7 does not have a convenient API for blurring, it does have fast new methods for making an image snapshot of a view. You will use these methods to give the **Clue Sheet** its own frosted glass effect.

Open **NewClueViewController.m** and import the UIImage helper category:

```
#import "UIImage+ImageEffects.h"
```

Add the following method:

```
- (void)updateImageView
{
  // 1
  UIView *snapshotView = [self.parentViewController.view
        resizableSnapshotViewFromRect:self.contentView.frame
        afterScreenUpdates:YES withCapInsets:UIEdgeInsetsZero];

  // 2
  UIGraphicsBeginImageContextWithOptions(
                   self.contentView.bounds.size, YES, 0.0f);
  BOOL result = [snapshotView
             drawViewHierarchyInRect:self.contentView.bounds
             afterScreenUpdates:YES];
  UIImage *snapshotImage =
               UIGraphicsGetImageFromCurrentImageContext();
  UIGraphicsEndImageContext();

  // 3
  if (result) {
    UIColor *tintColor = [UIColor colorWithWhite:0.97
                                     alpha:0.82];
    UIImage *blurredImage = [snapshotImage applyBlurWithRadius:4
                   tintColor:tintColor saturationDeltaFactor:1.8
                   maskImage:nil];
    _imageView.image = blurredImage;
  }
}
```

Here's how this works, step-by-step:

1. Create a new UIView by making a snapshot of the parent view controller's view, but only the section that is covered by the actual clue sheet (i.e. the contentView).

2. Draw this snapshot into a new graphics context in order to convert it to a UIImage.

3. Apply blur to the image using the helper method and place it into an image view.

The _imageView instance variable already exists; it is a leftover from the appearance customizations of the iOS 6 version of this app. You still need to create it, so add the following lines to viewDidLoad:

```
_imageView = [[UIImageView alloc]
                        initWithFrame:self.contentView.bounds];
[self.contentView insertSubview:_imageView atIndex:0];
self.contentView.clipsToBounds = YES;
```

This creates a new UIImageView that is exactly as big as the Clue Sheet's content view and places it behind the text view and the buttons. You set clipsToBounds to YES so that the image view also gets rounded corners.

Now all that's left is calling the new updateImageView method. Add the following line to the bottom of viewDidAppear:

```
[self updateImageView];
```

Build and run to see the effect:

Nice! Feel free to play with the parameters to applyBlurWithRadius:tintColor: saturationDeltaFactor:maskImage: to try out different effects.

Back to iOS 6

At the beginning of this tutorial, you set the **Deployment Target** of the project to 7.0. Because of this, the app no longer runs on iOS 6.1 or earlier. However, you can make your app support older iOS versions with a little bit of effort.

For new apps it makes sense to go iOS 7-only, but if you have an existing app on the App Store then you may not want to abandon iOS 6 just yet. The easiest solution is to make an iOS 7-only version of your app, with the **Deployment Target** set to 7.0, and upload that to the App Store. The App Store will still allow users with iOS 6 devices to download the previous version — but not the new one. The downside of this approach is that any new features or bugs fixes won't be ported back to your iOS 6 app. If you want to be backward compatible with iOS 6, then you need to make your app support both versions of the OS.

Go into the **Project Settings** screen and set the **Deployment Target** back to **6.1**. Choose the iOS 6.1 simulator from the scheme picker at the top. If you can't find the 6.1 simulators, you may need to install them first by going to **Xcode\Preferences\Downloads** and selecting **iOS 6.1 Simulator**.

Build and run your app, and... crash.

> **Note:** At this point you may get an error message, "iOS Simulator failed to install the application." If you receive this error, choose the **Reset Content and Settings...** option from the simulator menu bar to reset the simulator, and try again.

The app crashes immediately on the following line from `viewDidLoad` in **MyMapsViewController.m**:

```
self.tableView.separatorInset = UIEdgeInsetsZero;
```

That's because the `separatorInset` property doesn't exist on iOS 6. To fix this issue you can wrap it in an if-statement:

```
if ([self.tableView respondsToSelector:
                              @selector(separatorInset)]) {
   self.tableView.separatorInset = UIEdgeInsetsZero;
}
```

You will have to do this for every iOS 7-only API that the app uses.

There is another statement in the `tableView:willDisplayCell:` method in **MyMapsViewController.m** that will cause the app to crash, so wrap that in an `if` block as well:

```
if ([self.tableView respondsToSelector:@selector(tintColor)]) {
    cell.tintColor = cell.textLabel.textColor;
}
```

Build and run your app; it will look like the following under iOS 6:

You'll probably agree that the new graphics of the iOS 7 version don't work quite so well here. Notice that the navigation bar and tab bar are now brown; on iOS 6, the tint color changes the entire bar, not just the text on the buttons. But it's not just the colors that are different. Many views now have slightly different sizes and positions.

When making your backward compatible you need to make a decision: will you make the iOS 6 version look like the iOS 7 version? Or will you retain the original look?

Regardless of which option you choose, there are two ways to deal with this situation:

- Detect at runtime which version of iOS is running and make the necessary adjustments to your views. Your code will be littered with "*if (on iOS 6)*" statements.

- Create two storyboards, one for iOS 6 and one for iOS 7. This is a cleaner approach, but now you need to keep the two storyboard files in sync. You also need to remove the storyboard name from the **Info.plist** file so it's no longer loaded automatically and instead load the correct storyboard manually in the **UIApplicationDelegate** method `application:didFinishLaunchingWithOptions:`.

Having two separate storyboards may appear overkill, but recall how many small tweaks you made to the UI over the course of this chapter. For example, grouped style tables look quite different on iOS 6, so the cells from the iOS 7 storyboard will have the wrong metrics for iOS 6. Rather than trying to fix these metrics from code, it might be less work to have two storyboards.

If you don't want two use separate storyboards, there are several ways to tackle the problem of adjusting the positions and sizes of your views:

- If you're using Auto Layout, you can make outlets for your constraints and change their `constant` property depending on the OS version. Alternatively, you can always create the constraints in code instead of through Interface Builder.

- If your app does not use Auto Layout, then you may be able to use the new **Delta X/Y/Width/Height** options in the **Size inspector** to add/subtract from your view's position and size. For example, if you set delta X = 100, then iOS 6 adds 100 points to the X position of that view. This option isn't available when Auto Layout is enabled.

The good news is that asset catalogs will also work on iOS 6, so if you want both versions to share the same images, then it's safe to put them in an asset catalog. That goes for the icon and launch images as well. If the iOS 6 version needs to use different images, then you have to give them names that are different from the iOS 7 version.

As you can see, making your app support iOS 7 as well as earlier versions of the OS can be quite involved. After you've made all your changes, a number of intensive testing sessions to catch any bugs that may have crept in is **not** an optional step before you ship!

Where to go from here?

Phew, that was quite the ride. You've seen how to modernize an app so that it looks and feels good on iOS 7. Many of the changes were quite small, but it still took some effort to get everything updated.

The app ended up having a completely different visual style, but it still managed to retain some of its personality. Maybe your own apps don't need such an extreme makeover, but you will need to tweak your icons, fonts and colors. If you have apps on the App Store that could do with a dust off, then it's smart not to wait too long.

Switching to Auto Layout is probably the single biggest change that you can make. Auto Layout takes some getting used to, but it also makes it easier to support new technologies such as Dynamic Type.

To learn more about transitioning to iOS 7, go to the developer portal and download the **The iOS 7 UI Transition Guide**. This goes through all the changes between the UIKit controls in minute detail. It also has good suggestions for maintaining compatibility with iOS 6. Curl up by the fire some night and have a read through it; it will be worth your time.

> **Note:** As you update your apps to iOS 7, a new requirement to keep in mind is 64-bit compatibility. The new iPhone 5s has a 64-bit processor while older models only have 32-bit CPUs. For new projects Xcode will automatically build both 32- and 64-bit executables. However, for existing projects that you're importing from Xcode 4, you may need to enable a build option. Go to **Project Settings** and under **Build Settings**, **Architectures** choose "Standard Architectures (including 64-bit)". You can read more about developing for 64-bit in the **64-Bit Transition Guide for Cocoa Touch**, available from the iOS Dev Center.

Credits: The treasure map images are public domain images taken from Wikipedia.

Challenges

The difference between a good and a great app is all in the details. In this challenge you will implement a subtle but sweet animation effect.

Challenge 1: Swipe to go back

Navigation controllers in iOS 7 have a cool new feature: in addition to tapping the back button you can now use a left-to-right pan gesture to go back. This gesture is interactive and you can move back and forth, as shown below:

This is the **Award Type** screen. As you pan back, you'll see the **Award** cell from the **New Map** screen has remained selected. It stays that way until the screen is fully visible and then it fades out.

The automatic de-selection of cells is a feature of `UITableViewController` that you can enable or disable by setting the `clearsSelectionOnViewWillAppear` property accordingly (it's set to `YES` by default). This has been around since iOS 3.2, so it's hardly new.

However, if you've been playing close attention since upgrading to iOS 7 then you may have noticed that the built-in Settings app does something slightly different. When you swipe back, it doesn't wait to perform the fade out, but instead the amount of fading coincides with how far you've panned. It turns out this is a simple feature to add.

The code that you use to fade out a selected cell is:

```
[self.tableView deselectRowAtIndexPath:indexPath animated:YES];
```

When the user pans back to the **New Map** view controller, its `viewWillAppear:` method is called. That's a good place to perform the fade out of the **Award** row.

Now when you pan back from the award type picker controller, the **Award** row should fade out accordingly. It looks pretty sweet:

Note: This transition is one of the new *interactive transition* types in iOS 7, which means the animation between the two view controllers doesn't happen at a set speed — it's a function of how fast or slow the user pans. Therefore, the deselect animation varies as the user pans the view controller.

To learn more about interactive transitions in iOS 7, check out Chapter 3, "Custom View Controller Transitions."

Section II: What's New in Xcode 5

In this section, you'll learn about the new features in Xcode 5 that are useful when making *any* type of app. In particular, you'll learn about unit testing, source control, continuous integration, and more.

Chapter 9: What's New in Xcode 5

Chapter 10: What's New in Objective-C and Foundation

Chapter 11: Unit Testing in Xcode 5

Chapter 12: Beginning Source Control in Xcode 5

Chapter 13: Intermediate Source Control in Xcode 5

Chapter 14: Beginning Continuous Integration in Xcode 5

Chapter 15: Intermediate Continuous Integration in Xcode 5

Chapter 9: What's New in Xcode 5

By Felipe Laso Marsetti

Along with introducing iOS 7, Apple introduced a new version of its IDE: Xcode 5.

Before you dive into the rest of the chapters of this book, we wanted to give you a quick whirlwind tour of what's new in Xcode. Specifically, you'll learn about:

- Asset catalogs

- Image slicing

- Auto Layout improvements

- Preview window

- Language improvements

- Documentation improvements

- Debugging improvements

- Source control improvements

- Performance improvements

Note that unlike the rest of the chapters in this book, rather than diving into a deep tutorial this chapter will be a quick article-style birds-eye overview. This is so that you have a good context over what's changed with the IDE as you proceed through the rest of the chapters.

Asset catalogs

Before Xcode 5, in order to support different devices and resolutions, you had to have different versions of your artwork with slightly different filenames. For example, you might have:

- **myImage.png** [normal resolution version]
- **myImage@2x.png** [retina resolution version]
- **myImage@2x~ipad.png** [a retina resolution version specifically for iPad]

Xcode 5 comes with a much more elegant solution to this problem – Asset catalogs.

Asset catalogs are a way for you to tie all of the various versions of an image asset to a single name in a nice visual interface:

This is the screenshot of an asset catalog that contains four image sets. For each of these set, you can specify different versions – for example, different versions for retina and non-retina devices.

Here's an example of what the `AppIcon` asset looks like when selected:

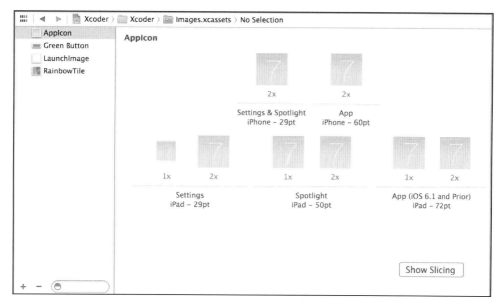

This asset has different versions of the images for iPad retina and non-retina, iPhone (retina-only as of iOS 7), and Settings and Spotlight each with its corresponding high-resolution version.

To add images to an asset catalog, simply drag the images into your project and then drag them to the asset catalog folder in the project navigator. Alternatively, you can click on the + button in the asset catalog viewer.

Notice that you no longer have to worry about putting keywords like @2x, ~iphone, ~ipad or −568h the image filenames. Your files can be named anything you wish - they can even share the same name inside a catalog!

To use an image from an asset catalog in code, you use the imageNamed: method of UIImage with the name of your asset set as shown in the following snippet:

```
UIImage *myImage = [UIImage imageNamed:@"RainbowTile"];
```

Asset catalogs are great because images no longer have to comply with a strict naming standard in order to work on all devices and resolutions. Also, if your project has iOS 7 as the deployment target, Xcode compiles your asset catalogs into a runtime binary file that reduces the download time of your app.

Image slicing

Image slicing is a new feature in Xcode 5 that allows you to "slice" your images into parts to ensure proper scaling of your images at run time. This means that a single image can be used by multiple views — and at multiple resolutions.

The following screen shot shows image slicing in action:

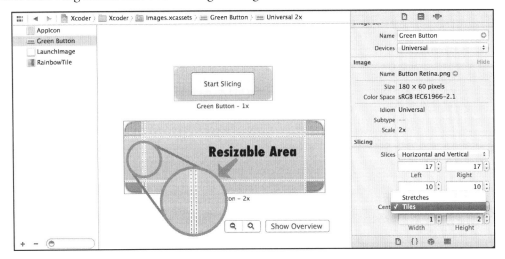

Here you see a button that is sliced into nine segments. There are three sets of lines for each direction: two outer slice handles and one inner slice handle. The outer handles let you adjust the size of the end caps while the inner handle lets you adjust the size of the center.

The end caps you set in the editor will be left untouched when your image is drawn while the center can be tiled or stretched. This setting is accessed via the attributes inspector under the *Slicing* section (shown in the previous screenshot).

Here's an image that shows you the difference between a tiled and stretched asset:

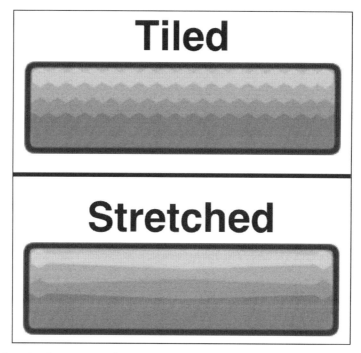

Xcode immediately shows you what your scaled image will look like — and it's even smart enough to use the same slicing scheme for both the retina and non-retina versions of your image.

Image Slicing is great because it allows you to easily use small images that can stretch to any size while still looking great. Also, you no longer have to take a trial-and-error approach to creating resizable end caps and sliced images. All you have to do is drag the slice handles, set the center mode and use the image in your project.

Auto Layout improvements

Auto Layout was introduced in iOS 6 as Apple's replacement for the antiquated "springs and struts" layout technology. While Auto Layout was designed to be intuitive and allow you to easily develop interface layouts for all screen-sizes, orientations and languages, it was quite painful to work with inside Interface Builder itself. As a result, many developers had to resort to workarounds or by using Auto Layout in code.

Fortunately, Xcode brings some new features to Auto Layout that make working with Auto Layout in Interface Builder much easier:

• Interface Builder no longer changes your constraints automatically as you move items

- But you can ask Interface Builder to calculate constraints automatically when you choose

- You can now easily set up constraints between two elements by control-dragging between them

- There are new controls to solve common Auto Layout problems, such as the **Pin** and **Resolve Auto layout Issues** buttons in interface builder, which let you clear constraints, reset to the suggested constraints in Interface Builder, add missing constraints, updates constraints, update frames, and more

- The interface to create and set up constraints is now a more visual and intuitive experience, offering popovers for setting up offsets and spacing between views and elements

The following screenshot shows some of the new Auto Layout functions available in Xcode 5:

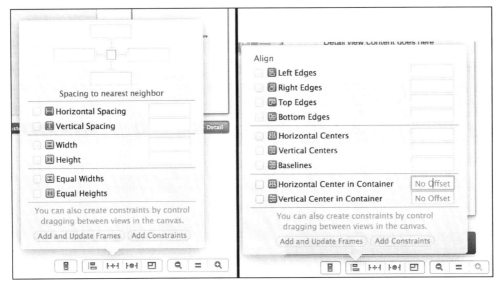

Notice how there are interfaces for pining and aligning elements, each one letting you specify several rules and constraints much quicker. Setting up complex views with multiple constraints used to take a long time and had to be done one click at a time. Now, you can easily see what you are changing and can do so for multiple values at once.

With the new Auto Layout features in Xcode 5, using Auto Layout in practice becomes a lot more feasible and less frustrating – so you no longer have an excuse to avoid Auto Layout!

Note: For an in-depth look at the new features of Auto Layout in Xcode 5, check out Chapter 7, "Transitioning to iOS 7 – What's New with Auto Layout". You may also enjoy our "Beginning and Intermediate Auto Layout" chapters in iOS 6 by Tutorials.

Preview window

Xcode 5 introduces a new way to preview your view controllers on different OS, orientation, and screen size combinations right from Interface Builder:

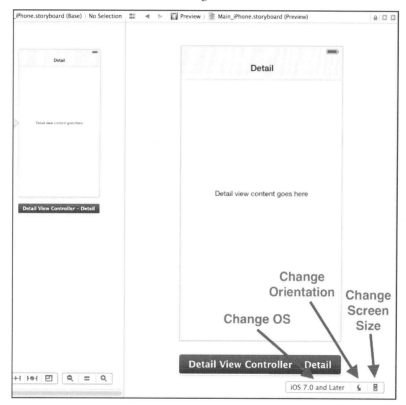

The next page shows an example of previewing an app on iOS 6 and iOS 7 devices using the preview window:

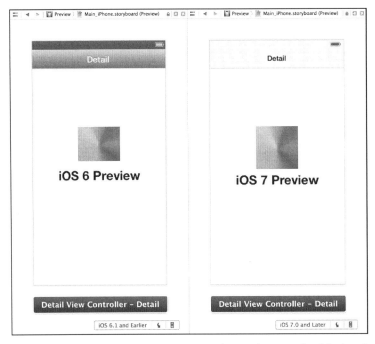

To view the preview pane, click the **Assistant Editor** button, highlighted in blue:

Then select **Preview** from the **jump bar**, as shown:

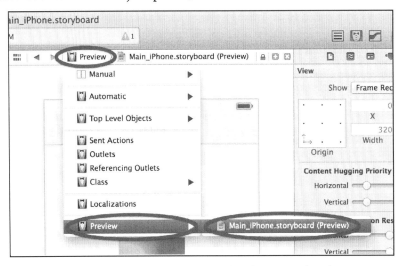

You will find the preview window especially helpful if you are developing an app that supports both iOS 6 and iOS 7 that you want to make sure looks great on both platforms.

Automatic configuration

If you've been developing iOS applications for a while, you're probably familiar with the tedious (and often painful) process of setting up certificates, provisioning profiles and entitlements.

Have you ever thought to yourself, "There should be an easier way to do this?" Well you're in luck – with Xcode 5, now there is!

Check out Xcode 5's new automatic configuration feature, by visiting the new Accounts tab inside the Xcode preferences window:

Then sign in with your developer account, and Xcode will set up certificates, provisioning profiles, and entitlements on your behalf. Additionally, Xcode will be fully aware of any developer programs you are enrolled in and any teams you belong to.

You can setup new profiles and certificates while viewing the details of a developer's account, as shown on the next page:

You can also easily switch between any teams that you are a member of from the General tab of your target settings, as shown here:

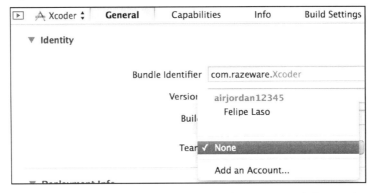

One of the real gems of automatic configuration is the new Capabilities tab in target settings. Capabilities allow you to automatically configure and enable services for your app, such as iCloud, Game Center, in-app purchases, background modes, and Passbook as easily as flipping a switch:

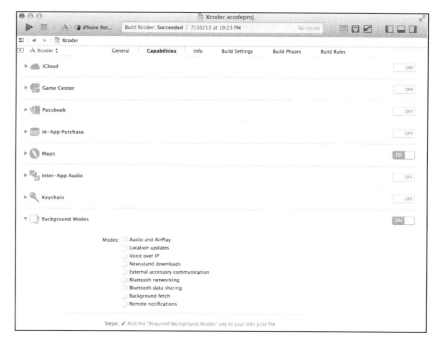

When you enable a specific feature from within the Capabilities tab, Xcode will automatically link the necessary frameworks and makes any required changes to your info.plist file. This is a welcome respite from the manual configuration of the past.

The new management features of accounts and capabilities, along with automated provisioning and configuration means that less time is spent configuring your project, and more time is spent where it counts — making great apps.

Language improvements

Previous versions of Xcode supported both LLVM and GCC, but Xcode 5 marks the complete transition to LLVM only. To celebrate this happy occasion, several new features and enhancements have been introduced, including modules.

Modules

Modules are a new and efficient way to include frameworks in your apps. Rather than the old days of adding the library and importing the header, you just need to add one line:

```
@import CoreData;
```

Modules also permit you to import specific headers from a framework, as shown:

```
@import Accelerate.vecLib;
```

It's good practice to use modules as much as possible moving forward, as it will improve compile-time performance, reduce the need to manage precompiled header files, and provide automatic linking of the imported frameworks.

Other language features

In addition, there are three other language features you should be aware of:

1. LLVM 5's Auto-Vectorizer makes use of the vector features of the modern ARM and Intel processors in iOS and OS X hardware.

2. Xcode 5 supports all C++ 11 updates and features, such as:

    a. The `auto` keyword

    b. The `nullptr` keyword

    c. Smart Pointers

    d. Lambdas

    e. Generalized Constant Expressions (`constexpr`)

    f. Strongly-typed enums

    g. Type traits and `static_assert`

    h. And more (see the C++11 Wikipedia entry for the full list of features)

3. Xcode 5 now includes the command line tools in the package by default — which means that when you update Xcode, the command line tools are automatically updated as well.

> **Note:** For more detailed information on the new language features, check out Chapter 10, "What's New with Objective-C and Foundation".

Documentation improvements

Xcode 5 brings two big improvements with documentation: a new documentation window, and doxygen comment parsing.

Documentation window

Documentation is now a first-class citizen in Xcode. Rather than being inside the Xcode Organizer, documentation now has its own window:

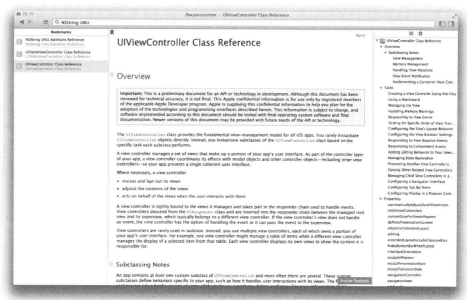

You can access the new documentation window from the **Help\Documentation and API Reference** menu (or the **Option + Command + ?** keyboard shortcut). You'll find it's is a convenient and fast documentation browser, including tabs and bookmarking functionality.

Doxygen comment parsing

Xcode 5 also contains a new new feature to parse and extract any doxygen-style comments in your source files. This makes it much easier to generate documentation for your source code – and the extracted comments are even used in code completion and quick-help popups!

Here's an example of a method declaration for `setCarouselItems:` and the corresponding comment:

```
/*! This is the description of what the method does.
 * \param items An array of items to be added to the carousel
 * \param animated Indicate whether setting the items should be animated or not
 * \returns the return value of your method, if available.
 */
- (BOOL)setCarouselItems:(NSArray *)items animated:(BOOL)animated;
```

And here's the resulting documentation when you option-click on a line that calls `setCarouselItems::`:

```
34        [self setCarouselItems:@[@"A", @"B", @"C"] animated:YES];
35
36    UIBarButt
          (inse    Declaration   - (BOOL)setCarouselItems:(NSArray *)items animated:
37    self.navi                   (BOOL)animated;
38    self.deta
39    }           Description   This is the description of what the method does.
40
41  - (void)didRe  Parameters    items       An array of items to be added to the carousel
42  {
43    [super di                   animated    Indicate whether setting the items should be animated or
44    // Dispos                                not
45  }
46                  Returns   the return value of your method, if available.
47  - (void)inser
48  {             Declared in   MasterViewController.h
```

As an Objective-C and iOS developer you've never really had a standard, official way to document your source code like Java or Ruby developers can.

With support for doxygen-style comments available by default in Xcode 5, Objective-C development can take a big step forward in making projects and custom code much easier to use and understand.

So be a tidy coder and start developing good habits by commenting your code!

Debugging improvements

Since GCC has been removed from Xcode 5, and by association GDB, LLDB has taken the reins as the debugger of choice. The debugging features added to Xcode 5 are probably some of the best improvements yet.

Data Tips

First on the list are data tips, which allow you to see the value of your variables as you step through your code. An example of a data tip is shown in the following screenshot:

```
35  - (void)configureView
36  {
37      if (self.detailItem)
38      {
39          NSString *labelValue = [[self.detailItem
                                  valueForKey:@"timeStamp"] description];
41          self.detailDescriptionLabel.text = labelValue;      Thread 1: breakpoint 1.1
42      }
43  }
                         ▶@"2013-07-21 16:07:16 +0000"  ◉ ❻
```

Quick Look

Quick Look in data tips is a feature clearly inspired by the Finder. Quick Look displays a graphical representation of variable values, which means you no longer have to rely on using po from the debug console. It can display images, Bezier paths, colors and several other preview types all within the editor itself.

Here are some examples of the available data tips in action:

UIBezierPath

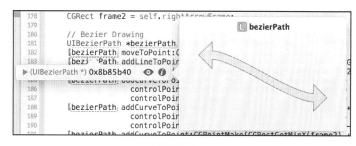

UIColor

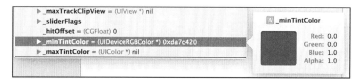

CGRect

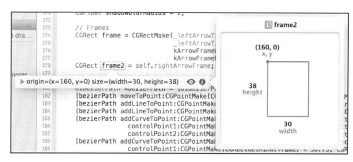

UIImageView

NSString

```
-  (void)configureView
{
    if (self.detailItem)
    {
        NSString *labelValue = [[self.detailItem
                      valueForKey:@"timeStamp"] description];
        self.detailDescriptionLabel.text = labelValue;    Thread 1: breakpoint 1.1
    }
}                           ▶@"2013-07-21 16:07:16 +0000" ◉ ◉
```

Debug Gauges

Debug gauges have been greatly enhanced as part of the improvements to the debugger interface. Little graphical gauges now appear in the debug navigator of Xcode and provide live feedback for crucial metrics such as memory and CPU usage, as illustrated:

You can monitor a wide range of metrics with both familiar and new widgets in Xcode 5, including OpenGL frame rates, iCloud activity, and energy consumption among others. Gauges add very little overhead to the system and require as little as 1% of a device's resources. This is a great help when you just want some quick performance statistics and don't want to go all the way into Instruments.

Clicking on a gauge presents you with a beautiful live report in the editor pane that shows you extended information about the selected metric. Here is a screenshot of the CPU Report in Xcode 5:

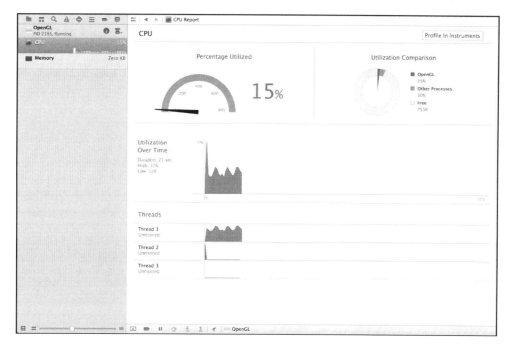

The CPU Report shows you the percentage of CPU currently being used by your process, as well as what's being used by the rest of the device. It also shows you the CPU utilization over time, along with the individual CPU utilization of each thread in your app.

However, debug gauges are still no replacement for Instruments — and that's why the debug reports contain a button in the top right corner labeled **Profile In Instruments**. This allows you to jump straight into Instruments for the currently selected metric.

Analyzing a single file

There's just one more thing to mention about debugging in Xcode 5: you can now analyze a single file by going to **Product > Perform Action > Analyze** *file name*, where *file name* is the name of the individual file to analyze. This should prove to be extremely useful when working with a very large project where compile and analysis performance tends to be sluggish.

Testing improvements

Testing methodologies and tools are now an integral part of Xcode 5, which now includes proper support for unit tests, the popular test-driven development workflow, and continuous integration services.

Unit testing

Xcode 5 includes a new native test framework, XCTest, which replaces OCUnit as the default test framework in Xcode. XCTest is derived from OCUnit but improved in the process, and is exclusive to iOS 7 and OS X Mavericks. Fortunately for you, OCUnit is still around and both frameworks can co-exist in the same project.

If you want to migrate to XCTest but already have existing tests in OCUnit, don't panic! Xcode 5 offers the ability to migrate your existing tests from the OCUnit framework to the XCTest framework. It's found under the menu item **Edit > Refactor > Convert to XCTest**, as shown:

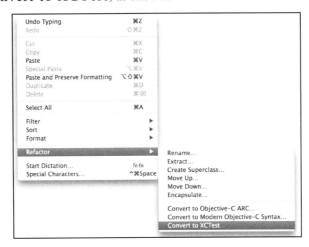

The following image shows the new test navigator in Xcode 5, located just to the right of the **Warnings and Errors** navigator:

This test navigator offers a complete overview of all the tests in the current workspace. It's easy to add new test targets and test classes; as well, you can run individual tests or ad-hoc collections of tests as the need arises. The navigator displays the outcome of the last test run as well as the latest integration results.

Opening one of the test implementation files in the editor shows you which tests have been run, the result of the most recent integration, as well as any errors or warnings for the test. You can see this feature in action in the screenshot:

```objc
15   @implementation OpenGLTests
16
17   - (void)setUp
18   {
19       [super setUp];
20
21       // Set-up code here.
22   }
23
24   - (void)tearDown
25   {
26       // Tear-down code here.
27
28
29
30       [super tearDown];
31   }
32
33   - (void)testExample
34   {
35       XCTFail(@"No implementation for \"%s\"", __PRETTY_FUNCTION__);         ⓘ failed - No implementation for "-[OpenGLTests testExample]"
36   }
37
38   - (void)testViewSetup
39   {
40       NSString *myString = @"";
41
42       XCTAssertEquals(myString, myString, @"The objects aren't equal");
43   }
44
45   - (void)testShaderCompilation
46   {
47       XCTAssertEquals(@5, @5, @"The objects aren't equal");
48   }
49
50   - (void)testFramerateLock
51   {
52       XCTFail(@"No implementation for \"%s\"", __PRETTY_FUNCTION__);         ⓘ failed - No implementation for "-[OpenGLTests testFramerateLock]"
53   }
```

For those of you using continuous integration tools such as Jenkins and Hudson, you'll be happy to know that those tests can now be run directly from the command line with the `xcodebuild test` command. To use it open a Terminal window, navigate to the folder with the .xcodeproj file and run this command:

```
xcodebuild test –scheme Xcoder –destination platform='iOS
Simulator',OS=latest,name=iPad
```

This tells the xcodebuild tool to run your project's test target (provided you have one) on the specified scheme and destination; in this case it's the iPad simulator running the latest version of iOS. Your results should look similar to the following screenshot:

```
Test Case '-[XcoderTests testExample]' failed (0.000 seconds).
Test Suite 'XcoderTests' finished at 2013-07-21 16:56:40 +0000.
Executed 1 test, with 1 failure (0 unexpected) in 0.000 (0.000) seconds
Test Suite 'XcoderTests.xctest' finished at 2013-07-21 16:56:40 +0000.
Executed 1 test, with 1 failure (0 unexpected) in 0.000 (0.000) seconds
Test Suite 'All tests' finished at 2013-07-21 16:56:40 +0000.
Executed 1 test, with 1 failure (0 unexpected) in 0.000 (0.001) seconds
** TEST FAILED **
```

For help and information on the `xcodebuild` command run `man xcodebuild` in a Terminal window.

> **Note**: To learn more about Unit Testing in Xcode 5, check out Chapter 11, "Unit Testing in Xcode 5".

Continuout Integration and Bots

If you aren't currently using a continuous integration server because you're concerned with potential overhead and maintenance issues, then you might be interested in the brand new Xcode service in OS X Mavericks Server.

The new Xcode service includes a feature called Bots, which makes continuous integration and automated unit testing a breeze. These bots are processes run from the Xcode service which automate the tasks of building, analyzing, testing and archiving the current version of a project in a repository.

Bots can be run automatically, in one of two configurations:

- **On Commit:** On each commit to your repository, the bot will checkout the code, analyze it, build it and run any tests.

- **Periodically:** On a defined schedule — hourly, daily or weekly – the bots run a full integration and are even nice enough to sign and archive the application for you. This is intended to emulate a production environment as closely as possible.

You also have the option of running a manual integration process any time you wish. However, automation is where it's at — once you automate your integration process you'll wonder why you've been avoiding it all this time.

Bots keep a full history of integration runs; this data is visible in Xcode 5 on the development workstation, which means you don't need access to the integration server to access integration history.

Builds and tests will run just fine on the simulator, but the bots can also run builds and tests on physical iOS devices that are connected to the server. No more hunting down test hardware — just leave it plugged in to the server and it will always be there when it's time to build. How convenient is that?

> **Note:** To learn more about Integration, check out Chapter 14, "Beginning Continuous Integration with Xcode 5".

Source control improvements

Source control is also hugely improved in Xcode 5, and is now a central part of the development workflow.

Xcode 5 has moved its source control menu from **File\Source Control** to a top-level **Source Control** menu. You'll also see a few additional options, such as viewing history and viewing and switching branches:

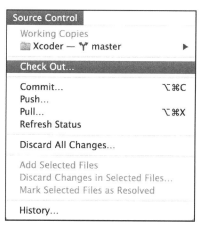

Source control functionality is now baked directly into the code editor. You can right-click on any line of code and select **Show Blame for Line** to view a popover detailing the person who committed the offending line of code, along with the revision's SHA, date and description as shown:

```
145  - (void)setupGL
146  {
147      [EAGLContext setCurrentContext:self.context];
148
149      [self loadShaders];
150
151      self.effect = [[GLKBaseEffect alloc] init];
152      self.effect.light0.enabled = GL_TRUE;
153      self.effect.light0.diffuseColor
154
155      glEnable(GL_DEPTH_TEST);
156
157      glGenVertexArraysOES(1, &_verte
158      glBindVertexArrayOES(_vertexAr
159
160      glGenBuffers(1, &_vertexBuffer)
161      glBindBuffer(GL_ARRAY_BUFFER, _vertexBuffer);
162      glBufferData(GL_ARRAY_BUFFER, sizeof(gCubeVertexData), gCubeVertexData, GL_STATIC_DRAW);
163
```

Felipe Laso Marsetti   1b9196581bba
Jul 10, 2013, 10:23 PM   Show 21 modified files

Initial Commit

Open in Blame   Open in Comparison

From inside the popup, you can immediately open the revision in Blame or Comparison mode in the Version Editor.

> **Note:** For an in-depth look at source control in Xcode 5, check out Chapter 12, "Beginning Source Control in Xcode 5".

Performance improvements

Last but not least, one of the nicest changes you'll notices in Xcode 5 is increased performance. Search, incremental builds, tab creation and device discovery are all significantly faster. The following chart shows these performance improvements visually:

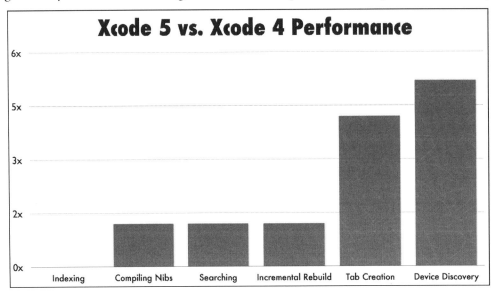

As stated in WWDC Session 400 – What's New in Xcode 5, these performance gains are almost exclusively the result of building Xcode 5 on top of ARC, instead of the antiquated garbage collection technology of earlier versions of Xcode.

> **Note:** To learn more about ARC, check out Chapter 2 and 3 of *iOS 5 by Tutorials*, "Beginner and Intermediate ARC".

Where to go from here?

The future is here, and its name is Xcode 5. This chapter was designed to bring you up to speed quickly with the new features of Xcode 5, seeing as you'll be using it throughout this book — and ostensibly for all your future iOS and Mac development projects as well!

There's a wealth of changes, updates, new features, and enhancements in Xcode 5, all designed to simplify your life as an Objective-C developer, and to help you write fast, efficient, high-quality code. Apple's dedication to helping the iOS and OS X development community produce the best apps possible is evident in great new features such as XCTest, bots, source control integration and automatic configuration.

For a more in-depth look at the topics mentioned in this chapter, please refer to this book's table of contents, or Apple's own Xcode 5 documentation.

Chapter 10: What's New in Objective-C and Foundation

By Matt Galloway

Objective-C is the most common language for developing iOS and OS X apps. Sure, you can use third party frameworks that allow you to develop apps using other languages such HTML & Javascript or C#, but if you want to write blazingly fast, super efficient native apps then you need to use Objective-C.

You'd be forgiven for thinking that Objective-C is fairly constant as it's been around since the early eighties. However, think back over the last few years, since the release of the initial iPhone SDK in 2008, and you'll recall many advances in the language that we all know and have come to love.

One of the biggest changes came about in 2011 when Apple announced Automatic Reference Counting, or ARC. This delivered a much stricter, but more developer friendly, memory management model. Naming conventions were formalized into a set of rules that ARC adheres to. This made developing both iOS and desktop apps much easier. Suddenly, a great deal of boilerplate code for memory management, and the headaches that went with it, disappeared in one fell swoop.

Objective-C is constantly evolving, and since Apple drives the majority of its development, iOS and OS X benefit handsomely. Staying on top of the newest changes to the language will make you a better developer, as you'll be aware of the latest tools and improvements, many of which directly affect the performance of your apps.

So what's new with Objective-C in iOS? Perhaps a better question is what's new in both iOS 7.0 *and* Xcode 5. The compiler is part of the Xcode tool-chain, whereas the runtime and system libraries are part of the OS; both of these have seen many improvements in the latest release.

On the tool-chain side of things you have the new `instancetype` return type and modules with an aim to vastly improve the compile time of your apps. The the system libraries include a few new classes as well as several improvements to the Foundation classes.

In this chapter you'll learn about some of the new shiny bits in both Objective-C and Foundation and why you should start using them. Note that unlike other chapters in this book, this chapter will be an article rather than a tutorial so you can get an overview of the new features as quickly as possible. Let's get started!

> **Note:** Did you know that Apple isn't responsible for the original implementation of Objective-C? Brad Cox and Tom Love of Stepstone originally created it in the early 1980s. Their idea was to port various elements of the Smalltalk language to C.
>
> Objective-C first gained popularity in 1988 when Steve Jobs licensed it through his company NeXT and then used it to develop the original AppKit and Foundation frameworks. The rest, as they say, is history.

Modules

Chances are good that you've written the `#import` statement a thousand times or more:

```
#import <UIKit/UIKit.h>
#import <MapKit/MapKit.h>
#import <iAd/iAd.h>
```

This syntax harkens back to the roots of Objective-C: vanilla C. The `#import` statement is a pre-processor directive that works in a similar fashion to `#include`. The only difference is that `#import` doesn't re-import headers that have already been imported; it's a one-shot deal.

When the pre-processor meets an `#import` directive, it literally replaces that single line with the entire contents of the header file being imported. It does this recursively, through a potentially large number of header files.

The `UIKit` umbrella header, `UIKit.h`, imports all of the other headers included in the `UIKit` framework. This means that you don't have to manually import each header file in the framework, such as `UIViewController.h`, `UIView.h` or `UIButton.h`.

Curious about the size of the UIKit framework? Go through and count all the lines in the entirety of `UIKit`'s headers, you'll find it amounts to over 11,000 lines of code!

In a standard iOS app, you'll import UIKit in most of your files, meaning every single file ends up being 11,000 lines longer. That's less than ideal; more lines of code means longer compile times.

Original solution: Pre-compiled Headers

Pre-compiled header files, or PCH files, attempt to address this problem by providing a mechanism for pre-computing and caching much of the work required during the pre-processing phase of compilation. You've probably seen the stock PCH file that's generated by the templates bundled with Xcode; it looks like this:

```
#import <Availability.h>

#ifndef __IPHONE_5_0
#warning "This project uses features only available in iOS SDK
5.0 and later."
#endif

#ifdef __OBJC__
    #import <UIKit/UIKit.h>
    #import <Foundation/Foundation.h>
#endif
```

The #warning in there notifies the developer if the app they're building targets an SDK prior to iOS 5. The UIKit and Foundation umbrella header files are part of this stock PCH, since every file in your app will use Foundation and most will use UIKit. Therefore these are generally good additions to the PCH file so that the pre-computation and caching will benefit the compilation of every file in your app.

"So what's wrong with that?" you might ask. There's nothing technically wrong with the PCH as-is — if it isn't broke, don't fix it. However, you may be missing out on a host of performance benefits that result from a well-maintained, highly tuned PCH file. For instance, if several areas of your app use the Map Kit framework, you may see an improvement in compilation time by simply adding either the Map Kit umbrella header file or the individual header files of the Map Kit classes you use to the PCH file.

We're all guilty of being lazy developers though, and nobody has time to tune their PCH file for each project they work on. That's why **modules** were developed as a feature of LLVM.

> **Note:** LLVM is a collection of modular and reusable compiler and toolchain technologies bundled with Xcode. LLVM has several components; the most

important ones for Objective-C developers are **Clang**, the native C, C++ and Objective-C compiler; and **LLDB**, the native debugger — which is the developer's best friend.

New solution: Modules

The first public appearance of modules in Objective-C was in a talk given by Apple's Doug Gregor at the 2012 LLVM developers' meeting. It's a fascinating talk, and it's highly recommended for anyone interested in the workings of their compilers. You can find the video of the session online at http://llvm.org/devmtg/2012-11/#talk6.

Modules encapsulate frameworks in much cleaner ways than ever before. No longer does the pre-processor need to replace an `#import` directive with the entire contents of the file verbatim. Instead, a module wraps a framework into a self-contained block, which is pre-compiled in the same manner as a PCH file and delivers the same improvements in compilation speed. However, you no longer have to state which frameworks you're using in a PCH file; you get the speed boost simply by using modules.

But there's more to modules than just that. I'm sure you recall the numerous steps you go though the first time you use a new framework in an app; it tends to go something like this:

1. Add `#import` line to the file using the framework.

2. Write code that uses the framework.

3. Compile.

4. Watch as errors are spat out during linking.

5. Remember that you forgot to link the framework.

6. Add the linking of the framework to the project build phase.

7. Compile again.

It's incredibly common to forget to link the framework, but modules solve this issue neatly as well. (Is there anything that modules can't do?)

A module tells the compiler not only which header files make up the module, but also what needs to be linked. This saves you from having to manually link the framework yourself. It's only a small thing, but anything that makes developing code easier is a good thing!

How to use modules

Modules are extremely easy to use in your projects. For existing projects, the first thing to do is enable them. You can find this option by searching for *modules* in the project's **Build Settings** (making sure to select **All**, not **Basic**) and then changing the **Enable Modules** options to **Yes**, like so:

All new projects created with Xcode 5 have this enabled by default, but you should definitely enable it on all your existing projects.

The **Link Frameworks Automatically** option can be used to enable or disable the automatic linking of frameworks as described earlier. There's little reason why you'd want to disable this though.

Once modules are turned on, you can start using them in your code. To do that, it's simply one small change to the syntax you're used to. Instead of the usual `#import` syntax, you simply use `@import`:

```
@import UIKit;
@import MapKit;
@import iAd;
```

It's still possible to import the parts of a framework that you need. As an example, if you wanted to import just `UIView`, you would write this:

```
@import UIKit.UIView;
```

Yup — it really is that simple! Well, sorry, that's not exactly the truth. It's even *simpler* than that. Technically, you don't *need* to convert all your `#import` lines to `@import` lines, as the compiler will implicitly convert them for you under the hood. However, it's always good practice to start using new syntax as often as you can.

Before you start getting too excited about modules, there is one little caveat, unfortunately. As of Xcode 5.0, it's not possible to use modules with your own frameworks or third-party frameworks. This will probably come in time — but for now it's an unfortunate downside. Nothing's perfect – not even Objective-C!

New return type - instancetype

A new type has been added to Objective-C, aptly named `instancetype`. This can only be used as a return type from an Objective-C method and is used as a hint to the compiler that the return type of the method will be an instance of the class to which the method belongs.

> **Note:** This feature is not strictly new in Xcode 5 and iOS 7, but has been stealthily dropped into recent Clang builds over time. However, Xcode 5 marks the first time that Apple has started using it throughout their frameworks. You can read more about this language feature on the official Clang website: http://clang.llvm.org/docs/LanguageExtensions.html#objective-c-features.

Why is `instancetype` useful? Consider the following code:

```
NSDictionary *d = [NSArray arrayWithObjects:@(1), @(2), nil];
NSLog(@"%i", d.count);
```

While this is clearly incorrect, the compiler would historically do absolutely nothing to inform you of the error. Try it for yourself if you still have a copy of Xcode 4.6 lying around on a floppy somewhere. You'll notice that no warning is generated, even though the code is clearly wrong! The code will even run without complaint as both `NSDictionary` and `NSArray` instances respond to `count`.

The reason this works at runtime is thanks to the powerful, dynamic nature of Objective-C. The type is purely a guide to the compiler. The `count` method is looked up at runtime on whatever class the `dictionary` variable happens to be. In this case, the `count` method exists, so the compiler believes all is well. However, this may come back to bite you later if you added code that uses another method that `NSArray` doesn't have in common with `NSDictionary`, such as `objectAtIndex:`. At first, it wouldn't be clear exactly where the issue lies.

But why does the compiler not figure out that the instance returned by `+[NSArray arrayWithObjects:]` is not an instance of `NSDictionary`? Well, that's because its method signature is as follows:

```
+ (id)arrayWithObjects:(id)firstObj, ...;
```

Notice the return type is `id`. The `id` type is an umbrella type meaning *any* Objective-C class; it doesn't even have to be a subclass of `NSObject`. It literally has no type information other than the fact it's an instance of an Objective-C class. For this to be useful, the compiler doesn't bother warning you when you implicitly cast `id` to a concrete type, such as `NSDictionary*` in the example above. If it *did* generate a warning, the `id` type would be largely useless.

But why is the return type of that method `id` in the first place? That's so you can successfully subclass the method and still use it without issue. To demonstrate why, consider the following subclass of `NSArray`:

```
@interface MyArray : NSArray
@end
```

Now consider the use of your new subclass in the code below:

```
MyArray *array = [MyArray arrayWithObjects:@(1), @(2), nil];
```

Ah — now you see why the return type of `arrayWithObjects:` must be `id`. If it were `NSArray*`, then subclasses would require to be cast to the necessary class. This is where the new `instancetype` return type comes in.

If you look at the header file for `NSArray` in the iOS 7.0 SDK, you'll notice the method signature for this method has changed to the following:

```
+ (instancetype)arrayWithObjects:(id)firstObj, ...;
```

The only difference is the return type. This new return type provides a hint to the compiler that the return value will be an instance of the class the method is called on. So when `arrayWithObjects:` is called on `NSArray`, the return type is inferred to be `NSArray*`; if called on `MyArray`, the return type is inferred to be `MyArray*` and so on.

This works around around the problem with the umbrella `id` type, while maintaining the ability to subclass successfully. If you compile the original code in Xcode 5, you'll now see the following warning:

```
warning: incompatible pointer types initializing 'NSDictionary
*' with an expression of type 'NSArray *' [-Wincompatible-
pointer-types]
  NSDictionary *d = [NSArray arrayWithObjects:@(1), @(2), nil];
                ^       ~~~~~~~~~~~~~~~~~~~~~~~~~~~~~~~~~~~~~~~~
```

w00t — now *that's* helpful! You now have the opportunity to fix the problem before it turns into a crash later down the line.

Initializers are also candidates for using this new return type. The compiler has warned you for some time now if you set the return type of an initializer to that of an incompatible type. But presumably it's just implicitly converting the `id` return type to `instancetype` under the hood. You should still use `instancetype` for initializers though, because it's better to be explicit for habit's sake.

Strive to use `instancetype` as much as possible going forward; it's become a standard for Apple — and you never know when it will save you some painful debugging time later on.

No more explicit bridging — sometimes

Ever since ARC was introduced, you've had to use strange looking *bridge* casts to cast between pointers to Objective-C class instances and raw pointers. For example, if you were storing `NSString` objects in a Core Foundation array, then you'd use something such as the following to obtain elements of that array:

```
CFMutableArrayRef cfArray = CFArrayCreateMutable(NULL, 0, NULL);
CFArrayAppendValue(cfArray, @"Foo");
CFArrayAppendValue(cfArray, @"Bar");
CFArrayAppendValue(cfArray, @"Baz");

NSString *obj =
    (__bridge NSString*)CFArrayGetValueAtIndex(cfArray, 1);
```

But an improvement to the compiler that comes bundled with Xcode 5 means you no longer need the explicit bridging cast in cases like this. The final line above can be replaced with the much more succinct, easier to read version below:

```
NSString *obj = CFArrayGetValueAtIndex(cfArray, 1);
```

This minor tweak means that a lot of extraneous code can now be removed. Remember, anything that makes your life easier during development is a good thing!

The bridging cast is no longer required because Core Foundation has been checked to ensure that all methods follow the strict naming conventions imposed by the Cocoa frameworks. For example, this means the compiler knows that the `CFArrayGetValueAtIndex` function returns an object not owned by the caller.

However, his doesn't mean *all* bridging casts are redundant. If the `Core Foundation` method returns an object that's owned by the caller, then you still need to use a bridging cast to inform the compiler whether or not you want ARC to manage the returned object. For instance, the compiler has no clue of your true intentions in the following code:

```
NSMutableArray *array = CFArrayCreateMutable(NULL, 0, NULL);
```

Since `CFArrayCreateMutable` returns an object owned by the caller, there is no way for the compiler to know whether or not you want that object to be managed by ARC. You may end up casting back to a `CFMutableArrayRef` at a later date and then release it yourself using `CFRelease`, which would cause the following compile-time error:

```
error: implicit conversion of C pointer type 'CFMutableArrayRef'
(aka 'struct __CFArray *') to Objective-C pointer type
'NSMutableArray *' requires a bridged cast

NSMutableArray *array = CFArrayCreateMutable(NULL, 0, NULL);
                        ^~~~~~~~~~~~~~~~~~~~~~~~~~~~~~~~~~~~~
```

You'll also find other places where bridging casts are still necessary, such as casting an Objective-C class instance pointer to a `void` pointer. Hopefully as ARC and the compiler are refined, some of these cases will be eliminated and explicit bridge casts will no longer be required.

New Foundations

The remaining part of this chapter is dedicated to various new bits of functionality in `Foundation`, the core framework of all Objective-C development. It's hard to develop Objective-C applications without `Foundation`, as all iOS apps require its use. Finding new gems in `Foundation` is a big part of the fun of getting your hands on a new release of the iOS SDK!

One of the major improvements in this release of `Foundation` lies in networking; so much, in fact, that there's an entire chapter dedicated to it in this book. Read more about networking-specific changes in Chapter 16, "Networking with NSURLSession".

The rest of this section outlines other interesting additions and changes to `Foundation`.

NSArray

Trying to retrieve an object from an instance of `NSArray` will throw an exception if the index you supply is beyond the length of the array. You'll also often find a need to access the first and last objects of an array, such as when you're using a mutable array to hold a queue. In a first-in-first-out (FIFO) queue you pop objects from the front of the array, and in a first-in-last-out (FILO) you pop objects from the end of the array.

However, when you retrieve the first or last objects from an array, you must always ensure that you're not going to read past the end of the array, which could easily occur if the array were empty. This leads to a lot of tedious code to ensure a call to `objectAtIndex:` won't throw an exception, like so:

```
NSMutableArray *queue = [NSMutableArray new];

// ...
if (queue.count > 0) {
    id firstObject = [queue objectAtIndex:0];
    // Use firstObject
}

// ...
if (queue.count > 0) {
    id lastObject = [queue objectAtIndex:(queue.count - 1)];
    // Use lastObject
}
```

In the case of retrieving the last object, you've always had the option of using the following method of `NSArray`:

```
- (id)lastObject;
```

Objective-C developers are the rejoicing the world over, as for the first time they have access to an equivalent method to retrieve the first object of the array:

```
- (id)firstObject;
```

This single, simple method turns out to be extremely useful. No longer do you have to account for an array being empty. If you've ever felt the sting of a crash because of an out of bounds exception then you'll definitely see this as a welcome addition.

> **Note:** If you look at the header for `NSArray` carefully, you'll see that `firstObject` has actually been around since iOS 4.0 but it wasn't made public until iOS 7. Therefore you *could* have accessed the method prior to iOS 7, but that would have required declaring the `firstObject` selector in one of your own header files to inform the compiler that it does in fact exist. That's certainly not a recommended approach, so it's good that Apple finally brought it out of hiding.

The previous code snippet can now be rewritten to use these two utility methods and forego the length checks, as illustrated below:

```
NSMutableArray *queue = [NSMutableArray new];
// ...

id firstObject = [queue firstObject];
// Use firstObject

id lastObject = [queue lastObject];
// Use lastObject
```

NSData

Data is one of those things you deal with a lot when you're programming. NSData is the Foundation class that encapsulates raw bytes and provides methods for manipulating those bytes, as well reading and writing data to and from a file. But one very common task for which there's been no native implementation is **Base64** encoding and decoding. At least that was the case until the release of iOS 7.

Base64 is a group of binary-to-text encoding schemes that represent binary data in ASCII format. These schemes are commonly used where there's a need to encode binary data to be stored on or transferred over media designed to deal solely with textual data. This ensures the data remains intact without modification during transport. The most common use of **Base64** encoding is handling attachments in email, as well as encoding small images that form part of a JSON response returned by a web based API.

Prior to iOS 7.0, Base64 encoding and decoding tasks required you to implement your own method or include part of a third party framework. In typical Apple fashion, it's now very easy to use this functionality. There are four core Base64 methods as follows:

```
- (id)initWithBase64EncodedString:(NSString *)base64String
     options:(NSDataBase64DecodingOptions)options;

- (NSString *)base64EncodedStringWithOptions:
     (NSDataBase64EncodingOptions)options;

- (id)initWithBase64EncodedData:(NSData *)base64Data
     options:(NSDataBase64DecodingOptions)options;

- (NSData *)base64EncodedDataWithOptions:
     (NSDataBase64EncodingOptions)options;
```

The first two methods deal with strings, while the latter two deal with UTF-8 encoded data. Both pairs of methods perform the same action, but sometimes using one over the other will prove more effective. If you were to Base64 encode a string and then write it to a file, you may decide to use the pair that handles UTF-8 encoded data. On the other hand, if you were to Base64 encode a string and then use that in some JSON, you may decide to use the pair that handles strings.

So if you've ever included a Base64 method or two in your project, now is the time to remove that unnecessary code and use Apple's implementations instead!

NSTimer

Timers often find homes in apps that perform periodic tasks. As useful as they may be, the problem is that they may fire off constantly when several timers are in use. This means the CPU is constantly active; it would be much more efficient if the CPU woke up, performed a batch of tasks and then went back to sleep. To solve this issue, Apple has added a `tolerance` property to `NSTimer` to help accommodate this behavior.

The `tolerance` property provides the system with a guide as to how late a timer is permitted to fire after it's schedule time. The underlying system will then group actions accordingly to reduce CPU overhead. The methods for accessing this new property are as follows:

```
- (NSTimeInterval)tolerance;
- (void)setTolerance:(NSTimeInterval)tolerance;
```

You may find you never need to use this property, but if you're firing several timers in very close succession, you may find it useful to benchmark your app's CPU usage using Instruments while tinkering with this setting.

NSProgress

It's not often that entirely new classes get added to `Foundation`. It's a pretty stable framework, mainly because new core classes aren't required too often. However, iOS 7.0 presents an entirely new class named `NSProgress`.

In essence, `NSProgress` aims to deliver progress reporting throughout Objective-C code, neatly separating the progress of individual components. For example, if you perform a few different tasks on some data, then each task can monitor its own progress and report back to its parent task.

The structure of NSProgress

The simplest way of using `NSProgress` is to use it to report progress on a set of tasks. For example if you have 10 tasks to achieve, then you can report progress as each task finishes. As each task finishes the progress goes up by 10%. Then, using Key Value Observing (KVO) on the `NSProgress` instance, you will be notified about this increase in progress. The following diagram shows the various method calls to achieve this.

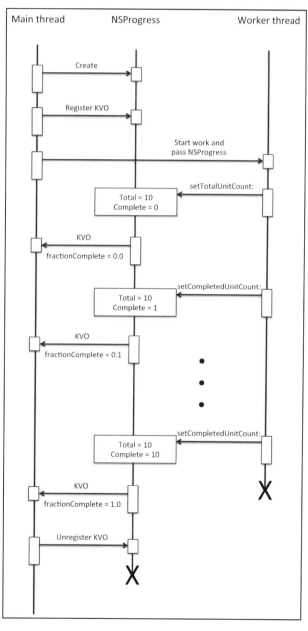

Each time the progress increases, KVO fires a notification back to the main thread. At this point, you would update your UI to show the progress marching on. For example you might use it as an opportunity to update a progress bar, or set the text on a label to give an indication of the progress.

But there is more to NSProgress than just this. Apple have made it incredibly powerful, mainly through the use of a child-parent relationship structure. The structure of NSProgress is much like a nested tree: each instance can have one parent and many children. Each instance has a total number of units of work to be performed, and as the task progresses the completed number of units is updated to reflect the current state. In doing so, the parent (if one exists) is notified of the progress as well.

To reduce the need to pass around NSProgress instances, each thread has its own NSProgress instance and child instances can be created directly from this instance. Without this functionality, every task that wanted to report progress in this way would have to be altered to take an NSProgress parameter.

Reporting progress

Using NSProgress is simple. It all starts with the following method:

```
+ (NSProgress *)progressWithTotalUnitCount:(int64_t)unitCount;
```

This creates a new instance of NSProgress as a child of the current instance and initializes it with the total number of units of work that will be performed overall. For example, if the task were to loop through an array, then you would probably initialize the NSProgress instance with the count of the array, like so:

```
NSArray *array = /* ... */;

NSProgress *progress =
    [NSProgress progressWithTotalUnitCount:array.count];

[array enumerateObjectsUsingBlock:
    ^(id obj, NSUInteger idx, BOOL *stop) {
        // Perform an expensive operation on obj
        progress.completedUnitCount = idx;
    }];
```

As the iteration progresses, the above code updates the instance of NSProgress to reflect the current progress.

Receiving progress updates

You can determine the progress of the task at any point through the following property:

```
@property (readonly) double fractionCompleted;
```

This returns a value from 0 to 1, indicating the total progress of the task. When there are no child instances in play, `fractionCompleted` is simply the completed unit count divided by the total unit count.

Key Value Observing (KVO) is the best way to be notified when the `fractionCompleted` property changes its value. Doing so is simple. All you need to do is register as an observer of the `fractionCompleted` property of the relevant `NSProgress` object like so:

```
[_progress addObserver:self
            forKeyPath:@"fractionCompleted"
               options:NSKeyValueObservingOptionNew
               context:NULL];
```

Then, override the method that KVO uses to notify you of changes, like so:

```
- (void)observeValueForKeyPath:(NSString *)keyPath
                      ofObject:(id)object
                        change:(NSDictionary *)change
                       context:(void *)context
{
    if (object == _progress) {
        // Handle new fractionCompleted value
        return;
    }

    // Always call super, incase it uses KVO also
    [super observeValueForKeyPath:keyPath
                         ofObject:object
                           change:change
                          context:context];
}
```

In this method you would handle the change in `fractionCompleted` value. For example, you might change the value of a progress bar or a label to indicate the current level of completion.

Of course, it's important to remember to unregister from KVO once you're done, like so:

```
[_progress removeObserver:self
            forKeyPath:@"fractionCompleted"
               context:NULL];
```

You must always unregister and your app will crash if you don't unregister by the time the registered object (self in this example) is deallocated. So ensure that you unregister as a last resort in `dealloc` if necessary.

Reporting progress on a set of tasks

The power of `NSProgress` is quite apparent when child instances come into play and you need to provide an overall progress for a sequence of tasks. For example, consider the following set of tasks:

1. Download a large JSON encoded file from the Internet.

2. Parse the JSON into an Objective-C model object.

3. Process the object.

4. Save the object to a local database.

A naïve approach to providing the progress for this set of tasks would consider that there are 4 total units of work to do, and after each one is done the number of completed units increases by 1. This would mean that as the set of tasks progressed, the progress would jump from 0% to 25%, to 50%, to 75%, and finally to 100%.

But wouldn't it be better if the progress of each individual task was reported so that the progress goes smoothly through from 0% to 25% as the file is downloaded, from 25% to 50% as the JSON is parsed, and so on and so forth. This sort of behavior is possible with `NSProgress` without the need for reams of additional code.

Just as long as each task creates its own `NSProgress` instance using `progressWithTotalUnitCount:` and sets the completed unit count accordingly, then it's relatively straightforward to implement this kind of progress measurement.

All that you'd have to do to implement progress reporting for all four tasks is the following:

```
NSProgress *progress =
    [NSProgress progressWithTotalUnitCount:4];

[progress becomeCurrentWithPendingUnitCount:1];
```

```
// Download data
[progress resignCurrent];
progress.completedUnitCount = 1;

[progress becomeCurrentWithPendingUnitCount:1];
// Parse JSON to model object
[progress resignCurrent];
progress.completedUnitCount = 2;

[progress becomeCurrentWithPendingUnitCount:1];
// Process object
[progress resignCurrent];
progress.completedUnitCount = 3;

[progress becomeCurrentWithPendingUnitCount:1];
// Save object to local database
[progress resignCurrent];
progress.completedUnitCount = 4;
```

The beauty of this model is that it doesn't actually matter if the sub-tasks report their own progress through NSProgress. If they don't then this will still work, but the progress will jump from 0%, to 25%, to 50%, to 75%, to 100%. That's fine. But if each sub-task does report progress through an NSProgress, just like you're doing, then the overall progress your main task reports, will go up smoothly. Read on to find out how that works.

You'll have noticed a couple of methods not yet mentioned:

```
- (void)becomeCurrentWithPendingUnitCount:(int64_t)unitCount;
- (void)resignCurrent;
```

Recall the discussion earlier about each thread having its own NSProgress instance. Before you execute a task that will report its progress back to the caller, call becomeCurrentWithPendingUnitCount: and indicate how much of your total work is to be regarded as completed by this sub-task. So in the example above, each sub-task is assigned a single unit of the overall four units.

As each sub-task progresses and reports via its own instance of NSProgress, the parent NSProgress reflects the total progress of the current task. So when the download is half way through, the overall progress will be 12.5%.

It's worth noting that you don't need to worry whether each sub-task supports NSProgress. If it does, then progress will be reported to the parent. But if it doesn't, then the progress simply won't update until that sub-task finishes and sets the number of completed units on the main task's instance of `NSProgress`.

Unequal sub-task weights

In the example above, it's unlikely that each sub-task will take exactly the same amount of time. It's also unlikely that your app knows in advance how long each task will take — there's no `NSPsychic` class just yet. :]

If your sub-tasks are known to take unequal time, then you probably have a rough idea of the proportion of time each subtask will take. In the example above, the file download will likely take the most time, then the processing of the data, then the parsing of the JSON, then finally the save to a local database. The weighting could be assigned as follows:

1. 9 – Download.

2. 5 – Processing.

3. 2 – Parsing.

4. 1 – Saving.

To achieve this weighting with `NSProgress`, set up the main task's progress with some large total count and then assign a fraction to each sub-task in unequal amounts. Taking the weights above and applying them to the example, you would do the following:

```
NSProgress *progress =
    [NSProgress progressWithTotalUnitCount:17];

[progress becomeCurrentWithPendingUnitCount:9];
// Download data
[progress resignCurrent];
progress.completedUnitCount = 9;

[progress becomeCurrentWithPendingUnitCount:2];
// Parse JSON to model object
[progress resignCurrent];
progress.completedUnitCount = 11;

[progress becomeCurrentWithPendingUnitCount:5];
// Process object
[progress resignCurrent];
progress.completedUnitCount = 16;

[progress becomeCurrentWithPendingUnitCount:1];
```

```
// Save object to local database
[progress resignCurrent];
progress.completedUnitCount = 17;
```

Notice how you set the pending unit count of each sub-task according to the weight of each task, and then set the completed unit count after each sub-task appropriately.

In this example, once the download was half way through, the progress of the main task would be 6 / 20 = 30%. Similarly, half way through the processing sub-task the progress would be 16.5 / 20 = 82.5%.

Weighting like this gives you much smoother display in your progress UI elements. How to weight each sub-task depends entirely on the tasks; there is no right answer. You will need to experiment with your own tasks to find a combination that works for your specific situation.

That wraps it up for NSProgress! If you'd like to see this in action, check out the sample project called **Progressive** included in the resources for this chapter. Take a look around the app; it uses Key Value Observing (KVO) on the current NSProgress instance's fractionCompleted property to update a label indicating the current progress of an overall task.

Challenges

In this chapter you've learned about several new features of Objective-C and its associated frameworks. You should always aim to stay up-to-date with advances in both the language and core system frameworks such as Foundation. If you do so, then you'll be able to make use of the latest and greatest offerings from Apple.

Go forth and make your apps compiler faster using modules. Make them more resilient to awkward bugs arising from umbrella id return types by using instancetype instead. And finally, start using all the fun new methods and classes found in Foundation!

Before you can truly use NSProgress in your own apps, you really need to prove that you're able to use it. So, I have a couple of challenges for you! In the resources for this chapter you'll find a starter project called **ProgressChallenge**.

Open that in Xcode, build and run, then take a look around the app as it stands. You'll see that it displays a list of tutorials from raywenderlich.com. When you tap on a row, it downloads the sample project ZIP file and unzips it. Once a download and unzip has completed, if you tap on a row it'll show you the list of files in the sample project.

You'll notice on each cell there is a handy progress bar. But it doesn't do anything yet! The KVO is all wired up (see `DownloadCell`) but it doesn't do anything yet because there's no `NSProgress` wired up.

Take a look in **ViewController.m**. You'll notice in `tableView:didSelectRowAtIndexPath:` that an `NSProgress` is created. Take time to familiarize yourself with how it's then subsequently used. It's made the current progress with a pending unit count of 1 and then after the processor is started, it's resigned as current. This means that any progress created inside the processor will use this progress as its parent. Therefore this progress will report the progress of the processor.

You're now going to add some extra progress logic in over the course of a couple of challenges.

Challenge 1: Download progress

Take a look at the `Downloader` class. It has an instance variable for an `NSProgress` instance, but it doesn't set one up yet. Your task is to set one up and use it to report the download progress. I've left a few comments with what you'll need to do:

- Create an `NSProgress` instance in `startWithHandler:`. In doing so, make sure its parent is the current thread's progress, i.e. the return value of +[`NSProgress currentProgress`].

- In `connection:didReceiveResponse:` you can find out how many bytes the download will be by inspecting `response.expectedContentLength`. Use that to set the total unit count on the progress.

- As data is downloaded, `connection:didReceiveData:` is called. Set the completed unit count in here to the total number of bytes that have been downloaded so far.

- When the download has completed successfully or failed, you need to set the completed unit count to the total unit count just as a backup to ensure the progress is now definitely 100%.

Once you have done this, build and run the app. You should see the progress bar go from 0% to 100% as the download proceeds. But that's just the download progress. The processor downloads and then unzips the file. You now need to report the overall progress of these two sub-tasks. The challenge continues…

Challenge 2: Processor progress

Take a look inside the `DownloadProcessor` class. This performs the download of a tutorial's starter project and then unzips it. Currently only the download portion of work reports any progress (challenge 1). Your task here is to add in progress reporting of the download plus unzip process.

Once again I have left comments explaining what you'll need to do. The process goes like this:

• Create an `NSProgress` instance in `startWithHandler:`. Initialize it with a pending unit count of something sensible. I chose the download to take 80% of the overall progress and the unzip to take 20%. To achieve this you would initialize the progress with a total unit count of 10 and then assign 8 units to the download and 2 to the unzip.

• The download you're saying will take 80% of the overall time, so you need to make the progress you've just created the current progress, setting the pending unit count to 8. Then after the call to `-[Downloader startWithHandler:]`, resign as current.

• Inside the completion block of the downloader, you should set the completed unit count accordingly (8 in this case).

• Then you need to wrap the unzip operation with another set of becoming / resigning current progress, this time with a pending unit count of 2.

After you have done this, build and run the app and you will see the progress go from 0% to 80% as the download progresses. Then from 80% to 100% as the unzip progresses.

> **Note:** Unfortunately, `SSZipArchive` does not report progress itself yet, which is understandable since `NSProgress` is new to iOS 7.0! This means that the overall progress jumps from 80% to 100% rather than moving smoothly along. I'm sure that as `NSProgress` becomes the de-facto way to report progress, libraries such as this will embrace it.

Congratulations - if you've completed these challenges then you sure do know your `NSProgress`!

Chapter 11: Unit Testing in Xcode 5

By Greg Heo

One of the most important aspects of a solid software development methodology is unit testing. After all, unit testing can help you find bugs and crashes, and according to Apple crashes are the *number one* reason that apps are rejected during the review process.

Unit tests aren't a silver bullet, but Apple includes them as part of their development toolset to help you produce apps that are not only stable, but ones that provide a consistent and enjoyable user experience. These are the apps that will send your users rushing back to the App Store to give you that coveted five-star review!

The iOS 7 SDK includes an upgraded unit testing framework and makes building and running unit tests from Xcode even easier. By the time you're done this chapter, you'll understand how to add tests to your existing apps — and hopefully develop a new love of writing tests!

Unit testing fundamentals

In the past, Xcode included an open source unit testing framework called OCUnit. Now in Xcode 5, Apple has released their own unit testing framework, called XCTest.

If you're already familiar with OCUnit, don't worry. XCTest is built on top of OCUnit and has a very similar API. Rest assured that rewiring your brain to think in XCTest terms is as simple as replacing `STFail` with `XCTFail`, `STAssert` with `XCTAssert`, and so on. If you're already familiar with the basics, feel free to skim the next section and skip ahead to the section titled **The starter project**.

But if you're new to unit testing, before you begin it's important to have a basic understanding of how unit testing works – things like test suites, test cases, and assertions. Once you understand these basics, you'll be ready to try it out for yourself!

High-level overview

There are four levels in the hierarchy of unit tests:

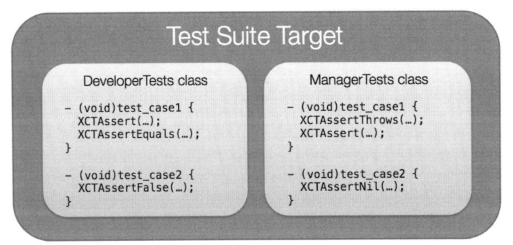

From top to bottom, they are:

1. **Test suite.** This is the entire collection of tests for your project. In Xcode, the test suite is set up as a separate build target.

2. **Test case classes.** As you might expect in an object-oriented system, tests are grouped into classes. Each test class usually corresponds to a single class in your app. For example, the `DeveloperTests` class could contain tests for the `Developer` class.

3. **Test case methods.** Each test case class contains multiple methods to test various features of the class. Just as methods and functions should be as short as possible and do one thing well, each test case should test one specific outcome — and test it fully.

4. **Assertions.** Assertions check specific conditions against an expected result. If the condition does not match the expected result, Xcode throws an error to indicate an assertion failure. For example, you could assert that your `Developer` class responds to the `writeKillerApp:` message; if it doesn't, the assertion will fail and an exception will be thrown.

Theory is all well and good, but sometimes it's easier to illustrate things with a short example. Create a new iOS project with the **Empty Application** template called **EmptyApp**.

The Xcode template automatically includes a test target called **EmptyAppTests,** in addition to the actual **EmptyApp** app target, as shown below:

Note that test case classes are contained a single **.m** file with no associated header file. Open **EmptyAppTests.m** and take a look at the source code for the first test case.

Test case methods must start with the word **test** so the test runner can find them. In your example project, the test class contains a single test called testExample.

The setUp and tearDown methods act like bookends around the test cases. By containing all the object setup routines and repetitive code to setUp, your test case methods stay dry, clean, and efficient. In a similar manner, cleanup activities such as closing file handles or cancelling pending network requests should live in the tearDown method.

The test runner calls the setUp, testExample, and tearDown methods in order. If you have a second test method testSecondExample declared, the test runner would call setUp, testSecondExample, and finally tearDown. If you have multiple test methods, then setUp and tearDown are called *multiple times* in a single test session — once per test case method!

The moral of this story is don't put anything too slow or processor-intensive in your setUp or tearDown — or you'll be facing some long waits when you run your test suite!

Creating your first test

The testExample method has a single call to XCTFail, which as the name suggests, will always fail. That's not terribly useful; you can write a better test than that!

Delete the entire testExample method and add the following method:

```
- (void)test_addition_twoPlusTwo_isFour
{
```

```
    XCTAssert(2 + 2 == 4, @"2 + 2 should be 4 but %d was
returned instead", 2+2);
}
```

A common and useful naming standard for test cases is
`unitOfWork_stateUnderTest_expectedBehavior`. In this example, the unit of work
being tested is addition, the test state is 2 + 2, and the expected behavior is that the result
is 4.

> **Note:** Check out this blog post by Roy Osherove for more details on naming
> standards for unit tests: http://osherove.com/blog/2005/4/3/naming-standards-
> for-unit-tests.html

All XCTest assertions begin with the prefix **XCT**. **XCTAssert** is the simplest assertion
available for your unit tests; the first parameter is an expression that is expected to
evaluate to true, while the NSLog-style parameters following the expression define the
message displayed if the assertion fails.

Ensure the current target for your project is **iPhone Simulator** and run the tests by
either navigating to **Product > Test** in the menu or by hitting **Command-U**. The
simulator will start and execute your test suite. If you have notifications enabled, you'll
see a confirmation message.

To confirm the success of your first unit test from within Xcode, switch to the **Test
Navigator**, indicated by the arrow below:

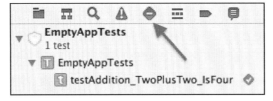

Huzzah! The verdant checkmark of success is displayed next to your unit test.

You'll also see diamond-shaped icons in the margins next to the code, as shown:

```
 15   @implementation EmptyAppTests
 16
 17   - (void)setUp
 18   {
 19       [super setUp];
 20       // Put setup code here; it will be run once, before the first test case.
 21   }
 22
 23   - (void)tearDown
 24   {
 25       // Put teardown code here; it will be run once, after the last test case.
 26       [super tearDown];
 27   }
 28
 29   - (void)test_addition_twoPlusTwo_isFour
 30   {
 31       XCTAssert(2 + 2 == 4, @"2 + 2 should be 4 but %d was returned instead", 2+2);
 32   }
```

These icons show the test status inline with your test code. The green checkmark next to the @implementation line means the test class as a whole passed, while the checkmark next to test_addition_twoPlusTwo_isFour means that this individual test passed.

As a bonus, these icons are buttons too; clicking the one next to the @implementation line will run all tests in the class, while the button next to the test method will run just that single test case. Try this now for yourself.

Now that you've seen what tests look like and how to execute them, it's time to get started with this chapter's sample project – which is sadly a bit test-starved at the moment!

The starter project

The starter project you'll use for the remainder of this chapter is the classic board game **Reversi**. Two players, represented by black and white pieces, take turns placing their pieces on an 8x8 board. You capture your opponent's pieces by surrounding them with pieces of your own color. The winner is the player with the most pieces at the end of the game.

> **Note:** To see how the game was built, check out our two-part *How to Develop an iPad Board Game App* tutorial: http://www.raywenderlich.com/29228/how-to-develop-an-ipad-board-game-app-part-12

Find the starter project in the chapter resources, build and run the app, and click the **Vs Computer** button at the bottom of the screen. Feel free to play a game or two against the computer to get a feel for the rules and the game's UI.

Did you manage to win a game? Or did you get schooled by your AI opponent? Either way, your job isn't to play games all day — it's time to add some useful tests to the project!

Adding support for tests

The GameBoard class is the first thing that needs some unit tests. Briefly, the GameBoard class encapsulates the basic logic of the 8x8 playing board. Each of the 64 game squares has a state – empty, black piece, or white piece – and a GameBoard instance lets you get and set this state for each square.

Open **GameBoard.h** and have a look at the methods contained within. Before writing any tests for existing code, it's a good idea to check out the module's header to get a feeling for the interface and functions of the module.

Inside **GameBoard.h**, you'll see the following two methods:

```
// gets the state of the cell at the given location
// raises an NSRangeException if the column or row are out of
bounds
- (BoardCellState) cellStateAtColumn:(NSInteger)column
andRow:(NSInteger)row;

// sets the state of the cell at the given location
// raises an NSRangeException if the column or row are out of
bounds
- (void) setCellState:(BoardCellState)state
forColumn:(NSInteger)column andRow:(NSInteger)row;
```

`cellStateAtColumn:andRow:` and `setCellState:forColumn:andRow:` form a very familiar getter/setter pattern. Your first test should perform the following actions:

1. Initialize a `GameBoard` instance

2. Set the cell state

3. Get the cell state

4. Assert that the cell state you specified in the setter is the same cell state that is returned from the getter.

The first step is to create a test class for `GameBoard`. Right-click on the **ReversiGameTests** group in the project navigator, select **New File…**, and select **iOS\Cocoa Touch\Objective-C test case class**. Name the class **GameBoardTests**, and make it a subclass of **XCTestCase**.

Ensure that your new test case class is added to the **ReversiGameTests** target as shown in the image below:

This is a critical step; your tests will not run unless they are added to the correct target!

Open **GameBoardTests.m** and delete `testExample`; you won't need it.

Add the following import to the top of **GameBoardTests.m**:

```
#import "GameBoard.h"
```

This simply allows you to access the `GameBoard` class from within your test class.

You'll need a `GameBoard` instance for every test that you write, so it will be a bit neater to use an instance variable instead of redeclaring it throughout your tests.

Update the `@interface` line in **GameBoardTests.m** as follows:

```
@interface GameBoardTests : XCTestCase {
    GameBoard *_board;
}
```

Now that you have your `_board` instance variable, you can start using it in your tests.

The setUp method is a perfect place to initialize GameBoard as it's called first in sequence. Modify the implementation of setUp in **GameBoardTests.m** to appear as follows:

```
- (void)setUp
{
    [super setUp];

    _board = [[GameBoard alloc] init];
}
```

Now every test case method you write in this class will have access to an initialized GameBoard in the _board instance variable.

The first test

That's all the setup you need to write your first test case. Add the following method to **GameBoardTests.m**:

```
- (void)test_setAndGetCellState_setValidCell_cellStateChanged
{
    [_board setCellState:BoardCellStateWhitePiece
                forColumn:4
                  andRow:5];

    BoardCellState retrievedState =
      [_board cellStateAtColumn:4 andRow:5];
    XCTAssertEqual(BoardCellStateWhitePiece,
                   retrievedState,
                   @"The cell should be white!");
}
```

The code above sets the board cell at (4,5) with a white piece, then immediately retrieves the state of the same cell. The XCTAssertEqual assertion then checks that the two are equal; if they aren't, you'll see an exception raised — and you'll know that you have some investigation to do.

The name of the above test method follows the naming format I suggested earlier. By just the method name, you can easily read that it tests the setter and getter by setting a valid cell location, and expects the cell to have changed state.

Now to see if your test works as designed. Make sure either the iPhone or iPad iOS Simulator is set as the current scheme, and run the test either via the **Product > Test** menu item, or by hitting **Command-U**.

Switch to the Test Navigator and you should see a green checkmark indicating the test passed, as shown below:

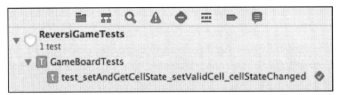

It seems like a simple test, but it provides great value in guarding against regression errors.

Internally, the GameBoard class uses a simple two-dimensional array to keep track of the 8x8 grid. But if you ever changed the array to a vector or matrix representation, this test will serve as a regression test ensuring the fundamentals of the interface are still working.

As a side benefit, writing tests for existing classes is a great way to understand how the code works. Analyzing the class's methods helps you discern their intended functions and guides you in writing your tests.

Testing for exceptions

Testing that the code is functioning as designed helps ensure correctness. But the corollary is to ensure that your apps "fail early and fail loudly"— and that inconsistent game states or invalid conditions are caught and raised as soon as possible to aid in debugging.

The comments on both cellStateAtColumn:andRow: and setCellState:forColumn:andRow: in **GameBoard.h** state they will throw an exception if the column or row passed in is out of bounds. Looks like you've found two more conditions to test.

Add the following two test methods to **GameBoardTests.m**:

```
- (void)test_setCellState_withInvalidCoords_exceptionThrown
{
    XCTAssertThrowsSpecificNamed(
      [_board setCellState:BoardCellStateBlackPiece
              forColumn:10
              andRow:7],
      NSException,
      NSRangeException,
      @"Out-of-bounds board set should raise an exception");
}
```

```
- (void)test_getCellState_withInvalidCoords_exceptionThrown
{
    XCTAssertThrowsSpecificNamed(
      [_board cellStateAtColumn:7 andRow:-10],
      NSException,
      NSRangeException,
      @"Out-of-bounds board access should raise an exception");
}
```

In the code above, `test_setCellState_withInvalidCoords_exceptionThrown:` attempts to set the state an out-of range cell (10,7), while `test_setCellState_withInvalidCoords_exceptionThrown:` attempts to get the state of a different out-of-range cell (7,-10). Once again, the method names make it clear that the tests are for invalid board coordinates, and that a thrown exception is the expected result.

`XCTAssertThrowsSpecificNamed` takes the following four items as arguments:

• an expression that should throw an exception

• the expected class of the exception

• the expected name of the exception

• the message to display when the test fails.

Hit **Command-U** to run the tests; you should see the results shown below:

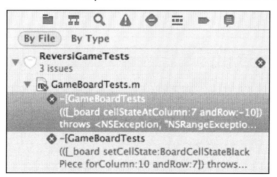

What's this? You were expecting the tests to pass with flying colors, but two failures are noted in the Issue Navigator, one for each test. The test failures are also reported inline with the test code, as shown on the next page:

```
40   - (void)test_setCellState_withInvalidCoords_exceptionThrown
41   {
42       XCTAssertThrowsSpecificNamed([_board setCellState:BoardCellStateBlackPiece
            forColumn:10 andRow:7],
43                                    NSException,
44                                    NSRangeException,
45                                    @"Out-of-bounds board set should raise an
                                        exception");
46   }  ([_board setCellState:BoardCellStateBlackPiece forColumn:10 andRow:7]) throws <NSException, "NSRangeExcepti...
47
48   - (void)test_getCellState_withInvalidCoords_exceptionThrown
49   {
50       XCTAssertThrowsSpecificNamed([_board cellStateAtColumn:7 andRow:-10],
51                                    NSException,
52                                    NSRangeException,
53                                    @"Out-of-bounds board access should raise an
                                        exception");
54   }  ([_board cellStateAtColumn:7 andRow:-10]) throws <NSException, "NSRangeException">) failed: throwing <NSEx...
```

The full test failure message is:

```
[GameBoardTests
test_getCellState_withInvalidCoords_exceptionThrown] failed:
(([_board cellStateAtColumn:7 andRow:-10]) throws <NSException,
"NSRangeException">) failed: throwing <NSException,
"NSGenericException", "row or column out of bounds"> - Out-of-
bounds board access should raise an exception
```

If you break apart the message above, you'll see that it tells you what the expected behavior was (throws <NSException, "NSRangeException">) and what actually happened (throwing <NSException, "NSGenericException">). In this case, NSRangeException was expected, but you received an NSGenericException instead.

Looks like you have some investigating to do!

Troubleshooting test failures

Time to track down the issue behind your test failures. Open **GameBoard.m** and find cellStateAtColumn:andRow: and setCellState:forColumn:andRow:. You'll notice they both call a helper method checkBoundsForColumn:andRow: to do the array bounds checking.

The comments in **GameBoard.h** state the following:

```
// raises an NSRangeException if the column or row are out of
bounds
```

However, the implementation of checkBoundsForColumn:andRow: throws an NSGenericExpression if an out of bounds condition is met. Generally, you treat the header comments as a public API specification, but in this case the code and the specifications don't match. What to do?

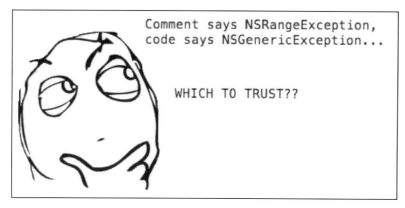

One possibility is to update the comment and the associated test to match the current implementation. In this case though, the specification noted in the comments makes more sense: a bounds check should follow the lead of NSArray and raise an NSRangeException.

Update the implementation of checkBoundsForColumn:andRow: in **GameBoard.m** to raise an NSRangeExpression instead, as shown below:

```
- (void)checkBoundsForColumn:(NSInteger)column
andRow:(NSInteger)row
{
    if (column < 0 || column > 7 || row < 0 || row > 7)
        [NSException raise:NSRangeException
                    format:@"row or column out of bounds"];
}
```

Re-run the tests using **Command + U** and the Test Navigator should display all of your tests with a pass result.

Specifications in comments are always a little dangerous since it's very easy for them to fall out of sync with the code. However, your tests can also do double duty as specifications. Since they're written in code, there's less risk of them not matching the implementation — as long as you run the tests regularly!

In addition, your tests provide a great high-level overview of the code, especially when they follow the suggested naming format. This comes in really handy when you're revisiting code that you haven't touched in a while — much like in the scenario in the next section.

Tests as bug insurance

A crash report has just come in for your app: one of your testers reports the app crashes when she launches the app and taps on the board *before* starting the game with either the "2 Player" or the "vs computer" button.

Confirm the bug for yourself: start up the app, and immediately tap on the game board without touching anything else on the screen. Boom — the app crashes with the following message displayed in the console output:

```
ReversiGame[1842:a0b] *** Terminating app due to uncaught
exception 'NSRangeException', reason: 'row or column out of
bounds'
```

Well, it seems the crash is reproducible, but what's throwing an NSRangeException? The call stack offers up the following information:

```
2 CoreFoundation +[NSException raise:format:] + 139
3 ReversiGame -[GameBoard checkBoundsForColumn:andRow:] + 142
4 ReversiGame -[GameBoard cellStateAtColumn:andRow:] + 76
5 ReversiGame -[ReversiBoard flipOpponentCountersForColumn:
andRow:withNavigationFunction:toState:] + 281
6 ReversiGame -[ReversiBoard makeMoveToColumn:andRow:] + 245
7 ReversiGame -[BoardSquare cellTapped:] + 192
```

That looks promising. Reading from the bottom up:

- **Lines 7 and 6**: the tap triggers the code to process the player's move.

- **Line 5**: the game logic checks for any to see if any of the opponent's pieces are surrounded and should be flipped.

- **Lines 4 and 3**: the code then calls cellStateAtColumn:andRow: and checkBoundsForColumn:andRow:

- **Line 2**: the underlying framework raises an out of bounds exception.

> **Note**: Need to brush up on debugging app crashes? Check out these tutorials:
>
> My App Crashed, Now What?
> http://www.raywenderlich.com/10209/my-app-crashed-now-what-part-1
>
> Demystifying iOS Application Crash Logs
> http://www.raywenderlich.com/23704/demystifying-ios-application-crash-logs

This is a perfect opportunity to write a test that will reproduce these crash conditions.

Not only will your new test validate that you have fixed the issue, but it will serve as a *regression test* to ensure that this bug stays fixed. There's nothing worse than fixing a bug, only to find months later that adding a feature or refactoring the code reintroduces the exact same bug.

Determining what to test

You know you need a test — but what should you test? ReversiBoard is the implementation of the generic GameBoard class, so it makes sense to start your troubleshooting efforts there.

Create another new class using the **iOS\Cocoa Touch\Objective-C test case class** template. Name the class **ReversiBoardTests**, and make it a subclass of **XCTestCase**.

As before, delete the boilerplate testExample method.

Add the following import to **ReversiBoardsTests.m** so your test class can access ReversiBoard:

```
#import "ReversiBoard.h"
```

Change the @interface line of **ReversiBoardTests.m** as shown below:

```
@interface ReversiBoardTests : XCTestCase {
    ReversiBoard *_reversiBoard;
}
```

Adding _reversiBoard as an instance variable means that you won't have to instantiate this variable throughout your test methods.

Now modify the implementation of setUp in **ReversiBoardTests.m** to initialize _reversiBoard as shown below:

```
- (void)setUp
{
    [super setUp];

    _reversiBoard = [[ReversiBoard alloc] init];
}
```

Testing the negative case

In the previous test you wrote, the *presence* of an exception was the expected result. This time, it's the *absence* of an exception that forms the basis of your test.

Add the following method to **ReversiBoardTests.m**:

```
- (void)test_makeMove_inPreGameState_nothingHappens
{
    [_reversiBoard setToPreGameState];

    XCTAssertNoThrowSpecificNamed(
        [_reversiBoard makeMoveToColumn:3 andRow:3],
      NSException,
      NSRangeException,
      @"Making a move in the pre-game state should do nothing");
}
```

In the code above, the test sets the game to the pre-game state; that is, the state before the player makes a choice to play either a two-player game or a game against the computer opponent. The test then makes a valid move on the game board to simulate the action of a player tapping the board.

The XCTAssertNoThrowSpecificNamed assertion is the inverse counterpart to XCTAssertThrowsSpecificNamed. The above test will fail if the specified exception is raised, and it will pass if the specified exception isn't raised.

You haven't yet fixed the bug, so running the test now should fail — but that's a good thing. Writing the test *before* fixing the bug means that you're validating your test's ability to reproduce the bug.

Hit **Command+U** to run the tests, and you should see a test failure with the following message:

```
test failure: -[ReversiBoardTests
test_makeMove_inPreGameState_nothingHappens] failed:
(([_reversiBoard makeMoveToColumn:3 andRow:3]) does not throw
<NSException, "NSRangeException">) failed
```

The test picked up on the thrown exception and failed as you had hoped. That's good news; you know that your test successfully creates the conditions to reproduce the bug. Once you attempt to fix the bug, this same test will show you if you've successfully squashed the bug — or if you still have some more debugging to do.

Correcting the code

Open **ReversiBoard.m** and find the `makeMoveToColumn:andRow:` method.

Think for a minute about how to correct this particular bug. It makes sense to allow moves only *after* the user has selected a game mode. There isn't much point in running the gameplay logic in the pre-game and post-game states.

Fortunately, there's a property that indicates the current state of the game: `gameState`.

Add the following lines to the very top of `makeMoveToColumn:andRow:` in **ReversiBoard.m**:

```
if ([self gameState] != GameStateOn)
    return;
```

The conditional above checks the current game state. If the state is anything other than `GameStateOn` — meaning a game is not in progress — the method terminates immediately.

Build and run your app, and test your bug fix manually by tapping on the screen before you select a game mode.

Finally, run the tests using **Command+U** and your Test Navigator should display nothing but green checkmarks. Looks like you squashed that bug!

Exploratory-style tests only cover obvious issues in the code, but regression-style tests written while fixing bugs provide some assurance that once you've fixed a bug, it should stay fixed — and if not, the test will catch it before the code is shipped!

Not only is your code more robust with each bug fix, but it also has a higher chance of *staying that way* thanks to your unit tests.

Where to go from here?

Testing is a *huge* task in the development life cycle, but this chapter has given you a good foundation on which to tackle unit test development in your apps. You've covered the following basic — yet critical — concepts in building intelligent unit tests:

- Which assertions to use, and where to use them

- Adding tests to an existing app

- Using tests as living specifications and living documentation

- Verifying bugs and bug fixes

- Guarding against future regressions

The integration of XCTest within Xcode makes it easier than ever to build and maintain your app test suite. The complete realm of iOS testing is quite large, and you would do well to build on your knowledge by reading up on the following iOS testing concepts:

- **Mock objects** are simulated objects that are just real enough to run your tests. Check out OCMock (http://ocmock.org/) for an Objective-C implementation.

- **UI testing** allows you to simulate user input such as touches and text entry. Have a look at the Automation task in the Instruments app.

- **Continuous integration (CI) systems** will run your unit tests automatically. To learn more about the new CI features in OS X Server, check out Chapter 14 and 15, "Beginning and Intermediate Continuous Integration in Xcode 5".

But before you get too deep into more advanced testing concepts, the following challenges are a great way to show yourself that you've mastered the concepts in this chapter.

> **Note:** There's a quick reference of the XCTest assertions at the end of this chapter for your testing convenience.

Challenges

The GameBoard class still has methods without any test coverage – your task is to write more unit tests to provide a complete test suite for your app. Don't worry if you get stuck; you can look up a set of sample solutions in the resources for this chapter.

Challenge 1: Testing clearBoard

clearBoard clears all pieces from the board. Since there's already a test for the getter and setter methods, you can assume those methods work and there's no need to test setting pieces on the board again.

Your test case method for clearBoard will have the following steps:

1. Set at least one black piece on the board

2. Set at least one white piece on the board

3. Call clearBoard

4. Check that the locations where you placed the black and white pieces are now empty (i.e. they have the BoardCellStateEmpty state)

Remember to name the test case following the suggested format used above: the unit of work or method name, what is being tested, and the expected result.

Challenge 2: Testing the scorekeeper

countCellsWithState: counts the number of pieces on the board having a specific state. This method calculates the final score, so it's important to make sure it works correctly!

Your test case for countCellsWithState: will perform the following actions:

1. Set some black and white pieces on the board.

2. Keep track of the number of pieces added.

3. Compare your counts with what is returned from countCellsWithState:.

countCellsWithState: takes a state as a parameter, so the full message will look like the following:

```
[_board countCellsWithState:BoardCellStateWhitePiece]
```

Again, make sure you name your test cases appropriately. Happy testing!

XCTest Assertions Reference

All assertions below take a variable-length argument (format...) as the last parameter which contains the NSLog style message to display on test failure.

`XCTFail(format...)`	Unconditional failure. Use to mark sections of code that shouldn't be reached.
`XCTAssertNil(exp, format...)` `XCTAssertNotNil(exp, format...)`	The expression should be nil or not nil. Use on Objective-C objects.
`XCTAssert(exp, format...)` `XCTAssertTrue(exp, format...)` `XCTAssertFalse(exp, format...)`	The expression should be a true-ish value or not. XCTAssert and XCTAssertTrue are the same.
`XCTAssertEqualObjects(a1, a2, format...)`	Objective-C objects a1 and a2 should be equal. Uses the isEqual: message under the hood.
`XCTAssertEqual(a1, a2, format...)`	Parameters a1 and a2 should be equal. Use to compare C scalars, unions, and structs such as CGRect or CGPoint instances. Uses NSValue to do the comparison under the hood.
`XCTAssertEqualWithAccuracy(a1, a2, delta, format...)`	Parameters a1 and a2 are equal to within the given delta. Use with floats and doubles where decimal values may not be exact.
`XCTAssertThrows(exp, format...)` `XCTAssertThrowsSpecific(exp, exception, format...)` `XCTAssertThrowsSpecificNamed(exp, exception, exceptionName, format...)`	The expression should cause an exception to be thrown. The more detailed versions let you specify the class and exception name.
`XCTAssertNoThrow` `XCTAssertNoThrowSpecific` `XCTAssertNoThrowSpecificNamed`	The "not" versions of the above assertions that will fail if the exception is thrown.

Chapter 12: Beginning Source Control in Xcode 5

By Felipe Laso Marsetti

Source control is the practice of managing and tracking changes to files. The files can be anything from a Word document or PDF, to an Objective-C header or implementation file, but in this chapter we're mainly going to focus on using source control to manage your Xcode projects.

Whether you're an independent developer or part of a larger team, it's very important to use source control in your apps.

• **If you're working in a team**, it's almost a necessity to allow multiple people to work on the same codebase and not step on each other's toes.

• **If you're working on your own**, source control is still extremely useful. It allows you to revert recent changes to code to get back to a good, known state, track diferent versions of your apps, and much more.

Think of source control like Time Machine for your programming projects; it gives you the security to change your code without fear of breaking the main codeline, and the accountability of a change history so that you can figure out "what, who, and when" if things do happen to go wrong.

Xcode has source control integration built right in (both in the user interface and command line), making it easy to use in your projects. The source control system Xcode uses is called Git, which is a free and open source distributed source control system that is easy to learn, lightweight and very fast.

This chapter will give you a crash course on the Git source control system and guide you through the creation of a project that will be stored on GitHub, which is a repository host as well as a team collaboration tool.

If you're already familiar with the basics of Git and have created and checked out a repository before, feel free to jump ahead to the next chapter, which deals with remote repositories and merging.

Getting started

The best way to learn about source control is to use it; it's time for you to get your feet wet and actually use Xcode with Git.

Open Xcode and create a new iOS **Master-Detail Application** named **ControllingSource** with your own Organization Name and Company Identifier, targeted for **iPhone** and that uses **Core Data**, as below:

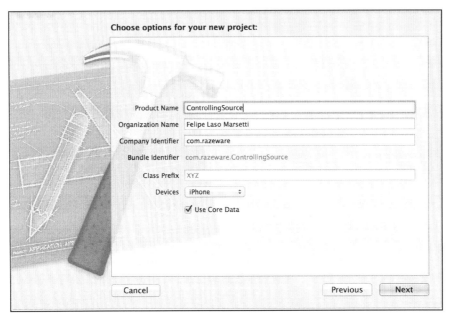

Click **Next**, but before you click anything else be sure to check the option at the bottom of the window called **Create git repository**:

Then choose a directory to save your project and click **Create**. Your project is now under git source control!

To prove this for yourself, select any file in the project navigator, open the file inspector and scroll down until you see the Source Control section. There's quite a bit of info in here, as shown by the following screenshot:

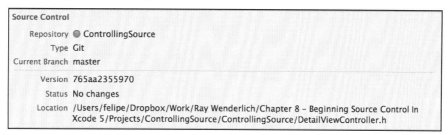

Let's go over each of the items in this pane:

- **Repository**: the name of the Git repository, which defaults to the name of the project.

- **Type**: the type of the repository, which is Git. At the time of writing this chapter, Xcode supports both Git and Subversion source control systems, although Git tends to be more popular in the iOS development community.

- **Current branch**: The fundamental unit in Git is a *commit*. A commit consists of changes to one or more files, and is identified by a unique alphanumeric ID called a *hash* or *SHA*. A commit also records the timestamp and the name of the person who made the change.

  A branch is a pointer to a specific commit that represents a state of the repository. The default branch in Git when you create a new repository is called *master*, which is what you see here. You will learn more about branches in the next chapter.

- **Version**: You're probably used to thinking of versions as sequential numbers, like version 1.0 of an app or version 10.9 of OS X. As previously mentioned, commits in Git are identified by a commit ID, a unique 40-character SHA1 hash that points to the exact state of your working directory when a commit is made. Here Xcode shows the first twelve characters of the commit's hash, which are generally enough characters to be unique.

- **Location**: The location of the file on your drive.

Git settings

Before you continue working with git, you should configure git with your name and email address so that your changes are tracked properly. To do this, open a Terminal window and enter the following commands:

```
git config --global user.name "YOUR NAME HERE"
git config --global user.email "EMAIL"
```

These commands will save your name and email to your local ~/.gitconfig file; these settings only apply to you, not any other accounts accounts on your computer.

To verify your changes, type in the following command in Terminal:

```
git config -l
```

This will list all of the Git configuration options that are currently set. As you can see, there are many more settings you can configure and customize from Terminal; to learn more about them you can type the following command in Terminal:

```
git config -help
```

Adding Git to an existing project

If you have an existing project that you'd like to place under source control there is no way to do so within Xcode. However, it's easy to set things up manually. To see how this is done, follow the steps below to create a sample project *without* Git, and then add it after the fact.

Create a new Xcode project called **ExistingProject** with the same settings as the ControllingSource project, but this time don't click the check box for creating a Git repository. Select a file and verify it is not under source control in the File Inspector:

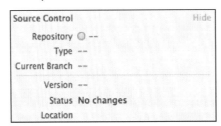

Now open the Terminal application, type cd with a space afterwards, then drag the project folder to the terminal window. You should see something similar to what's shown in the screenshot below:

```
● ● ●                    ⬆ felipe — bash — 80×24
Last login: Sat Aug 10 15:35:40 on ttys000
Felipes-MacBook-Pro:~ felipe$ cd /Users/felipe/Dropbox/Work/Ray\ Wenderlich/Chap
ter\ 8\ -\ Beginning\ Source\ Control\ In\ Xcode\ 5/Projects/ExistingProject
```

Hit **Return** on your keyboard, then type ls -la followed by another Return. This lists the items in the **ExistingProject** directory as illustrated below:

```
○ ○ ○                  ExistingProject — bash — 80×24
Felipes-MacBook-Pro:ExistingProject felipe$ ls -la
total 0
drwxr-xr-x    5 felipe   staff   170 Aug 10 15:26 .
drwxr-xr-x    5 felipe   staff   170 Aug 10 15:35 ..
drwxr-xr-x   15 felipe   staff   510 Aug 10 15:25 ExistingProject
drwxr-xr-x    5 felipe   staff   170 Aug 10 15:26 ExistingProject.xcodeproj
drwxr-xr-x    5 felipe   staff   170 Aug 10 15:26 ExistingProjectTests
Felipes-MacBook-Pro:ExistingProject felipe$ █
```

If the project were under git source control you'd see a hidden directory named *.git*. Since there isn't one, initialize a Git repository for this project by typing `git init` and hitting Return; Git will respond with the following:

```
○ ○ ○                  ExistingProject — bash — 80×24
Felipes-MacBook-Pro:ExistingProject felipe$ git init
Initialized empty Git repository in /Users/felipe/Dropbox/Work/Ray Wenderlich/Ch
apter 8 - Beginning Source Control In Xcode 5/Projects/ExistingProject/.git/
Felipes-MacBook-Pro:ExistingProject felipe$ █
```

If you see **Initialized empty Git repository** like you see here, that means the command was successful.

Type `git status` to see should get the current status of your working directory.

```
○ ○ ○                  ExistingProject — bash — 80×24
Felipes-MacBook-Pro:ExistingProject felipe$ git status
# On branch master
#
# Initial commit
#
# Untracked files:
#   (use "git add <file>..." to include in what will be committed)
#
#       .DS_Store
#       ExistingProject.xcodeproj/
#       ExistingProject/
#       ExistingProjectTests/
nothing added to commit but untracked files present (use "git add" to track)
Felipes-MacBook-Pro:ExistingProject felipe$
```

The output above shows that none of the files or folders in your project directory are being tracked by Git. There's also a helpful message noting that you can use `git add` to specify what files and directories to include in the next commit.

However, note that the output shows a file called `.DS_Store`, which is a special hidden file created by OS X that contains attributes about a folder such as positions of icons within the folder. This is typically something you don't want to track in source control, because it is specific to your particular machine and has nothing to do with the project itself.

So before adding files for tracking and making your first commit, it would be wise to learn how to exclude certain files from your repository automatically. You can do this with a special file called `.gitignore`.

The .gitignore file

The **.gitignore** file contains rules that indicate which files not to track or show in the staging area. Git will check each filename against the list of rules in .gitignore, and ignore the file if there is a match.

Open any text editor and add the followings lines to a new file:

```
# Xcode
.DS_Store
*/build/*
*.pbxuser
!default.pbxuser
*.mode1v3
!default.mode1v3
*.mode2v3
!default.mode2v3
*.perspectivev3
!default.perspectivev3
xcuserdata
profile
*.moved-aside
DerivedData
.idea/
*.hmap
```

This ignores many of the common types of files that you don't typically want in your git repositories. This is a good starter default .gitignore; you may want to keep a local copy to reuse in future projects.

> **Note:** The fine folks at GitHub maintain an extensive collection of gitignore files for many tools and languages that might come in handy. You can find them here:
>
> https://github.com/github/gitignore

Save the file in your **ExistingProject** project directory and name it `.gitignore`.

Go back to the terminal window and type `git status` once again:

```
● ● ○                     ⬜ ExistingProject — bash — 80×24                      ⤢
Felipes-MacBook-Pro:ExistingProject felipeS git status
# On branch master
#
# Initial commit
#
# Untracked files:
#   (use "git add <file>..." to include in what will be committed)
#
#       .gitignore
#       ExistingProject.xcodeproj/
#       ExistingProject/
#       ExistingProjectTests/
nothing added to commit but untracked files present (use "git add" to track)
Felipes-MacBook-Pro:ExistingProject felipeS
```

This time, there is no .DS_Store file as you specified it as one of the files to be ignored in **.gitignore**. It's usually a good idea to track and commit .gitignore so other users of the repository can use the same settings and prevent them from committing unwanted files as well.

> **Note:** This is a good starter default .gitignore; you may want to keep a local copy to reuse in future projects. The fine folks at GitHub maintain an extensive collection of gitignore files for many tools and languages.

A command line commit

With your .gitignore ready, it's time to stage your files and make your first commit. Enter this command in the terminal to add all the untracked files to the staging area:

```
git add .
```

Now enter `git status` one more time and notice how everything in your project is in the staging area but not yet committed.

To commit your files, enter the following command:

```
git commit -m "Initial commit."
```

This tells Git to commit everything in the staging area (which, at the moment is everything in your project) along with the quoted message specified with the −m flag.

Now enter `git status` to view the state of your repository. It should show that your repository HEAD is pointing to the default `master` branch, there's nothing to commit, and that your working directory is clean, as below:

Quit Xcode 5 and re-open **ExistingProject**. Select any item in the project and open the File Inspector; you should see details similar to the following:

Just as with your ControllingSource project, you now have an Xcode project with a Git repository initialized, a .gitignore file and the first commit.

Committing changes in Xcode 5

Now that you've learned how to put an existing project under source control and how to change your Git settings, it's time to make some code changes in Xcode and learn how to commit them.

Open the **ControllingSource** project and have a look at the project navigator. The files could stand to be organized a little better than they are currently. To start, group the view controllers together to make them easier to manage.

Select the four view controller files in the project navigator and right-click to open the context menu. Select **New Group From Selection** to group the files together and name the group **View Controllers**.

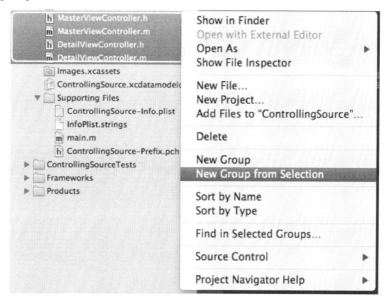

While you're at it, group the layout resources into a group and name it **Resources**, as so:

Note that the project file has an **M** next to it. This indicates that the project file, or something within the project, has been modified.

To commit the changes, right-click on the project file and select **Source Control Commit**, as shown:

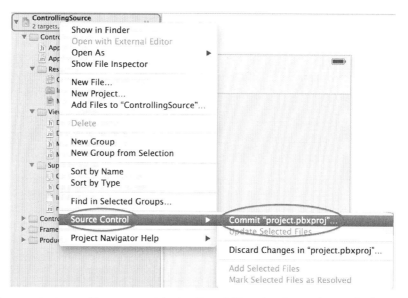

A drop-down window will appear with the list of files that have changed, the option to select what files to commit and a field for a commit message. Add a comment describing the reason for the commit, such as "Organize project navigator", and click **Commit**.

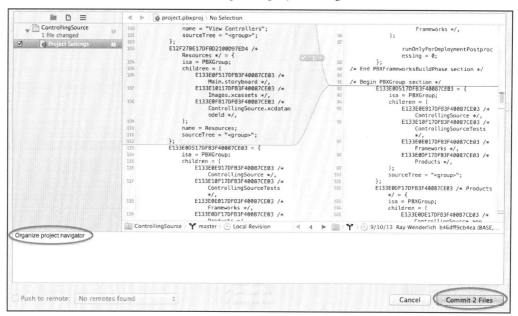

Now that you've committed some changes, how can you view what was changed? One way to view your commit logs is with the version editor. Click and hold on the version editor button and select **Log**, as shown on the next page:

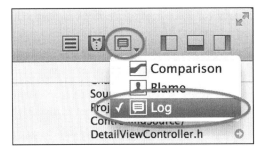

In the version editor you can see the abbreviated commit hash, the name of the person who made the commit, the date, and the files modified in the commit, as so:

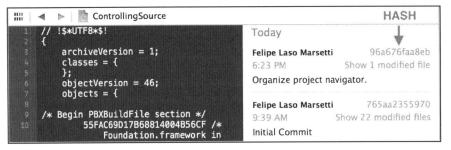

The commit list on the right hand side shows a high-level view of the history of the file, and you can click on the "Show 1 modified file" text to see what was changed in each commit.

Let's try out the other two verion editor options. Click and hold the version editor button again, but this time select **Comparison**. You should see the following:

The **Comparison** view shows the current state of the file side-by-side with the last committed state; this can be useful to review your latest changes with the previous revision.

You can try the last version editor option if you'd like (**Blame**), but the blame view is unavailable for project files so it won't show anything interesting. For other types of files, you will find it useful because it annotates lines and blocks of code with the relevant commit information, such as name, date, and message. This view is very helpful to see when certain portions of the code were changed, and more importantly, who to blame (or congratulate!) for those changes.

Viewing your project history

You've already seen how to review your commit logs with the version editor, which shows details on a file-by-file basis. You can also see the history of the project as a whole from the top-level repository view.

From the main menu, select **Source Control\History**, as shown below:

You'll see a screen with all the commits made to your project, and similar to the version editor's log view, the commit's hash, contact information, date and changed files, as shown on the next page:

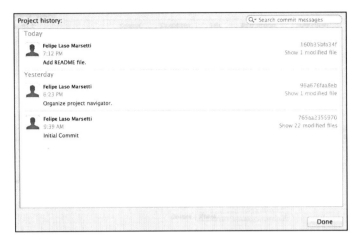

This view is particularly helpful if you want to get an overview of the changes to the project as a whole rather than on an per-file basis.

Adding the project to GitHub

Recall that Git is a distributed and decentralized system. That means all your commits are being made locally; if you delete the top-level project directory, the Git repository would disappear too. Your entire project is only an errant right-click away from impending doom! What to do?

Having a server component means you can easily share your code and collaborate with others. You can host a repository on your own server, or use a hosted service like GitHub. If you don't have a GitHub account, head to github.com to get one. After signing up, you'll need to configure a set of keys to be able to communicate with the repository via SSH.

SSH setup

GitHub uses a pair of keys — one public and one private — in order to communicate securely with your computer. First, find out if you already have an SSH keypair by typing the following commands in a Terminal window:

```
cd ~/.ssh
ls
```

If you see a file named `id_rsa.pub` or `id_dsa.pub` then you've already generated your SSH keys. In that case skip straight to the section titled **Adding your SSH key to GitHub**.

If you don't see either of those files, or you get a "No such file or directory" error, then type the following command in Terminal to generate a pair of SSH keys:

```
ssh-keygen -t rsa -C "YOUR EMAIL"
```

You'll then be prompted to enter a passphrase; this is optional but highly recommended to secure your keys. Once that's done, your SSH keys are ready to be added to GitHub.

Adding your SSH key to GitHub

If not already there, navigate to the .ssh directory in your home folder and open the id_rsa.pub file (or id_dsa.pub file if you have that one) in a text editor. Copy the contents of the file and go to your account settings on github.com.

Select the **SSH Keys** option then click the **Add SSH key** button, as below:

Paste the contents you copied from the `.pub` file into the Key section and give it a title, as shown below:

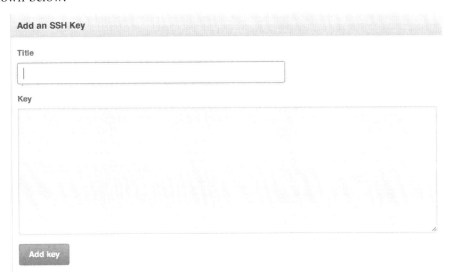

As far as a name goes, you can just use the name of the computer this key corresponds to — although note that you can reuse the same key on multiple computers.

Creating a new repository on GitHub

With your keys set up you can now create a new repository and push your project to GitHub.

On the GitHub home page, click on the **New Repository** button to create a new repository, as shown below:

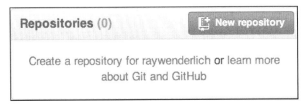

You'll be taken to a page where you can input some info for your repository.

The owner should default to your account; note that you can belong to more than one GitHub team. For the repository name type **ControllingSource**, give it a description, and make it a public repository; private repositories require a paid GitHub account. Ensure the options to initialize the repository with a readme, gitignore or license file remain unselected as shown below:

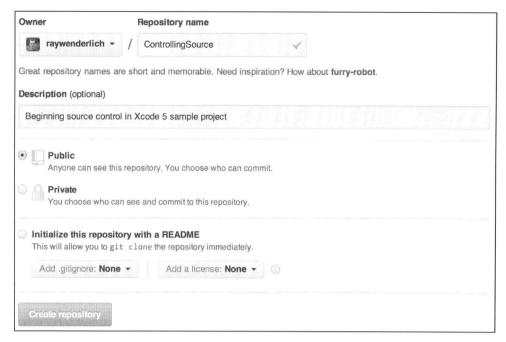

Finally, click the **Create repository** button; you'll see a screen with some instructions on how to create a new repository or take an existing repository and push it to GitHub.

Rather than spend more time on the command line, you'll be using Xcode 5 to add the GitHub repository as a remote and push to it.

The only thing you need to do is to copy the SSH address from GitHub for use in a moment:

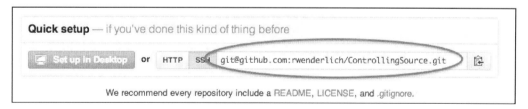

Pushing the changes to GitHub

Go back to Xcode and click the **Source Control** menu item. Select the **master** branch and choose the **Configure ControllingSource** option, as shown on the next page:

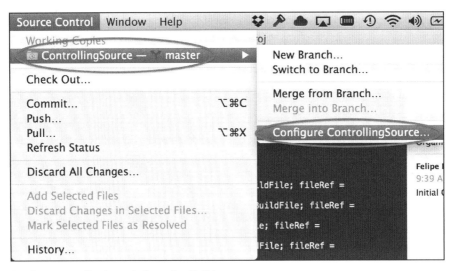

Click the "Remotes" tab and then the "+" button, as so:

Type **ControllingSource** for the remote repository name, paste the SSH address you copied from your GitHub repository, and click **Add Remote**, as shown below:

Create a new Remote:

Name: ControllingSource

Address: git@github.com:raywenderlich/ControllingSource.git

Cancel   Add Remote

Back in the configuration window, click **Done** and select the **Source Control** menu item again; this time select the **Push** option:

In the popup, you should see a dropdown titled "Push local changes:" along with a selection of branches to push to GitHub. Select the only branch available — **master** — and click **Push**, as below:

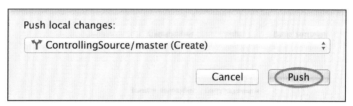

Go to your repository on github.com and refresh the page to see the results. The resulting table shows the branch you committed to, the number of commits, all of the files in the project as well as all of the contributors to the project:

That's the end of the line — you've pushed your repository to GitHub and it's now stored safely on the server.

From here on out, if you want to make changes you can follow these same two steps:

1. Go to **Source Control\Commit** to commit your changes locally.

2. Go to **Source Control\Push** to push your changes to Github.

Challenges

Source control is a practice that every developer should follow. Regardless of how many people are involved or what type of projects you work on, source control is a huge time-saver — and even sometimes a lifesaver!

Apple is making a strong push in Xcode 5 to encourage the use of source control, just as they are with unit testing and continuous integration. There are a lot of enhancements and new features with source control in Xcode 5, many of which you have seen in this chapter.

So far, you've only learned the basics of working with source control. In the next chapter, you'll work with an app on a remote repository and learn about working with multiple branches, merging and more.

But first, it's time for you to try a quick challenge to make sure you understand what you've learned so far.

Challenge 1: Your own commit

This is a quick and simple challenge that mimics what you'll do most frequently while developing. You'll make a change, commit and push the, and verify the change is visible on GitHub.

1. Open Main.storyboard and modify the color of the prototype cell's label and background in addition to the label and background color of the detail view controller.

2. Commit your changes from within Xcode and give the commit and appropriate message.

3. Push your changes to Github and verify that your commit is visible from your repository's website.

If you get stuck please refer to previous sections of the chapter where you are shown how to commit and push changes in your repository. Feel free to use the sample project as a starting point for the challenge.

Chapter 13: Intermediate Source Control in Xcode 5

By Felipe Laso Marsetti

In the previous chapter, you learned about the benefits of source control the basics of Git and GitHub, and how to use some of the source control features in Xcode 5.

In this chapter you will delve deeper into the world of Git and source control and learn more about remote repositories, how to work with branches, pulling, merging, and more.

Working with remote repositories

Before you get in to branching and merging, it's important to have a firm understanding of how to work with remote repositories. This section will show you three things:

1. **Local->Remote.** How to move a project that has a variety of local branches to a remote repository.

2. **Remote->Local.** How to check out a local copy of a project from a remote repository.

3. **Viewing repositories**. How to view and track the repositories that you are working with in Xcode.

Let's start with the first: moving a project with many local branches to a remote repository.

From local to remote

Included in the book's source code for this chapter you will find a starter project called **ControllingSource Starter**. Open it up in Xcode and take a look at the branches that already exist. These branches represent the following imaginary situation:

- I have worked on a branch called **FileOrganization**. This organizes everything in the project navigator, cleans up unnecessary code from source files, and organizes properties and method declarations alphabetically.

- Marin has worked on **ModelUpdates** in order to make the necessary changes to the Core Data model that will be used in the application.

- Ray made a branch called **RefactorClassNames** that renames MasterViewController and DetailViewController into class names that actually make sense and better describe what each controller does.

- Charlie and Ray have been working on the **master** branch. Charlie first added a README file to the project and Ray added a property list containing famous quotes to be used in the application.

This should give you a better idea of how the starter project is setup and what each branch contains.

If you worked through the previous chapter you already have a GitHub account along with SSH keys on your computer, but if not, refer to that chapter to create your GitHub account and SSH keys.

Go to the GitHub web site and add a new repository to your account. Name it **Intermediate_ControllingSource**, give it a description, and make sure you don't initialize it with a README, gitignore, or license file. Your screen should look like the one below:

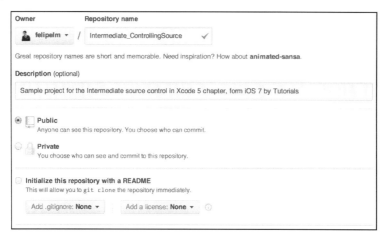

When your repository is ready, copy the SSH URL given to you by GitHub and open the starter project in Xcode 5.

Go to the **Source Control** menu, select the current working copy's branch and click **Configure ControllingSource...**, as below:

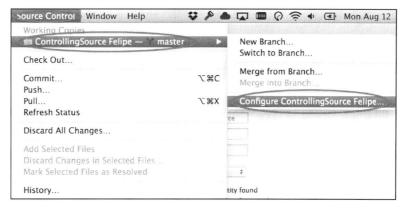

In the dropdown window select the **Remotes** tab and click the **+** icon to add a new remote repository to your local project, as so:

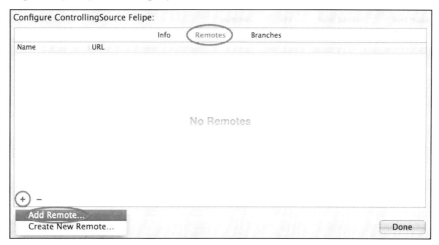

Name the remote repository **Intermediate_ControllingSource** and paste in the SSH URL you acquired from GitHub. Then click the **Add Remote** button, shown below, and then click the **Done** button from the previous dropdown window:

Now that your local repository is linked to your new GitHub repository, go to the **Source Control** menu item and click **Push...**.

You should already be in the master branch so leave the dropdown as is and click **Push,** as shown below:

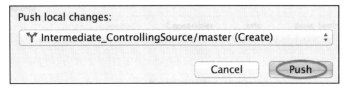

Notice how the branch's name has the word **Create** in parenthesis. This indicates that the master branch doesn't exist in the remote repository; your push operation will create a new branch.

Now go to the **Source Control** menu item and select the **Switch to Branch...** option, as so:

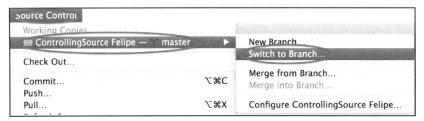

The dialog below will show your local branches, and after a brief pause, your remote branches as well. Your master branch should show up in the list, as in the screenshot below:

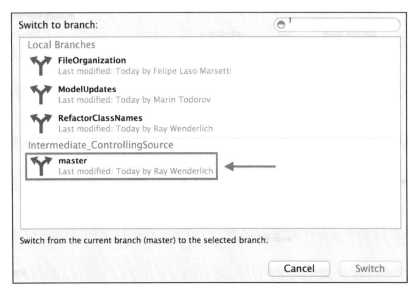

These are three branches that I set up for you in the starter project. Note that you've successfully published the master branch to your remote repository — but your other branches are still local-only.

Switch to each one of the local branches in turn and push them to GitHub just as you did with the master branch. When you're done, your screen should look like the one below:

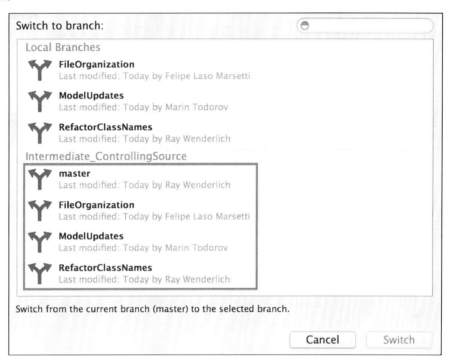

Just to verify that everything is correctly pushed to GitHub, open your repository page on the web. The info bar should list 4 branches, as shown below:

Click on the text, and you'll see all four branches listed:

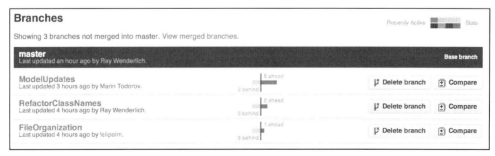

From remote to local

Many times when you join a project, your company or team will already have a repository hosted on a server. In this scenario you'll set yourself up with read/write access to the repository you'll be working on and make a local clone of the repository on your computer. Yes, you already have a local copy of the repository, but here you're simulating starting from scratch.

Close Xcode and delete the project folder; at this point, your project is gone. Copy your repository's SSH URL from GitHub and re-open Xcode 5.

Go to **Source Control** and select **Check Out…**:

From there go to the **Repositories** tab and enter the repository's URL that you copied from GitHub, as shown below:

Click **Next** and you'll be prompted to select the branch you wish to check out. Select the **master** branch, as so:

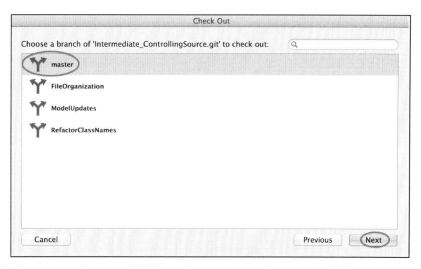

Select the directory where you'd like to check out the local copy of the repository and Xcode 5 will open your project from the local copy of the **master** branch that you checked out. Pretty painless!

Viewing repositories

To view your repositories in Xcode, open Xcode **Preferences** and select the **Accounts** tab.

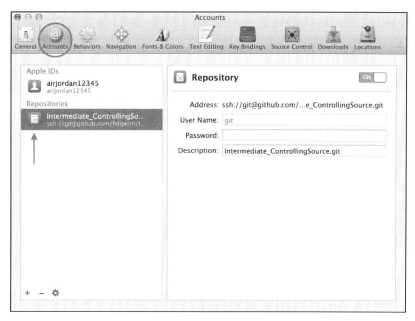

From here you can turn the repository on or off, change the description, or even change the credentials you use for authentication. Your project is set up for SSH keys, so you're not using credentials at present.

You can also view your repositories by selecting **Source Control\Check Out**. This shows you all of your repositories as well as recent repositories and favorite repositories. You can favorite a repository by clicking the star to the left of the repository.

Now that you have a fresh clone of the repository, it's time to start looking at the workflow of commits, branches, and merges.

A branch-based workflow

Why use branches?

Branches are part of the core Git workflow and an essential tool in your development cycle. They give you the security to keep work compartmentalized: a stable branch to build from and merge to (usually **master**), and the ability to separate chunks of work, new features, and bug fixes from the rest of the code.

What if you want to add a great new feature to your app, or fix a bug reported by one of your users? You certainly don't want to be committing those changes to your master branch in case something breaks.

With a branch-based workflow you can create a branch for each bug fix, new feature, or component you work on, and merge or rebase when it's ready and tested.

Creating a new branch

To try this out, you're going to create a new branch based on an existing one. A new branch starts from the current commit of the current branch. Right now, that's at the most recent or HEAD of the **master** branch.

Go to the **Source Control** menu item, hover over your **master** branch and select **New Branch…**, as below:

Name the branch **MyBranch** and click **Create**.

Now you have a brand-new working branch named **MyBranch** and Xcode has automatically checked it out for you and has switched you to this branch.

Discarding changes in your working directory

Sometimes you'll make a set of changes to a particular file, or set of files, that you want to revert wholesale. Instead of having to manually delete these changes or undo your way back to the file's original state, you can discard your changes with Git and revert a file to the last committed version.

Open **AppDelegate.h** and delete the UIKit import line:

```
#import <UIKit/UIKit.h>
```

The project navigator should reflect this change by showing you an **M** next to the file, as shown below:

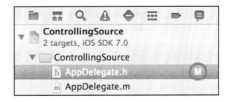

Now open **AppDelegate.m** and delete the unused UIApplicationDelegate methods:

```
- (void)applicationWillResignActive:(UIApplication *)application
- (void)applicationDidEnterBackground:(UIApplication
*)application
- (void)applicationWillEnterForeground:(UIApplication
*)application
- (void)applicationDidBecomeActive:(UIApplication *)application
```

Now there should be an **M** in the project navigator next to both files.

Right-click **AppDelegate.h** and select **Source Control\Discard changes...** as shown below:

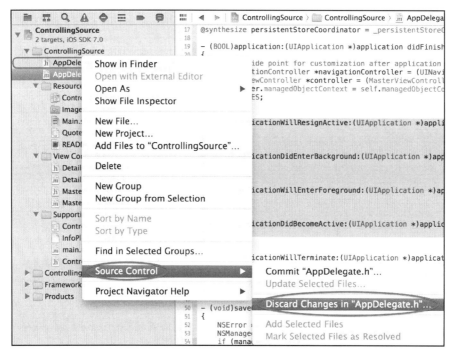

When prompted, click **Discard Changes**. Notice the **M** that was next to **AppDelegate.h** disappears, and your UIKit file is restored to its former glory. You can also command-select multiple files and right-click to discard the changes in the selected files.

However, to revert *all* of the changes you made, select **Source Control\Discard All Changes...**.

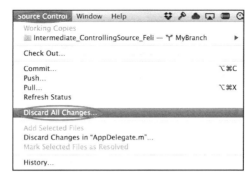

Then select **Discard All Changes** again from the prompt. Check out **AppDelegate.m**; the lines you deleted have now been restored, and your project navigator should no longer have an **M** anywhere.

Deleting a branch

When deleting a branch there are a two things to remember. One, you can't delete the branch you're currently working on. Two, it's quite possible to have a local and a remote version of the same branch, so deleting the branch locally will not delete it remotely. The reverse case is true as well; deleting a branch remotely won't delete your local branch.

Switch back to the **master** branch and go to **Source Control > Configure…**. In the **Branches** tab, select the **MyBranch** local branch and click the '-' icon on the bottom left portion of the dropdown, as shown below:

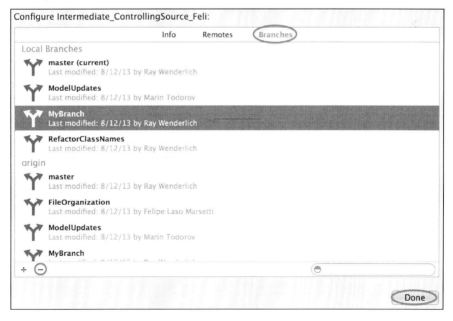

Finally, click **Delete Branch**. **MyBranch** no longer exists on your local machine.

At the moment, Xcode doesn't support deleting remote branches; you can use a separate Git client (see the end of this chapter for recommendations) or the command line to do this instead.

Pulling remote changes

So far, you've learned how to push changes you have made to a remote repository. But what if you want to pull changes that your team members have committed to the remote repository to your local copy?

This is done with a concept in Git called **pulling**, as you might expect. Let's take a look at how it works.

Making a change via GitHub

Since you are working alone in this project you are going to use the GitHub web site to edit a file and make a commit to simulate a remote change from a team member. Yup, you can do that with GitHub. It's pretty versatile!

Go to GitHub and open your repository's page. From there go to the **ControllingSource** folder and select **AppDelegate.m**. Click the Edit button and remove the following unused methods from the **UIApplicationDelegate** protocol:

```
- (void)applicationWillResignActive:(UIApplication *)application
- (void)applicationDidEnterBackground:(UIApplication
*)application
- (void)applicationWillEnterForeground:(UIApplication
*)application
- (void)applicationDidBecomeActive:(UIApplication *)application
```

Scroll to the bottom of the edit page, enter a commit message, and click **Commit Changes**.

Pulling changes in Xcode 5

With this new commit in place you now have something to merge into your local repository. Remember that when pulling, you automatically merge the HEAD branch with your local copy. Should there be any conflicts between your copy and the remote copy, you'll be prompted to resolve them yourself; otherwise, any updates from the remote repository will be merged into your local branch.

Back in Xcode make sure you're on the **master** branch and open up **AppDelegate.m**. The file should still have the methods you just removed via GitHub since you haven't yet merged the remote changes into your local copy.

To pull the changes down, go to **Source Control\Pull...**.

From the dropdown select the **origin/master** branch and click **Pull**:

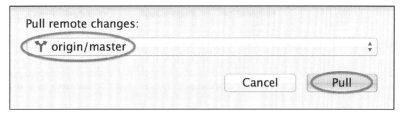

Now look at **AppDelegate.m**; the changes you made remotely have been merged with your local file. Take a look at the logs in the version editor as well; you'll see the commit action and accompanying message for the changes made via GitHub, as shown on the next page:

Today

Felipe Laso Marsetti   47533b1150a6
11:22 AM   Show 1 modified file
Cleanup AppDelegate.m file

August 12, 2013

Felipe Laso Marsetti   038ffb8a58cc
7:12 PM   Show 22 modified files
Initial Commit

Merging vs. Rebasing

Merging and rebasing are two key elements of source control in Git. Unfortunately, Xcode 5 only supports merging — not rebasing. However, it's good to know what their differences are and when you would use one over the other.

Should you merge or rebase?

In short, it depends.

Merging takes all of the changes that you have committed in a branch and merges those changes into another branch. For example, say you make commits A and B in your branch and your colleague makes commits Q and R in her branch. Your team lead merges both branches into master, and the resulting history ties together master, your branch, and you colleague's branch.

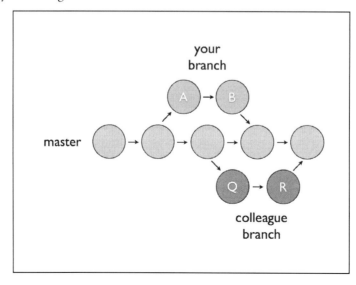

On the other hand, a rebase is usually used to bring your working branch back up to date. Let's say commit C is the latest one in master and you create a new branch. You add commits Q, R, and S to your branch. In the meantime, your colleague adds an emergency hotfix to master in commit D.

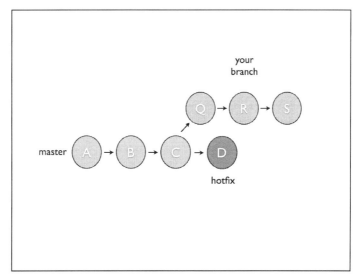

You want to incorporate the hotfix into your branch, but you don't want to merge your code into master yet. Instead, you can rebase your branch on the current master so it's as if you started your working branch off commit D rather than C.

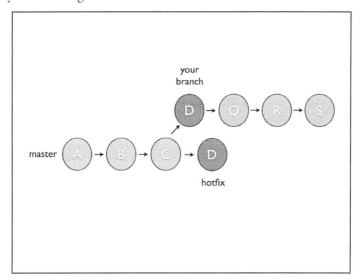

Choose to merge when you have a feature on a separate branch and want to bring that code into master or another branch. Choose to rebase when you want to stay in sync with the main branch when you're working on a long-lived side branch.

Merging into master

Now that you have a bit more knowledge about merging and rebasing, it's time to merge some of the branches in your repository.

In this Xcode project, I have set up a branch called FileOrganization that organizes the file and folder structure in your project navigator in addition to cleaning up your source files alphabetically and removing unused code.

In Xcode, go to the **Source Control** item and switch to the **FileOrganization** branch, as shown below:

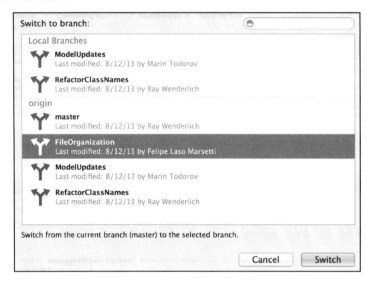

Now go back to the **Source Control** menu, select the branch, and select **Merge into Branch…**. From the available options, select the **master** branch and click **Merge**.

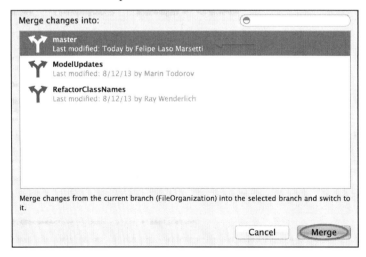

A new dropdown pane will appear with the destination file from the master branch on the left hand side, and the source file from the FileOrganization branch on the right.

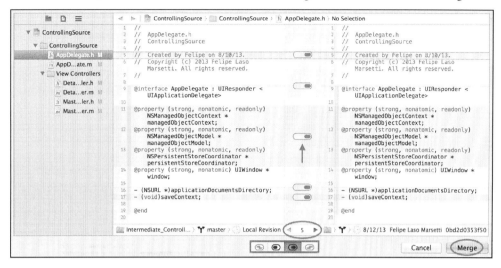

Note the arrow in the image above; the switches between the two files allow you to accept or reject individual changes from the source file to the destination file. By default, Xcode assumes you want to merge all changes, so you'll notice the switches are all to the right.

The circled number with arrows on each side lets you step through each detected change and conflict one at a time.

Finally, the buttons at the bottom let you (from left to right):

1. Resolve the selected conflict using the changes from the file on the left and then those from the file on the right.

2. Resolve the selected conflict using only the changes from the file on the left.

3. Resolve the selected conflict using only the changes from the file on the right.

4. Resolve the selected conflict using the changes from the file on the right and then the changes from the file on the left.

There are no conflicts or anything else in your way, so simply click **Merge**.

Go to **Configuration\Source Control** menu item and delete the **FileOrganization** branch from your local repository. If you want, you can also delete the branch from the remote repository via GitHub.

Since the branch containing your changes has been merged into the master branch, you no longer need to keep a copy of it remotely. If you are working on a team project it may cause confusion and increase the clutter when viewing all the branches available in the origin (in this case, Github).

Merging into another branch

Next you will merge the **ModelUpdates** branch not into master, but into the **RefactorClassNames** branch. The reason why you merge it into RefactorClassNames first and not directly into master is because ModelUpdates is a branch created from RefactorClassNames.

This will put the code back into its original branch before you merge things into master.

> **Note:** There is no rule that says you must merge everything into master; you can branch off something other than master and merge your work into any branch. Master is usually kept with stable, tested code and is treated as production-ready.

First, switch to the **ModelUpdates** branch to retrieve a local copy.

Note that in the previous example, you merged *into* a branch. For this next merge you'll try it the other way and merge *from* a branch.

Switch to the **RefactorClassNames** branch and select **Source Control\Merge from Branch...**. From the dropdown, select the **ModelUpdates** branch and click **Merge**.

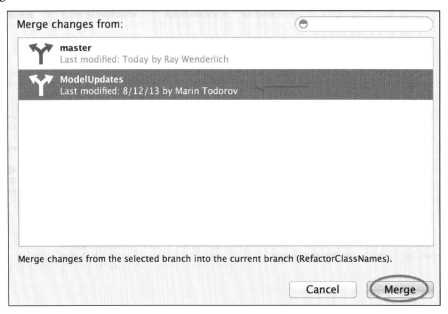

You should get a couple of merge changes. Once again resolve them with all the switches set to the branch, meaning you are selecting to keep the changes from the **ModelUpdates** branch, and click **Merge**.

Delete the **ModelUpdates** branch locally and, if you want, remotely. ModelUpdates has been merged into the RefactorClassNames branch so by deleting ModelUpdates locally and from the origin, you will prevent confusion and keep your repository clean.

Merge conflicts and resolution

Currently the merges of your **master** and **RefactorClassNames** are stored in your local repository; you haven't yet updated them on the server. Push your newly merged **RefactorClassNames** branch to GitHub.

After that's done switch to the **master** branch and push that up to GitHub as well.

Now you're ready for the final merge! In the **Source Control** menu, select **Merge from branch** and then **RefactorClassNames** to merge. Aha — there's a conflict that needs to be resolved.

There are two question mark symbols and nine switches for the changes made in the project file. Leave the switches as they are and focus on each of the question marks, starting with the first one.

Merge conflicts in the project file can be especially tricky to deal with. In this case, the master branch includes the reorganized file groupings. Click the button on the far left as indicated below:

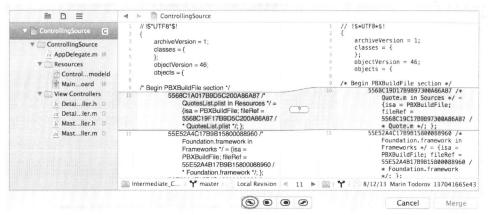

This resolves the conflict by accepting the change on the left before the change on the right. Repeat the process for the second question mark.

Once that's done, click the **Merge** button to finish the process, as below:

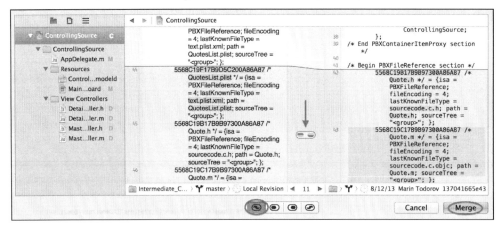

You've finished merging all of the branches that contained different portions of work. You now have an organized set of files and project navigator, a core data model with corresponding class files, an updated storyboard and the README and property list file to make your app work.

Push the master branch to GitHub and delete the **RefactorClassNames** branch locally and remotely. As with the previous merges, you delete the branch to keep the repository clean and avoid keeping unnecessary code around. Should you ever need to revert back to the branch's state before the merge, you can do so by checking out the commit prior to the merge.

Finishing the app

With your project merged and up to date, it's time to wrap up the code itself. This app lets users add random quotes from a plist file into a standard table view.

Open **Quote.m** and add the following code inside the implementation:

```objc
- (void)awakeFromInsert
{
    [super awakeFromInsert];

    NSString *quotesFilePath = [[NSBundle mainBundle]
                                  pathForResource:@"QuotesList"
                                ofType:@"plist"];

    NSArray *quotesArray =
```

```
                [NSArray arrayWithContentsOfFile:quotesFilePath];
        NSUInteger quoteIndex = arc4random() % [quotesArray count];
        NSDictionary *quoteDictionary = quotesArray[quoteIndex];

        [self setPrimitiveValue:quoteDictionary[@"personName"]
                        forKey:@"personName"];
        [self setPrimitiveValue:quoteDictionary[@"famousQuote"]
                        forKey:@"famousQuote"];
}
```

This method is called when you insert a new quote object into Core Data; it retrieves the property list file with the famous quotes, fetches a random quote and stores it in the newly inserted Quote object.

Switch to **QuoteListViewController.m** and update `insertNewObject:` as follows:

```
- (void)insertNewObject:(id)sender
{
    NSManagedObjectContext *context =
[self.fetchedResultsController managedObjectContext];
    NSEntityDescription *entity =
[[self.fetchedResultsController fetchRequest] entity];
    [NSEntityDescription insertNewObjectForEntityForName:[entity
name] inManagedObjectContext:context];

    NSError *error = nil;

    if (![context save:&error])
    {
        NSLog(@"Unresolved error %@, %@", error, [error
userInfo]);
        abort();
    }
}
```

Finally, update `configureCell:atIndexPath:` as shown:

```
- (void)configureCell:(UITableViewCell *)cell
atIndexPath:(NSIndexPath *)indexPath
{
    Quote *quote = [self.fetchedResultsController
objectAtIndexPath:indexPath];
    cell.textLabel.text = quote.personName;
}
```

These two methods handle the insertion and display of the quotes.

Commit these changes and push them to GitHub. Now run your app and click the plus button; a list of famous people will appear. Select the name of a famous person from the list and you'll see a random quote from that person.

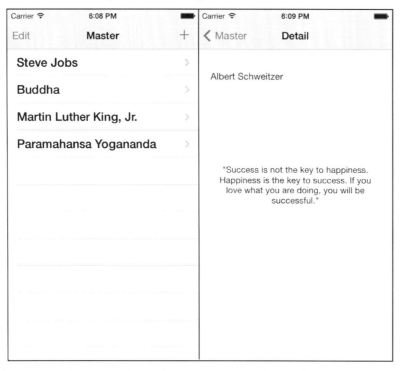

Congratulations! You've merged together a simple app, learned about Git source control with Xcode 5, and also learned a bit about GitHub too.

Where to go from here?

Despite many of the enhancements made to Source Control in Xcode 5, there are still a lot of missing features and shortcomings that prevent Xcode from being the go-to source control tool. Xcode is fine for basic tasks like checking out a repository, making a new branch, viewing history and logs, switching branches and pushing or committing changes, but it can't yet do everything that Git offers.

If you don't want to learn how to use Git from the command line and prefer GUI clients then check out the following clients:

• Tower Git

- Source Tree

- Gitbox

From here on out the sky is the limit when it comes to Git. There is always something new to learn and master. Check out the Git website and read through Pro Git; you won't be disappointed.

Challenge

Finally, here's a challenge for you to test and practice your git skills:

1. Create a branch called Enhancements and add 5 new quotes of your preference to the property list.

2. Commit the updated property list file and give the commit a descriptive message.

3. Add a .gitignore file to the project and commit that change, still in the Enhancements branch.

4. Push the Enhancements branch to Github and verify that it is visible remotely in your repository page.

5. Merge the **Enhancements** branch into **master** and push these changes to Github.

6. Delete the enhancements branch locally and from the remote repository (it's redundant and you no longer need to keep it around. This makes for a cleaner project repository).

7. Switch to the master branch and update the README file to give a better description of your project. Commit the changes once you are done.

8. Push the updated master branch to Github, and go to your repository's main page and make sure the new description is visible.

Chapter 14: Beginning Continuous Integration in Xcode 5

By Chris Wagner

All development shops struggle with the day-to-day management of builds and releases. Whether it's a one-person development shop, or a global distributed team, it's always challenging to keep the builds clean and an even bigger challenge to keep release day from disintegrating into mild chaos.

Xcode 5 and OS X Server for Mavericks combine to create a simple yet powerful build environment that leverages a new Xcode service and automations known as bots. Many iOS and Mac developers are familiar with open-source continuous integration servers such as Jenkins or Hudson; while these servers are powerful and worthy options, they often lack the ease-of-use and polish of a well-designed commercial product. Setting up one of these servers could take from several hours, to days, to even weeks in some cases.

Apple's offering, on the other hand, has greatly reduced the time required to construct a full integration environment; one that you will build yourself in this very chapter! In this chapter you'll learn how to set up OS X Server, install the Xcode Service, create a bot to run a build task, and integrate the bot with your Git repositories. By the end, you'll have a continuous integration server that will be of immediate benefit to you and your development team.

What is continuous integration?

The idea of continuous integration first became popular as a tenant of the extreme programming movement (see note below). The idea behind continuous integration is that when developers integrate their collective changes to the codebase early and often, they are less likely to enter that dreaded state of merge hell, where every new code addition results in a slew of conflicts, and every bug fix seems to break something else.

The more frequently you can verify that the project still builds and functions correctly, the better your development team can work as a whole.

> **Note:** So what's this *extreme programming* stuff? Essentially, it's a software methodology spun off as a branch of agile programming. It's designed to improve software quality and the responsiveness to changing customer requirements by creating more frequent releases with shorter development cycles.
>
> The path to creating frequent releases is made possible through automation of build and validation processes, so that any changes that affect the project in a detrimental manner are detected early — and fixed long before they affect anyone else.
>
> To learn more about Extreme Programming, check out this page:
>
> http://en.wikipedia.org/wiki/Extreme_programming

Continuous integration can be defined in many ways, but it generally boils down to the following practices:

1. **Source Control**: Have somewhere to store your projects' code base that is accessible by all team members. Popular examples of source control systems include Git, Subversion, and Mercurial. To learn more about using source control in your projects, check out Chapter 12 and 13, "Beginning and Intermediate Source Control in Xcode 5."

2. **Automated Builds**: The process of building your project should be automated, stipulating that human intervention is not required to generate the product.

3. **Automated Tests**: When a build completes, all of your projects' unit and integration tests should be run. If any of the tests fail then the build is considered a failure. To learn more about adding unit tests to your projects, check out Chapter 11, "Unit Testing in Xcode 5."

4. **Build Every Commit**: Every commit should be considered guilty until proven innocent. A developer should be careful to make sure their commit works before submitting to the baseline project; if the commit breaks the build, then all subsequent commits cease until the build is fixed. This process ensures regressions are caught soon and are fixed quickly.

5. **Access to Builds**: The final product of the build, which in the case of iOS development is the `.ipa` archive, should be easily accessible to all team members.

This allows quality assurance teams and/or key stakeholders to have immediate access to builds without the development team as a proxy.

6. **Publishing Build Status**: Everyone on the team should be aware of the build's status. A large display in a development area can be used to keep everyone aware of what's going on, or notifications can be sent to the team when a build fails. Whatever the medium, this information should always be readily available to the team.

7. **Automated Deployment**: In a world run by App Stores, this generally pertains to internal or quality assurance builds. The App Store submission process *may* be a candidate for automation, but it's likely that you'll manually choose an `.ipa` archive from those produced by your build system to submit to the App Store.

The benefits of continuous integration to development teams are substantial: a simplified development workflow, a replicated target environment, centralized builds providing code metrics such as test status and code coverage, easy product deployment, and above all, more time to write beautiful code and add features to delight your customers. What more could you ask for?

OS X Server

To set up continuous integration for your Xcode projects, you need a machine running OS X Server.

Unlike what you might expect, OS X Server is not a separate version of OS X, or a specific type of Mac hardware. Instead, it's just an app you can download from the Mac App Store and run on any modern Mac to make it a server. If you have a spare Mac Mini lying around, this makes for a particularly good candidate.

And the best part – if you're a member of the iOS developer program, OS X Server is free! You can get a redemption code on the iOS Dev Center.

The OS X Server app for Mavericks provides far more than just continuous integration support. It includes many server components useful for Macs running on your network, such as:

• **Caching**: Automatically cache downloaded and updated software on the server, with the goal of offering faster downloads to all other Macs on the network.

• **Calendar**: Share calendars, schedule meetings, book conference rooms and coordinate events.

• **Contacts**: Share contacts and keep them in sync across all Mac's on your network.

- **File Sharing**: Share files on Mac, iOS, and Windows with full permissions and access control managements. You can also monitor access and make use of Spotlight integration so that users can quickly find content on the network.

- **Mail**: An E-Mail server compatible with many of the popular email clients on Mac, iOS, and Windows. Includes support for push notifications, virus detection and junk mail filtering.

- **Messages**: Private instant messaging, hosted within the confines of your own network.

- **Profile Manager**: Create profiles to aid setting up and configuring user devices. Profiles can be sent out over-the-air via Push Notifications, and users can also install profiles via a self-service web portal. Users can reset their passcodes and remotely lock or wipe their Mac and iOS devices.

- **Time Machine**: Your server can act as the designated Time Machine backup location for every Mac on your network. This centralizes backups and eliminates the need for a separate backup drive for each Mac.

- **VPN**: Enable offsite users secure access to your local network. One specific use case for VPN pertaining to this chapter is access to the continuous integration system by offsite or remote team members. Depending on your network configuration you may need to take extra steps in exposing your OS X Server to the public Internet before the configured VPN service can be accessed. Detailed information on configuring the VPN service can be found by clicking the "Learn about" arrow in the VPN section of Server.

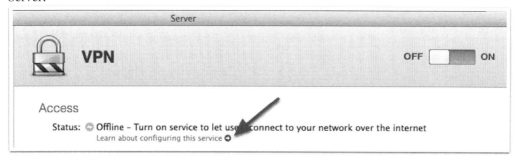

- **Websites**: Host website content with built-in support for PHP and Python web applications.

- **Wiki**: Host wiki powered websites where users can collaborate on the content.

- **Xcode Service:** Provide developer related services including bots and source control. The Xcode service is the focus of this chapter but it is also worth nothing that you can configure it to host Git repositories without the need to use bots.

You can think of running OS X Server as running your own mini iCloud, just for your network. And in true Apple fashion, many of these services are incredibly simple to enable, configure and begin using immediately.

Installing OS X Server

To install OS X Server, download the app from the Mac App Store. Once the installation process is complete, open **Server.app** from either your Applications folder or via Launchpad. You'll be presented with the following Server set up screen:

Click **Continue** to setup OS X Server locally; you'll be asked to accept the license agreement and then you'll be prompted to enter your system's administrative password. After that, you can sit in awe and watch the progress bar as Server is installed, or you can take a few minutes and do something fun.

As soon as setup completes, the app launches and presents the Server Tutorials window to you as seen below.

You may notice that there is an "Automate Xcode builds" section - you may want to glance through that tutorial if you are looking for a very brief introduction. Once you are done peeking at the Apple provided tutorials, close the window and you will land on the Server Overview shown below.

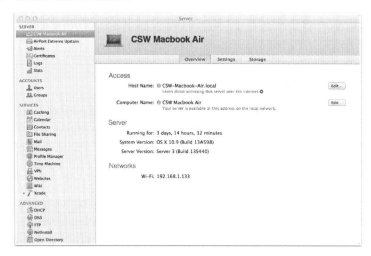

At this point you're ready to setup the Xcode service.

The Xcode Service

The Xcode service of OS X Server enables you to configure your server to perform development-related tasks. The service is only available in OS X Server for Mavericks, and requires that you have Xcode 5 installed. If you don't already have Xcode 5 installed on your OS X Server machine, it's as easy as searching for it on the Mac App Store and clicking Install.

The first step to enable the Xcode service is to select your Xcode installation. Locate the Xcode service in the Services group of the sidebar and click it, as so:

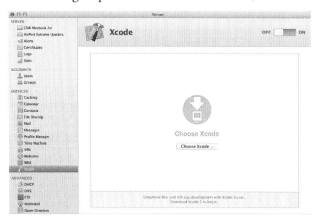

Click the button labeled **Choose Xcode...** and navigate to your Xcode installation, which is usually found in the **Applications** folder, as it is below:

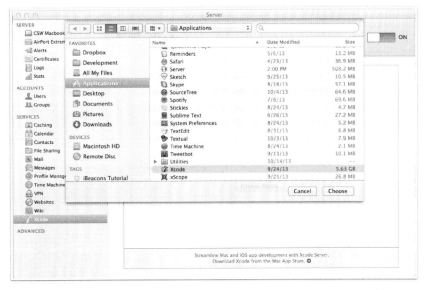

If you haven't previously launched Xcode on this machine, you may need to agree to a second license agreement and wait a short while for Xcode to finish its own setup process. Once that's done, the Xcode service settings are unveiled, as shown in the screenshot below:

On this screen you will find a switch at the top right to turn the service on and two tabs: **Settings** and **Repositories**. The **Settings** tab provides options to edit user level permissions of the bots that the service maintains, set which install of Xcode to use (same process as above), and add or remove Apple Developer teams. The last section is the device section where you can add devices to be used by bots when performing integrations. The **Repositories** tab is pictured below:

On this tab you are provided the options to add new repositories that the Xcode service is either hosting or is simply aware of.

Adding developer teams

Next you'll need to add a registered development team so that Server can add itself to your developer account and obtain its own a certificate signing request and necessary provisioning profiles. This is necessary being that bots will deploy apps to connected devices when running unit tests during integrations. In the **Builds** section on the right-hand pane click the **Add...** button and sign in with your developer account when prompted. If you belong to many teams, select the appropriate one to add; otherwise, a team will automatically be selected for you and you'll subsequently be asked if you want to add the server to your team, as shown in the screenshot below:

Choose **Add** to continue on.

OS X Server obtains new signing certificates for all App IDs belonging to the chosen teams. The server also adds itself as a team member on the developer portal; you can view added servers via a new Server tab in Member Center as shown below:

Adding devices

In order to be confident that your app works as designed, it's a good idea to run your test suite on physical devices rather than just on the simulator. Well, there's good news with that - continuous integration with OS X server has full support to run your test suite on physically connected devices automatically with each integration.

To add a device to the Xcode service you must first connect it to your Mac and choose "Trust" when prompted on your device. As soon as the system recognizes the device you should see it appear under the **Devices** section.

Once the device appears, click the corresponding **Add to Team** button and click the **Add** button to confirm you want to add the device to your team, a shown below:

> **Note:** If you've already added this device to your team in the iOS Provisioning Portal or in Xcode, you still need to complete this step.
>
> If the device has been previously added to your team this step will simply register the device with the Xcode service. Otherwise, it will register the device on the developer portal and consume one slot out of your one hundred available device slots.

The added device now appears in the **Devices** section of your Xcode server's settings screen along with the relevant team name. Every device that your Xcode server is aware of shows up here, regardless of which team it belongs to. That way, you can add several teams to the Xcode service and manage all devices and teams from this single settings pane.

> **Tip:** If you're curious about which provisioning profiles have been downloaded take a look in the following folder: **/Library/Server/Xcode/Data/ProvisioningProfiles**. Knowing they're stored in this location can also be helpful when trouble-shooting any issues, because provisioning and code signing *always* works flawlessly, right...*right?*

Starting the Xcode Service

The final step to enable your Xcode service is to start it. Simply toggle the large OFF/ON switch at the top right corner of the window. When the service has started (which may take about a minute) the status indicator changes from **Offline** to **Available on your local network at...** and the indicator turns green, as shown:

This section also gives you information about where the service is available and the name it's broadcasting on the network.

Xcode

Now that you have OS X Server and the Xcode service up and running, you need to tell Xcode about the service. Usually, you'll need to do this on the machines used by you and your team members. Best practices state that your continuous integration server should be a dedicated environment in order to provide a consistent, known, and reproducible environment where the software stack is built from the ground-up to avoid dependencies on local development machines.

However, it's entirely possible to setup a complete development environment on a single machine that runs the server app, but you do so at the risk of leaning too heavily on one single environment for your integration activities.

Adding OS X Server to accounts in Xcode

To add an OS X Server as an account in Xcode, launch Xcode and open the preferences window via the **Xcode/Preferences** menu item or via the **CMD+,** (command and comma) keyboard shortcut. Navigate to the Accounts pane, which is shown below:

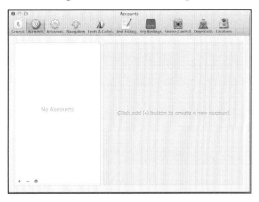

Click the **+** symbol in the bottom left corner of the window and choose **Add Server...** from the popup menu.

If your Xcode service is running and available on your local network, you should see it appear in the list as below:

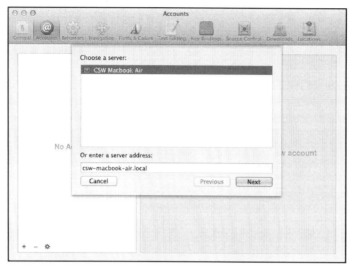

Select your server and choose **Next**; then enter the credentials for the server. Once you complete the authentication step, the server appears as an account entry, as shown below:

Alright, you've successfully connected to your OS X Server! Now you just need to set it up to do something interesting.

Bots

In order to instruct your OS X server to perform a specific task for a specific Xcode project scheme (like building a project or running unit tests), you create something called a **bot**. You can think of a bot as a little robotic servant who's happily performing tasks on your behalf in the background. Mwuahaha - feel the power!

Before you can create a bot, there are a few prerequisites you have to take care of. Here's what a bot requires:

1. OS X Server running on a local or remote machine.

2. A fully configured Xcode service.

3. The server added as an account in Xcode on your machine.

4. An Xcode project hosted in a repository the server has access to.

5. A shared Xcode scheme.

The good new is so far you've taken care of everything except setting up an Xcode project repository (step 4) and creating a shared Xcode scheme (step 5). Let's take care of that next.

Getting started

In this chapter, you will set up continuous integration for Reversi project you used in Chapter 11, "Unit Testing in Xcode 5." This project is an ideal candidate for continuous integration because it has unit tests ready to go.

In order to use the project, you need to host it in a repository. The easiest approach is to use Git with OS X Server since the necessary tools are already at your disposal.

The following steps will show you how to host the Reversi project on a git repository. However, to keep the focus on continuous integration this chapter will only provide a brief overview and assumes you have the Git command line tools installed and basic knowledge of Git. To learn more about Git and source control, check out Chapters 12-13, "Beginning and Intermediate Source Control in Xcode 5."

Initializing the Git Repository

The Reversi project can be found in the resources for this chapter. Open up Terminal.app and change to the project directory:

```
$ cd ~/Desktop/[REPLACE_WITH_PROJECT_NAME]/
```

Still in Terminal.app, enter the following command to initialize the Git repository:

```
$ git init
```

Commit the project files to the repository by typing the following commands:

```
$ git add .
$ git commit -m "Initial commit"
```

At this point you have a local repository created. Now you'll create a central repository for the code on your OS X server and push it there.

Adding a remote for the Git Repository

Exit Terminal.app and head back to Xcode to complete the remainder of the setup.

Open the project in Xcode; from the **Source Control** menu highlight the **ReversiGame** working copy and from the submenu select **Configure ReversiGame**. Select the **Remotes** tab from the configuration pane displayed, then press the **+** button. Choose **Create New Remote...** as shown:

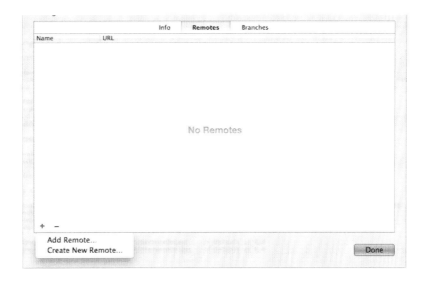

From the list, select the instance of OS X Server that you configured earlier. Set **Remote name** to **origin** and click **Create,** as below:

If you're presented with a confirmation alert, press **Confirm** to proceed with the setup, as so:

The remote now appears in the list of remotes in Xcode; you can now push your local repository to the remote to make it available to your bot. Click Done to close the configuration pane, then choose the **Source Control/Push...** menu item.

You'll see the remote listed with the master branch as **origin** in the drop down, as shown below:

Click **Push** to push your local changes to the remote; the pane will disappear once the process has completed.

A copy of your source code is now available both as a local working copy and as a remote copy on the server. Now your bot will have access to all of the files it needs to perform your build.

Creating the bot

Now comes the process of finally creating the bot itself. In Xcode, choose **Product/Create Bot...**; the **Create a new bot** dialog will be displayed like so:

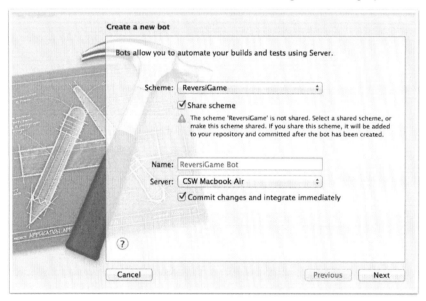

Ensure that the **ReversiGame** scheme is selected; Xcode will generate a name for your bot as the name of the scheme suffixed with **Bot**. You can change this if you like, but it's fine as-is. It is also required that the scheme be shared, a scheme contains important information about how to build the project and is needed by the bot, you will not be able to continue without sharing the selected scheme. Next, select your Xcode Server from the dropdown, and ensure that **Integrate immediately** is checked. When you've completed these changes, click **Next**. You'll be presented with the **Schedule bot integrations** screen, as shown below:

> **Note:** You may be prompted to authenticate in order to give access to your repository before seeing the following screen.

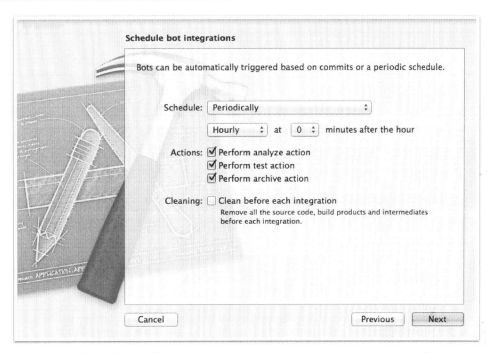

Here you can choose how often you want your bot to run, the actions it performs, and whether or not to perform a clean with each integration.

Schedule has three options: **On Commit**, **Periodically**, and **Manual**. On Commit tells your bot to run each time you push code changes to the remote server. Periodically is useful for regular processes, such as a nightly build, while Manual is ideal for bots that you want to run on demand, such as a release build.

Set the **Schedule** of your bot to **On Commit**.

You can also choose which actions to perform during each bot run:

• **Perform analyze action**: This tells the bot to run the static analyzer when it builds your project. You should run this with each integration task to catch memory leaks or other potential issues that aren't caught during the normal build process. You're likely familiar with the Analyze feature in Xcode; this just automates the task for you.

- **Perform test action**: This tells the bot to run your tests as part of your integration task; your bot can run these tests just as you run them manually in Xcode. It's critical to run these with each integration task to ensure regressions have not introduced.

- **Perform archive action**: This tells the bot to archive the build for later installation, distribution, or release. This option is best used with periodic or a manual bots since you don't want to generate an archive for each commit.

Since this bot will be performing a full integration build, check all three options.

The last option on the page is **Cleaning**. This simply instructs the bot to always clean its working directory before running the integration. Usually On Commit bots don't bother with performing a clean operation prior to a build since cleaning can be an expensive operation, and for each commit you're only really interested in whether the build succeeds and all tests pass. For any periodic and manual builds it's best to turn **Cleaning** on to ensure your builds are consistently created in a clean environment, instead of on top of whatever state the environment was from the last build.

However, check **Cleaned** for your bot so that you can see this option in action. Click **Next**, and you'll be taken to the **Choose a device...** screen, as below:

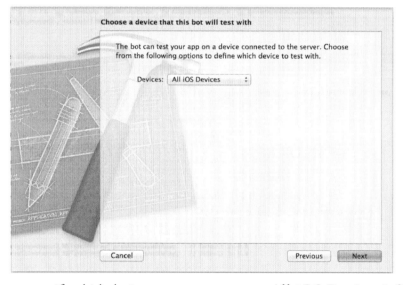

Here you can specify which devices to run your tests on. **All iOS Devices** informs the bot to perform the tests on all physically connected devices of which the Xcode Service is aware. You can also choose **All iOS Simulators** to instruct the bot to run on all available simulators. Otherwise you can choose **Specific Devices** and manually select the devices and/or simulators on which you'd like the bot to run tests.

Note: The integration will fail if a device was selected but not connected when the integration is run.

For this tutorial, choose **All iOS Devices** and click **Next**. You'll be taken to the very last setup screen for your bot: **Configure bot email notifications**, as shown below:

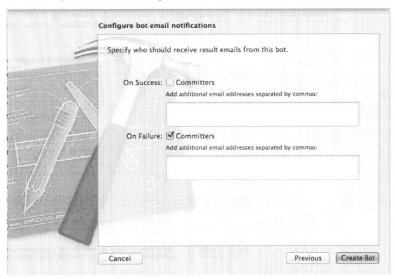

The options are pretty straightforward. The **On Success** option tells the bot to email the specified recipients when a build succeeds; the **On Failure** option instructs the bot to email people when the build fails. You can choose to send emails to only the **Committers;** that is, the authors of the commits made for this integration. The committer email addresses are obtained from the commit information if it is available. If you need to notify other people, you can specify a list of comma separated emails.

Generally, for a bot that runs On Commit, you want to send failure notifications to only the Committers; otherwise the inboxes of everyone on the project will fill up pretty quickly! Check **On Success** and **On Failure** and add your personal email address to the list. By default emails will be sent using the postfix server that is built in to OS X on your mac running OS X Server. If any custom settings are required you will need to enable the Mail service in OS X Server and configure it appropriately. For most users the default option is sufficient.

Be sure your test devices are connected to your remote server and click **Create Bot.** If your scheme was not already shared you will immediately be presented with a commit sheet to commit the Scheme to your repository, you must commit in order for the bot to be successfully created. Once the bot is created you'll be taken to the Summary view for

your bot and your integration will commence. While the integration is running you will
see an activity indicator along with the message "Integrating" in the Log Navigator of
Xcode as shown below:

Once the integration is complete, you'll see the results shown as below:

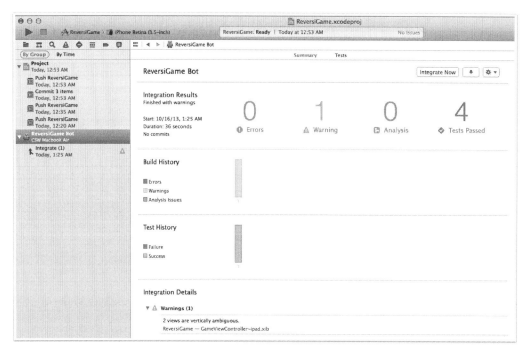

You've successfully created your first bot to perform one of the pillars of Continuous
Integration: integration builds on commit. This way, you'll know immediately if the
code you've added causes any problems. However, just because your code compiles
doesn't mean that it didn't break anything; well written unit tests will show you if you've
caused any untoward issues in the project.

To that end, you'll write a small unit test that fails, so that you can see how Xcode Server
responds when things don't go precisely as planned.

Triggering an integration

Open **ReversiBoardTests.m** and add the following test method that is guaranteed to
fail:

```
- (void)test_iLikeBreakingBuildsAndICannotLie
{
    XCTAssertTrue(false, @"The integration will fail");
}
```

Select **Source Control\Commit...** to commit your changes to the repository. Xcode will present you with the following commit dialog:

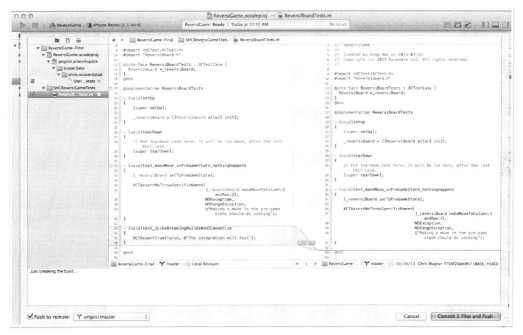

Uncheck all files except **ReversiBoardTests.m**, check the **Push to remote:** option in the bottom left corner of the window and ensure **origin/master** is selected in the dropdown. Enter a commit message, and click **Commit 1 File and Push**.

> **Note:** If you had other file changes you may wish to commit those, but for the purpose of this tutorial you only need to commit **ReversiBoardTests.m**

Switch to the **Log Navigator** by either typing **Cmd+8** or by clicking on the last icon in the navigator window. Keep an eye on your bot; after a few minutes you'll see it begin the integration. This is a good time to put your feet up and enjoy a frosty beverage while you wait. Once the integration is finished, you'll notice the red symbol indicating the build is broken.

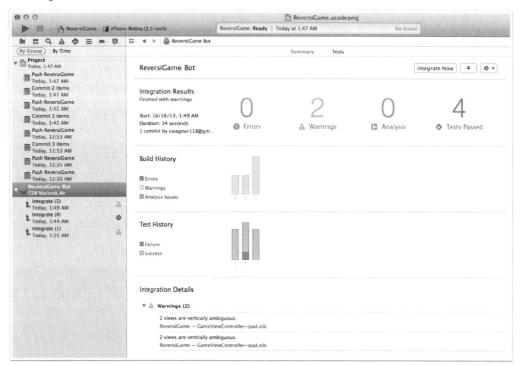

Every good developer knows that keeping the build server happy is paramount. Put down that frosty beverage and remove the failing test. Commit your changes, push them to the server, and you'll see another integration launch off. Once this integration finishes, you'll see the Summary view reports that the build passed, albeit with some warnings.

Where to go from here?

You've made it through the process of setting up OS X Server with the Xcode service, and you've successfully created a bot using Xcode. If you've never setup a continuous integration system then you may be thinking, "*That wasn't such a big deal, why is everyone freaking out about this?*"

Before continuous integration support with OS X server, it usually took several days to several weeks to get a continuous integration system up and running properly to fit the particular project and to work with all teams involved. If you've ever worked on building a continuous integration server in this manner, you'll understand immediately how Xcode Server and bots can make your life much, much easier. As well, the UI is much cleaner and streamlined compared to existing continuous integration software.

Now that you have the basics down, it's time to get serious and work with bots in detail. The next chapter deals with the following real-world integration concepts:

- The hardware you'll need to run a real continuous integration system

- The Log Navigator and bot information view in Xcode and web interface

- Displaying build status on a monitor for all to see

- Providing access to the latest builds of your app for QA and other internal teams

- Bot best practices from Apple

- Best practices from other continuous integration systems

- Making Xcode Schemes work for you

- Uploading builds automatically to TestFlight

- Uploading DSYM files automatically to Crashlytics

- Creating bots that build different branches of your project

It will be an action packed chapter — you should expect to learn a lot!

Challenges

There's just one challenge in this chapter – but it's a practical one if you're a GitHub fan!

Challenge 1: Integrating GitHub

1. You have learned how to create a bot with a repository hosted on your OS X Server. Now see if you can create a bot with a repository hosted on GitHub (http://github.com/).

   a. Hint 1: You need to create a GitHub account if you don't have one —they're free.

b. Hint 2: You need to either create a repository or fork an existing repository.

c. Hint 3: When you create a new Xcode project, use the option to create a local Git repository.

d. Hint 4: The Source Control menu in Xcode lets you add remotes to your local Git repository.

Good luck!

Chapter 15: Intermediate Continuous Integration in Xcode 5

By Chris Wagner

In the previous chapter you made a ton of progress – you've set up a system that ran the Xcode service on OS X Server, and created your first bot using Xcode to perform an automated build on every commit.

In this chapter, you'll take things even further and learn how to set up a real-world testing environment, set up a web-based scoreboard, automatically upload builds to TestFlight, and much more. Taking the time to set up a build environment like detailed in this chapter will pay huge dividends for you and your team in the long run!

In order to follow along with the tutorial in this chapter, you will have to have performed all of the steps in the previous chapter and have your project in the state where we left things off. However, if you're only interested in the theory and how-to then feel free to stick around. You'll be able to apply the topics covered to your existing projects as well. The requirement is that you have already setup OS X Server with the Xcode service, and know the basics of creating bots.

Hardware

If you followed through the setup of Xcode Server in the last chapter, you may have noticed that there wasn't any discussion of hardware requirements. This was intentional so that you could focus on the task at hand and not be distracted by what the ideal hardware setup looks like. However, to create a responsive and robust integration environment, you need to make sure it meets a few minimum specs.

The Mac

In order to run OS X Server your Mac must be capable of running OS X Mavericks; therefore it needs to fall into one of the following hardware classes:

- iMac (Mid-2007 or later)

- MacBook (Late 2008 Aluminum, or Early 2009 or newer)

- MacBook Pro (Mid/Late 2007 or newer)

- MacBook Air (Late 2008 or newer)

- Mac Mini (Early 2009 or newer)

- Mac Pro (Early 2008 or newer)

- Xserve (Early 2009)

- Have at least 2GB of RAM

- Have at least 10 GB of available disk space

An ideal setup for a server is usually a system that can be tucked away and left alone. Unfortunately, when Apple stopped making the Xserve hardware they left the market of rack-mounted servers altogether. The Mac mini is a great alternative for a server; there's even a version of the mini called **Mac mini with OS X Server** that's advertised as a server and comes with OS X Server pre-installed. At the time of writing, the server version of the Mac mini started at $999 and with additional configurations priced up to $1,999, as shown in the table below:

$999 Mac mini with Server	$1,999 Mac mini with Server
2.3Ghz Quad-Core Intel i7	2.6Ghz Quad-Core Intel i7
4GB 1600Mhz DDR3 SDRAM	16GB 1600Mhz DDR3 SDRAM
2x1TB Serial ATA Drive @ 5400RPM	2x256GB Solid State Drive

There's a happy medium in the non-server edition of the Mac mini; you get a memory boost over the introductory version of the Mac mini, but you'll take a hit on the drive hardware compared to the top-tier Mac mini, as illustrated below:

$1,149 Mac mini with Server

2.3Ghz Quad-Core Intel i7
8GB 1600Mhz DDR3 SDRAM
1TB Fusion Drive

This setup provides you with the best of both worlds: good performance at a reasonable price. The Fusion Drive automatically and dynamically moves frequently used files to Flash storage for quicker access, while infrequently used items move to the hard disk. As a result, you'll enjoy shorter startup times, and as the system learns how you work you'll see faster application launches and faster file access.

The best part? Fusion Drive manages all this automatically in the background, without any tweaking required on your part.

Your Mac hardware and configuration is ultimately dependent on your team's requirements, your budget, and the scale of projects that you work on. If you are a development shop writing many small projects that build quickly without a powerhouse system, you can likely get away with lower-end hardware. However, if your team works on large enterprise apps or games, you may benefit greatly from higher-end systems that can drastically reduce the time of your integration cycles.

The USB Hub

Connecting your test devices to your server seems simple enough; just get a USB hub with enough ports to cover the number of devices you intend to connect to it and you're done...right?

This setup is fine with iPhone and iPod Touch devices. However, the higher power requirements of the iPad will cause issues in a bare-bones configuration like this. iPads require greater amperage than is provided by most USB hubs; insufficient amperage means that your iPad may not charge while it's in use and plugged in.

A current generation Mac mini has 4 USB ports, which provides enough power to support four iPads; however, this leaves no USB ports for anything else. This might be sufficient for small development shops, but larger shops may want to test with multiple iPad hardware platforms running various versions of iOS. What to do?

If you're in this boat, then you'll need to check out the various USB hubs produced by a small number of vendors that meet these increased power requirements, such as **Cambrionix** - http://www.cambrionix.com. Always verify that the hub you're considering supports both charging and syncing, so that your bots can deploy apps while providing sufficient power to your plugged in devices. These types of USB hub aren't cheap, but it's a justifiable expense for any team that requires such a configuration.

The Display

Generally servers run as *headless* systems, meaning they run along happily without a connected monitor. For these types of server configurations, OS X Server provides remote access to permit remote management from other Macs. Setting up remote management is as easy as opening the **Sharing** options under **System Preferences** and turning **Remote Management** on. Once Remote Management is enabled you can use Remote Desktop (https://www.apple.com/remotedesktop/) to connect to your server. Depending on your network configuration you may need to take extra steps to ensure the route from your system to the server is unimpeded.

Headless systems work great for continuous integration servers as well, since the Xcode service provides a web interface for you to manage the Xcode installation on your server and monitor your bots.

You can view this web interface from any of the machines on your network, or you can set up an Apple TV and an oversized monitor can display this scoreboard to the entire development group using AirPlay. This keeps everyone informed of the current status of the integration build environment – and is a cool morale booster!

Reviewing and Managing Bots

Once you have a bot set up and running, you'll interact with it either in Xcode or through your web browser. Both are functionally equivalent; everything you can do in one interface, you can do in the other. Developers will likely spend most of their time interacting with bots using Xcode, whereas other members of the team such as QA or management are more likely to utilize the web interface to monitor build status.

> **Note:** The screenshots in the next section exist as examples only; your results will differ based on your own projects and how much you've been using bots to this point.

Xcode

Xcode's **Log Navigator** is the place to view information about your bots. It's found in the Navigators pane on the left side of the main Xcode window; you can hide or show or hide this pane using the **cmd+0** keyboard shortcut, or through the **View/Navigations/Show|Hide Navigator** menu item. Bot Summary View

Select a bot in the Log Navigator and you'll see the Summary page and its various sections, as shown below:

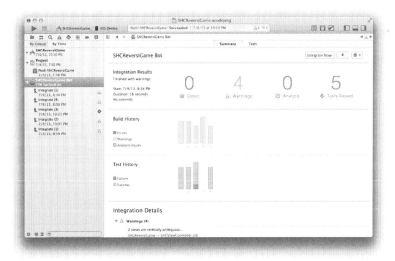

The title section displays the bot's name, and contains three buttons:

• **Integrate Now** — Manually kicks off this bot's integration task.

- **Download** — Downloads the Xcode archive file and .ipa of the most recent integration; this is only enabled when the last integration and archive task ran successfully.

- **Settings** — Displays a popup with three items: **Edit Bot**, where you can modify the bot's settings; **Delete Bot**, which deletes the bot from the OS X Server instance and from the Log Navigator in Xcode; and **View Bot in Browser,** which opens the bot's web interface.

Further down the page, the **Integration Results** section displays a brief summary of the most recent integration, as in the example below:

Here you can see the latest integration results and metrics. The summary section in this example indicates the integration task completed with warnings, shows the time, date, and duration of the integration task, and notes there were no commits as part of this task. The four key build indicators are displayed clearly on the right; in this example, the integration task completed with zero errors, four warnings, zero analysis issues and five tests passed.

The color of the indicator has meaning; it changes depending on the results of the latest integration, as shown in the image below:

These integration results show that one test failed during the run; as well, there was one commit performed as part of this integration.

The Build History section shows the running history of your project's integration runs. The colors and sizes of the stacked bars indicate the number of errors, warnings, and analysis issues encountered; however, if there were no integration issues then you'll see a simple green checkmark, as shown below:

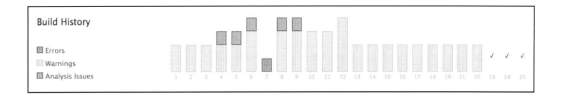

> **Note:** Build History only tracks errors, warnings and analysis issues, not tests. If a test fails during an integration run then the Build History will still show a green checkmark!
>
> So don't rely on the Build History alone to gauge the health of your build. Instead, you should look at the Test History section as well, as discussed below.

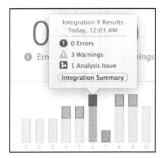

To see the exact number of errors, warnings, and analysis issues of an integration run, click on the relevant bar and you'll be shown a popup with the totals displayed. Click **Integration Summary** to jump straight to the integration's summary page for more detailed information on the build.

The **Test History** section shows a history of the relative number of test passes and test failures for your integrations, as demonstrated below:

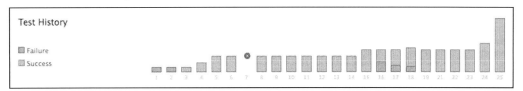

Just as in the **Build History** section, click on a specific bar to see more details about the test results, and click Integration Test Results to see a more detailed view of which tests passed and which failed, as shown on the next page:

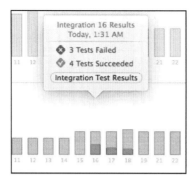

The **Test History** chart provides a good indicator of the health of your test suite. It also provides a measurement of the relative size of your test suite; generally the number of tests run should grow as the project goes on.

The **Integration Details** section provides detailed information on the issues encountered in your most recent integration, as in the example below:

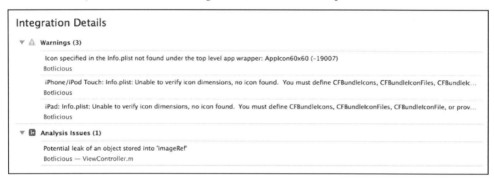

This section will only be populated if you have errors, warnings, analysis issues, or test failures from your last integration run. Often, you can double-click on the detail line to jump right to the offending line of code. How handy is that? Some issues listed here may not be code related however and therefore double-clicking on them has no action.

Bot Tests View

Click the **Tests** tab at the top of the screen. The first section displays the **Test History** chart that you're familiar with from the **Summary** pane, as below:

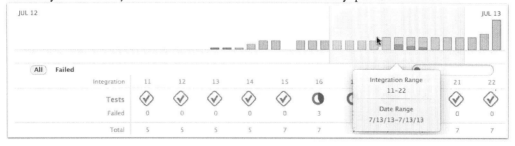

The highlighted grey area above is the **Integration Range** that is displayed below in more detail. Click and drag over the chart to set the integration range; the details of each integration run are displayed as such:

The Tests line shows whether all tests passed — indicated by a green checkmark — or whether some failed — indicated by a pie chart showing the proportion of tests that failed. The next two lines show you the number of failing tests and the total number of tests run respectively.

A tabular view below the Integration Range summary displays your integration runs in columns and your individual tests in rows, as shown below:

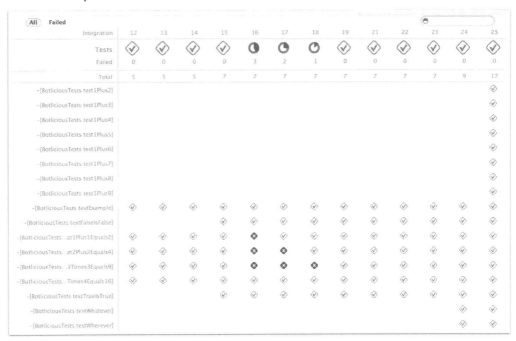

Red X's indicate failing tests, while green checkmarks indicate passing tests. A missing symbol indicates that the test didn't exist for that integration.

Filter the view by changing the scope selector at the top left from **All** to **Failed**; only tests that have failed in an integration run will be shown in the view, as shown on the next page:

When you have a lot of tests, this removes a significant amount of visual noise from the screen and lets you focus on the tests that have failed. You can also filter your test results by entering filter criteria in the search box on the top right. This filters your view to test names that match the search criteria as provided, like so:

To view a specific test, double-click on the test's row and Xcode will open the implementation of that test.

Double-clicking a column header lets you drill down into the test results related to that integration. This view shows you information about how the tests performed on each specific device in the integration run, as shown below:

In this example, you can see that all tests passed on the iPhone but one failed on the iPad.

In addition to **Tests**, there are three other tabs across the top of the screen:

Summary — similar to the bot summary view, except that it only shows information for the selected integration, minus the charts.

Commits — contains information about each commit included in this integration.

Logs — displays the same logs that you've seen in Xcode when you build your project. If you're getting obscure build failures and warnings, you'll want to check out the logs under this view.

Web Interface

As mentioned earlier, the web interface and Xcode interface for working with bots is nearly identical. In fact, the web interface boasts two excellent features that are absent in Xcode: the **Scoreboard,** and the ability to view all bots on your server besides those related to the open project.

Apple has provided not one, not two, but three different ways to access the web interface (which must be due to the fact it's so awesome that Apple wants to make it easy for you to get there):

2. Point your browser to http://{server-url}/xcode. ("server-url" may also be an IP address if you do not have a hostname or DNS configured for your network.)

3. Open Xcode, select a bot from the Log Navigator, then press the gear button and choose **View Bot in Browser**. You can also right-click on a bot in the Log Navigator and choose **View Bot in Browser.**

4. Open the OS X Server app, select the Xcode service on the Settings pane and click **View Bots** in the bottom left corner of the screen.

The landing page of the web interface displays a summary of the most recent integration, which integrations are queued, the latest downloads, and a list of all the bots on the server, as shown in the screenshot below:

The left hand side of the navigation bar at the top of the screen contains the Menu button along with a breadcrumb navigation trail. The right hand side of the navigation bar contains the **Scoreboard**, **Create Bot**, **Settings**, and **Logout** buttons.

Clicking on the name of a bot on the landing page takes you to the familiar summary view, as shown below:

The web version of the Summary page has almost all of the same information available in the Xcode interface. The main difference in the web version is that it lacks the handy Xcode-specific functions that let you jump straight to your code from the integration test results.

The scoreboard

Click the Scoreboard icon on the navigation bar (the first one on the right hand side) to see the Scoreboard in action, as shown:

You'll notice the scoreboard is a high contrast screen with only the most important information displayed. This is ideal for display in the development area of your shop, so that at a glance everyone can tell what's going on with the build. Access to Builds

Gone are the days where distributing interim builds for testing meant shipping them around manually or moving the distro to a secure shared location where other team members could retrieve it. The web interface displays the full list of integration products under the Archives tab, as shown below:

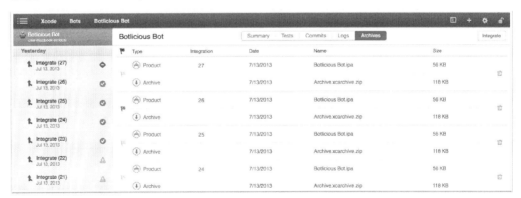

Now a team member only has to download the .ipa file in order to get their hands on the latest distribution. If they need the complete .xarchive, such as when submitting a release to the App Store, it's available as a compressed file. Automating distribution of interim or final releases means one more task taken off the plate of your development group!

Best practices for bots

Apple has given us a few best practices for building and working with bots in WWDC session 412 "Continuous Integration with Xcode 5". I'd put a fair bit of stock in what they have to say since they designed the technology!

Structure your code in workspaces

The first recommendation is to properly structure your code in Xcode workspaces. Why? Many apps have complicated source code structures where they pull in source code or frameworks from multiple sources and build any dependencies before building the app itself.

If you maintain a workspace that handles all of this for you, the Xcode service will have a much better chance of building your project successfully on the server without any intervention on your part.

To learn more about workspaces check out Apple's guide on the topic at https://developer.apple.com/library/ios/featuredarticles/XcodeConcepts/Concept-Workspace.html

Use role accounts for repositories

This one is more of a security best practice. Using role accounts for your remote repositories means you don't have to enter your personal repository credentials for OS X Server when checking out source code. You should create a specific role account for the server to provide access to your repositories. The process of creating specific accounts will vary based on what you use to host your repositories. If you are using OS X Server's repository feature you will need to manage User accounts on the server for anyone that needs access. If you use a provider such as GitHub you will need to create a new GitHub account for your server and be sure that account has access to your repositories.

In addition, favor SSH connections with private/public key pairs to HTTPS with username and password credentials. The pros of using SSH are the ease of set up whilst maintaining strong encryption and authentication. By default OS X supports the SSH protocol and enabling it is as simple as turning it on under the Settings tab for the server in question in Server.app or from the Sharing pane in System Preferences by checking "Remote Login" and choosing the allowed users. SSH is also efficient in that all data will be made as compact as possible before transferring.

Add must-have bots to every project

Apple recommends including a few specific bots to every one of your projects to facilitate your development workflow, and to disseminate information about your build results in a timely fashion.

- Always have an **On Commit** bot to build, test, and run the static analyzer on every commit. This provides the team with nearly real-time feedback about the project's health.

- Create a **Nightly Build** bot to build and archive your project every 24 hours. Testers can install this build each morning to keep in sync with development.

- Finally create an **On Commit** bot for every branch in your repository if you or your team use a branching workflow. This way you are assured that your branch work is solid before you merge it back with the main development line.

Best practices for release management

The following best practices are ones that have been established by different teams and online communities based on their experience.

Version Numbers

While there aren't any hard and fast rules about versioning your app throughout its lifecycle, **Semantic Versioning** (http://semver.org) is a good system that's understood by both developers and customers alike. The idea behind Semantic Versioning is that the version number is broken down into three parts, **Major**, **Minor**, and **Patch** and is presented as MAJOR.MINOR.PATCH.

- The **Major** version number should be incremented when the API of a framework changes or perhaps when a marketing team decides the product has seen enough enhancements to constitute a new Major version number.

- The **Minor** version number should be incremented when you add functionality that is backwards compatible or again, when a marketing team deems so.

- The **Patch** version number should be incremented when you make backwards-compatible bug fixes; the patch number is generally in full control of the development team.

The key thing is to choose a versioning system and be consistent in its application.

As well, all stakeholders should be in agreement as to changes in at least the major and minor release indicators. While Development might feel that a complete overhaul of the back-end of the app, moving to JSON from XML, and fixing that big list of bugs left over from iOS 5 constitutes a jump in the numbering from 1.7.1 to 2.0.0, Marketing may well see that nothing's changed in the GUI — which deserves no more than a jump to 1.8.0!

Your app versioning will likely be a manual process as designating a release as major, minor, or patch is a mostly subjective process. Just be sure that someone is responsible to maintain it — and to get agreement among stakeholders before bumping it.

Note: When your app passes the approval process of the App Store's review team, the version number is set in stone and cannot be re-used. However, you can opt to not release a specific version.

Build Numbers

Take a look at Xcode's build number by selecting **Xcode\About Xcode**; you'll see the following dialog:

The build number for the version shown in the screenshot is **5A11344j**. You may be asking yourself "*Why the heck would I ever want to know that?*" As a user of the product, you won't really need to know this — until the day you need support.

The version shown is a preview version of Xcode 5.0, but Apple releases several updates to Xcode before they're ready to release it to the general public. If Apple didn't maintain or advertise this build number, how in the world would a developer know the exact version they were using? Build numbers provide Apple with the exact revision of source code this release was built from, which allows them to track down and attempt to reproduce your reported issue with the specific release you're using.

> **Note:** In order to pinpoint the exact revision that a specific build was cut from you must note the build number or revision somewhere. In the case of using SVN you could very easily use the revision number of the repository as your build number. In the case of Git you might find the hash tags to be a little long to use as a build number. In this case you may choose to have an incrementing build number in the project and commit those changes with the build number as the commit message. You may also recall that your bots keep track of what commits were included in each integration, this is yet another way to track down the specific code that was used to cut a build.

The main difference between version numbers and build numbers is that the format of build numbers doesn't *really* matter. Yes, put your eyes back in their sockets. I'll say it again: it doesn't *really* matter. What *does* matter is that they are unique; they don't need to be sequential or carry any other significance. Theoretically you could even use *words* as build numbers, but the ideal case is to create a string composed of alphanumeric characters.

Since build numbers need to be unique and carry no specific meaning, it makes sense to let an unattended, automated process create them for you. Hm — automated, unattended processes sound a lot like using bots! :]

Maintaining build numbers with bots

Ideally the bots that perform your archive task should maintain your build numbers, since it's not important to increment the build number when you don't actually generate an archive or IPA as you will not be releasing anything to QA or a customer that needs to be referenced. To do this, you need to modify your build settings and add a new build phase that runs a script to create your build number.

Select your project in the **Project Navigator**. Make sure you're in the **target** settings, not the **project** settings, and select the **Build Settings** tab. Change the scope to **All** and search for *version*, as shown in the screenshot on the next page.

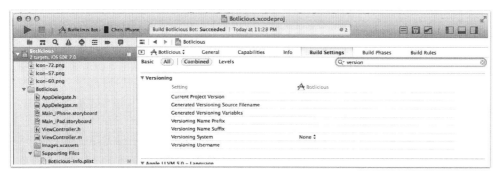

You should see a section called **Versioning**. Set the **Current Project Version** to 1 and change the **Versioning System** to **Apple Generic**.

Next, switch to the **Build Phases** tab as shown below:

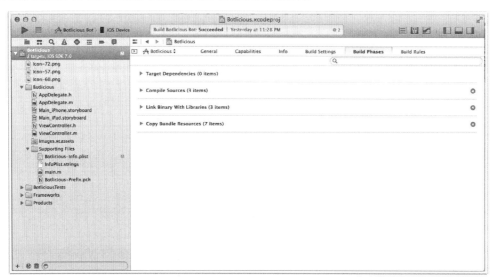

Select the **Editor/Add Build Phase/Add Run Script Build Phase** menu item, as so:

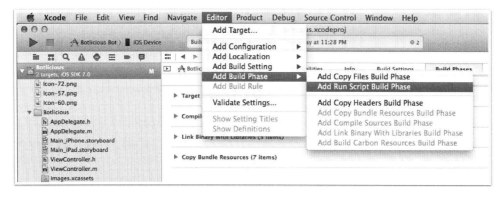

This adds a new Run Script section to the Build Phases pane, shown below:

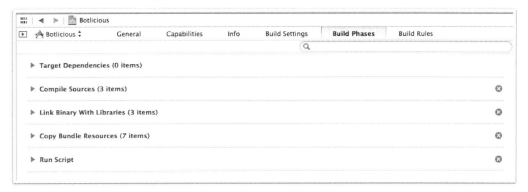

Your new script is there, but it's a little out of order. You want your build number generation task to occur before the copying of bundle resources, since your script will modify Info.plist. Click the **Run Script** phase and drag it above the **Copy Bundle Resources** phase; your build phase sequence should like the screenshot below:

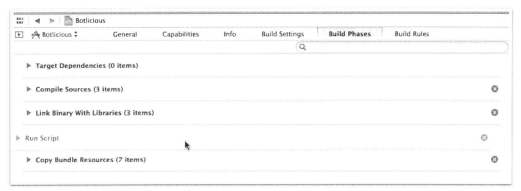

Double-click the **Run Script** phase and rename it **Bump Build Number**, like so:

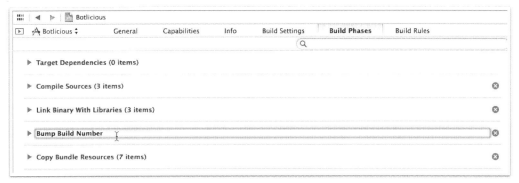

Expand the **Bump Build Number** phase to reveal the script editor, shown below:

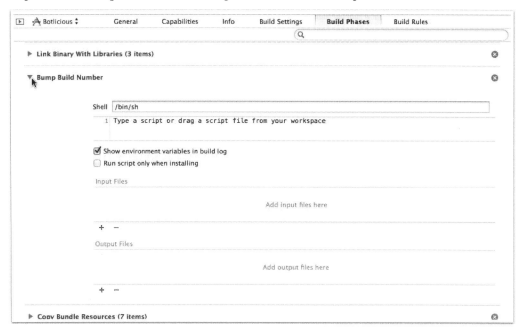

Replace the text `Type a script or drag a script file from your workspace` with the following script:

```
if [[ "$CONFIGURATION" == "Release" ]] &&
    [[ "$USER" == "_teamsserver" ]]
then
    echo "Bumping build number"
    agvtool bump -increment-minor-version
    NEW_BUILD_NUMBER=$(agvtool what-version -terse)
    /usr/libexec/Plistbuddy -c "Set CFBundleVersion
${NEW_BUILD_NUMBER}" ${PROJECT_DIR}/${INFOPLIST_FILE}
    git commit -a -m "Bump to build $NEW_BUILD_NUMBER"
    git config push.default simple
    git push
else
    echo "Setting build number to DEV"
    /usr/libexec/Plistbuddy -c "Set CFBundleVersion DEV"
${PROJECT_DIR}/${INFOPLIST_FILE}
fi
```

The script first checks to see if the Xcode configuration is set to **Release**; this is typical for Profile and Archive builds. It also checks that the user executing the script is **_teamsserver**. This is the account the Xcode service uses to perform its tasks. If both checks pass, it increments the build number using the `agvtool` command line tool, passing the parameters `bump` and `–increment-minor-version`.

> **Note:** `agvtool` (AppleGenericVersioningTool) is a command line tool that comes standard with the Apple Developer tools. It provides an interface to common operations for Xcode projects that use the Apple Generic Versioning system. You can find the manpage at https://developer.apple.com/library/mac/documentation/Darwin/Reference/Man Pages/man1/agvtool.1.html

The script then asks `agvtool` for the new build number and uses the `Plistbuddy` command line tool to modify the **Info.plist** file for the project, which sets the `CFBundleVersion` key to the new build number. Finally, it calls `git` to commit these modifications to the repository.

> Note: `Plistbuddy` is yet another command line tool that comes with the standard Apple developer toolset. This tool provides a command line interface for reading and writing `plist` files. It's manpage can be found at https://developer.apple.com/library/mac/documentation/Darwin/Reference/Man Pages/man8/PlistBuddy.8.html

If the build isn't using the **Release** configuration or is not being run by a bot, the script simply sets the build number to **DEV**.

You might be wondering why you set the build number to **DEV** for non-Release configurations. During app development, you're bound to experience crashes when running integrations. Setting the build number to **DEV** makes it easy filter out these crashes as a natural result of development. This also makes it obvious if a developer creates an archive manually, since there won't be a build number assigned.

> **Note:** The script provided in this example is a very basic way to manage your build numbers. You may want to develop a more sophisticated, custom script that meets your requirements. This script is by no means the definitive way to manage your build numbers, but it should give you a solid foundation to build on.
>
> **As well, this script shouldn't be used with any On Commit bots;** this will result in an infinite loop of integrations, since this script itself performs a

commit to the repository, which will trigger the On Commit bot — when this happens, it's turtles all the way down. You can regulate the script's execution by using configurations not named "Release" for **On Commit** bots so that the preconditions fail and set the build number to DEV. You could also change the preconditions to match a different configuration name.

Be stingy with distribution certificates and profiles

Once your bots are regularly creating archives and .ipa files, there's really no reason for any developer to manually create local builds for distribution. When at all possible, limit access to distribution certificates and distribution provisioning profiles. Restricting access to the distribution certificates and profiles will reduce any urge for developers to create adhoc builds that circumvent the defined build process. Even if you're the sole developer, you should opt to keep the distribution credentials on the bot server instead of your local development system.

There are always exceptions to any rule; for example, if you're debugging an issue with your builds or bot setup, you may find it's easier to do it locally as compared to on the server. Just be sure to remove the resources and retain the Xcode Archive in a secure place once you've solved the issues.

Only distribute bot-created builds

Disseminating manually-created builds really renders your whole continuous integration environment moot. When you distribute builds created from your local development machine, you're wasting the efforts you put into creating the bots in the first place. The more you rely on the bots, the easier your life will be and you'll find yourself with fewer tedious tasks on your plate. At first it may feel like the bots just add overhead but you'll soon find they become indispensible. The bots will guarantee a consistent and predictable output whereas each individual developer system may vary and produce a faulty build.

Automatically Upload to TestFlight

Although the Xcode service provides an excellent web interface to distribute your builds, it may still be desirable to use a beta distribution service such as **TestFlight** - http://www.testflightapp.com. Your bots can upload builds to TestFlight using Xcode Schemes and the TestFlight Upload API - https://testflightapp.com/api/doc.

In order to proceed with this section, you must already have a TestFlight account, and at least one registered device registered to verify things are working properly.

> **Note:** The steps involved in creating a TestFlight account and registering a device are beyond the scope of this chapter. However, they are both relatively straightforward operations; if you do run into problems TestFlight has a great support portal at http://help.testflightapp.com.

Setting Up TestFlight

Sign in to TestFlight; from the drop-down menu on the right-hand side of the screen select **+ Add Team.** You'll be presented with the following dialog:

Enter a team name and click **Save.**

Scroll to the very bottom of the next screen; Click **API** from the **Developer** section of the menu. Read through the information presented on this page, then click the **Get your API token** link as shown in the screenshot below:

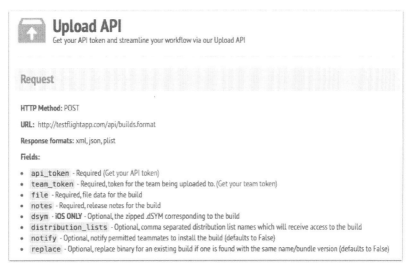

You'll see your token displayed as in the screenshot below; copy and store your API token so that you'll have it available for later.

Then go back to the **Team Info** page and click **Get your team token**, as below:

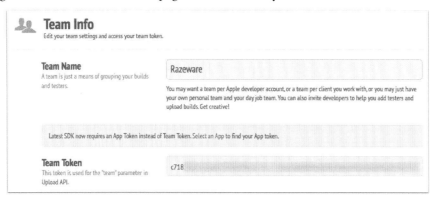

Copy and safely store your Team token somewhere. Now that you have your tokens, you'll need to create a distribution list so that your bot can grant permissions to the builds it uploads.

Select the **People** tab and press the **Add Distribution List** button, as shown below:

Enter **Everyone** as the **List Name**, select all the users you wish to include in this list and press **Save**, as so:

That's it for TestFlight. Now you just need to configure your Xcode Scheme to upload the .ipa file directly to TestFlight upon Archive.

Setup Xcode Scheme

Open your Xcode project and edit the scheme your bot uses to create the builds you want uploaded to TestFlight, as shown below:

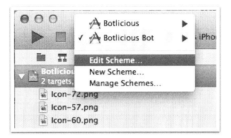

Expand the **Archive** task on the left, select **Post-actions**, and press the + button at the bottom of the pane. Choose **New Run Script Action** from the popup menu as shown below; this instructs Xcode to run a script on completion of the **Archive** task.

Use the **Provide build settings from** droplist to select your target, then paste the script below into the script editor:

```
API_TOKEN="YOUR_API_TOKEN"
TEAM_TOKEN="YOUR_TEAM_TOKEN"

xcrun -sdk iphoneos PackageApplication
"$ARCHIVE_PRODUCTS_PATH/$INSTALL_PATH/$WRAPPER_NAME" -o
"/tmp/${PRODUCT_NAME}.ipa"

echo "Uploading to TestFlight"

/usr/bin/curl "http://testflightapp.com/api/builds.json" \
-F file=@"/tmp/${PRODUCT_NAME}.ipa" \
-F api_token="${API_TOKEN}" \
-F team_token="${TEAM_TOKEN}" \
-F distribution_lists="Everyone" \
-F notes="Build uploaded automatically from Xcode."

echo "Uploaded to TestFlight"

#clean up ipa in tmp folder
/bin/rm -f "/tmp/${PRODUCT_NAME}.ipa"
```

Replace YOUR_API_TOKEN and YOUR_TEAM_TOKEN with their real-world counterparts that you safely stowed away earlier in this section. (You did save them somewhere you can find them...right?)

The script above performs the following actions:

1. Use the xcrun command line tool to generate an .ipa file from the Xcode Archive and place the .ipa file in the /tmp directory.

2. Use the curl command line tool to upload the .ipa file to TestFlight.

3. Delete the .ipa file from the /tmp directory.

Note that this script is executed every time the Archive task completes for this scheme. The Archive task should rarely, if ever, be run from a development system; your bots should be taking care of this task in a properly designed continuous integration environment. It's a good idea to have a separate scheme for tasks like this that is reserved exclusively for use by your bots.

To test the script, select the **Product\Archive** menu item in Xcode. Once the build finishes go back to TestFlight in your browser and view the **Apps** tab, where you'll see that your archive was uploaded, as so:

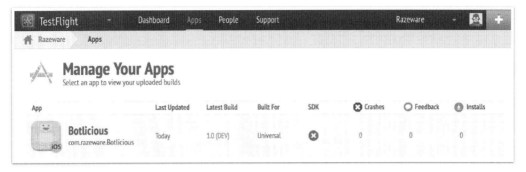

If you used the build numbering script from earlier you'll notice the build is labeled as **1.0 (DEV)**. This is a great indicator that a developer uploaded the build from their system directly.

Now, commit your changes to the repository and kick off an integration for the bot that uses the scheme you just configured. When the integration finishes, go back to TestFlight and you'll see the .ipa uploaded by your bot, in the screenshot below you will see that version 1.0 build 27 was uploaded.

Automatically Upload dSYM to Crashlytics

dSYM files are used to store the debug symbols for your app, and can be used to symbolicate your crash reports using services such as Crashlytics - http://crashlytics.com. When Crashlytics receives a crash report from a device, it automatically uses the uploaded dSYM files to symbolicate the report which lets you view the full stack trace for each thread running at the time of the crash and determine exactly which line, in which method, in which class, caused the crash.

Note: Setting up Crashlytics is beyond the scope of this chapter but thankfully the kind folks at Crashlytics have made it dead simple to integrate in your project. Check out http://try.crashlytics.com if you don't already have a Crashlytics account.

Open a project that's integrated the Crashlytics framework. Navigate to the **Build Settings** of your target and open the **Run Script** phase you added as part of the Crashlytics setup process; you'll see the following dialog:

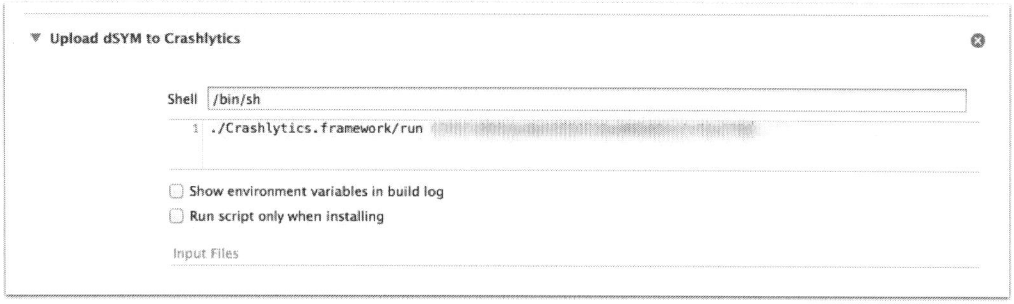

Modify the script above so that the dSYM upload is only performed when a bot runs the build and when the configuration is set to **Release,** as shown below:

```
if [[ "$CONFIGURATION" == "Release" ]] &&
    [[ "$USER" == "_teamsserver" ]]
then
    echo "Uploading dSYM to Crashlytics"
    ./Crashlytics.framework/run YOUR_UNIQUE_API_KEY
fi
```

Note: You must install the Xcode Crashlytics plugin on the server so that the dSYM upload can take place when your bot executes the run script in the Crashlytics framework.

To verify that the dSYM for your build was actually uploaded you can reference the Crashlytics website by navigating to your App, choose **Settings** and then **App,** a new window will appear where you will find a **Versions** tab, you can then expand the app version to reveal what builds Crashylytics has dSYM files for as shown below.

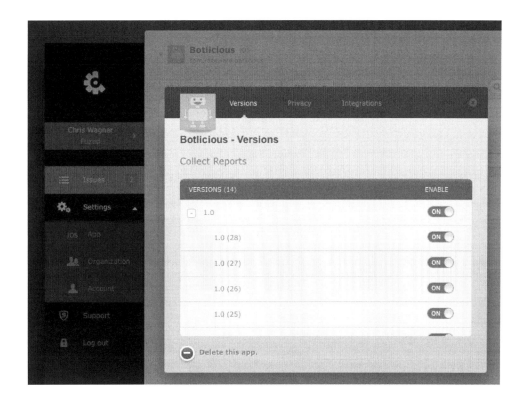

Some Things to Consider

While the new bots offering from Apple is fantastic, it is new technology and most importantly is limited to iOS and OS X development. If your development shop develops for other platforms like Android or Windows Phone it may not make sense to run an OS X Server with bots. You may prefer to have a single continuous integration system like Jenkins or Bamboo to orchestrate the builds for all of your platforms. And while Apple is known for releasing solid version 1.0 products, there is something to be said about mature systems when it comes to features, flexibility and community support. Always use the right tool for the right job.

Where to go from here?

Now that you've successfully completed this chapter you should have an excellent understanding of continuous integration systems and Xcode bots.

Continuous integration is a practice, not a set of rules; you'll find that each team and project you work with will have varying requirements. Some of the real-world scenarios you'll run into may include the following:

- How would you configure the OS X Server to support people in different parts of the world?

- How would you configure your Xcode workspace to properly load dependencies with CocoaPods?

- How do you ensure your bots clone all of the required sub-modules when using Git?

These are all very likely scenarios that have several different, yet equally valid solutions. As the development community starts to embrace bots and the Xcode service, some very elegant and powerful workflows are likely to emerge. Keep your ear to the ground as you develop, maintain and scale your own continuous integration environments!

Challenge

Your challenge for this chapter is to configure two bots that build two different branches of the same project hosted in a Git repository.

For example, take the example of a "master" branch that contains the most stable set of code, and a "development" branch that contains the latest, greatest, most bleeding-edge code from your developers that will later be validated and merged into the "master" branch. You'll need two bots, one to build against the "master" branch, and another to build against the "development" branch.

Hints:

1. You will need a Git repository that has two branches.

2. You will need one bot for each branch.

3. Creating a bot takes the current working branch as the one to be used by the bot.

Section III: Major New Features

In this section, you'll learn about the biggest and most important new features and frameworks in iOS 7 not already covered in this book. For example, you'll learn about a new way to write networking code, a new way to keep your app's data up to date, and much more.

Chapter 16: Networking with NSURLSession

Chapter 17: Beginning Multitasking

Chapter 18: Intermediate Multitasking

Chapter 19: JavaScript Core Framework

Chapter 20: AirDrop

Chapter 21: Peer-to-Peer Connectivity

Chapter 16: Networking with NSURLSession

By Charlie Fulton

Each new iOS release contains some terrific new networking APIs, and iOS 7 is no exception. In iOS 7, Apple has introduced NSURLSession, which is a suite of classes that replaces `NSURLConnection` as the preferred method of networking.

Why should you use `NSURLSession`? Well, it brings you a number of new advantages and benefits:

- **Background uploads and downloads**: With just a configuration option when the `NSURLSession` is created, you get all the benefits of background networking. This helps with battery life, supports UIKit multitasking and uses the same delegate model as in-process transfers. In the next chapter you will be creating an awesome application using this feature.

- **Ability to pause and resume networking operations**: As you will see later, with the `NSURLSession` API any networking task can be paused, stopped, and restarted. No `NSOperation` sub-classing necessary.

- **Configurable container**: Each `NSURLSession` is the configurable container for putting requests into. For example, if you need to set an HTTP header option you will only need to do this once and each request in the session will have the same configuration.

- **Subclassable and private storage**: `NSURLSession` is subclassable and you can configure a session to use private storage on a per session basis. This allows you to have private storage objects outside of the global state.

- **Improved authentication handling**: Authentication is done on a specific connection basis. When using `NSURLConnection` if an authentication challenge was issued, the challenge would come back for an arbitrary request, you wouldn't know exactly what request was getting the challenge. With `NSURLSession`, the delegate handles authentication.

- **Rich delegate model**: `NSURLConnection` has some asynchronous block based methods, however a delegate cannot be used with them. When the request is made it either works or fails, even if authentication was needed. With `NSURLSession` you can have a hybrid approach, use the asynchronous block based methods and also setup a delegate to handle authentication.

- **Uploads and downloads through the file system**: This encourages the separation of the data (file contents) from the metadata (the URL and settings).

NSURLSession vs NSURLConnection

"Wow, NSURLSession sounds complicated!", you might think.

Don't worry – using `NSURLSession` is just as easy as using its predecessor `NSURLConnection` for simple tasks. For an example, let's take a look at making a simple network call to get JSON for the latest weather in London.

Assume you have this `NSString` for constructing the `NSURL`:

```
NSString *londonWeatherUrl =
  @"http://api.openweathermap.org/data/2.5/weather?q=London,uk";
```

First here is how you make this call when using `NSURLConnection`:

```
NSURLRequest *request = [NSURLRequest requestWithURL:
[NSURL URLWithString:londonWeatherUrl]];

[NSURLConnection sendAsynchronousRequest:request
   queue:[NSOperationQueue mainQueue]
   completionHandler:^(NSURLResponse *response,
                       NSData *data,
                       NSError *connectionError) {
     // handle response
}];
```

Now let's use `NSURLSession`. Note that this is the simplest way to make a quick call using `NSURLSession`. Later in the chapter you will see how to configure the session and setup other features like delegation.

```
NSURLSession *session = [NSURLSession sharedSession];
```

```
[[session dataTaskWithURL:[NSURL URLWithString:londonWeatherUrl]
        completionHandler:^(NSData *data,
                            NSURLResponse *response,
                            NSError *error) {
        // handle response

}] resume];
```

Notice that you do not need to specify what queue you are running on. Unless you specify otherwise, the calls will be made on a background thread. It might be hard to notice a difference between these two, which is by design. Apple mentions that the `dataTaskWithURL` is intended to replace `sendAsynchronousRequest` in `NSURLConnection`.

So basically – `NSURLSession` is just as easy to use as `NSURLConnection` for simple tasks, and has a rich extra set of functionality when you need it.

NSURLConnection vs AFNetworking

No talk of networking code is complete without mentioning the `AFNetworking` framework. This is one of the most popular frameworks available for iOS / OS X, created by the brilliant Mattt Thompson.

> **Note:** To learn more about AFNetworking, checkout the github page found at: https://github.com/AFNetworking/AFNetworking. Also we have a tutorial for that:
>
> http://www.raywenderlich.com/30445/afnetworking-crash-course

Here is what the code for the same data task would look like using `AFNetworking 1.x`:

```
NSURLRequest *request = [NSURLRequest requestWithURL:
                            [NSURL
URLWithString:londonWeatherUrl]];

AFJSONRequestOperation *operation =
[AFJSONRequestOperation JSONRequestOperationWithRequest:request
    success:^(NSURLRequest *request,
            NSHTTPURLResponse *response,
```

```
              id JSON) {
    // handle response
} failure:nil];
[operation start];
```

One of the benefits of using `AFNetworking` is the data type classes for handling response data. Using `AFJSONRequestOperation` (or the similar classes for `XML` and `plist`) the success block has already parsed the response and returns the data for you. With `NSURLSession` you receive `NSData` back in the completion handler, so you would need to convert the `NSData` into `JSON` or other formats.

> **Note:** You can easily convert `NSData` into JSON using the `NSJSONSerialization` class introduced in iOS 5. To learn more, check out Chapter 23 of *iOS 5 by Tutorials*, "Working with JSON".

So you might be wondering if you should use `AFNetworking` or just stick with `NSURLSession`.

I think that for simple needs it's best to stick with `NSURLSession` – this avoids introducing an unnecessary third party dependency into your project. Also, with the new delegates, configuration, and task based API a lot of the "missing features" that AFNetworking added are now included.

However, if you would like to use some of the new 2.0 features found in AFNetworking like serialization and further `UIKit` integration (in addition to the `UIImageView` category) then it would be hard to argue against using it!

> **Note:** In the 2.0 branch of AFNetworking, they have converted over to using `NSURLSession`. See this post for more information:
>
> https://github.com/AFNetworking/AFNetworking/wiki/AFNetworking-2.0-Migration-Guide

Introducing Byte Club

In this chapter you'll explore this new API by building a notes and picture-sharing app on top of the Dropbox Core API for a top secret organization named Byte Club.

So consider this chapter your official invitation to Byte Club! What's the first rule of Byte Club you might ask? No one talks about Byte Club — except for those cool enough to have purchased this book. And definitely not those Android users; they're banned for life. :]

Head on in to the next section to get started building the app that will serve as your initiation into Byte Club.

Note that this chapter assumes you have some basic familiarity with networking in previous versions if iOS. It's helpful if you've used APIs like NSURLConnection or NSURLSession in the past. If you're completely new to networking in iOS, you should check out our iOS Apprentice series for beginner developers before continuing with this chapter.

Getting started

Byte Club is an exclusive group of iOS developers that joins together to perform coding challenges. Since each member works remotely on these challenges from across the world, members also find it fun to share panoramic photos of their "battle stations".

Here's a panoramic photo of Ray's office setup, for example:

Note: You might want to create your own panoramic photo of your office – it's fun, and it will come in handy later in this chapter.

In iOS 7, you can take a panoramic photo by opening **Photos** and selecting the tab named **Pano**.

If you like the results, you can set it as the wallpaper for your lock screen by opening **Settings** and selecting **Brightness & Wallpaper \ Choose Wallpaper \ My Panoramas**.

And of course – Byte Club has its own app to make this all happen. You can use the app to create coding challenges or share panoramic photos with other members. Behind the scenes, this is implemented with networking – specifically, by sharing files with the Dropbox API.

Starter project overview

The resources for this chapter include a starter project named Byte Club which includes the UI pre-made for you, so you can focus on the networking part of the app in this chapter. The starter project also includes some code to handle Dropbox authentication, which you'll learn more about later on.

Open up the project in Xcode and run it up on your device or simulator. You should see a screen like this:

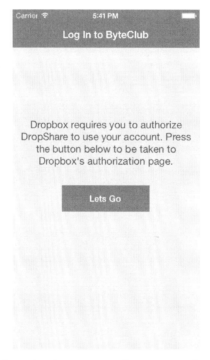

However, you won't be able to log in yet – you have to configure the app first, which you'll do in a bit.

Next open **Main.storyboard** and take a look at the overall design of the app:

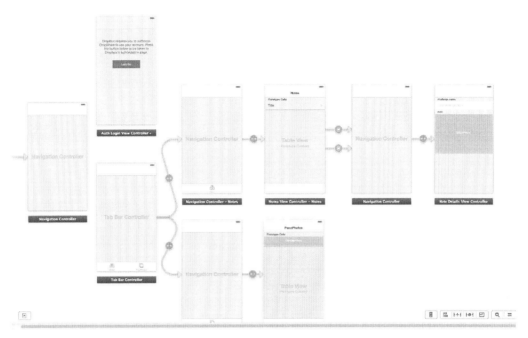

This is a basic `TabBarController` app with two tabs: one for code challenges, and one for panoramic photos. There's also a step beforehand that logs the user in to the app. You'll set up the login after you create your Dropbox Platform App below.

Feel free to look through the rest of the app and get familiar with what's there so far. You'll notice that other than the authorization component, there's no networking code to retrieve code challenges or panoramic photos – that's your job!

Creating a new Dropbox Platform app

To get started with your Dropbox App, open the Dropbox App Console located at
https://www.dropbox.com/developers/apps

Sign in if you have a Dropbox account, but if not, no sweat: just create a free Dropbox account. If this is your first time using the Dropbox API, you'll need to agree to the Dropbox terms and conditions.

After the legal stuff is out of the way, choose the **Create App** option. You'll be presented with a series of questions – provide the following responses.

- What type of app do you want to create?

    o   Choose: **Dropbox API app**

- What type of data does your app need to store on Dropbox?

  o   Choose: **Files and Datastore**

- Can your app be limited to its own, private folder?

  o   Choose: **No – My App needs access to files already on Dropbox**

- What type of files does your app need access to?

  o   Choose: **All File Types**

Finally, provide a name for your app, it doesn't matter what you choose as long as it's unique. Dropbox will let you know if you've chosen a name that's already in use. Your screen should look similar to the following:

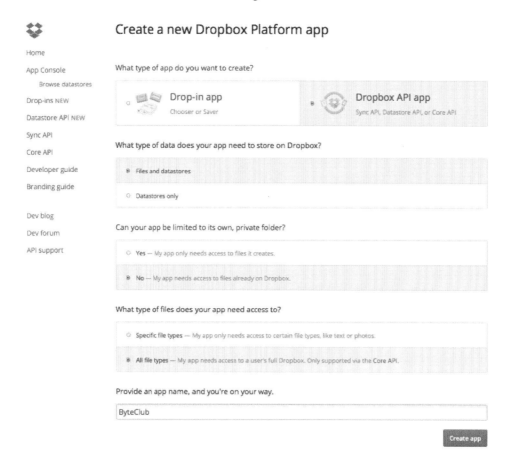

Click **Create App** and you're on your way!

The next screen you'll see displays the screen containing the **App key** and **App secret**:

Don't close this screen yet; you'll need the App Key and App Secret for the next step.

Open Dropbox.**m** and find the following lines:

```
#warning INSERT YOUR OWN API KEY and SECRET HERE
static NSString *apiKey = @"YOUR_KEY";
static NSString *appSecret = @"YOUR_SECRET";
```

Fill in your app key and secret, and delete the `#warning` line. You can close the Dropbox Web App page at this point.

Next, create a folder in the root directory of your main Dropbox folder and name it whatever you wish. If you share this folder with other Dropbox users and send them a build of the Byte Club app, they will be able to create notes and upload photos for all to see.

Find the following lines in Dropbox.m:

```
#warning THIS FOLDER MUST BE CREATED AT THE TOP LEVEL OF YOUR
DROPBOX FOLDER, you can then share this folder with others
NSString * const appFolder = @"byteclub";
```

Change the string value to the name of the Dropbox folder you created and delete the `#warning` pragma.

To distribute this app to other users and give them access tokens, you will need to turn on the "Enable additional users" setting for your Dropbox Platform App.

Go to the Dropbox app console at https://www.dropbox.com/developers/apps. Click on your app name, and then click the **Enable Additional Users** button. A dialog will appear stating that you have increased your user limit. Click **Okay** on the dialog to clear it. Your app page will now look like the following:

ByteClub

Settings	Details		
Status	Development		Apply for production
Development users	0 / 100		Unlink all users

> **Note:** You may notice that while you're developing your app, you can give access to up to 100 users. When you're ready to release your app for real, you have to apply for production status, which you can do by clicking the **Apply for production** button and sending Dropbox some additional information.
>
> Dropbox will then review your app to make sure it complies with their guidelines, and if all goes well they will then open your app's API access to unlimited users.

Dropbox authentication: an overview

Before your app can use the Dropbox API, you need to authenticate the user. In Dropbox, this is done by OAuth – a popular open source protocol that allows secure authorization.

The focus of this chapter is on networking, not OAuth, so I have already created a small API in Dropbox.m that handles most of this for you.

If you've ever used a third party twitter client app, like TweetBot, then you'll be familiar with the OAuth setup process from a user's perspective. The OAuth process is pretty much the same for your app.

Build and run your app, and follow the steps to log in. You will see a blank screen with two tabs, one for **Notes** and one for **PanoPhotos**, as shown:

OAuth authentication happens in three high level steps:

1. Obtain an OAuth request token to be used for the rest of the authentication process. This is the request token.

2. A web page is presented to the user through their web browser. Without the user's authorization in this step, it isn't possible for your application to obtain an access token from step 3.

3. After step 2 is complete, the application calls a web service to exchange the temporary request token (from step1) for a permanent access token, which is stored in the app.

If you're curious how this authentication step works, feel free to continue reading, where you'll learn more details about how this works. But if you want to dive right into NSURLSession, skip to the next section.

Dropbox authentication: the details

The starter project has also been set up to handle the OAuth authentication flow using PLAINTEXT OAuth authorization over https.

Here's a quick overview of how this works. In the App Delegate's application:didFinishLaunchingWithOptions:, the app checks to see if NSUserDefaults has a valid access token for the user (received from a previous successful login). If there is no token, then the app takes the following steps:

1. Displays the OAuthLoginViewController to ask the user to start logging in to DropBox (shown on next page).

2. Once the user taps the **Lets Go** button, `getOAuthRequestToken` in **OAuthLoginViewController.m** is called. This opens Safari with a special URL that starts the OAuth authentication process.

3. Once the user logs in, tap **Allow** to login to Dropbox and authorize Byte Club to access your account — don't worry, there's nothing malicious in the Byte Club app!

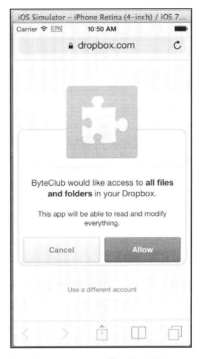

4. Upon authorization, the Dropbox server calls the URL provided by the client. In **OAuthLoginViewController.m** the starter app sends in the URL to call with the **oauth_callback** query parameter.

```
NSString *authorizationURLWithParams =
[NSString stringWithFormat:
@"https://www.dropbox.com/1/oauth/authorize?oauth_token=%@&oauth
_callback=byteclub://userauthorization",
  oauthDict[oauthTokenKey]];
```

5. The starter project is already set to handle this URL scheme:

6. Because of this, the app is launched and performs the final call to exchange the request token for a real user access token and secret. You can find this code in **AppDelegate.m**'s `exchangeRequestTokenForAccessToken` method.

After the initial login, the access token and secret are stored in `NSUserDefaults`. In a real app you would probably want to store this in the keychain.

The access token is the permanent token used to authorize all calls to the Dropbox API.

> **Note:** If you're even more curious, feel free to take a peek at the `Dropbox` class in the starter project; it uses `NSURLSession` and has no external dependencies.
>
> More details about OAuth 1 and 2 authentication to the Dropbox Core API can be found here: https://www.dropbox.com/developers/core/docs#request-token.
>
> Additionally, the following article was extremely helpful in getting PLAINTEXT over HTTPS OAuth working and is worth a read: https://www.dropbox.com/developers/blog/20/using-oauth-in-plaintext-mode

The NSURLSession suite of classes

Apple has described `NSURLSession` as both a new class and a suite of classes. There's new tools to upload, download, handle authorization, and handle just about anything in the `HTTP` protocol.

Before you start coding, it's important to have a good understanding of the major classes in the `NSURLSession` suite and how they work together.

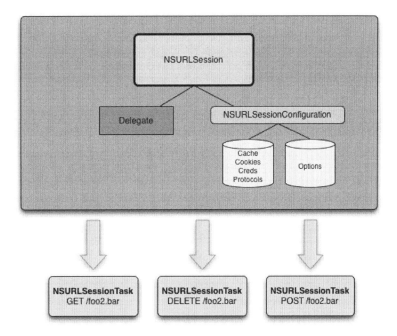

An `NSURLSession` is made using an `NSURLSessionConfiguration` with an optional delegate. After you create the session you then satisfy your networking needs by creating `NSURLSessionTask`'s.

NSURLSessionConfiguration

There are three ways to create an `NSURLSessionConfiguration`:

- `defaultSessionConfiguration` – creates a configuration object that uses the global cache, cookie and credential storage objects. This is a configuration that causes your session to be the most like `NSURLConnection`.

- `ephemeralSessionConfiguration` – this configuration is for "private" sessions and has no persistent storage for cache, cookie, or credential storage objects.

- `backgroundSessionConfiguration` – this is the configuration to use when you want to make networking calls from remote push notifications or while the app is suspended. Refer to Chaper 15 for more details.

Once you create a `NSURLSessionConfiguration`, you can set various properties on it like this:

```
NSURLSessionConfiguration *sessionConfig =
[NSURLSessionConfiguration defaultSessionConfiguration];
```

```
// 1
sessionConfig.allowsCellularAccess = NO;

// 2
[sessionConfig setHTTPAdditionalHeaders:
          @{@"Accept": @"application/json"}];

// 3
sessionConfig.timeoutIntervalForRequest = 30.0;
sessionConfig.timeoutIntervalForResource = 60.0;
sessionConfig.HTTPMaximumConnectionsPerHost = 1;
```

1. Here you restrict network operations to wifi only.

2. This will set all requests to only accept JSON responses.

3. These properties will configure timeouts for resources or requests. Also you can restrict your app to only have one network connection to a host.

These are only a few of the things you can configure, be sure to check out the documentation for a full list.

NSURLSession

NSURLSession is designed as a replacement API for NSURLConnection. Sessions do all of their work via their minions, also known as NSURLSessionTask objects. With NSURLSession you can create the tasks using the block based convenience methods, setup a delegate, or both. For example, if you want to download an image (*challenge hint*), you will need to create an NSURLSessionDownloadTask.

First you need to create the session. Here's an example:

```
// 1
NSString *imageUrl =
@"http://cdn2.raywenderlich.com/wp-
content/themes/raywenderlich/images/store/ios-apprentice/ios-
apprentice-bundle-v2_0b@2x.png";

// 2
NSURLSessionConfiguration *sessionConfig =
  [NSURLSessionConfiguration defaultSessionConfiguration];

// 3
NSURLSession *session =
```

```
[NSURLSession sessionWithConfiguration:sessionConfig
                                delegate:self
                           delegateQueue:nil];
```

Ok this is just a little different from what you have seen so far. Let's go over it step by step.

1. For this snippet we are downloading the same in two tasks.

2. You always start by creating an NSURLConfiguration.

3. This creates a session using the current class as a delegate.

After you create the session, you can then download the image by creating a task with a completion handler, like this:

```
// 1
NSURLSessionDownloadTask *getImageTask =
[session downloadTaskWithURL:[NSURL URLWithString:imageUrl]

    completionHandler:^(NSURL *location,
                        NSURLResponse *response,
                        NSError *error) {
      // 2
      UIImage *downloadedImage =
        [UIImage imageWithData:
          [NSData dataWithContentsOfURL:location]];
      //3
      dispatch_async(dispatch_get_main_queue(), ^{
        // do stuff with image
        _imageWithBlock.image = downloadedImage;
      });
}];

// 4
[getImageTask resume];
```

Ah ha! Now this looks like some networking code!

1. Tasks are always created by sessions. This one is created with the block-based method. Remember you could still use the NSURLSessionDownloadDelegate to track download progress. So you get the best of both worlds! (*hint for challenge*)

```
-URLSession:downloadTask
:didWriteData:totalBytesWritten
:totalBytesExpectedToWrite:
```

2. Here you use the location variable provided in the completion handler to get a pointer to the image.

3. Finally you could, for example, update `UIImageView`'s image to show the new file. (hint hint ☺)

4. You always have to start up the task!

5. Remember I said earlier that a session could also create tasks that will send messages to delegate methods to notify you of completion, etc.

Here is how that would look, using the same session from above:

```
// 1
NSURLSessionDownloadTask *getImageTask =
  [session downloadTaskWithURL:[NSURL URLWithString:imageUrl]];

[getImageTask resume];
```

1. Well this is certainly less code ☺ However, if you only do this you're never going to see anything.

You need to have your delegate implement some methods from the `NSURLSessionDownloadDelegate` protocol.

First we need to get notified when the download is complete:

```
-(void)URLSession:(NSURLSession *)session
    downloadTask:(NSURLSessionDownloadTask *)downloadTask
didFinishDownloadingToURL:(NSURL *)location
{
  // use code above from completion handler
}
```

Again you are provided with the location the file is downloaded to, and you can use this to work with the image.

Finally, if you needed to track the download progress, for either task creation method, you would need to use the following:

```
-(void)URLSession:(NSURLSession *)session
    downloadTask:(NSURLSessionDownloadTask *)downloadTask
    didWriteData:(int64_t)bytesWritten
totalBytesWritten:(int64_t)totalBytesWritten
totalBytesExpectedToWrite:(int64_t)totalBytesExpectedToWrite
{
  NSLog(@"%f / %f", (double)totalBytesWritten,
```

```
        (double)totalBytesExpectedToWrite);
}
```

As you can see, NSURLSessionTask is the real workhorse for "getting stuff done" over the network.

NSURLSessionTask

So far you have seen NSURLSessionDataTask and NSURLSessionDownloadTask in use. Both of these tasks are derived from NSURLSessionTask the base class for both of these, are you can see here:

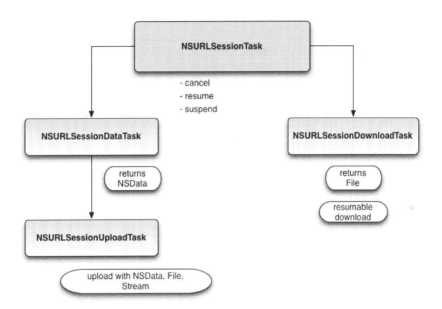

NSURLSessionTask is the base class for tasks in your session; they can only be created from a session and are one of the following subclasses.

NSURLSessionDataTask

This task issues HTTP GET requests to pull down data from servers. The data is returned in form of NSData. You would then convert this data to the correct type XML, JSON, UIImage, plist etc.

```
NSURLSessionDataTask *jsonData = [session
dataTaskWithURL:yourNSURL
```

```
        completionHandler:^(NSData *data,
                             NSURLResponse *response,
                             NSError *error) {
      // handle NSData
}];
```

NSURLSessionUploadTask

Use this class when you need to upload something to a web service using HTTP POST or PUT commands. The delegate for tasks also allows you to watch the network traffic while it's being transmitted.

Upload an image:

```
NSData *imageData = UIImageJPEGRepresentation(image, 0.6);

NSURLSessionUploadTask *uploadTask =
  [upLoadSession uploadTaskWithRequest:request
                             fromData:imageData];
```

Here the task is created from a session and the image is uploaded as NSData. There are also methods to upload using a file or a stream.

NSURLSessionDownloadTask

NSURLSessionDownloadTask makes it super-easy to download files from remote service and pause and resume the download at will. This subclass is a little different than the other two.

- This type of task writes directly to a temporary file.

- During the download the session will call URLSession:downloadTask:didWriteData:totalBytesWritten:totalBytesEx pectedToWrite: to update status information

- When the task is finished, URLSession:downloadTask:didFinishDownloadingToURL: is called. This is when you can save the file from the temp location to a permanent one.

- When the download fails or is cancelled you can get the data to resume the download.

This feature will be terribly useful when downloading a Byte Club location panoramic photo to your device's camera roll. You saw an example download task in the above snippet for downloading an image.

All of the above

All of the above tasks are created in a suspended state; after creating one you need to call its resume method as demonstrated below:

```
[uploadTask resume];
```

The `taskIdentifier` property allows you to uniquely identify a task within a session when you're managing more than one task at a time.

That's it! Now that you know the major classes in the `NSURLSession` suite, let's try them out.

Sharing notes with NSURLSession

OK, this isn't the Dead Poets Society, this is Byte Club! It's time to start seeing some of this network code in action.

You need a way to send messages to other members of Byte Club. Since you've already set up an access token, the next step is to instantiate `NSURLSesssion` and make your first call to the Dropbox API.

Creating an NSURLSession

Add the following property to **NotesViewController.m** just after the `NSArray *notes` line:

```
@property (nonatomic, strong) NSURLSession *session;
```

You will create all of your minions from the session above.

Add the following method to **NotesViewController.m** just above `initWithStyle`:

```
- (id)initWithCoder:(NSCoder *)aDecoder
{
    self = [super initWithCoder:aDecoder];
    if (self) {
        // 1
        NSURLSessionConfiguration *config =
[NSURLSessionConfiguration ephemeralSessionConfiguration];

        // 2
```

```
        [config setHTTPAdditionalHeaders:@{@"Authorization":
  [Dropbox apiAuthorizationHeader]}];

        // 3
        _session = [NSURLSession
  sessionWithConfiguration:config];
    }
    return self;
}
```

Here's a comment-by-comment explanation of the code above:

1. Your app calls `initWithCoder` when instantiating a view controller from a Storyboard; therefore this is the perfect spot to initialize and create the `NSURLSession`. You don't want aggressive caching or persistence here, so you use the `ephemeralSessionConfiguration` convenience method, which returns a session with no persistent storage for caches, cookies, or credentials. This is a "private browsing" configuration.

2. Next, you add the Authorization HTTP header to the configuration object. The `apiAuthorizationHeader` is a helper method that returns a string in the OAuth specification format. This string contains the access token, token secret and your Dropbox App API key. Remember, this is necessary because every call to the Dropbox API needs to be authenticated.

3. Finally, you create the `NSURLSession` using the above configuration.

This session is now ready to create any of the networking tasks that you need in your app.

GET Notes through the Dropbox API

To simulate a note being added by another user, add any text file of your choosing to the folder you set up in the root Dropbox folder. The example below shows the file **test.txt** sitting in the **byteclub** Dropbox folder:

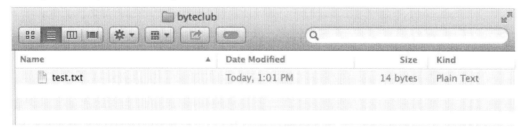

Wait until Dropbox confirms it has synced your file, then move on to the code.

Add the code below to the empty **notesOnDropBox** method in
NotesViewController.m:

```
[UIApplication
sharedApplication].networkActivityIndicatorVisible = YES;
// 1
NSURL *url = [Dropbox appRootURL];

// 2
NSURLSessionDataTask *dataTask =
[self.session dataTaskWithURL:url
           completionHandler:^(NSData *data,
                               NSURLResponse *response,
                               NSError *error) {
    if (!error) {
        // TODO 1: More coming here!
    }
}];

// 3
[dataTask resume];
```

The goal of this method is to retrieve a list of the files inside the app's Dropbox folder.
Let's go over how this works section by section.

1. In Dropbox, you can see the contents of a folder by making an authenticated GET
   request to a particular URL – like
   https://api.dropbox.com/1/metadata/dropbox/byteclub. I've created a convenience
   method in the Dropbox class to generate this URL for you.

2. NSURLSession has convenience methods to easily create various types of tasks. Here
   you are creating a data task in order to perform a GET request to that URL. When
   the request completes, your completionHandler block is called. You'll add some
   code here in a moment.

Remember a task defaults to a suspended state, so you need to call the resume method to
start the task.

That's all you need to do to start a GET request – now let's add the code to parse the
results. Add the following lines right after the "TODO 1" comment:

```
// 1
NSHTTPURLResponse *httpResp = (NSHTTPURLResponse*) response;
if (httpResp.statusCode == 200) {
```

```
    NSError *jsonError;

    // 2
    NSDictionary *notesJSON =
      [NSJSONSerialization JSONObjectWithData:data
        options:NSJSONReadingAllowFragments
        error:&jsonError];

    NSMutableArray *notesFound = [[NSMutableArray alloc] init];

    if (!jsonError) {
        // TODO 2: More coming here!
    }
}
```

There are two main sections here:

1. You know you made a HTTP request, so the response will be a HTTP response. So here you cast the NSURLResponse to an NSHTTPURLRequest response so you can access the statusCode property. If you receive an HTTP status code of 200 then all is well.

   Example HTTP error codes:

   400 - Bad input parameter. Error message should indicate which one and why.

   401 - Bad or expired token. This can happen if the user or Dropbox revoked or expired an access token. To fix, you should re-authenticate the user.

   403 - Bad OAuth request (wrong consumer key, bad nonce, expired timestamp...). Unfortunately, re-authenticating the user won't help here.

   404 - File or folder not found at the specified path.

   405 - Request method not expected (generally should be GET or POST).

   429 - Your app is making too many requests and is being rate limited. 429s can trigger on a per-app or per-user basis.

   503 - If the response includes the Retry-After header, this means your OAuth 1.0 app is being rate limited. Otherwise, this indicates a transient server error, and your app should retry its request.

   507 - User is over Dropbox storage quota.

   5xx - Server error.

2. The Dropbox API returns its data as JSON. So if you received a 200 response, then convert the data into JSON using iOS's built in JSON deserialization. To learn more about JSON and `NSJSONSerialization`, check out Chapter 23 in *iOS 5 by Tutorials*, "Working with JSON."

The JSON data returned from Dropbox will look something like this:

```
{
    "hash": "6a29b68d106bda4473ffdaf2e94c4b61",
    "revision": 73052,
    "rev": "11d5c00e1cf6c",
    "thumb_exists": false,
    "bytes": 0,
    "modified": "Sat, 10 Aug 2013 21:56:50 +0000",
    "path": "/byteclub",
    "is_dir": true,
    "icon": "folder",
    "root": "dropbox",
    "contents": [{
        "revision": 73054,
        "rev": "11d5e00e1cf6c",
        "thumb_exists": false,
        "bytes": 16,
        "modified": "Sat, 10 Aug 2013 23:21:03 +0000",
        "client_mtime": "Sat, 10 Aug 2013 23:21:02 +0000",
        "path": "/byteclub/test.txt",
        "is_dir": false,
        "icon": "page_white_text",
        "root": "dropbox",
        "mime_type": "text/plain",
        "size": "16 bytes"
    }],
    "size": "0 bytes"
}
```

So the last bit of code to add is the code that pulls out the parts you're interested in from the JSON. In particular, you want to loop through the "contents" array for anything where "is_dir" is set to false.

To do this, add the following lines right after the "TODO 2" comment:

```
// 1
NSArray *contentsOfRootDirectory = notesJSON[@"contents"];

for (NSDictionary *data in contentsOfRootDirectory) {
```

```
    if (![data[@"is_dir"] boolValue]) {
        DBFile *note = [[DBFile alloc] initWithJSONData:data];
        [notesFound addObject:note];
    }
}

[notesFound sortUsingComparator:
  ^NSComparisonResult(id obj1, id obj2) {
    return [obj1 compare:obj2];
}];

self.notes = notesFound;

// 6
dispatch_async(dispatch_get_main_queue(), ^{
    [UIApplication
sharedApplication].networkActivityIndicatorVisible = NO;
    [self.tableView reloadData];
});
```

There are two sections here:

1. You pull out the array of objects from the "contents" key and then iterate through the array. Each array entry is a file, so you create a corresponding DBFile model object for each file.

   DBFile pulls out the information for a file from the JSON dictionary – take a quick peek so you can see how it works.

   When you're done, you add all the notes into the self.notes property. The table view is set up to display any entries in this array.

Now that you have the table view's datasource updated, you need to reload the table data. Whenever you're dealing with asynchronous network calls, you have to make sure to update UIKit on the main thread.Astute readers will notice there's no error handling in the code above; if you're feeling like a keener (and most members of Byte Club are!) add some code here (and in subsequent code blocks you'll add) that will retry in the case of an error and alert the user.

Build and run your app; you should see the file you added to your Dropbox folder show up in the list, as shown in the following example:

It's a small thing, but it's living proof that you're calling the Dropbox API correctly.

The next step is to post notes and issue challenges to other club members, once again using the Dropbox API as your delivery mechanism.

POST Notes through the Dropbox API

Tap the plus sign in the upper right corner and you'll see the Note add/edit screen appear, as illustrated below:

The starter app is already set up to pass the `DBFile` model object to the `NoteDetailsViewController` in `prepareForSegue:sender:`.

If you take a peek at this method, you'll see that `NoteViewController` is set as the `NoteDetailsViewController`'s delegate. This way, the `NoteDetailsViewController` can notify `NoteViewController` when the user finishes editing a note, or cancels editing a note.

Open NotesViewController.m and add the following line to `prepareForSegue:sender:`, just after the line `showNote.delegate = self;`

```
showNote.session = _session;
```

`NoteDetailsViewController` already has an `NSURLSession` property named `session`, so you can set that in `prepareForSegue:sender:` before it loads.

Now the detail view controller will share the same `NSURLSession`, so the detail view controller can use it to make API calls to DropBox.

The **Cancel** and **Done** buttons are already present in the app; you just need to add some logic behind them to save or cancel the note that's in progress.

In NoteDetailsViewController.m, find the following line in

`(IBAction)done:(id)sender:`

```
    // - UPLOAD FILE TO DROPBOX - //
    [self.delegate
  noteDetailsViewControllerDoneWithDetails:self];
```

… and **replace** it with the following:

```
// 1
NSURL *url = [Dropbox uploadURLForPath:_note.path];

// 2
NSMutableURLRequest *request =
  [[NSMutableURLRequest alloc] initWithURL:url];
[request setHTTPMethod:@"PUT"];

// 3
NSData *noteContents = [_note.contents
dataUsingEncoding:NSUTF8StringEncoding];

// 4
NSURLSessionUploadTask *uploadTask = [_session
  uploadTaskWithRequest:request
  fromData:noteContents
  completionHandler:^(NSData *data,
```

```
  NSURLResponse *response,
  NSError *error)
{
  NSHTTPURLResponse *httpResp = (NSHTTPURLResponse*) response;

  if (!error && httpResp.statusCode == 200) {

      [self.delegate
noteDetailsViewControllerDoneWithDetails:self];
  } else {
      // alert for error saving / updating note
  }
}];

// 5
[uploadTask resume];
```

This implements everything you need to save and share your notes. If you take a close look at each commented section, you'll see that the code does the following:

1. To upload a file to Dropbox, again you need to use a certain API URL. Just like before when you needed a URL to list the files in a directory, I have created a helper method to generate the URL for you. You call this here.

2. Next up is your old friend NSMutableURLRequest. The new APIs can use both plain URLs and NSURLRequest objects, but you need the mutable form here to comply with the Dropbox API wanting this request to be a PUT request. Setting the HTTP method as PUT signals Dropbox that you want to create a new file.

3. Next you encode the text from your UITextView into an NSData Object.

4. Now that you're created the request and NSData object, you next create an NSURLSessionUploadTask and set up the completion handler block. Upon success, you call the delegate method noteDetailsViewControllerDoneWithDetails: to close the modal content. In a production-level application you could pass a new DBFile back to the delegate and sync up your persistent data. For the purposes of this application, you simply refresh the NotesViewController with a new network call.

5. Again, all tasks are created as suspended so you must call resume on them to start them up. Lazy minions!

Build and run your app and tap on the plus sign of the Notes tab. Enter your name in the **challenge name** field, and enter some text in the **note** field that offers up a challenge to Ray.

It should be similar to the example below:

When you tap **Done**, the `NoteViewController` will return and list your new note as shown below:

You've officially thrown down the gauntlet and issued a challenge to Ray; however, he has friends in very high places so you'd better bring your best game!

But there's one important feature missing. Can you tell what it is?

Tap on the note containing the challenge; the NoteDetailsViewController presents itself, but the text of the note is blank.

Ray won't find your challenge very threatening if he can't read it!

Right now, the app is only calling the Dropbox metadata API to retrieve lists of files. You'll need to add some code to fetch the contents of the note.

Open NoteDetailsViewController.m and replace the blank retreiveNoteText implementation with the following:

```
-(void)retreiveNoteText
{
    // 1
    NSString *fileApi =
      @"https://api-content.dropbox.com/1/files/dropbox";
    NSString *escapedPath = [_note.path
      stringByAddingPercentEscapesUsingEncoding:
      NSUTF8StringEncoding];

    NSString *urlStr = [NSString stringWithFormat: @"%@/%@",
      fileApi,escapedPath];

    NSURL *url = [NSURL URLWithString: urlStr];

    [UIApplication
sharedApplication].networkActivityIndicatorVisible = YES;

    // 2
    [[_session dataTaskWithURL:url completionHandler:^(NSData
*data, NSURLResponse *response, NSError *error) {

        if (!error) {
            NSHTTPURLResponse *httpResp = (NSHTTPURLResponse*)
response;
            if (httpResp.statusCode == 200) {
                // 3
                NSString *text =
                  [[NSString alloc]initWithData:data
                    encoding:NSUTF8StringEncoding];
                dispatch_async(dispatch_get_main_queue(), ^{
```

```
                    [UIApplication
  sharedApplication].networkActivityIndicatorVisible = NO;
                    self.textView.text = text;
            });

        } else {
            // HANDLE BAD RESPONSE //
        }
    } else {
        // ALWAYS HANDLE ERRORS :-] //
    }
    // 4
}] resume];
}
```

The code above (*sans* error checking) is explained in the notes below:

1. Set the request path and the URL of the file you wish to retrieve; the /files endpoint in the Dropbox API will return the contents of a specific file.

2. Create the data task with a URL that points to the file of interest. This call should be starting to look quite familiar as you go through this app.

3. If your response code indicates that all is good, set up the textView on the main thread with the file contents you retrieved in the previous step. Remember, UI updates must be dispatched to the main thread.

4. As soon as the task is initialized, call resume. This is a little different approach than before, as resume is called directly on the task without assigning anything.

Build and run your app, tap on your challenge in the list and the contents now display correctly in the view, as shown:

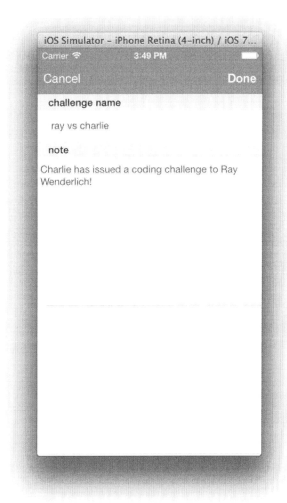

You can play the part of Ray and respond to the challenge by entering text to the note; the files will be updated as soon as you tap **Done**.

Share the app and the Dropbox folder with some of your coding friends and have them test out your app by adding and editing notes between each other. After all, Byte Club is much more fun with more than one person in it!

Posting photos with NSURLSessionTask delegates

You've seen how to use NSURLSesssion asynchronous convenience methods. But what if you want to keep an eye on a file transfer, such as uploading a large file and showing a progress bar?

For this type of asynchronous, time-consuming task you'll need to implement protocol methods from NSURLSessionTaskDelegate. By implementing this method, you can receive callbacks when a task receives data and finishes receiving data.

You might have noticed that the **PanoPhotos** tab is empty when you launch the app. However, the founding members of Byte Club have generously provided some panoramic photos of their own to fill your app with.

The photos folder in the chapter's resources contains some sample panoramic photos. Copy the **photos** directory of this chapter's resource package to your app folder on Dropbox. Your folder contents should look similar to the following:

Name	Date Modified	Size	Kind
▼ 📁 photos	Jul 27, 2013 9:08 AM	--	Folder
📷 Chris W Desk.jpg	Jul 10, 2013 9:19 PM	13.3 MB	JPEG image
📷 Feli Office 1.JPG	Jul 11, 2013 11:27 AM	8.1 MB	JPEG image
📷 Feli Terrace.JPG	Nov 18, 2012 4:49 PM	16.8 MB	JPEG image
📷 gregheo-balcony.jpg	Jul 11, 2013 3:17 PM	4.4 MB	JPEG image
📷 gregheo-office.jpg	Jul 11, 2013 3:17 PM	9.2 MB	JPEG image
📷 gregheo-roof.jpg	Jul 11, 2013 3:30 PM	4.8 MB	JPEG image
📷 Jamie-Balcony.jpg	Jul 11, 2013 11:55 AM	1 MB	JPEG image
📷 Marin_balcony.JPG	Jul 11, 2013 11:13 AM	8.1 MB	JPEG image
📷 mattg-coast.JPG	Jun 13, 2013 11:05 AM	10.5 MB	JPEG image
📷 Matthijs-Office-and-Cat.jpg	Jul 12, 2013 2:27 AM	7.2 MB	JPEG image
📷 Rays-Office.jpg	Jul 11, 2013 10:45 AM	6.2 MB	JPEG image
📄 ray vs charlie	Today 12:16 PM	71 bytes	Document
📄 test.txt	Today 11:50 AM	14 bytes	Plain...cument

The Dropbox Core API can provide thumbnails for photos; this sounds like the perfect thing to use for a UITableView cell.

Open PhotosViewController.m and add the following code to tableView:cellForRowAtIndexPath: just after the comment stating "GO GET THUMBNAILS":

```
[UIApplication
 sharedApplication].networkActivityIndicatorVisible = YES;
NSURLSessionDataTask *dataTask = [_session dataTaskWithURL:url
  completionHandler:^(NSData *data, NSURLResponse *response,
```

```
  NSError *error) {
    if (!error) {
      UIImage *image = [[UIImage alloc] initWithData:data];
      photo.thumbNail = image;
      dispatch_async(dispatch_get_main_queue(), ^{
        [UIApplication
sharedApplication].networkActivityIndicatorVisible = NO;
        cell.thumbnailImage.image = photo.thumbNail;
      });
    } else {
      // HANDLE ERROR //
    }
}];
[dataTask resume];
```

The above code displays the photo's thumbnail image in the table view cell...or at least it would, if the _photoThumbnails array wasn't currently empty.

Find refreshPhotos and replace its implementation with the following:

```
- (void)refreshPhotos
{
    [[UIApplication sharedApplication]
setNetworkActivityIndicatorVisible:YES];
    NSString *photoDir = [NSString
stringWithFormat:@"https://api.dropbox.com/1/search/dropbox/%@/p
hotos?query=.jpg",appFolder];
    NSURL *url = [NSURL URLWithString:photoDir];

    [[_session dataTaskWithURL:url completionHandler:^(NSData
      *data, NSURLResponse *response, NSError *error) {
        if (!error) {
            NSHTTPURLResponse *httpResp =
              (NSHTTPURLResponse*) response;
            if (httpResp.statusCode == 200) {

                NSError *jsonError;
                NSArray *filesJSON = [NSJSONSerialization
                  JSONObjectWithData:data
                  options:NSJSONReadingAllowFragments
                  error:&jsonError];
                NSMutableArray *dbFiles =
                  [[NSMutableArray alloc] init];
```

```
        if (!jsonError) {
            for (NSDictionary *fileMetadata in
                filesJSON) {
                DBFile *file = [[DBFile alloc]
                    initWithJSONData:fileMetadata];
                [dbFiles addObject:file];
            }

            [dbFiles
sortUsingComparator:^NSComparisonResult(id obj1, id obj2) {
                return [obj1 compare:obj2];
            }];

            _photoThumbnails = dbFiles;

            dispatch_async(dispatch_get_main_queue(), ^{
                [[UIApplication sharedApplication]
setNetworkActivityIndicatorVisible:NO];
                [self.tableView reloadData];
            });
        }
    } else {
        // HANDLE BAD RESPONSE //
    }
    } else {
        // ALWAYS HANDLE ERRORS :-] //
    }
}] resume];
}
```

This is very similar to the code you wrote earlier that loads the challenge notes. This time, the API call looks in the **photos** directory and only requests files with the .jpg extension.

Now that the _photoThumbnails array is populated, the thumbnail images will appear in the table view and update asynchronously.

Build and run your app and switch to the PanoPhotos tab; the thumbnails will load and appear as follows:

The photos look great — just beware of Matthijs's code-shredding cat!

Upload a PanoPhoto

Your app can download photos, but it would be great if it could also upload images and show the progress of the upload.

To track the progress of an upload, the PhotosViewController must be a delegate for both the NSURLSessionDelegate and NSURLSessionTaskDelegate protocols so you can receive progress callbacks.

Modify the PhotosViewController interface declaration in **PhotosViewController.m** by adding NSURLSessionTaskDelegate, as below:

```
@interface PhotosViewController ()<UITableViewDelegate,
UITableViewDataSource, UIImagePickerControllerDelegate,
UINavigationControllerDelegate, NSURLSessionTaskDelegate>
```

Next, add the following private property:

```
@property (nonatomic, strong)
  NSURLSessionUploadTask *uploadTask;
```

The above pointer references the task object; that way, you can access the object's members to track the progress of the upload task.

When the user chooses a photo to upload, didFinishPickingMediaWithInfo calls uploadImage: to perform the file upload. Right now, that method's empty – it's your job to flesh it out.

Replace uploadImage: with the following code:

```
- (void)uploadImage:(UIImage*)image
{
    NSData *imageData = UIImageJPEGRepresentation(image, 0.6);

    // 1
    NSURLSessionConfiguration *config =
[NSURLSessionConfiguration defaultSessionConfiguration];
    config.HTTPMaximumConnectionsPerHost = 1;
    [config setHTTPAdditionalHeaders:@{@"Authorization":
[Dropbox apiAuthorizationHeader]}];

    // 2
    NSURLSession *upLoadSession = [NSURLSession
sessionWithConfiguration:config delegate:self
delegateQueue:nil];

    // for now just create a random file name, dropbox will
handle it if we overwrite a file and create a new name..
    NSURL *url = [Dropbox createPhotoUploadURL];

    NSMutableURLRequest *request = [[NSMutableURLRequest alloc]
initWithURL:url];
    [request setHTTPMethod:@"PUT"];

    // 3
    self.uploadTask = [upLoadSession
uploadTaskWithRequest:request fromData:imageData];

    // 4
    self.uploadView.hidden = NO;
```

```
    [[UIApplication sharedApplication]
 setNetworkActivityIndicatorVisible:YES];

    // 5
    [_uploadTask resume];
}
```

Here's what's going on in the code above:

1. Previously, you used the session set up in `initWithCoder` and the associated convenience methods to create asynchronous tasks. This time, you're using an `NSURLSessionConfiguration` that only permits one connection to the remote host, since your upload process handles just one file at a time.

2. The upload and download tasks report information back to their delegates; you'll implement these shortly.

3. Here you set the `uploadTask` property using the `JPEG` image obtained from the `UIImagePicker`.

4. Next, you display the UIProgressView hidden inside of `PhotosViewController`.

5. Start the task — er, sorry, *resume* the task.

Now that the delegate has been set, you can implement the `NSURLSessionTaskDelegate` methods to update the progress view.

Add the following code to the end of PhotosViewController.m:

```
#pragma mark – NSURLSessionTaskDelegate methods

- (void)URLSession:(NSURLSession *)session
  task:(NSURLSessionTask *)task
  didSendBodyData:(int64_t)bytesSent
  totalBytesSent:(int64_t)totalBytesSent
  totalBytesExpectedToSend:(int64_t)totalBytesExpectedToSend
{
    dispatch_async(dispatch_get_main_queue(), ^{
        [_progress setProgress:
          (double)totalBytesSent /
          (double)totalBytesExpectedToSend animated:YES];
    });
}
```

The above delegate method periodically reports information about the upload task back to the caller. It also updates UIProgressView (`_progress`) to show `totalBytesSent /`

totalBytesExpectedToSend which is more informative (and much geekier) than showing percent complete.

The only thing left is to indicate when the upload task is complete. Add the following method to the end of PhotosViewController.m:

```
- (void)URLSession:(NSURLSession *)session
task:(NSURLSessionTask *)task didCompleteWithError:(NSError
*)error
{
    // 1
    dispatch_async(dispatch_get_main_queue(), ^{
        [[UIApplication sharedApplication]
setNetworkActivityIndicatorVisible:NO];
        _uploadView.hidden = YES;
        [_progress setProgress:0.5];
    });

    if (!error) {
        // 2
        dispatch_async(dispatch_get_main_queue(), ^{
            [self refreshPhotos];
        });
    } else {
        // Alert for error
    }
}
```

There's not a lot of code here, but it performs two important tasks:

1. Turns off the network activity indicator and then hides the _uploadView as a bit of cleanup once the upload is done.

2. Refresh PhotosViewController to include the image you just uploaded since your demo app is not storing anything locally. In a real world app, you should probably be storing or caching the images locally.

Build and run your app, navigate to the PanoPhotos tab and tap the camera icon to select an image.

> **Note:** If you're using the simulator to test the app, you obviously can't take a
> photo with your Mac, so just copy a panoramic photo to the simulator and
> upload that instead. To do this, ensure no other Xcode project is currently
> connected to the simulator and in Xcode select **Xcode \ Open Developer
> Tool \ iOS Simulator.**
>
> Drag one of the included panoramic photos from Finder to the simulator where
> the image will open in Safari. Then long press on the image and save the image to
> the photo library.

After selecting the image to upload, the `uploadView` displays in the middle of the screen
along with the `UIProgressView` as shown on the next page:

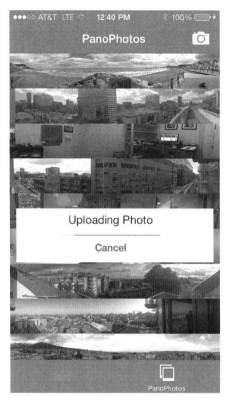

You might have noticed that an image upload can take some time due to the "better quality" scaling factor set on the upload task. Believe it or not, some users get a little impatient on their mobile devices! ☺ For those A-type personalities, you should provide a cancel function if the upload is taking too long.

The Cancel button on the uploadView has already been wired up from the storyboard, so you'll just need to implement the logic to cleanly kill the download.

Replace the cancelUpload: method in PhotosViewController.m with the code below:

```
- (IBAction)cancelUpload:(id)sender {
    if (_uploadTask.state == NSURLSessionTaskStateRunning) {
        [_uploadTask cancel];
    }
}
```

To cancel a task it's as easy as calling the cancel method, which you can see here.

Now build and run your app, select a photo to upload and tap **Cancel**. The image upload will halt and the uploadView will be hidden.

Challenges

Congratulations – you now have hands-on experience with they key networking classes in iOS 7. In particular, you have:

- Used `NSURLSession` to execute various `NSURLSessionTasks`

- Used both data tasks, and upload tasks

- Learned how to configure `NSURLSession` with `NSURLSessionConfiguration`

- Worked with a popular third party API and OAuth

Now it's time for some challenges so you can practice using `NSURLSession` on your own. As always, if you get stuck you can find the solutions in the resources for this chapter – but give it your best shot first!

Challenge #1: Save an image to camera roll

Think back to the beginning of this chapter where you learned that all worthy Byte Club members have a panoramic photo on their lock screen.

Your first challenge is to download one of the full resolution panoramic photos from the Byte Club app into your camera roll. If you complete this challenge, you will be ready to issue code challenges to anyone!

Hints:

1. Using the `StoryBoard`, create a new `UIViewController` that is loaded when a user taps on a thumbnail photo.

2. Create a new class for this `UIViewController` named `DownloadViewController`.

   a. Create public NSString property named to save the path

3. Set the class for the `UIViewController` on the storyboard to `DownloadViewController`.

4. Add `UIProgressView`, `UIImageView`, and `UILabel` and create outlets for them.

5. In `PhotosViewController.m`, import DownloadViewController, add a `prepareForSegue` method and set the **path** for the Destination `ViewController` (`DownloadViewController`) hint use the path property from the selected `DBFile` object.

```
int row = [self.tableView indexPathForSelectedRow].row;
DBFile *selectedThumbnail = _photoThumbnails[row];
```

6. Use `NSURLSessionDownloadTask` to use the Dropbox /files (GET) service. This takes a URL in format: https://api-content.dropbox.com/1/files/<root>/<path>

   a. Use the property created in step 2 to build the full URL.

7. An `NSURLSessionDownloadTask` will directly write the response data to a temporary file. When completed the delegate is sent `URLSession:downloadTask:didFinishDownloadingToURL:` this is where you can save the file permanently, use the location variable like we saw earlier to create the `UIImage` and then use `UIImageWriteToSavedPhotosAlbum` to save the image to the camera roll.

8. Update the UIImageView to show the full file.

Here is what my finished challenge looks like; man that cat still scares me!

Challenge #2: Pause and resume photo downloads

For this challenge, you'll add a mechanism to pause and/or cancel an in-progress download. You'll find the following method from `NSURLSessionDownloadTask` to be of use:

```
- (void)cancelByProducingResumeData:(void (^)(NSData
*resumeData))completionHandler;
```

Other hints for this challenge:

1. On the download screen, add a button to pause/cancel the download.

2. In the action for the above button, call `cancelByProducingResumeData` to save the `NSData`. Here's the Apple docs on this method:

```
"Cancel the download (and calls the superclass -cancel).  If
conditions will allow for resuming the download in the future,
the callback will be called with an opaque data blob, which may
be used with -downloadTaskWithResumeData: to attempt to resume
the download. If resume data cannot be created, the completion
handler will be called with nil resumeData."
```

3. Add another button to resume the download by loading the data from the file or memory.

4. Use the following `NSURLSession` method to resume the download:

```
/* Creates a download task with the resume data.  If the
download cannot be successfully resumed,
URLSession:task:didCompleteWithError: will be called. */
- (NSURLSessionDownloadTask *)downloadTaskWithResumeData:(NSData
*)resumeData;
```

If you have completed these challenges, congratulations and enjoy your lifetime membership in Byte Club! Just don't go telling any Android guys about it! :]

Chapter 17: Beginning Multitasking

By Pietro Rea

In the early days of iOS, only one app could run at a time. Tapping the Home button would terminate whichever app was currently running and take you back to Springboard. This one-at-a-time approach made sense for the first generation of mobile devices because they were still very limited in terms of memory and processing power.

However, iOS users wanted more out of their devices. They wanted to do multiple things at once such as listening to music while browsing the web, or playing a game while answering a phone call. Sounds reasonable, right?

Apple's philosophy on multitasking has been the same from the beginning: general concurrency is not the solution for mobile devices. According to Apple, users — whether they know it or not — care first and foremost about battery life, so letting apps run wild in the background is the last thing you want to do.

Balancing user demands against technical limitations, Apple proceeded to make multitasking available to third party developers on a service-by-service basis.

- Starting with iOS 4, apps could register for services such as background audio, voice over IP and GPS navigation.

- Starting with iOS 5, tapping the Home button would merely suspend an app rather than terminate it. The next time a suspended app was opened, it would continue right where it left off. This mechanism is the basis for **fast app switching**, a feature that lies at the core of the iOS experience to this day.

- Starting with iOS 6, Apple introduced the concept of State Preservation and Restoration. This feature made it easy for you to save the state of your app, allowing you to restore its state in the event your app was terminated since the last launch. This made apps appear to be continuously running even when they were not.

- Now in iOS 7, Apple has introduced many new and exciting multitasking APIs, intended to make it easy for you to download data or files from a remote web service periodically in order to keep your app's data up to date.

In this chapter, you will learn about all the new multitasking APIs in iOS 7. You will get hands-on experience by developing an app called NASA TV, that allows you to see the latest NASA news and download high quality videos:

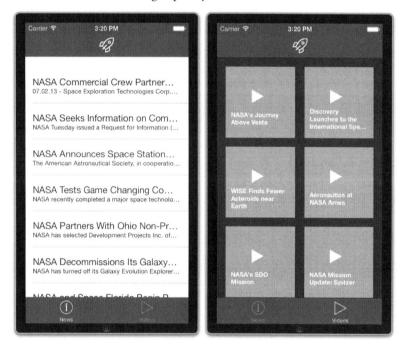

You will develop this app across two chapters:

1. **Chapter 17, Beginning Multitasking**: You are here! Learn how to keep your app's data up to date in the background with background fetching.

2. **Chapter 18, Intermediate Multitasking**: Learn how to download large files in the background and get notified of updates with silent push notifications.

Go grab your favorite caffeinated beverage and sip as you read – it's time for some multitasking!

Multitasking in iOS 7: an overview

The new multitasking APIs that come in iOS 7 are probably the most liberal multitasking APIs iOS developers have ever seen.

Although devices are more powerful and batteries longer-lasting these days, iOS 7 still exudes Apple's underlying philosophy of shunning concurrency in favor of task switching. You can definitely do more in the background in iOS 7, but you still need to be a good citizen and limit your background tasks to allow the device to go back to sleep.

Here are the new ways to do multitasking introduced in iOS 7:

Background fetch

Before iOS 7, if you opened a news app, a social networking app, or an online game, the first thing you would see was the old content. You would have to wait around impatiently as the app fetched new content and refreshed its UI after every launch.

Background fetch in iOS 7 removes this awkward wait and refresh period and allows apps to download their data in the background so they have the latest data ready as soon as you open the app. Using a set of prediction algorithms, iOS wakes up frequently-used apps and gives them some background processing time to update their content.

Background transfer

In iOS 6 and earlier, quitting an app in the middle of performing a lengthy download would stop the operation in its tracks. At best, the download would pause and resume when you re-opened the application. At worst, the download would be killed and you'd be forced to start all over.

The new `NSURLSession` class in iOS 7 supports background transfers, where lengthy uploads and downloads continue unhindered while the app is in the background. When complete, the download task calls back to your app delegate so you can update your UI if necessary and perform other post-transfer tasks.

Silent push notifications

In contrast to regular push notifications that lead to an app launch, silent push notifications trigger a background app refresh. They are event-driven and controlled externally from a web server whereas the new background fetch capabilities are scheduled by iOS.

For example, if you have an application that delivers sporadic or episodic content, such as a podcast, then you can keep the content up to date by sending out a silent push notification whenever new content is available. Similarly, if you have a file syncing application like Dropbox you can keep folders up to date across multiple devices with silent push notifications.

The new app switcher

To fully understand how the new multitasking features work, you need to understand the changes to the app switcher in iOS 7.

From iOS 4 to iOS 6, the app switcher – accessible from any screen by double-tapping the Home button – looked like this:

The old app switcher consisted of a row of icons showing the most recently used apps. From here you could remove an app from the list, which would also terminate the app process if it were still running.

The new app switcher in iOS 7 looks like this:

The new app switcher is still accessible by double-tapping the Home button and it still contains the row of icons at the bottom.

However, iOS 7 adds a screenshot of the app along with its icon. In the new app switcher world, it's your responsibility to keep your app's screenshot up to date — even if the user hasn't opened your app in a while. How do you accomplish this?

Essentially you need to instruct iOS to snapshot the UI of your app after you perform a refresh. Each time your app wakes up to perform a background execution task, the system provides you with a completion handler that you must call as soon as you finish execution of your background task.

Not only does calling this completion handler allow the device to sleep, it also takes a snapshot of your updated UI to display in the app switcher.

The app switcher also acts as the control center for multitasking. All background modes respect the app switcher; if the user kills your app from the app switcher, your app won't be able to perform background fetches, play music, or perform any other background tasks.

> **Note:** Even if your app is present in the app switcher, the user can opt-out of background transfers in Settings under **General/Background App Refresh**.

Getting started

In this chapter you will work on an app called **NASA TV**. Since this sample project includes a number of large video files, we have included the resources for this project as a separate download rather than included by default with the book. You can download the resources for this chapter here:

http://cdn1.raywenderlich.com/downloads/NASATV.zip

After you have downloaded the resources, you will find the starter project for the chapter inside. Build and run the app, and you will see the image on the following page:

Nothing shows up yet – this is because you haven't set up your web server yet. You'll do that soon.

NASA TV is a simple application with two tabs: the first tab will display the latest news stories from NASA, while the second tab will display the latest videos produced by NASA. The news stories will be published much more frequently than videos.

All the multitasking APIs introduced in iOS 7 require a web server. However, this chapter doesn't focus on backend services, so you will *simulate* a working backend server for your background fetch transfer activities. In the next chapter, you will use the backend service Parse to create silent push notifications.

You'll use a **MAMP** stack in this chapter to simulate your backend service. MAMP stands for **M**ac, **A**pache, **M**ySQL and **P**HP, which are four technologies that are frequently used together to create web services. You'll create a web service directly on your computer to simulate your web components of NASA TV.

> **Note:** MAMP is a spinoff of the common **LAMP** stack where the L stands for Linux. If you want to learn more about building a proper web service for your iOS apps you can read the following tutorials on this topic:
>
> http://www.raywenderlich.com/2941/how-to-write-a-simple-phpmysql-web-service-for-an-ios-app
>
> http://www.raywenderlich.com/19341/how-to-easily-create-a-web-backend-for-your-apps-with-parse

http://www.raywenderlich.com/44640/integrating-facebook-and-parse-tutorial-part-1

Setting up MAMP

To get some data into the blank NASA TV tabs, you'll need to get your MAMP stack up and running.

Head over to http://www.mamp.info and download the free version of MAMP. A paid version of MAMP is also available but the free one will work just fine for this chapter.

Once the download is complete, run the installer and the MAMP application will appear in the Applications folder. Start up MAMP and you'll see the following dialog:

You'll see there are two items in the **Status** box, which are turned off by default:

• **Apache server**: A web server that waits and listens for requests and serves up resources as needed.

• **MySQL server**: A database server works in a similar manner, but instead of serving resources over the network it serves up data from a database.

Before you can turn these servers on, you need to configure Apache to serve the NASA TV resources.

Launch your text editor of choice and open up the configuration file located at **/Applications/MAMP/conf/apache/httpd.conf**. Add the following configuration info to the bottom of the file:

```
Listen 44447

<VirtualHost *:44447>
    DocumentRoot "/Users/my_user_name/Desktop/NASA TV/MAMP"
```

```
    ServerName localhost:44447
    SetEnv APPLICATION_ENV development
    php_flag magic_quotes_gpc off

    <Directory "/Users/my_user_name/Desktop/NASA TV/MAMP">
        Options Indexes MultiViews FollowSymLinks
        AllowOverride All
        Order allow,deny
        Allow from all
    </Directory>
  </VirtualHost>
```

In the configuration options above, ensure you change BOTH entries for the path **/Users/my_user_name/Desktop/NASA TV/MAMP** to the directory where you downloaded the sample project for this chapter.

This sets up a new rule in Apache to listen to requests on port 44447 and map those requests to documents in **/Users/my_user_name/Desktop/NASA TV/MAMP**. This directory contains all the assets that the sample app will need, such as JSON files and NASA video clips.

Now go back to the MAMP app and click on the **Start Servers** button, which will turn the "Apache Server" status indicator to green. You won't use MySQL in this project, so don't worry if the "MySQL" indicator stays red.

If everything worked correctly, your default browser will open up and display a MAMP welcome screen. To verify that everything is hooked up correctly for your NASA TV app, go to **http://localhost:44447** in a web browser, where you will see the following text displayed:

> "Houston, Tranquility Base here. The Eagle has landed."
> **– Neil Armstrong**

This is the content of the index.html file found in the **NASA TV MAMP** directory. If you see that the eagle has landed, congratulations — your MAMP stack is serving up content as designed.

To make sure that you can resolve your own IP instead of using localhost all the time, find the IP of your computer in the Network pane in the System Preferences app, as so:

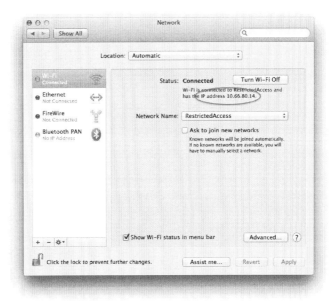

As a final test, open up the same test URL in your browser, substituting your machine's IP for localhost. If successful, you should see the same Neil Armstrong quote again.

A brief tour of the app

Now that your MAMP stack is up and running, you can modify your app to receive the content for NASA TV.

Open **AppDelegate.m** and modify the following line to reflect your computer's IP address:

```
NSUserDefaults* ud = [NSUserDefaults standardUserDefaults];
[ud setObject:@"http://10.66.80.14:44447"
      forKey:@"baseURLString"];
```

Build and run your project; check out the News and Video tabs and you'll see they're populated with relevant content. If you are testing the app on a physical device, make sure that the device is on the same Wi-Fi network as your Mac; otherwise, NASA TV won't be able to talk to your MAMP stack.

If at any point you are assigned a new IP address due to, for example, going to a new location, replace your new IP address in **AppDelegate.m** before continuing.

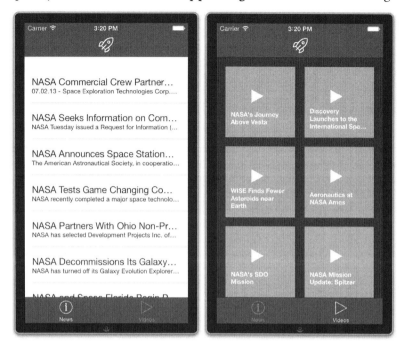

Before you go wild adding the multitasking features, take the following quick tour of the app to get acquainted with the architecture of NASA TV; that way you can see exactly how multitasking fits into the app as a whole.

Open up **Main.storyboard** and have a quick look at the scenes described:

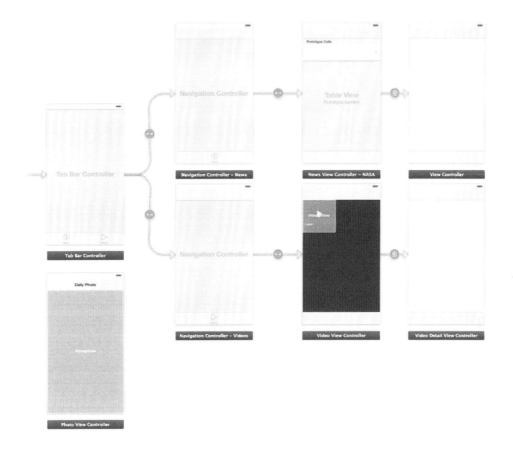

- **UITabBarController:** On the left is the root tab bar controller. The Video and News tabs each point to a `UINavigationController` instead of directly to the view controllers, which makes it easy to implement push/pop transitions.

- **NewsViewController:** This displays NASA news items in table form. A `UIRefreshControl` is attached to the table so the user can pull to refresh to check the latest and greatest updates from your favorite space agency.

- **NewsDetailViewController:** This view controller provides a simple way to display the press release information in each individual news item.

- **VideoViewController:** All available NASA videos are displayed here in a `UICollectionView`. If you want to know if there's a new video available, the attached `UIRefreshControl` provides pull to refresh functionality here as well.

- **VideoDetailViewController:** This view controller contains a `MPMoviePlayerController` that streams NASA video clips from the web server. All videos displayed here are provided with the sample project files in the directory **NASA TV MAMP/videos**.

- **PhotoViewController:** This view controller is floating in space (no pun intended) under the main `UITabBarController` and displays <u>NASA's Astronomy Picture of the Day</u>. This feature isn't yet implemented — but it gives you a hint as to what you'll be doing with silent push notifications in the next chapter.

As the final stop on this tour, open **NewsViewController.m** and take a look at `populateData`. `viewWillAppear:` and `refreshTableView:` both call this method which is attached to the table view's `UIRefreshControl`. That means that either switching to this tab or invoking pull to refresh will call `populateData` and refresh the data in the table.

Adding background fetching

It's time to add your first multitasking feature. Your first task is to integrate background fetch into `NewsViewController`.

The goal here is to keep the News feed up to date in the background so that there won't be an awkward pause when the user opens the app and retrieves the data from the server. This also keeps the app switcher snapshot up to date, making it more likely for your users to open NASA TV.

In Xcode, click on the project file and navigate to the new **Capabilities** tab. Set **Background Modes** on and then ensure **Background Fetch** is checked. This is equivalent to manually adding the `fetch` key to the `UIBackgroundModes` array in Info.plist.

Next, open **AppDelegate.m** and add the following implementation for `application:performFetchWithCompletionHandler:` at the bottom of the file:

```
- (void)application:(UIApplication *)application
      performFetchWithCompletionHandler:
      (void (^)(UIBackgroundFetchResult result))
      completionHandler {

UIViewController *rootVC = self.window.rootViewController;
UITabBarController *tbc = (UITabBarController *)rootVC;
```

```
    id selectedVC = tbc.selectedViewController;

    if ([selectedVC
         isMemberOfClass:UINavigationController.class]) {

        id topVC =
        [(UINavigationController *)selectedVC topViewController];

        if ([topVC isMemberOfClass:[NewsViewController class]]) {
            [(NewsViewController*)topVC
              populateDataWithCompletionHandler:completionHandler];
        }
    }
}
```

Xcode will warn you that `populateDataWithCompletionHandler:` is not defined. You'll take care of this shortly.

The system calls `application:performFetchWithCompletionHandler:` when it wakes up your application to perform a background fetch. The implementation shown above will only update the UI if `NewsViewController` is the currently selected tab. There's no need to waste resources updating the UI if `NewsViewController` is not currently visible

Note that this delegate method accepts a completion handler of type `(void(^)(UIBackgroundFetchResult result)`. Once the app has finished fetching data and refreshing the UI, you need to call this completion handler and report the correct `UIBackgroundFetchResult` to iOS using one of the following values:

• `UIBackgroundFetchResultNewData`: The background fetch succeeded and new data was retrieved. The new data will be available immediately after the next app launch and will also be shown in the app switcher snapshot. Hooray!

• `UIBackgroundFetchResultNoData`: The background fetch completed successfully but no new data was available. The next time the user launches the app there will be no visible change whatsoever. The user won't get to appreciate all the heavy lifting you did on their behalf. Bummer.

• `UIBackgroundFetchResultFailed`: Something went wrong and the background fetch failed. Maybe the web service that the background fetch was polling is unavailable or perhaps the request timed out. Mega bummer.

> **Note:** It's not difficult to guess why Apple asks for the background fetch result. Since battery life is limited, iOS is only going to wake a subset of all the apps that registered for background fetch. Background fetch result is *probably* one of the many factors that go into that decision — but only Apple knows for sure.

Next, open **NewsViewController.h** and add `populateDataWithCompletionHandler:` to the public interface as so:

```
#import <UIKit/UIKit.h>

@interface NewsViewController : UIViewController

- (void)populateDataWithCompletionHandler:
  (void (^)(UIBackgroundFetchResult))completionHandler;

@end
```

AppDelegate.m calls this method when there's a background fetch to perform.

Now open **NewsViewController.m** and rename `populateData` to `populateDataWithCompletionHandler:` so it matches the above method signature:

```
- (void)populateDataWithCompletionHandler:
  (void (^)(UIBackgroundFetchResult))completionHandler {
```

This is the same method that you inspected earlier, except now it accepts a parameter of an optional completion handler when it's executed from a background fetch.

Now add the add the following lines of code to `populateDataWithCompletionHandler:` at the bottom of `GetNewsWebOperation`'s success block within the `dispatch_async()` block:

```
//1
if (completionHandler) {
    //2
    if (hasNewEntries) {
        completionHandler(UIBackgroundFetchResultNewData);
        //3
        [UIApplication
          sharedApplication].applicationIconBadgeNumber++;
    }
    else {
        completionHandler(UIBackgroundFetchResultNoData);
```

```
        }
    }
```

You perform the following steps in the above code:

1. Check if a completion handler was passed in. If there's no completion handler available it means that `populateDataWithCompletionHandler:` was called from within `NewsViewController` and you don't have to do anything with regards to background fetching.

2. `hasNewEntries` is the second parameter passed in from `GetNewsWebOperation`'s successBlock. If you inspect **GetNewsWebOperation.m**, you'll see that `parseNewsData:` checks the incoming news items against the ones already stored in Core Data to set this flag.

   If there's nothing new coming back from the server, `hasNewEntries` is passed into the success block as NO. Otherwise, `hasNewEntries` is passed back as YES.

   This bit of information is necessary to differentiate between `UIBackgroundFetchResultNewData` and `UIBackgroundFetchResultNoData`.

3. Increment the application's icon badge number to give the user a visual cue that new data is available. In **AppDelegate.m**, `applicationWillEnterForeground:` sets this badge number back to zero so you don't have to do it yourself.

> **Note:** Notice that the completion handler executes *after* `[weakSelf.tableView reloadData]`. If you call the completion handler *before* the UI has had a chance to refresh, the app switcher snapshot will not reflect any changes. If your app switcher snapshot is still out of date even after you implement background fetching, this is probably why.

There's one more fetch status to report, `UIBackgroundFetchResultFailed`. Still in `populateDataWithCompletionHandler:` change `GetNewsWebOperation`'s failure block to the following:

```
[self.getNewsWebOperation setFailureBlock:^{
    [weakSelf.refreshControl endRefreshing];
    if (completionHandler) {
        completionHandler(UIBackgroundFetchResultFailed);
    }
}];
```

This simply executes the completion block (if one was passed in) with UIBackgroundFetchResultFailed. It's important that you don't forget this step because this is how you notify iOS that you are done fetching data and can go back to sleep.

You can't yet build and run your app as some methods in NewsViewController are still referencing populateData instead of populateDataWithCompletionHandler:

To fix this, update viewWillAppear: as shown below:

```
- (void)viewWillAppear:(BOOL)animated {
    [super viewWillAppear:animated];
    [self populateDataWithCompletionHandler:nil];
}
```

Also update refreshTableView: with the following method declaration:

```
- (void)refreshTableView:(id)sender {
    [self populateDataWithCompletionHandler:nil];
}
```

Build and run your app; you should have no errors or warnings at this point. The UI in the News tab won't have changed at all – all the code is there to handle background fetching, but there isn't yet anything to fetch!

The next step is to test that background fetching works properly. Background fetch can happen when your app is in one of two possible states:

1. **App suspended in background**: If NASA TV is suspended but still running in the background, iOS will simply wake it up to perform the background fetch.

2. **App not running at all**: The app is suspended in the background but for one reason or another was terminated by the system. The app still appears in the app switcher because the user hasn't *officially* closed it. NASA TV will have to launch again before doing the background fetch.

Xcode 5 makes it easy to test both scenarios. Before going any further, make a mental note of the top news item in NASA TV's news tab; it should read *NASA Commercial Crew Partner SpaceX Completes Two Human-Critical Reviews*.

Testing background fetch on app resume

If you have the app running, hit the Home button, or ⌘ + Shift + H if you're running in the simulator. If the app is not running, build and run and then hit the Home button. Xcode should still say "Running NASA TV on …". If it doesn't, try again.

Switch over to Finder and navigate to the **NASA TV MAMP** directory. Open **news.json** and **news-addendum.txt** in your favorite text editor. **news.json** contains an array of the 7 news items that populate NASA TV's "News" tab, ranging from id 1000 through 1006. **news-addendum.txt** has an additional three news items with ids 1007 through 1009.

Copy and paste the three news items from **news-addendum.txt** to the top of the root array in **news.json**. The end result should look like this:

```
[
 {
 "id" : 1009,
 "date" : "07.03.13",
 "title" : "Long-Running NASA/CNES Ocean Satellite Takes Final
Bow",
 "subtitle" : "The curtain has come down on a superstar of the
satellite oceanography world that played the 'Great Blue Way' of
the world's ocean for 11 1/2 years."
 },

 {
 "id" : 1008,
 "date" : "07.03.13",
 "title" : "NASA Selects Electrical Systems Engineering Services
Contract",
 "subtitle" : "07.03.13 – NASA has awarded a contract to ASRC
Federal Space & Defense (AS&D) of Greenbelt, Md., for the
Electrical Systems Engineering Services II (ESES II) for ..."
 },

 {
 "id" : 1007,
 "date" : "07.02.13",
 "title" : "NASA Makes the Grade on the SBA Procurement
Scorecard",
 "subtitle" : "07.02.13 – NASA has achieved an 'A' on the fiscal
year 2012 (FY12) Small Business Administration (SBA) Procurement
Scorecard."
 },
 {
 "id" : 1006,
 "date" : "07.02.13",
 "title" : "NASA Commercial Crew Partner SpaceX Completes Two
Human-Critical Reviews",
```

```
    "subtitle" : "07.02.13 - Space Exploration Technologies Corp.
  (SpaceX) of Hawthorne, Calif., recently completed two milestones
  for NASA's Commercial Crew Integrated Capability ..."
  },
  ...
```

Save **news.json**. Although copy-and-pasting is pretty low tech, what you just did effectively *simulates* three new news stories becoming available on your backend service.

> **Note:** If the resulting JSON structure is not absolutely perfect, the background fetch won't work. You can use a JSON validator like JSONLint if you're not sure you pasted the 3 new items in the right location.

Now open **AppDelegate.m** and add a breakpoint on the first line of `application:performFetchWithCompletionHandler:`. This step is optional, but it will help convince yourself that your code is truly being executed despite the fact NASA TV is not running in the foreground.

Open Xcode's Debug menu and select **Simulate Background Fetch**. If you can't find it, you're probably looking at the Simulator's Debug menu instead of Xcode's Debug menu.

At this point the debugger should stop at the breakpoint you set. Feel free to step through to trace the code, or select **Debug\Continue** to continue execution.

Once the code completes, the badge icon for NASA TV should bubble up to 1, as shown:

Now bring NASA TV back into the foreground and verify that three new items you added to **news.json** are instantly available without refreshing:

Great success!

Testing background fetch on app launch

In the last section you tested background fetch while the app was suspended in the background. Now you're ready to test background fetch when the app is launched instead of resumed from the background.

If you are running in the simulator, stop the app and click on **iOS Simulator\Reset Content and Settings...** from the main menu. If you are running NASA TV on an actual device, long-press on NASA TV's icon until it shakes then delete it. This erases the app and its data store.

Now go to **news.json** and delete the 3 items from the top that you added in the previous section (ids 1009, 1008 and 1007). Build and run the app, which should reinstall NASA TV on your simulator or device. At this point you've reverted all the changes you made in your previous test.

Hit the Stop icon in Xcode, then double tap the Home button and remove NASA TV from the app switcher by flicking its snapshot upwards.

Now repeat the steps from the previous section to add the news items from **news-addendum.txt** back into **news.json**. Remember that this simulates three new stories coming into the back end service connected to `NewsViewController`. The only difference is that this time the new stories came in while NASA TV was not running at all — not even in the background.

Xcode 5 has a great way to simulate launching in the background due to a background fetch. First, click on the "NASA TV" scheme in the top left corner of Xcode and select "Edit Scheme", as shown below:

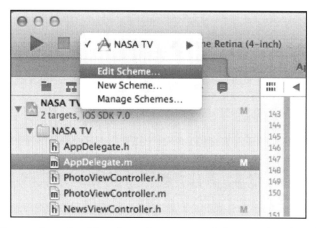

In the Scheme editor, select the "Run" configuration if it's not already selected and switch to the **Options** tab. Click on the checkbox next to "Launch due to a background fetch event", as so:

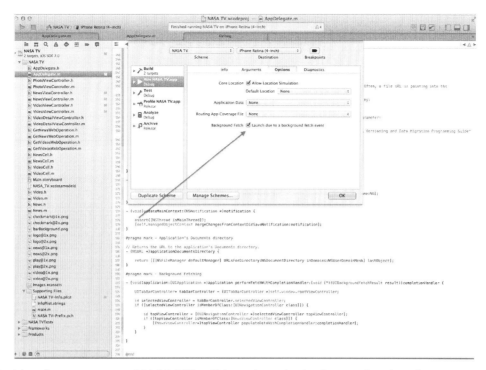

Build and run your app; NASA TV will launch in the background and perform a background fetch. You should not see any visible activity in your simulator or device. If you placed a breakpoint in `application:performFetchWithCompletionHandler:` then the debugger will pause at this point.

Resume the app if necessary and watch with bated breath as the NASA TV application badge icon bubbles up to one. Tap on NASA TV's icon to bring it to the foreground and verify that the new stories in the News tab are available immediately. Success yet again!

Once you're done, remember to edit your scheme and uncheck the background fetch checkbox from your Run configuration; otherwise NASA TV will keep launching in the background.

> **Note**: Another alternative is to create a separate scheme to test a background fetch from a background launch.
>
> Simply select "Duplicate Scheme" from the Scheme editor to create your new scheme and select the checkbox next to "Launch due to a background fetch event" in this duplicated Run configuration.
>
> This way, all you need to do is change schemes instead of modifying the normal Run configuration that you use all the time.

Challenges

You've successfully implemented background fetching on NASA TV. In doing so, you've also learned how to set up your own personal web server using MAMP. However, there is still a lot of ground to cover. Background fetching is only one of the three new multitasking APIs introduced in iOS 7. Completing this chapter's challenge is not required to continue to the next chapter but definitely work through it if you're looking for more practice implementing background fetching.

As always, you can find the complete solution in the resources folder you downloaded for this chapter. Remember not to rush to the solution if you get stuck! Work through the challenge as much as you can; that's where the real learning happens.

Challenge 1: Fetching videos in the background

The challenge for this chapter is to implement background fetch for the Videos tab. The solution will mostly follow what you already did for the News tab, except now we are only giving you hints rather than step-by-step instructions.

Here are a few hints:

- Modify `GetVideosWebOperation` so that the success block returns a BOOL property indicating if there were any new videos that weren't already in Core Data.

- Replace `VideoViewController`'s `populateData` with a public method that can accept the background fetch completion handler.

- Make sure you account for all three values of `UIBackgroundFetchResult` accurately.

- Modify the background fetching delegate method in `AppDelegate.m` so that the Videos tab takes care of the background fetch only if it is currently visible.

- Simulate new videos by copying JSON from **videos-addendum.txt** into **videos.json**.

- Test background fetching on app resume. Background fetching on app launch won't work the way you've set it up because by default the News tab is always visible on app launch.

If you got this working, congrats – you have a pretty good grasp of background fetching!

In the next chapter, you'll learn how to implement background transfers and silent push notifications, which will allow NASA TV to download videos for offline viewing and download NASA's Astronomy Picture of the Day as soon as it is available.

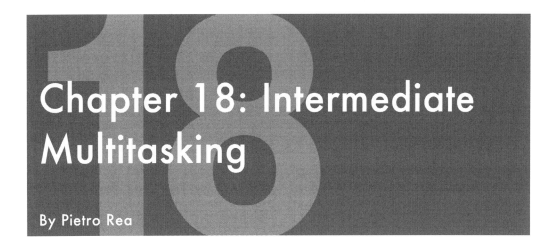

Chapter 18: Intermediate Multitasking

By Pietro Rea

In the previous chapter, you learned how to implement background fetching, which allows you to keep your app content up to date so the user always sees fresh content when they launch your app.

In this chapter, you'll learn about the other two multitasking APIs Apple introduced in iOS 7: background transfers and silent push notifications.

You'll continue to make modifications to the NASA TV application that you downloaded with this book's files. The changes in this chapter are not dependent on last chapter's changes, so if you didn't implement all of the functionality in the last chapter, don't worry – you can just begin with the starter project as-is.

Background transfers

In previous versions of iOS, quitting an app in the middle of an upload or download meant that your transfer would be paused — or killed altogether. In this chapter, you are going to focus on NSURLSession, which makes background transfers possible.

> **Note:** If you want to learn more about NSURLSession, make sure to read Chapter 16, "Networking with NSURLSession." It deals in depth with the new set of APIs in iOS 7 to perform common networking tasks.

Your first task in this chapter is to add the ability to download videos for offline viewing in NASA TV. An active download should continue even if the app isn't running in the foreground.

To start out, you're going to add a "Download" button and a progress bar to VideoDetailViewController. Open **Main.storyboard** and select the VideoDetailViewController scene on the far right.

Drag a UIBarButtonItem to the right side of VideoDetailViewController's navigation bar. In the Attributes inspector, change the UIBarButtonItem's Title property to **Download** as shown below:

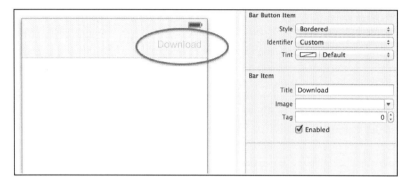

Similarly, drag a UIProgressView and place it to the left of the Download UIBarButtonItem you just dragged into the navigation bar. Change its default tint color under "View" to white.

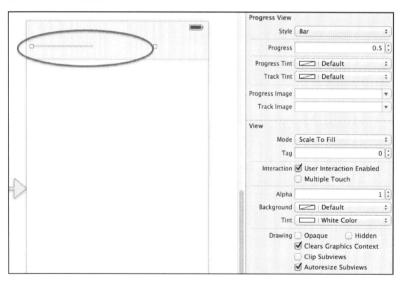

Next, connect the UIBarButton and UIProgressView to IBOutlets in code. Select the yellow View Controller icon on VideoDetailViewController's dock in the storyboard.

After that, select the **Assistant Editor** icon on the top right in Xcode; it looks like a butler wearing a bow tie. This will open **VideoDetailViewController.m** next to the storyboard.

Control-drag the Download button to the @interface section of **VideoDetailViewController.m** and name it **downloadButton**. Do the same with your **UIProgressView** (make sure you select the progress view inside the bar button item, not the bar button item itself) and name it progressView.

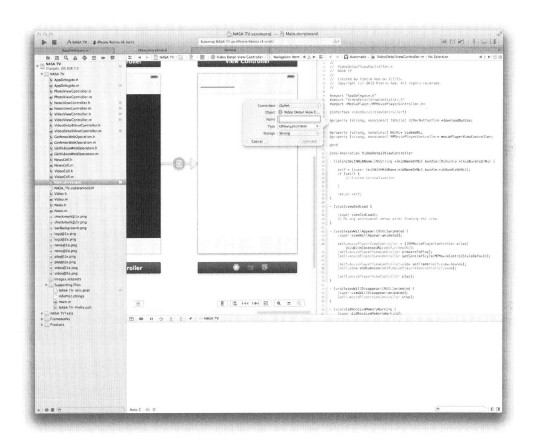

At this point, Xcode should have created two new properties for you:

```
@property (weak, nonatomic) IBOutlet
  UIBarButtonItem *downloadButton;

@property (weak, nonatomic) IBOutlet
  UIProgressView *progressView;
```

The download button is now connected to an `IBOutlet` in code, but it won't trigger anything when tapped. To fix this, control-drag from the button to the `@implementation` section in **VideoDetailViewController.m**.

This connection is going to be an action instead of an outlet. Name the `IBAction` method **downloadButtonTapped**; its code representation will look like the following:

```
- (IBAction)downloadButtonTapped:(id)sender {
}
```

Build and run your project; tap on the Videos tab to display the list of videos and then tap any video in the collection view. The `VideoDetailViewController` that is pushed into view should look similar to the one below:

Houston, we have liftoff! Well, not quite. The download button and the progress view look great but they don't do anything at the moment. You need to revisit **VideoDetailViewController.m** and add some code to perform those tasks.

Downloading videos

To add the code to download the video files, start by adding the following protocols to the @interface declaration in **VideoDetailViewController.m**:

```
@interface VideoDetailViewController() <NSURLSessionDelegate,
NSURLSessionTaskDelegate, NSURLSessionDownloadDelegate>
```

Those three protocols are necessary for monitoring the status of the download. Among other things, they allow you to update the UIProgressView that you just added to the user interface.

Next, add the following three properties to the @interface section:

```
@property (strong, nonatomic) NSURLSession* urlSession;
@property (strong, nonatomic)
NSURLSessionDownloadTask* downloadTask;
@property (strong, nonatomic) NSString* videosDirectoryPath;
```

The NSURLSession and NSURLSessionDownloadTask objects perform the heavy lifting in the download operation, while videosDirectoryPath points to the directory in the file system where the videos are going to be stored.

The methods that download and save the video are fairly large in size, so you're going to tackle it in small chunks. For now, just focus on making the progress view work properly when you tap on the download button.

Go to viewWillAppear: and add the following two lines to the top of the method:

```
- (void)viewWillAppear:(BOOL)animated {
    [super viewWillAppear:animated];

    self.progressView.progress = 0.0f;
    self.progressView.hidden = YES;
```

Those two lines ensure that the progress view is hidden and reset when the view controller first gets pushed into view.

Next, flesh out the implementation of downloadButtonTapped: as shown below:

```
- (IBAction)downloadButtonTapped:(id)sender {

    //1
    if ([self.video.availableOffline boolValue]) return;
```

```
    //2
    self.downloadButton.enabled = NO;
    self.progressView.hidden = NO;

    //3
    if (!self.urlSession) {

        NSURLSessionConfiguration* config =
        [NSURLSessionConfiguration defaultSessionConfiguration];

        self.urlSession =
        [NSURLSession
          sessionWithConfiguration:config
          delegate:self
          delegateQueue:[NSOperationQueue mainQueue]];
    }

    NSURLRequest *request = [NSURLRequest
                                requestWithURL:self.videoURL];

    self.downloadTask = [self.urlSession
                          downloadTaskWithRequest:request];

    //4
    [self.downloadTask resume];
  }
```

The method is short but it has important pieces that will come into play later. In the code above, you take the following actions:

1. Check if the current video's `availableOffline` property is set to `@(YES)` and if so, exit; this property indicates that a video has already been downloaded and prevents you from downloading it twice.

2. Disable the download button while the download operation is in progress to prevent launching a duplicate `NSURLSessionDownloadTask`; additionally, reveal the progress bar to show the download progress to the user.

3. Lazy instantiation of `NSURLSession`. The default configuration is fine for a simple download task but you'll have to change it to something else to enable background transfers. You'll deal with this a bit later.

4. Finally, start the download task.

Below `downloadButtonTapped:` add the following method implementation:

```objc
#pragma mark - NSURLSessionDownloadTask methods

- (void)URLSession:(NSURLSession *)session
      downloadTask:(NSURLSessionDownloadTask *)downloadTask
      didWriteData:(int64_t)bytesWritten
 totalBytesWritten:(int64_t)totalBytesWritten
totalBytesExpectedToWrite:(int64_t)totalBytesExpectedToWrite {

    dispatch_async(dispatch_get_main_queue(), ^{
        self.progressView.progress =
        (double)totalBytesWritten /
        (double)totalBytesExpectedToWrite;
    });
}
```

This method dispatches to the main thread to update the `UIProgressView` in `VideoDetailViewController`'s navigation bar so the user can see how the download is progressing.

Build and run your app; navigate to any video and tap **Download**; you should see the progress bar moving along from left to right. The download clearly finishes...but where's the video file?

`NSURLSessionDownloadTask` downloads the video into a temporary file — but if you don't immediately copy it to a permanent location, the file will simply vanish. Looks like you need to persist it somewhere.

Still in **VideoDetailViewController.m**, override the getter for the `videosDirectoryPath` property as shown below:

```objc
- (NSString*)videosDirectoryPath {

    if (!_videosDirectoryPath) {

        NSArray* paths =
        NSSearchPathForDirectoriesInDomains(NSCachesDirectory,
                                            NSUserDomainMask,
                                            YES);
        _videosDirectoryPath = [paths[0]
                                stringByAppendingPathComponent:
                                @"com.razeware.videos"];

        NSError* error;
        if (![[NSFileManager defaultManager]
```

```
            createDirectoryAtPath:_videosDirectoryPath
            withIntermediateDirectories:NO
            attributes:nil
            error:&error]) {

        /* Could not create directory */
        /* Handle NSFileManager error */
    }
  }
  return _videosDirectoryPath;
}
```

The code above creates a folder (if necessary) in your **Caches** directory and returns the directory reference to the caller. **Caches** is the recommended location to store files that may be regenerated or re-downloaded in the future.

Next, add the following method below the first `NSURLSessionDownloadTask` delegate method you implemented earlier:

```
- (void)URLSession:(NSURLSession *)session
    downloadTask:(NSURLSessionDownloadTask *)downloadTask
didFinishDownloadingToURL:(NSURL *)downloadURL {

    //1
    NSString* lastPathComponent =
    [downloadTask.originalRequest.URL lastPathComponent];

    //2
    NSString* destinationPath =
    [self.videosDirectoryPath
     stringByAppendingPathComponent:lastPathComponent];

    NSURL* destinationURL =
    [NSURL fileURLWithPath:destinationPath];

    //3
    NSError* error;

    BOOL copySuccessful =
    [[NSFileManager defaultManager]
     copyItemAtURL:downloadURL
     toURL:destinationURL
     error:&error];
```

```
        if (!copySuccessful) {
            /* Could not copy file to destinationURL */
            /* Handle NSFileManager error */
        }

        //4
        dispatch_async(dispatch_get_main_queue(), ^{
            self.video.availableOffline = @(YES);
            NSManagedObjectContext* moc =
            self.video.managedObjectContext;

            NSError* error;
            [moc save:&error];

            if (error) NSLog(@"Core Data error");

            //5
            self.progressView.hidden = YES;
            self.downloadButton.title = @"Downloaded";
        });
    }
```

That's a fair chunk of code, but it's explained comment by comment in the points below:

1. The video URLs are in the format http://192.168.1.111:44447/videos/video-name.mp4, where the path's lastComponent serves as the name of the file. The goal here is to extract the file name to build a reasonable file URL to which you can save the video permanently.

2. destinationPath represents the full file URL where the video is to be saved; it's the result of concatenating videosDirectoryPath to the video's file name. For example, **discovery.mp4** would be saved as …/Caches/com.razeware.videos/discovery.mp4.

3. This is where the magic happens. The first parameter is the URL for the downloaded video in its temporary location, and the second parameter gives the permanent location to save the video to before the file vanishes in a puff of digital smoke.

4. Update the videoAvailableOffline attribute of video to indicate that this video has been successfully downloaded, which downloadButtonTapped: uses to avoid re-downloading a video. This action must be dispatched to the main thread since the video that self.video points to was fetched on the main thread.

> **Note:** The Core Data details are not important for this chapter, but if you want to read more about using Core Data from multiple threads make sure to read Apple's Core Data Programming Guide.

5. Finally, hide the progress bar and change the text in the navigation bar from "Download" to "Downloaded". These small visual cues may seem unimportant now, but they will be helpful later when you're implementing background transfers.

Still in **VideoDetailViewController.m**, add the following empty method:

```
- (void)URLSession:(NSURLSession *)session
      downloadTask:(NSURLSessionDownloadTask *)downloadTask
 didResumeAtOffset:(int64_t)fileOffset
expectedTotalBytes:(int64_t)expectedTotalBytes {


}
```

This is a required `NSURLSessionDownloadTask` delegate method; you're not going to use it but it's included here to silence an Xcode warning.

You haven't yet taken care of the error handling. Although *nothing* ever goes wrong when downloading files over mobile networks, it's good practice to have it there just in case something glitches. ☺

If you encounter an error with the download, delete the temporary file from disk as the file will likely be of no use. Add the method implementation as shown below:

```
#pragma mark - NSURLSessionTaskDelegate methods

- (void)URLSession:(NSURLSession *)session
              task:(NSURLSessionTask *)task
didCompleteWithError:(NSError *)error {

    if (error) {
        NSString* lastPathComponent =
        [task.originalRequest.URL lastPathComponent];

        NSString* filePath =
        [self.videosDirectoryPath
         stringByAppendingPathComponent:lastPathComponent];

        [[NSFileManager defaultManager]
```

```
                removeItemAtPath:filePath error:nil];
        }
    }
```

If an error occurs, the above code generates the file URL from the video URL as you did before and deletes the temporary file.

Build and run your app. Try the following experiment: choose a video, download it, then (with the app still open) switch to Settings and go into Airplane mode or turn off Wi-Fi to simulate being offline. Switch back to your app and attempt to play your downloaded video — nothing happens! Why?

Enabling offline viewing

The video is present in the file system, but the movie player doesn't know how to find it. Solve this problem by modifying the code in `viewWillAppear:` as follows:

```
- (void)viewWillAppear:(BOOL)animated {
    [super viewWillAppear:animated];

    self.progressView.progress = 0.0f;
    self.progressView.hidden = YES;

    //1
    BOOL videoAvailableOffline =
    [self.video.availableOffline boolValue];

    NSURL* playbackVideoURL;

    //2
    if (videoAvailableOffline) {
        self.downloadButton.enabled = NO;
        self.downloadButton.title = @"Downloaded";

        /* Play local content if available */
        NSString* lastPathComponent =
        [self.videoURL lastPathComponent];

        NSString* videoPath =
        [self.videosDirectoryPath
         stringByAppendingPathComponent:lastPathComponent];

        playbackVideoURL = [NSURL fileURLWithPath:videoPath];
    }
```

```
    else {
        self.downloadButton.enabled = YES;
        playbackVideoURL = self.videoURL;
    }

    //3
    self.moviePlayerViewController =
    [[MPMoviePlayerController alloc]
     initWithContentURL:playbackVideoURL];

    [self.moviePlayerViewController prepareToPlay];

    [self.moviePlayerViewController
     setControlStyle:MPMovieControlStyleDefault];

    [self.moviePlayerViewController.view
     setFrame:self.view.bounds];

    [self.view addSubview:self.moviePlayerViewController.view];

    [self.moviePlayerViewController play];
}
```

Take a moment and go over the bits that you just added:

1. Recall that you had to update the `availableOffline` property when the download finished successfully. You have to unbox this `BOOL` because Core Data saves it as an `NSNumber`.

2. If the video is available locally, generate the file URL like you've been doing all along; otherwise, use the streaming URL in `self.video`. You can also use `availableOffline` to enable or disable the download button as needed, as there's no need to keep the download button active if you already have the video saved locally.

3. Here you're feeding `MPMoviePlayerController` a temporary variable named `playbackVideoURL` instead of `self.videoURL`. `playbackVideoURL` should have the correct URL based on whether or not the video is available locally.

Build and run NASA TV, navigate to any video and tap **Download**. After the download is complete, with the app still open switch to Settings and disable Wi-Fi, unplug the Ethernet cable, or do whatever you need to do to disconnect from the Internet. Switch back to your app, navigate to the same video and voila — your video now plays.

If you have a physical device, build and run your app on that as well; downloads are noticeably slower on physical devices, which will come in handy for your next task.

Re-enable your Internet connection, navigate to any video, and once again tap **Download**. However, this time quickly press the **Home** button before the download completes. Make a mental note of how far along the progress bar was when you quit NASA TV.

Wait about ten seconds, then restore your NASA TV app; the download should resume from exactly the same point at which you left it. That's not terribly pleasing to the user — but that's *exactly* what you're going to fix with background transfers.

Performing background transfers

Unlike other background modes, using background transfers does **not** require you to register for a special background mode in your application's `Info.plist`.

Add the following method to **AppDelegate.m**:

```
#pragma mark – Background Transfer

- (void)application:(UIApplication *)application
handleEventsForBackgroundURLSession:(NSString *)identifier
  completionHandler:(void (^)())completionHandler {

    NSDictionary* userInfo =
  @{@"completionHandler" : completionHandler,
    @"sessionIdentifier" : identifier};

    [[NSNotificationCenter defaultCenter]
     postNotificationName:@"BackgroundTransferNotification"
     object:nil
     userInfo:userInfo];
}
```

When a background transfer completes, the system calls `application:handleEventsForBackgroundURLSession:completionHandler:` which hands you a completion handler, just as was demonstrated in the previous chapter with background fetch.

In this case, the work to handle the background download work is done elsewhere. The delegate method delivers the completion handler by including it in the notification's `userInfo` dictionary.

An app can have several transfers queued up, so the NSURLSession identifier is posted as well so the receiver can identify which transfer completed.

Open **VideoDetailViewController.m** and add the following snippet of code to the bottom of viewWillAppear:

```
[[NSNotificationCenter defaultCenter]
 addObserver:self
 selector:@selector(handleBackgroundTransfer:)
 name:@"BackgroundTransferNotification"
 object:nil];
```

This simply adds an observer to the background transfer notification posted in **AppDelegate.m**.

Now scroll to the bottom of **VideoDetailViewController.m** and add the following:

```
#pragma mark - Background Transfers

- (void)handleBackgroundTransfer:(NSNotification*)notification {

    // 1
    NSString* sessionIdentifier =
    notification.userInfo[@"sessionIdentifier"];

    NSArray* components =
    [sessionIdentifier componentsSeparatedByString:@"."];

    NSString* videoID = [components lastObject];

    // 2
    if ([self.video.videoID integerValue] ==
        [videoID integerValue]) {

        // 3
        dispatch_async(dispatch_get_main_queue(), ^{
            self.downloadButton.title = @"Downloaded";
            self.progressView.hidden = YES;

            void(^completionHandler)(void) =
            notification.userInfo[@"completionHandler"];

            if (completionHandler) {
                completionHandler();
            }
```

```
            });
        }
    }
```

`handleBackgroundTransfer:` executes when a download complete notification arrives. There's a few new concepts introduced in this method:

1. Unpack the `NSURLSession` identifier from the notification's `userInfo` dictionary. The identifier is formatted similar to reverse DNS notation so the last component contains the video's ID.

2. If there are multiple downloads in progress, each one will have a `VideoDetailViewController` instance. Since it's possible that the video on the screen is not the same one identified in the notification, check that they match before continuing.

3. Perform the UI updates on the main thread: change "Download" to "Downloaded" and hide the progress bar. After that's done, execute the completion handler stored in the `userInfo` dictionary.

You've registered for the notification in `viewWillAppear:` so be sure to modify `viewWillDisappear:` to unregister for the notification as well:

```
- (void)viewWillDisappear:(BOOL)animated {
    [super viewWillDisappear:animated];
    [self.moviePlayerViewController stop];

    [[NSNotificationCenter defaultCenter]
    removeObserver:self];
}
```

The notifications and handlers now facilitate file transfers that will run to completion in the background. All that's left to do is configure `NSURLSession` to continue downloading the video in the background.

Go to `downloadButtonTapped:` and find the place where you lazy-load `NSURLSession`. Change that block of code as shown below:

```
    //3
    if (!self.urlSession) {

        NSString* sessionID =
        [@"com.razeware.backgroundsession."
         stringByAppendingFormat:@"%d",
         [self.video.videoID integerValue]];
```

```
NSURLSessionConfiguration* config =
[NSURLSessionConfiguration
 backgroundSessionConfiguration:sessionID];

self.urlSession =
[NSURLSession
 sessionWithConfiguration:config
 delegate:self
 delegateQueue:
 [NSOperationQueue mainQueue]];
}
```

Creating a background NSURLSessionConfiguration requires a session ID; this is the same ID that comes back in the delegate call application:handleEventsForBackgroundURLSession:completionHandler:.

In this case, you are using a reverse DNS notation and appending the video ID to the end. Make sure to create unique session IDs— these IDs will also show up in the debugger and help you track down the pertinent video if something goes wrong.

You're almost ready to test. But first add a breakpoint to **AppDelegate.m** inside application:handleEventsForBackgroundURLSession:completionHandler: and another one to **VideoViewController.m** inside handleBackgroundTransfer: right after the completion handler gets executed.

Build and run on your physical device; the slower download speed on the device gives you a little more time to quit the app mid-download to test your work.

Now navigate to any video, tap **Download** and press the **Home** button once the progress bar is halfway done.

Step away from your computer for a bit; maybe grab a sandwich or a coffee, or solve a Millennium Prize Problem, whatever you choose. When you come back, Xcode's debugger will be paused at the breakpoint you inserted in **AppDelegate.m,** as shown:

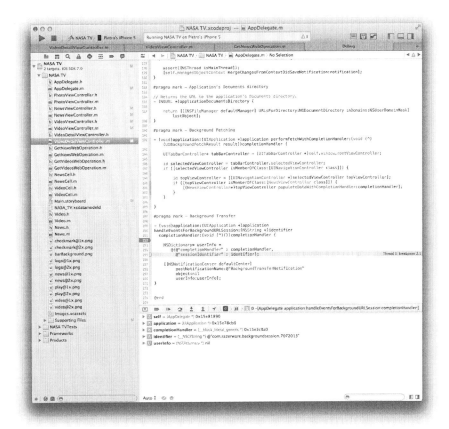

Click on **Continue** to move to the next breakpoint, which pauses the debugger immediately after executing the completion handler in **VideoDetailViewController.m.** Click on **Continue** once again to resume normal execution.

So that proves the completion handler was executed as expected — but was the app switcher screenshot updated? To find out, double-tap the **Home** button on your device to enter the app switcher and find the NASA TV screenshot, as shown on the next page:

Notice that the button in the top right reads "Downloaded", which means that the video has been copied permanently into the file system. At no point did you re-launch NASA TV to check on the download's progress, yet the app switcher snapshot tells you that the download completed successfully! This is your proof that the completion handler was called at the right moment.

Discretionary transfers

In the previous section you queued up a background transfer while the app was running in the foreground. However, it is also possible to start and finish a transfer entirely from the background, such as when the app wakes up for a background fetch operation or responds to a silent push notification.

Background transfers started from the background are **discretionary transfers**, which means they are power-managed and will only work over Wi-Fi.

You can optionally set foreground transfers to be discretionary by setting a BOOL property in NSURLSessionConfiguration named discretionary.

Keep discretionary transfers in the back of your mind as you implement background transfers. Users can easily see if your app is being a data hog by checking the Settings app, so it's up to you to determine whether the transfer is important enough.

Silent push notifications

The goal for traditional push notifications is to alert the user of something interesting going on — even if they're not using your app at the moment. This could be something like breaking news, a friend responding to a Facebook status or the latest issue of your favorite magazine becoming available.

Push notifications essentially *simulate* multitasking, making it seem like your app is constantly polling new information in the background and alerting you anytime something interesting happens. iOS 7 extends this concept by introducing silent push notifications, which allow third-party developers to trigger background refreshes without bothering the user.

When a device receives a silent push notification there is no visual indication that anything happened. But make no mistake: your app has been launched in the background and it is now fetching new content.

Unfortunately, push notifications won't work with the simulator, so you'll have to run NASA TV on a physical device in order to complete this section of the chapter.

> **Note:** If you want to learn more about traditional push notifications, you should read the following two-part tutorial that covers them in depth:
>
> Part 1: http://www.raywenderlich.com/32960/apple-push-notification-services-in-ios-6-tutorial-part-1
> Part 2: http://www.raywenderlich.com/32963/apple-push-notification-services-in-ios-6-tutorial-part-2

Certificates and provisioning

To send push notifications, you'll need to set up two things in the developer portal: a key and certificate to communicate with Apple's push notification servers, and a provisioning profile specific to your app.

If you're an old hand at this, you can set this up yourself and jump ahead to the next section. Otherwise, read on — creating the certificate and profile involves a fair number of steps but the whole process shouldn't take more than a few minutes.

The first thing you must do is to generate a *certificate signing request* file, also known as a CSR. You do this using the **Keychain Access** application on your Mac. This application ships with every Mac – it's in the Utilities folder inside Applications.

With Keychain Access open, select **Certificate Assistant \ Request a Certificate From a Certificate Authority...** from the Keychain Access menu.

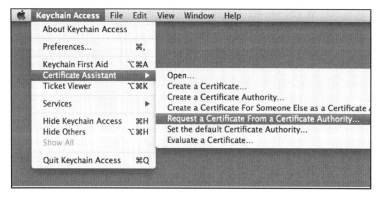

Type in your e-mail address and enter **NASA TV** as the common name. Select the "Saved to disk" radio button and leave the field "CA Email Address" blank as shown below:

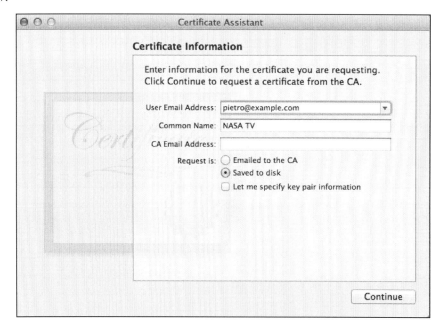

Click **Continue** when you're done entering your information, enter a filename of your choice and click **Save**. This will save a file with the extension **.certSigningRequest** to your desktop.

Now you need to create a unique App ID for NASA TV in Apple's developer portal. Log into Apple's iOS Developer Member Center and select **Certificates, Identifiers & Profiles**.

Select **Identifiers** under the iOS Apps heading, and then **App IDs**. This will show you a complete list of all your current App IDs. Click on the plus button in the top right corner to create a new App ID.

Enter **NASA TV** as the name of your new App ID, leave the App ID Prefix as the default value (Team ID), and under App ID Suffix select the radio box **Explicit App ID**. For Bundle ID, type in **com.razeware.NASA-TV** (but replace razeware with your own name or company name). This is the bundle ID that identifies NASA TV in Info.plist.

Finally, select the checkbox next to **Push Notifications** under the section called App Services.

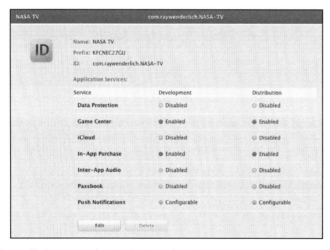

Double check all the information you just entered; if everything checks out, select **Continue** and then **Submit** to register your new App ID for NASA TV.

Back in the list of App IDs, select the ID you just created for NASA TV; it should say that Game Center and In-App Purchase are Enabled but that Push Notifications are Configurable.

Click **Edit** and scroll down to the Push Notification section. You should see two different "Create Certificate..." buttons: one for the Development SSL certificate and another one for the Production SSL certificate. In the **Development SSL Certificate** section, select **Create Certificate...**

> **Note:** The development certificate is used for testing push notifications with
> debug builds of the app. The production SSL certificate would be used with the
> release build submitted to the App Store.

To create the SSL certificate, you'll have to upload the **.certSigningRequest** file you
created using Keychain Access. Select **Continue** and then **Choose File...** and
navigate to the CSR on your Desktop. Then click **Generate**.

When the upload is complete, you can download the SSL certificate from the App ID
settings screen as shown here:

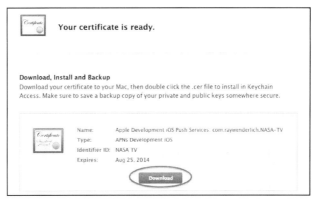

Double click on the downloaded SSL certificate to install it to your keychain. Open Keychain Access and find the certificate you just added under **My Certificates**; it's called *Apple Development iOS Push Services: com.razeware.NASA-TV*, as shown in the screenshot below:

Right-click on the certificate and select "Export Apple Development IOS Push Services…" and you'll be presented with the following dialog:

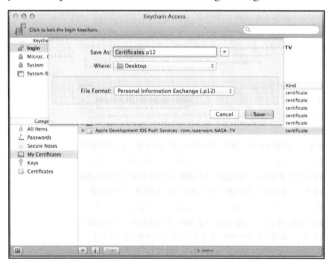

Select **Personal Information Exchange (.p12)** as the file format and click **Save**. At this point you will be given the option of entering a password to protect the .p12 file.

Don't enter any password; just select **OK**. You may be asked to enter your OS X password so that Keychain Access can export your certificate.

If everything went smoothly, you should have a .p12 saved and ready to be used to send push notifications.

The next step is to create a provisioning profile so that your device can register for and receive push notifications.

Note: A provisioning profile ties together a developer, an App ID and a set of devices that the application is allowed to run on. You could normally use your *wildcard* provisioning profile, which is not specific to any one App ID, to get any app to run on one of your development devices.

You can't do this here because a push notifications won't work if you sign your app with your wildcard provisioning profile. You have to create a provisioning profile using the push-enabled App ID you created a minute ago.

Once again, log into Apple's developer portal and select **Certificates, Identifiers & Profiles**.

In the **iOS** section, select **Provisioning Profiles** and click the plus button to create a new provisioning profile.

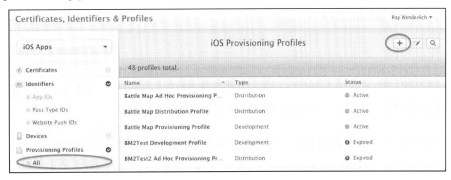

Select **iOS App Development** as the provisioning profile type and click **Continue**.

> **Note:** You won't need to create an App Store provisioning profile for the purposes of this chapter, but you'd need to create one if you were submitting NASA TV to the App Store.

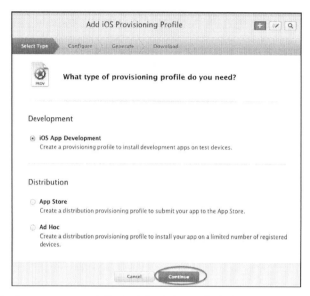

Select the App ID that you created for NASA TV and click **Continue**:

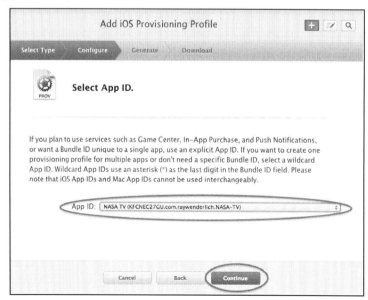

Next, select your iOS Development certificate(s) you wish to be able to sign this app and click **Continue**. As mentioned before, this certificate identifies you as a developer:

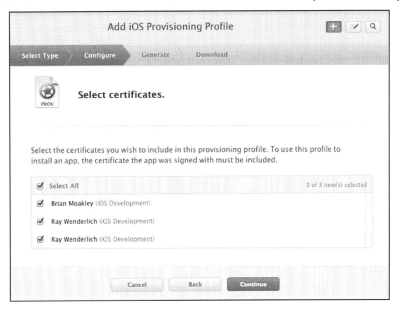

The next step asks you to choose the devices that will be tied to the new provisioning portal. Choose the device(s) that you will use to test silent push notifications and select **Continue**:

Note: Your device will only appear on the list above if it's already been added to your developer portal. If it hasn't, you can do this in Xcode's Organizer window.

Finally, choose a descriptive name for your provisioning profile such as **NASA TV Push-Enabled Development Profile** and click **Generate**:

Download your push-enabled provisioning profile from the next screen and install it in Xcode by double-clicking the downloaded file.

If all went well, you should see it your new provisioning profile in the Xcode account details. Open the **Preferences** window in Xcode and switch to the **Accounts** tab. Select your developer account and click the **View Details...** button, and you'll see your new provisioning profile, as shown below:

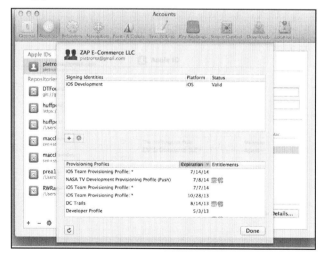

The final step is to match up the NASA TV project with the new provisioning profile.

Select the project file in the left-hand menu. Select the **Build Settings** tab and in the top right corner select **All** instead of Basic and **Levels** instead of Combined. This set of options should show you what the settings are at the project level as well as the individual target level.

Look for **Code Signing Identity** as well as **Provisioning Profile**.

Make sure the correct signing identity is selected for **Debug** at the target level. This should be the same development certificate that you used to create the push-enabled provisioning profile.

Also make sure that **Provisioning Profile** points to the push-enabled provisioning profile at the Target level.

Change these settings at the project level (second column) as well as the target level (third column). You'll know the settings are set correctly when the leftmost column **Resolved** has the correct values for **Code Signing Identity** and **Provisioning Profile** assigned.

Using Parse for push notifications

Push notifications, silent or otherwise, require a web server to talk to the Apple Push Notification Service (APNS). Instead of building a custom web service from scratch, you're going to take a shortcut and use **Parse**.

The first step in integrating Parse into NASA TV is to create a Parse account. Go to Parse's homepage and click **Sign Up** in the upper right hand corner.

Create an account with a username and password and click **Sign Up** again, shown in the screenshot on the next page.

Next, type **NASA TV** where it asks you to write your app's name and sign up as an **Individual Developer**. Next, click on **Start using Parse**, as shown below:

Ordinarily, you'd download and install Parse's SDK at this point. However, the starter project for NASA TV already contains the latest version of the SDK and required frameworks as of this writing.

Remember the .p12 certificate file that is sitting on your Desktop collecting dust? It's time to upload it to Parse.

Go to Parse, navigate to NASA TV's dashboard by selecting NASA TV in the top left drop down menu and click on the **Settings** tab in the top right corner.

Once in **Settings**, click on **Push notifications** on the left hand menu. You should see a screen similar to the one shown:

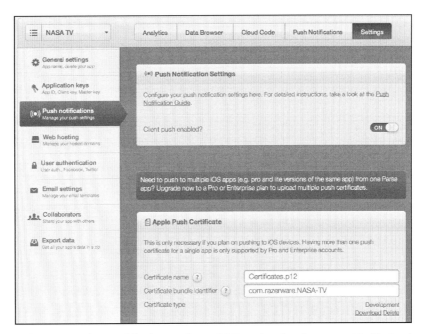

Turn the **Client push enabled** switch to **ON** and upload your .p12 file in the section named Apple Push Certificate. Verify that the certificate bundle identifier is **com.razeware.NASA-TV**. Also verify that the certificate type is Development.

Now that the setup is complete, you can now integrate the Parse SDK into NASA TV. Open **AppDelegate.m** and insert the following import statement at the top of the file:

```
#import <Parse/Parse.h>
```

After that, scroll down to `application:didFinishLaunchingWithOptions:` and add the following lines before the return statement:

```
[Parse setApplicationId:@"YOUR-APP-ID"
        clientKey:@"YOUR-CLIENT-KEY"];
```

You can find your application ID as well as your client key by navigating to NASA TV's **Settings** dashboard in Parse and selecting **Application keys** from the left hand menu, as shown on the next page:

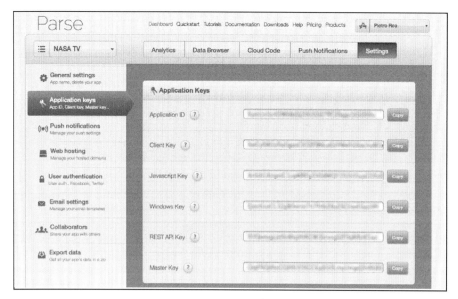

Before returning from application:didFinishLaunchingWithOptions: add the following line of code:

```
// Register for push notifications
[application registerForRemoteNotificationTypes:
    (UIRemoteNotificationTypeBadge |
     UIRemoteNotificationTypeAlert |
     UIRemoteNotificationTypeSound)];
```

registerForRemoteNotificationTypes: prompts iOS to ask the user if they would like to receive push notifications from NASA TV.

Next, scroll to the end of **AppDelegate.m** and add following two methods, which come straight from the Parse Push setup documentation:

```
#pragma mark - Push notification

- (void)application:(UIApplication *)application
didRegisterForRemoteNotificationsWithDeviceToken:
(NSData *)newDeviceToken {

    PFInstallation *currentInstallation =
    [PFInstallation currentInstallation];
    [currentInstallation setDeviceTokenFromData:newDeviceToken];
    [currentInstallation saveInBackground];
}

- (void)application:(UIApplication *)application
```

```
didReceiveRemoteNotification:(NSDictionary *)userInfo {
    [PFPush handlePush:userInfo];
}
```

The first delegate method shown above is required to implement silent push notifications. If the user elects to receive push notifications from NASA TV, their iOS device is assigned a device identifier token. This token comes back in the form of an opaque `NSData` called `newDeviceToken`.

You have to give this token to Parse using the `PFInstallation` object so that your device can start receiving push notifications from APNS.

The second delegate method handles regular push notifications and will help you verify that everything was set up properly with Parse.

Build and run your project on a physical device; you should see an alert view asking you if NASA TV can send you push notifications. Tap OK to accept.

> **Note:** You'll only see this push notification alert view once. If you select "Don't Allow" by accident, you'll have to go to the Notification Center section of the Settings app to change the setting.

Now go back to Parse and select the **Push Notifications** tab of the NASA TV app.

Click on the **Send a Push** button in the top-right. If you see "1 recipient" on the right side of the screen, as shown below, this means your device successfully uploaded its device token to Parse:

To send a push notification, type a short message under "Compose message" and click **Send Notification** at the bottom of the screen.

Your iOS device should immediately receive the push notification and present the message you just typed into Parse front and center, like so:

Implementing silent push notifications

Okay, so regular push notifications seem to be working correctly. Now it's time to implement silent push notifications.

When there's a new NASA photo of the day, you want the NASA TV app to stay up to date by downloading the photo in the background. You'll use a silent push notification to let the app know the photo is available.

Like background fetching, the first thing you have to do is register for remote notifications in Xcode. In Xcode, click on the project file and navigate to the new **Capabilities** tab, like so:

The switch next to **Background Modes** should already be set to ON from the last chapter. If, not, turn it on now.

Then select the checkbox next to **Remote notifications**. This is the same as adding the `remote-notification` key to the `UIBackgroundModes` array in Info.plist manually.

Next, open **AppDelegate.h** and add the following block property to the public interface:

```
@property (copy, nonatomic)
void(^silentRemoteNotificationCompletionHandler)
(UIBackgroundFetchResult);
```

Just like the other new background modes, you'll receive a completion handler to call when you've finished responding to the silent push notification. This property stores that completion handler for later use.

Now switch to **AppDelegate.m** and implement the method
`application:didReceiveRemoteNotification:fetchCompletionHandler:` at the bottom of the file:

```
- (void)application:(UIApplication *)application
didReceiveRemoteNotification:(NSDictionary *)userInfo
```

```
fetchCompletionHandler:
(void (^)(UIBackgroundFetchResult))completionHandler {

    //1
    self.silentRemoteNotificationCompletionHandler =
    completionHandler;

    //2
    UIStoryboard* sb =
    [UIStoryboard storyboardWithName:@"Main" bundle:nil];

    PhotoViewController* photoViewController =
    [sb instantiateViewControllerWithIdentifier:
     @"PhotoViewController"];

    UINavigationController *navController =
    [[UINavigationController alloc]
     initWithRootViewController:photoViewController];

    UITabBarController* rootViewController =
    (UITabBarController *)self.window.rootViewController;

    //3
    [rootViewController
     presentViewController:navController
     animated:YES
     completion:nil];
}
```

This new delegate method runs when your application receives a silent push notification. Just like the background fetching delegate method from the previous chapter, this method receives a completion handler of type (void(^)(`UIBackgroundFetchResult` result).

To see how the silent push notifications are handled, lets walk through the code step-by-step:

1. Save the completion handler in the public block property silentRemoteNotificationCompletionHandler. Instead of handing the completion handler to PhotoViewController, PhotoViewController will look for it here when it's done downloading NASA's photo of the day.

2. Instantiate an instance of `PhotoViewController` from the main storyboard. If you inspect **Main.storyboard**, you'll see that the `PhotoViewController` scene has no incoming or outgoing segues, so this is one of the few ways of getting a hold of one.

3. Finally, present the `PhotoViewController` from the root `UITabBarController`. The `PhotoViewController` is responsible for downloading NASA's daily photo and calling the completion handler.

Now switch to **PhotoViewController.m** and add the following import statement at the top of the file:

```
#import "AppDelegate.h"
```

Next, add the following properties and protocols to the top of the file, beneath the imports:

```
@interface PhotoViewController () <NSURLSessionDelegate,
NSURLSessionTaskDelegate, NSURLSessionDownloadDelegate>

@property (strong, nonatomic) NSURLSession* urlSession;
@property (strong, nonatomic)
  NSURLSessionDownloadTask* downloadTask;

@property (strong, nonatomic) NSString* photosDirectoryPath;

@end
```

The `NSURLSession` and download task will download the photo. `photosDirectoryPath`, on the other hand, will point to the directory that stores all of your daily photos.

Next, implement `viewWillAppear:` as follows:

```
- (void)viewWillAppear:(BOOL)animated {
    [super viewWillAppear:(BOOL)animated];

    //1
    NSString* baseURLString =
    [[NSUserDefaults standardUserDefaults]
     objectForKey:@"baseURLString"];

    NSString* urlString =
    [NSString stringWithFormat:@"%@%@",
     baseURLString, @"/photos/dailyphoto.jpg"];
```

```
        NSURL *photoURL = [NSURL URLWithString:urlString];

        NSURLRequest *request =
        [NSURLRequest requestWithURL:photoURL];

        //2
        NSString* sessionIdentifier =
        @"com.razeware.backgroundsession.dailyphoto";

        NSURLSessionConfiguration *configuration =
        [NSURLSessionConfiguration
         backgroundSessionConfiguration:sessionIdentifier];

        self.urlSession =
        [NSURLSession
         sessionWithConfiguration:configuration
         delegate:self
         delegateQueue:nil];

        //3
        self.downloadTask = [self.urlSession
                             downloadTaskWithRequest:request];

        [self.downloadTask resume];
  }
```

This should look almost identical to what you did for background transfers. In brief, each commented section does the following:

1. In reality, you'd be downloading the image straight from NASA's website. However, for the purposes of this tutorial you'll download an image from your local MAMP server.

2. Create a background NSURLSession with identifier **com.razeware.backgroundsession.dailyphoto**. It's important that the identifier is unique to avoid collisions with other background transfers elsewhere in the app.

3. Finally, recall that all NSURLSessionTask objects, including all of its subclasses, start in a suspended state. The instance method resume starts the operation.

Scroll to the bottom of the file and override the photosDirectoryPath getter as follows:

```
  - (NSString*)photosDirectoryPath {
```

```
    if (!_photosDirectoryPath) {

        NSArray* paths =
        NSSearchPathForDirectoriesInDomains(NSCachesDirectory,
                                            NSUserDomainMask,
                                            YES);
        _photosDirectoryPath =
        [paths[0] stringByAppendingPathComponent:
         @"com.razeware.photos"];

        NSError* error;
        if (![[NSFileManager defaultManager]
              createDirectoryAtPath:_photosDirectoryPath
              withIntermediateDirectories:NO
              attributes:nil
              error:&error]) {
          /* Could not create directory */
          /* Handle NSFileManager error */
        }

    }
    return _photosDirectoryPath;
}
```

The first time `self.photosDirectoryPath` is accessed, this getter method creates a directory called **com.razeware.photos** in **.../Library/Caches/**, just as you did for videos earlier in this chapter.

Now implement `URLSession:downloadTask:didFinishDownloadingToURL:` as shown below:

```
#pragma mark – NSURLSessionDownloadTaskDelegate methods

- (void)URLSession:(NSURLSession *)session
      downloadTask:(NSURLSessionDownloadTask *)downloadTask
didFinishDownloadingToURL:(NSURL *)downloadURL {

    NSString* lastPathComponent =
    [downloadTask.originalRequest.URL lastPathComponent];

    NSString* destinationPath =
    [self.photosDirectoryPath
     stringByAppendingPathComponent:lastPathComponent];
```

```
    NSURL* destinationURL =
    [NSURL fileURLWithPath:destinationPath];

    NSError* error;
    [[NSFileManager defaultManager]
     removeItemAtPath:destinationPath error:&error];

    BOOL copySuccessful =
    [[NSFileManager defaultManager]
     copyItemAtURL:downloadURL
     toURL:destinationURL
     error:&error];

    if (copySuccessful) {
        dispatch_async(dispatch_get_main_queue(), ^{
            UIImage *image = [UIImage imageWithContentsOfFile:
                                [destinationURL path]];
            self.imageView.image = image;
        });
    }
    else {
        NSLog(@"Error: %@", error.localizedDescription);
    }
}
```

The above delegate method runs when the download task completes. Inside the method you copy your newly downloaded photo from the temporary location in downloadURL to the permanent location in self.photosDirectoryPath.

Your downloaded photo is now safely ensconced in the file system and all is happy in the world. Not so fast, though — wasn't this part of a silent push notification? That's right – you still need to call the completion handler.

To tie this all together, implement URLSession:task:didCompleteWithError: as shown below:

```
#pragma mark - NSURLSessionTaskDelegate methods

- (void)URLSession:(NSURLSession *)session
            task:(NSURLSessionTask *)task
didCompleteWithError:(NSError *)error {

    //1
```

```
        AppDelegate* appDelegate =
        (AppDelegate*)[[UIApplication sharedApplication] delegate];

        void(^completionHandler)(UIBackgroundFetchResult) =
        appDelegate.silentRemoteNotificationCompletionHandler;

        //2
        if (error) {
            if (completionHandler) {
                completionHandler(UIBackgroundFetchResultFailed);
            }
            NSLog(@"Error : %@", error.localizedDescription);
        }
        else if (completionHandler) {
            [self postLocalNotification];
            completionHandler(UIBackgroundFetchResultNewData);
        }

        //3
        appDelegate.silentRemoteNotificationCompletionHandler = nil;
}
```

Despite this method's pessimistic name, it's called both on success and failure of the delegate. Here's how it works:

1. As promised, `PhotoViewController` retrieves the completion handler stored in `AppDelegate` once the download is complete.

2. Just as in background fetch, execute the completion handler passing in one of three possible `UIBackgroundFetchResult` values: new data, no data, or failure. If there is no error, call the completion handler with `UIBackgroundFetchResultNewData` and post a local notification to alert the user that their photo is ready. Otherwise, call the completion handler with `UIBackgroundFetchResultNoData`.

3. For safety, set the completion handler in `AppDelegate` to `nil`. You don't want to be calling a stale completion handler, do you?

> **Note:** The assumption here is that this particular silent push notification will only be sent out when a new photo is available; therefore in this case there's no need to implement `UIBackgroundFetchResultNoData`. However, this may not be true for all applications of silent push notifications.

Finally, implement `postLocalNotification` as shown below.

```
- (void)postLocalNotification {

    UILocalNotification* localNotification =
    [[UILocalNotification alloc] init];

    localNotification.fireDate = [NSDate date];
    localNotification.alertBody =
    @"Astronomy Picture of the Day Available";
    localNotification.applicationIconBadgeNumber++;

    [[UIApplication sharedApplication]
     presentLocalNotificationNow:localNotification];
}
```

To the user, this looks like a traditional remote push notification. In reality, it's the end of a journey that took you from silent push notification to background transfer to local notification. This pattern allows you to be 100% sure that the asset you downloaded is ready for viewing by the time the user sees the local notification.

Before you test out the code, add the following two download task delegate methods:

```
- (void)URLSession:(NSURLSession *)session
      downloadTask:(NSURLSessionDownloadTask *)downloadTask
      didWriteData:(int64_t)bytesWritten
 totalBytesWritten:(int64_t)totalBytesWritten
totalBytesExpectedToWrite:(int64_t)totalBytesExpectedToWrite {

}

- (void)URLSession:(NSURLSession *)session
      downloadTask:(NSURLSessionDownloadTask *)downloadTask
 didResumeAtOffset:(int64_t)fileOffset
expectedTotalBytes:(int64_t)expectedTotalBytes {

}
```

You're just adding them to satisfy the compiler, or else it will throw warnings. You can just leave them blank as you're not using them in this app.

Testing silent push notifications

Everything is in place to send your first silent push notification! Build and run your project on a physical device, and ensure your device is connected to Wi-Fi. Why? Since the photo download will be queued in the background, the download will work in discretionary mode and only work over Wi-Fi.

With NASA TV running in the foreground, press the **Home** button to go back to Springboard. Make sure Xcode still says "Running NASA TV on…"

Go back to Parse and navigate to NASA TV's push notification dashboard. Click **Send a Push**. This is where you sent the first push notification earlier in the chapter. Under **Compose message** flip the switch from Message to JSON, like so:

Every push notification has a JSON payload. The **Message** setting you used the first time around simply wrapped your message in a JSON dictionary.

The earlier message of "Houston, we have a problem." was actually sent in this format:

```
{
    "aps": {
        "alert": "Houston, we have a problem.",
        "sound": "default"
    }
}
```

The push notification information is contained inside a JSON dictionary called aps.

To send a *silent* push notification, the only thing you have to include in the aps dictionary is the content-available flag, shown below:

```
{
    "aps": {
        "content-available": 1
    }
}
```

Paste the silent push notification payload above into the **Compose message** field in Parse, then click **Send notification** at the bottom of the screen.

You should see the local notification pop up on your device's screen. In addition, NASA TV's app icon should have a badge of one.

> **Note:** Be patient if you don't immediately see the local notification after you send the silent push notification from Parse. The daily photo download is discretionary so it may be slow to complete.

Tapping on either the notification banner or the app icon reveals the photograph of the day ready to be viewed:

Great job! Silent push notifications don't have to be coupled with local notifications but in this case they worked well together to download the daily photograph and notify the user on completion.

Where To Go From Here?

Congratulations! You've successfully implemented background transfers and silent push notifications, which are two of the three new multitasking APIs in iOS 7. The previous chapter showed you how to implement the third — background fetching.

The new iOS 7 multitasking APIs enable you to do things that were never before possible in iOS. From auto-refreshing news feeds to downloads that continue even if your app crashes, the sky is the limit. ☺

However, as you well know — with great power comes great responsibility. Although not covered in the book, you should be aware that the new multitasking APIs can complicate issues of data protection and user privacy.

You should aim to keep your app snapshot up to date in the new app switcher, but take extra precautions if your snapshot could contain login credentials or other sensitive information such as data you'd normally have to log in to access.

Warnings aside, you now have the knowledge to leave your users feeling like your app "just works". So go out into the world and use the new multitasking APIs to anticipate your user's needs. They'll be glad you did.

Challenges

Completing this chapter's challenge will give you more practice with silent push notifications (and push notifications in general). As always, the complete solution is included in the resources folder you downloaded for this chapter.

Don't rush to the solution if you feel like you're getting stuck. Work through the challenge as much as possible before seeking help; that's where the real learning happens!

Challenge 1: "Unsilent" push notifications

If you've followed along with this chapter, you should have an app that's fully provisioned to receive push notifications from Parse. For this challenge, instead of downloading NASA's Astronomy Picture of the Day from a silent push notification, kick off the operation via a regular push notification.

Here are some hints:

- Identify the `UIApplicationDelegate` method that handles regular push notifications. It is one of the two methods that contains boilerplate code from the Parse SDK in **AppDelegate.m**.

- Copy the code that presents `PhotoViewController` into the app delegate method that handles regular push notifications. Remember that PhotoViewController has to be embedded in a `UINavigationController`.

- Go to Parse and send out a test push notification. There's no need to send raw JSON. The NASA TV app should show an alert view and a `PhotoViewController` should be presented behind it.

Challenge 2: Silent push notifications with metadata

Just because silent push notifications don't alert the recipient doesn't mean you can't send arbitrary information to your application embedded in the payload. You can think of this as another way to communicate between your application and your backend server — one that the user never gets to see! The only limitation is that the notification payload must not exceed 256 bytes.

In this challenge, add a custom field to the silent push notification — the name of the photo —and display it on `PhotoViewController`'s navigation bar.

This is the JSON payload you are going to send from Parse:

```
{
    "aps": {
        "content-available": 1
    },
    "photoTitle": "Nebula"
}
```

Your task is to display "Nebula" in `PhotoViewController`'s navigation bar when the app receives the silent push notification.

Here are some hints:

- The payload dictionary is passed to the app delegate method that handles silent push notifications. Extract `photoTitle` from this dictionary and store it in an `NSString`.

- Change `PhotoViewController`'s `title` property to `photoTitle` *after* presenting `PhotoViewController` from **AppDelegate.m**.

- Go to Parse and send the notification shown above while the app is in the foreground. Don't forget to send raw JSON instead of using Parse's message interface.

Chapter 19: JavaScript Core Framework

By Pietro Rea

Since the beginning of time (okay, okay, since the beginning of the mobile platform wars), mobile technology has been witness to an epic battle between native apps and web apps. In one corner, you have Objective-C powering native applications on iOS. In the opposite corner, you have the heavyweights HTML, CSS and JavaScript.

Before iOS 7, native and web apps hardly ever talked to each other; if they did, it was a pretty awkward conversation. If you wanted to render HTML or run JavaScript in iOS, you had to use a mostly self-contained `UIWebView`. All of that changes with the introduction of the JavaScriptCore framework in iOS 7.

In this chapter you'll explore the JavaScriptCore framework while you build a simple text adventure game that integrates Objective-C code with JavaScript elements. As well, you'll discover the potential memory management grues that lurk deep in the heart of this new framework.

> **Note:** Don't worry if you haven't worked much with JavaScript in the past. The syntax is simple and you'll be able to follow along with the chapter, learning along the way.

Introducing JavaScriptCore

JavaScriptCore is an Objective-C API that bridges JavaScript and Objective-C. With only a few lines of code, you can run JavaScript from Objective-C — and Objective-C from JavaScript.

This may sound like old news to you if you've already integrated native apps with web apps. Couldn't you do all of that before using a UIWebView?

You're absolutely right; in previous versions of iOS, you could pass a JavaScript string to your web view with the `stringByEvaluatingJavaScriptFromString:` message.

And if you wanted to run Objective-C from JavaScript, you could open a URL with a custom scheme (e.g. foo://) and handle it in the web view's delegate method `webView:shouldStartLoadWithRequest:navigtionType`.

However, as you continue reading this chapter you'll realize that JavaScriptCore is a superior way of interacting with JavaScript. Some of its benefits are:

• You can now use JavaScript outside of a `UIWebView`; there's no need to create a web view anymore if all you need to do is run a simple script.

• You can use modern Objective-C features such as blocks and collection subscripting. This is much better than the web view hacks you've undoubtedly used in the past.

• You can seamlessly pass values and objects between Objective-C and JavaScript, which wasn't possible in previous versions of iOS.

• You can create hybrid objects: native objects can have JavaScript values (including JavaScript functions) as properties. Imagine creating a native button that calls a

JavaScript function instead of Objective-C code when it's tapped. Oh yes, my friends — the future is now.

Integrating JavaScript with Objective-C can be useful in a lot of apps. Here are some cases where this might be useful:

- **Rapid development and prototyping**. If you have an area in your app that changes frequently (such as gameplay logic or some types of user interfaces) you may find you can develop and prototype these areas much faster with a higher level language like JavaScript rather than Objective-C. For games this is especially useful, as the easier you make it to iterate on gameplay, the better your game will be.

- **Team compartmentalization**. Since JavaScript is much easier to learn and use than Objective-C (especially if you develop a nice JavaScript sandbox), it can be handy to have one team of developers responsible for the Objective-C "engine/framework", and another team of developers write the JavaScript that uses the "engine/framework". Even non-developers can write JavaScript, so it's great if you want to get designers or other folks on the team involved in certain areas of the app.

- **JavaScript is interpreted**. Because JavaScript is interpreted at runtime, if you structure your use of it correctly you could set up your app so that you can tweak the JavaScript in real-time and see the results of your changes immediately in your app. This can be extremely handy in certain situations.

Note there are two things you cannot use JavaScript for: downloading and executing JavaScript code from a remote server (even if it is your own server that is returning JavaScript code as part of an in-app purchase), or allowing the end user to write their own JavaScript that your app executes.

Unfortunately at the time of writing this chapter, that is against the iOS Developer Program agreement section 3.3.2. That said – some apps seem to be doing this anyway – but consider it up to Apple's discretion and a matter of some risk.

JavaScriptCore overview

Before going further, you need to get you acquainted with the major classes and protocols of JavaScriptCore you'll cover in this chapter:

1. `JSValue`: An Objective-C object that represents a JavaScript entity. Keeping JavaScript's loose typing in mind, a JSValue can represent many primitive JavaScript values such as booleans, integers and doubles — even objects and functions.

2. `JSManagedValue`: Essentially a JSValue that's used to get around some tricky memory management situations. JSManagedValue helps Cocoa's reference counting and JavaScript's garbage collection play nicely with each other.

3. **JSContext:** Represents JavaScript's execution environment. You need a JSContext to evaluate and execute JavaScript. All instances of JSValue are tied to a JSContext. When you are getting or setting a JavaScript value or function through Objective-C, you'll need to go through the JSContext that initially loaded the script.

4. **JSExport:** This is a protocol rather than an object. As the name implies, you can use this protocol to export your native objects to JavaScript; native properties and methods become JavaScript properties and methods, just like magic.

5. **JSVirtualMachine:** Represents the object space, with its own heap and garbage collector. Most of the time you don't interact with the virtual machine unless you want to do something fancy with multithreading or memory management.

Getting started

In this chapter you will create a text-based adventure game named Xork using both JavaScript and Objective-C. Before getting started, locate the files that come with this chapter and open the starter project in Xcode.

The starter project is quite small; Xork includes one storyboard file, which itself contains one scene for XorkViewController, shown below:

`XorkViewController` contains two elements. The first is a `UITextView` subclass named `ConsoleTextView`. `ConsoleTextView` is the black Terminal-like console where the game text appears. Unlike a real terminal, you will not be typing any text into `ConsoleTextView`; it is simply for printing text returned by the game.

Sitting below the `ConsoleTextView` is a plain `UITextField`. This is where you will be issuing commands into the game such as "go north" and "take key".

Setting up the console

To get you acquainted with the game's user interface, start with a simple task: connect the input text field with `ConsoleTextView`.

The goal for now is to echo everything you type into the text field and print it on the console. The one special command you'll handle is `clear` which erases the console's contents.

In **XorkViewController.m**, replace the implementation of `textFieldShouldReturn:` with the code below:

```
- (BOOL)textFieldShouldReturn:(UITextField *)textField {

    //1
    NSString* inputString = textField.text;
    [inputString lowercaseString];

    //2
    if ([inputString isEqualToString:@"clear"]) {
        [self.outputTextView clear];
    }

    //3
    else {
        [self.outputTextView setText:inputString
                         concatenate:YES];
    }

    [self.inputTextField setText:@""];

    return YES;
}
```

`textFieldShouldReturn:` forwards commands typed into the text field to Xork. The JavaScript isn't in place yet, but you'll add it using the same pattern as above.

Looking at each commented step in turn:

1. Get the input string from the text view and convert it to a lower case string. This means that the commands "go north", "Go North" and "gO NoRtH" are all interpreted as the same command.

2. If the command is `clear`, erase the contents of the console. This is useful when the game's text has filled the screen and becomes uncomfortable to read.

3. For all other inputs, simply print the string to `ConsoleTextView`. Notice that you're using `setText:concatenate:` instead of setting the UITextView's text property directly. By default, the text view overwrites everything when you set its text property. Passing YES into `setText:concatenate:` preserves the text that was showing before.

Build and run your project; type anything you like into the UITextField to verify that it prints to the console correctly, like so:

After you've added some text, type `clear` into the text field and hit Return to see the screen clearing at work; this functions a little like Terminal.

Printing to the console from JavaScript

You've connected the text field to the `ConsoleTextView`, which is great, but you've only used Objective-C so far. Your second task is to get JavaScript to print "Hello World" to the console.

Before the introduction of Objective-C modules, you would have had to link the JavascriptCore framework in your project's Build Phases. The good news is that Xcode 5 uses modules by default so you can skip this step.

Create a new JavaScript file in Xcode by navigating to **File\New\File....** and select the **iOS\Other\Empty** template, like so:

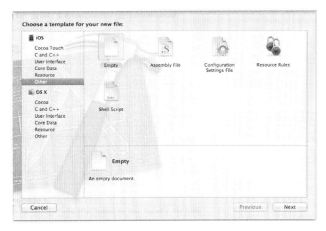

Name the file **hello.js** and select "Create".

> **Note:** You don't need to add **hello.js** to the Xork target because the JavaScript file is not going to be compiled with the rest of your Objective-C source code.

Next, you have to instruct Xcode to copy **hello.js** to the project bundle at runtime. If you omit this step, you won't be able to get a file path to **hello.js** and consequently you won't be able to execute the JavaScript that it contains. This copy operation happens automatically for assets like images and storyboard files, but as of this writing, Xcode won't do this automatically for JSON or JavaScript files.

Select your project file in the File Navigator and select the **Build Phases** tab. Click on the expandable arrow next to the menu **Copy Bundle Resources**, as shown below:

Select the plus icon to add a file, navigate to **hello.js** and select it to include it in the list.

Time to write your first JavaScript function!

Open **hello.js** and add the following function:

```
function startGame() {
    print("Hello World");
}
```

The code above defines the function `startGame()` which in turn calls the function `print()`. However, notice that `print()` itself is not defined anywhere in **hello.js**. So what is `print("Hello World")` going to do, if anything?

Here's where the magic happens: that JavaScript `print()` function will be defined with Objective-C code!

Open **XorkViewController.m** and add the following import:

```
@import JavaScriptCore;
```

In the same file, add the following property to the `@interface` section:

```
@property (strong, nonatomic) JSContext *context;
```

Recall that you need a `JSContext` object as an execution environment to run your own JavaScript. Scroll to the end of `viewDidLoad:` and add the following code:

```
//1
NSString *scriptPath = [[NSBundle mainBundle]
                        pathForResource:@"hello"
                        ofType:@"js"];

NSString *scriptString =
[NSString stringWithContentsOfFile:scriptPath
                          encoding:NSUTF8StringEncoding
                             error:nil];

//2
self.context = [[JSContext alloc] init];
[self.context evaluateScript:scriptString];

//3
__weak XorkViewController *weakSelf = self;

self.context[@"print"] = ^(NSString* text) {
    text = [NSString stringWithFormat:@"%@\n", text];
    [weakSelf.outputTextView setText:text concatenate:YES];
};
```

```
//4
JSValue *function = self.context[@"startGame"];
[function callWithArguments:@[]];
```

This part is important, so take a moment to review the above code step by step:

1. Grab the contents of hello.js and store it as a string.

2. Initialize a `JSContext` instance to evaluate and run the string containing the script. Note that your `startGame` method isn't called yet – hello.js just defines the method so you can call it later.

3. This is the secret sauce. Here you define the JavaScript function `print()` inside the `JSContext` — using Objective-C code. Block syntax means you have to use a weak reference to `self` to avoid a retain cycle.

   The print method takes an `NSString` as a parameter, and concatenates it to the text view.

4. Get a reference to the `startGame` function defined in hello.js, and then call it with an empty argument array since it doesn't take any arguments. This will run the `startGame` method in hello.js, which will then in-turn call the `print` method you defined in an Objective-C block earlier. Note that JavaScriptCore automatically handles the type conversion and seamlessly converts the "Hello World" into an NSString to pass to the block.

> **Note:** You can use modern Objective-C subscript notation with `JSContext`. That's because it implements `objectForKeyedSubscript:` and `setObject:forKeyedSubscript:`. You can use subscripting with `JSContext` to set and get values and functions.
>
> To learn more about Modern Objective-C, check out Chapter 2 in *iOS 6 by Tutorials*, "Programming in Modern Objective-C."

Build and run your project; you should see `Hello World` printed to the console, as below:

It doesn't seem like a big deal, but just think about what you've done. If you travelled back in time and told pre-iOS 7 developers of the JavaScript magic and type bridging your app just performed, they'd think you had gone crazy!

Building Xork

Now that you can call a JavaScript function from Objective-C and define a new JavaScript function from Objective-C, you can continue building Xork.

The game data for Xork is encoded in JSON and contains no executable code. The sample project files already have a file named **data.json** for this purpose. The game engine, on the other hand, contains the executable JavaScript that reads and interprets game data; this logic is contained in **xork.js**.

> **Note:** The separation of game data and game engine makes it very easy to write another text-based game of the same structure by merely swapping out **data.json** and keeping the game engine in **xork.js** intact. It also makes the game a lot easier to code.

Open **data.json** and take a quick look at its contents. The top-level object is a JSON array that contains several hashes (or "dictionaries" in Cocoa parlance). Each dictionary object looks similar to this:

```
{
    "trigger" : {
        "command" : {
```

```
            "action" : "go",
            "object" : "north"
        },
        "condition" : {
            "inventoryContains" : "key"
        },
        "print" : "You don't have the key to open the door"
    },
    "items" : [
        {
            "name" : "key",
            "description" : "This is a rusty key"
        }
    ],
    "name" : "Entrace",
    "description" : "There's a closed door to the north. The
doors are plated with gold and silver. There is a key on the
ground.",
    "adjacentRooms" : {
        "north" : "Throne Room"
    }
}
```

Each object represents a room in the game and contains the room's name, description, adjacent rooms, list of items and a trigger.

A **trigger** is the core logic unit in Xork. Before the game processes a command, it checks that the command you typed matches the trigger, if a trigger exists. If the command matches and the trigger's condition is true, Xork executes the command. If the trigger condition is false, the game prints the trigger's print property to the console and your command is not executed.

In the above example, the trigger command is go north. However, you can only go north if the inventoryContains condition matches key — meaning that you have the key in your inventory.

> **Note:** At the moment there is only one type of trigger condition, inventoryContains. As you can guess, this type of condition checks if you are currently carrying a particular object in your inventory.
>
> The game engine can be made more complex by adding different types of trigger conditions, but you'll keep it simple for now and leave it as-is.

The app currently loads JavaScript from **hello.js**. For the game to work properly, you need load the JavaScript from **xork.js** and the game data from **data.json**.

Back in **XorkViewController.m**, find the code you added to viewDidLoad: and replace it with the following:

```
//1
NSString *scriptPath = [[NSBundle mainBundle]
                        pathForResource:@"xork"
                        ofType:@"js"];

NSString *scriptString = [NSString
                          stringWithContentsOfFile:scriptPath
                          encoding:NSUTF8StringEncoding
                          error:nil];

//2
NSString *dataPath = [[NSBundle mainBundle]
                      pathForResource:@"data"
                      ofType:@"json"];


NSString *dataString = [NSString
                        stringWithContentsOfFile:dataPath
                        encoding:NSUTF8StringEncoding
                        error:nil];

NSData *jsonData = [dataString
                    dataUsingEncoding:NSUTF8StringEncoding];

NSError *error;
NSArray *jsonArray = [NSJSONSerialization
                      JSONObjectWithData:jsonData
                      options:0
                      error:&error];

if (error) {
    NSLog(@"%@", @"NSJSONSerialization error");
    return;
}

self.context = [[JSContext alloc] init];
[self.context evaluateScript:scriptString];
```

```
    __weak XorkViewController *weakSelf = self;

    self.context[@"print"] = ^(NSString* text) {
        text = [NSString stringWithFormat:@"%@\n", text];
        [weakSelf.outputTextView setText:text concatenate:YES];
    };


    //3
    JSValue *function = self.context[@"startGame"];
    JSValue *dataValue = [JSValue valueWithObject:jsonArray
                                        inContext:self.context];


    [function callWithArguments:@[dataValue]];
```

That's a fair bit of code, but most of it is similar to what you did to print out `Hello World`. Taking each commented section in turn:

1. Specify **xork.js** instead of **hello.js** as the file to load. The starter project already had **xork.js** set to be copied to the project bundle at runtime. That's an important step to remember in your own projects; otherwise the path will come back as `nil`.

2. Get the path for data.json and load it into an NSString. Convert it into an NSData instance so you can use it with NSJSONSerialization, which hands you an NSArray representation of the game data.

3. **xork.js** also has a function called `startGame()`. Unlike the **hello.js** version, this function takes an array of rooms. Convert the NSArray representation to a JavaScript object using `valueWithObject:inContext:`. Finally, call `startGame()` with `callWithArguments:` to start the game.

Earlier, you connected the app's text field to `ConsoleTextView` so that it would echo anything that was typed in.

Now that the game is ready to run and process user input, you need to redirect user input to the input processor. Find the `else` statement inside `textFieldShouldReturn:` shown below:

```
else {
    [self.outputTextView setText:inputString
                     concatenate:YES];
}
```

...and replace it with the following:

```
else {
```

```
        [self processUserInput:inputString];
    }
```

Add the following method just below `textFieldShouldReturn`:

```
- (void)processUserInput:(NSString *)input {
    JSValue *function = self.context[@"processUserInput"];
    JSValue *value = [JSValue valueWithObject:input
                                     inContext:self.context];

    [function callWithArguments:@[value]];
}
```

Instead of mindlessly echoing everything you type, the app forwards the input to the JavaScript function `processUserInput()`.

> **Note:** `processUserInput()` has already been implemented for you in the starter project. You'll cover it later in the chapter, but if you're curious you can open **xork.js** and take a look at that function to see how it works.

Build and run your project; you'll be greeted by the description of the first room of the game. However, you'll quickly realize that you can't do much:

It's clear the game and the native UI are communicating, but if you open **xork.js** and poke around `processUserInput()`, you'll see the only action implemented is `go`.

Unfortunately, you can't go anywhere without the key. Your next task is to implement some more actions, namely take so that you can get the darned key.

Extending the game logic

Open **xork.js** and find the function processCommand(action, object). Add the following else-if statement immediately before the closing else statement:

```
else if (action == "take") {
    take(object);
}
```

Next, find the function go() and implement take() below it:

```
function take(itemName) {
    //1
    var room = getCurrentRoom();

    //2
    if (room.hasItem(itemName)) {
        item = room.itemForName(itemName);
        inventory.addItem(item);
        room.removeItem(itemName);
        print("You picked it up. Woot!");
    }
    //3
    else {
        print("You can't pick that up.");
    }
}
```

A lot of this deals with the internals of the game, which you haven't encountered yet. This is what take() does, step-by-step:

1. A global array map contains all the rooms passed into startGame(). A global index currentRoom tracks your position in the map array as you navigate the game. The function getCurrentRoom() simply returns the Room object you're in according to the currentRoom index.

2. The Room object contains a hasItem() function that indicates whether or not a particular item is in the room. If it is, add the Item object to the global inventory array and remove it from the Room.

3. Alert the user if the item they want to take isn't in the room or doesn't exist.

Build and run your project; this time, you should be able to take the key and continue north:

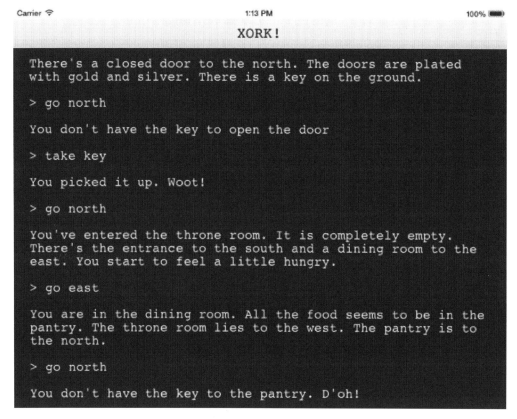

Enter the commands as shown above, and you'll find yourself in the Dining Room. However, the pantry door is locked and there is no key in sight.

Open and inspect **data.json**. Dining Room has a trigger for going north, which requires you to have an item called pantry key in your inventory.

However, none of the rooms have an item called pantry key. What are you going to do now?

Using JSExport

You're faced with a no-win situation — your very own Kobayashi Maru. You need to get into the pantry but can't find a pantry key to save your life.

To solve this conundrum, you're going to create a native Item object that mimics JavaScript's Item object using JSExport. Then you're going to insert the item into your game's inventory during runtime.

Add a new Objective-C class called **Item** that derives from **NSObject**. Open the newly created **Item.h** and replace its contents with the following:

```
#import <Foundation/Foundation.h>
@import JavaScriptCore;

//1
@protocol ItemExport <JSExport>

@property (strong, nonatomic) NSString* name;
@property (strong, nonatomic) NSString* description;

@end

//2
@interface Item : NSObject <ItemExport>

@property (strong, nonatomic) NSString* name;
@property (strong, nonatomic) NSString* description;

@end
```

Here you use JavaScriptCore's **JSExport** protocol to make your new class compatible with JavaScript. Looking at each step in turn:

1. The important bit here is that your class doesn't implement the **JSExport** protocol. Instead, the **Item** class specifies its own protocol that *inherits* from **JSExport**. In this case, this new protocol is called **ItemExport**. To make a native property or a method available to JavaScript, all you have to do is declare it inside in your **ItemExport** protocol.

2. Unfortunately, Xcode doesn't automatically synthesize inherited properties from a protocol so you have to repeat them in the **@interface** section or use **@synthesize** in the implementation file.

Add the following import to the top of **XorkViewController.m**:

```
#import "Item.h"
```

In the same file, add the following property to the **@interface** section:

```
@property (strong, nonatomic) JSManagedValue *inventory;
```

Now scroll to `viewDidLoad:` and add the following lines of code, just after the place where you populate the JSContext in the line `[self.context evaluateScript:scriptString]`:

```
//1
JSValue *value = self.context[@"inventory"];

//2
self.inventory = [JSManagedValue managedValueWithValue:value];
[self.context.virtualMachine addManagedReference:self.inventory
                                       withOwner:self];
```

Let's go over each step here:

1. Use subscript notation to get a `JSValue` reference to the inventory array used by the script. This is where you'll insert the pantry key.

2. For reasons discussed in the next section, the property that keeps track of the inventory array has to be a `JSManagedValue` instead of a `JSValue`. Use `managedValuewithValue:` to convert the inventory `JSValue` into a `JSManagedValue`. Finally, add a managed reference between the view controller and the managed value.

Next, scroll down to `textFieldShouldReturn:` and add the following else-if statement before the final else block:

```
else if ([inputString isEqualToString:@"cheat"]) {
    [self addPantryKeyToInventory];
}
```

The command `cheat` will not be forwarded to JavaScript. Instead, it will be handled by the native method `addPantryKeyToInventory`. Scroll to the bottom of the file and implement it as below:

```
- (void)addPantryKeyToInventory {
    //1
    Item* pantryKey = [[Item alloc] init];
    pantryKey.name = @"pantry key";
    pantryKey.description = @"Looks like a normal key. Hehe.";

    //2
    JSValue *inventory = [self.inventory value];
    JSValue *function = inventory[@"addItem"];
    [function callWithArguments:@[pantryKey]];
}
```

In this code, you do the following:

1. Create an `Item` object for the pantry key and set its name and description.

2. Get a reference to the inventory `JSValue` by calling `value` on its `JSManagedValue`. `xork.js` has the convenience method `addItem()`, which takes a JavaScript Item object as its argument. Finally, execute `addItem()` with `callWithArguments:` and pass in the native pantry key `Item` object you just created.

Build and run your project and enter the commands as shown below:

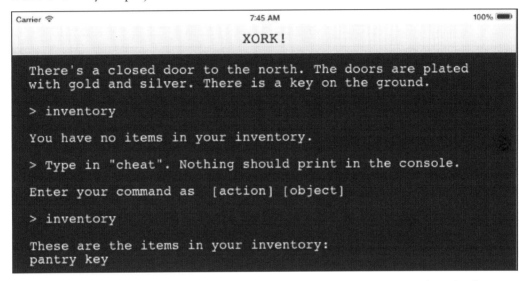

At startup, type `inventory` to print your inventory; you should have nothing at this point. Now type in `cheat`, which should not print anything to the console. Check your inventory again — you should now have a pantry key that materialized out of thin air.

Use this key to get into the Pantry once you've reached the Dining Room. Congratulations, you've beaten Xork!

Memory management gotchas

You've probably noticed that the integration between Objective-C and JavaScript is quite seamless. The truth is that these two languages are vastly different, especially in the way they handle memory management. As mentioned before, Objective-C uses reference counting whereas JavaScript uses garbage collection.

Although JavaScriptCore makes memory management a no-brainer for the most part, there are a few tricky situations to be aware of.

Capturing JSContext within a block

The first thing to be careful with is capturing certain JavaScriptCore objects inside an Objective-C block.

As you saw earlier in the chapter, you can define a JavaScript function using an Objective-C block. However, since this new function/block is not going to be used until a later point in time, it has to be kept around by copying it from the stack to the heap. In doing so, the block creates a strong reference to all the objects it captures.

JSContext keeps a strong pointer to all of the JSValues it manages. In addition, JSValue keeps a strong pointer to both its value and its context. This isn't usually a problem because the garbage collector breaks retain cycles. However, you don't want to make the problem worse by adding your own references to the block copying process.

To illustrate this problem and its solution, you're going to implement the version command in Xork, which will print the version of the app to the console.

Add the following code to viewDidLoad in **XorkViewController.m** after the definition of the print() function:

```
self.context[@"getVersion"] = ^{
    NSString* versionString = [[NSBundle mainBundle]
      objectForInfoDictionaryKey:@"CFBundleShortVersionString"];

    versionString = [@"Xork version "
      stringByAppendingString:versionString];

    JSContext *context = [JSContext currentContext];
    JSValue *version = [JSValue valueWithObject:versionString
                                      inContext:context];
    return version;
};
```

This block retrieves the app's NSBundle and wraps it in a JSValue. Notice that you're using [JSContext currentContext] instead of self.context to create the JSValue. Using currentContext removes the extraneous strong reference to JSContext when the block is copied to the heap.

Find processAction() in **xork.js** and add the following else-if statement immediately before the closing else statement:

```
else if (action == "version") {
    print(getVersion());
}
```

This else-if statement handles the command `version`. This simply retrieves the version string from `getVersion()` defined above and prints it to ConsoleTextView.

Build and run your project again; after the game starts, enter the command `version`. Your screen should look like the screenshot below:

To reiterate, use `[JSContext currentContext]` inside a block. If you don't, you won't just be leaking a few `JSValues`; you'll be leaking your entire `JSContext` and everything it contains.

Something else you want to avoid is to avoid capturing `JSValues` within blocks. Since `JSValue` has a strong reference to `JSContext`, it's as good as capturing `JSContext` itself.

Coming from a pure Objective-C world, you may want to do something like the following:

```
JSValue *name = [JSValue valueWithObject:@"bar"
                              inContext:self.context];


__weak JSValue *weakName = name;
__weak ViewController *weakSelf = self;


self.context[@"foo"] = ^{
    [weakSelf doSomething:weakName];
};
```

However, using `weak` is generally *not* the way to fix retain cycles with `JSValue`. You are essentially mixing weak/strong references with garbage-collected references, which is incorrect and doesn't solve your problem.

Apple's recommended way of capturing `JSValue` inside a block? **Don't**. You *never* want to capture a `JSValue` inside a block. What you should do instead is pass the `JSValue` into the block as an argument, like so:

```
__weak ViewController *weakSelf = self;
```

```
self.context[@"foo"] = ^(NSString *bar){
    [weakSelf doSomething:bar];
};
```

For this to make sense, the JSValue has to be available for use in JavaScript first. If this isn't the case, then create it and insert it from Objective-C using JSContext.

JSManagedValue and memory pitfalls

JavaScriptCore's Objective-C API gives you a great opportunity to experiment with hybrid objects. You need to be extra careful with memory management when you store JavaScript values in native instance variables.

JSValue inherits from NSObject, so it looks like a perfectly normal native object. When you create a custom object, you can reference other objects with instance variables and properties.

Therefore, you may be tempted to do this:

```
@interface XorkViewController () {
    JSValue *value;
}
```

Or this:

```
@property (strong, nonatomic) JSValue *value;
```

However, storing a JSValue in an instance variable makes it very easy to create retain cycles.

Not only is it dangerous from a memory management perspective, it's also incorrect. It just doesn't make sense to mix the strong/weak object lifecycle in Objective-C with garbage collected JSValues. JavaScriptCore provides you with another object for the purpose of creating hybrid Objective-C/JavaScript objects: JSManagedObject.

Before diving into the memory management implications of JSManagedObject, start with the following example in Xork.

The goal for this exercise is to create a native alert view that can be summoned from JavaScript. The alert view should have confirm and cancel buttons that trigger success and failure handlers in JavaScript. Sounds like a perfect job for a hybrid object!

Add a new Objective-C class called **XorkAlertView** that subclasses UIAlertView. Open **XorkAlertView.h** and change its contents as follows:

```
#import <UIKit/UIKit.h>
@import JavaScriptCore;

@interface XorkAlertView : UIAlertView

- (instancetype)initWithTitle:(NSString *)title
                      message:(NSString *)message
                      success:(JSValue *)successHandler
                      failure:(JSValue *)failureHandler
                      context:(JSContext *)context;

@end
```

The initializer takes a title, message, success and failure handlers as well as the
JSContext in which to execute the JavaScript handlers.

Now switch to **XorkAlertview.m** and add the following code:

```
#import "XorkAlertView.h"

@interface XorkAlertView() <UIAlertViewDelegate>

// 1
@property (strong, nonatomic) JSContext *ctxt;
@property (strong, nonatomic) JSManagedValue *successHandler;
@property (strong, nonatomic) JSManagedValue *failureHandler;

@end

@implementation XorkAlertView

- (instancetype)initWithTitle:(NSString *)title
                      message:(NSString *)message
                      success:(JSValue *)successHandler
                      failure:(JSValue *)failureHandler
                      context:(JSContext *)context {

    // 2
    self = [super initWithTitle:title
                        message:message
                       delegate:self
              cancelButtonTitle:@"No"
              otherButtonTitles:@"Yes", nil];
```

```
    // 3
    if (self) {
        // Initialization code
        _ctxt = context;

        _successHandler = [JSManagedValue
          managedValueWithValue:successHandler];
        [context.virtualMachine
          addManagedReference:_successHandler withOwner:self];

        _failureHandler = [JSManagedValue
          managedValueWithValue:failureHandler];
        [context.virtualMachine
          addManagedReference:_failureHandler withOwner:self];
    }
    return self;
}
@end
```

Taking the code step by step:

1. XorkAlertView's public initializer takes JSValue objects for the success and failure handlers. Internally these are stored in JSManagedValue instance variables.

2. The public initializer simply calls the usual UIAlertView initializer. Notice that XorkAlertView will be its own UIAlertViewDelegate. This is necessary so you know when to execute the success and failure handlers.

3. Convert the success and failure handlers into JSManagedValues and stored in _successHandler and _failureHandler.

A JSManagedValue by itself is a weak reference. You convert it into a *conditionally retained reference*, by inserting it to the JSVirtualMachine using addManagedReference:withOwner:.

A conditionally retained reference is retained as long as one of two conditions is true:

1. The JSManagedValue's JavaScript value is reachable from JavaScript.

2. The owner of the managed reference is reachable in Objective-C. Manually adding or removing the managed reference in the JSVirtualMachine determines reachability.

Add the following method below the custom initializer:

```
- (void)alertView:(UIAlertView *)alertView
clickedButtonAtIndex:(NSInteger)buttonIndex {
```

```
  if (buttonIndex == self.cancelButtonIndex) {
    JSValue *function = [self.failureHandler value];
    [function callWithArguments:@[]];
  }
  else {
    JSValue *function = [self.successHandler value];
    [function callWithArguments:@[]];
  }

  [self.ctxt.virtualMachine
    removeManagedReference:_failureHandler
              withOwner:self];

  [self.ctxt.virtualMachine
    removeManagedReference:_successHandler
              withOwner:self];
}
```

When the player taps on an alert view button, `alertView:clickedButtonAtIndex:` lets you know what the user chose. Depending on this selection, you execute either the success handler or failure handler without any arguments.

After the user makes their selection and the correct handler executes, the `XorkAlertView` instance will be deallocated. You need to remove the managed references to the `JSManagedValue` instance variables at the end of the method.

Your hybrid alert view is ready for prime time. Head over to **XorkViewController.m** and add the following import to the top of the file:

```
#import "XorkAlertView.h"
```

Scroll down to `viewDidLoad:` and add the following code just after the point where you set up your `JSContext`:

```
self.context[@"presentNativeAlert"] = ^(NSString *title,
                                        NSString *message,
                                        JSValue *success,
                                        JSValue *failure) {

  JSContext *context = [JSContext currentContext];
  XorkAlertView* alertView = [[XorkAlertView alloc]
                               initWithTitle:title

                                   message:message
```

```
                                    success:success
                                    failure:failure
                                    context:context];
    [alertView show];
};
```

This code defines a new JavaScript function `presentNativeAlertView()`, which creates a `XorkAlertView` and presents it to the user. The JavaScript caller needs to pass in the success and failure handlers, the title, and the message.

To test `XorkAlertView`, you'll mock up some save-game functionality. Saving usually prompts the user with some sort of alert asking "Are you sure?" This is where you'll present your `XorkAlertView`.

Scroll down to `textFieldShouldReturn:` and add the following else-if statement before the closing else statement:

```
else if ([inputString isEqualToString:@"save"]) {
    JSValue* function = self.context[@"saveGame"];
    [function callWithArguments:@[]];
}
```

This simply calls the function `saveGame()` from JavaScript without any arguments.

Now switch over to **xork.js** and implement `saveGame()` as well as the success and failure handlers for `XorkAlertView` at the bottom of the file:

```
function saveGame() {
    presentNativeAlert("Hello",
                       "Do you want to save the game?",
                       saveGameConfirm,
                       saveGameCancel);
}

function saveGameConfirm() {
    print('Yes');
}

function saveGameCancel() {
    print('No');
}
```

Executing `saveGame()` calls `presentNativeAlertView()`, which you just defined in Objective-C. The two handlers simply print out a message to the game console.

Build and run your project; type `save` and hit Return. A native alert view should come up asking for confirmation, as shown:

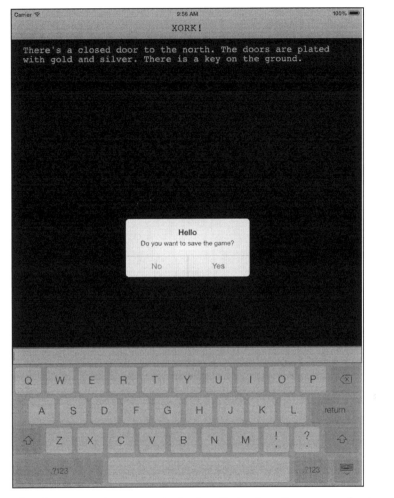

Select **Yes** on the alert view. As expected, the JavaScript handler runs and prints `Yes` to the console.

And with that, your adventure is complete!

Challenges

In this chapter you've learned the ins and outs of JavaScriptCore. You've learned different ways to call JavaScript from Objective-C as well different ways to expose

Objective-C to JavaScript. You've even navigated the murky waters of hybrid objects when you created `XorkAlertView`.

JavaScriptCore truly opens a whole new world of possibilities. There are scores of games and applications originally written for the web just waiting to be ported to iOS. There are also many opportunities to add lightweight JavaScript to your apps and reduce the amount of verbose Objective-C code.

If you already work on several platforms, you may find that JavaScriptCore reduces a lot of the redundancy in your different code bases. Even if you don't have a grandiose multi-platform app in your future, I leave you with the same challenge that an Apple engineer left us with at the end of his WWDC talk on JavaScriptCore: add some JavaScript to whatever app you're working on, even if it's just for a bit of configuration. You may be surprised how useful it can be.

But before you go, we have a challenge for you!

Challenge 1: Mmm, burritos!

Currently when you win the game, there's a burrito on the floor, but it's just sitting there tempting you. Let's make the endgame even tastier by letting the player eat that burrito!

Your challenge is to add a new command to the game called **eat** that takes an item name as a parameter. If the item name is in the room or inventory, and if the item name equals **burrito**, then the game should display **me-gusta.jpg** (in the resources for this chapter) onto the screen. Here are a few tips for how to accomplish this:

- Add a new full-screen image view to your storyboard, and connect it to an outlet. In `viewWillAppear:`, set it to hidden.

- Add a new Objective-C method to the JavaScript context called `showImage` that takes a single `NSString` as a parameter for the image name to display. This method should make the image view not hidden and display the image. For bonus points, make it fade out after some time.

- Update xork.js to add a new eat command that checks to see if the room or inventory contains the item, and if it's equal to **burrito** then call `showImage` with **me-gusta.jpg**.

Enjoy your tasty treat!

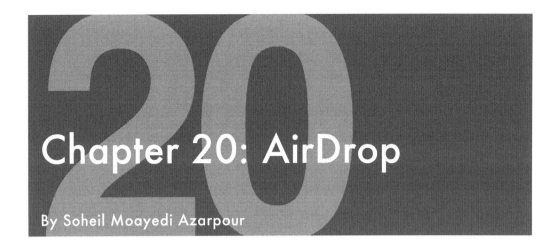

Chapter 20: AirDrop

By Soheil Moayedi Azarpour

iOS 7 introduces a new easy to use way to share your data with nearby devices called **AirDrop**.

AirDrop only works on newer devices like iPhone 5 or iPad 4th Gen – see the note at the end of this section for more details. Assuming you have two or more AirDrop-compatible devices, you can see AirDrop in action by opening up Photos, selecting a photo, and tapping the **Share** button.

If any AirDrop-compatible devices are in range, you will see them in the list as shown. You can then select the device and transfer your photos with a single tap!

On the other device, you will see an alert view that pops up with a thumbnail of the image you are willing to share. You can accept or decline to receive the image. If you tap on accept button, the image file will be downloaded into your Camera Roll and Photos app will launch and display the image.

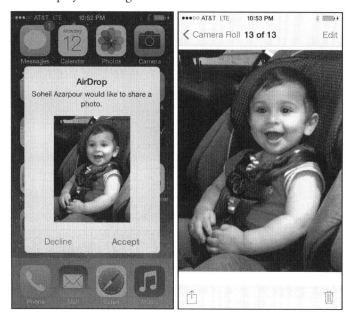

Depending on which option you choose, accept or decline, on the sending device you will see either a **Sent** or **Declined** confirmation text.

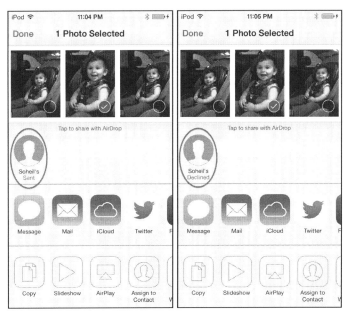

AirDrop works in two modes on the sending and receiving device: **Contacts Only** and **Everyone**. This preference is set in the **Control Center**, as shown below:

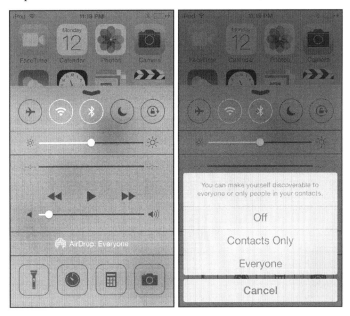

In Contacts Only mode, you must be logged into your iCloud account to receive AirDrop requests only from other users whose Apple IDs are in your list of contacts.

In Everyone mode, the sender's name shows up only if you have the other person's name in your contacts; otherwise, you simply see the sending device's name in your AirDrop activity view, as shown below:

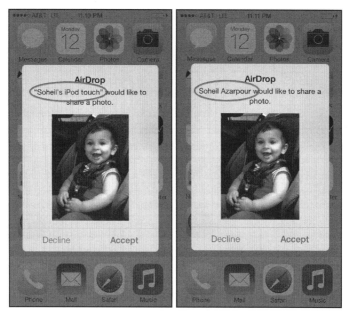

Due to security considerations, user confirmation is required to accept a file transfer. When a transfer is initiated, a dialog box is presented to the recipient and **Accept** must be tapped to receive the transfer. If the recipient doesn't want the file, or doesn't trust the sender, they can hit Decline to refuse the transfer.

AirDrop is not available when a device's screen is turned off. The receiving device must at least turn on its screen to appear as a peer on the sending device. Unlocking is not required. And both devices must have selected an appropriate mode (Contacts Only or Everyone). When the sending device taps on its peer, on the receiving device's lock screen you will see a notification similar to SMS or email notifications. You can swipe the notification to start the transfer. If the device has a passcode, you may be prompted to enter it first.

This is a very cool feature, and you may want support sharing data through AirDrop in your apps too.

Well, you're in luck – that's nice and easy to do in iOS 7!

This chapter will introduce you implement AirDrop in your apps in order to share various types of data, such as photos or URLs. You'll also learn how to register for particular file types so your app will get a chance to handle incoming files — a feature that you can use in other apps, even if they don't implement AirDrop.

> **Note:** AirDrop is supported on only newer devices; you'll need at least two iPhone or iPod Touch 5th generation, or iPad 4th generation devices to work with this tutorial. AirDrop requires you to enable both WiFi and Bluetooth. It appears Apple uses Bluetooth technology for discovery, that is when the action sheet appears, and then WiFi for actual data transmission. There's no simulator support for AirDrop, so you'll always need to test your app on your AirDrop-enabled device.

AirDrop Quick Start

Good news – adding AirDrop support is pretty easy, since it's already built into the existing `UIActivityViewController` class!

UIActivityViewController is a handy built-in view controller you can use to allow users to easily share photos, documents, URLs, and other kinds of data from your app. The user can select the method they want to share the data, from options like Twitter, Mail, or now AirDrop.

You can use UIActivityViewController to share NSString, NSAttributedString, UIImage, AVAsset, and NSURL data types. You may also share NSDictionary or NSArray objects that contain these data types.

So assuming you have an array of one of these data types, all you need to do is the following lines of code:

```
UIActivityViewController *controller =
  [[UIActivityViewController alloc]
    initWithActivityItems:objects applicationActivities:nil];
[self presentViewController:controller
                   animated:YES
                 completion:nil];
```

If the user chooses to send the data via AirDrop, once the other user receives the data, it will be opened in an app based on the type of data:

* NSString and NSAttributedString appear as new notes in **Notes.app**.

* UIImage and AVAsset are presented in **Photos.app**.

- NSURL is presented in **Safari.app**, unless it is a file URL, which will make the iOS to look for registered document types (UTI) and open the appropriate app.

It's as simple as that when it comes to sending data. When it comes to receiving data, it works the same way as it has in iOS in the past:

1. **Register document types**. You register your app to receive certain document types of data.

2. **User chooses app**. When the user receives a document (whether via email, a web link, AirDrop, etc.), the OS looks to see which app handles that type of document and asks the user what app he/she wants to use to open the file.

3. **Receive and process document**. If the user chooses to open the document in your app, you receive a URL to the data in an App Delegate callback.

The rest of this chapter walks you through how both send and receive data via AirDrop in a practical example project, but if this is enough to get you started, feel free to stop reading at this point and give it a shot in your app.

Getting started

The starter application for this chapter is a tab-based application called **DropMe**.

Unzip the starter package to a convenient location, open the project file in Xcode, and build and run the app. You'll be presented with the five screens on the following page:

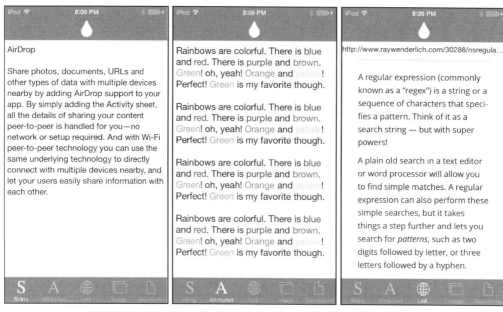

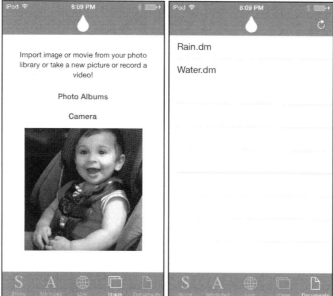

Each tab represents a type of data that you can share with AirDrop:

1. The **String tab** implements `StringViewController` and contains a `UITextView` where you can compose notes in plain text.

2. The **Attributed** tab also contains a `UITextView` — but this one has some magic in it. It leverages `NSAttributedString` to highlight the names of colors in the text.

3. The **Link** tab contains a `UIWebView` and a `UITextField` where users can enter a URL and view the web site.

4. The **Image** tab lets users take a picture or record a video, or alternatively they can choose a photo or video from the photo library.

5. The **Documents** tab allows users to view **DropMe** files in the app's User Documents directory. **DropMe** files are specific to this app. They are plain text files that have **dm** file name extension, e.g. **Water.dm**. You will learn how to register for specific file types later on in this chapter, so that whenever your users receives a .dm file, your app gets a chance to respond.

Right now the tabs don't support any AirDrop functionality — that's your job!

Each tab sends different types of data via AirDrop – but all of them will use the same basic code to share an array of objects using an `UIActivityViewController` like you saw in the AirDrop Quick Start section.

To keep things clean, let's put all of the code inside the `BaseViewController` class, which the view controllers for each tab derive from.

Add a new subclass of `UIViewController` to the project and name it `BaseViewController`. To do this in Xcode select File > New > File ... or use Command+Shift+N to add a new file.

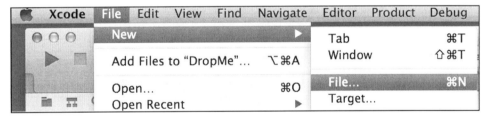

From the dialogue window select **Objective-C Class** template and click **Next**.

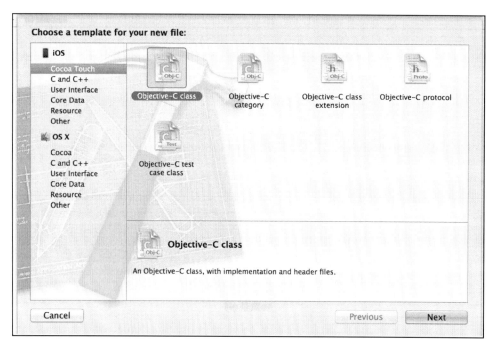

Enter **BaseViewController** in Class field and select **UIViewController** from the dropbox. Leave checkboxes unchecked and click **Next**.

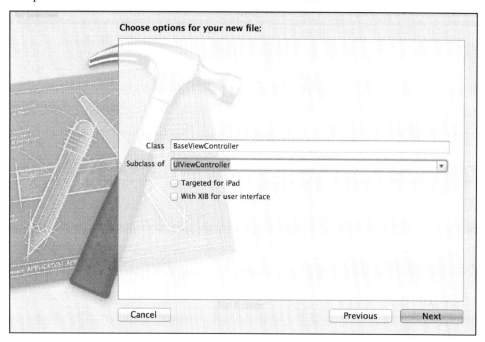

You will be prompted where to save it. Select **DropMe** folder and then click **Create**.

Your project navigator should look like this:

If Xcode didn't add the new files inside DropMe group automatically, you may drag them into that group. Open **BaseViewController.h** and add the following property:

```
/**
 * @property objectsToShare
 * @brief An array of objects that will be shared via AirDrop
when the activity view controller is presented.
 */


@property (nonatomic, strong) NSArray *objectsToShare;
```

objectsToShare holds a list of things to share via AirDrop. Each subclass will fill this with the appropriate set of objects.

Next, open **BaseViewController.m** and add the following two helper methods:

```
// Create a UIBarButton item with UIBarButtonSystemItemAction
and display it in the navigation bar.
- (void)displayActionButton
{
    UIBarButtonItem *actionButton = [[UIBarButtonItem alloc]
initWithBarButtonSystemItem:UIBarButtonSystemItemAction
target:self action:@selector(actionButtonTapped:)];
    [self.navigationItem setLeftBarButtonItem:actionButton
animated:YES];
}

// Remove the action bar button item.
- (void)hideActionButton
{
    [self.navigationItem setLeftBarButtonItem:nil animated:YES];
}
```

displayActionButton and hideActionButton will be called when the list of shareable objects changes. This pair of methods will initialize and display the action button, or remove it from the navigation bar.

Next, add the following custom setter method:

```
- (void)setObjectsToShare:(NSArray *)objectsToShare
{
    _objectsToShare = [objectsToShare copy];

    // If there is an object in the array to share, display the
    // action button; otherwise, hide the action button.
```

```
       if ([objectsToShare count])
           [self displayActionButton];
       else
           [self hideActionButton];
}
```

In order to have more control over what is being shared, you're providing a custom setter method for objectsToShare. The method will check the count of objects and hide or display the action button depending on whether there are any entries in the array.

Next up is the workhorse method to invoke the share sheet dialog.

Still working in **BaseViewController.m**, add the following method:

```objc
// Configure and present an instance of UIActivityViewController
for AirDrop only.
- (void)presentActivityViewControllerWithObjects:(NSArray
*)objects
{
    // 1 - Create an instance of UIActivityViewController with
the object.
    UIActivityViewController *controller =
[[UIActivityViewController alloc] initWithActivityItems:objects
applicationActivities:nil];

    // 2 - Exclude all activities except AirDrop.
    NSArray *excludedActivities = @[UIActivityTypePostToTwitter,
UIActivityTypePostToFacebook, UIActivityTypePostToWeibo,
UIActivityTypeMessage, UIActivityTypeMail, UIActivityTypePrint,
UIActivityTypeCopyToPasteboard, UIActivityTypeAssignToContact,
UIActivityTypeSaveToCameraRoll, UIActivityTypeAddToReadingList,
UIActivityTypePostToFlickr, UIActivityTypePostToVimeo,
UIActivityTypePostToTencentWeibo];
    controller.excludedActivityTypes = excludedActivities;

    // 3 - Present it.
    [self presentViewController:controller
                      animated:YES
                    completion:nil];
}
```

Here's what the above code does, comment by comment:

1. Creates an instance of UIActivityViewController, passing in the array of objects.

2. Excludes all other possible options that `UIActivityViewController` can present —
such as sharing via Twitter —since you want to limit the user to just AirDrop.

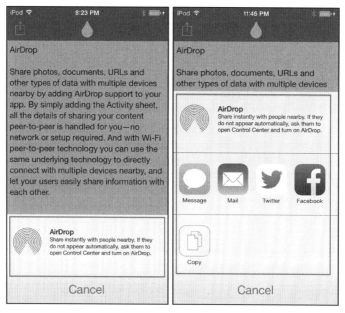

3. Displays `UIActivityViewController` as modal.

Finally, link the above method with the action button in the navigation bar by adding
this method:

```
- (IBAction)actionButtonTapped:(id)sender
{
    [self
presentActivityViewControllerWithObjects:self.objectsToShare];
}
```

When the action button is tapped, this method ties things together by calling
`presentActivityViewControllerWithObjects:` with the current list of objects to
share.

Believe it or not, this was the most important part of the app: presenting the
`UIActivityViewController` with the list of objects. Now let's use this base
functionality in each of the tabs, starting with plain text.

Sharing plain text

Open **StringViewController.m** and modify it as shown below. Each line noted below should be added to the top of the appropriate method:

```
- (void)viewDidLoad
{
    // Update object to be shared.
    self.objectsToShare = @[self.textView.text];
    ... the rest of the code ...
}
- (void)textViewDidBeginEditing:(UITextView *)textView
{
    self.objectsToShare = @[textView.text];
    ... the rest of the code ...
}

- (BOOL)textView:(UITextView *)textView
shouldChangeTextInRange:(NSRange)range replacementText:(NSString
*)text
{
    self.objectsToShare = @[textView.text];
    ... the rest of the code ...
}

- (void)textViewDidEndEditing:(UITextView *)textView
{
    self.objectsToShare = @[textView.text];
    ... the rest of the code ...
}
```

All you are doing here is setting and updating `objectsToShare` on the superclass in critical places. The object you'll share is simply the `NSString` text content of the text view.

Build and run your app; enter some text in the **String** tab and try to send it via AirDrop to another device. When the transfer completes, the receiving device will open the Notes.app, and save the transferred text as a new note, as shown on the next page:

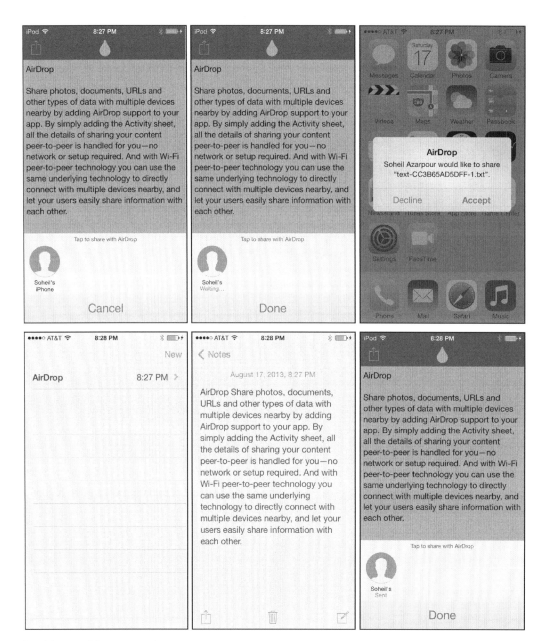

I told you this was easy!

Let's keep going with the rest – some are just as easy, and some are a tad more complex.

Sharing attributed string data

That does it for regular text. Now it's time to see how AirDrop handles transmission of attributed strings.

Open **AttributedStringController.m** and modify the following methods as indicated below:

```
- (void)viewDidLoad
{
    ... add this before [super viewDidLoad] ...
    self.objectsToShare = @[self.textView.attributedText];

    [super viewDidLoad];
}

- (void)textViewDidBeginEditing:(UITextView *)textView
{
    ... the rest of the code ...
    self.objectsToShare = @[textView.attributedText];
}

- (BOOL)textView:(UITextView *)textView
shouldChangeTextInRange:(NSRange)range replacementText:(NSString
*)text
{
    ... before return YES ...
    self.objectsToShare = @[attrStr];
    return YES;
}

- (void)textViewDidEndEditing:(UITextView *)textView
{
    self.objectsToShare = @[textView.attributedText];
    ... the rest of the code ...
}
```

The changes here are similar to the code for plain text, except you're using the `attributedText` property as the object to send via AirDrop.

Build and run your app again; type some text into the Attributed tab and be sure to include the name of a color or two to exercise the text highlighting. The app recognizes **red, blue, green, purple, brown** and **yellow** in its current state. Feel free to explore the code and add support for more colors.

Note: As of writing this chapter, AirDrop does not fully support NSAttributedString. That means on the receiving device you will get a plain text, which by default opens in **Notes.app**. If you need to transfer attributions, you need to wrap your NSAttributedString in a custom object, save it with a custom file type, and pass the file URL to AirDrop. On the receiving device, you need to register for your custom file type and take it from there.

Next, attempt to send it to another device via AirDrop. Success!

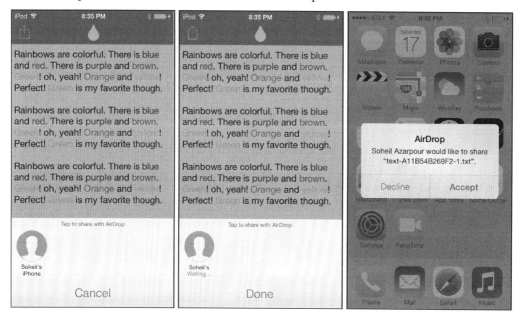

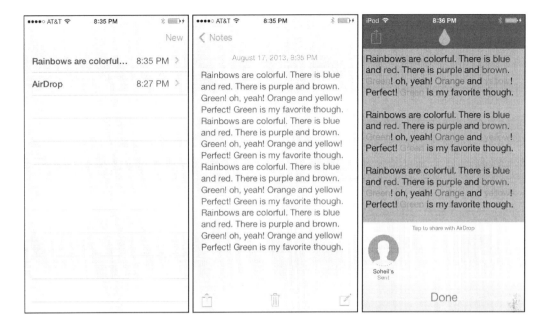

Sharing URLs

The third tab in your **DropMe** app contains a field to enter a URL and a UIWebView that displays the corresponding web page. When you send a URL via AirDrop, the receiving device will try to open the URL; for web links, Safari will be used as the launching app. If you try to send a file URL, the operating system detects that and launches the default associated app for the file type. This is covered in more detail in **Sharing Documents** section of this chapter.

Open **URLViewController.m** and modify the implementation as shown below:

```
- (void)loadURL:(NSURL *)URL
{
    self.objectsToShare = @[URL];
    ... the rest of the code ...
}


- (BOOL)webView:(UIWebView *)webView
shouldStartLoadWithRequest:(NSURLRequest *)request
navigationType:(UIWebViewNavigationType)navigationType
{
    if (navigationType == UIWebViewNavigationTypeLinkClicked)
    {
```

```
        self.textField.text = request.URL.absoluteString;
        self.objectsToShare = @[request.URL];
    }

    return YES;
}
```

The above code is similar to the previous implementation, but this time you're using an NSURL in objectsToShare; in this case since you are passing a web URL, AirDrop will launch Safari on the receiving device.

Build and run your app, enter a web URL with the http:// prefix and load up a web page. You should now be able to share a link with your friends over the air, as shown below:

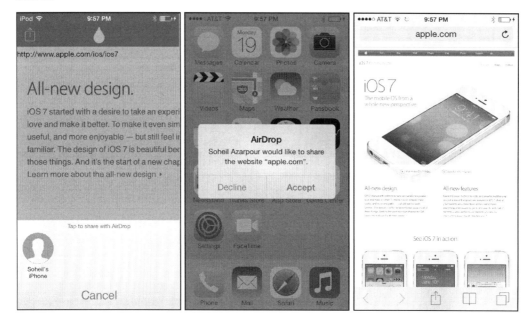

Sharing media and documents

Sharing photos and videos from the library is only a little more involved than sharing a string or a URL: you just need to share a UIImage directly, or an NSURL pointing to the media asset.

Open **ImageViewController.m** and replace the implementation of imagePickerController:didFinishPickingMediaWithInfo: with the following:

```objc
- (void)imagePickerController:(UIImagePickerController *)picker
didFinishPickingMediaWithInfo:(NSDictionary *)info
{
    // What did user pick? Is it a movie or is it an image?
    NSString *mediaType =
info[UIImagePickerControllerMediaType];

    // If it is an image...
    if ([mediaType isEqualToString:(NSString *)kUTTypeImage])
    {
        // Update UI and the object to share.
        self.imageView.image =
info[UIImagePickerControllerOriginalImage];
        self.objectsToShare =
@[info[UIImagePickerControllerOriginalImage]];
    }
    // else, if it is a movie...
    else if ([mediaType isEqualToString:(NSString
*)kUTTypeMovie])
    {
        // Get the URL to the movie for sharing
        NSURL *assetURL = info[UIImagePickerControllerMediaURL];
        self.objectsToShare = @[assetURL];

        // Update UI by taking a snapshot of the movie.
        self.imageView.image = [self
snapshotFromMovieAtURL:assetURL];
    }

    // Dismiss the picker.
    [picker dismissViewControllerAnimated:YES completion:nil];
}
```

When the standard image picker returns — either from the camera or the photo library — the code then calls `imagePickerController:didFinishPickingMediaWithInfo:` with the media asset information.

For an image, the `UIImagePickerControllerOriginalImage` key leads to a `UIImage` object. An image preview is displayed on screen, and the image itself is added to `objectsToShare`.

For a movie, the picker provides a URL pointing to the movie file directly. However, AirDrop recognizes this and sends the movie file rather than the URL.

Build and run your app, select an image or movie, and tap on the action button to AirDrop it to another device. The receiving device will display the thumbnail and a request to open the movie file, as shown in the following screenshot:

Sharing documents

The final use case in DropMe is sharing documents. I have set up this sample project to include two custom files in its bundle, **Rain.dm** and **Water.dm**. They are sample text files that I created with TextEdit. If the app is running for the first time ever, these sample files will be copied into the app's Documents directory so that user has something to start with. If you switch to **Documents** tab in the app, you will see these files listed.

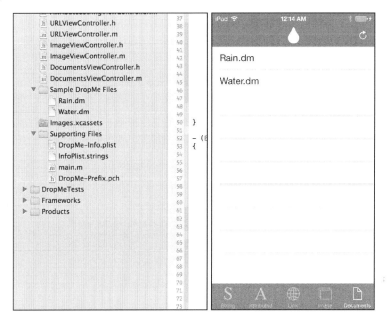

Open **DocumentsViewController.m** and make the following changes to the implementation:

```
- (void)updateDocumentsToShareWithDocument:(NSURL *)document
{
    ... insert at the end of the method implementation ...

    // Update object to share.
    self.objectsToShare = [self.toShare copy];
}

- (void)updateViewWithNotification:(NSNotification
*)notification
{
    self.objectsToShare = nil;
```

```
        ... the rest of the code ...
    }
```

The Documents tab displays the list of files in app's Documents directory that end with .dm. User can select one or more files to send via AirDrop.

As the user selects files in the list they're added to the `toShare` mutable array. That means setting up the `objectsToShare` is as easy as making a copy of the `toShare` array.

Build and run your app, select a few files from the list, and share them with another device as demonstrated below:

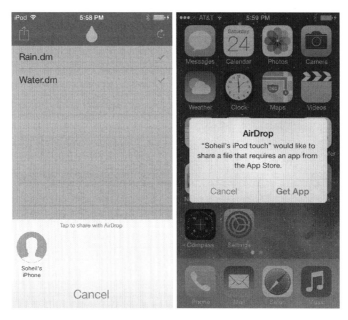

Registering UTIs

The interesting part of AirDrop is file sharing. You can share any data type — as long as you turn it into a file first. For example, you can turn your custom objects into `NSData`, save them locally in a temporary folder with a custom Uniform Type Identifier (UTI), and then pass the file URL to AirDrop.

> **Note:** A Uniform Type Identifier (UTI) is a unique ID for a type of data. Some of these are defined by Apple, and you can also make up your own and register it with iOS.

> For example, `public.text` represents text data, `com.apple.keynote.key` represents a Keynote presentation, and `com.razeware.battlemap.map` represents a custom UTI for Razeware's Battle Map 2 app.
>
> For more information and a list of registered UTIs, check out this guide:
>
> http://developer.apple.com/library/ios/ - documentation/Miscellaneous/Reference/UTIRef/Articles/System-DeclaredUniformTypeIdentifiers.html

The receiving device automatically launches the appropriate app for the type of data being shared so the user can view data. For example, when sending images, **Photos.app** launches and displays the shared image data.

However, if you AirDrop a file with an unknown UTI – as you just did with .dm files, or a data type that isn't native to iOS, your recipient will be prompted to download an app that is capable of handling the specified file.

This is actually a cool feature from an app developer's point of view – anything that encourages users to install your app is a good thing!

You can make your app handle known or custom UTIs. This functionality isn't tightly coupled with AirDrop – it's actually useful any time you want to share your app's data, whether via email or web links or AirDrop itself.

There are a few things that are important to understand about URL and UTI handling in regards to AirDrop:

• If your app is registered to handle a UTI, when you receive a file the app delegate will call `application:openURL:sourceApplication:annotation:`.

• When multiple files are transferred via AirDrop, the method above is invoked multiple times in quick succession, once for each file.

• The file URL of the object passed to AirDrop points to the **Inbox** folder, which is a folder in your app's sandbox under the **User Documents** directory. If that folder doesn't exist, iOS will create the directory for you.

• You should check the content of the **Inbox** folder on every launch or activation from background state to cover edge cases. For instance, when a large file is being transferred but the device's battery dies before the transfer is complete, your app will never be notified that the file is present on the receiving device.

So far your app is pretty good at *sending* content, but the final part of this tutorial will walk you through modifications that enable you to *receive* incoming file URLs from other devices that have the **DropMe** app installed.

URL Handling

When you use AirDrop to receive files, iOS treats those files as it would for attachments received in an email. For example, from the receiver's perspective, an NSString is just a text file with a .txt extension.

To invoke your app when someone transfers a specific data type via AirDrop, your app needs to register a UTI corresponding to that data type. You will add this functionality to your app to register as a handler for **dm** files so that when iOS attempts to open a dm file, your app will either launch automatically or show in the **Open in...** menu.

Xcode 5 has made registering UTIs much simpler than it used to be. Select the project from the Navigation Pane, and in the Editor area switch to the **Info** tab. Expand **Document Types** and then click on the + button to add a new document type.

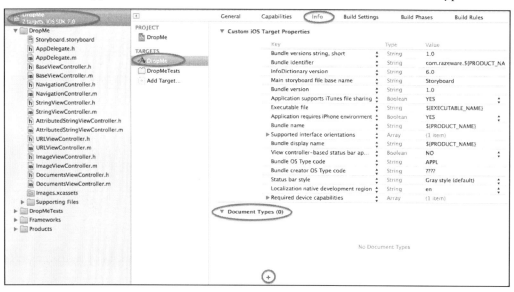

Since you're registering a new UTI that is not known by iOS, you have to provide some basic information. If you are adding a custom UTI that isn't already recognized by iOS, it's highly recommended that you add an icon for it so that the file type is distinguishable from others. The table below tells you the sizes you need for file icons. Icons for this project are included in the bundle.

Device	Size (pixels)
iPhone – non-retina	64x64
iPhone – retina	128x128
iPad – non-retina	320x320
iPad – retina	640x640

In the **Name** field enter "**DropMe File Type**" and in the **Types** field enter "**com.razeware.com.dropme.dm**". Drag and drop **fileIcon.png** file from the project navigator into the image placeholder. So far, it should look like the following:

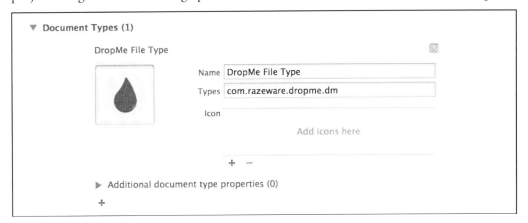

Next, expand the **Additional document type properties** section and click on the **Key** column. Enter "**CFBundleTypeRole**" in the **Key** column, leave **Type** as "**String**", and set the **Value** column to "**Editor**".

Repeat this by clicking the **+** button to add another key. This time, enter "**LSHandlerRank**" as the **Key**, leave **Type** as "**String**", and enter "**Owner**" in the **Value** column.

At this point, your two Additional document type properties should look like the following:

Key	Type	Value
CFBundleTypeRole	String	Editor
LSHandlerRank	String	Owner

This registers your app as a viewer for .dm files. You're registering the app as the owner, which means it can create and edit .dm files.

Since you are introducing a new file type, you need to give iOS some more information about the file type.

Expand **Exported UTIs** right below Document Type and click on the + button to add a new item.

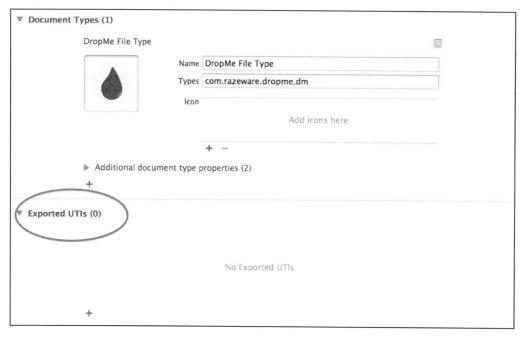

In the **Description** field enter "**DropMe File Type**" and in the **Identifier** field enter "**com.razeware.com.dropme.dm**". In **Conforms To** field enter "**public.text**" and for **Small Icon** select **fileIcon.png** from the drop down menu. It should look like the following:

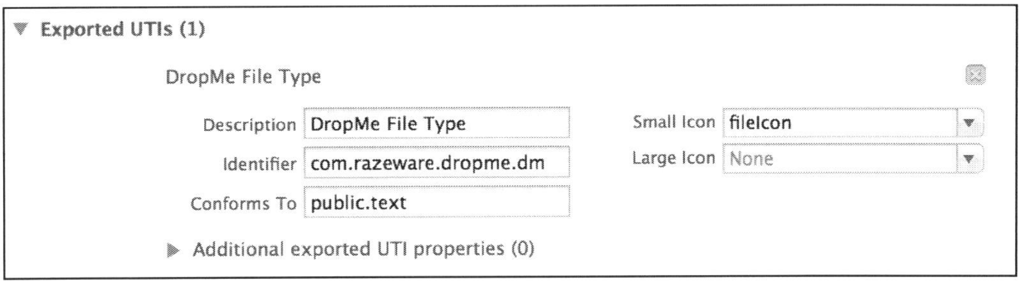

Next, expand **Additional exported UTI properties** section and click on the **Key** column. Enter "**UTTypeTagSpecification**" in the **Key** column and set **Type** as "**Dictionary**". Expand the dictionary by clicking on the disclosure triangle and click on the + button in front of it. Enter "**public.mime-type**" in the **Key** column and set the **Value** column to "**application/dropme**".

Repeat this by clicking the + button to add another key. This time, enter "**public.filename-extension**" as the **Key**, set **Type** as "**Array**", and click the + button in front of it. Leave **Key** column as "**Item 0**" and **Type** as "**String**". Enter "**dm**" in the **Value** column. Your Additional exported UTI properties should look like the following:

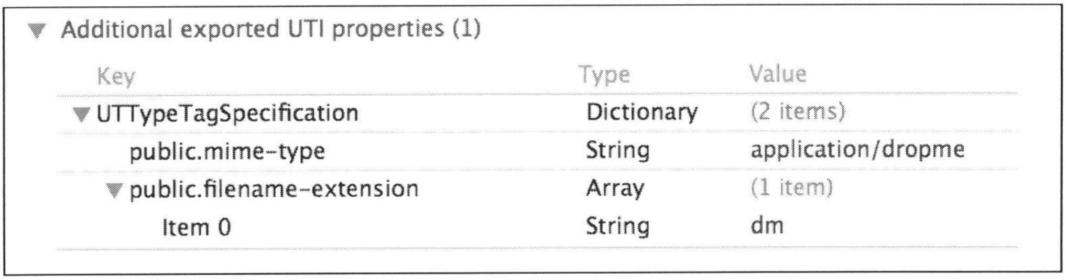

The Exported UTIs entry gives some information about com.razeware.dropme.dm to iOS. You tell the system that any file ending in .dm or with application/dropme mime type conforms to plain text and can be opened with DropMe app.

Now switch to **AppDelegate.m** and add the following methods:

```
// 1 called when app is opened via a URL
- (BOOL)application:(UIApplication *)application openURL:(NSURL
*)url sourceApplication:(NSString *)sourceApplication
annotation:(id)annotation
{
    // 2: Append the current date-time to the beginning of the
file to avoid conflicts.
```

```
    NSString *fileName = [NSString stringWithFormat:@"%@-%@",
[NSDate date], url.lastPathComponent];
    NSURL *destinationURL = [UserDocumentsDirectory()
URLByAppendingPathComponent:fileName];
    NSError *error = nil;
    BOOL success = [[NSFileManager defaultManager]
moveItemAtURL:url toURL:destinationURL error:&error];
    // 3
    if (!success)
    {
        NSLog(@"%@", error.localizedDescription);
    }
    else
    {
        // If successful, land user in Documents view
controller.
        UITabBarController *controller = (UITabBarController
*)self.window.rootViewController;
        [controller setSelectedIndex:4];

        // Send a notification so that interested classes can
update.
        [[NSNotificationCenter defaultCenter]
postNotificationName:DocumentsDirectoryContentDidChangeNotificat
ion object:self];
    }
    // 4
    return YES;
}
```

Looking at the code above comment by comment, you'll see that it does the following:

1. Implements the `UIApplication` delegate method
   `application:openURL:sourceApplication:annotation:`. It then asks if your
   app can open a resource file identified by the given URL. Since you have registered
   your app as the owner for .dm files, your app will be notified with a URL that points
   to a .dm file.

2. Extracts the file name from the URL and appends the current date to the end of the
   file name. This results in a unique filename to prevent possible conflicts with files that
   are transferred multiple times to your app.

3. If moving the file from **Inbox** to **User Documents** is successful, makes the
   Documents tab active and sends out a notification so that the UI has a chance to
   update itself.

4. Finally, `return YES`, signaling that your app can handle the URL.

Build and run your app, and install it on to two separate devices. Choose one of the sample files to share between the devices and send it. Behold! The receiving device should launch your app and land you in the Documents tab:

Congratulations – you now have made an app that can both send and receive data via AirDrop!

Where to go from here?

AirDrop offers a new way to share data between apps running on different devices. It abstracts out lots of low level and daunting networking jobs for you to find peers or transfer data.

Refer to `UIActivityViewController` class for more information and other cool things you can do with it, besides AirDrop.

You may have noticed that when you used AirDrop to share an image, user was presented with a thumbnail of the image. If you are sharing your own custom data type, you can also provide such nice features. To do so you need to either subclass `UIActivityItemProvider` objects, or have your custom object adopt `UIActivityItemSource` protocol. Refer to documentation for more information.

Challenges

You can do a lot more with AirDrop. Before you move on to the next chapter, it is worth putting some of your newfound knowledge to use.

Challenge 1: Add completion handler

The `UIActivityViewController` class provides a completion handler. The handler is called when user finishes interaction with the activity controller. The `UIActivityViewControllerCompletionHandler` is a `typedef` and defined as:

```
typedef void
(^UIActivityViewControllerCompletionHandler)(NSString
*activityType, BOOL completed);
```

When it gets called, it tells you what type of service the user picked. Because you excluded all other activities in your project, `activityType` will always return `UIActivityTypeAirDrop` if user completes AirDrop or `nil` if user cancels AirDrop. It will still return `UIActivityTypeAirDrop`, even if receiver denies AirDrop.

The `completed` flag is set to `YES` if service was performed; otherwise it is `NO`. It is also `NO` if user dismisses activity view controller regardless. Because of how AirDrop works, user always has to dismiss the activity view controller. That means in case of AirDrop you will always get `NO` for `completed`.

Now it's time for your first challenge – add a completion handler to the `BaseViewController` class and vibrate the phone if user used AirDrop. Here are a few hints:

• You'll need to add this before presenting the activity view controller.

• The format of the block is `^(NSString activityType, BOOL completed) { /* your code */ };`.

• To vibrate the phone, you need to import `AudioToolbox` framework.

• Vibration is a pre-defined system sound and this is how you call it:

```
AudioServicesPlaySystemSound(kSystemSoundID_Vibrate);
```

Challenge 2: Add iTunes file sharing

It is great that your app can now share documents via AirDrop, but there is still something missing: a very important and basic feature. You can't add or remove documents to your app via iTunes or from your computer.

Your challenge is to add iTunes file sharing support, so that users can add or remove files to the app's Documents directory via iTunes.

It is very easy. All you have to do is to set a flag in the app's **Info.plist**. The key is `UIFileSharingEnabled`.

Challenge 3: Add support for a public UTI

Now that your app supports iTunes file sharing, users may add any type of files to the app's Documents directory. But the app doesn't display them. It only displays **dm** files.

Wouldn't that be nice if your app could also display some other file types? Your last challenge is to add support for a public file type – PDF files. The goal is to enable the app to list PDF files in the app's Documents directory, and when a new PDF file is shared via AirDrop, your app is shown in **Open in** menu. Here are a few hints:

• You'll need to select the project from the Navigation Pane, and in the Editor area switch to the **Info** tab. Expand **Document Types** and add another **Document Type** by clicking on the **+** button.

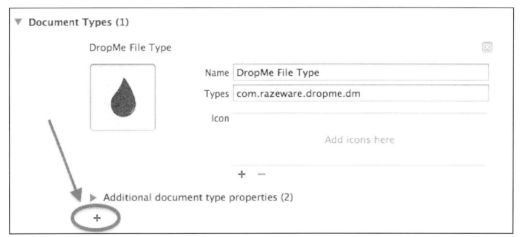

• Fill in the blanks in the same way you did for DropMe File Type. For **Name** field, enter "**PDF File Type**", and for **Types** field enter "**com.adobe.pdf**". Since it is a public file type, you can leave the icon blank.

- You'll need to add **Additional document type properties** too. Do it in the same way you did for DropMe file type. For **CFBundleTypeRole** enter **"Editor"**, and for **LSHandlerRank** enter **"Alternate"**, which hints the OS that your app is an alternative choice to view PDF files.

- You don't need to add **Exported UTIs** because PDF is a public file type.

- To display PDF files in the Documents view controller, you need to modify **DocumentsViewController.m**:

  a. The array of `acceptableFileTypes` should include `kUTTypePDF` – hint: cast to `(NSString *)`.

  b. The array of `acceptableFileExtensions` should include `@"pdf"`.

Chapter 21: Peer-to-Peer Connectivity

By Christine Abernathy

Have you ever been at a conference and needed to exchange some data with a fellow attendee, but ran into troubles due to a poor Internet connection?

Well, iOS 7 has introduced a new feature to help with that, through its new **Multipeer Connectivity** framework (also known as peer-to-peer connectivity). This gives you a way to share data with local users quickly and reliably – even without an Internet connection.

Behind the scenes, the framework handles finding the most efficient way to share data based on what's available, whether it be a local Wi-Fi network, peer-to-peer Wi-Fi, or a Bluetooth personal network.

With the Multipeer framework, you can allow users to share data in your app with nearby users.

For example, in this chapter you will develop an app called CardShare that allows users to share business cards with nearby users at conferences.

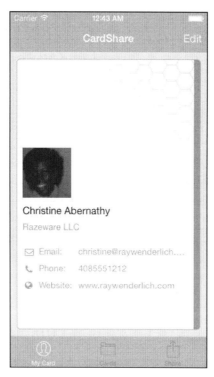

Here are a few reasons you might want to use the Multipeer Connectivity framework:

- If you have an app where users need to reliably share data in areas without an Internet connection

- If you want for users to be able to easily share data with other users based on physical location

- If you want for users to be able to share data with nearby users without having to set up a web backend

If any of this sound like something you might want to do in your app, keep reading for a hands-on guide for how to use it!

Peer-to-peer: an overview

Before you start coding, it's important to have a basic understanding of how multipeer connectivity works in iOS.

Consider two different users – Alice (the "advertiser"), and Bob (the "browser"), who are nearby each other. Let's consider how these users would initiate a peer-to-peer session:

1. **Alice: Advertise service.** Alice takes the role of an **advertiser**, and broadcasts the service that her app provides to the world.

2. **Bob: Search for service.** Bob takes the role of a **browser**, and searches for a nearby service to connect to.

3. **Bob: Send connection request.** Once the Bob finds Alice's service, he sends her a connection request.

4. **Alice: Accept or reject request.** Alice receives the request and can choose to either accept or reject the invitation. If Alice accepts the request, a peer-to-peer session is created between Alice and Bob and they can begin to exchange data, even without an Internet connection.

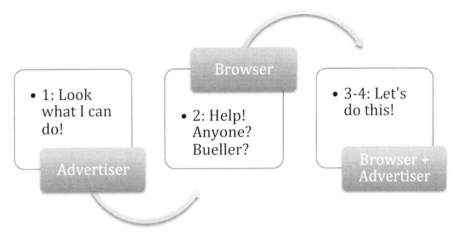

The Multipeer Connectivity framework comes with an easy to use API to make this all happen. It also includes some handy pre-built view controllers that can be used for advertising and browsing nearby devices. Of course, if you choose you can use lower-level interfaces in lieu of the built-in view controllers to create your own user experience.

The main classes in the Multipeer Connectivity framework are:

• `MCBrowserViewController`: Presents nearby devices to the user and enables that user to invite nearby devices to a session.

• `MCAdvertiserAssistant`: Handles advertising, presents incoming invitations to the user, and handles the users' responses.

• `MCNearbyServiceBrowser`: Searches for services offered by nearby devices and provides the ability to easily invite those devices to an `MCSession` (see below).

• `MCNearbyServiceAdvertiser`: Publishes an advertisement for a service specific to your app, and notifies its delegate about invitations from nearby peers.

- MCPeerID: Represents a peer in a Multipeer Connectivity session.

- MCSession: Facilitates the communication among all peers in a Multipeer Connectivity session.

Next, let's take a deeper look at the sample app you will be adding peer-to-peer connectivity to and dive into more detail about how it will work.

Getting started

The starter project for this chapter provides a shell app for CardShare that has the user interface pre-created, but no multipeer connectivity code.

Open up the project in Xcode, then build and run. The app should appear as below:

The **My Card** tab displays your contact card information. You can tap **Edit** to modify this information. Take a moment and enter your contact info; you'll need it later when sharing your contact details with other devices.

The **Cards** tab displays the list of cards that have been shared with you and saved to your device; it's empty at the moment since no cards have been shared, as shown below:

The **Share** tab displays cards that have been shared with you, and also allows you to initiate the card exchange, as shown in the screenshot below:

Tapping **Exchange** at this point doesn't do anything; you'll be adding code to implement the sharing functionality behind this action later.

Here's a sneak peek of multipeer discovery flow, using the same Alice and Bob example from earlier, which you will be implementing soon:

The first screenshot shows Bob searching for nearby devices. The second screenshot shows Alice accepting the invitation request. The third screenshot shows Bob seeing that the two devices are connected.

Once any available peers are connected, the corresponding flow of receiving a business card will look like this:

The first screenshot shows what Alice sees after Bob taps **Done** on his end. The second screenshot shows the incoming business card from Bob. The third screenshot shows Alice tapping Bob's business card and seeing the option to save it to her **Cards** list.

Overview of the starter code

Now that you have a sense of the inner workings of the UI, it's time for a high level tour of the starter code.

Open **Main.storyboard** file in Xcode to get your bearings. The layout is illustrated in the image below:

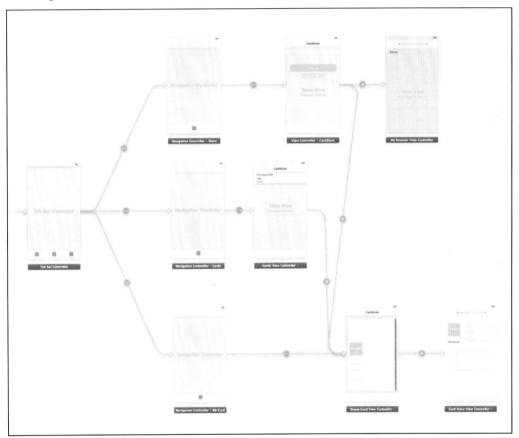

There's a single tab bar controller with three navigation controllers, one for each tab. The main classes in this app are as follows:

- `SingleCardViewController`: This is the root view controller of the navigation controller that belongs to the **My Card** tab; it displays your business card.

- CardEntryViewController: This serves as the view controller where you enter your contact details; it's accessible from SingleCardViewController.

- CardsViewController: This is the root view controller of the navigation controller that belongs to the **Cards** tab. It displays a list of your saved business cards; selecting an entry in the list navigates to SingleCardViewController.

- ShareViewController: This is the root view controller of the navigation controller that belongs to the **Share** tab. It contains two things: a button that initiates a peer browser when clicked, and a list of business cards that have been shared with you. Selecting a shared business card navigates to SingleCardViewController.

- MyBrowserViewController: This is the view controller for the customized peer browser.

- Card: This is the model for a business card. It implements the required protocols for serializing and de-serializing the card in order to persist it to disk.

- AppDelegate: This class contains logic to save and restore instances of the Card class from NSUserDefaults.

What you'll be adding

Your task is to implement the sharing features of this app, as described below:

1. Advertise your service when the app is launched.

2. Start browsing for peers when the share button is tapped.

3. Handle incoming invitations from a peer.

4. Share the business card once peer browsing is complete and connections to other peers have been established.

5. List incoming business cards, which can then be saved.

6. Create a customized browser for nearby devices.

Okay — you're now armed with enough information to get started with the coding. The next section details how to implement connections between devices using Multipeer Connectivity.

Peer-to-peer: the easy way

Like so many other things in iOS programming, there's more than one way to initiate connections between devices. The easiest method uses view controllers provided by the framework that implement a generic UI. The more involved method uses lower-level APIs that are more powerful and flexible — at the expense of requiring more coding on your part.

You'll first build the app using the easy method, as this is the fastest way to get you comfortable working with the Multipeer Connectivity framework.

The easy way uses `MCBrowserViewController` to display the peer browser and `MCAdvertiserAssistant` to handle incoming invitations.

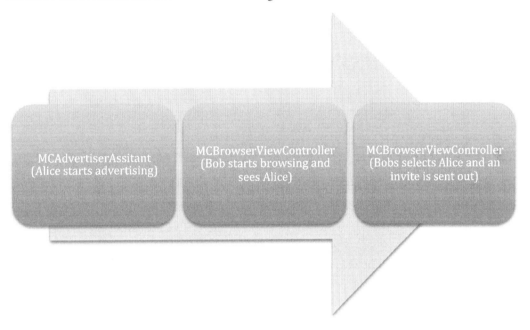

In this approach, Alice's device starts an instance of `MCAdvertiserAssistant` to serve as the advertiser at app launch. The advertiser is then left idle to wait for incoming browser invites.

Next, Bob's device initializes an instance of `MCBrowserViewController` to browse for nearby devices advertising the desired service. As nearby devices are discovered, they're displayed by the `MCBrowserViewController` instance. When a device is selected from the list, `MCBrowserViewController` sends an invitation to that device. This is how Bob sees Alice and sends her an invitation.

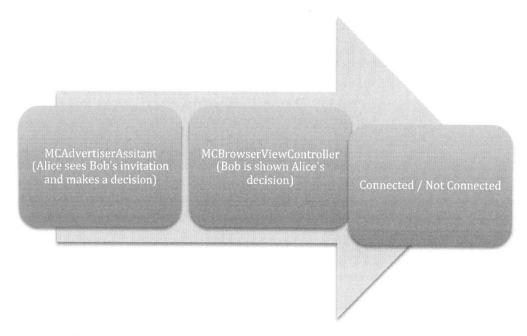

`MCAdvertiserAssistant` displays the invitation as an alert on Alice's device giving her a chance to accept or decline. Alice's decision is passed back to Bob's device where `MCBrowserViewController` displays the decision.

If Alice accepts the invitation, the devices are connected via an instance of `MCSession`. Otherwise, the peers are not connected. If `MCBrowserViewController` detects that a connection has been created with at least one peer, it enables the **Done** button on the view. Note that you can add code to handle both the **Cancel** and **Done** buttons of `MCBrowserViewController`.

Advertising a service

It's finally time to code! This app acts as both an advertiser and a browser – you will start by implementing the code to advertise a service.

Note that this app will set up the session management and communication logic in the App Delegate. In this manner, an event can be triggered from one view controller and terminate in the background while another view controller is onscreen.

You'll use `NSNotificationCenter` to post notifications about events of interest to your app, such as receiving a new business card. Observers, such as the list of cards received, can register for these notifications in order to update their respective views.

Okay – now you can start adding code.

Add the following to the top of **AppDelegate.h**:

```
#import <MultipeerConnectivity/MultipeerConnectivity.h>
```

Next, add the following line just below the import statements:

```
extern NSString *const kServiceType;
```

This simply declares a constant for the service type that's being advertised and searched for. Now you just need to assign a value to that constant.

Open **AppDelegate.m** and add the following line directly following the import statements:

```
NSString *const kServiceType = @"rw-cardshare";
```

Here "**rw**" acts as the service type identifier prefix and "**cardshare**" identifies the function of the service.

> **Note:** A service type should be a short text string in the same format as a Bonjour service type that describes the app's networking protocol. It can be up to fourteen characters in length, and must contain only lowercase ASCII letters, numbers and hyphens.
>
> The chosen string should also be easily distinguished from other unrelated services; a common practice is to prefix the string with your company's initials.

Open **AppDelegate.h** and add the following session and peer properties:

```
@property (strong, nonatomic) MCSession *session;
@property (strong, nonatomic) MCPeerID *peerId;
```

Now switch to **AppDelegate.m** and add the following to the class extension to specify the advertiser property:

```
@property (strong, nonatomic)
  MCAdvertiserAssistant *advertiserAssistant;
```

Now that all of the required properties are set up, you need some code to initialize and start the advertiser.

Add the code on the following page just above the `return YES;` statement in `application:didFinishLaunchingWithOptions:`

```
// 1
NSString *peerName =
self.myCard.firstName ? self.myCard.firstName :
    [[UIDevice currentDevice] name];
self.peerId = [[MCPeerID alloc] initWithDisplayName:peerName];
// 2
self.session =
    [[MCSession alloc] initWithPeer:self.peerId
                    securityIdentity:nil
                encryptionPreference:MCEncryptionNone];
self.session.delegate = nil;
// 3
self.advertiserAssistant =
[[MCAdvertiserAssistant alloc] initWithServiceType:kServiceType
                                     discoveryInfo:nil
                                           session:self.session];
// 4
[self.advertiserAssistant start];
```

There's a whole host of initializations happening here; first the peer, then the session, then the advertiser. The points below describe what's going on in the code, comment by comment:

1. First, initialize an MCPeerID object with a peer display name, which is either the first name on the user's business card if available, or alternatively the device name itself. It's best to keep the display name as short as possible.

2. Once the peer is set up, initialize an instance of MCSession and set the security and encryption-related parameters to nil; you'll learn more about those features later on in the chapter. The session's delegate is also set to nil; you'll implement the session's delegate methods later on, but for now this just keeps things simple.

3. Initialize an MCAdvertiserAssistant object with the service type identifier and MCSession instance you created in the previous step. discoveryInfo is a dictionary of string key/value pairs advertised to peer browsers. This allows you to give context to the data, such as the event where the card sharing is taking place, such as @{@"event": @"wwdc"}. For now, set discoveryInfo to nil.

4. Finally, call start on the MCAdvertiserAssistant instance to begin advertising the service.

Note: discoveryInfo is advertised using a Bonjour TXT record, meaning each key and value must be an instance of NSString less than 255 bytes and encoded

> in UTF-8 format. The total size of the TXT record is limited to 65,535 bytes, but Apple recommends limiting your TXT records to around 1300 bytes to fit inside a single Ethernet packet and improve network performance.

Browsing for a service

Setting up the advertiser didn't take much code; it's just as easy to set up the browser.

Open up **ShareViewController.m**; this is where a user initiates the sharing of cards.

The existing code in this file shows and hides a table view containing business cards that have been shared. Tapping an entry in the list transitions to `ShareViewController` and displays the selected card's details.

When no cards are present in the list, a button is displayed with its `action` parameter set to `addCardPressed:`. Your next step is to add some logic to this method to instantiate and display the browser view controller.

First, add an import declaration for the **Multipeer Connectivity** framework:

```
#import <MultipeerConnectivity/MultipeerConnectivity.h>
```

Next, add `MCBrowserViewControllerDelegate` to the list of protocols this class conforms to:

```
@interface ShareViewController ()
<UITableViewDataSource,
UITableViewDelegate,
MCBrowserViewControllerDelegate>
```

You need this protocol to handle dismissing the browser when the user taps **Cancel** or **Done** in the browser view controller.

Next, replace the existing `addCardPressed:` implementation with the following code:

```
- (IBAction)addCardPressed:(id)sender {
    AppDelegate *delegate = (AppDelegate *) [[UIApplication
sharedApplication] delegate];
    if (nil == delegate.myCard) {
        [[[UIAlertView alloc]
          initWithTitle:@""
          message:@"Please set up your business card first"
          delegate:nil
          cancelButtonTitle:@"OK"
          otherButtonTitles:nil] show];
```

```
        } else {
            MCBrowserViewController *browserViewController =
            [[MCBrowserViewController alloc]
             initWithServiceType:kServiceType
             session:delegate.session];
            browserViewController.view.tintColor =
            [UIColor whiteColor];
            browserViewController.delegate = self;
            [self presentViewController:browserViewController
                               animated:YES
                             completion:nil];
        }
    }
```

The original implementation of this method simply alerted the user if the contact details weren't filled in on their business card. The new code detects when the card information exists then creates an instance of MCBrowserViewController. It then uses a helper method to adjust the browser bar's tint information, sets its delegate and presents it to the user. This is a built-in view controller that will let the user select nearby devices.

Still working in the same file, add the following methods:

```
- (void)browserViewControllerDidFinish:
  (MCBrowserViewController *)browserViewController
{
    [browserViewController
      dismissViewControllerAnimated:YES completion:nil];
}

- (void)browserViewControllerWasCancelled:
  (MCBrowserViewController *)browserViewController
{
    [browserViewController
      dismissViewControllerAnimated:YES completion:nil];
}
```

Both of the above methods belong to the MCBrowserViewControllerDelegate protocol. Tapping the **Done** button calls browserViewControllerDidFinish:, while tapping **Cancel** calls browserViewControllerWasCancelled:.

Both method implementations simply dismiss the view controller at this point; later in this chapter you'll replace the current implementation of browserViewControllerDidFinish: with one that sends data to any connected peers.

Testing your app across devices

It's almost time to build and run to see your work in action, but there's a bit of setup to complete first.

To test this app, you'll need at least two devices: one acting as the browser and one playing the role of advertiser. The simulator can serve as one of the devices, but you'll need a physical device as a complement to the simulator. Make sure all your test devices are sitting on the same Wi-Fi network for now to keep things simple. If you prefer, you can also connect physical devices via Bluetooth.

Build and run your app on two devices, either simulated or physical. For the purposes of this test, call one of these devices Alice and the other Bob.

Since the apps advertise their services at startup, Alice is already advertising her service without having to do anything.

On Bob's device go to the **Share** tab, tap the **Exchange** button to initiate a browsing session and tap on Alice's name once it appears in the list of nearby devices.

On Alice's device you should see an invitation pop up from Bob. Alice is a polite user, so **Accept** the invitation from Bob.

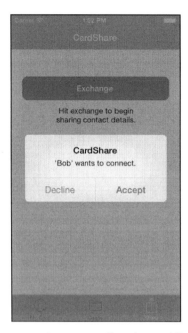

Back on Bob's device, the browser view controller shows Alice as connected and enables the **Done** button. Tap **Done** to dismiss the view controller.

Play around with a few different discovery scenarios until you're comfortable with the concepts of the browser and the advertiser. If you run into any issues such as the advertiser not showing up then quit the apps on the test devices, and restart them.

Now that your devices can connect to each other, you can move on to the more interesting work of sharing data between them!

Sending Data

Currently, an instance of `MCSession` initializes both the advertiser and the browser alike. Implementing the relevant methods of the `MCSessionDelegate` protocol will notify you of events such as a peer connecting or data arriving; you can act on these events to share data between devices.

Let's try this out. Open **AppDelegate.h** and declare a string constant to identify your app's notifications:

```
extern NSString *const DataReceivedNotification;
```

Next, open **AppDelegate.m** and add the following code to set the value of this identity string:

```
NSString *const DataReceivedNotification =
  @"com.razeware.apps.CardShare:DataReceivedNotification";
```

Add the line below to include `MCSessionDelegate` in the list of protocols your app delegate conforms to:

```
@interface AppDelegate () <MCSessionDelegate>
```

Find the statement in `application:didFinishLaunchingWithOptions:` where the delegate of the `MCSession` property is set to `nil` and replace it with the following:

```
self.session.delegate = self;
```

Now add the required delegate methods as shown below:

```
- (void)session:(MCSession *)session
  didReceiveData:(NSData *)data fromPeer:(MCPeerID *)peerID
{
    Card *card = (Card *)[NSKeyedUnarchiver
      unarchiveObjectWithData:data];

    [self.cards addObject:card];

    [[NSNotificationCenter defaultCenter]
      postNotificationName:DataReceivedNotification object:nil];
```

```
    }

    - (void)session:(MCSession *)session
      didReceiveStream:(NSInputStream *)stream
      withName:(NSString *)streamName fromPeer:(MCPeerID *)peerID
    {
    }

    - (void)session:(MCSession *)session
      didFinishReceivingResourceWithName:(NSString *)resourceName
      fromPeer:(MCPeerID *)peerID atURL:(NSURL *)localURL
      withError:(NSError *)error
    {
    }

    - (void)session:(MCSession *)session
      didStartReceivingResourceWithName:(NSString *)resourceName
      fromPeer:(MCPeerID *)peerID
      withProgress:(NSProgress *)progress
    {
    }
    - (void)session:(MCSession *)session peer:(MCPeerID *)peerID
      didChangeState:(MCSessionState)state
    {
    }
```

The Card class implements NSCoding, so you can un-archive a Card from an NSData using NSKeyedUnarchiver – that's exactly what
session:didReceiveData:fromPeer: does. It then adds the new Card instance to the array containing all shared business cards. Finally, the default notification center posts an NSNotification using the identity string defined earlier so anyone who is interested in this event can know about it.

The remainder of the method implementations is left empty at this point to keep the complier happy.

Sending card data to the peer

The delegate methods are in place — now you need to implement the logic that actually sends the data to the peer.

Add the following method to **AppDelegate.m**:

```
-(void)sendCardToPeer
```

```
{
    NSData *data = [NSKeyedArchiver
      archivedDataWithRootObject:self.myCard];
    NSError *error;
    [self.session sendData:data
                    toPeers:[self.session connectedPeers]
                    withMode:MCSessionSendDataReliable
                    error:&error];
}
```

The above method archives the `Card` instance stored in `myCard` using
`NSKeyedArchiver` and then calls `sendData:toPeers:withMode:error:` on the
`MCSession` instance stored in `session` property. The array provided to the `toPeers`
parameter contains all the peers connected to the session.

The `withMode` parameter controls the transmission mode, and can be one of two
options: `MCSessionSendDataUnreliable` for when speed trumps reliability, and
`MCSessionSendDataReliable` for when reliability matters most.

Next, you need to make this method public since it will be invoked from outside the app
delegate.

Add the following method declaration to **AppDelegate.h**:

```
- (void)sendCardToPeer;
```

Now you'll enhance the app to handle sending the user's business card and respond to
incoming business cards from nearby devices.

Open **ShareViewController.m** and add the following method:

```
- (void) sendCard {
    AppDelegate *delegate =
    (AppDelegate *) [[UIApplication sharedApplication]
                       delegate];
    [delegate sendCardToPeer];
    [self showMessage:@"Card sent to nearby device"];
}
```

This method simply instructs the app delegate to distribute the user's business card to
any connected peers. It then displays an alert to the user to inform them that their card
has been sent.

Still in **ShareViewController.m**, replace the existing implementation of
`browserViewControllerDidFinish:` with the following:

```
- (void)browserViewControllerDidFinish:
(MCBrowserViewController *)browserViewController
{
    [browserViewController
     dismissViewControllerAnimated:YES
     completion:^{
         [self sendCard];
     }];
}
```

This calls `sendCard` when the instance of `MCBrowserViewController` is dismissed using the **Done** button.

You can also make the app a little smarter: if the user taps the Exchange button when already connected to a nearby device, the card can be sent immediately instead of displaying the browser.

Replace the implementation of `addCardPressed:` with the following:

```
- (IBAction)addCardPressed:(id)sender {
    AppDelegate *delegate =
    (AppDelegate *) [[UIApplication sharedApplication]
                     delegate];
    if (nil == delegate.myCard) {
        [[[UIAlertView alloc]
          initWithTitle:@""
          message:@"Please set up your business card first"
          delegate:nil
          cancelButtonTitle:@"OK"
          otherButtonTitles:nil] show];
    } else {
        if ([[delegate.session connectedPeers]
             count] == 0) {
            MCBrowserViewController *browserViewController =
            [[MCBrowserViewController alloc]
             initWithServiceType:kServiceType
             session:delegate.session];
            browserViewController.view.tintColor =
            [UIColor whiteColor];
            browserViewController.delegate = self;
            [self presentViewController:browserViewController
                               animated:YES
                             completion:nil];
        } else {
            [self sendCard];
```

```
            }
        }
    }
```

In the code above, you've added a secondary `if` block to determine if the session already has any connected peers. If so, immediately call `sendCard`.

Receiving card data from the peer

All that's left to do at this point is display the incoming business cards.

Still in **ShareViewController.m,** add the following to the bottom of `viewDidLoad`:

```
[[NSNotificationCenter defaultCenter]
    addObserver:self
        selector:@selector(dataReceived:)
            name:DataReceivedNotification
        object:nil];
```

The above code simply observes the data arrival notification.

To unregister from observing the notification, override `dealloc` and add the following line:

```
[[NSNotificationCenter defaultCenter] removeObserver:self];
```

Now add the `dataReceived:` method, which is called when the notification is received:

```
- (void)dataReceived:(NSNotification *)notification
{
    [self showHideNoDataView];
    [self.tableView reloadData];
}
```

The above code hides the Exchange button and shows the table view with reloaded data in preparation for displaying the incoming card data.

Next, modify `viewWillAppear:` to call `dataReceived:` as shown below:

```
- (void)viewWillAppear:(BOOL)animated
{
    [super viewWillAppear:animated];
    [self dataReceived:nil];
}
```

This code reloads the view whenever the view is displayed so the cards are displayed.

Build and run your app, launch the peer browser and instantiate a connection between two devices.

Tap **Done** and your business card data should now appear on the receiving device's **Share** tab. Tap on any incoming card to display its details and tap **Add To Cards** to save the card data. Now move to the **Cards** tab to see the newly saved card, as shown in the screenshot below:

That's the easy way to send data via a peer-to-peer connection; the controllers and views are all set up for you, and you just need to call the key methods to instantiate sessions and send data between peers. But this method is a bit limiting; the real power can be found underneath by managing your peer connections programmatically.

Sending other types of data

You're not limited to sharing only NSData objects; you can also send the following data to any connected peer:

- URL content:
  sendResourceAtURL:toPeer:withTimeout:completionHandler: sends the content pointed to by an instance of NSURL over the current session. On the receiving

end, implement `session:didReceiveResourceAtURL:fromPeer:` delegate method to process the incoming data.

- **Streaming content:** Stream content between peers by calling `startStreamWithName:toPeer:error:` on an active session; this creates an instance of `NSOutputStream` that lets you communicate with the connected peer. On the receiver, implement `session:didReceiveStream:withName:fromPeer:` to process the incoming stream.

You've now covered how to set up discovery of nearby devices as well as sending and receiving data once the connection has been established.

Peer-to-peer: the programmatic way

That's it for the easy way to implement peer-to-peer connectivity in your apps. If that's all you need, feel free to stop reading here and move on to the next chapter!

But if you're looking for more power and customization, keep reading. The **Multipeer Connectivity** framework provides additional APIs that support programmatic discovery and customize the experience beyond what's provided by `MCBrowserViewController` and `MCAdvertiserAssitant`. As an example, you could customize the way the nearby devices are presented to the user. You could even customize the browser behavior when a nearby device has been found, such as immediately sending out an invite without waiting for user interaction.

`MCNearbyServiceBrowser` and `MCNearbyServiceAdvertiser` provide methods to handle programmatic discovery for the browser and advertiser respectively. The `MCNearbyServiceBrowserDelegate` protocol supports your custom browser by enabling you to respond to finding nearby devices, while `MCNearbyServiceAdvertiserDelegate` helps you handle browser invitations programmatically.

You'll have to do the heavy lifting in your code to construct your browser's UI, present nearby devices and initiate invitations to peers. On the advertiser end, the UI work involves presenting the invitation to the user, getting the user's response, and calling a handler to pass the user response to the browser.

However, once the peers are connected, sending data works exactly the same as before.

Your code changes will involve swapping out the current browser and advertiser set up code and replacing it with the programmatic version. You'll also implement the required delegate methods to manage the discovery flow.

For kicks, you'll use a flag to switch between the non-programmatic and the programmatic peer discovery. This allows you to switch between the two and compare the functionality against each other.

Open **AppDelegate.h** and add the following global constant below the existing constant declarations:

```
extern BOOL const kProgrammaticDiscovery;
```

Next, switch to **AppDelegate.m** and set the value of the flag by adding the following line just above the class extension:

```
BOOL const kProgrammaticDiscovery = YES;
```

Note that you are going to implement your custom user interface to look quite similar to the built-in interface. However, for your own apps you can obviously style this however you like – that is the entire benefit of this approach.

Setting up your advertiser

You'll approach things a little differently this time around by working on the advertiser-related code first.

Still in **AppDelegate.m**, add the following block definition for the advertiser's invitation handler:

```
typedef void(^InvitationHandler)(BOOL accept, MCSession
*session);
```

When a browser sends an invitation it passes an invitation handler block to the relevant advertiser delegate method. You'll need to save and call this handler block to inform the browser of the users' response, which you'll implement a little later.

Modify the app delegate's class extension as shown below:

```
@interface AppDelegate ()
<MCSessionDelegate,
MCNearbyServiceAdvertiserDelegate,
UIAlertViewDelegate>

@property (strong, nonatomic) MCAdvertiserAssistant
*advertiserAssistant;
@property (strong, nonatomic) MCNearbyServiceAdvertiser
*advertiser;
@property (copy, nonatomic) InvitationHandler handler;
```

```
@end
```

The code above adds the necessary protocols and properties to help manage the discovery flow from the advertiser's end. The `MCNearbyServiceAdvertiserDelegate` protocol methods respond to peer invites and you'll react to this by presenting a `UIAlertView` with accept and reject buttons.

You'll implement a single `UIAlertViewDelegate` protocol method to determine which button was tapped and call the invitation handler with the necessary response.

Next, locate the following section of code in `application:didFinishLaunchingWithOptions:`

```
self.advertiserAssistant =
[[MCAdvertiserAssistant alloc] initWithServiceType:kServiceType
                                     discoveryInfo:nil

session:self.session];
[self.advertiserAssistant start];
```

...and replace it with the following code:

```
if (kProgrammaticDiscovery) {
    // 1
    self.advertiser =
    [[MCNearbyServiceAdvertiser alloc]
        initWithPeer:self.peerId
      discoveryInfo:nil
        serviceType:kServiceType];
    // 2
    self.advertiser.delegate = self;
    // 3
    [self.advertiser startAdvertisingPeer];
} else {
    self.advertiserAssistant =
    [[MCAdvertiserAssistant alloc]
        initWithServiceType:kServiceType
            discoveryInfo:nil
                session:self.session];
    [self.advertiserAssistant start];
}
```

If `kProgrammaticDiscovery` is set, then the following actions are taken:

1. `initWithPeer:discoveryInfo:serviceType:` initializes the advertiser with a peer, a nil for the `discoveryInfo` parameter and the `serviceType` identifier for the

service being provided. Remember, only browsers searching for a service with the same identifier will see this advertiser.

2. Sets the advertiser's delegate to the app delegate.

3. Calls `startAdvertisingPeer` to commence the process of advertising this service.

Next, add the following code to **AppDelegate.m**:

```
- (void)advertiser:(MCNearbyServiceAdvertiser *)advertiser
didReceiveInvitationFromPeer:(MCPeerID *)peerID
withContext:(NSData *)context invitationHandler:(void (^)(BOOL,
MCSession *))invitationHandler
{
    self.handler = invitationHandler;

    [[[UIAlertView alloc]
        initWithTitle:@"Invitation"
            message:[NSString
                stringWithFormat:@"%@ wants to connect",
                    peerID.displayName]
            delegate:self
    cancelButtonTitle:@"Nope"
    otherButtonTitles:@"Sure", nil] show];
}
```

The above code is your advertiser delegate method that's called when an invitation is received from a peer. The `handler` property stores the invitation handler block passed to this method so that it can be used later to inform the browser of the user's decision.

The code then displays an instance of `UIAlertView` asking whether or not to accept the decision, and finally sets the delegate of the alert view to the app delegate.

All that's left on the advertiser's end is to determine what the user's response was.

Add the code below to **AppDelegate.m**:

```
- (void)alertView:(UIAlertView *)alertView
clickedButtonAtIndex:(NSInteger)buttonIndex
{
    BOOL accept = (buttonIndex == alertView.cancelButtonIndex) ?
NO : YES;

    self.handler(accept, self.session);
}
```

The above code implements the `alertView:clickedButtonAtIndex:` delegate method, determines which button the user tapped and calls `handler` with the result.

Build and run your app and walk through the discovery process again. You'll see the same browser interface you know and love. However, you'll notice the following subtle change in the invitation alert display:

The alert title and button text is different from that shown by `MCAdvertiserAssistant`.

Setting up your custom browser

That takes care of the advertiser; it's time to turn your attention to the browser. In your current implementation, `ShareViewController` sets up an instance of `MCBrowserViewController` and displays it to the user to initiate the browsing process.

You'll switch this around a bit to use your own custom browser. The starter project contains a view controller you've not seen yet, `MyBrowserViewController`; you'll use this to implement a custom browser.

The storyboard links `ShareViewController` to `MyBrowserViewController` via a push segue; however, there's currently no code to trigger that segue — you'll be adding this yourself.

The very first thing to take care of is establishing your custom browser using the relevant **Multipeer Connectivity** framework APIs. The process, outlined below, closely mimics the implementation of the stock view controllers provided by Apple:

1. `MyBrowserViewController` displays a `UITableView` that lists nearby peers.

2. When a nearby peer is found, the app automatically sends an invitation to that peer. This differs from the stock view controller that waits for the user to select a peer.

3. The remote peer device presents the invitation to the user who chooses whether or not to accept the invitation.

4. The browser then executes `session:didReceiveData:fromPeer:`, a method of the `MCSessionDelegate` protocol to detect changes to the session; a connected session means the invite was accepted, while a disconnected session means the invite was rejected.

5. The `session:didReceiveData:fromPeer:` method implementation then posts a notification to inform any observers of the session change.

6. The `MyBrowserViewController` instance registers for that notification; once the notification is received it updates the browser table view with the peer's decision.

7. If a minimum number of peers have joined the session, the controller displays a **Done** button to the user.

8. If a maximum number of peers have joined a session, the controller automatically triggers the **Done** button.

9. Tapping **Done** or **Cancel** in the custom browser stops the browser from looking for nearby devices.

10. A new adopted protocol, `MyBrowserViewControllerDelegate`, responds to the manner in which custom browser is dismissed. The methods that do this are based on those found in the `MCBrowserViewControllerDelegate` protocol.

11. Finally, the implementation modifies `ShareViewController` to conform to the `MyBrowserViewControllerDelegate` protocol and to implement the requisite methods. If the user dismisses the view controller with the **Done** button, the user's business card is then distributed to connected peers.

The completed custom browsing experience looks like this:

Now that you have a good sense of the flow, you can get started on the coding.

Connecting to the custom browser

Open **MyBrowserViewController.h** and import the header file for **Multipeer Connectivity** as shown below:

```
#import <MultipeerConnectivity/MultipeerConnectivity.h>
```

Switch to **MyBroserViewController.m** and add the following properties to the class extension:

```
@property (strong, nonatomic) MCNearbyServiceBrowser *browser;
@property (strong, nonatomic) NSString *serviceType;
@property (strong, nonatomic) MCPeerID *peerId;
@property (strong, nonatomic) MCSession *session;
```

Next, add the following method:

```
- (void)setupWithServiceType:(NSString *)serviceType
session:(MCSession *)session peer:(MCPeerID *)peerId
{
    self.serviceType = serviceType;
    self.session = session;
    self.peerId = peerId;
}
```

This is used to set up the browser-related properties when the view controller is presented via the appropriate segue:

Switch to **MyBrowserViewController.h** and add the following public declaration:

```
- (void)setupWithServiceType:(NSString *)serviceType
  session:(MCSession *)session peer:(MCPeerID *)peerId;
```

Switch to **ShareViewController.m** and import the custom browser header:

```
#import "MyBrowserViewController.h"
```

Next, modify the following code to include your custom browser's protocol along with the other protocols:

```
@interface ShareViewController ()
<MCBrowserViewControllerDelegate,
MyBrowserViewControllerDelegate,
UITableViewDataSource, UITableViewDelegate>
```

Now add the implementation of the protocol method below:

```
- (void)myBrowserViewControllerDidFinish:
(MyBrowserViewController *)browserViewController
{
    [browserViewController
     dismissViewControllerAnimated:YES
     completion:^{
        [self sendCard];
    }];
}

- (void)myBrowserViewControllerWasCancelled:
(MyBrowserViewController *)browserViewController
{
    [browserViewController
        dismissViewControllerAnimated:YES completion:nil];
}
```

Just as before, tapping **Done** dismisses the custom browser and distributes the business card to any connected peers, while tapping **Cancel** simply dismisses the custom browser.

Next, replace the existing addCardPressed: method with the following code:

```
- (IBAction)addCardPressed:(id)sender {
```

```
    AppDelegate *delegate =
    (AppDelegate *) [[UIApplication sharedApplication]
delegate];
    if (nil == delegate.myCard) {
        [[[UIAlertView alloc]
          initWithTitle:@""
          message:@"Please set up your business card first"
          delegate:nil
          cancelButtonTitle:@"OK"
          otherButtonTitles:nil] show];
    } else {
        if ([[delegate.session connectedPeers]
            count] == 0) {
          if (kProgrammaticDiscovery) {
              [self
              performSegueWithIdentifier:@"SegueToMyBrowser"
                              sender:self];
          } else {
              MCBrowserViewController *browserViewController =
              [[MCBrowserViewController alloc]
                initWithServiceType:kServiceType
                session:delegate.session];
              browserViewController.view.tintColor =
              [UIColor whiteColor];
              browserViewController.delegate = self;
              [self
              presentViewController:browserViewController
                          animated:YES
                        completion:nil];
          }
        } else {
            [self sendCard];
        }
    }
}
```

The implementation above is similar to the previous one; if the
kProgrammaticDiscovery flag is set, then segue to the custom browser. Otherwise,
just use the Apple-provided view controller that you used in the first half of this tutorial.

Then, replace the existing prepareForSegue: implementation with the following:

```
- (void)prepareForSegue:(UIStoryboardSegue *)segue
               sender:(id)sender
{
```

```
    if ([segue.identifier
        isEqualToString:@"SegueToMyBrowser"]) {
      AppDelegate *delegate =
      (AppDelegate *) [[UIApplication sharedApplication]
delegate];
      MyBrowserViewController *browserViewController =
      (MyBrowserViewController *)
        segue.destinationViewController;
      [browserViewController
       setupWithServiceType:kServiceType
       session:delegate.session
       peer:delegate.peerId];
      browserViewController.delegate = self;
    } else if ([segue.identifier
              isEqualToString:@"SegueToCardDetail"]) {
      SingleCardViewController *singleCardViewController =
      (SingleCardViewController *)
      segue.destinationViewController;
      singleCardViewController.card = self.selectedCard;
      singleCardViewController.enableAddToCards = YES;
    }
  }
```

The above implementation determines which segue is being run. If it represents the custom browser's segue, setupWithServiceType:session:peer: is called on the custom browser to setup its properties with the relevant values.

Build and run your app then tap **Exchange** from the Share tab. You'll see your brand spanking new browser interface.

At this point it's not too interesting as you haven't added any logic to search for and show nearby devices. You'll tackle that next.

Searching for nearby devices

Switch back to **MyBrowserViewController.m**. Modify the following in the class extension to adopt the `MCNearbyServiceBrowserDelegate` protocol:

```
@interface MyBrowserViewController ()
<UIToolbarDelegate,
MCNearbyServiceBrowserDelegate>
```

Now add the following code to the very end of `viewDidLoad` in **MyBrowserViewController.m**:

```
self.browser = [[MCNearbyServiceBrowser alloc]
initWithPeer:self.peerId
serviceType:self.serviceType];

self.browser.delegate = self;

[self.browser startBrowsingForPeers];
```

The above code creates an instance of `MCNearbyServiceBrowser`, using the `peerId` property as the peer and the `serviceType` property as the service type. The current class is set as the `MCNearbyServiceBrowserDelegate` delegate. Finally it calls `startBrowsingForPeers` to begin searching for nearby devices.

Next up is to implement the methods of the `MCNearbyServiceBrowserDelegate` protocol. Add the following method to **MyBrowserViewController.m**:

```
- (void)browser:(MCNearbyServiceBrowser *)browser
didNotStartBrowsingForPeers:(NSError *)error
{
    NSLog(@"Error browsing: %@", error.localizedDescription);
}
```

This is an extremely basic implementation that simply logs the error description to Xcode's console.

Before diving into the other protocol method implementations, note that there are three lists of data you'll track in order to display peer devices to your user:

• Nearby devices that the browser has detected.

• Nearby devices that have declined an invitation to connect.

• Nearby devices that have accepted an invitation to connect.

You'll manipulate these lists from the browser delegate methods and from methods notified about an advertiser's invitation decision.

Add the delegate method that gets called when a peer is found:

```
- (void)browser:(MCNearbyServiceBrowser *)browser
      foundPeer:(MCPeerID *)peerID
withDiscoveryInfo:(NSDictionary *)info
{
    [self.nearbyPeers addObject:peerID];
    [self.tableView reloadData];
}
```

This method adds the discovered peer to the array of nearby peers and reloads the table view to display the device.

Now add the delegate method that gets called when a peer disconnects:

```
- (void)browser:(MCNearbyServiceBrowser *)browser
      lostPeer:(MCPeerID *)peerID
{
    [self.nearbyPeers removeObject:peerID];
```

```
    [self.acceptedPeers removeObject:peerID];
    [self.declinedPeers removeObject:peerID];

    if ([self.acceptedPeers count] <
        (self.minimumNumberOfPeers - 1)) {
        [self showDoneButton:NO];
    }

    [self.tableView reloadData];
}
```

This method removes the peer that is no longer connected from each of the peer arrays. If the number of connected peers is below the desired threshold, it hides the **Done** button and reloads the table view.

Add the following statement to the top of **both** the cancelButtonPressed and doneButtonPressed methods:

```
[self.browser stopBrowsingForPeers];
self.browser.delegate = nil;
```

The code instructs the browser to stop browsing for peers when the **Done** and **Cancel** buttons are tapped then sets the browser delegate to nil.

Now replace the table view data source method that creates the cells with this one:

```
- (UITableViewCell *)tableView:(UITableView *)tableView
       cellForRowAtIndexPath:(NSIndexPath *)indexPath
{
    static NSString *CellIdentifier = @"NearbyDevicesCell";
    MyBrowserTableViewCell *cell = (MyBrowserTableViewCell*)
    [tableView
        dequeueReusableCellWithIdentifier:CellIdentifier];
    if (cell == nil) {
        cell = [[MyBrowserTableViewCell alloc]
                initWithStyle:UITableViewCellStyleDefault
                reuseIdentifier:CellIdentifier];
        cell.selectionStyle = UITableViewCellSelectionStyleNone;
        cell.accessoryType = UITableViewCellAccessoryNone;
        cell.accessoryView = nil;
    }
    // 1
    MCPeerID *cellPeerId = (MCPeerID *)
    self.nearbyPeers[indexPath.row];
```

```objc
    // 2
    if ([self.acceptedPeers containsObject:cellPeerId]) {
        if ([cell.accessoryView isKindOfClass:
             [UIActivityIndicatorView class]]) {
            UIActivityIndicatorView *activityIndicatorView =
            (UIActivityIndicatorView *)cell.accessoryView;
            [activityIndicatorView stopAnimating];
        }
        UILabel *checkmarkLabel =
            [[UILabel alloc]
                initWithFrame:CGRectMake(0, 0, 20, 20)];
        checkmarkLabel.text = @" √ ";
        cell.accessoryView = checkmarkLabel;
    }
    // 3
    else if ([self.declinedPeers containsObject:cellPeerId]) {
        if ([cell.accessoryView isKindOfClass:
             [UIActivityIndicatorView class]]) {
            UIActivityIndicatorView *activityIndicatorView =
            (UIActivityIndicatorView *)cell.accessoryView;
            [activityIndicatorView stopAnimating];
        }
        UILabel *unCheckmarkLabel =
            [[UILabel alloc]
                initWithFrame:CGRectMake(0, 0, 20, 20)];
        unCheckmarkLabel.text = @" X ";
        cell.accessoryView = unCheckmarkLabel;
    }
    // 4
    else {
        // 5
        UIActivityIndicatorView *activityIndicatorView =
        [[UIActivityIndicatorView alloc]

initWithActivityIndicatorStyle:UIActivityIndicatorViewStyleGray]
;
        activityIndicatorView.hidesWhenStopped = YES;
        [activityIndicatorView setColor:
         [(AppDelegate *)[[UIApplication sharedApplication]
                         delegate] mainColor]];
        [activityIndicatorView startAnimating];
        cell.accessoryView = activityIndicatorView;
        // 6
        [self.browser
```

```
        invitePeer:cellPeerId
        toSession:self.session
        withContext:[@"Making contact"
 dataUsingEncoding:NSUTF8StringEncoding]
        timeout:10];

    }
    // 7
    cell.textLabel.text = cellPeerId.displayName;

    return cell;
}
```

Each cell in the table view displays the peer's name, an indicator of an active connection, and the status of the invitation: accepted or declined. The points below explain the code in detail, comment by comment:

1. Retrieve the relevant peer from the `nearbyPeers` array based on the current cell's index path.

2. Check if the peer has accepted an invitation to join a session using the `acceptedPeers` array. If so, display a checkmark as a label in the cell's `accessoryView`, and stop any animated activity indicators.

3. If a peer has declined an invitation, display an X as a label in the cell's `accessoryView`. As before, stop any animated activity indicators, just in case you've interrupted an in-progress connection.

4. If the connection is neither accepted nor declined, then invite the peer to join a session in follow-on code.

5. Create an instance of `UIActivityIndicatorView` and assign it to the cell's `accessoryView`.

6. Send an invitation to the peer by calling `invitePeer:toSession:withContext:timeout:` on the instance of `MCNearbyServiceBrowser`. The `withContext` parameter can be any arbitrary piece of data to pass to the peer, such as the nature of the connection request.

7. Set the cell's display label to the peer's display name.

Once you've sent the invitation to the remote peer, you need to notify the browser of any response received so the browser can update the interface accordingly.

Open **AppDelegate.h** and declare the following constant string:

```
extern NSString *const PeerConnectionAcceptedNotification;
```

Next, switch to **AppDelegate.m** and provide a value for the identity string:

```
NSString *const PeerConnectionAcceptedNotification =
@"com.razeware.apps.CardShare:PeerConnectionAcceptedNotification
";
```

Modify `session:peer:didChangeState:` as shown below to trigger the notifications:

```
- (void)session:(MCSession *)session peer:(MCPeerID *)peerID
  didChangeState:(MCSessionState)state
{
    if (state == MCSessionStateConnected
        && self.session) {
        [[NSNotificationCenter defaultCenter]
         postNotificationName:PeerConnectionAcceptedNotification
         object:nil
         userInfo:@{
                     @"peer": peerID,
                     @"accept" : @YES
                     }];
    } else if (state == MCSessionStateNotConnected
               && self.session) {
        if (![self.session.connectedPeers
             containsObject:peerID]) {
            [[NSNotificationCenter defaultCenter]

postNotificationName:PeerConnectionAcceptedNotification
             object:nil
             userInfo:@{
                         @"peer": peerID,
                         @"accept" : @NO
                         }];
        }
    }
}
```

The method above responds to changes in the state of the session. When the browser sends out an invite to a peer, the remote peer's session state changes from `MCSessionStateNotConnected` to `MCSessionStateConnecting`. When the invitation is accepted, the remote peer's session state changes to `MCSessionStateConnected`.

When the invitation is rejected, the state of the remote peer session changes back to `MCSessionStateNotConnected`. The `userInfo` key of the posted notification is used to send an instance of `NSDictionary` containing a pointer to the remote peer and invitation decision. Observers can then extract the dictionary's values and process the invitation accordingly.

Switch back to **MyBrowserViewController.m** and add the following just below the call to `super` in `viewDidLoad`:

```
[[NSNotificationCenter defaultCenter]
    addObserver:self
        selector:@selector(peerConnected:)
            name:PeerConnectionAcceptedNotification
          object:nil];
```

This registers to receive the notification.

To unregister from observing the notification, override `dealloc` and add the following line:

```
[[NSNotificationCenter defaultCenter] removeObserver:self];
```

Next, add the following method:

```
- (void) peerConnected:(NSNotification *)notification
{
    MCPeerID *peer =
    (MCPeerID *)[notification userInfo][@"peer"];

    BOOL nearbyDeviceDecision =
    [[notification userInfo][@"accept"] boolValue];
    if (nearbyDeviceDecision) {
        [self.acceptedPeers addObject:peer];
    } else {
        [self.declinedPeers addObject:peer];
    }

    if ([self.acceptedPeers count] >=
        (self.maximumNumberOfPeers - 1)) {
        [self doneButtonPressed:nil];
    } else {
        if ([self.acceptedPeers count] <
            (self.minimumNumberOfPeers - 1)) {
            [self showDoneButton:NO];
        } else {
            [self showDoneButton:YES];
        }
        [self.tableView reloadData];
```

```
      }
   }
}
```

The above method receives the notification that contains the peer and the invite decision. If the user accepted the invitation, it adds the peer to the acceptedPeers array, but if the user declined the invite, it adds the peer to declinedPeers.

It then checks if the number of connected peers is above a maximum threshold to trigger the **Done** button action.

Otherwise if checks if it needs to show or hide the **Done** button based on the peers that are currently connected. Then it reloads the table view to show either a checkmark of cross as the visual indicator of the invite response.

Build and run your app and walk through the discovery process and try accepting or rejecting the automatically sent invites.

Securing your session

At this point just about any Tom, Dick and Harry can show up on your browser's doorstep and send you unwanted data if you're thumb-happy and accept their invitation.

Fear not, several tools are available at your disposal to keep your data secure. When you initialize an MCSession object, you can choose the mechanisms by which you secure both your identity and your data.

Authentication

You can authenticate a session by passing an instance of NSArray containing a SecIdentityRef, and optionally a list of certificates, as the securityIdentity parameter in the initWithPeer:securityIdentity:encryptionPreference: method of MCSession.

A SecIdentityRef is a **Core Foundation** type that represents an identity. To find out more, it's highly recommended that you check out the **Certificate, Key, and Trust Services Reference**[1] on Apple's Developer Center:

http://developer.apple.com/library/ios/#documentation/Security/Reference/certifkeytrus tservices/Reference/reference.html#//apple_ref/doc/uid/TP30000157

Encryption

You can also control the manner in which the session is encrypted by using `MCEncryptionOptional`, `MCEncryptionRequired` or `MCEncryptionNone` as the arguments to the `encryptionPreference` parameter of `initWithPeer:securityIdentity:encryptionPreference:`.

If one peer wishes to communicate with `MCEncryptionRequired`, then any potential peer needs to implement either that encryption level or the `MCEncryptionOptional` level.

Test out these combinations by modifying the session initialization logic.

Open **AppDelegate.m** and modify the session initialization code from:

```
self.session =
    [[MCSession alloc] initWithPeer:self.peerId
                   securityIdentity:nil
              encryptionPreference:MCEncryptionNone];
```

... to this:

```
self.session =
    [[MCSession alloc] initWithPeer:self.peerId
                   securityIdentity:nil
              encryptionPreference:MCEncryptionRequired];
```

Build and run your changes on only one device to create an encryption level mismatch. Try connecting to your nearby test device. The connection should be rejected. Now build the updated code on your other test device. Retry the connection. You should now be able to connect the devices.

Next, modify the initialization logic to the following:

```
self.session =
    [[MCSession alloc] initWithPeer:self.peerId
                   securityIdentity:nil
              encryptionPreference:MCEncryptionOptional];
```

Build and run your changes on only one device to create a level mismatch. In this scenario you should be able to connect the two test devices since one requires encryption and the other prefers encryption but can accept unencrypted connections.

Reset your encryption preference back to `MCEncryptionNone`.

Challenges

At this point, you have hands-on experience connecting to and communicating with nearby devices using the **Multipeer Connectivity** framework.

There's quite a bit more to explore with this new framework; to that end, here are three challenges for you to exercise what you've learned and delve into few more details of the API.

The three challenges range from easy to hard, but they all offer valuable insight into the framework. Don't worry if you try one and get stuck: you can always take a peek at the solutions that can be found in the resources for the chapter.

Challenge 1: Filtering advertisers

By default, browsers won't see advertisers with a service identifier that doesn't match theirs. However, there could be scenarios where the identifiers match but you want to allow users another layer to filter out advertisers. One scenario could be at a conference where a presenter only wants to see and send out business cards to attendees who know a "secret" code that they'll give out. These could be the attendees who actually attended their session.

Your first challenge is to add a way to filter out advertisers who don't have a given code. Here are a few hints:

- You can initialize the advertiser to send out the code in the `discoveryInfo` parameter. For `MCAdvertiserAssistant` modify the `initWithServiceType:discoveryInfo:session:` method and for `MCNearbyServiceAdvertiser` modify `initWithPeer:discoveryInfo:serviceType:`.

- Controlling advertisers presented to a browser can be implemented through the `browserViewController:shouldPresentNearbyPeer:withDiscoveryInfo:` delegate method in `MCBrowserViewControllerDelegate` for the built-in browser controller. Or it can be implemented through the `browser:foundPeer:withDiscoveryInfo:` delegate method in `MCNearbyServiceBrowserDelegate` for programmatic browser discovery.

Challenge 2: Session cleanup

The sample project opens the session but you may have noticed that it could use some cleanup. Your second challenge is to disconnect the session when appropriate. Modify the sample project so that a peer disconnects its session after receiving business cards from all connected peers.

Here are a few hints to help you out:

- Keep track of whether the user has sent out their business card. Set this flag in `sendCardToPeer`.

- Keep track of the list of peers that the user has received business cards from.

- Whenever a new business card is received, update your list of peers business cards have been received from and check if it's time to disconnect. Add this logic to `session:didReceiveData:fromPeer:`.

- Whenever a nearby device disconnects their session, check if it's time to disconnect. Add this logic to `session:peer:didChangeState:`.

- Your disconnect check should be based on whether the user has sent out a business card and received business cards from all currently connected peers.

- To disconnect perform a complete teardown of the session, peer, advertiser as well as associated delegates. After disconnecting, create new peer, session and advertiser instances to get ready for any follow up discovery flows.

Challenge 3: Stream the data

The sample project sends the business card data at all once using an instance of `NSData`. Your challenge is to use a stream of bytes to transfer the data instead. Hint: `NSInputStream` and `NSOutputStream` are your best friends for this task.

Here are some additional hints:

- Modify `sendCardToPeer` to replace the `sendData:toPeers:withMode:error:` call with logic to set up an output byte stream.

- An input stream of the business card data is the source for your sender's output stream. Create the business card data stream using `inputStreamWithData:` on `NSInputStream`.

- Create the output stream by calling `startStreamWithName:toPeer:error:`. Then set up the output stream delegate and schedule the stream to run in the main run loop. Finally, open the stream.

- Implement the `stream:handleEvent:` method of the `NSStreamDelegate` protocol to fill up your output stream with business card data when there's space available.

- On the business card receiving end, implement the `session:didReceiveStream:withName:fromPeer:` delegate method.

- In the implementation, configure your input stream as well as its delegate and schedule it to run in the main run loop.

- Modify `stream:handleEvent:` to read incoming data bytes as they become available.

- Once all the data bytes are in, call your existing `session:didReceiveData:fromPeer:` implementation that already has all the required logic to process the business card data.

- When initializing your browser, set the `maximumNumberOfPeers` property to 2 to ensure data is streamed between only two devices.

Section IV: Minor New Features

In this section, you'll learn about some minor improvements to existing APIs you know and love, such as AVFoundation, MapKit, and Core Location.

Chapter 22: What's New in AVFoundation

Chapter 23: What's New in MapKit

Chapter 24: What's New in Core Location

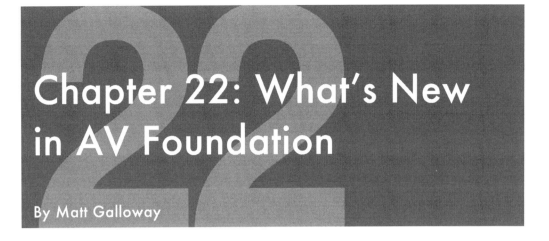

Chapter 22: What's New in AV Foundation

By Matt Galloway

Adding audio and video support can result in a much richer user experience in your apps, but working with digital media is often a complicated endeavor. Fortunately, Apple offers tools that ease this burden for developers, such as the AV Foundation framework.

iOS 4 introduced **AV Foundation** as a way to manage camera and microphone input, process digital media, and send output to the disk or the screen — a process collectively known as **media graph processing.** iOS 6 introduced even more advanced features in AV Foundation such as the ability to natively perform face detection in live video without the need to leverage Core Image.

iOS 7 brings even more improvements to AV Foundation, such as:

- Barcode reading support

- Speech synthesis

- Improved zoom functionality

You'll be introduced to these features as you work through this chapter's sample project: a QR code reader.

But it's not just a normal QR code reader – there's a twist! After you scan a QR code, the app will speak the code to you using AVFoundation speech synthesis. In addition, you'll make use of the improved zoom functionality to get a better shot.

Read on; you'll be pleasantly surprised how easy it is to implement these features.

> **Note:** To follow along with this project, you need to own, beg, borrow, or steal an iOS device that has a camera installed. The simulator just won't cut it for this project – sorry!

Getting started

Open Xcode and create a new project by navigating to **File\New\Project...** Select the **iOS\Application\Single View Application** template and click **Next**. Name the project **ColloQR**, choose **iPhone** for Devices, and click **Next**. Finally, choose a convenient location to save the project.

> **Note:** Wondering why the app is named "ColloQR"? Well, it's an unapologetically cheesy portmanteau of "Colloquy" and "QR" — namely, a QR code reader that has a conversation with you!

You now have a project with a single storyboard and a single view controller. It's pretty bare at the moment. To start, you'll put the view controller into a navigation controller so that it can at least have a title.

Open **Main.storyboard**, select the view controller in the scene, and select **Editor\Embed In\Navigation Controller**. Finally, select the navigation bar that appears and set its title to **ColloQR**.

The base project is all set up —it's time to get cracking on the camera work!

Working with the camera

First you need to import the AV Foundation framework in order to work with its juicy new features. Open **ViewController.m** and add the following import to the top of the file:

```
@import AVFoundation;
```

Next, add the following instance variables to the implementation declaration:

```
@implementation ViewController {
```

```
    AVCaptureSession *_captureSession;
    AVCaptureDevice *_videoDevice;
    AVCaptureDeviceInput *_videoInput;
    AVCaptureVideoPreviewLayer *_previewLayer;
    BOOL _running;
}
```

Here's a quick rundown of these instance variables:

1. _captureSession – AVCaptureSession is the core media handling class in AV Foundation. It talks to the hardware to retrieve, process, and output video. A capture session wires together inputs and outputs, and controls the format and resolution of the output frames.

2. _videoDevice – AVCaptureDevice encapsulates the physical camera on a device. Modern iPhones have both front and rear cameras, while other devices may only have a single camera.

3. _videoInput – To add an AVCaptureDevice to a session, wrap it in an AVCaptureDeviceInput. A capture session can have multiple inputs and multiple outputs.

4. _previewLayer – AVCaptureVideoPreviewLayer provides a mechanism for displaying the current frames flowing through a capture session; it allows you to display the camera output in your UI.

5. _running – This holds the state of the session; either the session is running or it's not.

Your instance variables are declared; now your need to initialize them. Add the following method to **ViewController.m**:

```
- (void)setupCaptureSession {
    // 1
    if (_captureSession) return;

    // 2
    _videoDevice = [AVCaptureDevice
            defaultDeviceWithMediaType:AVMediaTypeVideo];
    if (!_videoDevice) {
        NSLog(@"No video camera on this device!");
        return;
    }

    // 3
```

```
        _captureSession = [[AVCaptureSession alloc] init];

        // 4
        _videoInput = [[AVCaptureDeviceInput alloc]
                        initWithDevice:_videoDevice error:nil];

        // 5
        if ([_captureSession canAddInput:_videoInput]) {
            [_captureSession addInput:_videoInput];
        }

        // 6
        _previewLayer = [[AVCaptureVideoPreviewLayer alloc]
                            initWithSession:_captureSession];
        _previewLayer.videoGravity =
            AVLayerVideoGravityResizeAspectFill;
    }
```

The above method sets up the capture session. The following points explain the code comment by comment:

1. If the session has already been created, then exit early as there's no need to set things up again.

2. Initialize the video device by obtaining the type of the default video media device. This returns the most relevant device available. In practice, this generally references the device's rear camera. If there's no camera available, this method will return nil and exit.

3. Initialize the capture session so you're prepared to receive input.

4. Create the capture input from the device obtained in comment 2.

5. Query the session with `canAddInput:` to determine if it will accept an input. If so, call `addInput:` to add the input to the session.

6. Finally, create and initialize a preview layer and indicate which capture session to preview. Set the gravity to "resize aspect fill" so that frames will scale to fit the layer, clipping them if required to maintain the aspect ratio.

> **Note:** Video gravity modes are similar to `UIView`'s content modes, only with fewer options as not all of `UIView`'s content modes make sense for video.

Your preview layer is ready to roll, but you need somewhere for it to live.

Creating the preview view

Open **Main.storyboard**, drag a UIView onto the view controller, and make it fill the entire view. Next, add an outlet for the new view, name it previewView and wire it up. This serves a container for the preview layer.

Back in **ViewController.m**, modify viewDidLoad as shown below:

```
- (void)viewDidLoad {
    [super viewDidLoad];

    [self setupCaptureSession];

    _previewLayer.frame = _previewView.bounds;
    [_previewView.layer addSublayer:_previewLayer];
}
```

The code above creates the capture session, sets up the preview layer to fill the container view and adds it as a sublayer.

Next, add the following two methods to **ViewController.m**:

```
- (void)startRunning {
    if (_running) return;
    [_captureSession startRunning];
    _running = YES;
}

- (void)stopRunning {
    if (!_running) return;
    [_captureSession stopRunning];
    _running = NO;
}
```

These methods start and stop the session if required. The _running instance variable prevents unnecessary actions, like starting running sessions, or stopping terminated sessions.

The app should be a good citizen and start and stop the session as necessary. In your app, sessions run only when the view controller is on screen.

Add the following two methods to **ViewController.m**:

```
- (void)viewDidAppear:(BOOL)animated {
    [super viewDidAppear:animated];
    [self startRunning];
```

```
    }

    - (void)viewWillDisappear:(BOOL)animated {
        [super viewWillDisappear:animated];
        [self stopRunning];
    }
```

The above methods hook into the standard `UIViewController` methods to ensure the session only runs when the view controller is visible. However, that's only half of the solution; you also need to stop the session when the app is put into the background and restart it when the app comes back to the foreground.

Add the following notification registrations to `viewDidLoad:` in **ViewController.m**:

```
    [[NSNotificationCenter defaultCenter]
        addObserver:self
            selector:@selector(applicationWillEnterForeground:)
                name:UIApplicationWillEnterForegroundNotification
            object:nil];

    [[NSNotificationCenter defaultCenter]
        addObserver:self
            selector:@selector(applicationDidEnterBackground:)
                name:UIApplicationDidEnterBackgroundNotification
            object:nil];
```

The code above takes care of starting and stopping the session depending on whether the app is in the foreground or background.

Next, add the following implementation of the registered selectors to **ViewController.m**:

```
    - (void)applicationWillEnterForeground:(NSNotification*)note {
        [self startRunning];
    }

    - (void)applicationDidEnterBackground:(NSNotification*)note {
        [self stopRunning];
    }
```

Now the session will start and stop as required.

Build and run your project; as noted at the beginning of this chapter, you will need to run your app on a physical device that has at least one camera. The simulator is a pretty useful tool, but it can't simulate video capture devices.

Once your app is running, you'll see the camera's images displayed on-screen, similar to the image below:

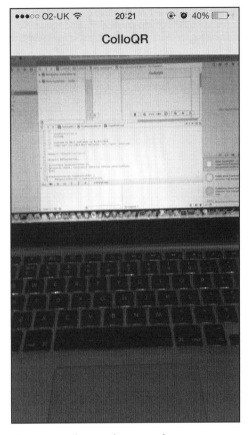

If you see the exact same image as above, then you have your camera pointed at the author's laptop — and that's just plain creepy!

The video capture is working well; it's time to do something with that video input.

Detecting machine readable codes

In addition to processing and displaying video, AV Foundation detects and decodes a comprehensive list of 1-D and 2-D barcodes:

1. QR code

2. Aztec

3. EAN13

4. EAN8

5. UPC-E

6. PDF417

7. Code 93

8. Code 39

9. Code 39 mod 43

You have probably seen some of these codes in action, even though you may not have known their names. EAN13 is a common standard in Europe for marking items, whereas UPC-E is favored in the United States. PDF417 is used by some mail services and is also the standard for airline boarding passes.

However, the QR code is probably pretty familiar to mobile users; that's the type of code you'll read in your app.

Open **ViewController.m** and add the following instance variable to the implementation block:

```
AVCaptureMetadataOutput *_metadataOutput;
```

`AVCaptureMetadataOutput` provides a callback to the application when metadata is detected in a video frame. AV Foundation supports two types of metadata: machine readable codes and face detection.

You need a way to capture and process that metadata. Add the following code to the end of `setupCaptureSession` in **ViewController.m**:

```
_metadataOutput = [[AVCaptureMetadataOutput alloc] init];

dispatch_queue_t metadataQueue =
    dispatch_queue_create("com.razeware.ColloQR.metadata", 0);

[_metadataOutput setMetadataObjectsDelegate:self
                                      queue:metadataQueue];

if ([_captureSession canAddOutput:_metadataOutput]) {
    [_captureSession addOutput:_metadataOutput];
}
```

Here you initialize the output with a delegate and then add it to the session. Just as you did with the inputs, you need to query `canAddOutput:` first to see if it's okay to add an output to your session.

AV Foundation is designed for high throughput and low latency; therefore any processing and analysis tasks should be moved off of the main thread if at all possible.

Similar to the delegate object, `AVCaptureMetadataOutput` requires that you provide a dispatch queue to make delegate callbacks. This frees the media subsystem to continue processing frames from the camera. If callbacks were executed in a synchronous manner, a long-running delegate callback would block frame processing until it was complete.

This might not be an issue in a simple one-input one-output system. However, asynchronous processing of callbacks is key in a multi-output system so that long-running callbacks on one output don't cause frame drops in other outputs.

In **ViewController.m**, modify the class continuation category declaration as shown below:

```
@interface ViewController ()
    <AVCaptureMetadataOutputObjectsDelegate>
```

Next, add the following method to **ViewController.m** to implement the delegate declared:

```
- (void)captureOutput:(AVCaptureOutput *)captureOutput
        didOutputMetadataObjects:(NSArray *)metadataObjects
        fromConnection:(AVCaptureConnection *)connection
{
    [metadataObjects
        enumerateObjectsUsingBlock:^(AVMetadataObject *obj,
                                     NSUInteger idx,
                                     BOOL *stop)
        {
            NSLog(@"Metadata: %@", obj);
        }];
}
```

The metadata output calls the above method every time it detects new metadata. At this point, the code simply logs each piece of metadata as it's detected. This is sufficient for testing purposes; you'll flesh out the rest of this implementation later.

There's one last tweak before you can build and run. Add the following line to `startRunning` in **ViewController.m,** immediately underneath the line `[_captureSession startRunning];`:

```
_metadataOutput.metadataObjectTypes =
    _metadataOutput.availableMetadataObjectTypes;
```

This sets the types of metadata in which your app is interested; in this case you'll detect all available types of metadata.

Build and run your app; pass your camera over the following QR code while keeping an eye on the Xcode console:

Once your device processes the QR code above, you should see the following output displayed:

```
2013-07-03 21:57:03.758 ColloQR[1262:1303] Metadata:
<AVMetadataMachineReadableCodeObject: 0x15e515d0> type
"org.iso.QRCode", bounds { 0.2,0.1 0.5x0.8 }, corners { 0.2,0.9
0.2,0.1 0.7,0.1 0.7,0.9 }, time 31399588077583, stringValue "W00t! A
QR code!"
```

There you are — your first scanned QR code. Feel free to try this out on any other QR codes nearby, or perform a quick Internet search.

Look closely at the output above and you'll see the metadata includes more information than just the contents of the code in `stringValue`, including the bounds and corners of the QR image.

You're not done yet! Many code readers provide visual feedback to the user to indicate if the code is properly positioned and capable of being read; next you'll use the bounds and corner metadata to draw an overlay on the camera view to achieve this.

Drawing overlays

The bounds metadata defines a rectangle that exactly contains the image, while the corner metadata defines the coordinates of the image's corners. The diagram below displays the difference between the two:

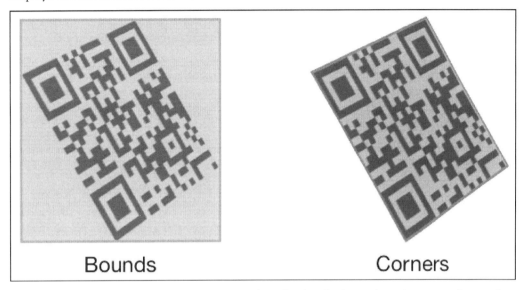

When the camera and the image are aligned perfectly, the bounds and corners depict the same region. However, holding the camera perfectly parallel to the image is nearly impossible, so it's useful to read and display both pieces of metadata.

Open **ViewController.m** and add the following instance variable to the implementation block:

```
NSMutableDictionary *_barcodes;
```

This provides dictionary storage for all detected barcodes, keyed by the barcodes' contents.

Add the following line to `viewDidLoad` in **ViewController.m**:

```
_barcodes = [NSMutableDictionary new];
```

`_barcodes` provides you with a dictionary to index the detected barcodes, but you also need to store the metadata associated with each barcode. It sounds like a class would be perfect for this job.

Add the following class definition to the top of **ViewController.m**, directly under the imports:

```objc
@interface Barcode : NSObject
@property (nonatomic, strong)
    AVMetadataMachineReadableCodeObject *metadataObject;
@property (nonatomic, strong) UIBezierPath *cornersPath;
@property (nonatomic, strong) UIBezierPath *boundingBoxPath;
@end

@implementation Barcode
@end
```

> **Note:** Technically you could put this class in its own file, but to keep this tutorial simple just store it in **ViewController.m**.

Add the following method to **ViewController.m**:

```objc
- (Barcode*)processMetadataObject:
            (AVMetadataMachineReadableCodeObject*)code
{
    // 1
    Barcode *barcode = _barcodes[code.stringValue];

    // 2
    if (!barcode) {
        barcode = [Barcode new];
        _barcodes[code.stringValue] = barcode;
    }

    // 3
    barcode.metadataObject = code;

    // Create the path joining code's corners

    // 4
    CGMutablePathRef cornersPath = CGPathCreateMutable();

    // 5
    CGPoint point;
    CGPointMakeWithDictionaryRepresentation(
        (CFDictionaryRef)code.corners[0], &point);
```

```
// 6
CGPathMoveToPoint(cornersPath, nil, point.x, point.y);

// 7
for (int i = 1; i < code.corners.count; i++) {
    CGPointMakeWithDictionaryRepresentation(
        (CFDictionaryRef)code.corners[i], &point);
    CGPathAddLineToPoint(cornersPath, nil,
                         point.x, point.y);
}

// 8
CGPathCloseSubpath(cornersPath);

// 9
barcode.cornersPath =
    [UIBezierPath bezierPathWithCGPath:cornersPath];
CGPathRelease(cornersPath);

// Create the path for the code's bounding box

// 10
barcode.boundingBoxPath =
    [UIBezierPath bezierPathWithRect:code.bounds];

// 11
return barcode;
}
```

The above method retrieves existing `Barcode` objects from the dictionary — or creates new `Barcode` dictionary entries as required — and creates paths to represent the bounds and corners of the stored `Barcode` objects.

The points below explain the method in further detail, comment by comment:

1. Query the dictionary of `Barcode` objects to see if a `Barcode` with the same contents is already cached.

2. If not, create a new `Barcode` object and add it to the dictionary.

3. Store the barcode's metadata in the cached `Barcode` object for later.

4. Instantiate `cornersPath` to store the path joining the four corners of the code.

5. Convert the first corner coordinate to `CGPoint` instances using some CoreGraphics calls.

6. Begin the path at the corner defined in Step 5.

7. Loop through the other three corners, creating the path as you go.

8. Close the path by joining the fourth point to the first point.

9. Create a `UIBezierPath` object from `cornersPath` and store it in the `Barcode` object.

10. Create the bounding box path using `bezierPathWithRect:`.

11. Finally, return the `Barcode` object.

That takes care of calculating the image's corner and bounds paths. Now you just need some code that will iterate through the cached `Barcode` objects and draw these paths on-screen.

Still working in **ViewController.m**, replace the contents of `captureOutput:didOutputMetadataObjects:fromConnection:` with the following:

```
// 1
NSMutableSet *foundBarcodes = [NSMutableSet new];

[metadataObjects enumerateObjectsUsingBlock:
^(AVMetadataObject *obj, NSUInteger idx, BOOL *stop) {
    NSLog(@"Metadata: %@", obj);
    // 2
    if ([obj isKindOfClass:
                  [AVMetadataMachineReadableCodeObject class]])
    {
        // 3
        AVMetadataMachineReadableCodeObject *code =
            (AVMetadataMachineReadableCodeObject*)
 [_previewLayer transformedMetadataObjectForMetadataObject:obj];
        // 4
        Barcode *barcode = [self processMetadataObject:code];
        [foundBarcodes addObject:barcode];
    }
}];

dispatch_sync(dispatch_get_main_queue(), ^{
    // Remove all old layers
    // 5
    NSArray *allSublayers = [_previewView.layer.sublayers copy];
```

```
        [allSublayers enumerateObjectsUsingBlock:
        ^(CALayer *layer, NSUInteger idx, BOOL *stop) {
            if (layer != _previewLayer) {
                [layer removeFromSuperlayer];
            }
        }];

        // Add new layers
        // 6
        [foundBarcodes enumerateObjectsUsingBlock:
        ^(Barcode *barcode, BOOL *stop) {
            CAShapeLayer *boundingBoxLayer = [CAShapeLayer new];
            boundingBoxLayer.path = barcode.boundingBoxPath.CGPath;
            boundingBoxLayer.lineWidth = 2.0f;
            boundingBoxLayer.strokeColor =
                [UIColor greenColor].CGColor;
            boundingBoxLayer.fillColor =
                [UIColor colorWithRed:0.0f
                                green:1.0f
                                 blue:0.0f
                                alpha:0.5f].CGColor;
            [_previewView.layer addSublayer:boundingBoxLayer];

            CAShapeLayer *cornersPathLayer = [CAShapeLayer new];
            cornersPathLayer.path = barcode.cornersPath.CGPath;
            cornersPathLayer.lineWidth = 2.0f;
            cornersPathLayer.strokeColor =
                [UIColor blueColor].CGColor;
            cornersPathLayer.fillColor =
                [UIColor colorWithRed:0.0f
                                green:0.0f
                                 blue:1.0f
                                alpha:0.5f].CGColor;
            [_previewView.layer addSublayer:cornersPathLayer];
        }];
    });
```

Here's a description of what's happening in the above code, comment by comment:

1. Create an NSMutableSet so you can easily enumerate the detected barcodes.

2. Process only the objects of type AVMetadataMachineReadableCodeObject. Recall that you configured the metadata output in startRunning to accept all metadata types; you need to filter out anything that's not a machine readable code.

3. Transform the image's bounds and corner coordinates — that are represented in relative coordinates — into the coordinate space of your containing view. In the relative coordinate system, an **x** value of 1.0 is the right hand side of the frame, while an **x** coordinate of 0.5 is in the middle of the frame. The preview layer has the very handy `transformedMetadataObjectForMetadataObject:` to do this task for you, which saves you from handling a ton of coordinate math.

4. Call the method you just wrote to process the barcode data, and add it to the set.

5. Remove all sublayers from the preview view by shipping a dispatch back to the main queue where the UI work is performed.

6. Finally, enumerate all the detected barcodes and add a `CAShapeLayer` for the bounding box path and corner path of each one. The shape layers have different colors to be visually distinct and have an alpha value of 0.5 so that the original code image can be seen through the drawn shapes.

You've done well to get through the overlay code — you deserve to see the fruits of your labors!

Build and run your app, hover the camera over a QR code of your choice, and you should see something similar to the image below:

Move the camera around to view the QR code from different angles and see for yourself how the bounding box and corners relate to one another.

Displaying the codes on-screen is pretty cool, but this is the 21ˢᵗ century, after all —
what if your app could *speak* the contents of the code to you?

Adding Speech Synthesis

iOS 7 brings speech synthesis to AV Foundation; modifying your app to speak the
contents of barcodes is the last step in creating your fully pimped-out code reader.

Open **ViewController.m** and add the following instance variable to the
implementation block:

```
AVSpeechSynthesizer *_speechSynthesizer;
```

Now add the following line of code to `viewDidLoad` in **ViewController.m**:

```
_speechSynthesizer = [[AVSpeechSynthesizer alloc] init];
```

This one line of code is all that you need to initialize the speech synthesizer. Seriously —
it's that simple to implement speech synthesis in your app.

The speech synthesizer controls playback and queuing of individual speech items, or
"utterances". The metadata output triggers the callback every time the video frame
updates – but you don't want your synthesizer to speak every time there's a frame
update. Otherwise, your app will sound like that guy in the office down the hall that
never…stops….talking.

Tracking barcode changes

Add the following line to the very top of
`captureOutput:didOutputMetadataObjects:fromConnection:` in
ViewController.m:

```
NSSet *originalBarcodes =
    [NSSet setWithArray:_barcodes.allValues];
```

The above set stores all detected barcodes before processing the new frame. Comparing
the cached set of barcodes against the newly detected barcodes allows you to cast out the
ones that haven't changed.

Add the following code immediately after the `enumerateObjectsUsingBlock:`
enumerator section in `fromConnection:`, just after the closing " `}];` "

```
NSMutableSet *newBarcodes = [foundBarcodes mutableCopy];
```

```
[newBarcodes minusSet:originalBarcodes];
```

Think about this in terms of a Venn diagram; if you take the set of current barcodes, subtract the set of original barcodes, then all you're left with is the set of new barcodes.

Add the following code immediately below the lines you just added:

```
NSMutableSet *goneBarcodes = [originalBarcodes mutableCopy];
[goneBarcodes minusSet:foundBarcodes];

[goneBarcodes enumerateObjectsUsingBlock:
^(Barcode *barcode, BOOL *stop) {
    [_barcodes
        removeObjectForKey:barcode.metadataObject.stringValue];
}];
```

The code above puts a bit of set theory into action: take the set of original barcodes, subtract the set of current barcodes, and you're left with the set of old barcodes that are no longer onscreen. Then you simply enumerate through the set of old barcodes and remove them from the dictionary cache.

Creating utterances

Finally, add the following code to the end of the `dispatch_sync` block:

```
[newBarcodes enumerateObjectsUsingBlock:
^(Barcode *barcode, BOOL *stop) {
    AVSpeechUtterance *utterance =
        [[AVSpeechUtterance alloc]
            initWithString:barcode.metadataObject.stringValue];
    utterance.rate =
        AVSpeechUtteranceMinimumSpeechRate +
            ((AVSpeechUtteranceMaximumSpeechRate -
                AVSpeechUtteranceMinimumSpeechRate) * 0.5f);
    utterance.volume = 1.0f;
    utterance.pitchMultiplier = 1.2f;

    [_speechSynthesizer speakUtterance:utterance];
}];
```

The code above enumerates through the remaining set of barcodes, sets the rate, volume and pitch of the speech, and then finally calls `speakUtterance:` to speak the barcode data to you!

> **Note:** Consult the AV Foundation framework documentation for more information on the parameters for `AVSpeechUtterance` and their respective ranges of acceptable values.

All that's left to do is indicate you need to use the audio hardware to play your utterances. Add the following code to the end of `startRunning` in **ViewController.m**:

```
[[AVAudioSession sharedInstance]
    setCategory:AVAudioSessionCategoryPlayback
    withOptions:0
        error:nil];
[[AVAudioSession sharedInstance] setActive:YES error:nil];
```

AVAudioSession provides all of the necessary routines to enable the audio hardware interfaces for your app. The code above indicates that the audio session should be active when the camera is active.

Finally, add the following code to the end of `stopRunning` in **ViewController.m**:

```
[[AVAudioSession sharedInstance] setActive:NO error:nil];
```

Similarly, when your session is not active, the audio session is inactivated.

Build and run your app; it won't *look* any different, but hover the camera over a barcode and your device will speak the barcode contents to you. Admittedly, the speech synthesis is no Siri, but it's cool nonetheless!

You can display barcodes on the screen, add overlays of bounds and corner paths and use speech synthesis to speak the contents of the barcodes spoke to you — all that's left to do is add zoom capability to your app.

Zooming images

iOS 7 now contains the ability to instruct the session to grab frames directly from the camera at a specific zoom factor.

Applying a transform to the preview layer was the only way to accomplish this in earlier versions of iOS. However, this wasn't ideal because the image would pixelate as you zoomed. However, the frames of video that come from the sensor are usually much larger than the screen size, so this pixelation isn't necessary. The new zoom APIs in iOS

7 keep your images crisp while zooming by chopping out the required middle portion of the video frame to perform the zoom.

This keeps them crisp because no transform is being applied, rather just the desired pixels are chopped from the middle of the frame. Obviously once you hit the limit where the number of pixels cropped is smaller than the screen size, a transform will have to be applied to zoom further.

Implementing pinch-to-zoom in your app is a good way to showcase this new feature. Open **ViewController.m** and add the following instance variable to the implementation block:

```
CGFloat _initialPinchZoom;
```

This holds the initial zoom factor during a pinch gesture.

Next, add the following code to the end of `viewDidLoad`:

```
[_previewView addGestureRecognizer:
    [[UIPinchGestureRecognizer alloc]
        initWithTarget:self
              action:@selector(pinchDetected:)]];
```

Recall that `previewView` is a `UIView` that displays the camera preview layer. You add the gesture recognizer here so that the pinch gesture will work anywhere on the video display.

Add the following method to **ViewController**:

```
- (void)pinchDetected:(UIPinchGestureRecognizer*)recogniser {
    // 1
    if (!_videoDevice) return;

    // 2
    if (recogniser.state == UIGestureRecognizerStateBegan) {
        _initialPinchZoom = _videoDevice.videoZoomFactor;
    }

    // 3
    NSError *error = nil;
    [_videoDevice lockForConfiguration:&error];

    if (!error) {
        CGFloat zoomFactor;
        CGFloat scale = recogniser.scale;
```

```
        if (scale < 1.0f) {
            // 4
            zoomFactor = _initialPinchZoom -
              pow(_videoDevice.activeFormat.videoMaxZoomFactor,
                1.0f - recogniser.scale);
        } else {
            // 5
            zoomFactor = _initialPinchZoom +
              pow(_videoDevice.activeFormat.videoMaxZoomFactor,
                (recogniser.scale - 1.0f) / 2.0f);
        }

        // 6
        zoomFactor = MIN(10.0f, zoomFactor);
        zoomFactor = MAX(1.0f, zoomFactor);

        // 7
        _videoDevice.videoZoomFactor = zoomFactor;

        // 8
        [_videoDevice unlockForConfiguration];
    }
}
```

Here's a description of the above code block, comment by comment:

1. Check if there's a valid video device. If not, then bail. This is merely a safeguard in the event that the capture session wasn't successfully created or you start pinching before the camera preview is ready.

2. Capture the initial zoom factor at the start of the gesture recognition. videoZoomFactor is your first taste of the new zoom API; it defines the zoom factor to apply to the video frames.

3. Lock the video device for configuration. You must always obtain a lock before editing the state of a device.

4. If the lock was created without error, then calculate the direction of zoom. A scale value less than 1.0 indicates an inward pinch, so the camera should zoom out.

5. A scale value scale greater than 1.0 indicates an outward pinch, and the camera should zoom in accordingly. The math used in Steps 4 and 5 simply make the zoom animation feel natural.

6. Limit the zoom factors to sensible minimum and maximum values.

7. Set the zoom factor on the video device.

8. Finally, unlock the video device as you're done with configuration. Always make sure that your lock and unlock actions are balanced; or the device might end up locked indefinitely!

Once again, AV Foundation wraps some very complex actions in a very straightforward API.

Build and run your app one final time; watch how the image scales in a natural fashion and maintains image quality as you zoom in and out.

> **Note:** `rampToVideoZoomFactor:withRate:` provides another mechanism to gradually change the zoom factor via the rate parameter instead of setting it immediately. This is especially helpful when zooming automatically to a detected feature.

Challenges

AV Foundation does a lot of heavy lifting for you, but you still need to know how to use it! To that end, there are a few challenges below to test your knowledge on the workings of AV Foundation. Completing these challenges will show that you're well on your way to understanding the use of AV Foundation.

Challenge 1: Zoom Slider

Not everyone likes pinch gestures to zoom as they don't give a great deal of precision. Your challenge is to add a slider to the UI that changes the zoom factor.

As a hint, you'll find the following function useful:

```
CGFloat ZoomFactorCalc(CGFloat maxZoomFactor,
                       CGFloat sliderValue)
{
    CGFloat factor = pow(maxZoomFactor, sliderValue);
    return MIN(10.0f, factor);
}
```

To use this function, provide the maximum zoom factor supported by the device you're using, along with a `sliderValue` from 0.0 to 1.0. It will return the required scaling value for the camera zoom using similar math to what you've already seen in the tutorial.

Once you've finished this challenge, you should end up with a UI similar to this:

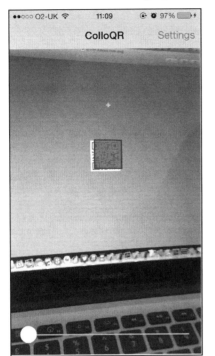

The slider at the bottom of the screen controls the zoom; sliding it all the way to the left zooms all the way out, and sliding it all the way to the right zooms all the way in.

> **Hint:** Make sure you add the slider as a child of the root view in the view controller — not the view used to display the preview layer!

Challenge 2: Alter the utterance settings

The speech synthesis in your app accepts parameters to control the speed, volume and pitch of the spoken words. It would be a great idea to include the ability to control these settings so the user could have some control over the speech engine.

Your task in this challenge is to add a speech settings menu that allows the user to change the speed, volume and pitch of the utterances.

Your hint for this task is to use `NSUserDefaults` to save the settings and read them back in when building an utterance.

The below image gives an example of how your settings screen might look — but see how creative you can be in your implementation!

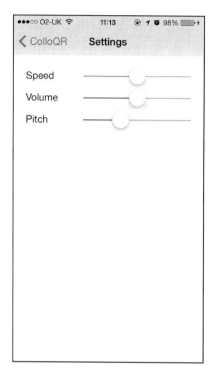

For bonus points, read up on how to change the base voice used for speech synthesis. Check out the header file of AVSpeechSynthesisVoice for details on how to go about this.

Challenge 3: Area of interest

You don't always want to pick up barcodes in the entire visible range of your camera; in fact, it's more efficient to only use a small section of the view to scan barcodes since AV Foundation won't need to scan the whole frame each time it's refreshed.

For example, you could restrict the scan to the half-height, half-width center portion of the frame. In this case, AV Foundation would only need to scan a quarter of the pixels in the frame.

Still need a few hints? Okay, here they are:

- Add a plain `UIView` in your storyboard indicating the area that you want the user to be able to scan a QR code in, color it black with 25% transparency, and connect it to an outlet.

- You want to set the `rectOfInterest` method of `AVCaptureMetadataOutput` to restrict the scan area. However, you can't just pass the frame of the view directly – you'll need to use the `metadataOutputRectOfInterestForRect:` method of `AVCaptureVideoPreviewLayer` to convert the coordinates first.

The screenshots below suggest a possible UI for this challenge:

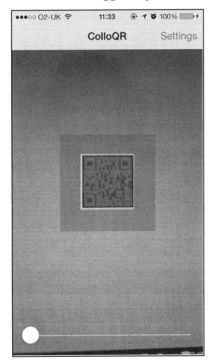 

The gray overlay box in the center of the view shows the active scan area for the barcodes. The screenshot on the left shows a QR being detected inside the box, while the right screenshot shows the same QR code outside the detection area.

Chapter 23: What's New in Map Kit

By Matt Galloway

Map Kit is one of the most commonly used frameworks in iOS, as many mobile apps use maps extensively. From navigation, to finding a good restaurant or pub, mobile apps often need to display data on a map.

The core functionality of Map Kit has not changed much since its introduction in iOS 3. However, over the years Apple has been quietly adding feature after feature. In iOS 6 we started to see the first really interesting additions, such as the introduction of a search API to look up points of interest, as well as the ability for apps to register themselves as route providers.

The biggest changes over the years were vector map tiles and Flyover; a mode where you can view select major cities in 3D. Flyover allows you to change the viewing angle and behave as though you're a bird in the sky above the city skyline! This was cool eye candy, but it was never available to third party apps — until iOS 7 came along.

On top of this, iOS 7 brings about a change in the way overlays on map views are handled. You no longer provide a view for each overlay, but instead you create a renderer that efficiently draws the overlay section by section.

iOS 7 also delivers a handful of new APIs:

• **Directions:** to obtain directions between two locations

• **Snapshots:** to asynchronously render a section of a map as an image

• **Cameras**: to set and manipulate the viewing angle of a map

In this chapter you're going to create an app that searches for a location, and then generates a route to get you there. The route will be based on the airport nearest to your current location, and the one nearest your destination. You'll learn all about the new APIs and see how the overlay handling has changed.

Fasten your seatbelts, ladies and gentlemen, and observe the no-smoking signs; you're now en-route to great destinations with Map Kit and iOS 7!

Getting started

The resources for this chapter include a starter project called **FlyMeThere** that has the user interface pre-made so you can keep focused on MapKit. Open up the project in Xcode and have a look around to get acquainted with the app.

Open **ViewController.m** and you'll see that `loadAirportData` loads data from a file called **airports.csv**. This file contains the latitude, longitude, name and city of all major airports in the world. Each airport's data is loaded into an instance of the model class **Airport** and stored in an array within the view controller.

> **Note:** The airport data is kindly supplied by OurAirports (http://www.ourairports.com/data/). I've supplied the latest file with the project but feel free to grab an updated version if there is one. Please be aware that if the file format has changed then the parsing code will no longer work.

As it stands now, you can search for points of interest, and you can even choose from a list of the discovered points. But once you select a point of interest, the app doesn't do anything. That's expected. You're going to add a whole load of functionality now that will make use of the basis in this starter project.

Searching for points of interest

Performing point of interest searches is *technically* not a new addition to iOS — it was added in iOS 6.1 as the only real feature of interest in that rather minor update. Consider yourself forgiven if you overlooked it.

The code for performing these searches is already present in the starter project. To see how it works, open **ViewController.m** and look at `startSearchForText:`. This method executes the search operation and then hands the results to a `UIActionSheet` to display and handle selection of the desired result.

The classes used to search are `MKLocalSearchRequest` and `MKLocalSearch`. First, you create an instance of `MKLocalSearchRequest` to encapsulate what you wish to search for. In the case of this app, you set `naturalLanguageQuery` to the `searchText` string passed to `startSearchForText:`.

The `MKLocalSearch` class executes the actual search; you create an instance of it using the local search request as described above. The search operation actually happens asynchronously, so it starts and executes the passed-in completion block once the search completes.

Build and run your app and perform a search. You'll see something like image below:

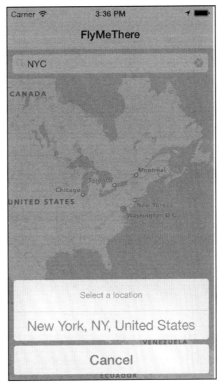

As it sits right now, the app isn't terribly exciting. Time to get cracking on adding some new features!

Enabling 3D mode

At the moment, you'll notice that you can't change the viewing angle of the map, also known as the **pitch**. By default, rotation of map views is enabled, but changing the pitch is not.

Fortunately it's very easy to enable pitching.

Add the following line of code to the end of `viewDidLoad` in **ViewController.m**:

```
_mapView.pitchEnabled = YES;
```

Build and run your app again and zoom in to your location. Then use a two-finger pan, up or down, to change the viewing angle. The map's pitch will change, as shown below:

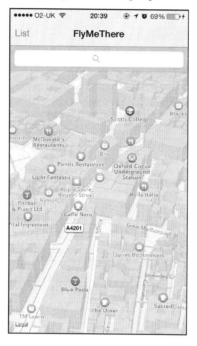

> **Note:** The two-finger pan gesture is much easier to do on an actual device, so I recommend you try this on an actual device instead of the simulator.
>
> However, if you don't have a device to test with, here's how you can perform the two finger up-or-down pan gesture in the simulator. Hold down the option (⌥) key and move the mouse so that the two touches are almost touching each other and in a horizontal line. Then hold down the shift key and drag the mouse up or down.

Try zooming right in on a location you know and changing the pitch. Then move around the map, zoom a bit and rotate the map. Pretty neat eh? That's the first new bit of Map Kit — and you only had to add a single line of code to get there.

Aside: Location simulation

During the course of this chapter, you may find that you want to run the app as if your device were located in a different city, in order to test out some of the different Map Kit features. Fortunately, Xcode has a rather handy feature to do just that.

To change your virtual location while an app is running, click on the **Location** icon situated on the toolbar of the Debug area, right next to the debugger controls. A menu will pop up with a list of pre-filled locations; simply select the one you want from the list and then the app will think you're in that location, as shown below:

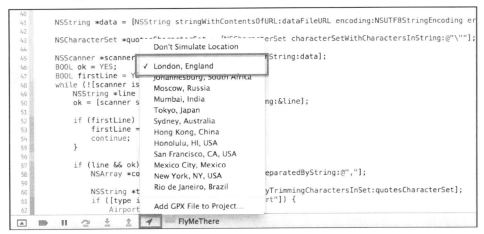

Calculating the route

The next feature you'll add is the route calculation feature. When the user selects a location, the app will determine which airport is closest to the device and which airport is closest to the destination. This will form the flying leg of the journey. For example, to calculate a route London to New York, the app will route you from London's Heathrow airport to New York's LaGuardia airport.

Later on in the chapter, you'll use the new directions API to provide directions from the user's current location to the departing airport, and from the destination airport to the actual destination. That means you need to calculate three legs of the journey separately:

1. Current location to departing airport via the directions API

2. Departing airport to destination airport via airplane

3. Destination airport to actual destination via directions API

The airport-to-airport calculation is the easiest, so you'll tackle this first.

Note: The app will not take into account actual airline routes. It simply chooses the nearest airport to both the source and destination, even if no airline actually flies between those cities! There is data out there that describes every airline route, but using it is beyond the scope of this chapter.

The sample project contains a model to hold the route. Open **Route.h;** you'll see it has properties representing the start and destination points, the departing and destination airports, as well as the three sections of the route. You'll populate the two `MKRoute` properties later using the new directions API; the `flyPartPolyline` is the bit you'll implement now.

Aside: Geodesic polylines

Now is a good time now to introduce one of the new features of Map Kit in iOS 7.0. The `flyPartPolyline` property in your app is an instance of `MKGeodesicPolyline`. Polylines have been part of Map Kit since iOS 4.0, but until now it was only possible to draw straight lines between two points on a map. The **geodesic polyline** describes a line between two points that follows the curvature of the earth.

Confused? Consider the following screenshot:

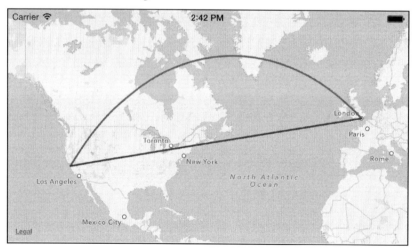

The blue line is the original `MKPolyline` class that has been around since iOS 4.0. However, in real life you can't follow a perfectly straight line between two points, as you're forced to follow the curvature of the earth as you travel. Flat Earth proponents, stay out of this! ☺

The red line — which is the geodesic polyline — is the shortest distance you can travel when you take the curvature of the earth into consideration. Airplanes don't travel on the ground, but this path is still a pretty close approximation of the route an airplane would take between these two locations.

Finding the source and destination airports

Now that you have a model to hold the full route, it's time to start calculating it. Open **ViewController.m** and add the following method:

```objc
- (void)setupWithNewRoute:(Route*)route {
    // 1
    if (_route) {
        [_mapView removeAnnotations:@[_route.source,
                                      _route.destination,
                                      _route.sourceAirport,
                                      _route.destinationAirport]];
        [_mapView removeOverlays:
            @[_route.flyPartPolyline]];
        _route = nil;
    }

    // 2
    _route = route;

    // 3
    [_mapView addAnnotations:@[route.source,
                               route.destination,
                               route.sourceAirport,
                               route.destinationAirport]];

    // 4
    [_mapView addOverlay:route.flyPartPolyline
                   level:MKOverlayLevelAboveRoads];

    // 5
    MKMapPoint points[4];
    points[0] =
        MKMapPointForCoordinate(route.source.coordinate);
    points[1] =
        MKMapPointForCoordinate(route.destination.coordinate);
    points[2] =
        MKMapPointForCoordinate(route.sourceAirport.coordinate);
    points[3] =
MKMapPointForCoordinate(route.destinationAirport.coordinate);
```

```
    MKCoordinateRegion boundingRegion =
        CoordinateRegionBoundingMapPoints(points, 4);
    boundingRegion.span.latitudeDelta *= 1.1f;
    boundingRegion.span.longitudeDelta *= 1.1f;
    [_mapView setRegion:boundingRegion animated:YES];
}
```

Here's what the above method does:

1. Checks if there's an existing route displayed, and if so, removes it from the map. The reason for doing this will become apparent in just a moment.

2. Sets the new route to the instance variable.

3. Adds the annotations to the map. This bit of code ensures that pins are displayed for the source, destination and their respective airports.

4. Adds the geodesic polyline as an overlay.

5. Calculates the bounding box of all the points to be displayed and sets the map view's region based on the bounding box to show the entire route.

> **Note:** Bounding box is a term used in geometry; it refers to the smallest measure (area or volume) within which a given set of points lie.

Now it's time to find those airports and call the method you just created. Add the following method to **ViewController.m**:

```
- (void)calculateRouteToMapItem:(MKMapItem*)item {
    // 1
    [self performAfterFindingLocation:
     ^(CLLocationCoordinate2D userLocation) {
        // 2
        MKPointAnnotation *sourceAnnotation =
            [MKPointAnnotation new];
        sourceAnnotation.coordinate = userLocation;
        sourceAnnotation.title = @"Start";

        MKPointAnnotation *destinationAnnotation =
            [MKPointAnnotation new];
        destinationAnnotation.coordinate =
            item.placemark.coordinate;
        destinationAnnotation.title = @"End";
```

```
            // 3
            Airport *sourceAirport =
                [self nearestAirportToCoordinate:userLocation];
            Airport *destinationAirport =
        [self nearestAirportToCoordinate:item.placemark.coordinate];

            // 4
            Route *route = [Route new];
            route.source = sourceAnnotation;
            route.destination = destinationAnnotation;
            route.sourceAirport = sourceAirport;
            route.destinationAirport = destinationAirport;

            // 5
            CLLocationCoordinate2D coords[2] =
                {sourceAirport.coordinate,
                 destinationAirport.coordinate};
            route.flyPartPolyline =
                [MKGeodesicPolyline polylineWithCoordinates:coords
                                                      count:2];

            // 6
            [self setupWithNewRoute:route];

            // 7
            _searchBar.userInteractionEnabled = YES;
        }];
}
```

So what does this do?

1. First, you invoke `performAfterFindingLocation:` with a block containing the remainder of the implementation, since you need to determine the user's location before you can do anything else in this method.

2. Create annotations for the source and destination points.

3. Calculate the coordinates of the nearest airports by using the `nearestAirportToCoordinate:` method that I added to the starter project for you.

4. Create and set up an instance of `Route` using the various bits of data you've just sourced.

5. Create a geodesic polyline to join the two airports and add it to the route.

6. Invoke `setupWithNewRoute:` with the `Route` instance you created that contains the new route.

7. Finally, re-enable user interaction on the search bar so that a new search can be performed.

You're almost done, but there's just one final piece of the jigsaw. Still working in **ViewController.m**, add the following method:

```
- (MKOverlayRenderer*)mapView:(MKMapView *)mapView
        rendererForOverlay:(id<MKOverlay>)overlay
{
    if ([overlay isKindOfClass:[MKPolyline class]]) {
        MKPolylineRenderer *renderer =
            [[MKPolylineRenderer alloc]
                initWithPolyline:(MKPolyline*)overlay];

        if (overlay == _route.flyPartPolyline) {
            renderer.strokeColor = [UIColor redColor];
        } else {
            renderer.strokeColor = [UIColor blueColor];
        }

        return renderer;
    }
    return nil;
}
```

This is one of the new `MKMapViewDelegate` methods added in iOS 7; if you have previous experience with Map Kit then it'll look awfully familiar — it's a replacement for the method `mapView:viewForOverlay:`. In iOS 7 Apple parted ways with single-view overlays and switched to use a renderer instead. The renderer's job is simple: to draw sections of the overlay as and when they're required.

This is far more efficient than the single-view approach, as it would be incredibly expensive to draw an entire single view, especially if it covered the entire world. The rendering approach draws only the required section, and only when it's required.

Finally, find `actionSheet:clickedButtonAtIndex:` in **ViewController.m** and find the following two lines:

```
// TODO: Calculate route
_searchBar.userInteractionEnabled = YES;
```

Replace both of these lines with the following:

```
[self calculateRouteToMapItem:item];
```

This initiates the route calculation when the user selects a point of interest from the search results.

Build and run your app; search for a destination location and select a result from the list. Your map will look similar to the one below:

That's the geodesic polyline being drawn. Play around with different locations to see what the geodesic polyline looks like for various points on the globe.

> **Note:** If you search for somewhere a long distance away, especially changing hemisphere, you may find that the map will not show the entire route. This is because a map view will not zoom out further than when either dimension hits its limit. In the case of this app, that is when the vertical dimension fits in the north pole to the south pole. Zooming out further used to be possible pre-iOS 6, but it appears that since Apple introduced their own maps in iOS 6, it's no longer possible. There's not much you can do about this unfortunately. In your own apps you may want to consider detecting if this limit is hit (use the aspect ratio of the map view to determine) and act accordingly.

Using renderers over single views

Earlier, you were introduced to the fact that single-view overlays have been replaced with overlay renderers. If you're only using system-supplied overlays, then you don't need to do much to take advantage of renderers, as the `MKOverlayView` subclasses of system-supplied overlays such as `MKPolyline`, `MKCircle` and `MKPolygon` have been replaced with renderers. For example, `MKPolyline` had a corresponding view of `MKPolylineView`, which has been replaced with `MKPolylineRenderer`.

But what does using renderers mean for your app? You probably have some existing code in other projects that looks a lot like the following:

```
MKPolyline *polyline = [MKPolyline polylineWithPoints:points
                                                count:count];

[self.mapView addOverlay:polyline];

...

- (MKOverlayView*)mapView:(MKMapView *)mapView
         viewForOverlay:(id<MKOverlay>)overlay
{
    MKPolylineView *view =
        [[MKPolylineView alloc] initWithOverlay:overlay];
    view.strokeColor = [UIColor redColor];
    view.lineWidth = 5.0f;
    return view;
}
```

It's incredibly easy to convert this to using renderers; you would simply replace `mapView:viewForOverlay:` with the new delegate method, as follows:

```
- (MKOverlayRenderer*)mapView:(MKMapView *)mapView
         rendererForOverlay:(id<MKOverlay>)overlay
{
    MKPolylineRenderer *renderer =
        [[MKPolylineRenderer alloc] initWithOverlay:overlay];
    renderer.strokeColor = [UIColor redColor];
    renderer.lineWidth = 5.0f;
    return renderer;
}
```

The concept behind renderers is that users don't often view the entire region for which an overlay is valid. In FlyMeThere, you see the entire geodesic polyline, but if you zoom in on a portion of the map, then only a portion of the polyline is visible. Single-view overlays render the *entire* view, even if there isn't any data to display in the visible portion of the map.

Overlay renderers offer vast improvements over single view overlays. They draw the visible portion into a graphics context, as well as sections to either side of the visible portion to avoid rendering things on the fly while scrolling. As well, overlay renderers permit multiple sections of the map to be rendered at the same time; this means that the OS could use several background threads while rendering to make full use of the available system resources.

You're not just limited to system-supplied renderers either, you can create your own just as you could create your own single-view overlays. Simply subclass `MKOverlayRenderer` and implement a single method:

```
- (void)drawMapRect:(MKMapRect)mapRect
           zoomScale:(MKZoomScale)zoomScale
           inContext:(CGContextRef)context
```

Map Kit calls the above method to requests a section to be rendered. Map Kit informs you of the rectangle of the map that needs to be drawn, at what scale and into which graphics context. Then all you do is draw the overlay as indicated by the parameters.

It's not often that you have to make your own custom overlay; only Map Kit aficionados would really ever come close to needing custom overlays. However, if you ever do need use them, renderers will undoubtedly make your life a lot easier — and your app much more efficient!

Enough about renderers — time to get back to the FlyMeThere app!

Using the directions API

You now have the air leg of the journey; your next task is to generate the two routes from the source and destination to their respective airports using the destination API.

Open **ViewController.m** and add the following method:

```
- (void)obtainDirectionsFrom:(MKMapItem*)from
                          to:(MKMapItem*)to
           completion:(void(^)(MKRoute*, NSError*))completion
{
    // 1
    MKDirectionsRequest *request =
        [[MKDirectionsRequest alloc] init];
```

```
    // 2
    request.source = from;
    request.destination = to;

    // 3
    request.transportType = MKDirectionsTransportTypeAutomobile;

    // 4
    MKDirections *directions =
        [[MKDirections alloc] initWithRequest:request];
    [directions calculateDirectionsWithCompletionHandler:
    ^(MKDirectionsResponse *response, NSError *error) {
        MKRoute *route = nil;

        // 5
        if (response.routes.count > 0) {
            route = response.routes[0];
        } else if (!error) {
            error =
          [NSError errorWithDomain:@"com.razeware.FlyMeThere"
                               code:404
                           userInfo:@{NSLocalizedDescriptionKey:
                                    @"No routes found!"}];
        }

        // 6
        if (completion) {
            completion(route, error);
        }
    }];
}
```

This method queries the directions API then calls a completion handler when it's finished. Either a route will be found or an error will be returned.

Here is what you do in this method:

1. Create an instance of MKDirectionsRequest to describe the request.

2. Set the source and destination properties.

3. The transport type is optional; here it's set to automobile, but you may want to allow your user to change this. The available options are MKDirectionsTransportTypeAutomobile,

MKDirectionsTransportTypeWalking or MKDirectionsTransportTypeAny. Choosing MKDirectionsTransportTypeAny means both automobile and walking routes will be considered.

4. Queries of the directions API are performed asynchronously. You create an instance of MKDirections using an instance of MKDirectionsRequest and then start the query by passing it a block to call upon completion.

5. Even if the query was successful, it's still possible that there's no valid route between the starting point and the airport(I've been there; you can't get there from here.) If there is at least one route, use the first route returned; if there were no results, then generate an error.

6. Finally, call the method's completion handler.

Now find calculateRouteToMapItem: in **ViewController.m** and replace steps four through seven with the following:

```
// 1
MKMapItem *sourceMapItem =
    [self mapItemForCoordinate:userLocation];
MKMapItem *destinationMapItem = item;

// 2
MKMapItem *sourceAirportMapItem =
    [self mapItemForCoordinate:sourceAirport.coordinate];
sourceAirportMapItem.name = sourceAirport.title;

MKMapItem *destinationAirportMapItem =
    [self mapItemForCoordinate:destinationAirport.coordinate];
destinationAirportMapItem.name = destinationAirport.title;

__block MKRoute *toSourceAirportDirectionsRoute = nil;
__block MKRoute *fromDestinationAirportDirectionsRoute = nil;

// 3
dispatch_group_t group = dispatch_group_create();

// 4
// Find route to source airport
dispatch_group_enter(group);
[self obtainDirectionsFrom:sourceMapItem
                        to:sourceAirportMapItem
                completion:^(MKRoute *route, NSError *error) {
                    toSourceAirportDirectionsRoute = route;
```

```
                        dispatch_group_leave(group);
                }];

// 5
// Find route from destination airport
dispatch_group_enter(group);
[self obtainDirectionsFrom:destinationAirportMapItem
                        to:destinationMapItem
                completion:^(MKRoute *route, NSError *error) {
                    fromDestinationAirportDirectionsRoute = route;
                        dispatch_group_leave(group);
                }];

// 6
// When both are found, setup new route
dispatch_group_notify(group, dispatch_get_main_queue(),
^{
    if (toSourceAirportDirectionsRoute &&
        fromDestinationAirportDirectionsRoute)
    {
        Route *route = [Route new];
        route.source = sourceAnnotation;
        route.destination = destinationAnnotation;
        route.sourceAirport = sourceAirport;
        route.destinationAirport = destinationAirport;
        route.toSourceAirportRoute =
            toSourceAirportDirectionsRoute;
        route.fromDestinationAirportRoute =
            fromDestinationAirportDirectionsRoute;

        CLLocationCoordinate2D coords[2] =
            {sourceAirport.coordinate,
             destinationAirport.coordinate};
        route.flyPartPolyline =
            [MKGeodesicPolyline polylineWithCoordinates:coords
                                                  count:2];

        [self setupWithNewRoute:route];
    } else {
        UIAlertView *alert =
        [[UIAlertView alloc] initWithTitle:@"Oops!"
        message:@"Failed to find directions! Please try again."
                                delegate:nil
                       cancelButtonTitle:nil
```

```
                        otherButtonTitles:@"OK", nil];
        [alert show];
    }

    _searchBar.userInteractionEnabled = YES;
});
```

Here's what your modified code does:

1. Creates instances of `MKMapItem` to represent the source and destination.

2. Creates instances of `MKMapItem` to represent the airports. Why `MKMapItem`? Simply because the directions API accepts these objects as arguments.

3. Creates a dispatch group to connect two critical sections of code that need to complete before you proceed. There's more about dispatch groups in the note box below.

4. Requests the directions from the starting point to the departure airport. Retrieve the route in the completion block and signal the dispatch group that this task is done.

5. In a similar manner, it requests the directions from the destination airport to the final destination.

6. Finally, register a block with the dispatch group to be executed once the two directions API requests have completed. You instruct the group to execute this block on the main queue as it handles updates to the UI. The block creates an instance of `Route`; if no routes were found, then a `UIAlertView` is displayed.

> **Note:** The dispatch group is an often-overlooked yet powerful feature of Grand Central Dispatch (GCD), which allows you to group semi-related actions. In the code above, you need to perform two directions API requests, but can only continue processing once both have completed.
>
> Rather than blocking the UI, which would be highly inappropriate and provide a poor user experience, you simply use a dispatch group to keep track of the blocks that have entered and exited the group. When the number of blocks that have entered balances with the number of blocks that have exited, the group can notify you to proceed with code execution.
>
> It's a little like a semaphore and a critical section had a bit too much to drink one night, and this was the end result. In any case, try to find ways to use this pattern in your own apps to reduce your code and make it more readable.

You're almost there; there's just one more thing to do. Find `setupWithNewRoute:` in **ViewController.m** and replace it with the following code:

```
- (void)setupWithNewRoute:(Route*)route {
    if (_route) {
        [_mapView removeAnnotations:
            @[_route.source, _route.destination,
              _route.sourceAirport, _route.destinationAirport]];

        // 1
        [_mapView removeOverlays:
            @[_route.toSourceAirportRoute.polyline,
              _route.flyPartPolyline,
              _route.fromDestinationAirportRoute.polyline]];
        _route = nil;
    }

    _route = route;

    [_mapView addAnnotations:
        @[route.source, route.destination,
          route.sourceAirport, route.destinationAirport]];

    // 2
    [_mapView addOverlay:route.toSourceAirportRoute.polyline
                level:MKOverlayLevelAboveRoads];
    [_mapView
        addOverlay:route.fromDestinationAirportRoute.polyline
            level:MKOverlayLevelAboveRoads];

    [_mapView addOverlay:route.flyPartPolyline
                level:MKOverlayLevelAboveRoads];

    MKMapPoint points[4];
    points[0] =
        MKMapPointForCoordinate(route.source.coordinate);
    points[1] =
        MKMapPointForCoordinate(route.destination.coordinate);
    points[2] =
        MKMapPointForCoordinate(route.sourceAirport.coordinate);
    points[3] =
    MKMapPointForCoordinate(route.destinationAirport.coordinate);

    MKCoordinateRegion boundingRegion =
```

```
        CoordinateRegionBoundingMapPoints(points, 4);
    boundingRegion.span.latitudeDelta *= 1.1f;
    boundingRegion.span.longitudeDelta *= 1.1f;
    [_mapView setRegion:boundingRegion animated:YES];
}
```

Step 1 takes care of removing any existing path overlays from the map, while step 2 adds two more overlays to the map when a new route is set. These overlays represent your journeys from your starting point to the departure airport, and from the destination airport to your final destination.

The new overlays come directly from the instances of MKRoute found using the directions API; the MKRoute objects come with a handy polyline property that you can use to create a polyline that joins up all the points in the route.

Build and run your app; search for a destination and select it. Your map now boasts blue lines showing the route to and from the relevant airports. Depending on how close you are to your nearest airport, you may need to zoom in to the see the new routes and annotations, as below:

Map cameras

Before iOS 7.0, you could only look down on a map from one point at one certain zoom scale. You could manipulate the region displayed by setting the visible region, or by setting the center coordinate and the zoom scale, but that was all. Since iOS 7.0 delivers the ability to rotate the map and project it in 3D, it also needs a more complex method of managing the visible region — **cameras**.

A camera precisely describes the region of the map that is displayed, taking into account any rotation and whether or not it's 3D. This is all encapsulated in the new MKMapCamera class.

Think of a camera as describing a position somewhere above the ground. If the camera is pointing straight down, with the viewfinder showing north as up, west as left etc., then that camera is emulating the viewpoint of maps prior to iOS 7. The altitude of the camera gives rise to the zoom scale, while the position above the ground where the camera is placed forms the center coordinate of the visible region.

But cameras can do more than that. Consider the following diagram:

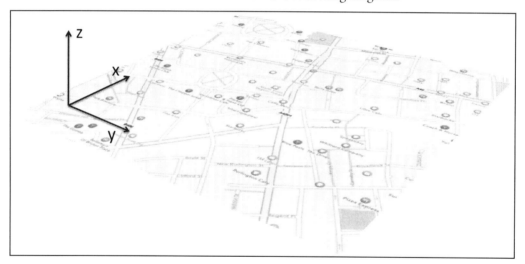

The above image demonstrates how a camera sees the world. A camera is positioned somewhere in space based on its x, y and z coordinates. If the map is rotated so that north is no longer north, that represents a rotation around the z-axis. Entering 3D mode represents a rotation around the y-axis.

Fortunately, you don't really need to worry about the camera's coordinates in space too much; Apple has made this process painless. You simply need to consider a **heading**, which describes the orientation of the map; and a **pitch**, which describes the viewing angle. If both of these are 0, then the camera is looking down from above, with north at the top of the map. In x-y-z coordinate space, heading represents the rotation about the z-axis and pitch represents the rotation about the y-axis.

Apple has provided a helper method for creating cameras, which makes things tremendously easy for you, the developer. It's much simpler to think of a camera's position being described by its position, altitude and focal point. This is illustrated in the following diagram:

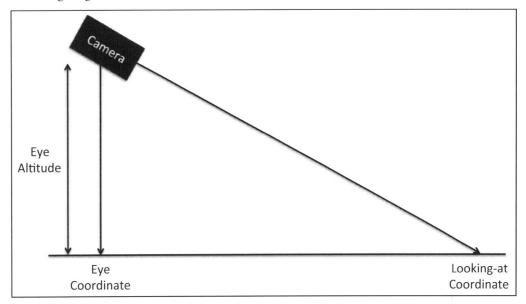

If the eye coordinate is equal to the looking-at coordinate, then the view will not be in 3D mode. However, if the looking-at coordinate changes, then you're working in 3D mode. In FlyMeThere, you're going to use cameras to let the user zoom in on the four points of interest in their route.

Adding cameras to your map view

Open **ViewController.m** and add the following method:

```
- (void)moveCameraToCoordinate:
        (CLLocationCoordinate2D)coordinate
{
    // 1
    MKMapCamera *camera =
        [MKMapCamera cameraLookingAtCenterCoordinate:coordinate
                              fromEyeCoordinate:coordinate
                                    eyeAltitude:1000.0];
```

```
    // 2
    camera.pitch = 55.0f;

    // 3
    [UIView animateWithDuration:1.0
                    animations:^{
                        // 4
                        _mapView.camera = camera;
                    }];
}
```

This method points the camera at a given coordinate, as follows:

1. Create an instance of MKMapCamera using the factory method mentioned earlier. The camera will be pointing straight down from an altitude of 1000 meters at the desired coordinate.

2. Set the pitch directly on the camera; this angles the view slightly and puts the map in 3D mode.

3. Animate the camera changes by wrapping the assignment of your new camera in a generic UIView animation block.

4. Finally, set your camera on the map view.

It really is as simple as that to create and setup a camera; all you need to do now is wire your method up to something in the app so that it can be used.

Open **Main.storyboard** and add four bar button items to the toolbar at the bottom of the **FlyMeThere** scene and set their titles, left to right, as follows:

• Start

• Airport A

• Airport B

• End

Add a flexible space bar button item to the left and right sides of the buttons to make things look pretty and to center the buttons. Your button bar should look like this:

Next, add the following four methods to **ViewController.m**:

```
- (IBAction)startTapped:(id)sender {
    [self moveCameraToCoordinate:_route.source.coordinate];
}

- (IBAction)airportATapped:(id)sender {
    [self
  moveCameraToCoordinate:_route.sourceAirport.coordinate];
}

- (IBAction)airportBTapped:(id)sender {
    [self
  moveCameraToCoordinate:_route.destinationAirport.coordinate];
}

- (IBAction)endTapped:(id)sender {
    [self moveCameraToCoordinate:_route.destination.coordinate];
}
```

Wire up the buttons you just added to these methods, matching the title of the button to the corresponding method name.

Finally, add the following line to the end of setupWithNewRoute:

```
    self.navigationController.toolbarHidden = NO;
```

This ensures that the toolbar will only be visible when a route is being displayed.

Build and run your app; search for a point of interest and selct it. You should see your toolbar appear; tap on each of the four buttons in turn and watch the map fly to the relevant point on the route, as shown on the next page:

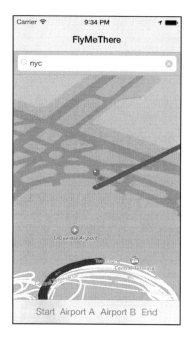 

Map snapshots

The final new API you're going to use in **FlyMeThere** is the map snapshots API. This is a handy API that lets you obtain a rendered image of a map. Previously, you had to use `UIView`'s `renderInContext:` to get a rendered view of a map. But this was a bit of a hack and prone to fail, as it was never really meant for rendering maps. You'll be using the map snapshots on the directions list screen.

Uh, wait, *what* directions list screen? Yeah, we haven't run across that screen yet. Eagle-eyed readers will have noticed the **List** button in the navigation bar; when tapped, it shows a list of the steps in your route. This data comes from the separate instances of `MKRoute` obtained using the directions API.

DirectionsListViewController.m is responsible for displaying the list of directions; open it up, take some time to look around it and understand how it works. In particular, note that the `steps` properties of the `MKRoute` instances are responsible for providing the lists of directions.

A picture is worth a thousand words, so you'll add a thumbnail to each of the table view cells showing a map relevant to that step of the route.

Open **DirectionsListViewController.m** and add the following instance variable to the implementation block:

```
@implementation DirectionsListViewController {
    NSMutableDictionary *_snapshots;
}
```

This acts as a cache and stores snapshots that have already been generated, preventing you from unnecessarily regenerating snapshots each time a cell is drawn on the screen.

Now find `viewDidLoad` and add the following line to the end:

```
_snapshots = [NSMutableDictionary new];
```

This simply initializes the instance variable.

Next, add the following method:

```
- (void)loadSnapshotForCellAtIndexPath:(NSIndexPath*)indexPath {
    // 1
    MKRouteStep *step = nil;
    switch (indexPath.section) {
        case 0: {
            step =
            _route.toSourceAirportRoute.steps[indexPath.row];
        }
            break;
        case 2: {
            step =
            _route.fromDestinationAirportRoute.steps[indexPath.row];
        }
            break;
    }

    // 2
    if (step) {
        // 3
        MKMapSnapshotOptions *options =
            [[MKMapSnapshotOptions alloc] init];
        options.scale = [[UIScreen mainScreen] scale];
        options.region = CoordinateRegionBoundingMapPoints(
                        step.polyline.points,
                        step.polyline.pointCount);
        options.size = CGSizeMake(44.0f, 44.0f);

        // 4
        MKMapSnapshotter *snapshotter =
            [[MKMapSnapshotter alloc] initWithOptions:options];
```

```
        [snapshotter startWithCompletionHandler:
         ^(MKMapSnapshot *snapshot, NSError *error) {
             if (!error) {
                 // 5
                 dispatch_async(dispatch_get_main_queue(), ^{
                     // 6
                     UITableViewCell *cell =
                         [self.tableView
                             cellForRowAtIndexPath:indexPath];

                     // 7
                     if (cell) {
                         cell.imageView.image = snapshot.image;
                         [cell setNeedsLayout];
                     }

                     // 8
                     _snapshots[indexPath] = snapshot.image;
                 });
             }
         }];
    }
}
```

This method creates a snapshot for the cell at the corresponding index path. Here's how it works:

1. You first retrieve the instance of MKRouteStep that corresponds to the given index path.

2. Then check the retrieved instance to ensure that a route step was actually found and it's not nil.

3. Create an instance of MKMapSnapshotOptions; this describes which region of the earth will be rendered as well as the size of image to create. You can either use a camera or set the map region manually to set the region to be rendered. The options also have a scale property that should be set to the result of [[UIScreen mainScreen] scale]. This ensures that the image will be nice and crisp on Retina screens.

4. Create the map snapshot asynchronously through the use of MKMapSnapshotter; you simply pass it the instance of MKMapSnapshotOptions created in the previous step, start it, and then pass it a completion block.

5. If the snapshot was created successfully, jump to the main queue and update the UI; the snapshots were generated asynchronously on a background queue so as not to block thread execution.

6. Ask the table view for the cell corresponding to the index path.

7. Since there's no guarantee a cell will still be on screen when this method is called due to scrolling or other UI factors, make sure you actually received a cell from the table view. If so, then set the thumbnail as the snapshot.

8. Finally, save the snapshot image to the cache.

Find `tableView:cellForRowAtIndexPath:` in **DirectionsListViewController.m** and replace the comment with the following:

```
UIImage *cachedSnapshot = _snapshots[indexPath];
if (cachedSnapshot) {
    cell.imageView.image = cachedSnapshot;
} else {
    [self loadSnapshotForCellAtIndexPath:indexPath];
}
```

This simply checks the cache to see if a snapshot already exists for the corresponding index path. If it does, then the thumbnail is set using the snapshot from the cache. Otherwise, it renders a snapshot.

Build and run your app; generate a route and then tap the **List** button. You'll see little thumbnail maps created for each route step, just as in the screenshot below:

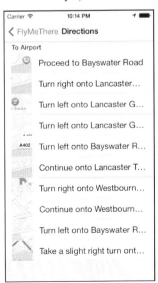

Printing maps is another common use case for map snapshots; simply render a map into an image, and add that image to a page to be printed. That's pretty slick, especially since this was only possible in previous versions of iOS by using ugly hacks.

Challenges

In this chapter you've seen how to use the new directions, camera and snapshot APIs of iOS 7, as well as the point-of-interest search feature that Apple introduced in iOS 6.1. You've seen how overlays have changed from simple single-view overlays to more complex — yet highly efficient — overlay renderers. Go forth and make cool map based apps!

What's that? You want more? Well, there are a *few* challenges for you...

Challenge 1: Rendering feedback

There were two interesting methods added to `MKMapViewDelegate` in iOS 7:

```
- (void)mapViewWillStartRenderingMap:(MKMapView*)mapView;
- (void)mapViewDidFinishRenderingMap:(MKMapView*)mapView
                    fullyRendered:(BOOL)fullyRendered;
```

These tell you when the map has started rendering and when it has finished. These are useful additions as they provide visual feedback to a user when the map is rendering.

Your challenge is to use these new delegate methods in **FlyMeThere** to display a spinner in the navigation bar while the map is rendering. After you have finished the app should look like this:

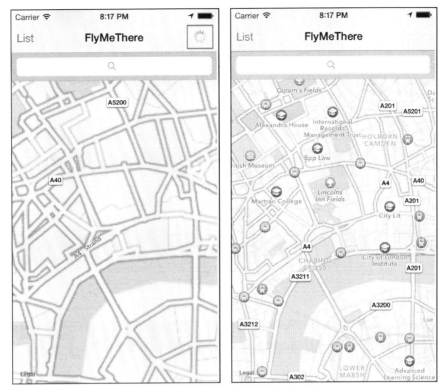

The screenshot on the left shows the map after a zoom in action where the map has not finished rendering to the new zoom scale. The screenshot on the right shows the fully rendered map.

Challenge 2: Smooth camera transitions

As the app currently stands, when you tap on one of the buttons to move the camera to one of the points of interest, the motion can end up being very confusing and can leave you feeling a little nauseous. The map flies away beneath you and you have absolutely no context about where you're moving to. But you can change that!

First off, add the following instance variable to **ViewController**:

```
NSMutableArray *_pendingMapCameras
```

Then add the following method:

```
- (void)goToNextMapCamera {
    if (_pendingMapCameras.count > 0) {
        MKMapCamera *nextCamera =
            [_pendingMapCameras lastObject];
```

```
        [_pendingMapCameras removeLastObject];

        [UIView animateWithDuration:1.0
                         animations:^{
                             _mapView.camera = nextCamera;
                         }];
    }
}
```

This method lets you move the map to the next camera in the _pendingMapCameras array. So this array can be used like a queue of cameras, animating from one to the next. You can use this to transition smoothly from one point to the next by creating several intermediate cameras and breaking the animation up in to smaller chunks.

You'll need to change moveCameraToCoordinate: to create cameras in between the current map location and the target in order to make the transition smoother.

Hint 1: Don't forget to initialize _pendingMapCameras! I suggest doing this in viewDidLoad.

Hint 2: You can find out when a camera animation has finished by implementing MKMapView's mapView:regionDidChangeAnimated: delegate method. When this gets called, animate to the next pending camera.

Try playing around with different pending cameras; you can make some really interesting animations this way! For bonus points, make the animation depend upon the distance between the current map location and the target. Different animations work best for different distances. If it's a very long distance then it looks nice to zoom right out, fly across the world, then zoom back in again. Doing the same for a very short distance would look silly.

Chapter 24: What's New in Core Location

By Chris Wagner

Many of us come to think of our iPhones as more than a piece of hardware; it becomes our virtual companion or assistant, performing tasks in the background to make our life easier. Our phones can remind us to of something we need to do when we arrive at a specific point, suggest we try a nearby cafe, or let us know a friend is nearby and available to meet up for a drink.

These features wouldn't be possible without Core Location and the hardware that supports the framework. When Apple introduced iOS 5 they also unveiled the Reminders app. At the time, it didn't seem overly impressive until Apple demonstrated how the reminders could be made location-aware and trigger when you arrive at or depart from a specific location. Now *that's* useful!

iOS 7 makes it possible for developers to do even more things with Core Location, so you can delight your users in new and exciting ways.

In this chapter you'll learn about a brand new feature in Core Location called **iBeacon**. This allows you to create an app that broadcasts its presence to iPhones.

Why is this cool? Well, imagine having an iBeacon at each piece of art in an art gallery, and having an app that displays information about individual art pieces as you draw near. Or having an iBeacon at each car in a car dealership, and an app that tells you more information about the car you're next to.

In this chapter, you'll try out iBeacon for yourself by developing an app that broadcasts a restaurant's location. You'll also develop a companion app that detects the nearby restaurants, provides the location details to the user, and allows the user to reserve a table.

Sound good? Then come on inside — your table awaits!

Overview

Rather than being an introduction to Core Location, this chapter assumes you are familiar with the basics and focuses on the new features of Core Location in iOS 7.

If you're completely new to Core Location, you might want to check out the **Location Awareness Programming Guide**[1] and the 2012 WWDC session **Staying on Track with Location Services**. iOS 5 by Tutorials also covers the new location APIs that were introduced in that release.

That being said, many of the existing features of Core Location will be covered in detail in this chapter, so you can choose to skip the background and just follow along with this chapter and learn along the way if you'd like.

[1] http://developer.apple.com/library/ios/documentation/UserExperience/Conceptual/LocationAwarenessPG/Introduction/Introduction.html

Region Monitoring

Since iOS 4, Core Location has provided the ability to monitor the entry and departure of regions via the `CLRegion` and `CLLocationManager` classes. What's a region, you ask? Well, a region is a defined area with a center based on a latitude and longitude coordinate pair and a radius measured in meters.

A big limitation of region monitoring is that each iOS app is restricted to monitoring a maximum of twenty regions at a time. Consider the Apple Store app; if you wanted to use Core Location's region notifications to greet customers as they approached a particular store, you would quickly realize that there are many more Apple stores than there are regions you can monitor.

Thankfully, iOS 7 provides you with a solution to overcome this type of situation: it's called **iBeacon**.

What's an iBeacon?

First, I hate to disappoint you, but it's iBeacon, not iBacon.

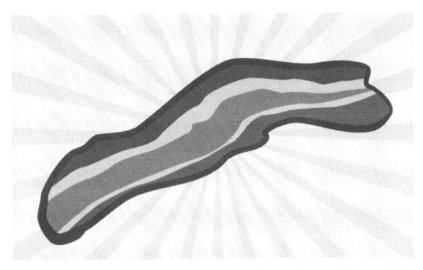

An iBeacon is really just a marketing name for the Bluetooth Low Energy (LE) advertising specification. iBeacons can run on various types of hardware, ranging from iOS devices to third-party Bluetooth LE emitters. When a Bluetooth LE device is emitting the appropriate information, an iOS device can listen for the emitter and developers can act upon this information.

Specifically, when an emitter is detected, your app is notified that the device has entered the iBeacon's region; conversely, you are also notified when the device has left the region. Additionally, the device can get an idea of how far it is from the emitter by measuring the **Received Signal Strength Indication**, or RSSI for short. The RSSI can be used to determine the closest iBeacon in the event that there are multiple iBeacons in the area, as well as giving your app a rough idea as to how close the device is to that emitter.

At this point you might be thinking of dozens of ways you can take advantage of this new feature. However, you might also be thinking, "I can do this without iBeacons by using the geo-fencing features of iOS 5.0!" And you would be correct — to a point.

Geo-fencing is a powerful feature, but it relies on GPS or GPS-like technologies that work using satellite or cellular tower signals. Both of these signals can attenuate significantly, or be completely unavailable when inside a building or riding the tube. Generally speaking, you can think of geo-fencing as a *macro*-level location monitoring technology, and iBeacons as a *micro*-level location monitoring technology.

Bluetooth LE is rated to work at a range of 50 meters, or 160 feet, though results may vary based on the environment. Bluetooth LE transmits data via radio waves, which are also subject to attenuation but do not require a clear line of sight like GPS. This means that you can confidently rely on signals from an iBeacon within a building, which is where micro-level location monitoring comes into its own.

Apple has made this technology extremely easy to work with, and if you're already familiar with Core Location it'll be even easier. As iBeacons rely on Bluetooth, you'll also need to learn about Core Bluetooth if you intend to use an iOS device as an iBeacon. Also, in addition to utilizing iBeacons within your own app, if you're a Passbook developer you can even make your pass listen for and respond to iBeacons. You can learn more about how to do this in Chapter 28, "What's New in PassKit, Part 2".

Apple has added just two classes to the Core Location framework to support iBeacons: `CLBeacon` and `CLBeaconRegion`. Let's go over these one by one.

CLBeacon

`CLBeacon` inherits from `NSObject` and represents the beacons encountered during region monitoring. The location manager provides instances of the `CLBeacon` class to its delegate as iBeacons are encountered. These instances contain information your app can use to determine which beacon was encountered.

The `CLBeacon` class provides the following properties:

- `proximityUUID`: A globally unique ID that is generally used to represent your company. To generate a unique id string use the `uuidgen` command-line tool via the Terminal app.

- `major` and `minor`: These properties can be used to identify individual beacon emitters. You might use the major value to represent a specific store, and the minor value to represent a specific department within the store.

- `proximity`: The relative distance to the beacon, you can use the value to determine which beacon is nearest if there are multiple beacons in the vicinity.

- `accuracy`: The accuracy in meters, you can use this value to differentiate between beacons with the same proximity value. You should however not use it as a precise location for the beacon.

- `rssi`: The average received signal strength of the beacon, measured in decibels since the range of the beacon was last reported.

Now let's move on to the second class related to iBeacons: `CLBeaconRegion`.

CLBeaconRegion

`CLBeaconRegion` inherits from `CLRegion` and defines a region based on a device's proximity to an iBeacon. When the system detects an iBeacon whose identifying information matches that of the defined `CLBeaconRegion`, it delivers a notification to your application. `CLBeaconRegion` is used both to determine what regions you're interested in monitoring, as well as to configure an iOS device to act as an iBeacon.

The `CLBeaconRegion` class has three initializers:

- `initWithProximityUUID:identifier:`
- `initWithProximityUUID:major:identifier:`
- `initWithProximityUUID:major:minor:identifier:`

Each initializer adds further identifying information to the region. The property names will look familiar, as they are the same on `CLBeacon`. It is important to use the appropriate initializer for your requirements, as the associated properties are read-only.

In order to configure an iOS device to act as an iBeacon there is one other method, `peripheralDataWithMeasuredPower:` that returns an `NSMutableDictionary`. This dictionary is used by a `CBPeripheralManager` to advertise the current device as a beacon.

Finally there is one other property that is mutable, `notifyEntryStateOnDisplay`, a `BOOL` that indicates whether beacon notifications are sent when they device's display is on.

How iBeacon works: a quick start

Want a quick overview of how things work before getting into the tutorial? This section is for you!

To configure an iOS device to act as an iBeacon, you follow these steps:

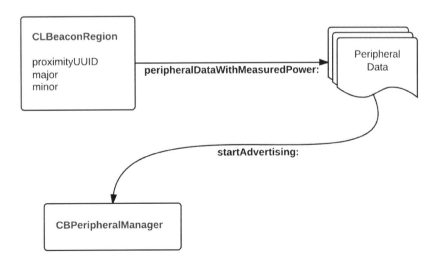

1. **Create a** `CLBeaconRegion`. Your `CLBeaconRegion` must be initialized with the identifiers you want to advertise, `proximityUUID`, `major`, and/or `minor`. The identifier string is used to differentiate between beacon instances within your application, it is not advertised and must not be `nil`.

```
NSUUID *uuid = [[NSUUID alloc] initWithUUIDString:@"41EAF359-
C87F-4AAF-92DC-9E4A17519AE1"];

NSString *identifier = @"com.razeware.beacon";

CLBeaconRegion *region = [[CLBeaconRegion alloc]
initWithProximityUUID:uuid major:2 minor:10
identifier:identifier];
```

2. **Obtain the peripheral data from** `CLBeaconRegion`. You request the data dictionary required for your peripheral manager directly from the region you initialize.

```
NSDictionary *peripheralData = [region
peripheralDataWithMeasuredPower:nil];
```

3. **Create a** `CBPeripheralManager`. To advertise you must leverage Bluetooth, initialize a `CBPeripheralManager` instance.

```
dispatch_queue_t queue =
dispatch_get_global_queue(DISPATCH_QUEUE_PRIORITY_BACKGROUND,
0);

CBPeripheralManager *peripheralManager = [[CBPeripheralManager
alloc] initWithDelegate:self queue:queue];
```

4. **Start advertising with** `CBPeripheralManager`. Pass the peripheral data dictionary to the `startAdvertising:` method.

```
[peripheralManager startAdvertising:peripheralData];
```

To start monitoring for nearby iBeacons, you follow these steps:

1. **Create a** `CLBeaconRegion`. An instance of `CLBeaconRegion` must be initialized with the `proximityUUID`, `major`, and `minor` values that you want to listen for. Also specify when and how you want to be notified when the region is entered or exited.

```
NSUUID *uuid = [[NSUUID alloc] initWithUUIDString:@"4B3E0C2E-
CE28-4E88-8D4E-89EB3E1F5B17"];
NSString *identifier = @"com.razeware.beacon";

CLBeaconRegion *region = [[CLBeaconRegion alloc]
initWithProximityUUID:uuid major:1 minor:2
identifier:identifier];
region.notifyOnEntry = entry;
region.notifyOnExit = exit;
region.notifyEntryStateOnDisplay = YES;
```

2. **Create a** `CLLocationManager`. To begin monitoring you must have an instance of `CLLocationManager` to register the `CLBeaconRegion` with it.

```
CLLocationManager *locationManager = [[CLLocationManager alloc]
init];
```

3. **Start monitoring**. To start monitoring for entry/exit of that region, use the `startMonitoringForRegion:` method of your location manager instance. Regions that you register with a location monitor persist between launches of your application.

```
[locationManager startMonitoringForRegion:region];
```

4. **Upon callback, respond accordingly**. Once an iBeacon is detected, your application will be launched and your `CLLocationManager` instance will receive a callback. At this point you can create notifications, change your UI, or use `startRangingBeaconsInRegion:` to receive updates when the relative distance of the iBeacon changes.

To receive the callbacks you must retain an instance variable or property in your AppDelegate

```
@interface AppDelegate () <CLLocationManagerDelegate>

@property CLLocationManager *_locationManager;

@end
```

And initialize the variable in `application:didFinishLaunchingWithOptions:`

```
_locationManager = [[CLLocationManager alloc] init];
_locationManager.delegate = self;
```

Your `locationManager:didEnterRegion:` delegate implementation may look like...

```
if ([region isKindOfClass:[CLBeaconRegion class]]) {
  CLBeaconRegion *beaconRegion = (CLBeaconRegion *)region;

  if ([beaconRegion.proximityUUID isEqual:_raysUUID]) {

    UILocalNotification *notification =
      [[UILocalNotification alloc] init];

    notification.alertBody = @"Welcome to Ray's!";

    [[UIApplication sharedApplication]
      presentLocalNotificationNow:notification];
  }
}
```

The rest of this chapter will walk you through a practical step-by-step example of adding iBeacon into an app. But before you begin, you need to make sure you have some test devices.

Devices supporting iBeacon

Only the most recent iOS devices contain Bluetooth LE hardware; therefore only devices with this hardware — and ones running iOS 7 — can support iBeacons. The following table indicates the first generation of each device that added support for Bluetooth LE. Given Apple's investment in this technology, it's safe to assume any future devices will also support Bluetooth LE.

Device	First to Support Bluetooth LE
iPad	3rd generation
iPad Mini	1st generation
iPhone	4S
iPod Touch	5th generation

To follow along with the rest of this chapter, you will need at least two devices from the above list, one of which needs to be an iPad (because the sample project was designed for an iPad). Unfortunately, the iOS Simulator cannot act as an iBeacon or monitor for iBeacons so beg, borrow, or steal some physical devices to use with this chapter's project.

Getting started

In this chapter you'll work with two apps:

1. **Wait List (the "restaurant's app")**: This is an iPad app that acts a digital waiting list for restaurants to keep track of guests waiting to be seated.

2. **Aroma (the "customer's app")**: This is an iPhone app that customers will use to find information on restaurants and to reserve a table. This is implemented using the new Multipeer Connectivity framework, which you can learn about in Chapter 19, "Peer-to-Peer Connectivity".

The resources for this chapter include starter projects for these two apps with most of the UI pre-made, but no iBeacon code added yet. That's your job!

Specifically, you will be making three improvements to these apps:

1. **Make Wait List act as an iBeacon**. You'll add support to Wait List so it broadcasts its location as an iBeacon while it is running so nearby customers can find the restaurant.

2. **Make Aroma search for nearby iBeacons**. Next, you'll modify Aroma to listen for nearby restaurants, alert customers when they're close to the restaurant and invite them in to enjoy a meal.

3. **Allow table reservations when within range**. You'll also improve Aroma so that it only allows the customer to reserve a table when they're within the restaurant's iBeacon region, which means they are also in range for Multipeer Connectivity.

4. **Bid farewell on region exit**. Finally, you'll modify Aroma to bid the customer farewell on behalf of the restaurant as the guest exits the restaurant's iBeacon region.

Introducing Wait List

You'll find the starter project Wait List in the resources for this chapter. Open it in Xcode, and build and run it on your compatible iPad device.

When you first start the app you'll be presented with an empty list. Add a few guests to the list by tapping the **+** button in the top right corner. You'll be presented with the guest registration screen as shown below:

The **Name** and **Party Size** fields are required; **Arrival Time** and **Quoted Time** are both set to defaults (the current time, and 5 minutes respectively).

Mood also defaults to the Happy state; hopefully most of your guests will be arriving in a happy mood! The **Notes** field is optional and is empty by default.

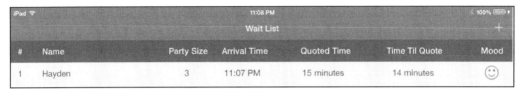

Once added, the guest shows up on the list and the **Time Til Quote** is calculated. All of the Time Til Quote labels are updated at an interval of 5 seconds with a tolerance of 5 seconds for power efficiency. Check out Chapter 8, "What's New In Objective-C and Foundation in Xcode 5", for more information on NSTimer's new tolerance property.

Once a guest is on the list, they need to be removed when they're seated, or when they give up in frustration and leave to find another restaurant. You may also need to edit their information if their party size or mood changes.

Tap a guest's row to bring up a menu of available actions, as shown below:

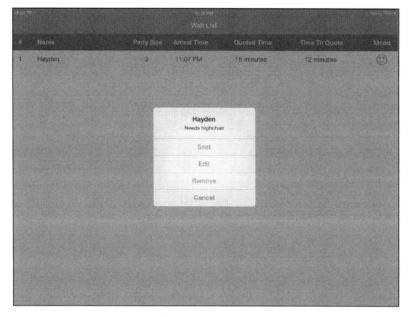

The **Seat** option removes the guest from the list. **Edit** opens the same view as when adding a guest, but pre-populated with the information of the selected guest. **Remove** deletes the selected guest from the list.

In this implementation, Seat and Remove are effectively the same operation, but it may be desirable to track metrics on seating and people leaving separately, so they are defined as two separate actions. Wait List is fairly simple, yet entirely workable for a restaurant in lieu of paper-based lists.

What you haven't seen yet is that Wait List is advertising itself as a Multipeer Connectivity peer, which allows guests to add themselves to the seating list right from within Aroma!

Introducing Aroma

Now find the Aroma starter project in the resources for this chapter and build and run it on your compatible iPhone or iPod Touch device.

This starter project comes pre-loaded with information about three restaurants. Ideally, these details would come from a web service, but that's beyond the scope of this tutorial. You can swipe left and right to scroll between the restaurants:

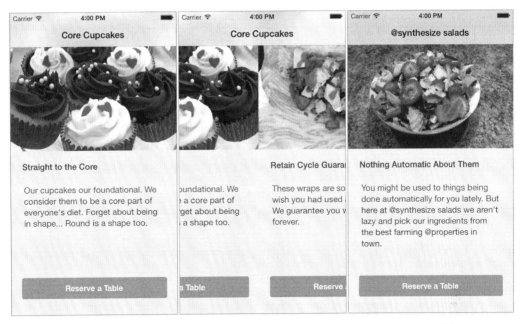

If you have Wait List running on your iPad, you can tap the **Reserve a Table** button to connect to Wait List and add yourself to the list. Select **Host Stand** as the peer, accept the connection in the Wait List app, then tap **Done** in Aroma to begin entering your information.

Aroma and Wait List use the default interfaces provided by the Multipeer Connectivity framework; they aren't pretty but they get the job done. However, you can customize or completely replace these views if you desire. To learn more, check out Chapter 19, "Peer-to-Peer Connectivity."

Feel free to look through the code of these two projects to get familiar with how things work. When you're ready, read on and get ready for your first taste of iBacon! Whoops, iBeacon!

Advertising as an iBeacon

In order to do anything with iBeacons, you'll need some kind of hardware emitting a beacon signal. You'll modify Wait List to act as an iBeacon that Aroma listens for.

The first step is to set up the project infrastructure – later you'll add the iBeacon code itself.

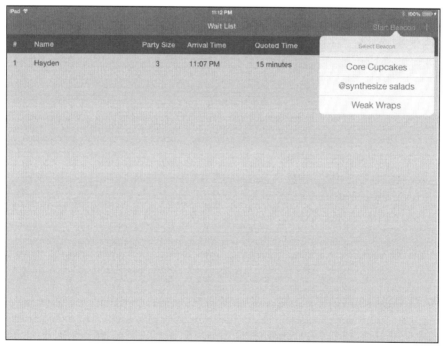

Selecting an option at this point does nothing — but fixing that is your next task.

First open **BeaconAdvertisingService.h** and take a look over the interface.

```
@interface BeaconAdvertisingService : NSObject
```

```
@property (nonatomic, readonly, getter = isAdvertising) BOOL
advertising;

+ (BeaconAdvertisingService *)sharedInstance;

- (void)startAdvertisingUUID:(NSUUID *)uuid
major:(CLBeaconMajorValue)major minor:(CLBeaconMinorValue)minor;
- (void)stopAdvertising;

@end
```

This class follows the Singleton design pattern that guarantees only one instance will be created while the application is running, given that you always use the sharedInstance method to access the singleton instance. The two other methods allow you to start and stop advertising of beacons; those are the interesting ones and what you will use next.

In order to do anything when an option is selected from the **Start Beacon** popover you need a delegate method to handle the selection of an item from the action sheet. Add the following to **WaitListTableViewController.m**

```
- (void)actionSheet:(UIActionSheet *)actionSheet
clickedButtonAtIndex:(NSInteger)buttonIndex
{
  switch (buttonIndex) {
    case 0: {
      NSUUID *cupcakesUUID = [[NSUUID alloc]
initWithUUIDString:@"EC6F3659-A8B9-4434-904C-A76F788DAC43"];
      [[BeaconAdvertisingService sharedInstance]
startAdvertisingUUID:cupcakesUUID major:0 minor:0];
      self.navigationItem.title = @"Core Cupcakes";
      break;

    } case 1: {
      NSUUID *saladsUUID = [[NSUUID alloc]
initWithUUIDString:@"7B377E4A-1641-4765-95E9-174CD05B6C79"];
      [[BeaconAdvertisingService sharedInstance]
startAdvertisingUUID:saladsUUID major:0 minor:0];
      self.navigationItem.title = @"@synthesize salads";
      break;

    } case 2: {
      NSUUID *wrapsUUID = [[NSUUID alloc]
initWithUUIDString:@"2B144D35-5BA6-4010-B276-FC4D4845B292"];
```

```
        [[BeaconAdvertisingService sharedInstance]
  startAdvertisingUUID:wrapsUUID major:0 minor:0];
        self.navigationItem.title = @"Weak Wraps";
      break;
    }
    default:
      break;
  }
}
```

Each `case` statement in the `switch` block creates an `NSUUID` instance based on a pre-generated UUID string. It then passes the `NSUUID` instance to the advertising service to start advertising that UUID along with `major` and `minor` values of `0`. Finally, it sets the title of the view to the selected restaurant.

Build and run your app; you'll see the view title change as you select different restaurants. You may also notice that **Start Beacon** never changes to **Stop Beacon**. To fix this you'll have to flesh out the `BeaconAdvertisingService` class. It's finally time for some iBeacon code!

Advertising as an iBeacon

Open **BeaconAdvertisingService.m** and take a quick look at it. The implemented methods are unrelated to the iBeacon feature itself, but they help support the application. The `sharedInstance` method follows the standard GCD approach for creating a singleton, there is an empty `init` and then three unimplemented methods that do relate specifically to iBeacon, you get to implement these soon! The last is a big one, but it's relatively simple `bluetoothStateValid:` returns a `BOOL` designating if the device's Bluetooth radio is available and in a state which it can be utilized. If the state is invalid it will write to the error pointer provided and return `NO`.

On to the implementation! Start by adding the following line to the `init` method before the return.

```
_peripheralManager = [[CBPeripheralManager alloc]
initWithDelegate:self
queue:dispatch_get_global_queue(DISPATCH_QUEUE_PRIORITY_DEFAULT,
0)];
```

This allocates and initializes a `CBPeripheralManager` instance by setting its delegate to `self` using a default priority dispatch queue, and then assigns it to the `_peripheralManager` instance variable. A `CBPeripheralManager` manages published services for the devices Generic Attribute Profile (GATT) database and to advertise them to other devices. This class is not only used for iBeacon but also for other Bluetooth LE accessories. In order to use any of the methods on the class the hardware must be turned on and in the `CBPeripheralManagerStatePoweredOn` state.

Now implement the `peripheralManagerDidUpdateState:` delegate method with the following:

```
- (void)peripheralManagerDidUpdateState:(CBPeripheralManager
*)peripheral
{
  NSError *bluetoothStateError = nil;
  if (![self bluetoothStateValid:&bluetoothStateError]) {
    dispatch_async(dispatch_get_main_queue(), ^{
      NSString *title = @"Bluetooth Issue";
      NSString *message =
              bluetoothStateError.userInfo[@"message"];

      UIAlertView *bluetoothIssueAlert = [[UIAlertView alloc]
                initWithTitle:title
                      message:message
                     delegate:nil
            cancelButtonTitle:@"OK"
            otherButtonTitles:nil];

      [bluetoothIssueAlert show];
    });
  }
}
```

This delegate method is called by the `CBPeripheralManager` when it's state changes, it is important to let the user know if the Bluetooth peripheral is not in a valid state and why. The `bluetoothStateValid:` method is used; if the state is not valid then display an error message using the message from the `NSError` instance.

One more particularly interesting delegate method for this application is `peripheralManagerDidStartAdvertising:error:`. This method is called when you call the `startAdvertising:` method to begin advertising the local device's peripheral data. If advertising is successful the error parameter will be `nil`.

For this app, if advertising has started you need to update the `advertising` property, and if it fails to start you should alert the user.

Add the `peripheralManagerDidStartAdvertising:error:` method to
BeaconAdvertisingService.m:

```objc
-(void)peripheralManagerDidStartAdvertising:(CBPeripheralManager
*)peripheral error:(NSError *)error
{
  dispatch_async(dispatch_get_main_queue(), ^{
    if (error) {
      NSString *title = @"Cannot Advertise Beacon";
      NSString *message = @"There was an issue starting the
advertisement of your beacon.";

      UIAlertView *alert = [[UIAlertView alloc]
                            initWithTitle:title
                                  message:message
                                 delegate:nil
                        cancelButtonTitle:@"OK"
                        otherButtonTitles:nil];
      [alert show];
      NSLog(@"Start Advertising Error: %@", error);

    } else {
      NSLog(@"Advertising!");
      self.advertising = YES;
    }
  });
}
```

Things are really starting to take shape, but you still haven't really done anything
particularly interesting with iBeacons themselves. At this point everything is in place to
implement your `startAdvertisingUUID:major:minor:` method, which is a
convenience method to check the state of `CBPeripheralManager` create a
`CLBeaconRegion` instance and instruct `CBPeripheralManager` to begin advertising the
beacon's peripheral data.

As this is completely new, I'll walk you through the different sections of the
implementation first, and then you'll add it. Replace the stub implementation with the
following:

```objc
- (void)startAdvertisingUUID:(NSUUID *)uuid
                       major:(CLBeaconMajorValue)major
                       minor:(CLBeaconMinorValue)minor
{
  NSError *bluetoothStateError = nil;
```

```
if (![self bluetoothStateValid:&bluetoothStateError])
{
  NSString *title = @"Bluetooth Issue";
  NSString *message =
                   bluetoothStateError.userInfo[@"message"];

  UIAlertView *alert = [[UIAlertView alloc]
                   initWithTitle:title
                         message:message
                        delegate:nil
               cancelButtonTitle:@"OK"
               otherButtonTitles:nil];
  [alert show];
  return;
 }
}
```

This verifies that the Bluetooth state is valid. If it isn't then there's no reason to continue so you return.

Next add this to the bottom of the method:

```
CLBeaconRegion *region;
if (uuid && major && minor) {
  region = [[CLBeaconRegion alloc]
           initWithProximityUUID:uuid
                           major:major
                           minor:minor
                      identifier:kBeaconIdentifier];
} else if (uuid && major) {
  region = [[CLBeaconRegion alloc]
           initWithProximityUUID:uuid
                           major:major
                      identifier:kBeaconIdentifier];
} else if (uuid) {
  region = [[CLBeaconRegion alloc]
           initWithProximityUUID:uuid
                      identifier:kBeaconIdentifier];
} else {
  [NSException raise:@"You must at least provide a UUID to start
advertising"
              format:nil];
}
```

Now depending on what was passed in, you are going to create an instance of `CLBeaconRegion`. If all three values are passed in you use them, other wise you continue to degrade as makes sense. If no values are passed in then an exception is raised.

Continue by adding this to the end of the method:

```
NSDictionary *peripheralData =
            [region peripheralDataWithMeasuredPower:nil];


[_peripheralManager startAdvertising:peripheralData];
```

Now that you've a valid instance of `CLBeaconRegion`, you can request the peripheral data from it using `peripheralDataWithMeasuredPower:`. This method returns an instance of `NSDictionary,` which is to be passed to your `CBPeripheralManager` and informs it exactly what needs to be broadcast over the Bluetooth radio.

This method also has an optional parameter of measured power and by passing `nil` you're telling the peripheral manager that you want it to use the default power level. In the case of Wait List and Aroma, this should be fine as it's not imperative that the iBeacon only be heard at certain distances.

> **Note:** This value becomes more important when you're working with ranges and you want to measure the distance between the device and an iBeacon. Depending on the environment that the iBeacon is in, it may be necessary to lower or raise this value; the value passed should represent the expected RSSI at a distance of 1 meter.
>
> So, if you calibrated your environment and found that when a receiving device is 1 meter away from the beacon it reads an average RSSI value of -35, you would set this value to -35.

That's it for this method. The last piece of the puzzle is to implement `stopAdvertising`, and it's an easy one. Replace the empty method stub with the following:

```
- (void)stopAdvertising {
    [_peripheralManager stopAdvertising];
    self.advertising = NO;
}
```

Here you inform the peripheral manager to stop advertising, and then update the `advertising` property accordingly so that observers are made aware.

Build and run your app; tap the Start Beacon button and select a restaurant. You'll notice the button text changes to Stop Beacon, as shown below:

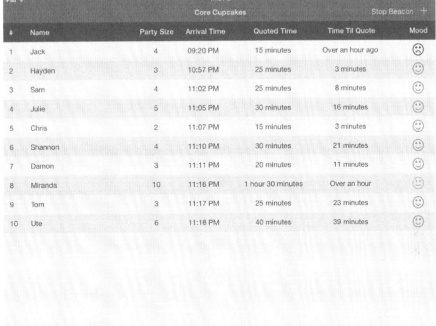

#	Name	Party Size	Arrival Time	Quoted Time	Time Til Quote	Mood
1	Jack	4	09:20 PM	15 minutes	Over an hour ago	☹
2	Hayden	3	10:57 PM	25 minutes	3 minutes	☺
3	Sam	4	11:02 PM	25 minutes	8 minutes	☺
4	Julie	5	11:05 PM	30 minutes	16 minutes	☺
5	Chris	2	11:07 PM	15 minutes	3 minutes	☺
6	Shannon	4	11:10 PM	30 minutes	21 minutes	☺
7	Damon	3	11:11 PM	20 minutes	11 minutes	☺
8	Miranda	10	11:16 PM	1 hour 30 minutes	Over an hour	☺
9	Tom	3	11:17 PM	25 minutes	23 minutes	☺
10	Ute	6	11:18 PM	40 minutes	39 minutes	☺

Your iPad is now acting as an iBeacon. In the next section you'll modify Aroma so that it detects your iPad's advertisement. For convenience, you can find the completed version of Aroma in the resources for this chapter.

Limitations on iBeacon and device state

One unfortunate limitation with advertising an iBeacon from an iOS device is that Apple requires the app to be running in the foreground; if your device goes to sleep or is interrupted by another foreground process such as a phone call, then advertising will halt. With Wait List this is a pretty big deal; it's very likely the iPad will go to sleep on it's own unless the user enables the relevant setting to prevent it. Another option would be to disable the idle timer in your code so the app won't permit the device to sleep.

However, neither of these solutions can guard against the scenario of a bored employee who closes the app to play Angry Birds. Because of these situations, it's recommended that you use **Guided Access** when appropriate to prevent the device from sleeping or being turned off, as well as preventing the app from being closed.

Hopefully cost-effective third party beacons will soon be available, which will resolve the issue entirely for applications like Wait List. There are certainly cases where you still want an iOS device to act as a beacon, but for many applications it may make more sense to use a standalone beacon device. There are a few players entering the market in this space notably KST (http://www.kstechnologies.com/products/ibeacon-alpha-program-participants-only) and Estimote (http://estimote.com/). More manufacturers are expected to reveal themselves and enter the market soon.

Listening for iBeacons

Open the Aroma Xcode project. Right-click on the **iBeacon** group in the **Project Navigator** and choose **New File...** from the popup menu. Create a new **Objective-C class** named **BeaconMonitoringService** and make it a subclass of **NSObject**. Once the files have been created, open **BeaconMonitoringService.h** and replace the contents with the following:

```
#import <Foundation/Foundation.h>

@import CoreLocation;

@interface BeaconMonitoringService : NSObject

+ (BeaconMonitoringService *)sharedInstance;
- (void)startMonitoringBeaconWithUUID:(NSUUID *)uuid
                                major:(CLBeaconMajorValue)major
                                minor:(CLBeaconMinorValue)minor
                           identifier:(NSString *)identifier
                              onEntry:(BOOL)entry
                               onExit:(BOOL)exit;

- (void)stopMonitoringAllRegions;

@end
```

Here you import the Core Location framework and declare the class method `sharedInstance` which returns the singleton instance of the `BeaconMonitoringService`. The other two methods start and stop region monitoring.

This time you're going to jump straight into the implementation of this service class. Open **BeaconMonitoringService.m** and replace its contents with the following:

```
#import "BeaconMonitoringService.h"

@implementation BeaconMonitoringService {
    CLLocationManager *_locationManager;
```

```
    }

@end
```

Next add the implementation of sharedInstance and override init:

```
+ (BeaconMonitoringService *)sharedInstance {
    static dispatch_once_t onceToken;
    static BeaconMonitoringService *_sharedInstance;
    dispatch_once(&onceToken, ^{
        _sharedInstance = [[self alloc] init];
    });

    return _sharedInstance;
}

- (instancetype)init {
    self = [super init];
    if (!self) {
        return nil;
    }

    _locationManager = [[CLLocationManager alloc] init];

    return self;
}
```

Here you use the standard GCD approach for creating a singleton, override the init method to create an instance of CLLocationManager and assign it to the _locationManager instance variable. The CLLocationManager is responsible for handling the delivery of location events to your application. It will also be used to manage the registration and un-registration of regions that your app is to monitor.

Now it's time to implement startMonitoringBeaconWithUUID:major:minor:identifier:onEntry:onExit: . Add the following method to **BeaconMonitoringService.m**:

```
- (void)startMonitoringBeaconWithUUID:(NSUUID *)uuid
                                major:(CLBeaconMajorValue)major
                                minor:(CLBeaconMinorValue)minor
                           identifier:(NSString *)identifier
                              onEntry:(BOOL)entry
                               onExit:(BOOL)exit
{
```

```
        CLBeaconRegion *region = [[CLBeaconRegion alloc]
                              initWithProximityUUID:uuid
                                             major:major
                                             minor:minor
                                        identifier:identifier];
    region.notifyOnEntry = entry;
    region.notifyOnExit = exit;
    region.notifyEntryStateOnDisplay = YES;
    [_locationManager startMonitoringForRegion:region];
}
```

This is really just a convenience method that creates an instance of CLBeaconRegion, sets the notification properties as necessary and informs the _locationManager to start monitoring for the region. That's really all it takes to get a location manager listening for an iBeacon.

There is, of course, more work to be done in order to react when an iBeacon is discovered, and you'll implement that soon. But first you need to finish the service implementation.

Add the stopMonitoringAllRegions method as below:

```
- (void)stopMonitoringAllRegions {
    for (CLRegion *region in _locationManager.monitoredRegions)
    {
        [_locationManager stopMonitoringForRegion:region];
    }
}
```

Again, super simple stuff. The location manager keeps track of the regions it's monitoring, so you simply iterate through the regions and inform the location manager to stop monitoring each instance as it's presented. If you were dealing with other types of regions like CLCircularRegion you may want to verify the region is actually of the CLBeaconRegion type before stopping the monitoring. But Aroma only monitors for iBeacons, not geo-fencing, and therefore you can safely remove them all.

That's it for the BeaconMonitoringService class. Your task now is to use it to monitor for beacons.

Open **AppDelegate.m** and import the class header:

```
#import "BeaconMonitoringService.h"
```

Replace the contents of didFinishLaunchingWithOptions: with the following:

```
[[BeaconMonitoringService sharedInstance]
                    stopMonitoringAllRegions];
NSArray *restaurants =
        [[RestaurantDetailService sharedService] restaurants];


for (Restaurant *restaurant in restaurants)
{
  [[BeaconMonitoringService sharedInstance]
      startMonitoringBeaconWithUUID:restaurant.uuid
                    major:0
                    minor:0
                identifier:restaurant.name
                  onEntry:YES
                  onExit:YES];
}


return YES;
```

When the app launches you ask the monitoring service to stop monitoring all regions. This is mostly a sanity check and balancing call to ensure that you're only ever monitoring the regions you're interested in. If the RestaurantDetailService class started returning a different set of restaurants, you'd want to ensure that you had stopped monitoring any existing restaurants.

Next you ask the RestaurantDetailService's singleton object for an array of all the restaurants that it knows about; the starter project includes the same UUIDs that the Wait List app advertises. Then you iterate over those restaurants and begin monitoring for their iBeacons.

Now that each restaurants' iBeacon is being monitored by Aroma, you'll need to respond to the delegate methods that get called when certain events occur. First, though, you'll need an instance of CLLocationManager to inform you of these events.

Open **AppDelegate.h** and replace it's contents with the following:

```
#import <UIKit/UIKit.h>

@import CoreLocation;

@interface AppDelegate : UIResponder <UIApplicationDelegate>

@property (strong, nonatomic) UIWindow *window;

@property (strong, nonatomic, readonly) CLLocationManager
*locationManager;
```

```
@end
```

Return to **AppDelegate.m** and add the following two lines to the top of `didFinishLaunchingWithOptions:`

```
_locationManager = [[CLLocationManager alloc] init];
_locationManager.delegate = self;
```

Here you create an instance of `CLLocationManager`, assign it to the `_locationManager` instance variable maintained by the property you just declared and set the manager's delegate.

The compiler should be warning you that `self` does not conform to the `CLLocationManagerDelegate` protocol. To address this, add the following class extension above `@implementation AppDelegate` in **AppDelegate.m** to declare the class conforms to the protocol:

```
@interface AppDelegate () <CLLocationManagerDelegate>
@end
```

There are three specific delegate methods you're interested in.

- `locationManager:didDetermineState:forRegion:`
- `locationManager:didEnterRegion:`
- `locationManager:didEnterRegion:`

While the method names seem pretty descriptive, you're probably asking yourself "Who calls these, and how does my app respond to them? They aren't part of the UIApplicationDelegate protocol."

A valid question, to be sure. Normally when your app is in the background or has been closed entirely, it's informed of an event via the **UIApplicationDelegate** protocol. Once you being monitoring a region, iOS launches your application in the background once the region is detected, which subsequently calls `application:didFinishLaunchingWithOptions:`. Recall that you initialized an instance of `CLLocationManager` in that method and assigned its delegate to `self`. So therefore it's the `CLLocationManager` instance that's calling the delegate methods.

Add the first of the three delegate methods to **AppDelegate.m**:

```
- (void)locationManager:(CLLocationManager *)manager
      didDetermineState:(CLRegionState)state
              forRegion:(CLRegion *)region {
  if ([region isKindOfClass:[CLBeaconRegion class]]) {
```

```
    CLBeaconRegion *beaconRegion = (CLBeaconRegion *)region;
    Restaurant *restaurant =
        [[RestaurantDetailService sharedService]
            restaurantWithUUID:beaconRegion.proximityUUID];
    if (restaurant) {
      NSDictionary *userInfo =
            @{@"restaurant": restaurant,
              @"state": @(state)};
      [[NSNotificationCenter defaultCenter]
            postNotificationName:@"DidDetermineRegionState"
                        object:self
                      userInfo:userInfo];
    }
  }
}
```

This method begins by verifying the region is an instance of `CLBeaconRegion`. It then asks the `RestaurantDetailService` for the `Restaurant` instance that matches the regions UUID. If a restaurant is returned, it then posts a notification containing the `Restaurant` instance and `state` in the `userInfo` dictionary. Later on you'll be listening for this notification and making use of the `userInfo` object's contents.

Next, add the second delegate method:

```
- (void)locationManager:(CLLocationManager *)manager
        didEnterRegion:(CLRegion *)region {
    if ([region isKindOfClass:[CLBeaconRegion class]]) {
      CLBeaconRegion *beaconRegion = (CLBeaconRegion *)region;
      Restaurant *restaurant =
                [[RestaurantDetailService sharedService]
                restaurantWithUUID:beaconRegion.proximityUUID];
      if (restaurant) {
        UILocalNotification *notification =
                            [[UILocalNotification alloc] init];
        notification.userInfo =
            @{@"uuid": restaurant.uuid.UUIDString};
        notification.alertBody =
            [NSString stringWithFormat:@"Smell that? Looks like
you're near %@!",
                                        restaurant.name];
        notification.soundName = @"Default";
        [[UIApplication sharedApplication]
            presentLocalNotificationNow:notification];
```

```
        [[NSNotificationCenter defaultCenter]
            postNotificationName:@"DidEnterRegion"
                          object:self
                        userInfo:@{@"restaurant": restaurant}];
    }
  }
}
```

This method starts in the same manner as the previous one: obtain the corresponding `Restaurant` instance for the given region. Then it posts a local notification with the UUID string in the `userInfo` dictionary, a message indicating the restaurant's name, and the default alert sound to play. Next it posts a notification with the `userInfo` dictionary containing the `Restaurant` instance; again, you'll be listening for this notification later.

The `userInfo` dictionary of the local notification contains the restaurant's details to display if the user responds to the notification. This bit was implemented for you in the starter project; you'll find the relevant code at the foot of **AppDelegate.m** in `application:didReceiveLocalNotification:`.

Now add the third and final delegate method:

```
- (void)locationManager:(CLLocationManager *)manager
        didExitRegion:(CLRegion *)region {
    if ([region isKindOfClass:[CLBeaconRegion class]]) {
      CLBeaconRegion *beaconRegion = (CLBeaconRegion *)region;
      Restaurant *restaurant =
          [[RestaurantDetailService sharedService]
              restaurantWithUUID:beaconRegion.proximityUUID];
      if (restaurant) {
        UILocalNotification *notification =
            [[UILocalNotification alloc] init];
        notification.alertBody = [NSString stringWithFormat:
                                   @"We hope you enjoyed the
smells and more of %@. See you next time!",
                                    restaurant.name];
        [[UIApplication sharedApplication]
            presentLocalNotificationNow:notification];
        [[NSNotificationCenter defaultCenter]
            postNotificationName:@"DidExitRegion"
                          object:self
                        userInfo:@{@"restaurant": restaurant}];
    }
  }
```

```
}
```

The few differences between this implementation and the previous one are that a different message is presented, there's no `userInfo` dictionary created for the notification and a sound isn't used as it isn't critical that the user responds to this notification.

At this point Aroma is monitoring for all the iBeacons Wait List advertises, so you're all set to give it a try.

Build and run your app, and make sure Bluetooth is enabled on both devices. Once both apps have launched, you can either close Aroma or put the device to sleep. On Wait List, tap **Start Beacon** and choose **@synthesize salads**. You should see the following notification displayed on your device running Aroma:

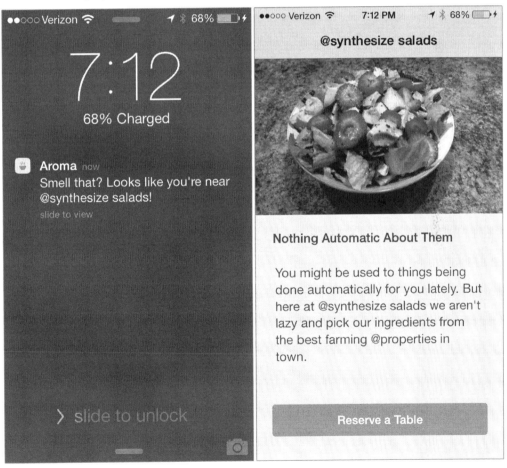

Just like that, the device running Aroma alerts you to let you know you're near the restaurant; sliding the notification takes you straight to the restaurant's detail page. Feel free to try turning on the iBeacons for the other restaurants to see their notifications in action too.

> **Note:** Be sure that your device is not in **Do Not Disturb** mode otherwise you may not see the notifications.

Now stop the running iBeacon or move the device running Aroma away from the iPad running Wait List; eventually you'll receive the exit notification below:

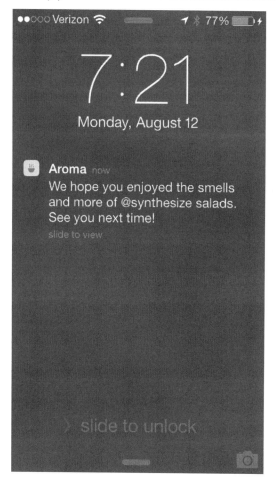

You've probably noticed it takes a minute or so to receive the exit region notification when you stop an iBeacon. There's nothing in the Apple documentation to state why this would occur, but it's assumed that exit notifications are not immediate in the event that you're loitering on the edge of a region, as this would result in persistent enter/exit notifications. Also be aware that restarting the beacon before the exit notification is received will not trigger another enter region notification.

Updating app state based on location

You've learned a lot of what iBeacons has to offer; they're relatively simple yet incredibly powerful and lend themselves to tons of neat real-world applications. But remember that you were trying to design an app to make your user's life easier, not just tell them when they're in range of one of their favorite restaurant.

Currently the **Reserve a Table** button is permanently visible on the detail page of each restaurant whether or not you're within range for Multipeer Connectivity. That doesn't make sense, and could be misleading to the user. The **Reserve a Table** button should only appear when the user is within the region of the respective restaurant.

The app delegate will post notifications when particular location updates take place. You'll listen for these notifications and invoke some handler methods when these notifications come through.

Add the following handler method to **RestaurantDetailViewController.m**:

```objc
-(void)handleDidDetermineRegionStateNotification:(NSNotification
*)note
{
    Restaurant *r = note.userInfo[@"restaurant"];
    if (r == _restaurant) {
        CLRegionState state =
                    [note.userInfo[@"state"] integerValue];
        switch (state) {
            case CLRegionStateInside:
                _reserveATableButton.hidden = NO;
                break;
            case CLRegionStateOutside:
                _reserveATableButton.hidden = YES;
                break;
            case CLRegionStateUnknown:
                _reserveATableButton.hidden = YES;
                break;
        }
    }
}
```

This method handles the notification posted when the state of a region has been determined. Based on the state of the region, either show or hide the **Reserve a Table** button depending on which restaurant's region you've detected.

Still working in the same file, add the following method:

```
- (void)handleDidEnterRegionNotification:(NSNotification *)note
{
    Restaurant *r = note.userInfo[@"restaurant"];
    if (r == _restaurant) {
        _reserveATableButton.hidden = NO;
    }
}
```

This method simply displays the button when your device enters a region.

Now add the final method of this trio, as below:

```
- (void)handleDidExitRegionNotification:(NSNotification *)note {
    Restaurant *r = note.userInfo[@"restaurant"];
    if (r == _restaurant) {
        _reserveATableButton.hidden = YES;
    }
}
```

This method hides the button when your device exits a region.

Now you need to register for the actual notifications. Add the following to `viewDidLoad`:

```
[[NSNotificationCenter defaultCenter] addObserver:self
selector:@selector(handleDidEnterRegionNotification:)
name:@"DidEnterRegion" object:nil];

[[NSNotificationCenter defaultCenter] addObserver:self
selector:@selector(handleDidExitRegionNotification:)
name:@"DidExitRegion" object:nil];

[[NSNotificationCenter defaultCenter] addObserver:self
selector:@selector(handleDidDetermineRegionStateNotification:)
name:@"DidDetermineRegionState" object:nil];
```

Don't forget that you have to balance this out by implementing `dealloc` to unregister for the notifications. Add the following method:

```
- (void)dealloc {
```

```
    [[NSNotificationCenter defaultCenter] removeObserver:self
  name:@"DidEnterRegion" object:nil];

    [[NSNotificationCenter defaultCenter] removeObserver:self
  name:@"DidExitRegion" object:nil];

    [[NSNotificationCenter defaultCenter] removeObserver:self
  name:@"DidDetermineRegionState" object:nil];
  }
```

One caveat to this approach is that you're not guaranteed to receive the notification when the view is loaded; therefore you don't know whether to show or hide the buttons when the view appears. To alleviate this, use the `CLLocationManager` property of the application delegate to request the state of the region for the restaurant being viewed.

Add the following instance variable to the implementation block of `RestaurantDetailViewController`:

```
CLLocationManager *_locationManager;
```

Next, add the following code to `viewDidLoad`:

```
_locationManager = [(AppDelegate *)
  [UIApplication sharedApplication].delegate locationManager];
CLBeaconRegion *region = [[CLBeaconRegion alloc]
  initWithProximityUUID:_restaurant.uuid major:0 minor:0
  identifier:_restaurant.name];
[_locationManager requestStateForRegion:region];
```

Here you assign the app delegate's `locationManager` property to the local `_locationManager` instance variable, then create a region that represents the current restaurant and ask the location manager for its state. This method is asynchronous; therefore once the delegate method is called, you'll receive the relevant notification and your `handleDidDetermineRegionStateNotification:` method updates the **Reserve a Table** button accordingly.

Build and run your app; you'll notice that the Reserve a Table buttons are hidden when Aroma is not within the restaurant's region. Open Wait List and start an iBeacon while Aroma is still open; you'll see the Reserve a Table button appear. As an added bonus, the app scrolls to the detail page of the restaurant whose region you just entered. This feature was already present in the sample project; if you want to take a look and see how this was done, check out the application delegates' `aapplication:didReceiveLocalNotification:` method.

> **Note:** Due to the way exit notifications work, the Reserve Table button may take some time to disappear once you have left the region or the beacon has stopped advertising.

You're now armed with the knowledge required to enhance your existing apps to take full advantage of iBeacons; if you're like me, your head is probably already full of ideas!

You can find the final version of Aroma in the resources for this chapter.

Scaling considerations

The tutorial in this chapter used UUIDs to represent each individual restaurant. Recall that an app can only monitor twenty regions at a time; this is also true for UUIDs. Once your app becomes a hit (we can all dream, can't we?) and more than twenty restaurants want to use your system you have a big scaling problem.

To alleviate this, it would be wise to consider using a *single* UUID and then taking advantage of the `major` and `minor` values. The major value could represent a restaurant id, and the minor could be reserved for later uses, such as different locations of a restaurant in the same city. The underlying storage for both the `major` and `minor` fields is `uint16_t` — a 16bit unsigned integer — which means you have the range from 0 to 2^{16}, or 0 to 65,536 values to choose from. If you went this route you'd be able to support just over 65,000 restaurants before running into any issues.

If you consider that you also get twenty separate UUIDs to monitor, that takes you up to a gargantuan 1,310,720 restaurants. Furthermore, say you decided to use the `major` value to represent the chain and the `minor` value the specific location; you're now looking at 2^32 combinations which is over 4.2 billion. Then multiply *that* by 20 again and you're now at over 85 billion combinations.

That sure is a heck of a lot more than twenty geo-fences!

Where to go from here?

The tutorial covered most of what you need to know to get up and running with iBeacons. However there is one topic that's hasn't been covered: **ranging**.

`CLLocationManager` has another suite of methods specific to iBeacons. Just as you can monitor iBeacons, you can *range* them as well using `startRangingBeaconsInRegion:`.

This begins reporting iBeacons as they're discovered to its delegate via `locationManager:didRangeBeacons:inRegion:`. You can then view the iBeacons passed to this method and compare their RSSI values and accuracies to calculate which iBeacon is the closest. Remember though that that radio signals can and do attenuate, and you shouldn't rely on the provided values to determine precise locations of iBeacons.

However, it's generally safe to use the information to get a good idea of which iBeacon is nearest, which can be important in an environment where multiple beacons are advertised, such as museums with multiple exhibits using iBeacons as virtual tour guides to display information about the exhibits to the visitor. Be sure to check out the above APIs if your application needs to distinguish between multiple iBeacons in the same vicinity.

Challenge

Your challenge for this chapter is to introduce a new restaurant with its own UUID that Wait List advertises and Aroma listens for. The restaurant will be called "Bitmask Bites"; its image is already included in the project and is named "Bites".

Hints:

1. Update `RestaurantDetailService` to include the new restaurant information in Aroma.

2. Generate a new UUID string using the `uuidgen` command-line tool.

3. Use the same UUID in Wait List to create the iBeacon.

Section V: Bonus Chapters

Good news – we have some bonus chapters for you! In these chapters you'll learn about the new inter-app audio feature in iOS 7, learn about some neat updates to PassKit, and finally, learn how to add iAds into your apps.

These bonus chapters come as an optional PDF download, which you can download for free here:

• http://www.raywenderlich.com/store/ios-7-by-tutorials/bonus-chapters

We hope you enjoy the bonus chapters!

Chapter 25: Beginning Inter-App Audio

Chapter 26: Intermediate Inter-App Audio

Chapter 27: What's New in PassKit, Part 1

Chapter 28: What's New in Passkit, Part 2

Chapter 29: Introduction to iAd